The Princeton Review®

Catholic High School Entrance Exams (HSPT®/COOP®/TACHS®) PREP

3rd Edition

The Staff of The Princeton Review

PrincetonReview.com

Penguin Random House

The Princeton Review
110 East 42nd St, 7th Floor
New York, NY 10017
E-mail: editorialsupport@review.com

Published in the United States by Penguin Random House LLC, New York, and in Canada by Random House of Canada, a division of Penguin Random House Ltd., Toronto.

ISBN: 978-0-525-57042-4
ISSN: 2693-678X

Editor: Selena Coppock
Production Editors: Emma Parker, Sarah Litt
Production Artist: Gabriel Berlin
Printed in the United States of America.

10 9 8 7 6 5 4 3 2 1

Third Edition

Acknowledgments

The Princeton Review would like to give a special thanks to Anne Goldberg-Baldwin and Kevin Baldwin for their hard work on the revisions for this edition.

Contents

Get More (Free) Content at PrincetonReview.com/prep

As easy as 1·2·3

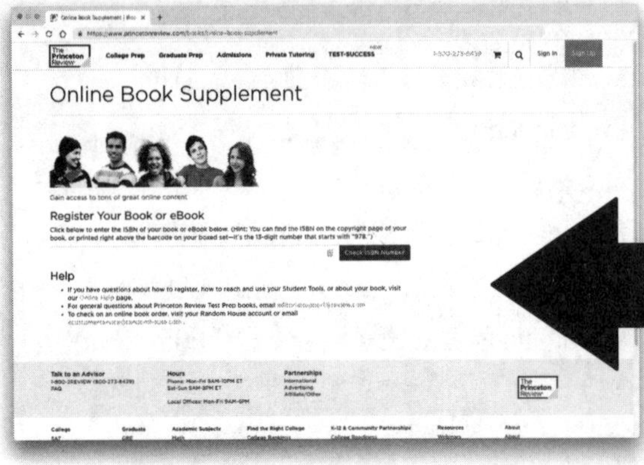

1 Go to PrincetonReview.com/prep and enter the following ISBN for your book:

9780525570424

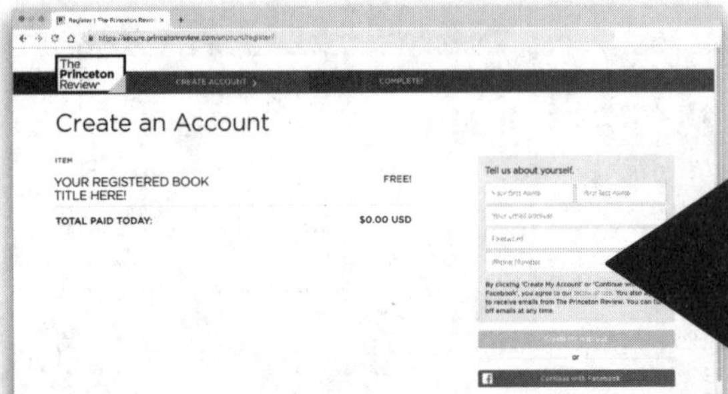

2 Answer a few simple questions to set up an exclusive Princeton Review account. *(If you already have one, you can just log in.)*

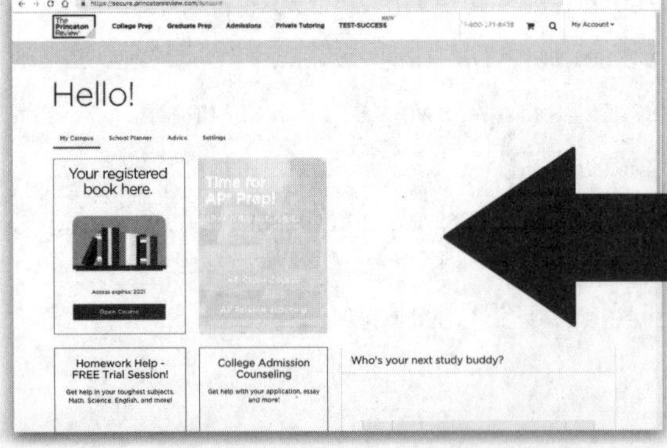

3 Enjoy access to your **FREE** content!

Once you've registered, you can...

- Get our take on any recent or pending updates to the HSPT, the COOP, or the TACHS
- Take a full-length practice PSAT, SAT, and/or ACT
- Get valuable advice about the college application process, including tips for writing a great essay and where to apply for financial aid
- If you're still choosing between colleges, use our searchable rankings of *The Best 386 Colleges* to find out more information about your dream school
- Access comprehensive study guides and additional, printable bubble sheets
- Check to see if there have been any corrections or updates to this edition

Need to report a potential **content** issue?

Contact **EditorialSupport@review.com** and include:

- full title of the book
- ISBN
- page number

Need to report a **technical** issue?

Contact **TPRStudentTech@review.com** and provide:

- your full name
- email address used to register the book
- full book title and ISBN
- Operating system (Mac/PC) and browser (Firefox, Safari, etc.)

Look for These Icons Throughout the Book

PROVEN TECHNIQUES

APPLIED STRATEGIES

WATCH OUT

ANOTHER APPROACH

GOING DEEPER

An Introduction for Parents

Congratulations on taking the first step in helping your child prepare for the HSPT, the COOP, or the TACHS! There are ways, besides using this book, in which you can increase your child's performance on these tests and improve his or her chances of admission to a given private secondary school. We've compiled a few suggestions that you can follow to help your child have a healthy and productive educational experience during the application and admission process.

THE RIGHT PERSPECTIVE

Many parents and students have the false impression that doing poorly on a standardized test means that the student has not learned mathematics or English. It's important for you and your child to know that standardized tests such as the HSPT and the COOP are not intelligence tests. Nor are they really tests of what your child has learned in primary school. While many of the problems involve mathematics or English language mechanics, what the tests really measure are *extremely narrow* skills, which bear only a passing resemblance to the skills taught in school. Certainly, knowing the basics of mathematics and English language mechanics is important and will be covered in this book, but what is just as important is for students to learn how these basic skills are tested on the HSPT and the COOP. Learning how to do well on standardized tests is a skill unto itself that many students have never learned. This explains why many students who are perfectly capable in math and English still score poorly on these tests.

It's important that your child understand what these tests truly measure. Placing too much emphasis on standardized tests can lead to one stressed-out kid! While a little anxiety can be motivational, too much anxiety can be hurtful to the learning experience.

HOW YOU CAN HELP YOUR CHILD

First and foremost, be supportive and involved. Preparing for these tests and applying to private school can be intimidating. The more you can accompany your child through the process, the more comfortable he or she will feel. Help your child learn vocabulary. Review the practice tests together and help reinforce the basic skills outlined in this book. You'll probably find it an interesting experience, and it will help you to get to know your child better as well as make the educational process fun.

Second, understand that standardized tests are very different than tests that are taken in school. The expected rules that apply to school tests may not apply here. Many students, for instance, actually hurt their scores by trying to answer every question. On timed tests like these, accuracy is much more important than speed. Students should adopt a strategy that will get them the greatest number of points, which usually means slowing down and doing fewer problems.

Finally, be understanding. Your child may not yet have learned how to take standardized tests or how to perform well on them. This is especially intimidating. Imagine how a good student who scores poorly on a standardized test must feel, despite the fact that he or she knew the material tested. Remember that test-taking is a skill that can be learned. It simply takes expert instruction, practice, and time (the first two of which we will provide in this book!).

Of course, a little cajoling is also in order. Make sure that your child is committed to spending the time necessary to work through this book thoroughly and accurately.

Encourage your child to read something every day and to look up the difficult vocabulary words. With a bit of concentrated time and effort—and a lot of support—almost all students can learn to perform well on these tests.

WHAT COUNTS AS A GOOD SCORE? WHAT ABOUT THE ADMISSIONS PROCESS?

The writers of the HSPT and the COOP do not publicly release data on the performance of everyone who takes the test, so there is no way to know how students do in relation to one another. Moreover, each school has its own policies regarding the significance of these tests. Most consider a number of factors, in addition to test scores, when making admissions decisions. There is, therefore, no way to know exactly what score will qualify a student for admission at a particular school. You should simply try to help your child perform his or her best by giving him or her all the support and attention you can. You should, however, contact the schools to which your child is interested in applying to learn more about their admissions criteria.

What Are the SSAT and the ISEE?

The SSAT and the ISEE are two other common tests used by private high schools for admissions purposes. Although this book will provide some overlap in preparation for these tests, we highly recommend that you purchase *SSAT and ISEE Prep*, which is specifically designed to prepare students for these tests.

We hope that you find this book to be a useful, accessible, and helpful tool in your preparations, and we wish you the very best of luck in your child's future success.

An Introduction for Students

HOW DO I USE THIS BOOK?

This book will review the basic concepts, question types, and problem-solving techniques you'll need to improve your score on either the HSPT or the COOP. The practice tests will help you get used to the timing and pace of the tests. The more quality time you put into studying this book, the better you'll do. Learning to take standardized tests is like learning to play any sport: the first time you try you may feel clumsy, but with practice you can always improve.

STUDY RULES

Set aside a time when you can concentrate with no distractions. It's a good idea to have a place (such as your room or a library) where you always study. Have a few sharpened pencils and a dictionary handy.

As you read each chapter, try the techniques and do all the exercises. Check your answers against the answer keys, and note any questions you get wrong. Review your errors carefully, and work through them. Remember: Now is the chance to make all the errors you want (and learn from them) so that you won't make them on the actual test!

When Should I Start to Study?

We suggest that you start studying for the test about a month before it's given. If you're starting earlier than that, we suggest that you do two things from now until the test to help improve your score: Read as much as you can and learn new vocabulary words.

Reading

Both the HSPT and the COOP—as well as almost every other standardized test you're ever going to take—place a lot of weight on reading comprehension. How do you get better at reading? By reading. The more you read, the better you'll be at it. Follow these tips to get started:

- Try to find a short article or story every day to read. Perhaps download the app of a trusted, interesting newspaper or news source and enable notifications so that you are given articles to read each day. After you read it, try to explain it to a friend or parent. By trying to explain it to someone else, you'll see how much of it you really understood.
- Pick something to read that is just a bit above your current reading level. It can be an adventure book, a weekly magazine, a newspaper, or a long-form essay or article online or in print.
- Mark any words you don't know. Try to figure out what a word means from the context (the sentence and paragraph it's in); if you can't, look up the word. Write down these words and definitions on index cards to help you remember them. Carry those cards with you everywhere—you never know when you'll have some free time to flip through your vocabulary index cards and you want to be prepared.

When You Take a Practice Test

The study plans on pages 15 and 327 advise you on when to take the practice tests. Here are some tips for getting the most out of them:

- Time yourself correctly. Use a timer, watch, or stopwatch that will make a noise, or have someone else time you. You want to get a feel for exactly how much time you'll have for each section.
- Take the practice test in one sitting, just like the real thing. It's important to build up your endurance for the actual test.
- Take the practice tests using the answer sheet with bubbles to fill in (you can find this in the back of this book or in your Student Tools online), just like on the real test. You should practice filling in your bubbles thoroughly and checking to make sure that you're filling in the correct bubble for a given question.

THE DAY OF THE EXAM

No matter how much you prepare for the test, if you don't do all of these things the day of the exam, you are likely to run out of steam and do poorly.

- Wake up refreshed from a good night's sleep.
- Eat a good breakfast.
- Arrive early to the testing session.
- Remind yourself that you do not need to solve every problem to get a good score. Pace yourself!

And one more thing: Good luck!

Chapter 1
General Test-Taking Skills

Whether you are taking the HSPT, the COOP, or the TACHS, there are certain test-taking skills that you should learn and follow. These alone, without other review, will already improve your score on any standardized test.

PACING

One of the most important test-taking skills is pacing, or how you spend your time. Of course, you want to do as many problems as you can so that you can get as high a score as possible. But on standardized tests, accuracy is more important than speed.

This may sound a little confusing: Although you should fill in every single bubble on the answer sheet, you shouldn't feel that you have to work every single problem on the test. You're better off if you slow down and work at a steady pace to make sure that you get as many problems correct as you can. Most "dumb mistakes" are caused by working too quickly, so make sure that you aren't rushing and doing sloppy work. When you have only a few minutes left, quickly fill in the remaining bubbles with your Letter Of The Day (LOTD). Why? Read on and we'll explain.

Most students think that they need to answer every problem on the test to get a great score, and most students hurt their score because they try to do too many problems. There are two reasons why you shouldn't try to do every single problem.

First, it's very hard to find time to answer every question correctly. So, naturally, people rush, then make careless errors and lose points. Almost everyone is better off *slowing down,* using the whole time to work on fewer problems and answering more of those problems correctly. Think about it this way: You'll get a higher score if you do *only 75 percent* of the problems on this test and answer them correctly than if you do all of the problems and answer about half correctly. Weird, huh?

Second, some questions are easier than others, but they're all worth the same number of points. So why waste time working on hard problems when there are easier ones you can do?

In short, if you follow this advice, your score will improve:

- **Slow down.** Make sure you work slowly and carefully enough to make sure that you get most of the problems correct. If you find that you are making lots of mistakes, slow down even more. It may feel funny, but it will help your score.
- Guess at any problems that you don't have time to try. This means that you should **absolutely fill in every bubble on your answer sheet.** You are not penalized for wrong choices, and you will probably get a few extra points by random chance.
- If you find that a problem is too hard or isn't making sense, **skip it and go on to an easier one.** You can always go back if you have time. If you don't, you're better off making your best guess.

PROCESS OF ELIMINATION

Another very important test-taking skill is Process of Elimination. This is a strategy in which you don't have to know the answer to the question to get the correct answer. Have a look at the following problem.

1 **What is the capital of Malawi?**

A Washington

B Paris

C Tokyo

D London

E Lilongwe

(Don't worry—you won't see any questions like this on your test. It's just an example.)

How did you know the answer was (E)? Because you knew that it couldn't be (A), (B), (C), or (D). That's Process of Elimination. When you are solving a problem, always cross off the choices you know are wrong, for whatever reason. Especially on the English and reading comprehension sections of the test, you'll often find that you can cross off every answer except one—the right one! Even if you can't always narrow the choices down to only one, you will certainly cross off a few choices and improve your chances of guessing correctly. **Using Process of Elimination whenever you need to will improve your chances of getting the correct answer.**

BALLPARKING

In mathematics sections, another great tool is Ballparking. This means "take a guess and see which answers are in the ballpark." This can help you save time and make a good guess when you don't know or don't have time to figure out the correct answer.

Have a look at the following problem:

2 What is $\frac{1}{2}$ of 1022?

A 51

B 52

C 511

D 512

Before you try to solve this, look at the answer choices. Which ones are in the ballpark? Certainly not (A) and (B). These can be eliminated. If you're out of time or have a hard time solving the problem, you can now guess between (C) and (D).

If you can eliminate choices for any reason, you improve your odds by making a correct guess, and you will improve your chances of getting the right answer.

Chapter 2
Vocabulary

VOCABULARY

Having a good vocabulary will not only help you better understand what you read, but it will help you understand the world around you. As you get older, a broad vocabulary will help you prepare for college and beyond. You should also learn the meanings of words that you come across in school or in your readings that you don't know. Here are some pointers for using vocabulary.

- Every time you find an unfamiliar word, write the word on the front of an index card and write its definition and a sample sentence on the back. Then quiz yourself to practice memorizing the meanings of your words. Remember to include a sample sentence—it's easier to learn words in context.
- Pick five words each day and use them every chance you get. Your friends may think you are a little strange when you walk around saying things like, "*Bob's Burgers* was an unusually mediocre episode last night." But you'll certainly learn those words. (By the way, mediocre means "of moderate or low quality.")

VOCABULARY YOU SHOULD KNOW

Ab through An

Abandon
Abbreviation
Abdicate
Abhor
Abrupt
Abundant
Abyss
Acclaimed
Accord
Acknowledge
Acute
Adamant
Adapt
Adept
Adhesive
Admire
Admonish
Adversary
Affiliation
Agenda
Aggrandize
Aggravate
Aggregate
Agile
Ail
Aimless
Akin
Alarmed
Allege
Aloof
Alter
Altruism
Ambiguous
Ambivalent
Ameliorate
Amiable
Amorphous
Analyze
Ancient
Androgynous
Anguish
Animosity
Annex

An through Ca

Antagonistic
Antipathy
Anxious
Apprehension
Approximate
Arbitrary
Arid
Ascertain
Aspect
Aspiration
Assail
Assent
Assert
Assess
Assured
Astonish
Astute
Audible
Auspicious
Austere
Authentic
Authoritative
Banal
Barrage
Barren
Barrier
Bashful
Bastion
Belligerent
Bemoan
Benevolent
Benign
Bequest
Betray
Bewilder
Biased
Blatant
Blunt
Bombastic
Brash
Brazen
Brittle
Candid
Capricious

Ca through Cu

Cascade
Cater
Cautious
Censor
Chagrin
Chasm
Chronic
Chronicle
Coalesce
Coerce
Commodities
Compassion
Compel
Competent
Composure
Comprehensive
Conceal
Concise
Condemn
Condescending
Condone
Confer
Confine
Conform
Confound
Congenial
Conniving
Consensus
Conspicuous
Consume
Contemplation
Contented
Contradiction
Contrite
Controversial
Conventional
Cordial
Corpulent
Counsel
Counterfeit
Credible
Creed
Crucial
Cunning

Da through Dr

Dawdle
Debate
Debt
Deceive
Decline
Decree
Defensive
Defiant
Deficient
Deft
Dejection
Deliberate
Delicate
Depict
Despair
Desolate
Detest
Detrimental
Deviate
Devotion
Differentiate
Dignity
Dilute
Disavow
Discreet
Disgraced
Dismayed
Disparage
Dispel
Disperse
Display
Disputed
Dissect
Distasteful
Distort
Diversity
Docile
Domestic
Dominate
Dormant
Doubtful
Drastic
Dread
Drenched

Du through Fl

Dubious
Duration
Eager
Economize
Egotist
Egress
Elegant
Elegy
Elongate
Eloquent
Embodiment
Embryonic
Emphasize
Endeavor
Enigma
Entrust
Envy
Ephemeral
Epitome
Equity
Equivalent
Eradicate
Erratic
Esoteric
Essential
Esteem
Euphemism
Evacuate
Evade
Exalt
Exasperate
Excavate
Excel
Exemplify
Exhilarating
Exile
Exquisite
Fatigue
Feasible
Feeble
Feign
Fickle
Flaccid
Flatter

Fl through Hi

Fleeting
Flotsam
Flourish
Fluctuate
Foolhardy
Foreseen
Forge
Formulate
Fortunate
Foster
Fragile
Frank
Frugal
Fundamental
Furious
Gap
Generous
Genial
Genuine
Germane
Glean
Glint
Graceful
Gratified
Grievances
Gullible
Haphazard
Hardship
Extend
Extent
Extinct
Extol
Extravagant
Facet
Fallacy
Fallow
Falter
Fathom
Feisty
Hasten
Haughty
Hazard
Hesitate
Hideous

Hi through Le

Hinder
Hoard
Homely
Ignoble
Illuminate
Illustrate
Immaculate
Impasse
Imply
Impulsive
Inane
Incident
Incidental
Incision
Incisive
Incite
Indifferent
Indignant
Infiltrate
Ingenuity
Ingress
Inhabit
Initial
Innate
Innocuous
Innovate
Inquiry
Insight
Insinuate
Insipid
Insolent
Integrity
Integrate
Intermission
Intricate
Inundate
Invoke
Irate
Jeer
Jest
Jubilant
Justify
Keen
Kinetic
Lament
Laudatory
Lavish
Legacy

Le through Om

Legend
Legitimate
Lenient
Liberate
Limber
Linger
Lofty
Lucrative
Luminous
Lure
Malicious
Meager
Meander
Meddle
Menace
Mentor
Merge
Meticulous
Mimic
Mirage
Misery
Model (adjective)
Modify
Molten
Moral
Morose
Muddled
Mundane
Mystify
Myth
Nag
Navigate
Negate
Neglect
Noncommittal
Nostalgic
Notorious
Novel
Novice
Noxious
Null
Obscure
Obstacle
Obstinate
Obstruct
Obtuse
Occupy
Ominous

Om through Re

Omit
Opaque
Optimistic
Opulent
Ostentatious
Overbearing
Overt
Pacify
Pact
Palpable
Paltry
Parody
Parsimonious
Particle
Partisan
Patron
Peak
Permeate
Perpetuate
Perplexed
Persevere
Persist
Pragmatic
Precise
Predicament
Prediction
Predominate
Prejudiced
Presume
Pretentious
Prevalent
Primary
Pristine
Prominent
Prone
Prophesy
Prototype
Provoke
Prudent
Pungent
Puny
Puzzled
Ratify
Ravenous
Recalcitrant
Reckless
Refute
Reject

Re through Ro

Reluctant
Reminisce
Remote
Rendezvous
Renounce
Renown
Personify
Pervasive
Pessimistic
Petty
Pigment
Pilfer
Pinnacle
Pious
Placate
Plausible
Plea
Plight
Plunder
Pompous
Porous
Replenish
Replete
Replica
Reprehensible
Repress
Reprimand
Reproach
Repudiate
Repugnant
Reservations (about something)
Residual
Resilience
Restore
Resume
Reticent
Reveal
Revere
Reverent
Robust
Rouse
Routine

Ru through Ta

Rue
Ruminate
Ruse
Rustic
Ruthless
Salvage
Satire
Savor
Scant
Scarce
Scorn
Seclude
Sedate
Seldom
Sequence
Shrewd
Simulate
Sincere
Sinister
Solemn
Solitary
Somber
Soothe
Specific
Speck
Spirited
Spontaneous
Sporadic
Stagnate
Stature
Steadfast
Stringent
Subside
Succinct
Sullied
Superb
Superfluous
Suppose
Surrogate
Tact
Tangible
Taper

Ta through Za

Task
Taunt
Tenacious
Terse
Testify to
Thrivc
Thwart
Timid
Tiresome
Toil
Torment
Tragedy
Trifle
Trite
Ultimate
Uncouth
Undermine
Unique
Unruly
Uproot
Utilitarian
Utilize
Vacillate
Vend
Veneration
Versatile
Vibrant
Viewpoint
Vigilant
Vigorous
Vivacious
Vivid
Voracious
Vow
Voyage
Wane
Wax (verb)
Weary
Wily
Wrath
Writhe
Zany

Part I
Cracking the HSPT

Chapter 3
What Is the HSPT?

The High School Placement Test (HSPT) is a 2 1/2 hour, five-section test designed to help Catholic high schools make admissions decisions. Your score of 200 to 800 will be based on how many of the 298 questions you get right. The HSPT is fairly vocabulary-intensive, so concentrate on Chapter 2 and begin learning vocabulary as soon as possible. The test changes from year to year, so the information presented in this book is the most accurate for the year it was printed. When this book went to press, STS (Scholasic Testing Service, Inc.) announced that the HSPT could be taken as a web-based test starting in the fall of 2020. For more information about this, visit **ststesting.com**.

There are two types of HSPT exams: closed and open. The closed exam is administered by the school but scored by Scholastic Testing Service, Inc. (STS). Those scores are used in computing nationwide percentiles. The open exam is administered and scored by the school, so STS does not deal with student results.

Along with the basic HSPT, you may be offered an optional test in Catholic religion, science, or mechanical aptitude, depending on the type of school to which you are applying. The score on these optional tests does not count toward your HSPT score, and very few schools ask for them, so we won't cover these areas in this book.

Here is the format of the HSPT:

- Verbal skills (16 minutes)
- Quantitative skills (30 minutes)
- Reading comprehension and vocabulary (25 minutes)
- Mathematics (45 minutes)
- Language (25 minutes)

Be sure to review Chapter 1 of this book ("General Test-Taking Skills") to learn the basic techniques that will help you score high on HSPT—and most any standardized test. Also review "An Introduction for Students" (page xi) for basic strategy on how to approach this book. Chapters 4 through 8 will take you through each of the test sections in detail and will review the types of problems you'll likely see. Make sure to take the practice tests in the back of the book and study the explanations to find out which areas you need to review the most to earn a high score on the HSPT. Good luck!

HSPT Study Plan

If you are taking the HSPT, follow this nine-session study plan.

Session 1

- Before you do anything else, besides reading this introduction, take the first practice HSPT in this book. Correct it and pay particularly close attention to your mistakes.
- Write down anything you notice that you had difficulty with, such as "triangle problems." This will help you remember to pay extra attention to those concepts when you study those chapters.
- If you got more than 25% incorrect in any section, tell yourself to slow down and do fewer problems. You are much better off doing only 75% of the questions and getting more of them correct than doing all of the problems and getting many of them wrong.

Session 2

- Read Chapter 1: General Test-Taking Skills

Session 3

- Read Chapter 3: What Is the HSPT?
- Read Chapter 2: Vocabulary

Session 4

- Read Chapter 4: Verbal Skills

Session 5

- Read Chapter 5: Quantitative Skills

Session 6

- Read Chapter 6: Reading Comprehension and Vocabulary

Session 7

- Read Chapter 7: Mathematics

Session 8

- Read Chapter 8: Language Skills

Session 9

- Take the second practice HSPT test in this book. Correct the test, "ooh" and "ahh" over how much your score improved, and then review the concepts in the book for the questions you answered incorrectly.
- Use any additional days before the test to continue to review the concepts and test-taking techniques covered in the book.

Chapter 4
Verbal Skills

WHICH ONE IS NOT LIKE THE OTHERS?

Several of the questions in the verbal skills section of the HSPT will give you four words and ask you which word does not belong with the other words. Here's a typical example:

1. Which word does *not* belong with the others?

a. pencil
b. chalk
c. ruler
d. pen

Here's How to Crack It

All of the choices will usually have something to do with each other—in this case, each of these objects is something that you might use at school. So we have to find something else that three of these words have in common. Then we'll know which one of them is the one that does *not* belong.

The best way to approach this is to make a sentence. Think of a sentence that will tell us what three of the words have in common.

A pencil, a pen, and chalk are all things that you can write with.

A ruler, however, is not something that you can write with. Therefore, the answer is (C).

Common Tricks

In the above example, the words all seemed related because they were all things you might find at school. We had to make a more exact sentence to figure out which one did not belong. There are two other common ways that a word will seem like it belongs with the others, even when it doesn't.

Read the following question:

2. Which word does *not* belong with the others?

a. Shovel
b. Hammer
c. Tool
d. Screwdriver

Here's How to Crack It

What kind of sentence could you make for this problem?

A shovel, a hammer, and a screwdriver are all types of tools.

In this case, tool is related to shovel, hammer, and screwdriver because these objects are all types of tools. However, it does not belong with the others because the words *shovel, hammer,* and *screwdriver* are names for tools; the word tool is the name of a category, not a name for a tool. This makes (C) the best answer.

Now try this one:

3. Which word does *not* belong with the others?

a. trunk
b. tree
c. branch
d. leaf

Here's How to Crack It

What kind of sentence could you make for this question?

A branch, a leaf, and a trunk are all parts of a tree.

All of the words in this problem seem to fit together because they are all related to trees. However, the words *branch, leaf,* and *trunk* all refer to parts of a tree; the word tree does not refer to a part of a tree. Therefore, the answer is (B).

That's all there is to it!

ANALOGIES

What Is an Analogy?

An analogy is just a fancy word that means two pairs of objects have the same relationship. For instance kittens/cat and puppies/dog are analogies. Each pair of words has the same relationship: Kittens are baby cats, just as puppies are baby dogs. On the HSPT, the way you express this analogy is by saying "Cat is to kittens as dog is to puppies."

Your job will be to complete the analogy to make a sentence like the one above. Here's an example of how an analogy question will appear on the HSPT.

4. Apple is to fruit as beef is to

a. restaurant
b. vegetable
c. meat
d. cow

Here's How to Crack It

Make a Sentence

Just as with the last question type, the best way to figure out the relationship between words is to make a sentence. In this case, to find the relationship between the first two words, we should make a sentence with them. Then we can try to use that same sentence for each of the answer choices to see which one fits best.

Step 1: Cross out the words "is to" and "as."

Step 2: Make a sentence using the first two words in the problem. In this case, we can make the sentence "An apple is a kind of fruit."

Step 3: Try using the same sentence with each of the answer choices and see which one works best. So you'd say, "Beef is a kind of ____."

Is beef a kind of restaurant? No, so cross off A. Is beef a kind of vegetable? No, so cross off (B). Is beef a kind of meat? Yes. Is beef a kind of cow? No, so cross off (D).

The best answer is (C). It is the only choice that works with the sentence we made to define the words *apple* and *fruit.*

Making Good Sentences

Of course, some sentences you can make will be more helpful than others. If we had said, "Apple and fruit both have five letters," that wouldn't have been very useful to us in solving the problem.

When you make a sentence for the first two words, try to use one word to define the other. For example, the sentence "An apple is a kind of fruit" defines apple.

HSPT Analogy Exercise

Answers can be found in Chapter 9.

Try making sentences from the following words.

mansion / house ______________________________

leaf / tree ______________________________

desert / sand ______________________________

engine / automobile ______________________________

bread / baker ______________________________

brush / painter ______________________________

Synonyms and Antonyms

Other questions in the verbal skills section will ask you to identify synonyms and antonyms of words. A synonym is a word that has the same meaning as another word. Here's a trick that should help you remember: synonym = same. An antonym is a word that has the opposite (anti) meaning of another word.

Here's an example of a synonym problem.

5. Hinder most nearly means

a. look up
b. play
c. hold back
d. protect

Here's How to Crack It

If you know the meaning of the word:

Step 1: Cover the answer choices with your hand. If you read the answer choices first, you might get confused.

Step 2: State what the word means to you in your own words.

Step 3: Uncover the answer choices and see which choice most closely matches what you said.

In this case, let's cover up the answer choices. In your own words, what does the word *hinder* mean? Maybe you came up with something like "stop" or "prevent." Now uncover the answer choices and see which best matches your word. Chances are good that you came up with something very close to "hold back"; therefore, the answer is (C).

If you "sort of" know what the word means:

Maybe you have a sense of what the word means but can't quite put your finger on it. Perhaps you can think of a saying that uses the word—even if you're not sure what the word means—and you should still be able to get the right answer or at least come up with a good guess. If either of these is the case, use the "side of the fence" trick. This is when you ask yourself whether the word is a positive word or a negative word. If the word is positive, you can eliminate any words that are not positive. If the word is negative, you can eliminate any words that are not negative.

Take a look at the following example.

6. Pretentious most nearly means

a. intelligent
b. arrogant
c. inventive
d. hidden

Here's How to Crack It

If you have a sense of the word *pretentious*—perhaps you've heard someone criticized as a really pretentious person—you may know that pretentious is a bad thing to be. It's a negative word. Since this question is asking for a synonym of the word *pretentious*, we know that the correct answer has to be another negative word.

Even if we don't know what *pretentious* means, we know that (A) and (C) are positive words, so they can be eliminated. Choice (D) really isn't positive or negative. If you know that (B) is also a negative word, you should guess (B), which is the correct answer.

If you know the meaning of the word, remember the steps we just went over:

Step 1: Cover the answer choices with your hand. If you read all the answer choices first, you might get confused.

Step 2: State what the word means to you in your own words.

Step 3: Uncover the answer choices and see which choice most closely matches what you said.

If you "sort of" know what the word means:

Maybe you have a sense of what the word means but can't quite put your finger on it. Perhaps you can think of a saying that uses the word—even if you're not sure what the word means—and you should still be able to get the right answer or at least come up with a good guess. If either of these is the case, use the "side of the fence" trick. This is when you ask yourself whether the word is a positive word or a negative word. If the word is positive, you can eliminate any words that are not positive. If the word is negative, you can eliminate any words that are not negative.

Try the following example:

7. Courteous means the opposite of

a. honest
b. unconcerned
c. rude
d. jealous

Here's How to Crack It

If you have a sense of the word *courteous*, you may know that it's a positive word. Since this question is asking us for an antonym, we know that the correct answer has to be a negative word.

Even if we don't know what the word *courteous* means, we know that (A) is another positive word, so eliminate it. Remember that we're looking for the opposite. Choice (B) really isn't positive or negative, so it probably isn't the answer. If you can get no further with this problem, you can take a great guess between (C) and (D). (In fact, the answer is (C).)

What if you have no idea what a word means?

Regardless of whether it's a synonym or antonym question, if you really have no idea what the word means, take your best guess and move on to the next question. Your time will be better spent on other problems in this section.

TRUE OR FALSE QUESTIONS

For a true or false question, you will be asked to read two sentences that describe people, places, or things. The third sentence will be something that we might or might not know for sure. Your job is to figure out whether the final sentence is true, false, or uncertain.

What Do "True," "False," and "Uncertain" Mean?

Look at these two statements.

- Jason scored a 92 on his math test.
- Lisa scored a 96 on her math test.

There are many things you might assume to be true, given these two statements. Here are some of them:

- Lisa is a better student than Jason.
- Lisa knows math better than Jason does.
- Lisa and Jason are in the same math class.

However, none of these choices really has to be true. Sure, they might be true, but we don't really know. These statements are all uncertain, since we can't know 100% that they are true or false. Lisa might not be a better student than Jason—maybe she just got lucky on this test, or maybe in most other subjects she scores much worse than Jason. Lisa might not be better at math—maybe she's just taking an easier math class than Jason is taking. We don't know whether they're in the same math class. We don't even know whether they're in the same grade or the same school! We can't make any assumptions on these questions.

What is something that we are certain is *true* given the information above? Lisa scored higher on her math test than Jason scored on his math test.

And what is something we are certain is *false* given the information above? Lisa scored lower on her math test than Jason scored on his math test.

How True or False Questions Appear on the HSPT

Read the following question.

8. Mary collected more shells than Carrie and Tim. Tim collected more shells than Tracy. Mary collected more shells than Tracy. If the first two statements are true, then the third is

a. True
b. False
c. Uncertain

Here's How to Crack It

The best way to approach true or false questions is to make a diagram.

Let's make a diagram showing who has more shells, putting those with the most shells to the left.

We know that Mary collected more shells than Carrie and Tim. We can draw this:

M > C + Tim

We also know that Tim collected more than Tracy. So we can add this fact to our diagram

M > C + Tim
Tim > Tracy

Since we know that Mary has more than Tim, and that Tim has more than Tracy, we know that Mary has more than Tracy, so the third statement is true.

Now try this one:

9. Mary collected more shells than Carrie and Tim. Tim collected fewer shells than Tracy. Mary collected more shells than Tracy. If the first two statements are true, then the third is

a. True
b. False
c. Uncertain

Here's How to Crack It

We can diagram the first sentence of this question the same way as before:

M > C + Tim

We now add the second sentence, which says that Tracy has more shells than Tim:

M > C + Tim
Tracy > Tim

We know that Mary has more than Carrie and Tim, and that Tracy has more than Tim, but we don't know whether Mary or Tracy has more shells. We only know that they each have more than Tim does. Therefore, the third statement is **uncertain**.

Now try some sample problems.

HSPT Verbal Skills Exercise

Answers can be found in Chapter 9.

1. Which word does *not* belong with the others?

a. sad
b. lonely
c. feeling
d. upset

2. Which word does *not* belong with the others?

a. oregano
b. parsley
c. spice
d. pepper

3. Librarian is to library as curator is to

a. museum
b. studio
c. mall
d. workshop

4. Prejudice is to unbiased as worry is to

a. adamant
b. active
c. blithe
d. unconcerned

5. Revolve most nearly means

a. push against
b. go forward
c. leave behind
d. turn around

6. Fortify means the *opposite* of

a. load
b. weaken
c. sail
d. clean

7. Bizarre most nearly means

a. lonely
b. unable
c. odd
d. able

8. Opaque means the *opposite* of

a. dirty
b. clear
c. normal
d. late

9. Alex bought more apples than Barry and Marcia. Marcia bought more apples than Elisa and Kim. Alex bought more apples than Kim. If the first two statements are true, then the third is

a. True
b. False
c. Uncertain

10. Alex bought more apples than Barry. Barry bought more apples than Marcia and Elisa. Elisa bought more apples than Alex. If the first two statements are true, then the third is

a. True
b. False
c. Uncertain

11. Alex bought more apples than Barry and Marcia. Elisa bought more apples than Marcia. Alex bought more apples than Elisa. If the first two statements are true, then the third is

a. True
b. False
c. Uncertain

Chapter 5
Quantitative Skills

Most of the questions in this section require you to do some amount of arithmetic. Let's take a moment to review the basics.

MATH VOCABULARY

Term	Definitions	Examples
integer	any number that does not contain either a fraction or a decimal	–4, –1, 0, 9, 15
positive number	any number greater than zero	$\frac{1}{2}$, 1, 4, 101
negative number	any number less than zero	$-\frac{1}{2}$, –1, –4, –101
even number	any number that is evenly divisible by two	–2, 0, 2, 8, 24 (*Note:* 0 is even)
odd number	any number that is not evenly divisible by two	–1, 1, 5, 35
prime number	any number that is evenly divisible only by one and itself	2, 3, 5, 7, 11, 13 (*Note:* 1 is not a prime number)
sum	the result of addition	The sum of 6 and 2 is 8.
difference	the result of subtraction	The difference between 6 and 4 is 2.
product	the result of multiplication	The product of 3 and 4 is 12.

HSPT Math Vocabulary Exercise

Answers can be found in Chapter 9.

1. **How many integers are there between –4 and 5?**

2. **How many positive integers are there between –4 and 5?**

3. **What is the sum of 6, 7, and 8?**

4. **What is the product of 2, 4, and 8?**

ORDER OF OPERATIONS

How would you do the following problem?

$$4 + 5 \times 3 - (2 + 1)$$

Whenever you have a problem such as this, remember the rule.

Please **E**xcuse **M**y **D**ear **A**unt **S**ally

Believe it or not, this sentence tells you the order in which you should solve the above problem. This stands for:

Parentheses
Exponents
Multiplication and **D**ivision (from left to right)
Addition and **S**ubtraction (from left to right)

Therefore, we need to solve the parentheses first.

$$4 + 5 \times 3 - (2 + 1)$$

becomes

$$4 + 5 \times 3 - 3$$

Next, we do multiplication and division to get

$$4 + 15 - 3$$

Finally, we add and subtract to get our final answer of 16.

HSPT Order of Operations Exercise

Answers can be found in Chapter 9.

1. $15 - 5 + 3 =$ ____

2. $15 - 2 \times 3 =$ ____

3. $2 \times (2 + 3) - 5 =$ ____

4. $20 + 3 \times 5 + 10 =$ ____

5. $(3 + 6) \times 3 \times 4 =$ ____

FRACTIONS

A fraction is just another way of representing division. For instance, $\frac{2}{5}$ actually means two divided by five (which is 0.4 as a decimal). Another way to think of this is to imagine a pie cut into five pieces: $\frac{2}{5}$ means two out of the five pieces. The parts of the fraction are called the numerator and the denominator. The numerator is the number on top; the denominator is the number on the bottom.

$$\frac{\text{numerator}}{\text{denominator}}$$

Reducing Fractions

Often you'll need to reduce your fractions after you have made a calculation. This means that you want to make the numbers as small as possible. To reduce a fraction, simply divide top and bottom by the same number. Don't spend too long trying to figure out the best number to divide by; use 2, 3, or 5, and keep dividing until you can't divide anymore.

For example, if you have the fraction $\frac{42}{18}$, you can divide the top and the bottom each by 3 to get $\frac{14}{6}$. Then you can divide top and bottom by 2 and get $\frac{7}{3}$. It can't be reduced any further than this, so this is your final answer.

Adding and Subtracting Fractions

To add or subtract fractions, the fractions have to have a common denominator. This means that they have to have the same number on the bottom (the denominators need to be the same). If the fractions already have a common denominator, you can add or subtract them by adding or subtracting the numbers on top.

$$\frac{4}{7}+\frac{2}{7}=\frac{6}{7}$$

If the fractions do not have a common denominator, the easiest way to add or subtract them is to use the Bowtie.

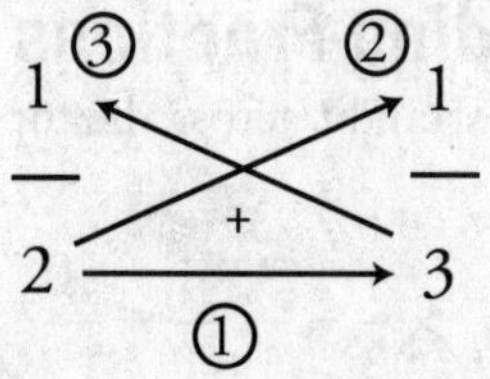

Step 1: Multiply the two bottom numbers together. Their product goes on the bottom of your two new fractions.

Step 2: Multiply diagonally from the bottom left to the top right. Write this product on the top right.

Step 3: Multiply diagonally from the bottom right to the top left. Write this product on the top left.

See—it looks like a bowtie! Now you have two fractions with a common denominator, and you can add or subtract them.

For example:

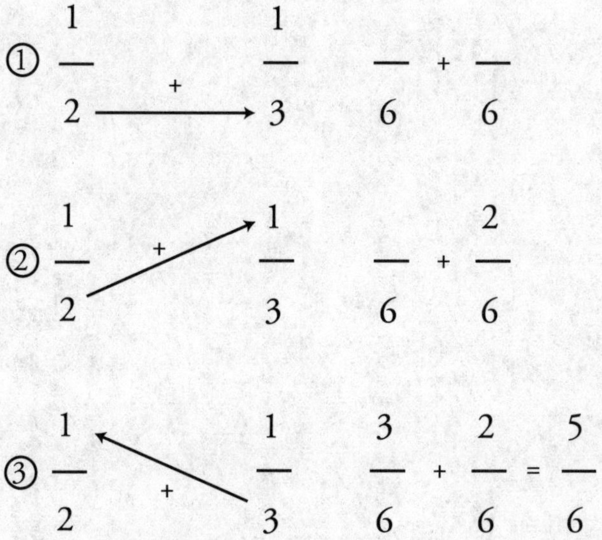

Multiplying and Dividing Fractions

To multiply fractions, multiply straight across the top and bottom.

$$\frac{3}{5} \times \frac{1}{3} = \frac{3 \times 1}{5 \times 3} = \frac{3}{15}$$

To divide fractions, flip the second fraction and multiply.

$$\frac{3}{5} \div \frac{1}{3} = \frac{3 \times 3}{5 \times 1} = \frac{9}{5}$$

HSPT Fractions Exercise

Answers can be found in Chapter 9.

1. Reduce $\frac{12}{60}$ = ____

2. $\frac{3}{8} + \frac{2}{3} =$ ____

3. $\frac{3}{4} - \frac{2}{3} =$ ____

4. $\frac{3}{4} \times \frac{3}{2} =$ ____

5. $\frac{1}{3} \div \frac{1}{2} =$ ____

DECIMALS

Remember that decimals are just another way of writing fractions. Be sure to know the names of all the decimal places.

3 4 . 8 5 7

3 = tens, 4 = units, 8 = tenths, 5 = hundredths, 7 = thousandths

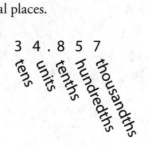

Adding Decimals

To add decimals, just line up the decimal places and add.

$$\begin{array}{r} 24.05 \\ +12.23 \\ \hline 36.28 \end{array}$$

Subtracting Decimals

To subtract decimals, just line up the decimal places and subtract.

$$\begin{array}{r} 24.05 \\ -\ 12.23 \\ \hline 11.82 \end{array}$$

Multiplying Decimals

To multiply decimals, count the total number of digits to the right of the decimal point in the numbers you are multiplying. Then multiply the numbers without the decimal points. Once you have your answer, add all of the decimal places you removed from the first two numbers back into the new number.

To solve 0.2×3.4, remove two decimal places and multiply.

$$\begin{array}{r} 34 \\ \times\ 2 \\ \hline 68 \end{array}$$

Now put back the two decimal places we removed to get 0.68.

Dividing Decimals

To divide decimals, move the decimal places in both numbers the same number of places to the right until you are working with only integers. But unlike when you're multiplying decimals, you don't have to put the decimals back in when you're dividing.

$$3.4 \div 0.2 = 34 \div 2 = 17$$

Converting Decimals to Fractions

Remember that multiplying by 10 means the same thing as moving the decimal point one place to the right, and dividing by 10 means the same thing as moving the decimal points one place to the left.

$$9 \div 10 = \frac{9}{10} = 0.9$$

$$5 \div 100 = \frac{5}{100} = 0.05$$

This is why the first place to the right of the decimal is called "tenths" and the second place to the right is called "hundredths." Nine-tenths = 0.9 = $\frac{9}{10}$. Five-hundredths = 0.05 = $\frac{5}{100}$. So to convert a decimal to a fraction, all you need to do is change the numbers after the decimal to their fraction form.

$$5.24 = 5 + \frac{2}{10} + \frac{4}{100}$$

HSPT Decimals Exercise

Answers can be found in Chapter 9.

1. **2.43 + 5.25 =** ____

2. **5.75 – 3.12 =** ____

3. **1.5 × 3 =** ____

4. **2.5 × 0.5 =** ____

5. **2.5 ÷ 0.5 =** ____

6. **What is 6.32 in fraction form?** ____

EXPONENTS, SCIENTIFIC NOTATION, AND SQUARE ROOTS

Exponents are just a short way of writing multiplication. 3^2 means to multiply two 3s together: 3×3. Likewise, 3^4 means to multiply four 3s together: $3 \times 3 \times 3 \times 3$. On the HSPT you will not see very complex exponents, so the best way to solve them is to write them out longhand and multiply.

Scientific notation is also a short way of writing big numbers. Whenever you see a number such as 3.44×10^2, this means that you should move the decimal point to the right the same number of places as the exponent to the right of the 10. In this case, you move the decimal two places to the right (10^2), and you get 344. Likewise, 4.355×10^2 is just another way of writing 435.5.

Square root is just the opposite of raising a number to the second power. $\sqrt{4} = 2$, since $2^2 = 4$. On the HSPT you will not have very big square roots. Your best bet is simply to memorize these common ones.

Since $2^2 = 4$, $\sqrt{4} = 2$

Since $3^2 = 9$, $\sqrt{9} = 3$

Since $4^2 = 16$, $\sqrt{16} = 4$

Since $5^2 = 25$, $\sqrt{25} = 5$

HSPT Exponents, Scientific Notation, and Square Roots Exercise

Answers can be found in Chapter 9.

1. $4^3 =$ ____
2. $2^4 =$ ____
3. $3.4 \times 10^2 =$ ____
4. $5.23 \times 10^4 =$ ____
5. $\sqrt{4} + \sqrt{16} =$ ____

SOLVE FOR *X*

To solve an equation, you want to get the variable (the x) on one side of the equation and put everything else on the other side.

To get only the variable on one side, follow these two steps.

Step 1: Move elements around using addition and subtraction. Put the variables on one side of the equation and numbers on the other. As long as you do the same operation on both sides of the equal sign, you aren't changing the value of the variable.

Step 2: Divide both sides of the equation by the coefficient, which is the number in front of the variable. If that number is a fraction, multiply everything by the denominator.

For example:

$$3x + 5 = 17$$

Subtract 5 from each side.

$$\begin{array}{rcr} 3x + 5 & = & 17 \\ -5 & = & -5 \\ \hline 3x & = & 12 \end{array}$$

Divide 3 from each side

$$\begin{array}{rcr} 3x & = & 12 \\ \div 3 & = & \div 3 \\ \hline x & = & 4 \end{array}$$

Always remember the rule of equations: *Whatever you do to one side of the equation, you must also do to the other side.*

HSPT Solve for *x* Exercise

Answers can be found in Chapter 9.

1. **If $4x = 20$ then $x =$** ____

2. **If $4x + 3 = 31$ then $x =$** ____

3. **If $6 = 8x + 4$ then $x =$** ____

4. **If $4x - 3 = 3x$ then $x =$** ____

PERCENT TRANSLATION

Everyone knows how easy it is to make a simple mistake on a percent problem. Should you write "5% of 100" as $\frac{5}{100}$ or as $\frac{100}{5}$ or as something else? To make sure to avoid silly mistakes, here's a foolproof method for solving percent questions.

Any percent problem can be translated word for word into an equation if you know the mathematical equivalent of the English words. For instance, "percent" means the same thing as "divided by 100," and "of" means the same thing as "multiply." Therefore, "5% of 100" can be written as $\frac{5}{100} \times 100$, which equals 5.

The chart below shows you the mathematical translation of the English words you will probably see. To solve any percent question, read the problem back to yourself and replace the words on the left side of the chart with the math symbols on the right. Then you can easily solve.

Percent	$\div$ 100
Of	$\times$
What	*x* (or any variable)
Is, Are, Equals	=

Here are two examples:

20% of 50 is?

20% of 50

↓ ↓ ↓

$$\frac{20}{100} \times 50$$

5 is what percent of 80?

5 is what percent of 80

↓ ↓ ↙ ↙ ↙

$$5 = \frac{x}{100} \times 80$$

$$5 = \frac{x}{100} \times 80$$

HSPT Percent Translation Exercise

Answers can be found in Chapter 9.

1. **30% of 60 =** ____

2. **40% of 200 =** ____

3. **15 is what percent of 60?** ____

4. **What is 25% of 10% of 200?** ____

COMPUTATION QUESTIONS

Several of the questions on the HSPT will ask you to perform basic arithmetic computations. Don't worry about variables here; you won't see any—just addition, subtraction, multiplication, and division. The trick here is to work carefully and in bite-size pieces to make sure that you don't make any careless errors.

Here's an example of a computation question.

10. What number is 4 more than $\frac{1}{4}$ of 32?

a. 6
b. 8
c. 10
d. 12

Here's How to Crack It

The most common mistakes in computation problems stem from trying to do the whole problem at once. Let's just take it one step at a time—in bite-size pieces—and get the right answer. First, let's solve $\frac{1}{4}$ of 32. $\frac{1}{4}$ of 32 is 8. So now the question reads: What number is 4 more than 8? 4 + 8 = 12. The answer is (D)

If you are careful and have mastered basic arithmetic, these questions shouldn't give you too much trouble.

HSPT Computation Exercise

Answers can be found in Chapter 9.

1. **What is three times the difference of 75 and 30?** ____

2. **What is $\frac{1}{8}$ of the sum of 50 and 14?** ____

3. **What is 16 more than half of 30?** ____

4. **What number is 160% of 40?** ____

5. **What number is 2 more than the difference of 6^2 and 5^2?** ____

SERIES QUESTIONS

A series is a list of numbers that follow a pattern. For instance, the numbers 2, 4, 6, 8 make a series because each number is 2 more than the number before it. On the HSPT, several questions will show you a series with a blank in it and ask you to figure out what number should fill the blank. What you need to do is figure out the pattern.

To see how to solve one, let's look at the following example.

11. What number should come next in this series: 1, 5, 9, ___?

Here's How to Crack It

Between the numbers, write the number that, by performing an operation like adding, subtracting, multiplying, or dividing, takes you from the first number to the next and so on.

1 (+ 4) 5 (+ 4) 9 ___

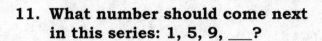

Since each number is 4 more than the previous number, the next number in the series must be 13.

Sometimes you will need to try more than one kind of operation between each pair of numbers. On more complicated problems, you may need to try subtraction, multiplication, and division.

Here's another example.

12. What number should come next in this series: 7, 5, 12, 10, 17, ___?

Here's How to Crack It

	−2		+7				−2		+7			−2
7		5		12	|	12		10		17	| 17	___

Since the series goes (– 2) then (+ 7), then the next element should be 2 less than 17, or 15.

Try this one.

13. What number should come next in this series: 2, 4, 5, 10, 11, 22, ___?

Here's How to Crack It

	×2	+1		×2	+1		×2	+1
2	4	5	5	10	11	11	22	___

This series goes (× 2) then (+ 1), so the next element should be 1 more than 22, or 23.

Sometimes the blank will be in the middle of the series rather than at the end. Follow the same technique, and double-check your answer by making sure that the number you put in the blank works with the number(s) that follow.

14. What number should fill the blank in this series: 3, 5, 10, 12, 24, ___, 52?

Here's How to Crack It

	+2	×2		+2	×2		+2	×2
3	5	10	10	12	24	24	___	52

This series goes (+2) then (× 2), so the missing number should be 2 more than 24, or 26. We can double-check this by making sure that 26 × 2 = 52, which it does.

That's all there is to series questions! Now give it a try.

HSPT Series Exercise

Answers can be found in Chapter 9.

1. **4, 8, 12, 16, 20, ___?**

2. **38, 32, 26, 20, ___?**

3. **6, 12, 16, 32, 36, 72, ___?**

4. **10, 5, 15, 10, 20, 15, ___?**

5. **7, 14, 12, 24, 22, 44, ___?**

6. **8, 16, 20, 40, ___, 88?**

7. **20, 18, 25, 23, ___, 28?**

COMPARISON PROBLEMS

The rest of the problems in this section of the HSPT will ask you to compare three values or three quantities. You may be asked to perform some simple arithmetic operations or do simple geometry. (For the geometry review, see Chapter 7.)

Here's an example of a question that asks you to compare three values.

15. Examine the following and find the best answer.

1. $\frac{6}{10}$
2. $\frac{40}{100}$
3. $\frac{9}{100}$

a. 1 > 2 > 3
b. 1 = 2 = 3
c. 2 > 1 = 3
d. 2 > 1 > 3

Here's How to Crack It

Solve for the values of (1), (2), and (3).

In this case, (1) = 0.6, (2) = 0.44, and (3) = 0.9

Once you have the values for (1), (2), and (3), carefully look at the answer choices to see which accurately represents their relationships. Use the Process of Elimination to cross off any choices that you know are wrong, and be sure to read carefully!

Since (1) is the largest, we can eliminate answers (B), (C), and (D). Therefore, (A) is the answer.

Here's another example of a question that asks you to compare three quantities.

16. Examine (A), (B), and (C) and find the best answer.

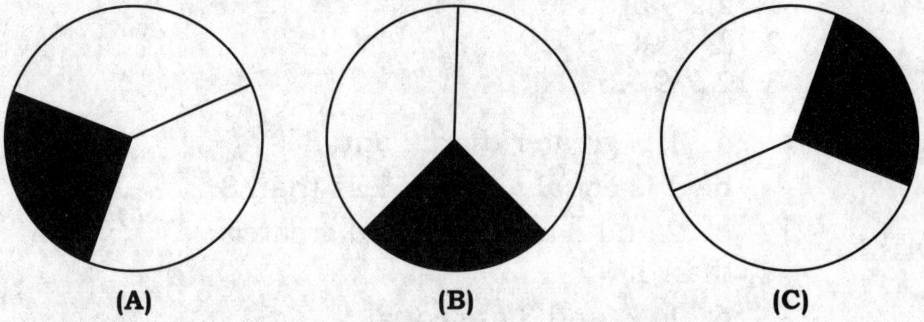

a. (A) is more shaded than (B)
b. (A) is less shaded than (B) and more shaded than (C)
c. (C) is more shaded than both (A) and (B)
d. (A), (B), and (C) are equally shaded

Here's How to Crack It

In this case, you should inspect circles A, B, and C. Figure out what the relationship is among them and use Process of Elimination to find the best choice. Since A and B are equally shaded, choices (A) and (B) can be eliminated. Since B and C are equally shaded, choice (C) can also be eliminated. Therefore, choice (D) must be the answer.

HSPT Comparison Exercise

Answers can be found in Chapter 9.

1. Examine the following and find the best answer.

1. $2(9 - 5)$
2. $(2 \times 9) - 5$
3. $2 \times 9 - 5$

a. 1 is greater than 2 and 3
b. 1 is equal to 2 and less than 3
c. 2 and 3 are equal and greater than 1
d. 1, 2, and 3 are equal

2. Examine the following and find the best answer.

1. 40% of 60
2. 60% of 40
3. 50% of 90

a. 1 is greater than 2 and 3
b. 1 is equal to 2 and less than 3
c. 2 and 3 are equal and greater than 1
d. 1, 2, and 3 are equal

3. Examine the following and find the best answer.

1. 2.3×10^2
2. 2,300
3. 2.3×10^3

a. 1 is greater than 2 and 3
b. 1 is equal to 2 and less than 3
c. 2 and 3 are equal and greater than 1
d. 1, 2, and 3 are equal

4. Examine the following and find the best answer.

1. the area of a square with side 6
2. the perimeter of a square with side 6
3. half the area of a square with side 8

a. 1 is greater than 2, which is less than 3

b. 1 is equal to 2 and less than 3

c. 2 and 3 are equal and greater than 1

d. 1, 2, and 3 are equal

5. Triangle *ABC* is isosceles. Angle *a* measures 40°. Find the best answer.

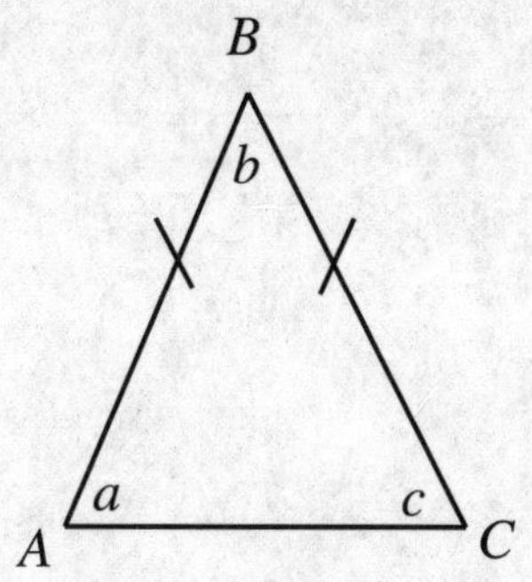

a. a is greater than $b + c$

b. a is less than $b + c$

c. a is equal to $b + c$

d. a, b, and c are all equal

Chapter 6
Reading Comprehension and Vocabulary

A WORD ABOUT TIMING

This section of the HSPT combines two very different question types: reading comprehension and reading vocabulary. How should you spend your time?

The reading vocabulary questions are very much like the synonym questions we discussed in Chapter 4. You should go through them very quickly, since you either know the word or you don't. This means you should spend the majority of your time on the reading comprehension. Slow down, take your time, and get your points on reading comprehension, because taking extra time on vocabulary probably won't help. Of your 25 minutes, the first five should be spent on the vocab, and the rest of time can be used on reading comprehension.

HOW TO THINK ABOUT READING COMPREHENSION

Reading the passages on the HSPT is different from most other kinds of reading that you will do in school. You might think that you have to read slowly enough to learn all the information in the passage. But there is much more information in the passage than you can learn in a short time, and you will be asked about only a few facts from the passage. So trying to understand all of the facts in the passage is not the best use of your time.

Most importantly, you don't get points for understanding everything in the passage. You only get points for answering questions correctly. Therefore, we're going to teach you the best strategy to get the most correct answers.

There is one more important thing to know, which works to your advantage: *The answer to every question can be found somewhere in the passage.* All you've got to do is find it. This means that you should think of reading comprehension like a treasure hunt: You need to use clues in the questions to find the answers in the passage and earn your points.

STRATEGY FOR ATTACKING READING COMPREHENSION

Step 1: Read the passage and label each paragraph. Don't try to learn every single fact in the passage; you can always go back later. It is important to only get a general idea of what the paragraph is about.

Step 2: Answer the general questions based on your paragraph labels.

Step 3: Answer the specific questions by looking back at the passage and finding the answer.

Important! In steps 2 and 3, answer your questions by using Process of Elimination. The test-writers will often try to disguise the correct answer by using different words that mean basically the same thing as the words used in the passage. You might not recognize these words right away as synonymous with the words used in the passage. Why do the test-writers do this? If they gave you the exact words straight out of the passage, that would be too easy. So your best bet is the cross off the choices that you know are wrong and pick from the choices that are left.

Now let's look at each step in more detail.

Step 1: Label Your Paragraphs

Every good treasure hunt needs a map, which will help you locate the answers in the passage. The best way to make a map is to label your paragraphs as you read. This will help you understand the main idea of the passage and at the same time make it easier to locate facts in the passage while you're reading.

After you finish each paragraph, stop for a moment and ask yourself, "What is this paragraph about?" Try to summarize the idea of this paragraph in seven or eight words, and quickly write this summary in the margin. This way, you'll have a guide to important parts of the passage when you have to answer a question.

After you have read the entire passage, take a moment and ask yourself, "What is this whole passage about?" Write a one sentence summary at the bottom of the page. This will help you answer any main idea questions you may see.

Try doing Step 1 for the following passage.

Contrary to popular belief, the first European known to lay eyes on America was not Christopher Columbus or Amerigo Vespucci, but a little-known Viking named Bjarni Herjolfsson. In the summer of 966, Bjarni sailed from Norway to Iceland, heading for the Viking settlement where his father Heriulf resided.

When he arrived in Iceland, Bjarni discovered that his father had already sold his land and estates and set out for the latest Viking settlement on the subartic island called Greenland. Discovered by an infamous murderer and criminal named

Erik the Red, Greenland lay at the limit of the known world. Dismayed, Bjarni set out for this new colony. ____________

Since the Vikings traveled without a chart or compass, it was not uncommon for them to lose their way in the unpredictable northern seas. Beset by fog, the crew lost their bearings. When the fog finally cleared, they found themselves before a land that was level and covered with woods. They traveled farther up the coast, finding more flat, wooded country. Farther north, the landscape revealed glaciers and rocky mountains. Without knowing it, Bjarni had arrived in North America. ____________

Though Bjarni realized this was an unknown land, he was no intrepid explorer. Rather, he was a practical man who had simply set out to find his father. Refusing his crew's request to go ashore, he promptly turned his bow back to sea. After four days' sailing, Bjarni landed at Herjolfsnes on the southwestern tip of Greenland, the exact place he had been seeking all along. ____________

What is this whole passage about? ____________

Your labels and passage summary should look something like this.

Paragraph 1: America was first visited by Bjarni Herjolfsson.

Paragraph 2: Herjolfsson wanted to follow his father to Greenland.

Paragraph 3: He got lost and ended up at America.

Paragraph 4: He turned around and finally reached Greenland.

Summary: How Bjarni Herjolfsson got lost and saw America before anyone else.

Now we have a good picture of the overall point of the passage, and we should be able to look back and find any details we need. So let's turn to the questions.

Step 2: Answer the General Questions

It's usually best to answer the general questions first. These questions ask you about the passage as a whole. There are several types of general questions, and they look like this:

Main Idea/Purpose

- The passage is mostly about
- The main idea of this passage is
- The best title for this passage would be
- The purpose of this passage is to
- The author wrote this passage in order to

Tone/Attitude

- The author's tone is best described as
- The attitude of the author is one of

General Interpretation

- The author would most likely agree that
- It can be inferred from the passage that
- The passage implies that
- You would probably find this passage in a
- This passage is best described as

To answer a main idea/purpose question, ask yourself, "What did the passage talk about most?" Look at the choices and cross off anything that was not discussed or that was only a detail of the passage.

To answer a tone/attitude question, ask yourself, "How does the author feel about the subject?" Cross off anything that was not discussed in the paragraph or that does not agree with the author's view.

Let's take a look at some general questions for this passage.

1. The passage is mostly about

a. the Vikings and their civilization

b. the waves of Viking immigration

c. the sailing techniques of Bjarni Herjolfsson

d. one Viking's glimpse of America

Here's How to Crack It

To answer this question, let's look back at our labels and our summary of the passage. We said that the main idea of the passage was how Bjarni Herjolfsson got lost and saw America before anyone else. Choices (A) and (D) are about the Vikings in general and not about Herjolfsson, so they can be eliminated. Choice (C) is about Herjolfsson, but his sailing techniques are not really discussed. This makes (D) the best choice.

2. Which of the following can be inferred from the passage?

a. The word *America* was first used by Herjolfsson.

b. Herjolfsson's discovery of America was an accident.

c. Herjolfsson was helped by Native Americans.

d. Greenland and Iceland were the Vikings' most important discoveries.

Here's How to Crack It

You should make quick work of this problem using Process of Elimination. The passage never says anything about Native Americans, so (C) can be eliminated.

Also, it doesn't say that Herjolfsson ever used the word *America*, so you can cross off (A). (If you're not positive whether this is true or not, quickly skim back and double-check this in the passage.) We're already down to two choices. Choice (D) is an extreme choice—meaning it uses strong language that makes something absolutely true or false—due to the word *most*, so it probably is not the answer. If you check the passage, you can see that (D) is never stated. Therefore, (B) is the best choice.

Step 3: Answer the Specific Questions

Specific questions ask you about a fact or detail mentioned in the passage. For these questions, look back at the passage to find your answer. These are different kinds of specific questions:

Fact

- According to the passage
- According to the author
- Which of these questions is answered by the passage?

Vocabulary in Context

- The word <u>pilfer</u> probably means
- What does the passage mean by <u>pilfer</u>?

Specific Interpretation/ Purpose

- The author mentions Mother Goose in order to
- From the information in the passage, Mother Goose would probably

To answer a **fact** question, look back at the passage and find the lines that mention the thing you are asked about. Use your passage labels to find the information quickly, or simply skim until you find it. Reread those lines to see exactly what the passage says. Then look for a choice that best restates what the passage says. Cross off anything that is never stated or that says the opposite of the information in the passage.

To answer a **Vocabulary in Context** question, look back at the passage and find the underlined word. It will probably be a word that you don't know. Cover the word with your finger. Reread the lines around that word, and think of the word that you should put there. If you can't think of the exact word, it's okay to simply note that the word should be a "positive word" or a "negative word."

To answer a **Specific Interpretation/Purpose** question, look back at the passage and find the lines that discuss the thing you are asked about. Use your passage labels or skim the passage. Reread those lines to see exactly what the passage says. The correct answer will always be very closely based on the information in the passage. For instance, if a passage tells us that John likes to play tennis, we can infer that he will probably play tennis if he is given the chance. Cross off any choices that are not stated in the passage or sound very far off from what the passage says.

3. According to the passage, Greenland was discovered by

a. Amerigo Vespucci
b. Bjarni Herjolfsson's father
c. Bjarni Herjolfsson
d. Erik the Red

Here's How to Crack It

To answer this question, we should look back at the passage and find the line that talks about the discovery of Greenland. If you skim for the word Greenland, you'll find it in the second paragraph: "Discovered by an <u>infamous</u> murderer and criminal named Erik the Red, Greenland lay at the limit of the known world." Therefore the answer is (D).

4. The word <u>infamous</u> probably means

a. lazy
b. strong
c. wicked
d. intelligent

Here's How to Crack It

Let's reread the line that mentions the word *infamous*: "Discovered by an <u>infamous</u> murderer and criminal named Erik the Red..." Since the word *infamous* describes a *murderer and criminal*, it must be a word that describes someone who is bad. Choices (B) and (D) are positive words, so you can eliminate them. Choice (C) sounds much more like a description of a bad person than (A), so the best choice is (C).

5. According to the passage, Bjarni Herjolfsson left Norway to

a. start a new colony
b. open a trade route to America
c. visit his relatives
d. map the North Sea

Here's How to Crack It

The end of the first paragraph discusses Herjolfsson's departure. There it states, "Bjarni sailed from Norway to Iceland, heading for the Viking settlement where his father resided." The correct answer will use different words, but it should restate the same idea. Can we find anything here about starting a colony? No, so (A) can be eliminated. Does it mention opening a trade route to America? No, so (B) can also be eliminated. (It's true that he does eventually reach America, but that isn't the reason why he left.) Does it mention visiting his relatives? Well, it does say that he wanted to find his father. So let's leave (C). Does this sentence mention mapping the North Sea? No. Choice (D) is incorrect, too, so (C) is the answer.

6. Bjarni's reaction upon landing in Iceland can best be described as

a. disappointed
b. satisfied
c. amused
d. fascinated

Here's How to Crack It

Where can we find a description of Bjarni Herjolfsson's arrival in Iceland? At the beginning paragraph. There it states, "When he arrived in Iceland, Bjarni discovered that his father had already sold his land and estates and set out for the latest Viking settlement on the subarctic island called Greenland." Feeling "dismayed," Bjarni left to look for the new colony. Since he had missed his father, he was unhappy. Which word best states this idea? Choice (A).

7. When the author says, "The crew lost their bearings," this probably means that

a. the ship was damaged beyond repair

b. the sailors did not know which way they were going

c. the sailors were very angry

d. the sailors misplaced their clothes

Here's How to Crack It

Let's reread the lines around "the crew lost their bearings": "Since the Vikings traveled without chart or compass, it was not uncommon for them to lose their way in the unpredictable northern sea. Beset by fog, the crew lost their bearings." Since the story says that the crew would often "lose their way" the best answer is (B).

PROCESS OF ELIMINATION

If you're stuck on which answer is correct, remember to use the Process of Elimination to cross off answers you know are wrong.

On general questions, you'll usually want to cross off answers that

- are not mentioned in the passage
- are too detailed—if the passage mentions something in only one line, it is a detail, not a main idea
- go against, or say the opposite of, information in the passage
- are too big—you can't say much in four or five paragraphs, so any answer that says something like, "The passage proves that the theory Einstein spent his entire life creating was right" is probably a wrong answer
- are too extreme—if a choice uses absolute terms such as "all," "every," "never," or "always," it's probably a wrong answer
- go against common sense

On specific questions, you should probably cross off answers that

- are extreme
- go against information in the passage
- are not mentioned in the passage
- go against common sense

If you look back at the questions in the sample reading comp passage above, you'll see that following guidelines eliminates many of the wrong answer choices. Use these guidelines when you take the HSPT.

What Kind of Answers Do I Keep?

Correct answers tend to be

- restatements or paraphrases of what is said in the passage
- traditional and conservative
- moderate, using words such as "may," "can," and "often"

HSPT Reading Comprehension Exercise

Answers can be found in Chapter 9.

Try the following reading comprehension passage. Don't forget to label your paragraphs!

Although many people associate indoor lighting with modern electrical wiring, practical indoor lighting existed thousands of years before Thomas Edison invented the light bulb. Rudimentary oil lamps, a primitive ancestor of the gaslight, were used in the caves in which prehistoric humans lived.

Approximately 50,000 years ago, cave-dwelling humans fashioned a basic oil-based lamp out of animal fat that was kept inside a stone base as well as a wick made out of a clothlike material. Due to the fact that animal fat smells awful when burned, the lamp gave off a terrible odor.

Thousands of years later, during the Egyptian era (around 1300 B.C.E.) the structure and design of the lamp changed. Instead of using only stone, the Egyptians used a form of decorated pottery with a papyrus-based wick and vegetable oil instead of the foul-smelling animal fat.

In times of need people burned whatever oil was plentiful. Because vegetable oil and animal fat are both edible, in times of hunger people did not burn lamps; they used the oil for food. But oil lamps brought with them other problems. Wicks for the lamps did not always burn away and had to be changed periodically. Soon the oil lamp gave way to the first candle, which became a popular source of light in Rome during the first century B.C.E.

1. What is this passage mostly about?

a. how Egyptians lit their homes
b. why the candle is better than the oil lamp
c. the history of indoor lighting
d. why vegetable oil replaced animal fat in oil lamps

2. It can be inferred that the author views the change from oil lamps to candles as

a. the most important discovery of human history
b. a mistake made by the Romans
c. important to the discovery of electricity
d. a step in the development of indoor lighting

3. The word <u>rudimentary</u> most likely means

a. expensive
b. basic
c. colorful
d. handy

4. The author mentions Thomas Edison in the passage in order to

a. explain his discoveries
b. compare him with other modern inventors
c. introduce someone that the author will discuss later
d. show that Edison was not the first to discover indoor lighting

5. The word <u>foul</u> probably means

a. awful
b. sweet
c. fruity
d. clean

6. People probably stopped burning animal fat in lamps because

a. vegetable oil was more plentiful
b. they needed the animal fat for cooking
c. animal fat smelled bad
d. burning animal fat was against the law

7. The author's tone can best be described as

a. angry
b. unconcerned
c. instructive
d. critical

READING VOCABULARY

The vocab section of this test should only take you about five minutes. As mentioned earlier, these questions are very much like the synonym questions in Chapter 4, and can be solved using the same techniques.

1. To recall an event

a. plan
b. leave
c. remember
d. attend

Here's How to Crack It

If you know the meaning of the word:

Step 1: Cover the answer choices with your hand. If you read the answer choices first, you might get confused.

Step 2: State what the word means to you in your own words.

Step 3: Uncover the answer choices and see which choice most closely matches what you said.

In this case, let's cover up the answers choices. In your own words, what does the word *recall* mean? Maybe you came up with something like "remember" or "think about." Now uncover the answer choices and see which best matches your word. Chances are good that you came up with something very close to (C).

If you "sort of" know what the word means:

Maybe you have a sense of what the word means but can't quite put your finger on it. Perhaps you can think of a saying that uses the word—even if you're not sure what the word means—and you should still be able to get the right answer or at least come up with a good guess. If either of these is the case, use the "side of the fence" trick. This is when you ask yourself whether the word is a positive word or negative word. If the word is positive, you can eliminate any words that are not positive. If the word is negative, you can eliminate any words that are not negative.

Take a look at the following example.

2. A <u>surplus</u> of food

a. basket
b. excess
c. lack
d. field

Here's How to Crack It

You might have a sense that the word *surplus* is positive, especially because the word *plus*, which you can see inside it. Then you may guess that the word *surplus* means something like "a lot." If so, you can eliminate (A) and (C), and take your best guess from the remaining choices. (The answer is (B).)

What if you have no idea what the word means?

You're on a learning roll! Now it's time to take a stroll!

If you have no idea what the word means, take your best guess and move on to the next problem. This is the perfect time to use the Process of Elimination or your LOTD.

Chapter 7
Mathematics

RATIOS AND PROPORTIONS

What Is a Ratio?

A ratio is a way of stating the relationship of two numbers in a reduced form. For instance, if there are 50 boys and 25 girls in a room, we can say that the ratio of boys to girls is 50 to 25. But we can also reduce this ratio just like a fraction: $\frac{50}{25} = \frac{2}{1}$. So we can also say that the ratio of boys to girls is 2 to 1. This is sometimes written as "The ratio of boys to girls is 2:1."

Of course, if we say that the ratio of boys to girls is 2 to 1, this doesn't tell us exactly how many boys and girls there are. The actual number could be 8 boys and 4 girls, or 10 boys and 5 girls, or 200 boys and 100 girls. Each of these can be reduced to the ratio 2 to 1.

But if we know one of the actual values, we can always solve for the other one. For instance, if we know that the ratio of boys to girls is 2 to 1, and there are 200 boys, we know that there must be 100 girls. Most of you can probably do that in your heads. But how do you calculate it?

Solving Ratio and Proportion Problems

The way you solve almost all ratio and proportion questions is by setting up two fractions and cross multiplying.

$$\frac{A}{B} = \frac{C}{D}$$

Whenever you set up two equal fractions, you know that $A \times D$ is equal to $B \times C$. The only thing you have to make sure to do is keep the same thing on top and bottom of each fraction.

In this case, if we know that the ratio of boys to girls is 2 to 1 and that there are 200 boys, we can figure out the number of girls by setting up these fractions.

$$\frac{\text{boys}\ 2}{\text{girls}\ 1} = \frac{200}{x}$$

Now we can cross-multiply: We know that $2x = 1 \times 200$. This means that $x = 100$.

Take a look at the following problem.

1. John has a bowl of red and blue marbles. The ratio of red to blue marbles is 5 to 4. If there are 35 red marbles in the bowl, how many blue marbles are in the bowl?

a. 16
b. 20
c. 28
d. 39

Here's How to Crack It

Let's set up our fractions with red marbles on top and blue marbles on the bottom. It will look like this:

$$\frac{\text{red}}{\text{blue}}\frac{5}{4} = \frac{35}{x}$$

Now we can cross-multiply. We know that $5x = 4 \times 35$. After we multiply, $5x = 140$. We can solve for x by dividing both sides by 5 to get $x = 28$. Therefore, there are 28 blue marbles in the bowl, which is (C).

AVERAGES

The formula we use to figure out the average is:

$$\text{average} = \frac{\text{sum total}}{\text{\# of things}}$$

For instance, if you take 3 tests on which you score 50, 55, and 57, the sum total of your scores is 50 + 55 + 57, or 162. Since there were 3 tests, the average must be $\frac{162}{3} = 54$.

Try the following problem.

2. During a certain month, David counted the number of apples he ate each week. He ate 2 apples during the first week, 4 apples during the second week, and 2 apples during the third week. The fourth week he ate no apples. On average, how many apples did David eat each week of the month.

a. 2

b. $2\frac{1}{2}$

c. $3\frac{1}{3}$

d. 7

Here's How to Crack It

The total number of apples David ate was 2 + 4 + 2 + 0, or 8. This sum total, over the number of weeks, will give us the average: $\frac{8}{4} = 2$.

PLUGGING IN THE ANSWER CHOICES

Very often you may think that you need to do a lot of complicated math to set up a problem. This is especially true on those long, wordy problems that give everyone a headache.

You know, however, that one of the answer choices given has to be the correct answer. All you've got to do is figure out which one. Therefore, the easiest way to solve many problems is by simply plugging in each answer choice until you find the one that works. Plugging in just means substituting numbers to figure out the answer quickly.

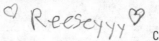

Take a look at the following problem.

3. If $x(x + 4) = 12$, which of the following could be the value of x?

a. −1
b. 0
c. 1
d. 2

Here's How to Crack It

You might think that you have to do some complicated algebra to solve this problem, but you really don't. Let's just try plugging in each answer choice for the value of x and see which one makes the equation work.

If we plug in −1 for x, does $-1(-1 + 4) = 12$? No. Cross off (A). If we plug in 0 for x, does $0(0 + 4) = 12$? No. Cross off (B). If we plug in 1 for x, does $1(1 + 4) = 12$? No. Cross off (C). If we plug in 2 for x, does $2(2 + 4) = 12$? Yes, so (D) is the answer.

4. David is five years older than his brother Jim, and Jim is twice as old as Ann. If David is 10 years older than Ann, how old is Jim?

a. 20
b. 15
c. 10
d. 8

Here's How to Crack It

The question asks how old Jim is, so this is what we'll be plugging in for. Let's start with (A). Could Jim be 20? We know that David is five years older than Jim, so if Jim is 20, then David is 25. We also know that Jim is twice as old as Ann, so Ann must be 10. But the last sentence says that David should be 10 years older than Ann, which he's not. Therefore (A) can't be the answer.

How about (B)? Could Jim be 15? We know that David is five years older than Jim, so if Jim is 15, then David must be 20. We also know that Jim is twice as old as Ann, so Ann must be $7\frac{1}{2}$. But the last sentence says that David should be 10 years older than Ann, which he's not. Therefore (B) can't be the answer.

Let's try (C). Could Jim be 10? We know that David is five years older than Jim, so if Jim is 10, then David is 15. We also know that Jim is twice as old as Ann, so Ann must be 5. Does this make David 10 years older than Ann? Yes. So (C) is the answer.

Here's a slightly harder problem. Trying to solve it using algebra is difficult, but by plugging in the answer choices, it becomes very easy.

5. If the average of 4 and *x* is equal to the average of 5, 4, and *x*, what is the value of *x*?

a. 1
b. 2
c. 6
d. 8

Here's How to Crack It

Let's start with (A), and plug 1 in for x. Does the average of 4 and 1 (which is 2.5) equal the average of 5, 4, and 1 (which is $\frac{10}{3}$)? No, so (A) can be eliminated. Let's try (B). Does the average of 4 and 2 (which is 3) equal the average of 5, 4, and 2 (which is $\frac{11}{3}$)? No. Choice (B) can also be eliminated. How about (C)? Does the average of 4 and 6 (which is 5) equal the average of 5, 4, and 6 (which is 5)? Yes. Choice (C) is the answer.

PLUGGING IN YOUR OWN NUMBERS

The problem with doing algebra is that it's just too easy to make a mistake. Whenever you see a problem with variables (*x*) in the answer choices, PLUG IN. Start by picking a number for the variable in the problem (or for more than one variable, if necessary); solve the problem using that real number; then see which answer choice gives you the correct answer.

Have a look at the following problem:

6. If *x* is a positive integer, then 20 percent of 5*x* equals

a. x
b. $2x$
c. $5x$
d. $15x$

Here's How to Crack It

Let's start by picking a number for *x*. Let's plug in the nice round number 10. When we plug in 10 for *x*, we change every *x* in the whole problem into a 10. Now the problem reads:

7. If 10 is a positive integer, then 20 percent of 5(10) equals

a. 10
b. 2(10)
c. 5(10)
d. 15(10)

Here's How to Crack It

Look how easy the problem becomes! Now we can solve: 20 percent of 50 is 10. Which answer says 10? Choice (A) does.

Let's try it again.

8. If 0 < x < 1, then which of the following is true?

a. $x > 0$

b. $x > 1$

c. $x > 2$

d. $2x > 2$

Here's How to Crack It

This time when we pick a number for x, we have to make sure that it is between 0 and 1, because that's what the problem states. So let's try $\frac{1}{2}$. If we make every x in the problem into $\frac{1}{2}$, the answer choices now read:

(a) $\frac{1}{2} > 0$

(b) $\frac{1}{2} > 1$

(c) $\frac{1}{2} > 2$

(d) $1 > 2$

Which one of these is true? Choice (A). Plugging In is such a great technique that it makes even the hardest algebra problems easy. *Anytime you can, plug in!*

GEOMETRY

Lines and Angles

On every line, all the angles must add up to a total of 180°.

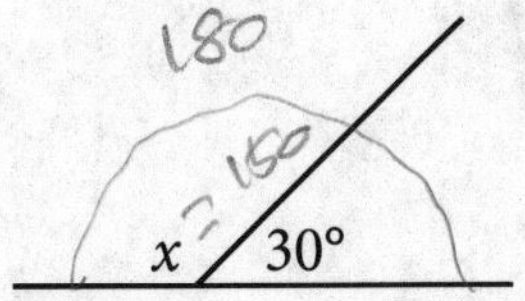

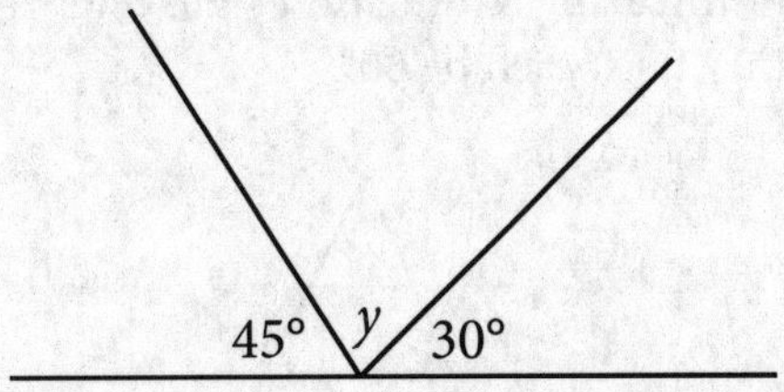

Since x and 30° must add up to 180°, we know that x must measure 180° – 30°, or 150°. Since 45°, y, and 30° must add up to 180°, we know that y must measure 180° – 45° – 30°, or 105°.

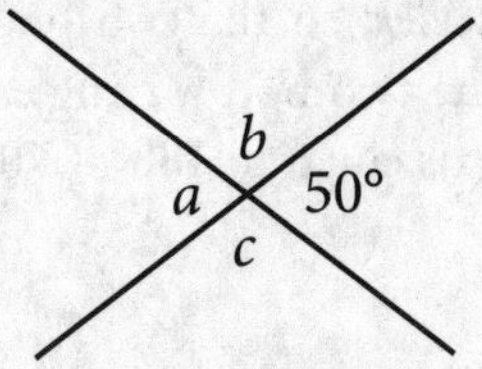

In this case, b and the angle measuring 50° are on a line together. This means that b must measure 130° (180° – 50° = 130°). Also, c and the angle measuring 50° are on a line together. This means that c must also measure 130° (180° – 50° = 130°). Finally, a must measure 50°, because $a + b$ (and we already know that b = 130°) must measure 180° (50° + 130° = 180°).

This explains why vertical angles (the angles opposite each other when two lines cross) are always equal. Angles b and c are both 130°, and angle a (which is opposite the angle 50°) is 50°.

In a triangle, all the angles must add up to 180°. In a four-sided figure, all the angles must add up to 360°.

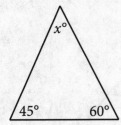

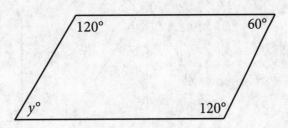

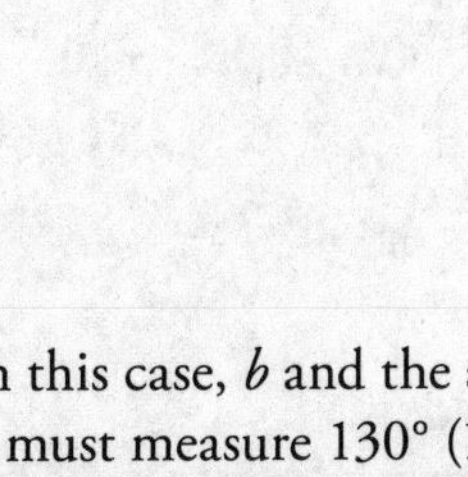

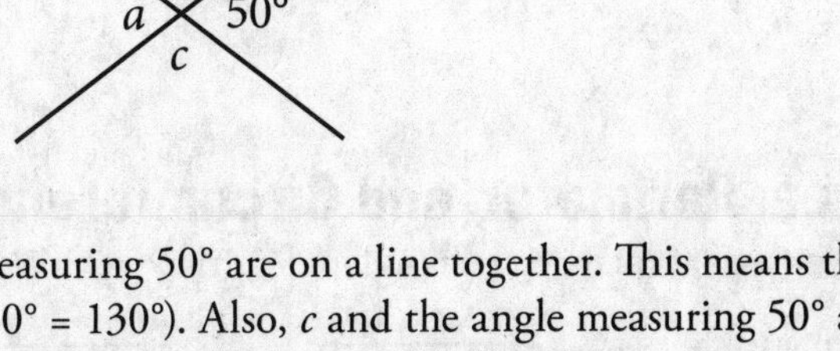

In this triangle, two of the angles are 45° and 60°. They make a total of 105°. The sum of the angles needs to equal 180°. Therefore angle x must be 180° – 105°, or 75°.

In the figure on the right, three of the angles have a total of 300°. Therefore y must be equal to 360° – 300°, or 60°.

A triangle is *isosceles* if it has two equal sides. This means that the two opposite angles are also equal. A triangle is *equilateral* if it has three equal sides. This means that all three angles are also equal. Since these angles must equally divide from 180°, they must each be 60°.

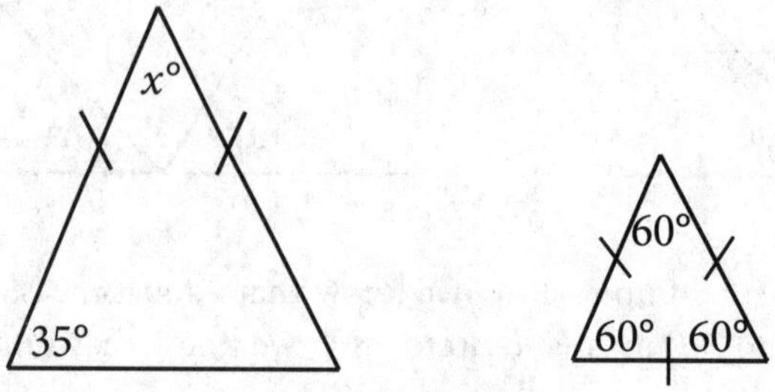

The triangle on the left is isosceles, so the two bottom angles must each be 35°. This makes a total of 70° for the two bottom angles. Since all of the angles must add up to 180°, we know that x is equal to 180° – 70°, or 110°.

Area, Perimeter, and Circumference

The area of a square or rectangle is length × width.

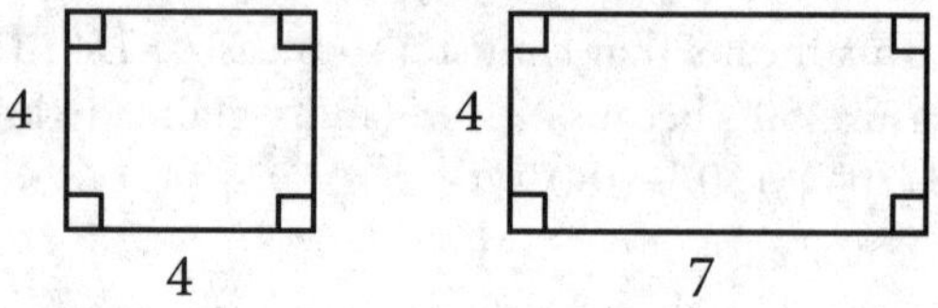

The area of this square is 4 × 4, or 16. The area of the rectangle is 4 × 7, or 28.

The area of a triangle is $\frac{1}{2}$ base × height.

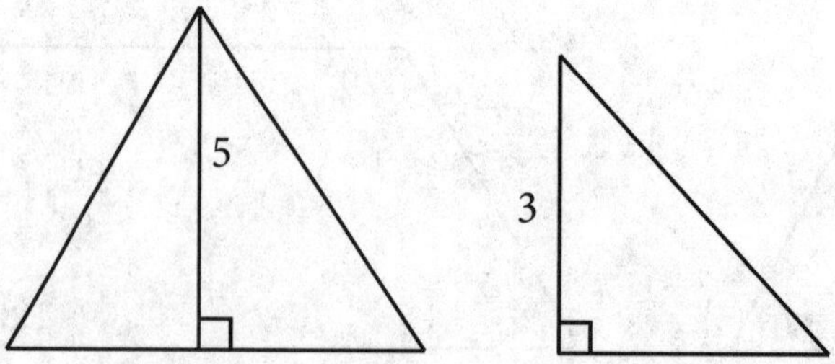

The area of the triangle on the left is $\frac{1}{2} \times 5 \times 8$, or 20.

The area of the triangle on the right is $\frac{1}{2} \times 3 \times 3$, or $4\frac{1}{2}$.

The perimeter of any object is the sum of the lengths of its sides.

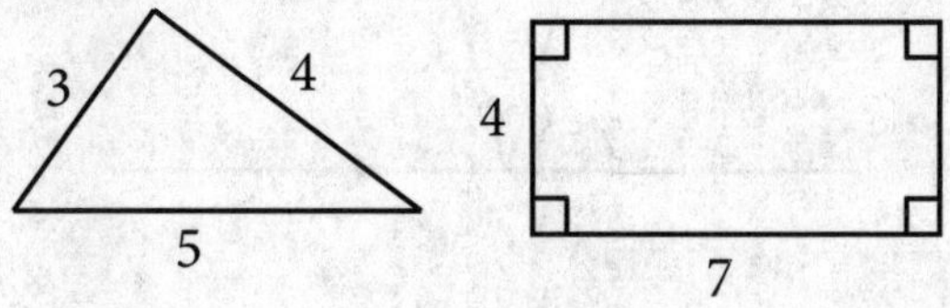

The perimeter of the triangle is 3 + 4 + 5, or 12. The perimeter of the rectangle is 4 + 7 + 4 + 7, or 22 (opposite sides are always equal to each other in a rectangle or a square).

The circumference of a circle with radius r is $2\pi r$. A circle with a radius of 5 has a circumference of 10π.

The area of a circle with radius r is πr^2. A circle with a radius of 5 has an area of 25π.

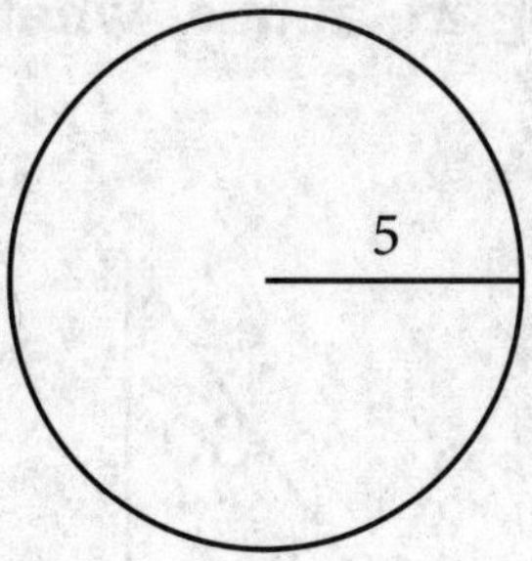

HSPT Geometry Exercise

Answers can be found in Chapter 9.

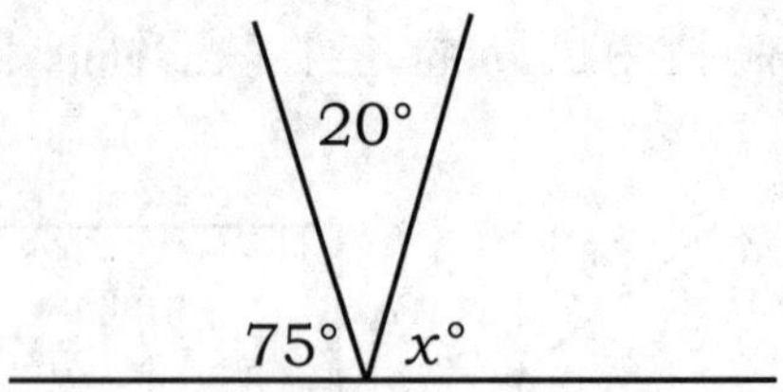

1. In the figure above, what is the value of *x*?

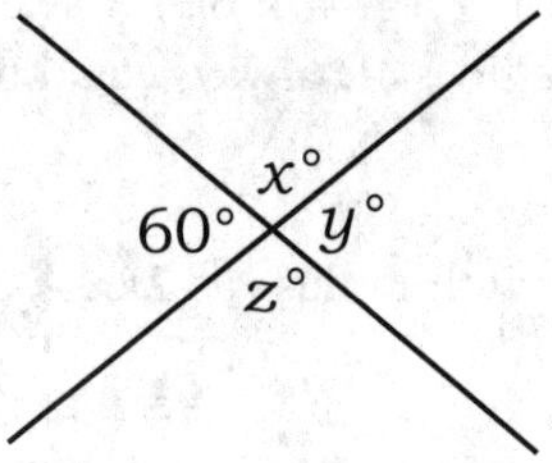

2. In the figure above, what is the value of *y* + *z*?

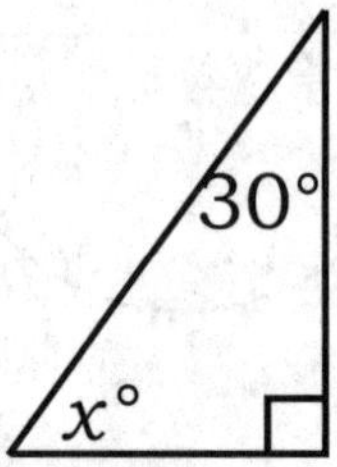

3. In the figure above, what is the value of *x*?

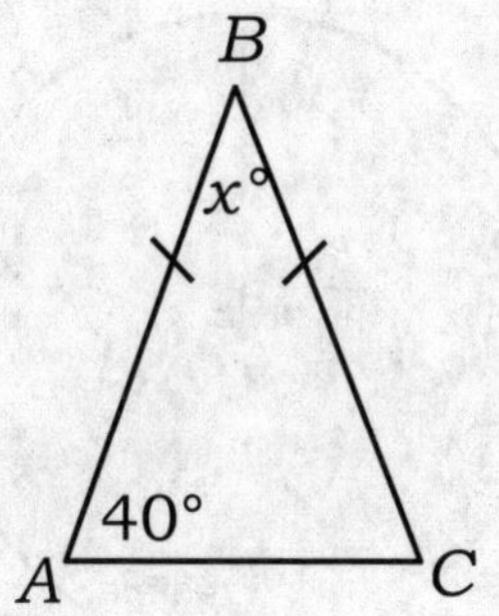

4. If triangle *ABC* is isosceles, what is the value of *x*?

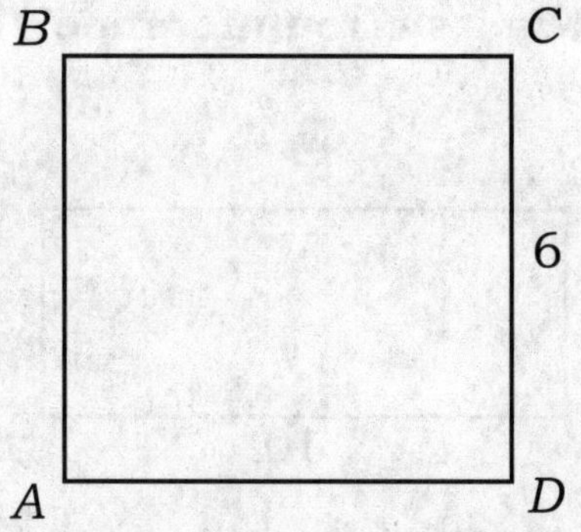

5. What is the area of square *ABCD* above?

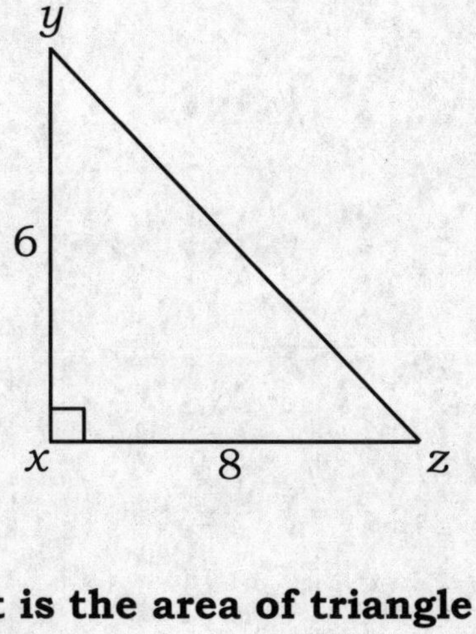

6. What is the area of triangle *XYZ* above?

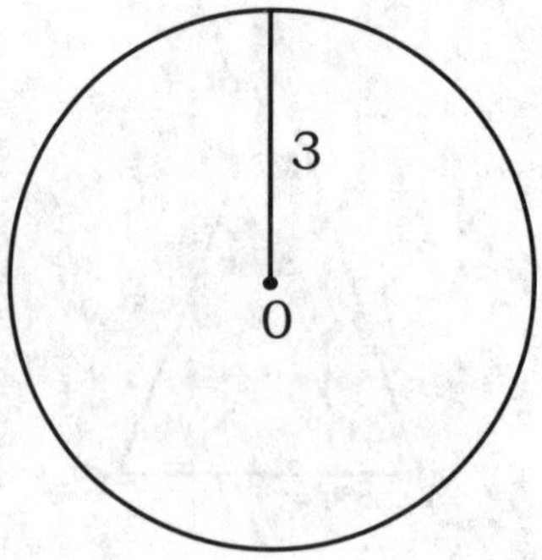

7a. What is the area of the circle above with center *O*?

7b. What is its circumference?

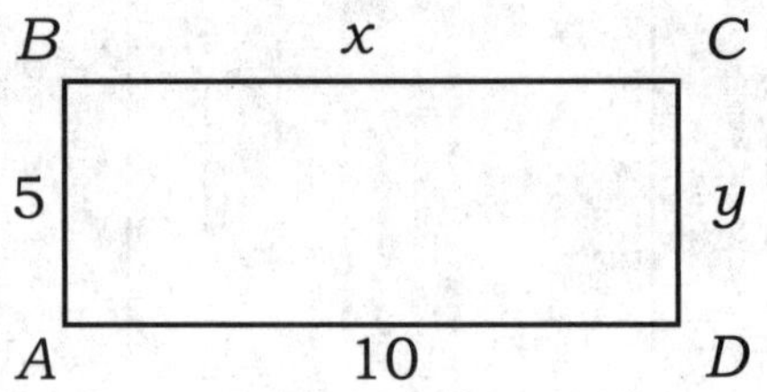

8a. If *ABCD* is a rectangle, x = ___ and y = ___.

8b. What is the perimeter of rectangle *ABCD*?

Chapter 8
Language Skills

USAGE QUESTIONS

Most of the questions in the language expressions section of the HSPT will ask you to look at four sentences and figure out which one, if any, contains an error. If the sentence contains no error, pick (D), "No mistake."

ERRORS

What kind of errors should you look for? The HSPT tests only a few kinds of errors. Learn them, and you'll know what to look for to greatly increase your score.

Subject/ Verb Agreement

What is wrong with the following sentences?

1. **The cats in the house watches the bird.**

2. **A wild dingo from Sydney were caught last year.**

To spot subject/verb agreement errors, always find the subject and the verb in the given sentence. To find the subject, ask yourself, "Who or what is acting or being described?" To find the verb, find the action word by asking yourself, "What is the subject doing?" Then make sure that the subject and the verb agree. Subjects and verbs have to agree in both number (singular or plural) and person (I, she, we, you). You may have to read around other parts of the sentence to make it clear to yourself.

What is the subject in sentence 1? It's the cats who are watching the bird. Can you say, "The cats **watches** the bird"? No. *Cats*, in this case, is plural—more than one cat—so the verb has to agree. It should be "The cats **watch** the bird."

What is the subject in sentence 2? A *wild dingo* is the thing being described. Can you say, "A wild dingo **were** caught last year"? No; *dingo* is singular, and the verb has to agree with a singular subject. It should be "A wild dingo **was** caught last year."

Verb Form and Tense

What is wrong with the following sentences?

3. Yesterday, John is going to the playground.

4. Patricia has took her hamster to the vet.

Verb Tense

The word *yesterday* in sentence 3 tells us that the verb should be in the past tense. You can see that this sentence has an error because it clearly says that the action happened yesterday, but the verb "is going" is in the present tense. The sentence should read "Yesterday, John **went** to the playground." *Went* is the past tense of the infinitive verb *to go*. To spot tense problems, look for words and phrases that indicate present or past, such as

- today (present)
- now (present)
- yesterday (past)
- last week (past)
- in 1956 (past)
- once (past)
- a long time ago (past)
- during the Second World War (past)

Verb Form

Sometimes the error will be in the verb form, such as in sentence 4. Recognizing correct verb form is as simple as knowing the proper present, past, and future forms of verbs. The HSPT will ask you not to identify and name verb forms, just to choose the correct version of the sentence. Usually, it should be obvious to you when a verb form is wrong because the sentence just won't make sense. The past tense form of the verb *to take* would be either *took* or *has taken*. You could say, "Patricia **took** her hamster to the vet" or "Patricia **has taken** her hamster to the vet." But *has took* is not a possible form. Make sure that you review proper verb forms as part of your preparation for the HSPT.

Adjective/ Adverbs

What is wrong with the following sentence?

5. Kim ran quick around the track.

What is the word *quick* describing? The way that Kim ran around the track. If a word describes a person or a thing, it should be an adjective like *quick*. But if a word describes an action (verb), it should be an adverb like *quickly*. Don't forget: Most adverbs end in *-ly*.

Remember this rule: Adjectives modify nouns; adverbs modify everything else.

Comparison Words

What is wrong with the following sentences?

6. He was one of the most greatest authors of his time.

7. She is intelligenter than he is.

Some questions on the HSPT will ask you to determine the right form of a comparison word. In the sentences above, *greatest* and *more intelligent* are the correct forms of the comparison words. For most adjectives that have only one syllable, we make them into comparison words by adding *–er* and *–est* to the end of the word, such as big, bigger, biggest and great, greater, greatest.

For most adjectives with more than one syllable, we make the comparison using the words more and most, as with intelligent, more intelligent, most intelligent and interesting, more interesting, most interesting.

Pronoun Agreement and Case

8. The dog ran away, but they soon came back.

9. Murray is a man which loves to play the piano.

10. Olivia gave the assignment to Peter and I.

Pronouns are words, such as *I, it, they, me,* and *she,* that take the place of nouns. Whenever you see pronouns in a sentence, check to make sure that they agree with the nouns they stand for and that they are in the proper case. Pronoun *agreement* means that singular pronouns stand in for singular nouns, and plural pronouns stand in for plural nouns. In sentence 8, the subject is "the dog," which is singular, but the pronoun "they" is plural. The sentence should read "The dog ran away, but it soon came back."

Another important rule to remember is to use the pronoun *who* for people and *which* or *that* for things. Therefore, sentence 9 should read "Murray is a man **who** loves to play the piano."

Pronoun *case* means that the subject of the sentence (the thing doing the action) needs a subject pronoun, and the object of a sentence (the thing receiving the action) needs an object pronoun. In the sentence "Mary threw the ball to John," Mary is the subject and John is the object. Below is a chart that tells you how to use a pronoun whether it is the subject or the object.

Subject	**Example**
I	I left the office.
You	You should get some rest.
He/she/it	He knew the best route to take.
We	We love to visit our grandparents.
They	They live in California.
Object	**Example**
Me	My boss told me to go home.
You	A good night's sleep would do you some good.
Him/her/it	Jenny refused to tell him the best route to take.
Us	Our grandparents love us.
Them	We visited them in California.

In sentence 10, does the word *I* describe someone who is giving the book (a subject) or someone to whom the book was given (an object)? Think about it this way: We say *I* gave it to *him,* but *he* gave it to *me.* In sentence 10, the word *I* describes someone who received the action, not someone who was performing the action. So the pronoun used should be the object pronoun, and the sentence should read "Olivia gave the assignment to Peter and *me.*" If you are confused about the correct answer, try this trick: Take away the word *Peter* and see what is left. You wouldn't say, "Olivia gave the assignment to I," but you would say, "Olivia gave the assignment to me."

Important note: Whenever a pronoun follows a preposition (such as *to, of, in, at, around, between,* and *from*), the pronouns are *always* in the object case.

Here are some common pronoun mix-ups. Don't forget them because recognizing them is a simple way to rack up points on the HSPT.

It's = it is	It's raining outside.
Its = belongs to it	The dog eats its bone.
You're = you are	You're a great friend.
Your = belongs to you	I love your shoes.
Who's = who is	Who's at the door?
Whose = belongs to who	Whose car is this?

Sentence Fragments

What is wrong with the following sentences?

11. Told me that I would have to see the dentist.

12. The elephant, after eating dinner, walking around the zoo.

Every sentence has to express a complete thought and have both a subject and a verb. What is the subject in sentence 11? Who or what told me to go to the dentist? There is no subject in this sentence, and therefore it is only a sentence fragment. Sentence fragments are not complete sentences and are never the correct answer on the HSPT.

Sentence 12 has a subject—the elephant—but the verb is in the wrong tense. It is also a fragment, so we know it's an error!

Parallelism

What is wrong with the following sentences?

13. Lawrence left the house and going to school.

14. Erica wanted to eat lunch, visit her friend, and to play soccer.

Whenever you read a sentence that contains a list of actions or objects, check to make sure that the items in the list are all in the same form. For instance, in sentence 13 there are two actions. The first action is that Lawrence left the house. So the second action must be in the same form; however, *left* and *going* aren't in the same form. The second part of the sentence should read "Lawrence went to school" to make this a parallel sentence.

In sentence 14, there are three things that Erica wanted to do: to *eat* lunch, *visit* her friend, and to *play* soccer. Are these three things in the same form? No. the first and the third things on the list use the infinitive verb forms—*to eat* and *to play*—but the second does not. To be parallel and correct, the sentence should read "Erica wanted to eat lunch, to visit her friend, and to play soccer." You could also say "Erica wanted to eat lunch, visit her friend, and play soccer."

Double Negative

What is wrong with the following sentence?

15. Paul has hardly seen no birds today.

In English, you should have only one negative word in the same phrase. When a sentence has two, it is called a double negative. All of the following are double negatives, and are always considered incorrect.

- can't hardly
- can't never
- barely none
- barely never
- won't never
- won't hardly
- hardly never
- hardly none
- hasn't got none

Capitalization and Punctuation

Always capitalize proper names, including names of the following:

- people (Jim)
- places (Alaska)
- holidays (Independence Day)
- months of the year (March)
- geographical features (Rocky Mountains)
- important words in the titles of books or movies (*All Quiet on the Western Front*)
- official titles when they are followed by a proper name (Chief Smith, Aunt Maggie)
- names of languages and peoples (French, Cuban)
- closings of letters (Sincerely, *but* Sincerely yours,)

Punctuation

Some of the questions will involve punctuation errors. Most of the punctuation problems on the HSPT involve problems with commas.

Remember to always use a comma in the following cases:

- between the name of a city and a state (Seattle, Washington)
- between the date and the year (April 19, 1999)
- between elements in a list (John, Amelia, Robert, and I)
- when addressing a person (Penelope, can you come here?)
- openings and closings of letters (Dear Bob,; Sincerely yours,)

A comma should NOT be used between a subject and its verb or between a verb and its object.

- INCORRECT: Alexandra, discovered a bone in her backyard.
- INCORRECT: David hit, the ball so hard that it broke a window.

HSPT Language Exercise

Answers can be found in Chapter 9.

1. **There is already many people in the auditorium.**

2. **Since my father's company has so much business, they are very busy.**

3. **My uncle often help my parents to make dinner.**

4. **Henry going to school, runs into his friend.**

5. **The giant mouse ran through the house and escaping from the cat.**

6. **I met her on March 1 2010.**

7. **Last year, Ines won the first prize and receives a beautiful trophy.**

8. **Roger finished his most biggest assignment.**

9. **Colin cleaned the bowl and gives it to his mother.**

10. **Rachel read the letter to my brother and I.**

SPELLING QUESTIONS

A few questions on the HSPT will ask you to identify which sentence, if any, contains a misspelled word. If none of the words is misspelled, choose (D), "No mistake." To approach these questions, read carefully through (A), (B), and (C). Pay close attention to the long or unusual words. If you find an error, pick it. If you can't find an error, pick (D).

COMPOSITION QUESTIONS

Other questions in the language section will ask you to find the sentence that is correctly written. For these questions, three of the choices will contain grammatical errors or awkward constructions.

Here's the procedure for attacking composition questions.

Step 1: Read all five sentences and eliminate any choice that breaks a rule of grammar.

Step 2: Reread the choices that are left, and cross off any choices that are awkward or don't make sense.

Step 3: Make your choice. The sentence you are left with may not sound great, but you should always pick the one that is the best of the bunch—the one that makes the most sense. If you can't get it down to only one sentence, that's okay. Cross off what you can, and guess from among the remaining choices.

SENTENCE COMPLETIONS

A few questions in the language section will ask you to complete a sentence by filling in a blank. Some of the questions in this section of the HSPT will test how well you can pick the correct word based on the "direction" of the sentence.

How would you fill in the blanks in the following sentences?

1. I really like you _____ you are very friendly.

2. I really like you _____ you are a very nasty person.

In sentence 1, you probably picked a word like "because." How did you know that this word was the right one to choose? Because the idea after the blank ("are very friendly") kept going in the *same direction* as the idea before the blank ("I really like you"). The sentence started out with a positive idea and continued with a positive idea.

In sentence 2, you probably picked something like "but," "although," or "even though." Why? Because the idea after the blank ("you are a very nasty person") went in the *opposite direction* from the idea before the blank ("I really like you"). The sentence started out with a positive idea and then changed to a negative idea.

Here are lists of same-direction and opposite-direction words.

Same-Direction

- and
- moreover
- in fact
- for instance
- for example
- so
- therefore
- because
- since

Opposite-Direction

- however
- but
- yet
- although
- though
- nevertheless
- nonetheless
- despite
- rather
- instead
- in contrast

Try the following example:

3. Fill in the blank.

Susie's mother wanted her to be a dancer; _____ Susie felt like becoming a doctor.

a. because,
b. however,
c. in fact,
d. rather,

Here's How to Crack It

In this case, the idea after the blank ("becoming a doctor") goes in the opposite direction from the idea before the blank ("be a dancer"). Therefore, we can eliminate (A) and (C). If you get no further, you have a great guess. The best choice is (B).

STRUCTURE QUESTIONS

A few questions in this section will ask you to choose which sentences fit best with our other sentences in a paragraph. You may be asked to find the following:

- Where does the sentence belong in the paragraph?
- Which sentence does not belong in the paragraph?

To answer these questions, make sure that the ideas are in a logical order from one sentence to the next.

To answer a question that asks you where a sentence belongs in the paragraph, read the sentence and ask yourself what the sentence is about. Then read the paragraph and ask yourself, "Where in the paragraph is this same idea discussed?"

To answer a question that asks you which sentence does not belong, read the paragraph and ask yourself what the paragraph is about. Then reread it, and find the sentence that does not discuss this same idea or suddenly changes the topic.

Take a look at the following examples.

4. Where should the sentence "At first it was rough" be placed in the paragraph?

1) Paper has a long and interesting history. 2) It was first made in China around 100 B.C.E. from bits of plants and tree bark. 3) This made it difficult to use for writing. 4) Soon, however, people found ways to make it flat and even. 5) Over the next few hundred years, paper was introduced to the rest of Asia, where it was used to keep government documents and religious inscriptions.

a. After sentence 1
b. After sentence 2
c. After sentence 3
d. After sentence 4

Here's How to Crack It

If we read the paragraph, we see that it discusses the history of paper, from early years to later years. The sentence "At first it was rough" belongs in the discussion of the early years of paper. Sentence 3 discusses the properties of early paper, so the new sentence should come right after sentence 2.

5. Which of the following sentences does not belong in the paragraph?

1) One of the most loved musical styles today is blues. 2) Blues originated in the early 1900s in America. 3) It was born from a combination of African-American work chants and gospel songs. 4) The blues got its name from the introduction of special "blue notes," which are created by "bending" normal notes up or down. 5) These blue notes give the song a certain sad sound that people recognize as part of the blues. 6) While some people like sad music, other people prefer happier songs. 7) In the 1920s, blues began to incorporate elements from jazz, dance music, and show tunes. 8) Today, blues has spread to many different countries and is one of the most popular types of music in the world.

a. Sentence 3
b. Sentence 4
c. Sentence 5
d. Sentence 6

Take a break from studying with a quick solo dance party!

Here's How to Crack It

If we read the paragraph, we see that it is about the musical style called blues. Each sentence talks about this idea except for sentence 6, which talks about whether people like happy or sad music. This makes (D) the best choice.

Chapter 9
Answers to HSPT Exercises

CHAPTER 4

HSPT Analogy Exercise

A mansion is a very large house.

A leaf is part of a tree.

A desert is full of sand.

An engine allows an automobile to run.

Bread is made by a baker.

A brush is used by a painter.

HSPT Verbal Skills Exercise

1. **C**
2. **C**
3. **A**
4. **D**
5. **D**
6. **B**
7. **C**
8. **B**
9. **A**
10. **B**
11. **C**

CHAPTER 5

HSPT Math Vocabulary Exercise

1. –3, –2, –1, 0, 1, 2, 3, 4 are all integers. That makes a total of 8.
2. 0, 1, 2, 3, 4, are all positive integers. That makes a total of 5.
3. $6 + 7 + 8 = 21$
4. $2 \times 4 \times 8 = 64$

HSPT Order of Operations Exercise

1. 13
2. 9 (Do multiplication first!)
3. 5 (Do parentheses, then multiplication!)
4. 45 (Do multiplication first!)
5. 108 (Do parentheses first!)

HSPT Fractions Exercise

1. $\frac{1}{5}$ (Divide the top and bottom by 12.)
2. $\frac{3}{8} + \frac{2}{3} = \frac{9}{24} + \frac{16}{24} = \frac{25}{24}$
3. $\frac{3}{4} - \frac{2}{3} = \frac{9}{12} - \frac{8}{12} = \frac{1}{12}$
4. $\frac{3}{5} \times \frac{3}{2} = \frac{3 \times 3}{5 \times 2} = \frac{9}{10}$
5. $\frac{1}{3} \div \frac{1}{2} = \frac{1}{3} \times \frac{2}{1} = \frac{2}{3}$

HSPT Decimals Exercise

1. 7.68
2. 2.63
3. 4.5
4. 1.25
5. 5
6. $\frac{632}{100}$

HSPT Exponents, Scientific Notation, and Square Roots Exercise

1. $4 \times 4 \times 4 = 64$
2. $2 \times 2 \times 2 \times 2 = 16$
3. 340
4. 52,300
5. This becomes $2 + 4 = 6$.

HSPT Solve for *X* Exercise

1. $x = 5$
2. $x = 7$
3. $x = \frac{1}{4}$
4. $x = 3$

HSPT Percent Translation Exercise

1. $\frac{30}{100} \times 60 = 18$
2. $\frac{40}{100} \times 200 = 80$
3. $15 = \frac{x}{100} \times 60 = 25\%$
4. $x = \frac{25}{100} \times \frac{10}{100} \times 200 = 5$

HSPT Computation Exercise

1. The difference of 75 and 30 is 45; $3 \times 45 = 135$.
2. The sum of 50 and 14 is 64; $\frac{1}{8} \times 64 = 8$.
3. Half of 30 is 15; $16 + 15 = 31$
4. $\frac{160}{100} \times 40 = 64$
5. $6^2 = 36$ and $5^2 = 25$; the difference of 36 and 25 is 11; $11 + 2 = 13$

HSPT Series Exercise

1. 4 (+ 4) 8 (+ 4) 12 (+ 4) 16 (+ 4) 20 (+ 4) 24
2. 38 (– 6) 32 (– 6) 26 (– 6) 20 (– 6) 14
3. 6 (× 2) 12 (+ 4) 16 (× 2) 32 (+ 4) 36 (× 2) 72 (+ 4) 76
4. 10 (– 5) 5 (+ 10) 15 (– 5) 10 (+ 10) 20 (– 5) 15 (+ 10) 25
5. 7 (× 2) 14 (– 2) 12 (× 2) 24 (– 2) 22 (× 2) 44 (– 2) 42
6. 8 (× 2) 16 (+ 4) 20 (× 2) 40 (+ 4) 44 (× 2) 88
7. 20 (– 2) 18 (+ 7) 25 (– 2) 23 (+ 7) 30 (– 2) 28

HSPT Comparison Exercise

1. **C** (1) is $2 \times 4 = 8$. (2) is $18 - 5 = 13$. (3) is $18 - 5 = 13$. Therefore, (2) and (3) are equal and greater than (1).
2. **B** (1) is $\frac{40}{100} \times 60 = 24$. (2) is $\frac{60}{100} \times 40 = 24$. (3) is $\frac{50}{100} \times 90 = 45$. So (1) is equal to (2) and less than (3).
3. **C** (1) is 230. (2) is 2,300. (3) is 2,300. So (2) and (3) are equal and greater than (1).
4. **A** The area of a square is one side squared, so (1) is $6 \times 6 = 36$. The perimeter of a square is the sum of all sides, which are equal, so (2) is $6 + 6 + 6 + 6 = 24$. (3) is $\frac{1}{2} \times 8 \times 8$ (one-half times one side squared) = 32. Therefore, (1) is greater than (2), which is less than (3).
5. **B** Since angle *a* measures 40° and the triangle is isosceles, we know that angle *c* is also 40°, and therefore angle *b* must be 100°. So angle *a* is less than angles *b* + *c*.

CHAPTER 6

HSPT Reading Comprehension Exercise

1. **C** If you summarized the passage well, you probably wrote something like "People have had indoor lighting way before Thomas Edison invented the electric light." Choice (A) is too precise, since the Egyptians are discussed in only one paragraph. Choices (B) and (D) are just details that are discussed in only one or two lines.

2. **D** In the final paragraph, the author says that "oil lamps brought with them other problems." Therefore, the Romans began to use candles. Choices (B) and (C) are not stated in the paragraph, so they can be eliminated. Choice (A) is extreme because of the term *most important.*

3. **B** If we reread the line that mentions the word *rudimentary,* it states, "<u>Rudimentary</u> oil lamps, a primitive ancestor of the gaslight..." Therefore, the word *rudimentary* must be something like *primitive.* This will eliminate (A), (C), and (D).

4. **D** If we skim the passage looking for Edison, we can find him mentioned in the first paragraph. It states that "practical indoor lighting existed thousands of years before Thomas Edison invented the light bulb." Does this sentence explain his discoveries or mention other inventors? No, so we can eliminate (A) and (B). Does the author later discuss Edison? No, so (C) can also be eliminated.

5. **A** The passage says that "the lamp gave off a terrible odor," and "foul-smelling" is used to describe the odor of the lamp.

6. **C** There is no evidence in the passage to support (A), (B), or (D). The passage does say that the "animal fat smells awful when burned," so (C) is the best answer.

7. **C** Nothing in the passage sounds angry, so we can eliminate (A). Choice (B) probably isn't right since someone who was unconcerned wouldn't have written the passage. If that's as far as you got, take a guess between (C) and (D). Critical means that the author disagrees with something, but there's nothing in the passage that shows disagreement, which rules out (D). Choice (C) is the best answer.

CHAPTER 7

HSPT Geometry Exercise

1. Since these angles must add up to 180°, $x = 85°$.
2. x and z must be 120° each, and y must be 60°, so $y + z = 180°$.
3. The angles in a triangle must add up to 180°. Since we already have angles 90° and 30°, the remaining angle must be 60°.
4. Since this triangle is isosceles, the two bottom angles measure 40° each. To make a total of 180°, $x = 100°$.
5. The area of this square is 6×6, or 36.
6. The area of a triangle is $\frac{1}{2}$ base × height, or $\frac{1}{2} \times 8 \times 6 = 24$.

7a. The area of this circle is $3^2\pi$, or 9π.

7b. The circumference of this circle is $2(3)\pi$, or 6π.

8a. Since this figure is a rectangle, $x = 10$ and $y = 5$.

8b. The perimeter is $10 + 5 + 10 + 5 = 30$.

CHAPTER 8

HSPT Language Exercise

1. Since "many people" is plural, it needs the plural verb form *are*: "There **are** already many people in the auditorium."
2. Since "my father's company" is singular, the pronoun and verb should be singular *it is* instead of the plural *they are:* "Since my father's company has so much business, it is very busy."
3. "My uncle" is singular, so it needs the singular verb form *helps:* "My uncle often **helps** my parents to make dinner."
4. This is a sentence fragment. A complete sentence would read: "On his way to school, Henry ran into his friend."
5. The first verb, "ran," is in the past tense; to maintain parallel form, the second verb, "escaping," should also be in the past tense: "The giant mouse ran through the house and **escaped** from the cat."

6. There should be a comma after the date and before the year: "I met her on March 1, 2010."

7. The first verb, "won" is in the past tense, and the second verb, "receives," is in the present tense. You know the sentence should be in the past tense because of the clue words "last year." To maintain parallel form, the verbs should both be in the same tense: "Last year, Ines won the first prize and **received** a beautiful trophy."

8. "Most biggest" is not a valid comparative form. The sentence should simply read "Roger finished his **biggest** assignment."

9. The first verb, "cleaned," is in the past tense, but the second verb, "gives," is in the present tense. To maintain parallel form, these verbs should both be in the same tense: "Colin cleaned the bowl and **gave** it to his mother."

10. Since "my brother and I" are the people being read to, not doing the reading, the pronoun should be objective: "Rachel read the letter to my brother and **me**."

Chapter 10
HSPT
Practice Test 1

Verbal Skills

Questions 1-60, 15 Minutes

1. Dog is to crate as human is to

a. park
b. porch
c. house
d. yard

2. Blatant is to obvious as outrageous is to

a. candid
b. extreme
c. false
d. bland

3. Ruminate most nearly means

a. move
b. bother
c. direct
d. ponder

4. Which word does *not* belong with the others?

a. run
b. walk
c. jog
d. halt

5. Meager means the *opposite* of

a. plentiful
b. pleading
c. measured
d. hostile

6. Mundane most nearly means

a. mobile
b. commonplace
c. factual
d. worldly

7. Which word does *not* belong with the others?

a. path
b. trail
c. park
d. route

8. Dull is to insipid as tart is to

a. faint
c. tainted
c. sharp
d. spoiled

9. Which word does *not* belong with the others?

a. toe
b. nose
c. person
d. ear

10. Team is to coach as orchestra is to

a. manager
b. violinist
c. conductor
d. soloist

11. Which word does *not* belong with the others?

a. tulip
b. daffodil
c. daisy
d. flower

12. Pragmatic most nearly means

a. flexible
b. practical
c. measured
d. novel

13. Act is to play as chapter is to

a. book
b. poem
c. movie
d. verse

14. Innocuous means the *opposite* of

a. virulent
b. harmless
c. benign
d. tame

15. Which word does *not* belong with the others?

a. gloves
b. earmuffs
c. sandals
d. snowshoes

16. Docile means the *opposite* of

a. dreamy
b. sweet
c. grouchy
d. wild

17. Which word does *not* belong with the others?

a. fish
b. trout
c. salmon
d. snapper

18. Feeble most nearly means

a. foolish
b. fickle
c. weak
d. timid

19. Omelet is to egg as pancake is to

a. cake
b. batter
C. fruit
D. syrup

20. Which word does *not* belong with the others?

a. granite
b. limestone
c. slate
d. pebble

21. Gullible most nearly means

a. gut-wrenching
b. credulous
c. playful
d. unwise

22. Buckle is to belt as lace is to

a. shoe
b. glove
c. shirt
d. sleeve

23. Stem is to leaf as trunk is to

a. petal
b. branch
c. root
d. bark

24. Which word does *not* belong with the others?

a. rake
b. hoe
c. tool
d. shovel

25. Spawn most nearly means

a. make
b. con
c. stop
d. trap

26. Rachel wrote her book report after Connie. Hoda wrote her book report after Alec. Rachel wrote her book report before Alec. If the first two statements are true, the third is

a. True
b. False
c. Uncertain

27. Which word does *not* belong with the others?

a. inch
b. centimeter
c. interval
d. yard

28. In a horse race, Devil's Advocate finished before Spirited Away. Incognito finished the race after Spirited Away. Incognito finished the race before Devil's Advocate. If the first two statements are true, the third is

a. True
b. False
c. Uncertain

29. Prevail most nearly means

a. outsmart
b. seek
c. succeed
d. send

30. Exonerate most nearly means

a. pardon
b. worship
c. raise
d. condemn

31. Soft is to touch as sour is to

a. cherry
b. food
c. garbage
d. taste

32. Which word does *not* belong with the others?

a. track
b. tennis
c. basketball
d. shoe

33. Eloquent means the *opposite* of

a. verbose
b. elegant
c. zany
d. inarticulate

34. Nurse is to hospital as teacher is to

a. school
b. student
c. lesson
d. class

35. Aloof most nearly means

a. curious
b. alert
c. detached
d. content

36. Which word does *not* belong with the others?

a. pound
b. weight
c. ounce
d. kilogram

37. Nick can do more push-ups than Delaynie and Kevin. Anne can do more push-ups than Nick. Kevin can do more push-ups than Delaynie. If the first two statements are true, the third is

a. True
b. False
c. Uncertain

38. Conniving means the *opposite* of

a. manipulative
b. congenial
c. uncertain
d. forthright

39. Lush most nearly means

a. expensive
b. luxurious
c. sterile
d. fragrant

40. Which word does *not* belong with the others?

a. leaf
b. bud
c. petal
d. root

41. Plainville has more inhabitants than Rehoboth, but fewer than Allentown. Bellingham has fewer inhabitants than Rehoboth. Allentown has more inhabitants than Bellingham. If the first two statements are true, the third is

a. True
b. False
c. Uncertain

42. Blade is to grass as wave is to

a. tide
b. ocean
c. ripple
d. tsunami

43. Which word does *not* belong with the others?

a. band
b. guitar
c. piano
d. drums

44. Toni, Katelyn, and David have the same number of plants. Giselle has fewer plants than Katelyn. David has fewer plants than Giselle. If the first two statements are true, the third is

a. True
b. False
c. Uncertain

45. Dubious most nearly means

a. doubtful
b. double
c. tired
d. intense

46. Ephemeral means the *opposite* of

a. expiring
b. fleeting
c. brushing
d. lasting

47. Which word does *not* belong with the others?

a. actor
b. director
c. theater
d. stage hand

48. Conspicuous most nearly means

a. joined
b. prominent
c. central
d. suitable

49. Comprehensive most nearly means

a. complete
b. understandable
c. confusing
d. valid

50. Which word does *not* belong with the others?

a. bumper
b. tire
c. trunk
d. car

51. Hinder means the *opposite* of

a. free
b. domesticate
c. practice
d. keep

52. Reminisce most nearly means

a. remake
b. manage
c. rematch
d. recollect

53. Undermine means the *opposite* of

a. challenge
b. aid
c. protect
d. damage

54. Ophelia is older than Everleigh and Lisa. Sean is older than Jimmy and Alexis. Ophelia is younger than Sean. If the first two statements are true, the third is

a. True
b. False
c. Uncertain

55. Novel most nearly means

a. new
b. bookish
c. plain
d. established

56. Shelly can skip rope more times than Kevin but fewer times than Jenna. Antoni can skip rope more times than Sheri and Jenna. Antoni can skip rope fewer times than Shelly.

a. True
b. False
c. Uncertain

57. Legitimate means the *opposite* of

a. solid
b. laughable
c. invalid
d. legal

58. Overt most nearly means

a. blatant
b. truncated
c. blunt
d. inane

59. Greg has more dogs than Farran but fewer than Trixie. Trixie has fewer dogs than Tyler. Greg has more dogs than Tyler. If the first two statements are true, the third is

a. True
b. False
c. Uncertain

60. Recalcitrant means the *opposite* of

a. reticent
b. insolent
c. stubborn
d. obedient

Quantitative Skills

Questions 1–52, 30 Minutes

1. What number should come next in this series: 2, 4, 8, 16, ___?

a. 24
b. 32
c. 34
d. 64

2. Examine the triangle below and find the best answer.

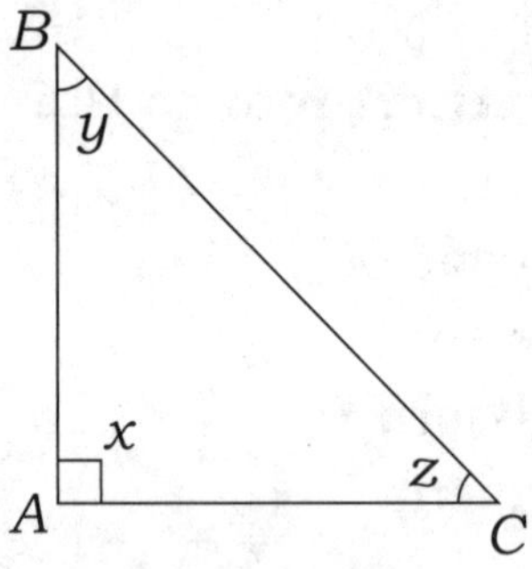

a. ∠y is equal to ∠z
b. $\overline{AB}$ is equal to $\overline{BC}$
c. $\overline{AB}$ is bigger than $\overline{AC}$
d. ∠y+∠z is equal to ∠x

3. What number divided by 3 is $\frac{1}{4}$ of 48?

a. 12
b. 18
c. 24
d. 36

4. Examine the following and find the best answer:

I. $\frac{1}{2}$ of 18

II. $\sqrt{81}$

III. $\frac{1}{3}$ of 27

a. I > II > III
b. I = III > II
c. I = II = III
d. II = III > I

5. What number should come next in this series: 96, 48, 24, 12, ___?

a. 4
b. 6
c. 8
d. 10

6. Examine A, B, and C to find the best answer.

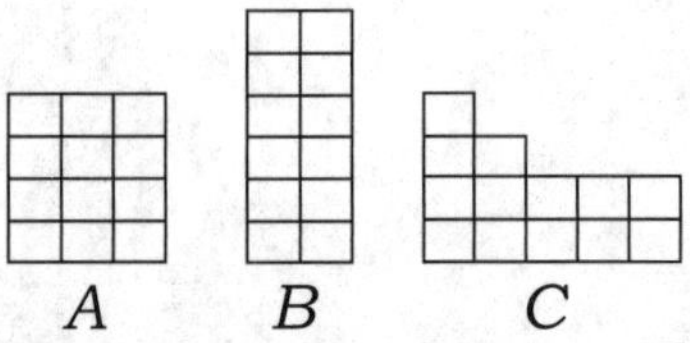

a. A has more squares than B but fewer than C
b. A, B, and C each have the same number of squares
c. C has more squares than A and B
d. B has more squares than A and C

7. What number should come next in this series: 8, 12, 20, 36, ___?

a. 60
b. 64
c. 68
d. 72

8. Examine the following to find the best answer:

I. 50% of 80
II. 25% of 120
III. 300% of 12

a. I is greater than II and III
b. III is less than II but greater than I
c. II is greater than I and III
d. I, II, and III are all the same

9. 25% of what number is 3 times 10?

a. 60
b. 75
c. 100
d. 120

10. What number should come next in this series: 1, –3, 9, –27, ___?

a. –81
b. –54
c. 54
d. 81

11. Examine the following to find the best answer:

I. -2^3
II. -3^2
III. 3^2

a. III is greater than I but less than II
b. II is less than I and III
c. II and III are equal but less than I
d. I, II, and III are the same

12. What number should come next in this series: 11, 15, 19, 23, ___?

a. 25
b. 26
c. 27
d. 28

13. $\frac{2}{3}$ of what number is $\frac{1}{4}$ of 48?

a. 12
b. 14
c. 16
d. 18

14. What number should come next in this series: 5, 6, 8, 11, ___?

a. 15
b. 17
c. 19
d. 20

15. What number is $\frac{1}{4}$ the product of 2, –3, and –4?

a. –6
b. –4
c. 4
d. 6

16. Examine the following to find the best answer:

I. $\frac{3}{8}$
II. $\frac{6}{16}$
III. $\frac{24}{64}$

a. I is greater than II, and II is greater than III
b. II is less than III, but greater than I
c. I, II, and III are all equal
d. I is less than II and III

17. What number is 200% of the sum of 3 and 12?

a. 15
b. 30
c. 36
d. 72

18. Examine the following to find the best answer:

I. $2(3 \times 9)$
II. $-2(-2 \times 10)$
III. $-3 \times 2 \times 10$

a. I is greater than II, and II is greater than III
b. I, II, and III are all equal
c. I is less than II but greater than III
d. III is greater than both I and II

19. What number should fill in the blank in this series: 48, –24, 12, ___, 3?

a. –6
b. –4
c. 3
d. 6

20. What number is $\frac{1}{10}$ of the product of 20 and 3?

a. 3
b. 6
c. 18
d. 60

21. Below is a circle with center *O*. Find the best answer.

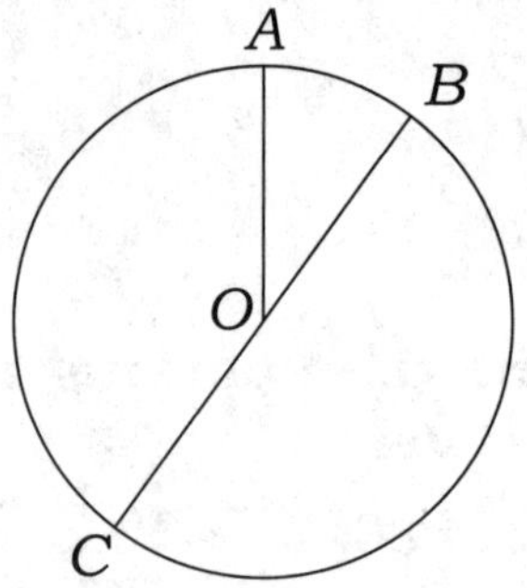

a. $OA > OB > CB$
b. $OA = OB > BC$
c. $BC > OB = OA$
d. $OA > OB = OC$

22. What number divided by 5 is 20% of 50?

a. 10
b. 25
c. 50
d. 75

23. What number should fill in the blank in this series: 6, 12, ___, 18, 15, 30?

a. 9
b. 10
c. 13
d. 15

24. Examine the following to find the best answer:

I. The square root of 100
II. 50% of 80
III. 250% of 15

a. I is greater than II, II is greater than III
b. I, II, and III are all equal
c. III is greater than II, II is less than I
d. I is less than II, II is greater than III

25. The difference of 25 and what number is 25% of 20?

a. 5
b. 10
c. 15
d. 20

26. What number should fill in the blank in this series: 4, 16, 8, ___, 3, 9?

a. 48
b. 52
c. 64
d. 72

27. Below are a rectangle and right triangle. Find the best answer.

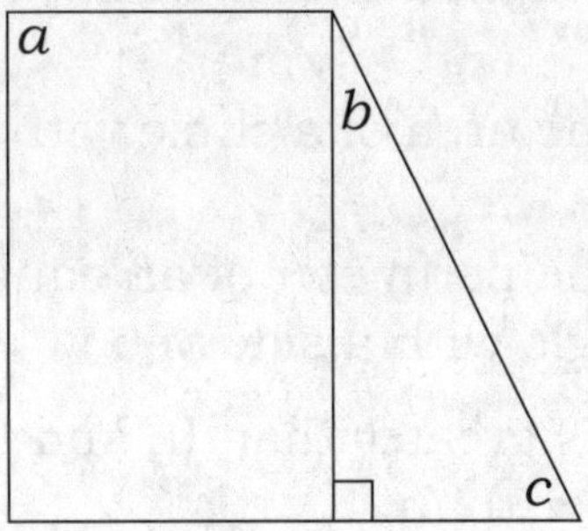

a. $a < b < c$
b. $a = b + c$
c. $b + a = c$
d. $a + c = b$

28. What number should come next in this series: 30, 15, 24, 12, ___?

a. 18
b. 20
c. 21
d. 24

29. What number is 75% of 40?

a. 20
b. 25
c. 30
d. 35

30. What number should come next in this series: 2, 8, 6, 12, 10, 16, 14, ___?

a. 18
b. 20
c. 22
d. 24

31. Examine the following to find the best answer:

I. The area of a square with a side of 4

II. The area of a circle with a radius of 4

III. The perimeter of an equilateral triangle with a side of 6

a. I is greater than II, and II is greater than III

b. I, II, and III are all equal

c. II is greater than III, III is less than I

d. I is less than II, and II is greater than III

32. What number is 5 more than the product of 3^2 and 50% of 10?

a. 35

b. 45

c. 50

d. 60

33. Examine the image below and find the best answer:

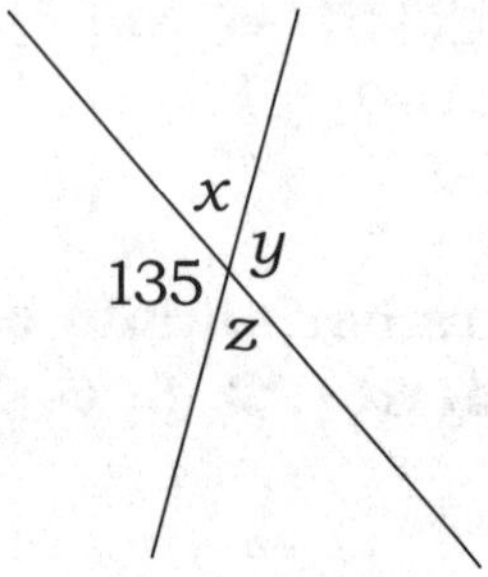

a. $x + y = y + z$

b. $x + z > y$

c. $z = y = x$

d. $y - x = z$

34. What number should come next in this series: 22, 44, 33, 66, ___?

a. 49

b. 55

c. 88

d. 132

35. What number should come next in this series: 3, 9, 4, 16, 11, 121, ___?

a. 32

b. 72

c. 110

d. 116

36. What number is 25% of 40% of 500?

a. 25

b. 50

c. 75

d. 100

37. Examine (A), (B), and (C) to find the best answer.

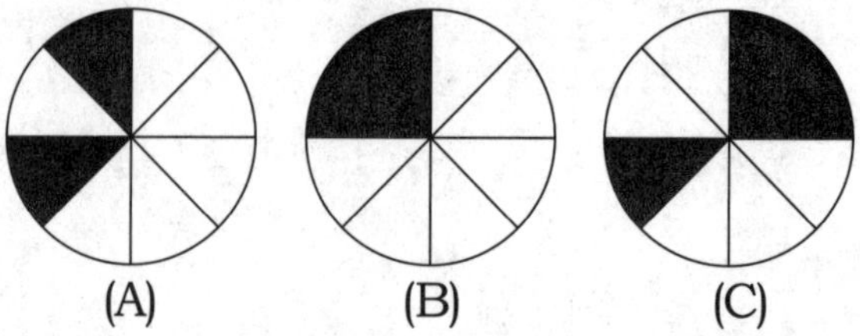

a. (A) is more shaded than (B)

b. (A) and (B) together are shaded equal to (C)

c. (C) is more shaded than (A) and (B)

d. (A) is more shaded than (C)

38. What number is $\frac{4}{5}$ of the median of 5, 25, and 30?

a. 20
b. 30
c. 48
d. 60

39. What number should fill in the blank in this series: 0, 7, 14, 21, ___, 35?

a. 24
b. 27
c. 28
d. 32

40. Examine the following to find the best answer:

I. 4.5×10^{-4}
II. .045
III. 4.5×10^{-3}

a. I is greater than II, II is greater than III
b. I, II, and III are all equal
c. II is greater than III, I is less than III
d. I is less than II, III is greater than II

41. What number comes next in this series: $\frac{1}{2}, \frac{1}{4}, \frac{1}{6}, \frac{1}{8}, \frac{1}{10}$ ___?

a. $\frac{1}{10}$
b. $\frac{1}{12}$
c. $\frac{1}{16}$
d. $\frac{1}{32}$

42. Examine the following to find the best answer if $x = 3$:

I. $3x^2$
II. $4x$
III. $\frac{x^3}{2}$

a. III is greater than II, I is greater than III
b. I, II, and III are all equal
c. II is greater than III, I is less than III
d. I is less than II, II is greater than III

43. What is 30% of 75% of 400?

a. 30
b. 90
c. 100
d. 150

44. What number leaves a remainder of 5 when divided by 6?

a. 30
b. 35
c. 36
d. 42

45. What number should come next in this series: 8, 15, 29, 57, ___?

a. 96
b. 100
c. 113
d. 124

46. Examine the following to find the best answer:

I. The perimeter of an equilateral triangle with a side of 18

II. The area of a square with side of 9

III. The area of a 45-45-90 triangle with base of 16

a. I, II, and III are all equal

b. II is greater that I but less than III

c. III is less than I but greater than II

d. I is greater than II, and II is greater than III

47. What number is 4 greater than the square root of 64?

a. 8

b. 9

c. 12

d. 15

48. What number should fill in the blank in this series: 10, 18, 15, ___, 20, 28?

a. 20

b. 21

c. 22

d. 23

49. Examine the following rectangles and triangles to find the best answer:

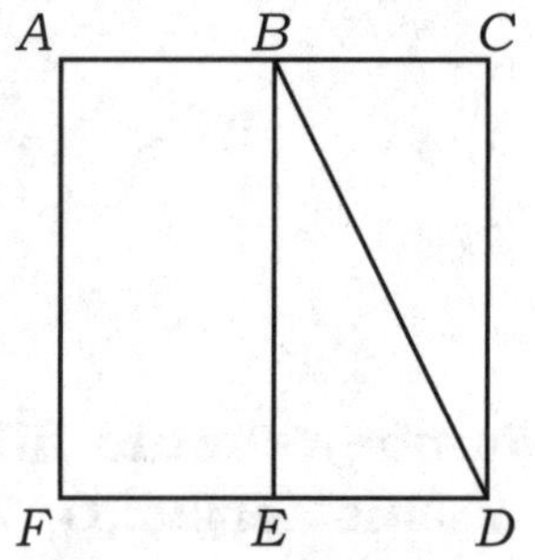

I. The area of ABEF

II. The area of BDE

III. The area of ACDF

a. I is greater than II and III

b. III is less than II and II greater than I

c. I, II, and III are equal

d. III is greater than the sum of I and II

50. What number is $\frac{1}{4}$ the average of 16, 20, 26, and 34?

a. 6

b. 8

c. 24

d. 96

51. What number should come next in this series: 2, 3, 4, 6, 8, 12, ___?

a. 12

b. 15

c. 16

d. 17

52. What number is 9 more than $\frac{1}{3}$ of 81?

a. 27

b. 30

c. 33

d. 36

Reading

Questions 1–40, 25 Minutes

Questions 1–8 refer to the following passage.

Passage 1 - The Westbeth

I had always imagined New York City as a bustling maze of concrete, with people swarming like bees around a honey comb. At each street corner, I envisioned the raucous car horns screaming by brightly colored hotdog stands and Halal carts and Broadway lights flashing their grand marquee, attracting audiences from far and wide to attend the next showstopping extravaganza.

But here I was, on a quiet cobblestone crosswalk without a car in sight as I walked up to the stone entryway of the unassuming Westbeth building. Ivy snaked up and wound around the windows, much in the way I was used to seeing back home on the brick <u>edifices</u> in New England. As I passed under the carved archway and into the foyer, the silence echoed against the marble, amplifying each footstep as I glanced around timidly for the elevator. My performance was on the twelfth floor. Who was going to come? Would they know there was a theater in this converted residence hall? Would they make the effort to come all the way to the top floor?

I stepped gingerly into the cramped elevator, praying the elevator would hold my weight as I manually closed the wire gate behind me. The rickety shaft stuttered and spurred up to the twelfth floor, coming to an abrupt halt at the top. The outer door rolled open, and I stepped into a bustling sanctuary of wonder. The Merce Cunningham Studio, the storied dance space I had dreamt about from history books, stood in front of me. The <u>din</u> of preshow excitement waved over me as other dancers, choreographers, lighting designers, and producers mingled in the entryway as I stepped out of the elevator. I ventured into the hallowed studio to find a seemingly infinite dance floor spreading the entire length of the room. The industrial, exposed beams of the cathedral roof stretched majestically over the stage floor as I took my first step onto the dance floor. Far from the multicolored marquee, this was the real New York, the one that I would treasure the rest of my artistic life.

1. When the story begins, the narrator describes New York as

a. boring
b. overwhelming
c. busy
d. ugly

2. The word <u>edifices</u>, as used in the passage, most nearly means

a. pathways
b. vines
c. buildings
d. streets

3. The narrator describes the Westbeth as "unassuming" probably because

a. it wasn't in New York
b. it wasn't flashy like the theaters on Broadway
c. it was falling apart
d. it reminded her of home

4. Which of the following is true of the Westbeth described in the second paragraph?

a. its architecture is older than the theaters'
b. it is on a quiet street
c. it is falling apart and needs repair
d. it is surrounded by flashing lights and food carts

5. The narrator describes the dance floor as "seemingly infinite" probably because

a. spanned the entire room
b. it stretched into space
c. it was oddly shaped
d. it was otherworldly

6. The word <u>din</u>, as used in the passage, most nearly means

a. darkness
b. silence
c. antiquity
d. clamor

7. The narrator "stepped gingerly into the cramped elevator" probably because

a. the elevator was old and insecure
b. the elevator was broken
c. the narrator was afraid of elevators
d. the narrator did not know how elevators work

8. The narrator finds the Westbeth remarkable for its

a. hustle and bustle
b. wealth of hidden opportunity
c. ivy crawling up its walls
d. showstopping extravaganzas

Questions 9–16 refer to the following passage.

Passage 2 – Marie Curie and Radiology

Marie Curie made history as the first woman to win the Nobel Prize, not once but twice, for her discoveries in Chemistry and Physics. Her contributions of discovering two new elements and isolating radioactive isotopes remain invaluable to the medical community. Any time someone has an X-ray for a broken bone, they should be thanking Marie Curie.

Madame Curie, born Maria Sklodowska, did her professional training in Warsaw, Poland, where she was born, and then continued on to Paris to continue her education and research. There, she met Pierre Curie, who invited her to collaborate in some scientific projects. Eventually the two married and continued to work on experiments in a Paris lab, where she eventually became known as Marie instead of Maria. Shortly thereafter, they discovered two new elements, polonium and radium. Marie Curie named the element "polonium" after her native country, Poland, and the couple named the element "radium" after the Latin word for "ray."

The Curies also coined the term "radioactivity" as well and were the first to discover that radiation killed tumor-forming cells more easily than healthy cells. To solidify their discovery, the team attempted to isolate the two elements. While it was relatively simple to isolate polonium, radium remained elusive. For this discovery, Pierre Curie and the couple's research partner Henri Becquerel were nominated for the Nobel Prize in 1908. Madame Curie was not initially nominated. However, a committee member and women's rights advocate alerted Pierre of the nomination, and he protested to add Marie to the nomination as well. This made her the first woman to be nominated for the Nobel Prize.

Upon the death of her husband in 1908, Marie Curie also became the first female professor at the University of Paris, where she decided to continue her husband's legacy. However, Marie realized that she would not get adequate lab space as she expected, so she bravely threatened to resign. As a result, in partnership with the Pasteur Institute and the University of Paris, Curie was able to implement the Curie Pavilion. She continued her research into isolating radium, for which she finally succeeded and won her second Nobel Prize in 1911.

Madame Curie died in 1934 due to the long-term effects of radiation from her research. However, her research has certainly continued her legacy in modern-day science. In the present day, X-rays serve as a powerful tool for many common ailments, from diagnosing broken bones to fighting cancer. For this, we should tip our hats to Madame Curie.

9. This passage is mostly about

a. the awards Marie Curie has won
b. how to isolate radium
c. why women's rights are so important
d. the important contributions of Marie Curie's research

10. According to the facts in the passage, Madame Curie contributed to the fields of

a. Medicine and Biology
b. Medicine and Immunology
c. Immunology and Chemistry
d. Chemistry and Physics

11. The word elusive, as used in the passage, most nearly means

a. difficult to isolate
b. hard to see
c. curious
d. invisible

12. It can be inferred from the passage that the University of Paris

a. is a corrupt institution
b. was not initially going to offer Curie a larger lab space
c. valued Louis Pasteur's research more than Pierre Curie's
d. did not have money to support the Curies

13. The author would most likely agree with which of the following statements?

a. Pierre Curie made more contributions to science than did his wife.
b. The theory of radiology is the most important discovery of the twentieth century.
c. It took longer for the Curies to isolate radium than plutonium.
d. The Curies did not deserve the Nobel Prize.

14. The word threatened, as used in the passage, most nearly means

a. endangered
b. understood
c. expressed an intent
d. advised

15. It can be inferred from the passage that radium

a. was difficult to isolate
b. was easier to work with than plutonium
c. looked like a light ray
d. was a complex compound

16. Curie's accomplishments help our modern-day ability to

a. isolate germs
b. take x-rays
c. sterilize scientific tools
d. understand how the atoms work

Questions 17–24 refer to the following passage.

Passage 3 – A Caffeinated Nation

Long before Starbucks, the U.S. has had a long love affair with that dark, bitter drink that occasionally gives people the jitters. However, coffee has not had quite as long a history in the U.S. as you might think. In fact, most people drank tea instead of coffee until the infamous Boston Tea Party in 1773, at which point coffee was seen as the patriotic drink of choice to protest the British Empire.

While there are earlier accounts of brewed drinks with the entire red coffee berry around 1000 A.D., the earliest form of our modern-day idea of coffee stems from Arabian practices in the 1300s. It was in Arabia that people first started to roast the coffee beans before brewing drinks with it, and the idea quickly spread through Africa. Colonial powers started to grow the coffee in Southeast Asia and the Caribbean in the 17th century as it grew in popularity. It soon became a powerful trading tool with Eastern Europe and eventually made its way to Italy and France. In the 18th and 19th centuries, the idea of the coffee house took hold, only furthering the drink's popularity.

Throughout all this time, though, there was little to no coffee consumption in the U.S., even though coffee plants were being grown in the nearby Caribbean. Why? The U.S. was still part of the British Empire in which most people consumed tea. This changed when King George III decided to place a tax on tea, which resulted in Boston residents throwing hundreds of pounds of tea into the harbor to protest. After this point, coffee became a drink of protest against the unfair tea tax. During the Civil War years, coffee grew in popularity and later became a popular social drink as it had already become across Europe.

Coffee remains one of our most precious commodities across the world, second only to oil. Large brands such as Starbucks have capitalized on the idea of specialty coffee, though many smaller independent coffee companies have sprouted up across the country as well. Many promote social awareness with fair trade. Others treat coffee as an artisan treat. Still others are mad scientists, inventing new and interesting recipes. All the while, this unique beverage has a rich and complex history, as rich and complex as its flavor.

17. This story is mostly about

a. how people first learned to roast coffee beans
b. the history of coffee houses
c. the Boston Tea Party's legacy
d. the history of coffee and its how popularity has grown in the U.S.

18. The word <u>stems</u>, as used in the passage, most nearly means

a. originates
b. spills
c. stalks
d. restricts

19. The people who first roasted coffee beans were the

a. Italians
b. French
c. Arabians
d. Americans

20. The author says that when it first arrived in the U.S., coffee was

a. different in taste than it is now
b. initially not very popular
c. immediately a household staple
d. a form of protest against the British Empire

21. It can be inferred from the passage that

a. Colonial powers helped to spread coffee consumption throughout the world.
b. scientists are performing experiments with coffee.
c. coffee tastes better when the beans are roasted first.
d. tea tastes better than coffee.

22. The word <u>sprouted up</u>, as used in the passage, most nearly means

a. germinated
b. emerged
c. budded
d. flowered

23. Which of the following can be inferred from the passage?

a. Coffee had more of an effect when the beans are roasted first.
b. Coffee houses furthered the popularity of coffee drinks.
c. Everyone who protests drinks coffee.
d. Starbucks is the only coffee shop that offers lots of options for coffee drinks.

24. According to the passage, which of the following is true?

a. There are a variety of coffee companies across the U.S.
b. Starbucks is the most influential coffee company in the U.S.
c. The Civil War made coffee popular initially.
d. There were people who secretly drank coffee before the Boston Tea Party.

Questions 25–32 refer to the following passage.

Passage 4 – The First American Space Launch in Almost a Decade

On May 30th, 2020, the first American space expedition in almost a decade launched in Florida, set for the International Space Station. While there have been quite a few space launches throughout latter half of the twentieth century in the United States, this one certainly was one for the history books.

First of all, the spacecraft was launched by the private company SpaceX instead of the government-sponsored NASA program. Up until this point, the only research, space travel, and innovation was done through NASA. All of the famous Apollo, Challenger, and Discovery missions were undertakings of NASA, as were the other innovations in technology that were developed for space research. However, SpaceX's quirky yet visionary founder, Elon Musk, has some ideas that fundamentally change how space research and travel occur. Musk, also the founder of the Tesla car company, memorably sent a Tesla with a dummy driver into space during one of SpaceX's test runs.

One of the most innovative achievements of the SpaceX's approach to space missions is sustainability. Previous missions have created space waste as propellers and launchers detach and float endlessly in space. However, SpaceX has created technology to reuse orbital rockets by allowing them to return to earth. This mission's Falcon 9, the orbital rocket that initially gets the spacecraft into space from earth, successfully came back to earth and impressively landed itself perfectly on a landing target on a barge ship. The Dragon 2, the spacecraft transporting the astronauts, also successfully attached to the International Space Station without a hitch, and will be reused for future missions as well.

What will SpaceX do next? Musk has stated that he wants to bring the cost of space travel down, increasing the average person's ability to travel to space one day. He also plans to build spacecrafts large enough to travel to Mars, possibly allowing for colonization in the future. Currently, Musk has plans to send two unmanned cargo ships to Mars in 2022 called the Starships. Does this mean that colonization on Mars is not too far off?

25. This passage is mostly about

a. SpaceX's revolutionary innovations in space travel
b. how SpaceX is a new version of NASA
c. space travel to Mars
d. sustainability and space

26. One of SpaceX's innovations was

a. traveling to Mars
b. reusing the Falcon 9 rocket
c. transporting astronauts to the International Space Station
d. orbiting the moon

27. The word <u>undertakings</u>, as used in the passage, most nearly means

a. travels
b. tasks
c. spacecrafts
d. tests

28. According to the passage, which of the following is true?

a. SpaceX has successfully transported civilians to Mars.
b. SpaceX is fully funded by the government.
c. SpaceX sent a car into space on a test launch.
d. SpaceX is a superior agency to NASA.

29. With which of the following would the author probably agree?

a. The Apollo missions were the greatest launches in the history of the U.S.
b. SpaceX will partner with the government to colonize Mars.
c. NASA and SpaceX will travel beyond Mars someday.
d. NASA contributed many technological innovations to society through its research.

30. According to the passage, one difference between NASA and SpaceX is that

a. SpaceX has plans to go to Mars
b. SpaceX has transported humans to space
c. SpaceX is privately owned
d. SpaceX has sent astronauts to the International Space Station

31. The word <u>hitch</u>, as used in the passage, most nearly means

a. connection
b. problem
c. hub
d. landing pad

32. According to the passage, what device successfully landed itself for reuse back on earth?

a. Falcon 9
b. Starship
c. Dragon 2
d. Apollo

Questions 33–40 refer to the following passage.

Passage 5 – The Legacy of Lester Horton

In the 1930s and 1940s, Lester Horton revolutionized the world of dance. He founded his own company, the Lester Horton Dancers, and theater, the Lester Horton Dance Theater, in Los Angeles in 1946. This was the first theater in the United States to feature only modern dance, which was <u>unprecedented</u> at the time. Not only was Horton a groundbreaking dancemaker, he also was the first to insist on having a racially integrated dance company, something truly radical at the time.

Not only was the theater space groundbreaking, but so was Horton's dance technique, which is still taught across the world today. To make his technique, Horton combined movements from Native American folk dance with elements of Balinese and Javanese upper body motions and Afro-Caribbean lower body motions. For instance, Horton incorporated upper body isolations found in Balinese and Javanese dance with hip rolls from Afro-Caribbean traditions to create a technique uniquely his own. He later documented these exercises as a set of warmups and strengtheners for the dancers in his company.

In addition to creating a unique movement vocabulary, Horton trained many famous dancers, including Alvin Ailey and Bella Lewitzky. Both Ailey and Lewitzky danced in Horton's company in the 40's and 50's, and they premiered many of Horton's works, from stage to film productions. While Lewitzky left the company in 1950, Ailey continued to dance for Horton until Horton's untimely death in 1953. Ailey led the company for a year before moving to New York to found his own company, bringing much of Horton's technique and vocabulary to a whole new audience.

Today, Lester Horton's influence <u>permeates</u> many dance genres and works. Many of Ailey's famous pieces of choreography feature Horton vocabulary, and many jazz dance teachers use the isolations and body movements of his exercises as part of their pedagogy. Whether you knew his name or not, it is almost certain that you have seen the effects of Horton's innovations in the world today.

33. According to the passage, where did Horton draw inspiration for his technique?

a. Ballet
b. Tap
c. Afro-Caribbean
d. Jazz

34. The word <u>unprecedented</u>, as used in the passage, most nearly means

a. interesting
b. unparalleled
c. strange
d. extraordinary

35. You would probably find this article in

a. a biology textbook
b. a diary
c. an instructional manual
d. an encyclopedia

36. What would be the best title for this passage?

a. The Rise of Alvin Ailey
b. Horton Technique: a Compendium
c. Horton the Revolutionary
d. The History of Jazz Dance

37. Which of the following can be inferred from the passage?

a. Jazz dance may borrow some of the concepts from Horton technique.
b. Jazz dance came before other modern dance techniques.
c. Horton technique is superior to other modern dance techniques.
d. Alvin Ailey was the lead dancer of Horton's company.

38. Bella Lewitzky was Horton's

a. director
b. dancer
c. mentor
d. teacher

39. The author would probably agree with which of the following statements?

a. Alvin Ailey was the best dancer in Horton's company.
b. Los Angeles was the epicenter of modern dance in the 1940s.
c. Horton technique is more revolutionary than other modern dance techniques.
d. Lester Horton made significant contributions to the field of modern dance.

40. The word <u>permeates</u>, as used in the passage, most nearly means

a. extends
b. passes through
c. pretends
d. intrudes

Vocabulary

41. Choose the best definition of the underlined word.

a <u>commonplace</u> object

a. shared
b. odd
c. ordinary
d. authentic

42. Choose the best definition of the underlined word.

To tread <u>lightly</u>

a. carefully
b. flippantly
c. carelessly
d. informallly

43. Choose the best definition of the underlined word.

The <u>apex</u> of the mountain

a. climax
b. highlight
c. emphasis
d. peak

44. Choose the best definition of the underlined word.

a <u>tacit</u> agreement

a. understood
b. unknown
c. legitimate
d. surefire

45. Choose the best definition of the underlined word.

a <u>whirlwind</u> tour

a. short-lived
b. quick
c. chaotic
d. thoughtless

46. Choose the best definition of the underlined word.

a <u>docile</u> animal

a. pliable
b. soft
c. beautiful
d. calm

47. Choose the best definition of the underlined word.

a <u>solid</u> plan

a. confident
b. malleable
c. definite
d. positive

48. Choose the best definition of the underlined word.

the <u>heart</u> of the city

a. center
b. region
c. mind
d. emotion

49. Choose the best definition of the underlined word.

to <u>feign</u> illness

a. assume
b. fake
c. mock
d. fantasize

50. Choose the best definition of the underlined word.

a <u>biased</u> subject

a. unfair
b. independent
c. defiant
d. influenced

51. Choose the best definition of the underlined word.

a <u>rigid</u> decision

a. harsh
b. inflexible
c. sound
d. correct

52. Choose the best definition of the underlined word.

a <u>senseless</u> murder

a. priceless
b. needless
c. ridiculous
d. feckless

53. Choose the best definition of the underlined word.

an unforeseen <u>circumstance</u>

a. job
b. place
c. post
d. situation

54. Choose the best definition of the underlined word.

a <u>deviant</u> habit

a. evil
b. reckless
c. abnormal
d. ingrained

55. Choose the best definition of the underlined word.

a <u>veiled</u> insult

a. impolite
b. weighted
c. implied
d. laced

56. Choose the best definition of the underlined word.

to find <u>common</u> ground

a. unique
b. public
c. collective
d. everyday

57. Choose the best definition of the underlined word.

to <u>defy</u> the naysayers

a. disobey
b. challenge
c. change
d. redesign

58. Choose the best definition of the underlined word.

a <u>foolproof</u> plan

a. thoughtless
b. safe
c. secure
d. infallible

59. Choose the best definition of the underlined word.

a <u>snide</u> comment

a. sarcastic
b. slippery
c. insinuating
d. off-color

60. Choose the best definition of the underlined word.

a <u>true</u> friend

a. verified
b. notarized
c. loyal
d. upward

61. Choose the best definition of the underlined word.

to <u>transcend</u> differences

a. ascend
b. excel
c. overcome
d. outdo

62. Choose the best definition of the underlined word.

a <u>trendy</u> dress

a. elegant
b. stylish
c. classy
d. smart

Mathematics

Questions 1–64, 45 Minutes

1. Which can be divided by 6 with no remainder?

a. 33
b. 34
c. 36
d. 44

2. Which of the following is the largest?

a. $\frac{1}{4}$
b. $\frac{2}{3}$
c. $\frac{1}{5}$
d. $\frac{3}{5}$

3. If you add two odd whole numbers, the result will always be:

a. Negative
b. Positive and Odd
c. Odd
d. Even

4. How many distinct prime factors does the number 21 contain?

a. 1
b. 2
c. 3
d. 4

5. The radius of a circle with an area of 25π is

a. 4
b. 5
c. 12.5
d. 25

6. Which of the following is the least common multiple of 5 and 8?

a. 20
b. 24
c. 40
d. 80

7. What is 2.085 + 5.43 rounded to the nearest 10th?

a. 7.5
b. 7.528
c. 7.53
d. 8.5

8. What is the greatest integer less than 0?

a. –0.9
b. –1.5
c. –2
d. –6

9. Which of the following is equal to 2.55×10^3?

a. .00255
b. .255
c. 255
d. 2550

10. What is the perimeter of an equilateral triangle with a side of 6?

a. 12
b. 18
c. 24
d. 36

11. Which of the following is closest in value to –2.7?

a. –2.292
b. –2.35
c. –3.03
d. –3.043

12. The ratio of 8.5 to 6 is the same as

a. 17 to 12
b. 8 to 9
c. 200 to 60
d. 3 to 2

13. Two positive integers have a sum of 12 and product of 32. Which of the following could be one of those two numbers?

a. 3
b. 6
c. 8
d. 12

14. At Douglas Summer Camp, the ratio of campers to counselors is 7:1. What fractional part of the people at the camp are counselors?

a. $\frac{1}{7}$
b. $\frac{1}{8}$
c. $\frac{6}{7}$
d. $\frac{3}{4}$

15. If $-3.2 < x < 2.4$, how many possible integer values for x are there?

a. 5
b. 6
c. 7
d. 8

16. What is the perimeter of a square with an area of 81?

a. 9
b. 27
c. 36
d. 81

17. 4^3 =

a. 12
b. 48
c. 64
d. 86

18. Which of the following is the reciprocal of 4?

a. $\frac{1}{4}$
b. 2
c. 16
d. 32

19. Which of the following is equal to 0.125?

a. $\frac{3}{16}$

b. $\frac{1}{8}$

c. $\frac{3}{8}$

d. $\frac{13}{25}$

20. Which of the following is equal to $3\sqrt{6^3}$?

a. 6^3

b. $\sqrt{6}$

c. 36

d. 6

21. If the area of a triangle is 48 and its height is 8, what is the base?

a. 8

b. 10

c. 12

d. 24

22. The ratio of basketball players to soccer players at Douglas High School is 3:5. If 65 students are playing soccer, how many students are playing basketball?

a. 30

b. 36

c. 39

d. 45

23. How many 2-inch cubes can fit into a cube with a side of 4 inches?

a. 4

b. 6

c. 8

d. 10

24. In Kayla's backpack there are 5 flavors of chapstick and two of them are cherry. If Kayla takes one chapstick out of her backpack at a time, what is the greatest number of times she must pull a chapstick out of her bag to make sure she gets a cherry flavor?

a. 1

b. 2

c. 3

d. 4

Problem Solving

25. $\frac{10}{.3} =$

a. 3
b. 13
c. 30
d. 300

26. Chris went grocery shopping one day. He bought two loaves of bread costing $3 each and one pound of lunch meat costing $7. If he had $17 to spend, how much money did he have left at the end of the day?

a. $2
b. $4
c. $7
d. $10

27. If $3x + 6 = 15$, then $x =$

a. $\frac{4}{3}$
b. $\frac{5}{3}$
c. $\frac{7}{3}$
d. $\frac{9}{3}$

28. What percent of 200 is 30?

a. 10
b. 15
c. 18
d. 22

29. $5\frac{5}{6} + 3\frac{2}{6} =$

a. 8
b. $8\frac{1}{6}$
c. 9
d. $9\frac{1}{6}$

30. Alyssa buys a bag of candy every day of the week, except for Mondays and Tuesdays, when she buys 3 bags of candy. If a bag of candy costs $0.85, how much does Alyssa spend on candy every week?

a. $5.95
b. $7.65
c. $9.35
d. $12.75

31. Kevin is looking at a map where 2 miles is 3.5 inches to plan a hike. If Kevin's hike is 16 miles, what is the length in inches on the map?

a. 16 in.
b. 32 in.
c. 56 in.
d. 64 in.

32. During a clearance sale, a suit that originally cost $125 was marked down 60%. What was the price of the suit during the sale?

a. $50
b. $60
c. $75
d. $125

33. $\frac{18}{5} \times \frac{10}{5} =$

a. 10
b. 12
c. 15
d. 18

34. If $x^2 + 6 = 31$, then x could be

a. 2
b. 4
c. 5
d. 9

35. $6.1 \times 4.3 =$

a. 10.4
b. 22.83
c. 24.23
d. 26.23

36. Nick scored 26, 28, 32, and x on his four English exams. If his average score for the four tests was 27, what was the value of test x?

a. 20
b. 22
c. 25
d. 27

37. 30% of 50 is equal to 25% of what number?

a. 50
b. 60
c. 75
d. 80

38. Which of the following is equal to $\frac{8}{5} \div \frac{1}{5} =$

a. 5
b. 7
c. 8
d. 10

39. Joanne goes to a coffee shop and buys 5 boxes of muffins. Each box contains 6 muffins. If Joanne brings the muffins to her office of 7 people (including Joanne) and each eats 3 muffins, how many will be left at the end of the day?

a. 9
b. 11
c. 13
d. 15

40. How many hours will it take a car traveling 60 miles per hour to travel 270 miles?

a. 3
b. 3.5
c. 4
d. 4.5

41. $7 - (2 + 4) + 2 \times 6 =$

a. 8
b. 13
c. 21
d. 66

42. John is twice as old as Eli, and Eli is 6 years younger than Alex. If John is 14, how old will Alex be in 4 years?

a. 13
b. 15
c. 17
d. 22

43. If $3^x = 9^2$**, then** $x =$

a. 3
b. 4
c. 5
d. 6

44. If the ratio of peppers to onions in Greg's garden is 3:7 and there are 63 onions in the garden, how many peppers are there?

a. 7
b. 9
c. 13
d. 15

45. $4\frac{1}{6} \div 8\frac{1}{3} =$

a. $\frac{1}{3}$
b. $\frac{1}{2}$
c. 1
d. 2

46. $2x + 9 = 8x - 9$**, then** $x =$

a. –5
b. –2
c. 0
d. 3

47. Connie has decided to save money to buy a new tablecloth. If the tablecloth costs $36 and Connie saves $2.25 a day, how many days will it take to have enough money purchase the tablecloth?

a. 16
b. 18
c. 19
d. 22

48. Jerry has four times as many ties as Matt. If the average number of ties between the two men is 10, how many ties does Matt have?

a. 3
b. 4
c. 5
d. 6

49. If an isosceles right triangle has a side of 6, what is the area of two of these triangles?

a. 18
b. 36
c. 40
d. 72

50. If $-6x + 3 > 0$, which of the following is true?

a. –3
b. 1
c. 3
d. 5

51. If a newspaper deliverer begins their route at 6:10 A.M. and finishes at 2:35 P.M., how long did it take them to complete their paper route?

a. 3 hours 30 minutes
b. 4 hours 45 minutes
c. 6 hours 20 minutes
d. 8 hours 25 minutes

52. If the average of 7, 10, x is equal to the average of 6 and x, what is the value of x?

a. 16
b. 18
c. 20
d. 22

53. Jim put 35 pennies and 15 nickels in a bowl. Approximately what percent of the coins in the bowl are nickels?

a. 25%
b. 30%
c. 50%
d. 85%

54. How many times greater is $3\frac{3}{4}$ than $\frac{3}{4}$?

a. 3
b. 4
c. 5
d. 6

55. If $\frac{5}{3x} + 6\frac{1}{6} = 7$, then $x =$

a. $\frac{5}{6}$
b. 2
c. 4
d. 5

56. The price of a toaster is reduced by 25%. If the new price of the toaster is $45, what was the original price?

a. $60
b. $80
c. $92
d. $102

57. $\frac{.6 + .8 + 1 + 1.2}{2} =$

a. 1.2
b. 1.4
c. 1.6
d. 1.8

58. If Jordan can run 4 miles in 45 minutes, how long would it take him to run 12 miles?

a. 1 hour and 30 minutes
b. 2 hours and 15 minutes
c. 3 hours
d. 3 hours and 45 minutes

59. $3\sqrt{3} \times 3\sqrt{27} =$

a. $\sqrt{81}$
b. 9
c. $9\sqrt{81}$
d. 81

60. $(45 - 49) \times 3 + 3^2 =$

a. –48
b. –3
c. 3
d. 27

61. Kenny gets $4.75 for every lawn he mows. He wants to earn enough money to buy a new pair of shoes that costs $33. How many lawns will Kenny have to mow to be able to purchase the shoes?

a. 5
b. 6
c. 7
d. 8

62. At Douglas High, 120 students take AP History and 90 take AP Music Theory. Of those students, 45 take both AP History and AP Music Theory. How many students take AP History but do not take AP Music Theory?

a. 75
b. 85
c. 90
d. 95

63. If $3(3x - 4) = 33$, then x =

a. 2
b. 3
c. 4
d. 5

64. Which of the following is the product of two distinct prime numbers?

a. 9
b. 10
c. 25
d. 28

Language

Questions 1–60, 25 minutes

For questions 1-40, check the sentences for errors of usage, capitalization, or punctuation. If there is no error, choose (D).

1. **Choose the sentence with the correct grammar.**
   a. Retail stores try to make their clothing look as appealing as possible.
   b. The Washington Monument is the city's most sought out attraction.
   c. Most individuals require silence while they study.
   d. No mistake.

2. **Choose the sentence with the correct grammar.**
   a. There are seven kinds of fruit at the Farmer's Market.
   b. Today's computers are most more powerful than computers historically.
   c. It is necessary to listen to the entire album very intent.
   d. No mistake.

3. **Choose the sentence with the correct grammar.**
   a. Jenna purchased a new pot from a boutique shop.
   b. Adam left the ice cream on the counter and it melted.
   c. Many skillets are made from iron.
   d. No mistake.

4. **Choose the sentence with the correct punctuation.**
   a. I often have to look up words, in the dictionary.
   b. At the grocery store I purchased tomatoes, berries, and apples.
   c. Once I found a leak in the ceiling.
   d. No mistake.

5. **Choose the sentence with the correct capitalization.**
   a. Most of the cars in the united states are imported.
   b. Last year there was an inspiring exhibit at the Museum of Natural Science.
   c. If you install your own fence, Make sure to have a good shovel to dig your holes.
   d. No mistake.

6. Choose the sentence with the correct punctuation.

a. I was startled, when the doorbell rang.
b. Many of Jims questions are hypothetical and have no answers.
c. “That’s amazing,” he said. “I wish I had known that.”
d. No mistake.

7. Choose the sentence with the correct grammar.

a. I never realized my sister was scheduling a surprise party.
b. John goes to the library when he needed to study.
c. Even though Alex owns cars, he learned to fix them.
d. No mistake.

8. Choose the sentence with the correct grammar.

a. Most doesn’t realize how hard being a barber is.
b. He showed my family and me how to cook paella.
c. Max go to baseball games last summer.
d. No mistake.

9. Choose the sentence with the correct punctuation.

a. Doctors spend long times in school for training.
b. Fredrick Douglass was an expert, at speaking.
c. Teachers sometimes have trouble reading students’ handwriting.
d. No mistake.

10. Choose the sentence with the correct punctuation.

a. Every time the apartments power went out the residents panicked.
b. They were looking forward to attending their friend’s party.
c. The man in line forgot his wallet and didnt have enough money to purchase his food.
d. No mistake.

11. Choose the sentence with the correct grammar.

a. Jerry typically are very calm.
b. Michael ask, “What time should I arrive?”
c. My father owns a large coin collection.
d. No mistake.

12. Choose the sentence with the correct grammar.

a. Ethan knew his dog was incredibly smart.
b. Sometimes I has more troubles waking up in the morning in winter.
c. My sister makes and excellent painting.
d. No mistake.

13. Choose the sentence with the correct capitalization.

a. The mayor was known to be kind.
b. Chris went to the store to buy granny smith apples.
c. My father took me to National Football League game.
d. No mistake.

14. Choose the sentence with the correct punctuation.

a. Nick disliked the movie, that he saw last week.
b. "Isn't he cute?" asked Delaynie when her parents met her dog, Sunny, for the first time.
c. George Walker became the first African American composer, to win the Pulitzer Prize.
d. No mistake.

15. Choose the sentence with the correct grammar.

a. I make sure to wash my hands for 20 seconds when I get home.
b. Ella Fitzgerald had a beautiful singing voice.
c. My brother was unaware that cheetahs are so fast.
d. No mistake.

16. Choose the sentence with the correct grammar.

a. Frank donated blood every time their was a national disaster.
b. Hardly anyone believed Jackie Robinson would play Major League Baseball.
c. It is dangerous to drive when it rained.
d. No mistake.

17. Choose the sentence with the correct grammar.

a. My kids are not allowed to have eaten dessert unless they finish their dinner.
b. Kevin forgot his wallet and could wouldn't pay his friend back.
c. It is possible that Charlie wouldn't make it to the event on time.
d. No mistake.

18. Choose the sentence with the correct punctuation.

a. LeBron James won several championships, even after losing many times.
b. Whenever the postal worker delivers our mail, the dog across the street starts barking.
c. "Tammy, please bring that plate to the table," my mother stated.
d. No mistake.

19. Choose the sentence with the correct grammar.

a. Yesterday, my parents order Indian food for dinner.
b. The cleanup crew is pick up garbage left on the ground after the concert.
c. My teacher taught me the importance of creative writing.
d. No mistake.

20. Choose the sentence with the correct grammar.

a. Duke Ellington was the first jazz musician to receive the Medal of Freedom.
b. Dan didn't know which tie matched his suit.
c. My mother cooked us a healthy meal every night.
d. No mistake.

21. Choose the sentence with the correct grammar.

a. The lake near my house have beautiful hiking trails.
b. It was hard to hear the performance louder than the audience.
c. Sarah found the fruit she had just purchased spoiled.
d. No mistake.

22. Choose the sentence with the correct grammar.

a. Anne walks her dog many miles last month.
b. It is important to read to your children when they are young.
c. Learn to dance is not always easy.
d. No mistake.

23. Choose the sentence with the correct grammar.

a. My grandfather's health has been getting better.
b. My neighbor purchased a new car from her brother.
c. Public transportation can be slower, but helps the environment.
d. No mistake.

24. Choose the sentence with the correct grammar.

a. The Mayor always meets with people at the coffee shop.
b. No one know how hard my sister works.
c. Brady felt bad that he would have to miss his lesson tomorrow.
d. No mistake.

25. Choose the sentence with the correct grammar.

a. The President gives an impassioned speech to his country yesterday.
b. The airline did not explain why Joe's flight got delayed.
c. The cold temperature today was a record-breaking.
d. No mistake.

26. Choose the sentence with the correct grammar.

a. I can't believe I earned 25 point at bowling on my first try.
b. Travis leave his journal at school yesterday.
c. There are fewer cookies in the jar than when I looked this morning.
d. No mistake.

27. Choose the sentence with the correct grammar.

a. They has every reason to be skeptical.
b. Karamo win the teacher-of-the-year award.
c. Anne's dog is cuter than Anthony's.
d. No mistake.

28. Choose the sentence with the correct grammar.

a. Michael and I have been friends for over ten years.
b. It's so nice to see a familiar face.
c. There is a large pile of garbage sitting in the corner.
d. No mistake.

29. Choose the sentence with the correct grammar.

a. Unlike dogs, cat enjoy quiet time by themselves.
b. Paulina is a stellar caregiver to Marco.
c. Stella delegated the tasks to my sister and I.
d. No mistake.

30. Choose the sentence with the correct grammar.

a. My mother is more outgoing than I.
b. I would rather watch a movie with a close friend than go to a busy shopping center.
c. Plastic comprises almost half of the world's garbage.
d. No mistake.

31. Choose the sentence with the correct punctuation.

a. While it is important to brush your teeth, it is equally important to wash your face.
b. I wanted to go to the concert, but I got food poisoning.
c. Not only is Shelly a great singer, she is also a wonderful dancer.
d. No mistake.

32. Choose the sentence with the correct punctuation.

a. My dentist asked me "sir do you brush your teeth?"
b. Before I could meet the governor, the FBI ran a background check on me.
c. I sent letters to my grandmother, father and cousin.
d. No mistake.

33. Choose the sentence with the correct capitalization.

a. My best friends, Eli, Chris, and John, surprised me for dinner.
b. Mark called the customer service line in Texas.
c. Katie and Michael went on vacation to India.
d. No mistake.

34. Choose the sentence with the correct grammar.

a. Without knowing, the waiter spilled the drink.
b. Jason couldn't understand why his roommate wouldn't not do dishes.
c. The weather change so quickly that no one had time to grab umbrellas.
d. No mistake.

35. Choose the sentence with the correct grammar.

a. Kayla love Korean food, but wasn't as fond of Thai food.
b. Kevin missed his car payment and had to pay a penalty.
c. Sandy feel she wouldn't make it to the concert.
d. No mistake.

36. Choose the sentence with the correct grammar.

a. The chef did know the meatball recipe because his mother did not trust him yet.
b. Dan knew that he was a terrible cook, and that is why he often ordered out.
c. Sharon often says thing that she shouldn't have said.
d. No mistake.

37. Choose the sentence with the correct grammar.

a. The soccer team doesn't knew where Andrew went.
b. The lawyer forgot to renew his license next week.
c. Karen's two sons take music lessons on Tuesdays.
d. No mistake.

38. Choose the sentence with the correct grammar.

a. The company lost a lot of money last month.
b. The flowers were well maintained also not arranged well.
c. Brian doesn't do well in heat of the summer.
d. No mistake.

39. Choose the sentence with the correct grammar.

a. He decided to attending the parade that starts at 1 P.M.
b. The waves were so big the surfers are nervous.
c. The baseball players were unhappy about taking a pay cut.
d. No mistake.

40. Choose the sentence with the correct grammar.

a. The family was worried but they are not sad.
b. Sheri spent all her money when she was buying her hat.
c. Kyle is in the kitchen cooking a grilled cheese sandwich.
d. No mistake.

Spelling

For questions 41–50, look for errors in spelling. If there are no errors, choose (D).

41. Choose the incorrect spelling.

a. The rain roared as it pelted the roof.
b. Modern environmentalists understand the importance of sustainability.
c. Nikhil's parents took their spots in the stands as the game began.
d. No mistake.

42. Choose the incorrect spelling.

a. Lenny lead the protest last night.
b. Jenny enjoys hiking on the weekends.
c. The people jeered at the rude baseball star.
d. No mistake.

43. Choose the incorrect spelling.

a. Go to the principle's office now!
b. There are several disadvantages to this plan.
c. Tan delivered so much more than he initially promised.
d. No mistake.

44. Choose the incorrect spelling.

a. The other team's record is intimidating.
b. The museum was filled with many beautiful pieces.
c. Thank you very much for the complement.
d. No mistake.

45. Choose the incorrect spelling.

a. Both children agreed it was best not to argue with each other.
b. Would you like a peace of pie?
c. The director asked the actor to make a different character choice.
d. No mistake.

46. Choose the incorrect spelling.

a. Your correct in stating that the garage door does not work.
b. Kevin entered the concert hall with a great deal of confidence.
c. Jamail started taking guitar lessons three years ago.
d. No mistake.

47. Choose the incorrect spelling.

a. The poorly patched hole in the ceiling is unmistakably visible.
b. Anne thoroughly enjoys tending to her vegetable garden.
c. Doctor Harris often shares her wealth of knowledge with others.
d. No mistake.

48. Choose the incorrect spelling.

a. Chelsea fumbled for her keys in her purse.
b. I think I ate to much for dinner.
c. I don't think Taylor fully understood the consequences of her actions.
d. No mistake.

49. Choose the incorrect spelling.

a. Jason is an ambitious student who wants to become a doctor someday.
b. Michael was pinning for Kelly after their breakup.
c. Joshua worried he would not be able to pay rent next month.
d. No mistake.

50. Choose the incorrect spelling.

a. The community enjoys the positive affects of the mural in the public square.
b. The band opened for the headliner last night.
c. The runner broke the world record at the world championships this year.
d. No mistake.

Composition

51. Choose the sentence that is correct and most clearly written.

a. Kelly, after debating for weeks, the red pants were chosen.
b. After debating for weeks, the red pants were chosen by Kelly.
c. The red pants were decided upon by Kelly after debating for weeks.
d. Kelly chose the red pants after debating for weeks.

52. Choose the sentence that is correct and most clearly written.

a. Occasionally, I like to go horseback riding, but I do not get to go regularly.
b. On occasion, though I do not get to go very regularly, going horseback riding is enjoyable to me.
c. I enjoy going horseback riding, occasionally, I do not get to go regularly.
d. I do not get to do so regularly, occasionally, though I like to go horseback riding.

53. Choose the sentence that is correct and most clearly written.

a. His compassion, Ted is the articulate mayor of Alltown.
b. Ted, the mayor of Alltown, is compassionate and is articulate.
c. Ted is the mayor of Alltown; he is compassionate and articulate.
d. Ted is the mayor of Alltown, and he is compassionate, and he is articulate.

54. Where should the following sentence be placed in the paragraph below?

His fame did not come without controversy, however.

1) Born in 1935, Elvis Presley was an iconic singer, dancer, and actor in the United States. 2) His many songs range from rock and roll to gospel to ballads and many styles in between. 3) Presley's gyrating hips and curled upper lip made him appealing to the coming-of-age generation in the 50's while simultaneously inappropriate and unsettling to older generations. 4) When he appeared on the Ed Sullivan Show in 1956, television producers found his dance moves so risqué that camera crews were ordered to only film him from the waist up. 5) Even with such controversy, Elvis Presley eventually became known as the King of Rock and Roll.

a. After sentence 1
b. After sentence 2
c. After sentence 3
d. After sentence 4

55. Where should the following sentence be placed in the paragraph below?

Regardless of their true origins, Corgis are herding dogs.

1) The history of the Pembroke Welsh Corgi breed has uncertain origins, so many legends have cropped up to help explain the breed. 2) Earliest legends of the breed allege that Corgis were the cavalry of fairies and wee-folk of the British Isles. 3) Regardless of their true origins, Corgis are herding dogs. 4) Because Corgis are low to the ground and agile, they generally heard cattle, ducks, and sheep. 5) In fact, Corgis are less likely to be injured by cattle winding up to kick because they are lower to the ground, so they can roll out of a kick easier and the cattle cannot wind up as far.

a. After sentence 2
b. After sentence 3
c. After sentence 4
d. After sentence 5

56. Fill in the blank.

Tanissa remembered that she forgot to water the plants, ________ it turns out that none of the plants had begun to wither yet.

a. because
b. but
c. moreover
d. so

57. Fill in the blank.

Finding the proper type of shampoo for one's hair can make it healthy and hydrated; ______, it can allow the hair's natural texture to shine.

a. nevertheless,
b. yet,
c. moreover,
d. in contrast,

58. Fill in the blank.

Most people feel that one or two elegant pieces can elevate any wardrobe, ______ they might be more expensive.

a. even though
b. in fact
c. therefore
d. despite

59. Which sentence does not belong in the following paragraph?

1) While many people assume that tomatoes are vegetables, they are actually fruits. 2) To be considered a fruit, there must be seeds present. 3) In 1753, the tomato was officially classified as the *Lycopersicon esculentum.* 4) This may seem surprising since most people would slice a tomato into a veggie salad instead of a fruit salad. 5) Similarly, cucumbers and peppers are actually considered fruits instead of vegetables from a botanical point of view.

a. Sentence 2
b. Sentence 3
c. Sentence 4
d. Sentence 5

60. Which sentence does not belong in the following paragraph?

1) There are few animals that can live without oxygen, but there are certain species of bacteria that actually use anaerobic respiration. 2) This means that instead of needing oxygen for respiration, the bacteria use carbon dioxide. 3) These bacteria can be found in a variety of places, from the digestive tracts of cows and sheep to coastal waters rich in algae. 4) Instead of producing carbon dioxide like aerobic respirators, these bacteria largely produce methane or hydrogen sulfide. 5) In fact, oxygen is poisonous to these bacteria and exposure to it can kill them. 6) Some prokaryotes are considered facultatively anaerobic, meaning they can switch between aerobic and anaerobic respiration and fermentation.

a. Sentence 2
b. Sentence 3
c. Sentence 5
d. Sentence 6

Chapter 11
HSPT
Practice Test 1: Answers and Explanations

ANSWER KEY

Verbal Skills

1. C	31. D
2. B	32. D
3. D	33. D
4. D	34. A
5. A	35. C
6. B	36. B
7. C	37. C
8. C	38. D
9. C	39. B
10. C	40. D
11. D	41. A
12. B	42. B
13. A	43. A
14. A	44. B
15. C	45. A
16. D	46. D
17. A	47. C
18. C	48. B
19. B	49. A
20. D	50. D
21. B	51. A
22. A	52. D
23. B	53. B
24. C	54. C
25. A	55. A
26. C	56. B
27. C	57. C
28. B	58. A
29. C	59. B
30. A	60. D

Quantitative Skills

1. B	27. B
2. D	28. C
3. D	29. C
4. C	30. B
5. B	31. D
6. C	32. C
7. C	33. A
8. A	34. B
9. D	35. D
10. D	36. B
11. B	37. C
12. C	38. A
13. D	39. C
14. A	40. C
15. D	41. B
16. C	42. A
17. B	43. B
18. A	44. B
19. A	45. C
20. B	46. B
21. C	47. C
22. C	48. D
23. A	49. D
24. D	50. A
25. D	51. C
26. C	52. D

Reading

1. C	33. C
2. C	34. D
3. B	35. D
4. B	36. C
5. A	37. A
6. D	38. B
7. A	39. D
8. B	40. A
9. D	41. C
10. D	42. A
11. A	43. D
12. B	44. A
13. C	45. B
14. C	46. D
15. A	47. C
16. B	48. A
17. D	49. B
18. A	50. D
19. C	51. B
20. B	52. B
21. A	53. D
22. B	54. C
23. B	55. C
24. A	56. C
25. A	57. A
26. B	58. D
27. B	59. A
28. C	60. C
29. D	61. C
30. C	62. B
31. B	
32. A	

Mathmatics

1. C	33. B
2. B	34. C
3. D	35. D
4. B	36. B
5. B	37. B
6. C	38. C
7. A	39. A
8. C	40. D
9. D	41. B
10. B	42. C
11. C	43. B
12. A	44. B
13. C	45. B
14. B	46. D
15. B	47. A
16. C	48. B
17. C	49. B
18. A	50. A
19. B	51. D
20. D	52. A
21. C	53. B
22. C	54. C
23. C	55. B
24. D	56. A
25. C	57. D
26. B	58. B
27. D	59. D
28. B	60. D
29. D	61. C
30. C	62. A
31. C	63. D
32. A	64. B

Language

1. D	31. D
2. A	32. B
3. D	33. D
4. B	34. A
5. B	35. B
6. C	36. B
7. A	37. C
8. B	38. A
9. C	39. C
10. B	40. C
11. C	41. D
12. A	42. A
13. C	43. A
14. B	44. C
15. D	45. B
16. B	46. A
17. C	47. D
18. D	48. B
19. C	49. B
20. D	50. A
21. C	51. D
22. B	52. A
23. D	53. C
24. A	54. B
25. B	55. A
26. C	56. B
27. C	57. C
28. D	58. A
29. B	59. B
30. D	60. D

ANSWERS AND EXPLANATIONS

Verbal Skills

1. **C** A dog lives in a crate. A human lives in a house. The correct answer is (C).
2. **B** Blatant and obvious are synonyms. Outrageous and extreme are also synonyms. The correct answer is (B).
3. **D** Ruminate means to think about. Ponder most closely matches, meaning to think about something. The correct answer is (D).
4. **D** The question asks which word does *not* belong. Run, walk, and jog are all words that are types of moving. To halt means to stop moving. The correct answer is (D).
5. **A** Meager means insufficient or skimpy. The opposite of this would be sufficient or plentiful. The correct answer is (A).
6. **B** Mundane means normal or everyday. Commonplace also means normal and everyday. The correct answer is (B).
7. **C** The question asks which word does *not* belong. Path, trail, and route are all things that people walk on in a certain direction. While a park may have paths in it, there is no direction suggested by merely a park. The correct answer is (C).
8. **C** Dull and insipid are synonyms. Tart means sharp or bitter. The correct answer is (C).
9. **C** The question asks which word does *not* belong. Toe, nose, and ear are all appendages of a person. A person is an entire being. The correct answer is (C).
10. **C** A team is directed by a coach. An orchestra is directed by a conductor. The correct answer is (C).
11. **D** The question asks which word does *not* belong. Tulip, daffodil, and daisy are all types of flowers. A flower is the overarching category. The correct answer is (D).
12. **B** Pragmatic most nearly means practical. The correct answer is (B).
13. **A** An act is a part of a play. A chapter is a part of a book. The correct answer is (A).
14. **A** Innocuous means harmless, so the opposite would mean something close to "harmful." Eliminate harmless, benign, and tame, which are all synonyms of innocuous. Virulent means harmful and persistent. The correct answer is (A).
15. **C** The question asks which word does *not* belong. Gloves, earmuffs, and snowshoes are all equipment meant for cold weather. Sandals are meant for warm weather. The correct answer is (C).
16. **D** Docile means sweet or submissive, so the opposite of this would be something like "wild" or "untamed." This matches (D). The correct answer is (D).

17. **A** The question asks which word does *not* belong. Trout, salmon, and snapper are all types of fish. Fish is an overall category. The correct answer is (A).

18. **C** Feeble means weak or brittle. The correct answer is (C).

19. **B** An omelet is made with eggs. A pancake is made with batter. The correct answer is (B).

20. **D** The question asks which word does *not* belong. Granite, limestone, and slate are all types of stone. A pebble could be made of granite or limestone or slate but, in this context, it is the thing that doesn't belong. The correct answer is (D).

21. **B** Gullible means easily believing. The closest word to this is credulous. The correct answer is (B).

22. **A** A buckle holds a belt together. A lace holds a shoe together. The correct answer is (A).

23. **B** A stem is the central part of a plant that leaves come off from. A trunk is the central part of a tree that branches come off from. The correct answer is (B).

24. **C** The question asks which word does *not* belong. Rake, hoe, and shovel are all types of tools. Tools is the overarching category and therefore does not belong. The correct answer is (C).

25. **A** To spawn most nearly means "to generate." The closest word to this meaning is *make.* The correct answer is (A).

26. **C** The question states that *Rachel wrote her book report after Connie. Hoda wrote her book report after Alec. Rachel wrote her book report before Alec.* Since the first two statements do not have any people in common, it is impossible to know if the third statement is true or not. Therefore, the third statement is uncertain. The correct answer is (C).

27. **C** The question asks which word does *not* belong. Inch, centimeter, and yard are all ways of measuring length. Interval describes the type of measurement which most likely does not belong with a length. The correct answer is (C).

28. **B** The question states that *Devil's Advocate finished before Spirited Away. Incognito finished the race after Spirited Away.* Draw a diagram with the horses in order of finish: Devil's Advocate, then Spirited Away, then Incognito. Therefore, Incognito finished after Devil's Advocate, not before. The correct answer is (B).

29. **C** To prevail means "to win" or or "to outlast." The closest to this meaning is "to succeed." The correct answer is (C).

30. **A** Exonerate means to exculpate or remove guilt. Pardon is the closest to this meaning. The correct answer is (A).

31. **D** Soft is a type of touch. Sour is a type of taste. The correct answer is (D).

32. **D** The question asks which word does *not* belong. Track, tennis, and basketball are all sports. Though it is advisable to wear sneakers while playing sports, shoe is not a sport. The correct answer is (D).

33. **D** Eloquent means "well spoken." The *opposite* must be "not well spoken." Inarticulate matches this meaning. The correct answer is (D).

34. **A** A nurse works in a hospital. A teacher works in a school. Note that a student does not work at the school; rather, they attend a school. The correct answer is (A).

35. **C** Aloof means uninterested and detached. This matches (C). The correct answer is (C).

36. **B** The question asks which word does *not* belong. Pound, ounce, and kilogram are all types of weight. Weight is the overall category. The correct answer is (B).

37. **C** Make a diagram for this question. The questions states that *Nick can do more push-ups than Delaynie and Kevin.* Place Nick above Delaynie and Kevin, but it is unclear in which order Delaynie and Kevin should go. The question then states that *Anne can do more push-ups than Nick.* Place Anne above Nick. Since the third statement asks about Delaynie and Kevin, there is no information as to which order they should be placed, and therefore the answer is uncertain. The correct answer is (C).

38. **D** Conniving means scheming. The opposite would be to be transparent. The best answer here is *forthright.* The correct answer is (D).

39. **B** Lush means luxurious and deluxe. This matches (B). The correct answer is (B).

40. **D** The question asks which word does *not* belong. Leaf, bud, and petal are all parts of a plant that are above ground, while the roots are below ground. The correct answer is (D).

41. **A** Make a diagram for this question. The question states that *Plainville has more inhabitants than Rehoboth, but fewer than Allentown.* The diagram from most to least should be Allentown, Plainville, Rehoboth. The question then states that *Bellingham has fewer inhabitants than Rehoboth.* Place Bellingham after Rehoboth on the diagram, so it should have the fewest inhabitants. The third statement, *Allentown has more inhabitants than Bellingham,* is therefore true. The correct answer is (A).

42. **B** A blade of grass is a small little bit of a larger area. A wave is a small part of the larger ocean. The correct answer is (B).

43. **A** The question asks which word does *not* belong. Guitar, piano, and drums are all different instruments. A band is not an instrument. The correct answer is (A).

44. **B** Make a diagram for this question. The question states that *Toni, Katelyn, and David have the same number of plants.* The question then states that *Giselle has fewer plants than Katelyn.* Therefore, Giselle should have fewer plants than everyone. The third statement, *David has fewer plants than Giselle* is therefore false. The correct answer is (B).

45. **A** Dubious means doubtful. The correct answer is (A).

46. **D** Ephemeral means fleeting, so the *opposite* must be something like "not fleeting." Lasting matches this definition. The correct answer is (D).

47. **C** The question asks which word does *not* belong. Actor, director, and stage hand are all people who work at a theater. The theater itself is a building. The correct answer is (C).

48. **B** Conspicuous means visible and easily spotted. This matches the definition of *prominent*, which means easily visible, at the forefront. The correct answer is (B).

49. **A** Comprehensive means complete. This matches (A). The correct answer is (A).

50. **D** The question asks which word does *not* belong. Bumper, tire, and trunk are all parts of a car. A car is the whole object. The correct answer is (D).

51. **A** Hinder means to stop or impede. The *opposite* of hinder would be something like "allow." The closest to this meaning is *free.* The correct answer is (A).

52. **D** Reminisce means to remember. This most closely matches *recollect.* The correct answer is (D).

53. **B** Undermine means to impede or undercut. The *opposite* of undermine would be something like "to help." *Aid* most closely matches "to help." The correct answer is (B).

54. **C** Make a diagram for this question. The question states that *Ophelia is older than Everleigh and Lisa.* Place Ophelia above Everleigh and Lisa, but do not rank Everleigh and Lisa yet. The question then states that *Sean is older than Jimmy and Alexis.* Place Sean above Jimmy and Alexis, but do not rank Jimmy and Alexis yet. The third statement that *Ophelia is younger than Sean* is uncertain because each of the first two statements does not contain any names in common. The correct answer is (C).

55. **A** Novel means new. This matches (A). The correct answer is (A).

56. **B** Make a diagram for this question. The question states that *Shelly can skip rope more times than Kevin but fewer times than Jenna.* From most to least, the order should be Jenna, Shelly, Kevin. The question then states that *Antoni can skip rope more times than Sheri and Jenna.* Place Antoni above Jenna, so the list now reads Antoni, Jenna, Shelly, Kevin. It is not clear where to place Sheri, but it is not relevant to the third statement. The third statement that *Antoni can skip rope fewer times than Shelly* is false according to the diagram. The correct answer is (B).

57. **C** Legitimate means valid or authentic. Therefore, the *opposite* would have to mean "invalid." This matches (C). The correct answer is (C).

58. **A** Overt means over-the-top. Blatant is the closest in meaning because it means obvious. The correct answer is (A).

59. **B** Make a diagram for this question. The question states that *Greg has more dogs than Farran but fewer than Trixie.* From most to fewest dogs, the diagram should read Trixie, Greg, Farran. The question then states that *Trixie has fewer dogs than Tyler.* Place Tyler at the beginning of the list with the most dogs. The third statement that *Greg has more dogs than Tyler* is therefore false. The correct answer is (B).

60. **D** Recalcitrant means stubborn. The *opposite* of this would be something like "cooperative." *Obedient* is the closest to this meaning. The correct answer is (D).

Quantitative Skills

1. **B** Find the pattern in the series. $2 \times 2 = 4$. $4 \times 2 = 8$. $8 \times 2 = 16$. $16 \times 2 = 32$. The correct answer is (B).

2. **D** The question is asking what *must* be true, not what *could* be true. Eliminate (A) because it is not something that *must* be true. Eliminate (B) because the two legs of the triangle do not have to equal each other. Eliminate (C) because it is not necessarily true that one leg is greater than the other. Choice (D) is true because the sum of angles y and z must equal 90 degrees since x is a 90 degree angle. The correct answer is (D).

3. **D** Translate English into math: $\frac{x}{3} = \frac{1}{4} \times 48$. Simplify the right-hand side to find that $\frac{1}{4} \times 48 = 12$. The equation should now read $\frac{x}{3} = 12$. Multiply by 3 on each side to find that $x = 36$. The correct answer is (D).

4. **C** Evaluate each of the answers to know the order of the Roman numerals. Evaluate the first Roman numeral: $\frac{1}{2}$ of 18 is 9. Next, evaluate the second Roman numeral: $\sqrt{81} = 9$. Since Roman numerals I and II are equal, eliminate (A), (B), and (D). The correct answer is (C).

5. **B** Find the pattern in the series. $96 \div 2 = 48$. $48 \div 2 = 24$. $24 \div 2 = 12$. $12 \div 2 = 6$. The correct answer is (B).

6. **C** Count the number of squares in each figure: Figure A has 12 squares, Figure B has 12 as well, and Figure C has 13 squares. Eliminate (A) because Figures A and B have the same number of squares. Eliminate (B) because Figure C has more squares than (A) and (B). Keep (C) because this fits. Eliminate (D) because Figure B does not have more squares than Figure (A). The correct answer is (C).

7. **C** Find the pattern in the series. $8 \times 2 - 4 = 12$. $12 \times 2 - 4 = 20$. $20 \times 2 - 4 = 36$. $36 \times 2 - 4 = 68$. The correct answer is (C).

8. **A** Evaluate each of the Roman numerals. 50% of 80 is 40. 25% of 120 is 30. 300% of 12 is 36. Keep (A) because 40 is greater than 30 and 36. Eliminate (B) because 36 is not less than 30, nor is it greater than 40. Eliminate (C) because 30 is not greater than 40 or 36. Eliminate (D) because none of the values are equal. The correct answer is (A).

9. **D** Translate English into math to find the equation, $\frac{25}{100} \times x = 3 \times 10$. Simplify $\frac{25}{100}$ and 3×10 to find the equation is equal to $\frac{1}{4} \times x = 30$. Multiply by 4 on both sides to isolate x, which yields 120. The correct answer is (D).

10. **D** Find the pattern in the series. $1 \times -3 = -3$. $-3 \times -3 = 9$. $9 \times -3 = -27$. $-27 \times -3 = 81$. The correct answer is (D).

11. **B** Evaluate each of the Roman numerals. $-2^3 = -8$ since the negative sign is not inside parentheses. $-3^2 = -9$, also because the negative sign is not enclosed by parentheses. $3^2 = 9$. Eliminate (A) because while III is greater than I, it is not less than II. Keep (B) because II is more negative and therefore less than both I and III. Eliminate (C) and (D) because none of the values are equal to each other. The correct answer is (B).

12. **C** Find the pattern in the series. 11 + 4 = 15. 15 + 4 = 19. 19 + 4 = 23. 23 + 4 = 27 The correct answer is (C).

13. **D** Translate English into math to find the equation, $\frac{2}{3} \times x = \frac{1}{4} \times 48$. Simplify the righthand side of the equation to find that $\frac{2}{3} \times x = 12$. Multiply by the reciprocal, $\frac{3}{2}$ to isolate *x*. $x = 18$. The correct answer is (D).

14. **A** Find the pattern in the series. 5 + 1 = 6. 6 + 2 = 8. 8 + 3 = 11. 11 + 4 = 15. The correct answer is (A).

15. **D** Translate English into math. $\frac{1}{4}$ the product of 2, –3, and –4 should read $\frac{1}{4}(2 \times -3 \times -4)$. Work inside the parentheses first: $2 \times -3 \times -4 = 24$. The equation now should read $\frac{1}{4}(24)$. Multiply the numerators and denominators to find the final product is 6. The correct answer is (D).

16. **C** Simplify the fractions first to compare them. $\frac{3}{8}$ is as simplified as it can be, but $\frac{6}{16}$ can be reduced to $\frac{3}{8}$. From this, eliminate (A), (B), and (D) because the two fractions are equal. The correct answer is (C).

17. **B** Translate English into math so that the equation will read $x = \frac{200}{100} \times (3 + 12)$. Simplify $\frac{200}{100}$ to $\frac{2}{1}$ or just 2, and work inside the parentheses: 3 + 12 = 15. The equation now reads $x = 2(15)$, so $x = 30$. The correct answer is (B).

18. **A** Evaluate the Roman numerals to be able to compare them. The first Roman numeral, 2(3 × 9) can be rewritten 2(27), or 54. The second Roman numeral, –2(–2 × 10) can be rewritten –2(–20), which is 40. Eliminate (B) because these two values are not equal. Eliminate (C) because 54 is not less than 40. Evaluate the third Roman numeral: –3 × 2 × 10 = –60. Eliminate (D) because –60 is not greater than either of the other two numbers. The correct answer is (A).

19. **A** Find the pattern in the series. 48 ÷ –2 = –24. –24 ÷ –2 = 12. 12 ÷ –2 = –6. –6 ÷ –2 = 3. The correct answer is (A).

20. **B** Translate English into math to find the expression $\frac{1}{10} \times (20 \times 3)$. Simplify inside the parentheses so that 20 × 3 = 60. $\frac{1}{10} \times (60) = 6$. The correct answer is (B).

21. **C** Choose the statement that *must* be true, not what *could* be true. Eliminate (A) and (D) because OA cannot be greater than OB if they are both radii. Eliminate (B) because while OA = OB, a radius cannot be greater than the diameter. Keep (C) since the diameter BC is greater than the radii OA and OB, which are both equal to each other. The correct answer is (C).

22. **C** Translate English into math to find the equation $\frac{x}{5} = \frac{20}{100}(50)$. Simplify $\frac{20}{100}$ to $\frac{1}{5}$, so the equation will read $\frac{x}{5} = \frac{1}{5}(50)$. Simplify $\frac{1}{5}(50)$ to 10. The equation now reads $\frac{x}{5} = 10$. Multiply both sides by 5 to find that $x = 50$. The correct answer is (C).

23. **A** Find the pattern in the series. There are groups of two numbers: $6 \times 2 = 12$, ___ $\times 2 = 18$, and $15 \times 2 = 30$. Therefore, $9 \times 2 = 18$. The correct answer is (A).

24. **D** Evaluate the Roman numerals to be able to compare the values. The square root of 100 is 10. 50% of 80 is 40. Eliminate (A) since 10 is not greater than 40. Eliminate (B) because 10 and 40 are not equal. Eliminate (C) because 40 is not less than 10. The correct answer is (D).

25. **D** Translate English into math to create the equation $25 - x = \frac{25}{100}(20)$. Simplify the righthand side of the equation. $\frac{25}{100}$ is equal to $\frac{1}{4}$. $25 - x = \frac{1}{4}(20)$. Now multiply the righthand side of the equation to find that $25 - x = 5$. Subtract 25 from both sides to find that $-x = -20$. Multiply by -1 to find that $x = 20$. The correct answer is (D).

26. **C** Find the pattern in the series. There are groups of two numbers: $4^2 = 16$, $8^2 =$ ___, and $3^2 = 9$. Therefore $8^2 = 64$. The correct answer is (C).

27. **B** Choose the statement that *must* be true, not what *could* be true. Eliminate (A) because angle A must be a right angle since it is a rectangle, which must be greater than both angles B and C, which must be less than 90 degrees since they are the smaller angles of a right triangle. Keep (B) because angles B and C must add together to 90 degrees since they are part of a right triangle, and angle A is also 90 degrees. Eliminate (C) because adding angle A to anything else would be greater than angle C, which is already established as less than 90 degrees. Eliminate (D) for this same reason. The correct answer is (B).

28. **C** Find the pattern in the series. There is an alternating pattern: $30 \div 2 = 15$. $15 + 9 = 24$. $24 \div 2 = 12$. Therefore, $12 + 9 = 21$. The correct answer is (C).

29. **C** Translate English into math to find the equation $x = \frac{75}{100}(40)$. Simplify $\frac{75}{100}$ to $\frac{3}{4}$. $x = \frac{3}{4}(40)$. Continue to simplify. 40 divided by 4 is 10, and $10 \times 3 = 30$. Therefore, $x = 30$. The correct answer is (C).

30. **B** Find the pattern in the series. There is an alternating pattern: 2 + 6 = 8. 8 – 2 = 6. 6 + 6 = 12. 12 – 2 = 10. 10 + 6 = 16. 16 – 2 = 14. Therefore, the next step in the pattern is 14 + 6 = 20. The correct answer is (B).

31. **D** Evaluate the Roman numerals to compare the values. In the first Roman numeral, the area of a square with a side of 4 is $4^2 = 16$. The area of a circle with a radius of 4 is $4^2\pi = 16\pi$, which is larger than 16. Eliminate (A) because I is not greater than II. Eliminate (B) because the values are not equal. Now evaluate the third Roman numeral. The perimeter of an equilateral triangle with a side of 6 would be 6 + 6 + 6 = 18. Eliminate (C) because 16π is not greater than 18. Keep (D) because 16 is less than 16π, and 16π is greater than 18. The correct answer is (D).

32. **C** Translate English into math to find the equation, $x = 5 + \left(3^2\left(\frac{50}{100} \times 10\right)\right)$. Use PEMDAS to do the correct order of operations. Work inside the innermost parentheses first: $\frac{50}{100}$ can be simplified to $\frac{1}{2}$, and $\frac{1}{2}$ of 10 is 5. Now the equation reads $x = 5 + (3^2(5))$. Next, work the exponents to find that $3^2 = 9$. $x = 5 + (9(5))$. Parentheses indicate multiplication. $x = 5 + 45$. Finally, add: 5 + 45 = 50. The correct answer is (C).

33. **A** Choose the statement that *must* be true, not what *could* be true. Use the information about vertical angles and supplementary angles to find the values for the other angles. Since 135 degrees is opposite *y*, *y* must also equal 135 degrees. Angles *x* and *z* are supplementary to 135, so they must equal 180 – 135, or 45 degrees. Evaluate (A): 45 + 135 = 135 + 45, which is true. Keep (A). Eliminate (B): 45 + 45 is not less than 135. Eliminate (C): $45 \neq 135 \neq 45$. Eliminate (D): $135 - 45 \neq 45$. The correct answer is (A).

34. **B** Find the pattern in the series. There is an alternating pattern: 22 × 2 = 44. 44 – 11 = 33. 33 × 2 =66. 66 – 11 = 55. The correct answer is (B).

35. **D** Find the pattern in the series. There is an alternating pattern: $3^2 = 9$. 9 – 5 = 3. $4^2 = 16$. 16 – 5 = 11. $11^2 = 121$. Therefore, 121 – 5 = 116. The correct answer is (D).

36. **B** Translate English into math to find the expression, $\frac{25}{100} \times \frac{40}{100} \times 500$. First, simplify the fractions: $\frac{25}{100}$ can be simplified to $\frac{1}{4}$, and $\frac{40}{100}$ can be simplified to $\frac{2}{5}$. Now, the expression reads $\frac{1}{4} \times \frac{2}{5} \times 500$. Continue to simplify: cancel a 5 from both the numerator (from 500) and the denominator, so the equation now reads $\frac{1}{4} \times \frac{2}{1} \times 100$. Continue to simplify: take a 4 out of the numerator (from 100) and the denominator. $\frac{1}{1} \times \frac{2}{1} \times 25$. Now multiply 2 × 25 = 50. The correct answer is (B).

37. **C** Evaluate the figures first and then compare. Figure A has $\frac{2}{8}$ or $\frac{1}{4}$ of the circle shaded. Figure B has the same, $\frac{2}{8}$ or $\frac{1}{4}$, shaded. Figure C has $\frac{3}{8}$ shaded. Now evaluate the answer choices. Eliminate (A) because Figures A and B are equal. Eliminate (B) because Figures A and B together would be $\frac{4}{8}$ or $\frac{1}{2}$ which is not equal to 3/8. Keep (C) because $\frac{3}{8}$ is greater than $\frac{2}{8}$. Eliminate (D) because Figure A is not more shaded than Figure C. The correct answer is (C).

38. **A** First find the median, or middle number: 25. Now, find $\frac{4}{5}$ of 25, which is 20. The correct answer is (A).

39. **C** Find the pattern in the series. 0 + 7 = 7. 7 + 7 = 14. 14 + 7 = 21. 21 + 7 = 28. 28 + 7 = 35. The correct answer is (C).

40. **C** Evaluate the Roman numerals first and then compare. 4.5×10^{-4} can be rewritten as 0.00045. Leave the second Roman numeral as is. The third Roman numeral, 4.5×10^{-3} can be rewritten as 0.0045. Eliminate (A) because 0.00045 is not greater than 0.045. Eliminate (B) because 0.00045 is not equal to 0.045 and 0.0045. Keep (C) because 0.045 is greater than 0.00045, and 0.0045. Eliminate (D) because while 0.00045 is less than 0.045, 0.0045 is not greater than 0.045. The correct answer is (C).

41. **B** Find the pattern in the series. Add 2 to the denominator: $\frac{1}{2}, \frac{1}{2+2} = \frac{1}{4}, \frac{1}{4+2} = \frac{1}{6}, \frac{1}{6+2} = \frac{1}{8}, \frac{1}{8+2} = \frac{1}{10}$. Therefore, $\frac{1}{10+2} = \frac{1}{12}$. The correct answer is (B).

42. **A** Evaluate the Roman numerals first and then compare. If $x = 3$, $3(3)^2 = 3(9) = 27$. The second Roman numeral reads 4(3) = 12. Eliminate (B) because 27 and 12 are not equal. Eliminate (D) because 27 is not less than 12. Now evaluate Roman numeral III. $\frac{3^3}{2} = \frac{27}{2} = 13.5$. Eliminate (C) because 12 is not greater than 13.5. Choice (A) works: 13.5 is greater than 12, and 27 is greater than 13.5. The correct answer is (A).

43. **B** Translate English into math to find the equation, $x = \frac{30}{100} \times \frac{75}{100} \times 40$. Simplify the fractions first: $\frac{30}{100}$ can be simplified to $\frac{3}{10}$, and $\frac{75}{100}$ can be simplified to $\frac{3}{4}$. Now the equation will read $x = \frac{3}{10} \times \frac{3}{4} \times 400$. Now, continue to simplify. Take a 4 out of the numerator and the denominator, so the equation will now read $x = \frac{3}{10} \times \frac{3}{1} \times 100$. Continue to simplify by taking a 10 out from the numerator and denominator: $x = \frac{3}{1} \times \frac{3}{1} \times 10$. Multiply across the numerators and denominators to find that $x = 90$. The correct answer is (B).

44. **B** Test the answers here. 30 ÷ 6 = 5 with no remainder, so eliminate (A). 35 ÷ 6 = 30, R5. This works. Eliminate (C) and (D) as well since they are multiples of 6, and will thus have no remainder. The correct answer is (B).

45. **C** Find the pattern in the series. (8 × 2) – 1 = 15. (15 × 2) – 1 = 29. (29 × 2) – 1 = 57. Therefore, (57 × 2) – 1 = 113. The correct answer is (C).

46. **B** Evaluate the Roman numerals first and then compare. The perimeter of an equaliteral triangle with a side of 18 is 18 + 18 + 18 = 54. The area of a square with a side of 9 is $9^2 = 81$. Eliminate (A) because 54 and 81 are not equal. Eliminate (D) because 54 is not greater than 81. Now evaluate III. The area of a 45-45-90 triangle with a base of 16 is $(\frac{1}{2})(16)(16) = 128$. Eliminate (C) because 128 is not less than 54. Choice (B) works: 81 is greater than 54, but less than 128. The correct answer is (B).

47. **C** Translate English into math to find the equation, $x = 4 + \sqrt{64}$. The square root of 64 is 8, so the equation should read $x = 4 + 8 = 12$. The correct answer is (C).

48. **D** Find the pattern in the series. There is an alternating pattern: 10 + 8 = 18. 18 – 3 = 15. 15 + 8 = 23. 23 – 3 = 20. 20 + 8 = 28. The correct answer is (D).

49. **D** Choose the statement that *must* be true, not what *could* be true. It is not clear in this figure if it is to scale, so do not trust it. However, the question stem does state that these are rectangles, so it is okay to assume that there are right angles. Roman numeral I is the lefthand slender rectangle. Roman numeral II is the triangle inside the rectangle. Roman numeral III is the entire large rectangle. Eliminate (A) and (B) because III cannot be less than I. Eliminate (C) because I and III cannot be equal. Keep (D) because I and II are still less than the area of III. The correct answer is (D).

50. **A** Translate English into math to find the equation, $x = \frac{1}{4}\left(\frac{16 + 20 + 26 + 34}{4}\right)$. Simplify inside the parentheses first: 16 + 20 + 26 + 34 = 96. $\frac{96}{4} = 24$. Now, the equation reads $x = \frac{1}{4} \times 24$. Multiply $\frac{1}{4} \times 24$ to find that x is 6. The correct answer is (A).

51. **C** Find the pattern in the series. 2 + 1 = 3. 3 + 1 = 4. 4 + 2 = 6. 6 + 2 = 8. 8 + 4 = 12. 12 + 4 = 16. The correct answer is (C).

52. **D** Translate English into math to find the equation, $x = 9 + \left(\frac{1}{3}\right)81$. First, multiply: $\left(\frac{1}{3}\right)81 = 27$. Therefore, $x = 9 + 27 = 36$. The correct answer is (D).

Reading

1. **C** The question asks how the narrator describes New York when the story begins. The first paragraph describes New York City as *a bustling maze of concrete, with people swarming like bees around a honey comb.* This description describes a *busy* city. This matches (C). Eliminate (A), (B), and (D), which do not mean *busy.* The correct answer is (C).

2. **C** The question asks what the word *edifices* most nearly means in the context of the passage. An edifice is a building, which matches (C). The correct answer is (C).

3. **B** The question asks why the narrator describes the Westbeth as "unassuming," which means modest. In the second paragraph, the passage states that she was *on a quiet cobblestone crosswalk without a car in sight.* Eliminate (A) since it never says the Westbeth is not in New York. Keep (B) since this is consistent with the description of a quiet street. Eliminate (C) because the passage never states the building is falling apart. Eliminate (D) because, while the narrator does say the ivy reminded her of what she *was used to seeing back home on the brick edifices in New England,* it does not answer the question about why she describes the building as *unassuming.* The correct answer is (B).

4. **B** The question asks which of the following is true about the Westbeth in the second paragraph. Go to the answer choices to see which is supported by the second paragraph. Eliminate (A) because the passage never states that the Westbeth's architecture is *older than the theaters',* though it does imply that the building is old. Eliminate (C) because the passage never states the building *needs repair.* Eliminate (D) because the *flashing lights and food carts* are in the first paragraph. The correct answer is (B).

5. **A** The question asks why the narrator describes the dance floor as "seemingly infinite." The passage states in the third paragraph that the dance floor spreads *the entire length of the room.* This matches (A). Eliminate (B) since the floor does not actually stretch into space. Eliminate (C) because it is not known that it is *oddly shaped,* only that it is large. Eliminate (D) because the passage does not state that it is *otherworldly.* The correct answer is (A).

6. **D** The question asks what the word *din* most nearly means in the context of the passage. The passage states that *The <u>din</u> of preshow excitement waved over me as other dancers, choreographers, lighting designers, and producers mingled in the entryway as I stepped out of the elevator.* Since there are a lot of other people mingling, the answer must be something that means "hubbub." Eliminate (A), (B), and (C), which are not synonymous with hubbub. *Clamor* is the closest to the meaning of "hubbub." The correct answer is (D).

7. **A** The question asks why the narrator "stepped gingerly into the cramped elevator." In the third paragraph, the passage states that the narrator *stepped gingerly into the cramped elevator, praying the elevator would hold her weight.* It then goes on to state that *The rickety shaft stuttered and spurred up to the twelfth floor.* Evaluate the answer choices and eliminate answers that are inconsistent with this information. Keep (A) since *old* and *insecure* are consistent with this information. Eliminate (B) because, though it is not working well, the elevator is not broken. Eliminate (C) because it

never says that the narrator is afraid of elevators, perhaps just nervous with this particular one. Eliminate (D) because the narrator knows how to use the elevator. The correct answer is (A).

8. **B** The question asks why the narrator finds the Westbeth remarkable. The passage in the third paragraph states that the narrator *stepped into a bustling sanctuary of wonder.* She goes on to describe the room as *the hallowed studio.* Eliminate (A) because while this might be true of the people preparing for the show, it is not necessarily describing the Westbeth itself. Keep (B) because it fits with the adjectives and her excitement to perform there. Eliminate (C) because the ivy reminded her of other buildings back home, but this does not make it remarkable. Eliminate (D) because this describes the Broadway theaters, not the Westbeth. The correct answer is (B).

9. **D** The question asks what the passage is mostly about. The passage is about Marie Curie and her numerous achievements and contributions to science. Eliminate (A) because it is not only about the awards Curie won. Eliminate (B) because it is a detail of the passage, not a main idea. Eliminate (C) because the passage as a whole is not about women's rights, though Curie is a pioneer for women in science. Keep (D), which is consistent with the prediction. The correct answer is (D).

10. **D** The question asks which fields Marie Curie contributed to. The first sentence in the first paragraph states that *Marie Curie made history as the first woman to win the Nobel Prize, not once but twice, for her discoveries in Chemistry and Physics.* This matches (D). The correct answer is (D).

11. **A** The question asks what the word *elusive* most nearly means in the context of the passage. The passage states in the third paragraph that *While it was relatively simple to isolate polonium, radium remained elusive.* This means it was difficult to isolate radium and that the Curies were not immediately successful. This matches (A). Eliminate (B) and (D) because while atoms are *hard to see* or *invisible* to the naked eye, neither matches the meaning of the sentence. Eliminate (C) because *curious* does not mean *difficult to isolate.* The correct answer is (A).

12. **B** The question asks what can be inferred about the University of Paris from the passage. The passage states in the fourth paragraph that *Marie realized that she would not get adequate lab space as she expected* from the University of Paris. Eliminate (A) because it is too extreme. Keep (B) as it matches the text. Eliminate (C) because the passage never states whose research the University of Paris valued more. Eliminate (D) because it is not stated in the passage. Curie ultimately does receive the funding, so this proves that the University did in fact have enough money to fund her. The correct answer is (B).

13. **C** The question asks which statement the author would probably agree with. Use the answer choices to locate key words in the passage. Eliminate (A) because the passage never states that *Pierre Curie made more contributions to science than did his wife.* Eliminate (B) because it is extreme when it says the *most* important discovery. Keep (C) because it did take Curie longer to successfully isolate radium. In the fourth paragraph, the passage states that *She continued her research into isolating radium, for which she finally succeeded* after she had already isolated polonium. Eliminate (D) because the passage never states that the Curies *did not deserve the Nobel Prize.* The correct answer is (C).

14. **C** The question asks what the word *threatened* most nearly means in the context of the passage. The passage states that *Marie realized that she would not get adequate lab space as she expected, so she bravely threatened to resign. Threatened* in this context must mean something like "notified with intent" to resign. Eliminate (A) since in this context threatened does not mean endangered. Eliminate (B) because *understood* does not match the prediction. Keep (C) since this matches the prediction. Eliminate (D) because, while *advised* does mean "notified with intent," it does not make sense in the context of the sentence. The correct answer is (C).

15. **A** The question asks what can be inferred about radium from the passage. The passage states that *While it was relatively simple to isolate polonium, radium remained elusive.* This means it was difficult to isolate radium and that they were not immediately successful. This matches (A). Eliminate (B) because the opposite is true. Eliminate (C) because it never mentions what radium actually looks like. Eliminate (D) because it is unknown how complex the compound was. The correct answer is (A).

16. **B** The question asks what Curie's accomplishments help us to do in the modern day. The passage states in the last paragraph that *In the present day, X-rays serve as a powerful tool for many common ailments, from diagnosing broken bones to fighting cancer.* This matches (B). The correct answer is (B).

17. **D** The question asks what the story is most about. The passage talks about the history of coffee and its growing popularity in the United States. Eliminate (A) because the passage never states *how people first learned to roast coffee beans.* Eliminate (B) because *coffee houses* are only a detail of the passage, not the main point. Eliminate (C) because the Boston Tea Party, while an important part of the story, is not the main point of the passage. Keep (D) as it matches the prediction. The correct answer is (D).

18. **A** The question asks what the word *stems* most nearly means in the context of the passage. The passage states in the second paragraph that *the earliest form of our modern-day idea of coffee stems from Arabian practices in the 1300s.* In the context of the passage, *stems* must mean something like "rooted in." This matches only (A). The correct answer is (A).

19. **C** The question asks which people were the first to roast coffee beans. The passage states in the second paragraph that *It was in Arabia that people first started to roast the coffee beans before brewing drinks with it.* This matches (C). The correct answer is (C).

20. **B** The question asks what the author says about coffee when it first arrived in the United States. The passage states in the third paragraph that *Throughout all this time, though, there was little to no coffee consumption in the U.S., even though coffee plants were being grown in the nearby Caribbean. Why? The U.S. was still part of the British Empire where most people consumed tea.* Since *most people consumed tea* and *there was little to no coffee consumption in the U.S.*, it must not have been immediately popular. Eliminate (A) since the passage does not mention *taste.* Keep (B) as it matches the prediction. Eliminate (C), which is the opposite of what happened. Eliminate (D) because this happened after the Boston Tea Party, not *when it first arrived in the United States.* The correct answer is (B).

21. **A** The question asks what can be inferred from the passage. Use the answer choices to locate key words in the passage with which to answer the question. The passage states in the second paragraph that *Colonial powers started to grow the coffee in Southeast Asia and the Caribbean in by the 17th century as it grew in popularity. It soon became a powerful trading tool with Eastern Europe and eventually made its way to Italy and France.* This supports (A), so keep it. Eliminate (B) because there are not scientists performing experiments with coffee, rather the passage describes how some coffee companies are inventing new and interesting recipes. Eliminate (C) because the passage never mentions *taste.* Eliminate (D) because that is an opinion that is never stated in the passage. The correct answer is (A).

22. **B** The question asks what the word *sprouted up* most nearly means in the context of the passage. The passage states in the fourth paragraph that *Large brands such as Starbucks have capitalized on the idea of specialty coffee, though many smaller independent coffee companies have <u>sprouted up</u> across the country as well.* In this context, *sprouted up* must mean something like the companies "started" or "were founded." Eliminate (A), (C), and (D) because *germinated, budded,* and *flowered* are all too literal to be used to describe a company. The correct answer is (B).

23. **B** The question asks what can be inferred from the passage. Use the answer choices to locate key words to find information in the passage with which to answer the question. The passage states in the second paragraph that *In the 18th and 19th centuries, the idea of the coffee house took hold, only furthering the drink's popularity.* Eliminate (A) the passage never states this information and it does not answer the question. Keep (B) as it matches the prediction. Eliminate (C) since not *everyone who protests drinks coffee.* Eliminate (D) because it is too extreme to state that *Starbucks is the only coffee shop that offers lots of options for coffee drinks.* The correct answer is (B).

24. **A** The question asks which of the following statements is true, according to the passage. Use the answer choices to locate key words to find information in the passage with which to answer the question. The passage states in the last paragraph that *Large brands such as Starbucks have capitalized on the idea of specialty coffee, though many smaller independent coffee companies have <u>sprouted up</u> across the country as well.* It goes on to describe some of the independent coffee companies. Keep (A) as it matches the text. Eliminate (B) because the passage never states that Starbucks is *the most influential coffee company in the U.S.* Eliminate (C) because the Civil War was not what made coffee popular initially. Eliminate (D) because the passage never states that people *secretly* drank coffee. The correct answer is (A).

25. **A** The question asks what the passage is mostly about. The passage introduces SpaceX, the innovations it has made thus far, and some plans it has for the future. Keep (A) as it is consistent with the prediction. Eliminate (B) because the passage never states that SpaceX is a *new version of NASA.* Eliminate (C) because this is only part of SpaceX's future plans, not the main idea. Eliminate (D) because it is too broad and is not focused on SpaceX. The correct answer is (A).

26. **B** The question asks for one of SpaceX's innovations. The passage states in the third paragraph that *This mission's Falcon 9, the orbital rocket that initially gets the spacecraft into space from earth, successfully came back to earth and impressively landed itself perfectly on a landing target on a barge ship.* Eliminate (A) because traveling to Mars has not happened yet. Keep (B) because the passage supports *reusing the Falcon 9 rocket.* Eliminate (C) because it is not clear that only SpaceX transported astronauts to the International Space Station. Eliminate (D) because it is not clear that only SpaceX orbited the moon. The correct answer is (B).

27. **B** The question asks what the word *undertakings* most nearly means in the context of the passage. The passage states in the second paragraph that *All of the famous Apollo, Challenger, and Discovery missions were <u>undertakings</u> of NASA, as were the other innovations in technology that were developed for space research.* In the context of the passage, *undertakings* should mean something like "activities" or "missions." Eliminate (A) because while these charges could be space travels, they do not have to be. Keep (B), since a *task* is a "charge." Eliminate (C) because a *spacecraft* is not a "charge." Eliminate (D) because *tests* are not "charges" or "missions." The correct answer is (B).

28. **C** The question asks which of the following statements is true, according to the passage. Use the key words in the answer choices to locate relevant information in the passage. Eliminate (A) because these are only future plans. Eliminate (B) because the passage states that SpaceX is *privately funded.* Keep (C) because the passage states in the second paragraph that *Musk, also the founder of the Tesla car company, memorably sent a Tesla with a dummy driver into space during one of SpaceX's test runs.* Eliminate (D) because the passage never states that one company is superior to the other. The correct answer is (C).

29. **D** The question asks which of the following statements the author would probably agree with. Use the key words in the answer choices to locate relevant information in the passage. Eliminate (A) because the author never calls the Apollo missions *the greatest launches in the history of the U.S.* Eliminate (B) because it is unknown whether the government will *partner* with SpaceX to *colonize Mars.* Eliminate (C) because the passage never mentions *space travel beyond Mars.* Keep (D) because the passage states in the second paragraph that *All of the famous Apollo, Challenger, and Discovery missions were <u>undertakings</u> of NASA, as were the other innovations in technology that were developed for space research.* The correct answer is (D).

30. **C** The question asks for a difference between NASA and SpaceX found in the passage. Eliminate (A) because it is unknown whether NASA has plans to go to Mars. Eliminate (B) because the passage never states that SpaceX is the only company to have *transported humans to space.* Keep (C) because the passage states at the beginning of the second paragraph that *the spacecraft was launched by the private company SpaceX instead of the government-sponsored NASA program.* Eliminate (D) because it never states that SpaceX was the only company to have *sent astronauts to the International Space Station.* The correct answer is (C).

31. **B** The question asks what the word *hitch* most nearly means in the context of the passage. In the third paragraph, the passage states that *The Dragon 2, the spacecraft transporting the astronauts, also successfully attached to the International Space Station without a hitch, and will be reused for future missions as well.* In the context of the passage, *hitch* must mean something like "problem" or "setback." This matches (B). The correct answer is (B).

32. **A** The question asks what device successfully landed itself for reuse back on earth. The passage states in the third paragraph that *This mission's Falcon 9, the orbital rocket that initially gets the spacecraft into space from earth, successfully came back to earth and impressively landed itself perfectly on a landing target on a barge ship.* This matches (A). The correct answer is (A).

33. **C** The question asks where Horton drew inspiration for his technique. The passage states in the second paragraph that *Horton combined movements from Native American Folk Dance with elements of Balinese and Javanese upper body motions and Afro-Caribbean lower body motions.* This matches (C). The correct answer is (C).

34. **D** The question asks what the word *unprecedented* most nearly means in the context of the passage. The passage states in the first paragraph that *This was the first theater in the United States to feature only modern dance, which was unprecedented at the time.* In the context of the passage, *unprecedented* should mean something like "groundbreaking." Eliminate (A) because *interesting* is not necessarily "groundbreaking." Eliminate (B) because *unparalleled* does not necessarily mean "groundbreaking." Eliminate *strange* because it does not mean "groundbreaking." Keep (D) because *extraordinary* is most closely related to "groundbreaking." The correct answer is (D).

35. **D** The question asks where you would probably find this article. The article is informative and gives an overview about Horton's work. Eliminate (A) because it would not be in a biology textbook, as it is the wrong subject. Eliminate (B) because it not a personal reflection. Eliminate (C) because it is not an instructional manual, even though it is informative. Keep (D) because informative overviews are the majority of encyclopedia entries. The correct answer is (D).

36. **C** The question asks for the best title for this passage. Eliminate (A) because Alvin Ailey is a detail of the passage, not the main focus. Eliminate (B) because this is not a compendium of exercises. Keep (C) because it talks about Horton and his revolutionary contributions as a dance maker. Eliminate (D) because, though Horton had an influence on jazz dance, the article is not about jazz dance. The correct answer is (C).

37. **A** The question asks which statement can be inferred from the passage. Use the key words in the answer choices to locate relevant information in the passage. Keep (A) because the passage states in the fourth paragraph that *many jazz dance teachers use the isolations and body movements of his exercises as part of their pedagogy.* Eliminate (B) because it is clear that jazz dance came *after* Horton's technique. Eliminate (C) because the author never states that Horton technique *is superior.* Eliminate (D) because the passage never states that Ailey was the *lead* dancer of Horton's company. The correct answer is (A).

38. **B** The question asks who Bella Lewitzky was in relation to Horton. The passage states in the third paragraph that *Horton trained many famous dancers, including Alvin Ailey and Bella Lewitzky.* This matches (B). The correct answer is (B).

39. **D** The question asks which statement the author would probably agree with. Use the key words in the answer choices to locate relevant information in the passage. Eliminate (A) because the passage never states that Ailey was the *best* dancer in Horton's company. Eliminate (B) because the passage never states that Los Angeles was the *epicenter* of modern dance in the 1940s. Eliminate (C) because the author never compares Horton technique to that of any other modern dance. Keep (D) because the passage talks about Horton's many contributions to the field of modern dance. The correct answer is (D).

40. **A** The question asks what the word *permeates* most nearly means in the context of the passage. The passage states in the last paragraph that *Today, Lester Horton's influence permeates many dance genres and works.* Therefore, *permeates* must mean something like "pervades" or "infiltrates." Keep (A) because it matches the prediction. Eliminate (B) because it is too literal. Eliminate (C) because the Horton's influence cannot *pretend* dance genres. Eliminate (D) because *intrudes* has a negative connotation. The correct answer is (A).

Mathematics

1. **C** Divide each answer choice by 6. If the answer choice is able to be evenly divided by 6, it is the correct answer. Choice (C) is the only answer that is divisible by 6. The correct answer is (C).

2. **B** All of the answer choices are fractions. First, round each answer choice to the nearest whole number; (A) and (C) would round down to zero and can be eliminated. Find a common denominator between (B) and (D). With a common denominator of 15, the numerator of (B) is 10, and the numerator for (D) is 9. The correct answer is (B).

3. **D** Choose 2 odd numbers and add them to make eliminations. Choose 3 and 5, which adds to 8. This eliminates (A), (B), and (C), as the number is not odd or negative. The correct answer is (D).

4. **B** Identify all the factors of 21, which are 1, 3, 7, and 21 (1×21, 3×7). Of these numbers, the only prime numbers are 3 and 7. The correct answer is (B).

5. **B** The equation for circumference is πr^2. To find the radius, identify r^2, which is the square root of 25. 25π can be rewritten as $\pi 5^2$, which makes the radius 5. The correct answer is (B).

6. **C** Make a list of all the multiples of 5 and 8. The multiples of 5 (5, 10, 15, 20, 25, 30, 35, 40) and 8 (8, 16, 24, 32, 40) line up for the first time at 40. The correct answer is (C).

7. **A** Line up the decimals and add the numbers together to get 7.515. This number needs to be rounded to the nearest 10th, meaning the first decimal place. This rounds to 7.5. The correct answer is (A).

8. **C** Identify answer choices that are not integers, eliminating (A) and (B). Of (C) and (D), the answer closest to 0 is (C), making it the greatest integer. The correct answer is (C).

9. **D** When multiplying by 10^3, move the decimal place three digits to the right. Moving 2.55 3 to the right makes it 2,550. The correct answer is (D).

10. **B** An equilateral triangle means that all sides are the same length. If one side is 6, all 3 sides are 6. Add them together to get 18. The correct answer is (B).

11. **C** Identify the numbers that are closest above and below the target of –2.7, eliminating (A) and (D). Choice (B) is .35 away from –2.7, and choice (C) is .32 away. The correct answer is (C).

12. **A** A ratio needs to remain similar, meaning if you multiply or divide one number you must do the same to the other. Choice (A) is the same ratio as 8.5 to 6 if you multiply each by 2. The correct answer is (A).

13. **C** All answer choices are integers that could add with another integer to a sum of 12. Look at what answer choice divides evenly into 32. The only integer that goes into 32 is 8. The correct answer is (C).

14. **B** If for every 7 campers there is 1 counselor, that is a total of 8 people. One counselor out of 8 people is a fraction of $\frac{1}{8}$. The correct answer is (B).

15. **B** List all the integers between –3.2 and 2.4 (–3, –2, –1, 0, 1, 2). There are 6 integers between the listed values. The correct answer is (B).

16. **C** All sides of a square are the same length. To find the length of the sides in a square, square root the area. The square root of 81 is 9. There are 4 sides, so multiply 9 by 4 to get 36. The correct answer is (C).

17. **C** The equation 4^3 is the same as $4 \times 4 \times 4$, which equals 64. The correct answer is (C).

18. **A** To get the reciprocal, place 1 over the number given. Here, the reciprocal of 4 is $\frac{1}{4}$. The correct answer is (A).

19. **B** Use ballparking to eliminate some answer choices. Choice (C) and (D) are close to $\frac{1}{2}$, which is 0.5, and can be eliminated. Use (B) to divide and convert to a decimal. $\frac{1}{8}$ is the same as 0.125. The correct answer is (B).

20. **D** The equation asks for the cube root of a number that is being cubed. The cube root and cubed number cancel each other out, leaving you with 6. The correct answer is (D).

21. **C** The equation for the area of a triangle is $\frac{1}{2}bh$. Plug in the information given to set up the equation $\frac{1}{2}b(8)=48$. Solve for b, which is 12. The correct answer is (C).

22. **C** Set the 3:5 ratio of basketball players to soccer players against the 65 soccer players in the question. The equation will be $\frac{3}{5} = \frac{x}{65}$. Solve for x. The correct answer is (C).

23. **C** Find the volume of a cube with a side of 4. The volume is 64. Next, find the volume of the cube with sides of 2. The volume of that cube is 8. Divide 64 by 8 to find how many of the smaller cube fit in the larger cube. The correct answer is (C).

24. **D** Two out of the 5 chapsticks in Kayla's backpack are cherry. It is possible that the first 3 times she pulls a random chapstick out of her backpack it is not cherry. The fourth time would leave only 2 chapsticks, both cherry, meaning she would pull that flavor. The correct answer is (D).

25. **C** Dividing by a decimal is the same as multiplying by the tenths digit. Multiply 10 by 3. The correct answer is (C).

26. **B** Calculate how much money Chris spent on groceries. Two loaves of bread at $3 each is $6 plus the $7 on lunch meat, totaling $13. If Chris had $17 and spent $13, he has $4 left. The correct answer is (B).

27. **D** All of the answer choices are fractions with the same denominator. Since each fraction would first have to be multiplied by 3, it cancels the denominator leaving only the numerator. Find the answer choice whose numerator adds to 6 to equal 15. The correct answer is (D).

28. **B** To find the percentage, divide 30 by 200 to get .15, which is the same as 15%. The correct answer is (B).

29. **D** Use process of elimination to narrow down the answers. Add the fractions together to find that $\frac{5}{6}+\frac{2}{6}=1\frac{1}{6}$. The correct answer must have a fraction; eliminate (A) and (C). Add 5 + 3 together to get to 8, and then add the remaining $1\frac{1}{6}$. The correct answer is (D).

30. **C** The question states that 5 days a week Alyssa buys a bag of candy and twice a week she buys 3 bags of candy. This means Alyssa buys 11 bags of candy a week. Calculate the cost per week by multiplying $0.85 by 11 to get $9.35. The correct answer is (C).

31. **C** The question sets up a ratio where 3.5 inches equals 2 miles. Set up the equation $\frac{3.5}{2}=\frac{x}{16}$. Solve for x. The correct answer is (C).

32. **A** Multiply $125 by 60% (0.6) to find the amount off is $75. Subtract $75 from $125 to find the new price of $50. The correct answer is (A).

33. **B** Multiply the numerators and denominators into each other to get $\frac{180}{15}$. Simplify this to 12. The correct answer is (B).

34. **C** Plug each answer choice in for x until the equation balances. The correct answer is (C).

35. **D** Multiply the two integers together to know the correct answer must be over 24. Eliminate (A) and (B). Ballpark how much the decimals will add, as 6×0.3 would add at least another 1.8 to 24; the only possible option is 26.23. The correct answer is (D).

36. **B** Plug each answer choice in for x and find the average to see if it matches 27. The correct answer is (B).

37. **B** Work the equation in steps. First, find that 30% of 50 is 15. Next, 25% is the same as $\frac{1}{4}$, so to find what 15 is $\frac{1}{4}$ of, multiply 15 by 4 to get 60. The correct answer is (B).

38. **C** When dividing by a fraction, multiply by the reciprocal. $\frac{8}{5} \times \frac{5}{1}$ means that the 5's will cancel out. The correct answer is (C).

39. **A** Joanne purchases 5 boxes of muffins with 6 muffins in each, totaling 30 muffins. If the 7 people in her office eat 3 muffins each, they will eat 21 muffins, leaving 9. The correct answer is (A).

40. **D** Each hour the car will drive 60 miles. Multiply 60 by 4 to know the car will have travelled 240 miles in 4 hours, which means it will take even longer to reach 270 miles. The correct answer is (D).

41. **B** Solve the equation using PEMDAS to get 13. The correct answer is (B).

42. **C** John is 14 years old, which is twice as old as Eli who is 7. Alex is 6 years older than Eli making him 13. In 4 more years Alex will be 17. The correct answer is (C).

43. **B** Solving 3^2 is the same as 9, so 9×9 is the same as $3^2 \times 3^2$. When you multiply numbers with exponents, add the exponents to get 3^4. The correct answer is (B).

44. **B** Place the ratios equal to each other, $\frac{3}{7} = \frac{x}{63}$ and solve for x. The correct answer is (B).

45. **B** Turn the mixed fractions into improper fractions, then multiply by the reciprocal. $\frac{25}{6} \times \frac{3}{25} = \frac{1}{2}$. The correct answer is (B).

46. **D** Isolate x by subtracting $2x$ from each side $9 = 6x - 9$. Next, add 9 to both sides: $18 = 6x$. Divide each side by 6: $3 = x$. The correct answer is (D).

47. **A** Divide the cost of the tablecloth by the amount saved each day: 33 ÷ \$2.25 = 16. The correct answer is (A).

48. **B** For the average number of ties between 2 people to be 10, the total amount of ties must be 20. If Jerry has 4 times as many ties, plug in the answer choices for the amount of ties Matt has and check if the sum of both comes out to 20. If Matt has 4 ties, Jerry would have 16, which would be 20 ties total. The correct answer is (B).

49. **B** An isosceles right triangle will have sides of the same length. Two of these triangles makes a square. Find the area of a square with side lengths 6. The correct answer is (B).

50. **A** Plug in the answer choices for x. Only a negative number will make the equation work. The correct answer is (A).

51. **D** First, add up the whole hours (e.g. 7 A.M., 8 A.M., 9 A.M., 10 A.M., 11 A.M., 12 P.M., 1 P.M.) which is 7 hours. The correct answer has to be larger than 7 hours, which leaves (D). The correct answer is (D).

52. **A** Plug in the answer choices and find the average for each set of numbers. If x is 16, the average of 7, 10, and 16 is 11. The average of 6 and 16 is also 11. The correct answer is (A).

53. **B** There are a total of 50 coins in the bowl and 15 are nickels. Divide 15 by 50 to find the percent. The correct answer is (B).

54. **C** Start with $\frac{3}{4}$ and continue adding $\frac{3}{4}$ until the number reaches $3\frac{3}{4}$. The correct answer is (C).

55. **B** Test the answer choices to find the correct answer. Start with one of the middle choices: try (B). Does $\frac{5}{3(2)} + 6\frac{1}{6} = 7$? Simplify and create an improper fraction to find that $\frac{5}{6} + \frac{37}{6} = \frac{42}{6} = 7$. This works, so there is no need to check the other choices. The correct answer is (B).

56. **A** The new reduced price of the toaster is $45, which equals 75% of the original price. Test the answers to find which answer which one reduced by 25% equals $45. Try one of the middle answers: try (B). 25% of $80 is $20, so the resulting price would be $60. This is too much, so the answer must be (A). 25% of $60 is $45. The correct answer is (A).

57. **D** First, treat the numerator numbers like they are in parentheses and find the sum first before dividing. .6 + .8 + 1 + 1.2 = 2.34. Then, divide by 2 to find that 3.6 divided by 2 is 1.8. The correct answer is (D).

58. **B** Find the ratio between the amount of miles in the example and the length the question asks for: 12 miles is 3 times the 4 mile example. Multiply the time it takes Jordan to run 4 miles by 3 as well: 45 × 3 = 135. Convert 135 minutes into hours. The correct answer is (B).

59. **D** Use the rules of roots and exponents to answer this question. Multiply numbers outside of the radical together to find that 3 × 3 = 9. The numbers under the radical can be multiplied together as well: 3 × 27 = 81. The square root of 81 is 9. 9 × 9 is 81. The correct answer is (D).

60. **D** Solve the following equation using PEMDAS, starting with parentheses first: 45 – 49 = –4, so the expression will then read (– 4) × 3 + 3^2. Next, do the exponents: 3^2 = 9. The expression will now read (– 4) × 3 + 9. Next comes multiplication: (– 4) × 3 = –12. The expression is now –12 + 9 = –3. The correct answer is (B).

61. **C** Test the answer choices, starting with one of the middle choices: try (B). $4.75 × 6 lawns = 28.5, which is not enough. Eliminate (A) and (B). Try (C): $4.75 × 7 lawns = 33.25, which is enough to buy the shoes. The correct answer is (C).

62. **A** If 45 students take both classes, those same 45 students are counted in the 120 AP History students. Subtract 120 – 45 and the amount of students who only take AP History is 75. The correct answer is (A).

63. **D** Use PEMDAS and test the answers: try (B). If x = 3, then 3(3(3) – 4) = 33. Start inside the parentheses: 3(3) – 4 = 9 – 4 = 5. Now, the equation reads 3(5) = 33. This is not correct; eliminate (A) and (B). Since 15 is so much less than 33, perhaps try (D). If x = 5, then 3(3(5) – 4) = 33. Start inside the parentheses: 3(5) – 4 = 15 – 4 = 11. Now, the equation reads 3(11) = 33. This is a true statement, so (D) works. The correct answer is (D).

64. **B** Test the answers. 3 × 3 = 9, but the question asks for *distinct* prime numbers. Remember that *distinct* means *different*. Eliminate (A). Try (B): 2 × 5 = 10, which works. Keep (B). Try (C): 5 × 5 = 25, but again, these are not *distinct* prime numbers. Eliminate (C). Try (D): Try (D): 4 × 7 = 28, but 4 is not prime. Similarly, 2 × 14 = 28, and 14 is not prime. Eliminate (D). The correct answer is (B).

Language

1. **D** All sentences are correct as written. The correct answer is (D).

2. **A** Eliminate (B) because it is not necessary to use *most* and *more* at the same time. Eliminate (C) because to listen *intently* should be an adverb. The correct answer is (A).

3. **D** All sentences are correct as written. The correct answer is (D).

4. **B** Eliminate (A) because there is no need for a comma. Eliminate (C) because it is in need of a comma after *once.* The correct answer is (B).

5. **B** Eliminate (A) because the *United States* should be capitalized. Eliminate (C) because *make* should not be capitalized. The correct answer is (B).

6. **C** Eliminate (A) because the sentence does not need a comma. Eliminate (B) because *Jims* needs an apostrophe to be *Jim's.* The correct answer is (C).

7. **A** Eliminate (B) because the tenses do not match. Eliminate (C) because the tenses do not match. The correct answer is (A).

8. **B** Eliminate (A) because *Most* and *doesn't* do not agree. Eliminate (C) because *go* should be *goes.* The correct answer is (B).

9. **C** Eliminate (A) because *long times* is not a countable amount. Eliminate (B) because there should not be a comma. The correct answer is (C).

10. **B** Eliminate (A) because there should be a comma after *out.* Eliminate (C) because *didn't* should have an apostrophe. The correct answer is (B).

11. **C** Eliminate (A) because *Jerry* and *are* do not agree. Eliminate (B) because *Michael* and *ask* do not agree. The correct answer is (C).

12. **A** Eliminate (B) because *I* and *has* do not agree. Eliminate (C) because the word *and* is incorrectly used as a connector. The correct answer is (A).

13. **C** Eliminate (A) because *mayor* should be capitalized. Eliminate (B) because *granny smith* should be capitalized. The correct answer is (C).

14. **B** Eliminate (A) because there should not be a comma after *movie.* Eliminate (C) because there should not be a comma after *composer.* The correct answer is (B).

15. **D** All sentences are correct as written. The correct answer is (D).

16. **B** Eliminate (A) because *Frank* and *their* do not agree. Eliminate (C) because the tenses do not match. The correct answer is (B).

17. **C** Eliminate (A) because the tenses do not match. Eliminate (B) because it is unnecessary to have both *could* and *wouldn't* together. The correct answer is (C).

18. **D** All sentences are correct as written. The correct answer is (D).

19. **C** Eliminate (A) because *yesterday* and *order* do not agree with regard to tense. Eliminate (B) because *is pick up* does not agree with *after the concert.* The correct answer is (C).

20. **D** All sentences are correct as written. The correct answer is (D).

21. **C** Eliminate (A) because *lake* and *have* do not agree. Eliminate (B) because *louder* should be *over.* The correct answer is (C).

22. **B** Eliminate (A) because the present tense does not match *last month.* Eliminate (C) because *Learn* should be *Learning.* The correct answer is (B).

23. **D** All sentences are correct as written. The correct answer is (D).

24. **A** Eliminate (B) because *one* and *know* do not agree. Eliminate (C) because the past tense and *tomorrow* do not match. The correct answer is (A).

25. **B** Eliminate (A) because the present tense and *yesterday* do not match. Eliminate (C) because *a* does not belong. The correct answer is (B).

26. **C** Eliminate (A) because *25 points* should be plural. Eliminate (B) because *leave* and *yesterday* do not match. The correct answer is (C).

27. **C** Eliminate (A) because *they* and *has* do not agree. Eliminate (B) because *Karamo* and *win* do not agree. The correct answer is (C).

28. **D** All sentences are correct as written. The correct answer is (D).

29. **B** Eliminate (A) because *dogs* and *cat* are not parallel. Eliminate (C) because *I* should be an object pronoun, not a subject pronoun. The correct answer is (B).

30. **D** All sentences are correct as written. The correct answer is (D).

31. **D** All sentences are correct as written. The correct answer is (D).

32. **B** Eliminate (A) because there should be a comma after *me.* Eliminate (C) because there should be a comma after *father.* The correct answer is (B).

33. **D** All sentences are correct as written. The correct answer is (D).

34. **A** Eliminate (B) because *wouldn't* and *not* are redundant. Eliminate (C) because the tenses do not agree. The correct answer is (A).

35. **B** Eliminate (A) because *Kayla* and *love* do not agree. Eliminate (C) because the tenses do not agree. The correct answer is (B).

36. **B** Eliminate (A) because the sentence contradicts itself with positives and negatives. Eliminate (C) because *thing* should be plural. The correct answer is (B).

37. **C** Eliminate (A) because the tenses do not agree. Eliminate (B) because *forgot* and *next week* do not agree. The correct answer is (C).

38. **A** Eliminate (B) because *also* is the incorrect transitional word. Eliminate (C) because it is missing the article *the* before *heat.* The correct answer is (A).

39. **C** Eliminate (A) because *attending* should be *attend.* Eliminate (B) because the tenses do not agree. The correct answer is (C).

40. **C** Eliminate (A) because the tenses do not agree. Eliminate (B) because the tenses are not parallel. The correct answer is (C).

41. **D** All sentences are correct as written. The correct answer is (D).

42. **A** Because it is past tense, the correct spelling should be *led. Lead* is the present tense. The correct answer is (A).

43. **A** The person who runs a school is a *principal,* not a *principle,* which is a guideline. The correct answer is (A).

44. **C** A person pays a *compliment,* but *complementary* things supplement each other. The correct answer is (C).

45. **B** *Peace* is living symbiotically, while a *piece* of piece is a slice. The correct answer is (B).

46. **A** *Your* is the possessive pronoun, but the sentence should contain the contraction *you're* instead. The correct answer is (A).

47. **D** All sentences are correct as written. The correct answer is (D).

48. **B** This sentence contains the preposition *to* instead of the adverb *too.* The correct answer is (B).

49. **B** The word *pinning* is to pin something to a surface, but *pining* is to long for someone. The correct answer is (B).

50. **A** The sentence needs the noun *effect,* not the verb *affect.* The correct answer is (A).

51. **D** Eliminate (A), (B), and (C) because they all contain the passive voice. Only (D) contains the active voice. The correct answer is (D).

52. **A** Keep (A) because it is complete and clear. Eliminate (B) because it switches from the passive to the active voice. Eliminate (C) because it is a run-on sentence. Eliminate (D) because it is a fragmented sentence. The correct answer is (A).

53. **C** Eliminate (A) because it is fragmented. Eliminate (B) because it is redundant to have *is* twice in a list. Keep (C) because it is direct. Eliminate (D) because it is a run-on sentence. The correct answer is (C).

54. **B** This sentence contains a transition, *however*, as well as the key word *controversy*. Eliminate (A) because there is nothing that needs a contrast. Keep (B) because there needs to be a transition between Presley's legacy and the controversy detailed in the third sentence. Eliminate (C) and (D) because the controversy has already been introduced in sentence 3. The correct answer is (B).

55. **A** Look for a key word. The sentence states that Corgis *are herding dogs*. This links it to sentence 3. This means it should come immediately after sentence 2 and before 3. The correct answer is (A).

56. **B** The two parts of the sentence show a contrast. The best transition to show a contrast of these options is *but*. The correct answer is (B).

57. **C** The two parts of the sentences are related in the same direction. Eliminate (A), (B), and (D) because they all indicate a change in direct. The correct answer is (C).

58. **A** The two parts of the sentence contrast each other. *Even though* is the only phrase that indicates a contrast. The correct answer is (A).

59. **B** Sentence 3 is tangential and does not flow with the rest of the paragraph. The correct answer is (B).

60. **D** Sentence 6 changes focus from bacteria to prokaryotes and introduces aerobic as well as anaerobic respiration, thus changing the topic. The correct answer is (D).

Chapter 12
HSPT
Practice Test 2

Verbal Skills

Questions 1–60, 15 Minutes

1. Conquer most nearly means

a. defeat
b. fear
c. dislike
d. calm

2. Country is to president as army is to

a. battle
b. general
c. soldier
d. weapon

3. Fortify means the *opposite* of

a. load
b. weaken
c. sail
d. clean

4. Which word does *not* belong with the others?

a. sad
b. lonely
c. feeling
d. upset

5. Compelling most nearly means

a. serious
b. interesting
c. insulting
d. funny

6. Gigantic is to large as hilarious is to

a. serious
b. interesting
c. insulting
d. funny

7. Opaque means the *opposite* of

a. dirty
b. clear
c. normal
d. late

8. Which word does *not* belong with the others?

a. oregano
b. parsley
c. spice
d. pepper

9. Fragile most nearly means

a. important
b. dangerous
c. clean
d. delicate

10. John has more marbles than Alice. Alice has fewer marbles than Kenny. John has more marbles than Kenny. If the first two statements are true, the third is

a. True
b. False
c. Uncertain

11. Generate most nearly means

a. imagine
b. create
c. project
d. lose

12. Juanita finished the race before Lucy. Mary finished the race after Lucy. Mary finished the race before Juanita. If the first two statements are true, the third is

a. True
b. False
c. Uncertain

13. Labor most nearly means

a. give
b. animal
c. work
d. science

14. Which word does *not* belong with the others?

a. touch
b. sight
c. sense
d. hearing

15. Abundant means the *opposite* of

a. meager
b. honest
c. foolish
d. tame

16. Morose most nearly means

a. content
b. new
c. flexible
d. sad

17. Which word does *not* belong with the others?

a. feather
b. bird
c. beak
d. wing

18. Robert read his paper before Weston. Abigail read her paper after Tyrone. Robert read his paper before Tyrone. If the first two statements are true, the third is

a. True
b. False
c. Uncertain

19. Portrait most nearly means

a. history
b. picture
c. investigation
d. device

20. Cage is to bird as jail is to

a. cell
b. crime
c. prisoner
d. warden

21. Strive most nearly means

a. follow
b. dive
c. try hard
d. divide

22. Which word does *not* belong with the others?

a. water
b. ocean
c. lake
d. river

23. Sentence is to paragraph as verse is to

a. rhyme
b. line
c. novel
d. poem

24. Valid most nearly means

a. possible
b. forgotten
c. old-fashioned
d. true

25. Ruthless means the *opposite* of

a. protective
b. merciful
c. small
d. healthy

26. Quest most nearly means

a. search
b. discovery
c. plan
d. talent

27. Which word does *not* belong with the others?

a. yard
b. length
c. mile
d. foot

28. Colleague most nearly means

a. cook
b. coworker
c. criminal
d. teacher

29. Chaos means the *opposite* of

a. act
b. motion
c. order
d. gravity

30. Which word does *not* belong with the others?

a. sandal
b. slipper
c. shoe
d. glove

31. Vacant most nearly means

a. future
b. open
c. empty
d. circular

32. Bread is to grain as jam is to

a. bread
b. fruit
c. knife
d. jar

33. Hat is to cap as shoe is to

a. sneaker
b. foot
c. lace
d. race

34. Prevalent means the *opposite* of

a. common
b. thick
c. subtle
d. rare

35. Which word does *not* belong with the others?

a. tool
b. hammer
c. knife
d. screwdriver

36. Contort most nearly means

a. polish
b. touch
c. sprint
d. twist

37. Which word does *not* belong with the others?

a. pear
b. apple
c. fruit
d. orange

38. Reprimand means the *opposite* of

a. praise
b. steal
c. give
d. forbid

39. Agnes can count faster than Louis and Jeremy. Lisa can count faster than Agnes. Jeremy can count faster than Lisa. If the first two statements are true, the third is

a. True
b. False
c. Uncertain

40. Tree is to trunk as flower is to

a. bee
b. stem
c. leaf
d. pollen

41. Which word does *not* belong with the others?

a. dog
b. mammal
c. cat
d. rabbit

42. Culpable most nearly means

a. guilty
b. careful
c. honest
d. skilled

43. Which word does *not* belong with the others?

a. peanut
b. cashew
c. shell
d. walnut

44. Mile is to distance as pound is to

a. weight
b. ounce
c. foot
d. kilogram

45. Ray, Eric, and Steve have the same number of baseball cards. Carl has fewer baseball cards than Eric. Steve has fewer baseball cards than Carl. If the first two statements are true, the third is

a. True
b. False
c. Uncertain

46. Erratic means the *opposite* of

a. abrupt
b. stable
c. jealous
d. upset

47. Conspicuous most nearly means

a. optional
b. new
c. obvious
d. expected

48. Mayville has more inhabitants than Suntown, but fewer than Lanville. Pinton has fewer inhabitants than Suntown. Lanville has more inhabitants than Pinton. If the first two statements are true, the third is

a. True
b. False
c. Uncertain

49. Esteem means the *opposite* of

a. respect
b. dislike
c. debate
d. certainty

50. Which word does *not* belong with the others?

a. speak
b. yell
c. sound
d. whisper

51. Indifferent means the *opposite* of

a. concerned
b. soft
c. casual
d. clever

52. Which word does *not* belong with the others?

a. flute
b. violin
c. orchestra
d. cello

53. Ollie is older than Quinn and Joseph. Sally is older than Steven and Joseph. Ollie is younger than Sally. If the first two statements are true, the third is

a. True
b. False
c. Uncertain

54. Cook is to kitchen as doctor is to

a. patient
b. hospital
c. medicine
d. needle

55. Which word does *not* belong with the others?

a. theater
b. stadium
c. arena
d. crowd

56. Howard can sing more songs than Bill but fewer than Enid. Adam can sing more songs than Becky and Enid. Adam can sing fewer songs than Howard. If the first two statements are true, the third is

a. True
b. False
c. Uncertain

57. Which word does *not* belong with the others?

a. book
b. cover
c. page
d. spine

58. Penelope has more cats than Uma but fewer than Michael. Michael has fewer cats than Petra. Penelope has more cats than Petra. If the first two statements are true, the third is

a. True
b. False
c. Uncertain

59. Tree is to forest as star is to

a. sun
b. sky
c. planet
d. constellation

60. Intentional means the *opposite* of

a. distracted
b. unhappy
c. accidental
d. hungry

Quantitative Skills

Questions 1–52, 30 Minutes

1. **What number should come next in this series: 4, 12, 20, 28, ____?**

a. 32
b. 34
c. 36
d. 38

2. **Examine the rectangle below and find the best answer.**

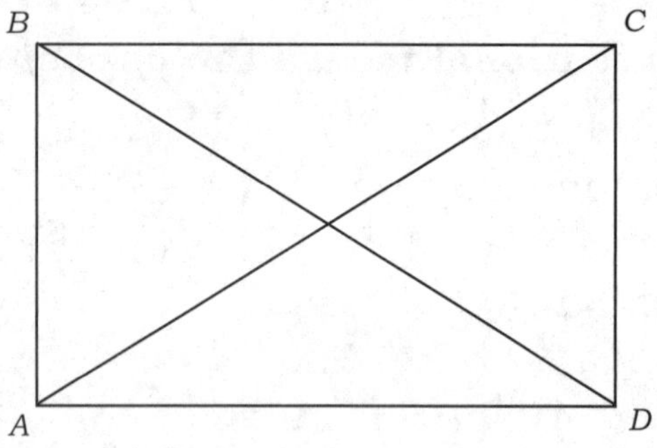

a. *AC* is bigger than *BD* and bigger than *AB*
b. *AC* is equal to *BD* and bigger than *AB*
c. *BC* is bigger than AB and bigger than *BD*
d. *AB* is equal to *CD* and equal to *BD*

3. **What number divided by 2 is $\frac{2}{3}$ of 39?**

a. 13
b. 26
c. 39
d. 52

4. **Examine the following to find the best answer.**

1. $\frac{1}{4}$ of 84
2. $\frac{1}{2}$ of 48
3. $\frac{1}{2}$ of 42

a. 1 > 2 > 3
b. 1 = 2 = 3
c. 2 > 1 = 3
d. 2 > 1 > 3

5. **What number should come next in this series: 3, 6, 12, 24, ____?**

a. 27
b. 30
c. 36
d. 48

6. Examine (A), (B), and (C) to find the best answer.

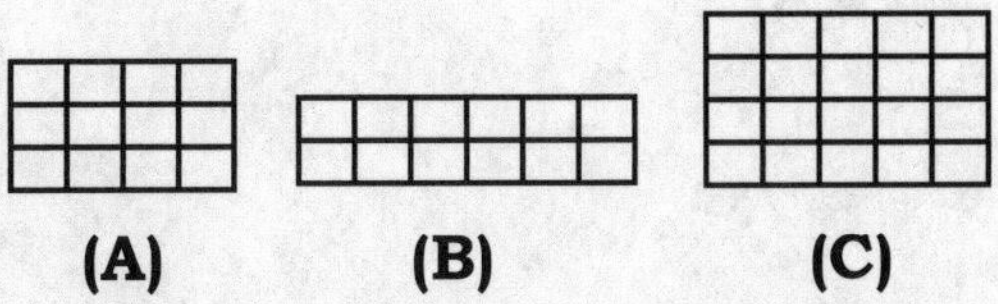

a. (A) has as many squares as (B) and fewer than (C)
b. (A) has more squares than (B) and fewer than (C)
c. (B) and (C) each have more squares than (A)
d. (A), (B), and (C) each have the same number of squares

7. What number should come next in this series: 4, 8, 12, 16, ____?

a. 18
b. 20
c. 22
d. 24

8. Examine the following to find the best answer.

I. 20% of 60
II. 60% of 20
III. 200% of 6

a. I is greater than II or III
b. I, II, and III are equal
c. I is equal to II and greater than III
d. II is less than I and III

9. 20% of what number is 5 times 3?

a. 15
b. 25
c. 50
d. 75

10. What number should come next in this series: 5, 8, 12, 15, 19, ____?

a. 21
b. 22
c. 23
d. 24

11. Examine the following to find the best answer.

I. 3^3
II. 4^2
III. 5^1

a. I. > II. > III.
b. I. = II. = III.
c. II. > I. = III.
d. II. > I. > III.

12. What number should come next in this series: 8, 5, 9, 6, 10, ____?

a. 7
b. 8
c. 9
d. 14

13. $\frac{2}{3}$ of what number is $\frac{1}{2}$ of 24?

a. 36
b. 18
c. 12
d. 6

14. What number should come next in this series: 4, 7, 9, 12, 14, 17, ____?

a. 18
b. 19
c. 20
d. 21

15. What number is $\frac{3}{4}$ of the product of 3, 4, and 5?

a. 45
b. 60
c. 75
d. 240

16. Examine the following to find the best answer.

1. $\frac{5}{10}$
2. $\frac{70}{100}$
3. $\frac{8}{100}$

a. 1 > 2 > 3
b. 1 = 2 = 3
c. 2 > 1 = 3
d. 2 > 1 > 3

17. What number is 200% of the difference between 12 and 3?

a. 3
b. 9
c. 12
d. 18

18. Examine the following to find the best answer.

1. $3(5 \times 9)$
2. $(3 \times 5) \times 9$
3. $3 \times 5 \times 9$

a. 1 is greater than 2 and 3
b. 1 is equal to 2 and less than 3
c. 2 and 3 are equal and greater than 1
d. 1, 2, and 3 are equal

19. What number should fill the blank in this series: 12, 18, 22, 28, ____, 38?

a. 28
b. 30
c. 32
d. 34

20. $\frac{5}{100}$ of the product of 5 and 4 is

a. 1
b. $\frac{1}{4}$
c. 4
d. 5

21. Below is a circle with center O. Find the best answer.

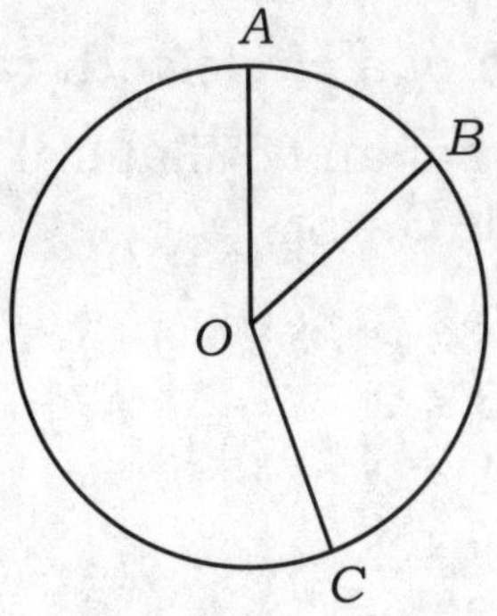

a. $OA > OB > OC$
b. $OA = OB > OC$
c. $OA = OB < OC$
d. $OA = OB = OC$

22. What number divided by 4 is 15% of 90?

a. 42
b. 48
c. 52
d. 54

23. What number should fill the blank in this series: 4, 8, 10, 20, 22, ____, 46?

a. 44
b. 42
c. 36
d. 32

24. Examine the following to find the best answer.

1. the smallest prime number bigger than 4
2. the square root of 25
3. 75% of 8

a. 1 is greater than 2 and 3
b. 1 is equal to 2 and less than 3
c. 2 and 3 are equal and greater than 1
d. 1, 2, and 3 are equal

25. The sum of 20 and what number is equal to the product of 6 and 8?

a. 22
b. 24
c. 28
d. 32

26. What number should fill the blank in this series:
$2, \frac{1}{2}, 3, \frac{1}{3}$ ____, $\frac{1}{4}$?

a. $\frac{1}{5}$
b. 3
c. 4
d. 5

27. Below is a square and a equilateral triangle. Find the best answer.

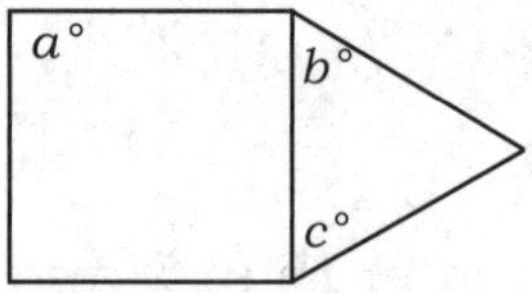

a. *a* is greater than *b* + *c*
b. *a* is less than *b* + *c*
c. *a* is equal to *b* + *c*
d. *a*, *b*, and *c* are all equal

28. What number should come next in this series: 30, 28, 25, 21, ____?

a. 18
b. 17
c. 16
d. 15

29. What number is 140% of 40?

a. 16
b. 32
c. 56
d. 64

30. What number should come next in this series: 2, 4, 3, 5, 4, 6, 5, ____?

a. 6
b. 7
c. 8
d. 9

31. Examine the following to find the best answer.

1. the area of a square with side 3
2. the area of a circle with radius 3
3. the area of an equilateral triangle with side 3

a. 1 > 2 > 3
b. 1 = 3 < 2
c. 3 < 1 < 2
d. 3 < 1 = 2

32. What number is 2 more than the difference of 3^3 and 3^4?

a. 3
b. 5
c. 29
d. 56

33. Examine the figure below and find the best answer.

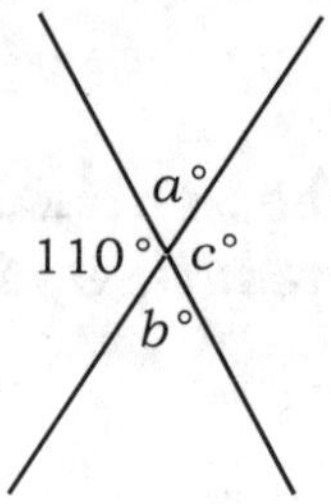

a. $a + c = b + c = a + b$
b. $a + c = b + c > a + b$
c. $a + b > a + c > b + c$
d. $a + b > a + c = b + c$

34. What number should come next in this series: 11, 22, 44, 88, ____?

a. 122
b. 124
c. 144
d. 176

35. What number should fill the blank in this series: 15, 30, 35, 50, 55, ____, 75?

a. 70
b. 65
c. 60
d. 55

36. 75% of 20% of 200 is

a. 30
b. 40
c. 45
d. 50

37. Examine (A), (B), and (C) to find the best answer.

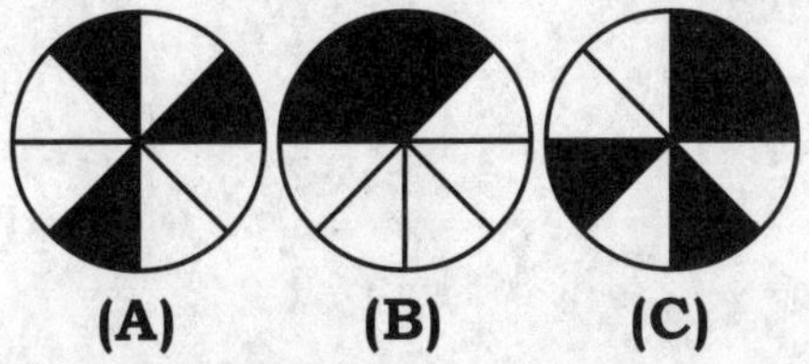

a. (A) is more shaded than (B)
b. (A) is less shaded than (B) and more shaded than (C)
c. (C) is more shaded than both (A) and (B)
d. (A), (B), and (C) are equally shaded

38. $\frac{3}{5}$ of the average of 20, 25, and 45 is

a. 14
b. 18
c. 22
d. 24

39. What number should fill the blank in this series: 20, 30, 45, 65, ____, 120?

a. 70
b. 80
c. 90
d. 110

40. Examine the following to find the best answer.

1. 6.5×10^{-3}
2. 0.0065
3. 650×10^{-4}

a. 1 is greater than 2 and 3
b. 1 is equal to 2 and less than 3
c. 2 and 3 are equal and greater than 1
d. 1, 2, and 3 are equal

41. What number should come next in this series: 1, 1, 2, 4, 3, 9, 4, ____?

a. 12
b. 14
c. 16
d. 18

42. Examine (a), (b), and (c) to find the best answer if

I. $2x^2$
II. $(2x)^2$
III. $2^2 \times x^2$

a. I is greater than II and III
b. I is equal to III and less than II
c. II and III are equal and greater than I
d. I, II, and III are equal

43. What is 40% of 20% of 600?

a. 24
b. 48
c. 60
d. 120

44. What number leaves a remainder of 3 when divided by 4?

a. 25
b. 31
c. 33
d. 37

45. What number should come next in this series: 15, 20, 18, 23, 21, 26, 24, ____?

a. 22
b. 26
c. 28
d. 29

46. Examine (a), (b), and (c) to find the best answer.

I. the area of a square with side 2
II. the area of a square with side 3
III. the area of half of a square with side 4

a. II > I > III
b. III > I > II
c. III > II > I
d. II > III > I

47. What number is 5 greater than the product of 15 and $\frac{1}{3}$?

a. 5
b. 10
c. 15
d. 20

48. What number should fill the blank in this series: 56, 51, 48, 43, 40, ____, 32?

a. 37
b. 36
c. 35
d. 34

49. Examine the following to find the best answer.

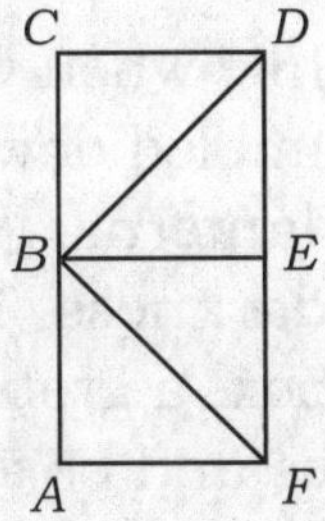

1. the perimeter of square *BCDE*
2. the perimeter of triangle *BDF*
3. the perimeter of rectangle *ACDF*

a. 2 > 1 > 3
b. 3 > 1 > 2
c. 3 > 2 > 1
d. 2 > 3 > 1

50. What number is $\frac{1}{6}$ of the average of 18, 24, 25, and 29?

a. 4
b. 5
c. 6
d. 7

51. What number should come next in this series: 110, 55, 50, 25, 20, ____?

a. 15
b. 10
c. 5
d. 0

52. What number is 16 more than 6^2?

a. 22
b. 36
c. 48
d. 52

Reading

Questions 1–62, 25 Minutes

Questions 1–8 refer to the following passage.

Passage 1 - Westward Journey

I do not remember crossing the Missouri River, or anything about the long day's journey through Nebraska. Probably by that time I had crossed so many rivers that I was dull to them. The only thing very noticeable about Nebraska was that it was still, all day long.

I had been sleeping, curled up in a red plush seat, for a long while when we reached Black Hawk. Jake roused me and took me by the hand. We stumbled down from the train to a wooden siding, where men were running about with lanterns. I couldn't see any town, or even distant lights; we were surrounded by utter darkness. The engine was panting heavily after its long run. In the red glow from the firebox, a group of people stood huddled together on the platform, encumbered by bundles and boxes.

I knew this must be the immigrant family the conductor had told us about. The woman wore a fringed shawl tied over her head, and she carried a little tin trunk in her arms, hugging it as if it were a baby. There was an old man, tall and stooped. Two half-grown boys and a girl stood holding oilcloth bundles, and a little girl clung to her mother's skirts. Presently a man with a lantern approached them and began to talk, shouting and exclaiming. I pricked up my ears, for it was positively the first time I had ever heard a foreign tongue.

1. When the story begins, the narrator is on a

a. plane
b. ship
c. rooftop
d. train

2. The narrator finds the rivers in Nebraska "dull" probably because

a. the narrator has never liked rivers
b. the narrator has seen too many rivers
c. the rivers in Missouri were much more interesting
d. they were all too small to be interesting

3. The word <u>roused</u>, as used in the passage, most nearly means

a. woke
b. saw
c. ran
d. told

4. The narrator finds Nebraska remarkable for its

a. cows
b. interesting scenery
c. silence
d. fields of corn

5. The word <u>tongue</u>, as used in the passage, most nearly means

a. song
b. mouth
c. language
d. handle

6. The people described in the second paragraph are carrying "bundles and boxes" probably because they

a. are farmers taking their goods to market
b. are coming back from a shopping trip
c. have recently arrived in this country from elsewhere
d. are paid to move other people's things

7. The narrator "stumbled down from the train" probably because the narrator

a. was still sleepy
b. was not wearing shoes
c. wore a cast on one leg
d. was very hungry

8. Which of the following is true of the family described in the final paragraph?

a. The family has four children—three boys and a girl.
b. The family has four children—two boys and two girls.
c. The family has three children—two boys and a girl.
d. The family has three children—all boys.

Questions 9–16 refer to the following passage.

Passage 2 - The Evolution of Electricity

Though electricity has only recently been used to drive machines, people have known about electricity for thousands of years. The ancient Greeks discovered that they could make objects cling together by rubbing cloth against amber. This, we now know, is due to static electricity.

Benjamin Franklin was one of the earliest people to investigate this curious phenomenon. His curiousity in electricity was sparked when he began to play with an electricity tube that was given to him by his friend Peter Collinson.

Franklin is widely regarded as the first person to realize that lightning was made of electrically charged air. As a way of testing his theory, he attempted to discover whether lightning would pass through a metal object. To show this, he used a kite to raise a key into the air on a stormy night. From this experiment, Franklin realized that this electricity could be guided to the ground by a metal wire or rod, thereby protecting houses, people, and ships from being hurt.

Many other people in the late 1700s to mid-1800s worked to discover more of the laws and uses of electricity. In 1779 Allesandro Volta, an Italian inventor, created the first battery. For the first time, a controlled and regular stream of electricity could be used. For his discovery, the volt was named after him.

Perhaps the most significant development was made by Michael Faraday. He discovered that when you move a magnet back and forth inside a wire coil, you will generate electricity inside the wire. With this knowledge he was able to build the first electric generator and the first electric motor (which is essentially an electric generator in reverse). Even today, the generators that we use to make electricity in our hydroelectric dams are almost identical to the one he created well over a century ago.

Later, Thomas Edison and Nikola Tesla improved the generator and created transformers, which change the voltage of an electrical current to adapt it to a particular purpose. While Edison advocated direct current (DC), Tesla argued for alternating current (AC), which we use today in our homes.

Without the hard work and intelligence of these people, we never would have developed the use of electricity. Almost our whole modern world—computers, radios, even lights—depends on their discoveries.

9. One of Franklin's discoveries was

a. how to protect houses from lightning
b. the battery
c. the electric generator
d. a hydroelectric dam

10. This passage is mostly about

a. what lightning really is
b. how a battery works
c. the early scientists who investigated electricity
d. how much the Greeks knew about electricity

11. With which of the following would the author probably agree?

a. The electric generator was the most important discovery of all time.
b. Modern electric motors are very different from Faraday's generator.
c. The discovery of electricity was very important to the development of the modern world.
d. Benjamin Franklin was a better writer than a scientist.

12. According to the passage, which of the following is true?

a. Thomas Edison was a good friend of Benjamin Franklin's.
b. The word volt is named after Michael Faraday.
c. Benjamin Franklin was the first person to know about the existence of electricity.
d. Faraday built the first electric generator.

13. The word <u>significant</u>, as used in the passage, most nearly means

a. readable
b. important
c. well-known
d. accidental

14. According to the passage, Edison and Tesla disagreed about

a. whether hydroelectric dams should be built
b. whether to use direct or alternating current
c. how a transformer should be designed
d. how to create electricity

15. According to the passage, what device can change the voltage of an electric current?

a. a generator
b. a transformer
c. an electric motor
d. a battery

16. The word advocated, as used in the passage, most nearly means

a. disagreed
b. promoted
c. imagined
d. threw away

Questions 17–24 refer to the following passage.

Passage 3 - The Flight of Amelia Earhart

After Charles Lindbergh made history with his flight across the Atlantic Ocean, New York publisher George Putnam wanted to have a woman make the same flight. He found Amelia Earhart.

At first, Putnam didn't trust her to fly the plane. Earhart made the transatlantic flight as a passenger with two male colleagues at the controls. However, Amelia decided that she wanted to be the pilot. She began to improve her flight skills, breaking record after record in speed and number of miles flown by a woman.

Finally in 1932, she decided that she wanted to make a solo transatlantic flight. She wanted to do it not only for herself, but to show that aviation was not exclusive to men. When she touched down in Ireland, she became an instant hero. She was showered with awards and attention from the international press.

Amelia began flying greater and greater distances. She flew across America, and then across the Pacific Ocean. Finally, she decided that she wanted to fly around the world at its widest point: the equator. This would be a journey longer than anyone had ever made.

On May 20, 1937, she took off from Oakland, California, with her navigator, Fred Noonan, in an attempt to fly around the globe. At that time, airplanes could not go very far on a tank of fuel. Moreover, her small Lockheed Electra 10E could not carry enough fuel to fly more than 6,000 miles. Therefore she had to make several small flights, stopping every few thousand miles in order to refuel.

After flying more than half the distance around the world, Amelia's plane was lost. Ten ships searched for more than two weeks, but no trace of the plane could be found. To this day, nobody is sure what became of Amelia Earhart.

17. According to the passage, who was the first person to make a transatlantic flight?

a. Fred Noonan
b. Charles Lindbergh
c. George Putnam
d. Amelia Earhart

18. The word colleagues, as used in the passage, most nearly means

a. coworkers
b. brothers
c. students
d. mechanics

19. What would be the best title for this passage?

a. "How to Make a Transatlantic Flight"
b. "The Amazing Story of Amelia Earhart"
c. "Modern American Airplanes"
d. "The Life of George Putnam"

20. The word aviation, as used in the passage, most nearly means

a. birdwatching
b. the flying of airplanes
c. airplane repair
d. going on vacation

21. You would probably find this article in

a. an encyclopedia
b. a science textbook
c. a book on European history
d. a book on the Lockheed Electra 10E

22. Which of the following can be inferred from the passage?

a. The Lockheed Electra 10E was the best airplane available in 1937.
b. Charles Lindbergh taught Earhart how to fly.
c. Amelia was never afraid of flying.
d. The equator represents the largest path around the earth.

23. With which of the following would the author probably agree?

a. The U.S. government should have looked harder for Earhart's plane.
b. Nobody is certain what happened to Earhart's plane.
c. Earhart could have flown around the world without stopping.
d. Earhart's plane must have run out of fuel and crashed into the Pacific Ocean.

24. Fred Noonan was Earhart's

a. teacher
b. sponsor
c. navigator
d. mechanic

Questions 25–32 refer to the following passage.

Passage 4 - Louis Pasteur vs The Germs

Louis Pasteur, born in 1822, is perhaps best known for having discovered the role of germs in disease. Before Pasteur, nobody was certain what caused most illnesses. Nobody thought that small creatures, invisible to the naked eye, could be the cause of so many dangerous diseases.

Pasteur, however, after spending many hours looking through a microscope, discovered that germs could reproduce very rapidly and be very dangerous to humans. This led him to conclude that doctors—who, up until that time, did not always wash their hands or their instruments—were spreading disease and that they needed to <u>sterilize</u> their equipment and scrub their hands. People began for the first time to use antiseptics, and this helped to greatly reduce the number of infections in hospitals.

Pasteur also discovered that heat could kill bacteria. He discovered this one day while experimenting with chickens. He realized that a certain bacteria, called anthrax, could live in sheep but could not live in chickens. The reason for this, he discovered, was that chickens had a body temperature of 44 degrees Celsius, or more than 100 degrees Fahrenheit. Today, we heat our dairy products to kill the germs, a process that we call pasteurization.

Finally, and most important, Pasteur discovered the principle of vaccination. Pasteur realized that animals could make defenses against diseases such as anthrax. The problem was to find a way to help their bodies make these defenses without making them sick. He realized that he could kill the anthrax germs by injecting them into chickens and then take those dead germs and inject them into sheep. Since the germ was dead, it would not make the sheep sick; but it still allowed the animal to make <u>antibodies</u> to protect it if it ever came into contact with live anthrax.

Today, people all over the world get vaccines and are free from dangerous diseases such as polio, thanks to Louis Pasteur.

25. This passage is mostly about

a. Louis Pasteur's childhood
b. the important discoveries of Louis Pasteur
c. how to make a vaccine
d. why it is important to wash your hands

26. It can be inferred from the passage that an antiseptic is

a. something that kills germs
b. a machine used to heat milk
c. a kind of bacteria
d. a kind of microscope

27. Pasteur's advice for doctors was that they should

a. read more books
b. wash their hands and equipment
c. begin to use anesthetics
d. be nicer to their patients

28. It can be inferred from the passage that sheep

a. have a body temperature of less than 44 degrees Celsius
b. are not as smart as chickens
c. could pass diseases on to other kinds of animals
d. often became ill with polio

29. The word <u>sterilize</u>, as used in the passage, most nearly means

a. rebuild
b. sell
c. check for safety
d. kill the germs

30. According to the facts in the passage, which of these might be pasteurized?

a. beef
b. cheese
c. broccoli
d. apples

31. With which of the following would the author probably agree?

a. 44 degrees Celsius is hot enough to kill any germ.
b. Receiving a vaccine is usually very painful.
c. Polio was the most dangerous disease of all time.
d. Pasteur made many important contributions to good health.

32. The word antibodies, as used in the passage, most nearly means

a. holes
b. defenses
c. wool
d. shepherds

Questions 33–40 refer to the following passage.

Passage 5 - A Chocolate-Covered History

The cocoa plant, from which chocolate is made, is native to Central and South America. Many of the native cultures—most notably the Aztecs, but even the ancient Mayans—cultivated and ate the fruit of the cocoa plant. In certain cultures, cocoa beans were even used as a form of money. The Aztecs made cocoa beans into a hot drink with no sugar at all. In fact, the Aztecs used chili peppers to make it spicy. It was bitter and strong, and they called it xocoatl.

When Spanish explorers arrived in South America, they discovered the cocoa bean and brought it back to Europe in huge quantities. This was how chocolate was introduced to Europeans. At the beginning, the Europeans drank it in the Aztec fashion—hot, spicy, and unsweetened.

It wasn't until the seventeenth century that Europeans began to add sugar instead of chili peppers to their cocoa, and chocolate became a sweet drink. At first, when cocoa was rare, chocolate was considered a delicacy; as trade with the Americas became more regular, chocolate became accessible to almost everyone.

The last step in the evolution of chocolate was its transformation from a drink to a solid bar. In the 1820s, a process was developed to press out some of the fat (the "butter") in the cocoa bean. The resulting powder could be mixed with sugar, recombined with the cocoa butter, and formed into solid bars. By the 1850s, what we know today as chocolate was finally available.

33. This story is mostly about

a. the evolution of chocolate
b. the importance of cocoa beans to the Aztecs
c. how to make xocoatl
d. when chocolate arrived in Europe

34. The word <u>fashion</u>, as used in the passage, most nearly means

a. clothes
b. way
c. house
d. cup

35. The people who brought chocolate to Europe were the

a. Mayans
b. Aztec
c. Spanish
d. Dutch

36. It can be inferred from the passage that

a. cocoa plants have never been grown in Europe
b. the Aztecs did not have sugar
c. Europeans began to add sugar to their chocolate in the fifteenth century
d. one ingredient in solid chocolate is cocoa butter

37. The author says that when it first arrived in Europe, chocolate was a "delicacy" because it was

a. very sweet
b. rare
c. difficult to make
d. inexpensive

38. According to the passage, which of the following is true?

a. Cocoa beans have been used as a form of money.
b. The Aztecs put sugar in their chocolate drink.
c. The first Europeans to discover the cocoa bean were the Germans.
d. The cocoa plant was originally grown in Asia.

39. Which of the following can be inferred from the passage?

a. Most Europeans didn't like chocolate until it was sweetened with sugar.
b. Chocolate was the most important discovery of European explorers in the Americas.
c. When chocolate first arrived in Europe, it was not available to everyone.
d. The Aztecs were the first people to drink chocolate.

40. The word <u>transformation</u>, as used in the passage, most nearly means

a. discussion
b. melting
c. change
d. cooking

Vocabulary

41. Choose the best definition of the underlined word.

a <u>malleable</u> substance

a. slimy
b. soft
c. interesting
d. bumpy

42. Choose the best definition of the underlined word.

an <u>impartial</u> jury

a. fair
b. whole
c. new
d. thankful

43. Choose the best definition of the underlined word.

a <u>meritorious</u> act

a. quick
b. silent
c. unknown
d. noble

44. Choose the best definition of the underlined word.

to <u>abdicate</u> the throne

a. seize
b. give up
c. envy
d. control

45. Choose the best definition of the underlined word.

a large <u>receptacle</u>

a. picture
b. table
c. container
d. tool

46. Choose the best definition of the underlined word.

an <u>inquisitive</u> mind

a. curious
b. normal
c. distracted
d. entertained

47. Choose the best definition of the underlined word.

a <u>cynical</u> attitude

a. silly
b. remarkable
c. distrustful
d. loyal

48. Choose the best definition of the underlined word.

the <u>dominant</u> part

a. youngest
b. largest
c. intelligent
d. hopeful

49. Choose the best definition of the underlined word.

a <u>tactful</u> remark

a. probable
b. crude
c. steady
d. polite

50. Choose the best definition of the underlined word.

a <u>thorough</u> investigation

a. complete
b. late
c. official
d. thoughtless

51. Choose the best definition of the underlined word.

an unintended <u>consequence</u>

a. interruption
b. result
c. discovery
d. section

52. Choose the best definition of the underlined word.

a <u>mediocre</u> performance

a. excellent
b. public
c. lengthy
d. average

53. Choose the best definition of the underlined word.

an <u>elaborate</u> project

a. original
b. complex
c. expensive
d. ordinary

54. Choose the best definition of the underlined word.

a recently discovered <u>paradox</u>

a. treasure
b. puzzle
c. witness
d. map

55. Choose the best definition of the underlined word.

the <u>pinnacle</u> of his career

a. peak
b. end
c. study
d. talent

56. Choose the best definition of the underlined word.

to <u>guarantee</u> a victory

a. dream
b. avoid
c. desire
d. promise

57. Choose the best definition of the underlined word.

a <u>grave</u> situation

a. serious
b. honorable
c. poor
d. customary

58. Choose the best definition of the underlined word.

to <u>imply</u> something else

a. add
b. reply
c. suggest
d. see

59. Choose the best definition of the underlined word.

a <u>sedate</u> individual

a. famous
b. calm
c. picky
d. dry

60. Choose the best definition of the underlined word.

to require great <u>exertion</u>

a. audience
b. preparation
c. effort
d. money

61. Choose the best definition of the underlined word.

a <u>mobile</u> home

a. popular
b. small
c. movable
d. country

62. Choose the best definition of the underlined word.

an <u>equitable</u> settlement

a. closed
b. fair
c. proud
d. lost

Mathematics

Questions 1–64, 45 Minutes

Mathematical Concepts

1. **Which can be divided by 8 with no remainder?**
   a. 38
   b. 56
   c. 65
   d. 81

2. **Which of the following is the largest?**
   a. $\frac{2}{3}$
   b. $\frac{1}{4}$
   c. $\frac{1}{3}$
   d. $\frac{2}{5}$

3. **If you add two even whole numbers, the result will be**
   a. odd
   b. prime
   c. even
   d. odd and positive

4. **How many distinct prime factors does the number 18 have?**
   a. 1
   b. 2
   c. 3
   d. 4

5. **The radius of a circle with a circumference of 16π is**
   a. 4π
   b. 4
   c. 8
   d. 16

6. **Which of the following is the least common multiple of 3 and 9?**
   a. 3
   b. 9
   c. 18
   d. 27

7. **What is 3.096 + 2.85 rounded to the nearest tenth?**
   a. 5.95
   b. 5.94
   c. 5.946
   d. 5.9

8. **What is the greatest integer less than –2.4?**
   a. –3
   b. –2.5
   c. –2
   d. –1

9. Which of the following is equal to 3.21×10^2?

a. 0.0321
b. 0.321
c. 32.1
d. 321

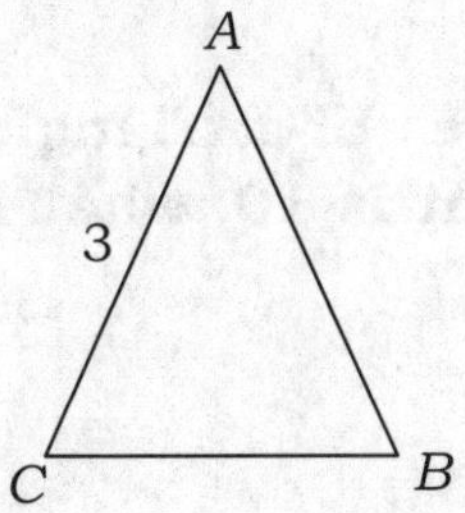

10. What is the perimeter of equilateral triangle *ABC*?

a. 3
b. 4.5
c. 6
d. 9

11. Which of the following is closest in value to –4?

a. –3.8
b. –4.01
c. –4.078
d. –4.101

12. The ratio of 3.5 to 2 is the same as the ratio of

a. 14 to 8
b. 7 to 6
c. 350 to 20
d. 6 to 4

13. Two positive integers have a sum of 18 and a product of 72. Which of the following could be one of the two numbers?

a. 6
b. 8
c. 10
d. 14

14. At Davis Junior High the ratio of students to teachers in each classroom is 18:1. What fractional part of the people in the classroom are teachers?

a. $\frac{1}{19}$
b. $\frac{1}{18}$
c. $\frac{18}{19}$
d. $\frac{18}{1}$

15. If $-5.2 < x < 3.4$, how many possible integer values for x are there?

a. 6
b. 7
c. 8
d. 9

16. What is the perimeter of a square with an area of 36?

a. 12
b. 18
c. 24
d. 36

17. 3^3 =

a. 91
b. 92
c. 27
d. 272

18. Which of the following is a pair of reciprocals?

a. $\left(\frac{1}{3}, \frac{9}{3}\right)$
b. $\left(1, \frac{1}{2}\right)$
c. $\left(\frac{1}{3}, -\frac{1}{3}\right)$
d. $\left(3, \frac{3}{3}\right)$

19. Which of the following is equal to 0.16?

a. $\frac{4}{25}$
b. $\frac{16}{10}$
c. $\frac{8}{5}$
d. $\frac{4}{10}$

20. Which of the following is equal to $2\sqrt{2^3}$?

a. 24
b. $2\sqrt{3}$
c. $4\sqrt{2}$
d. 2

21. If the area of a triangle is 30, and its height is 10, what is its base?

a. 3
b. 5
c. 6
d. 9

22. The ratio of piano students to guitar students at a certain music school is 2:4. If 80 students are learning the guitar, how many students are learning the piano?

a. 10
b. 20
c. 30
d. 40

23. How many 1-inch cubes can fit into a cube with side 3?

a. 3
b. 6
c. 9
d. 27

24. In Amy's bag are three cans of cola and one can of lemon-lime soda. If Amy randomly takes one can at a time out of her bag, what is the greatest number of cans she must take out of her bag to make sure that she gets a can of cola?

a. 1
b. 2
c. 3
d. 4

Problem Solving

25. $\frac{5}{0.25} =$

a. 0.2
b. 2
c. 20
d. 200

26. Mary went shopping one day. She spent $8 on a hat, $12 on a dress, and $2 on a scarf. If she had $30 to spend, how much money did she have left at the end of the day?

a. $8
b. $20
c. $22
d. $52

27. If $5x + 3 = 21$, then $x =$

a. $\frac{18}{5}$
b. $\frac{5}{18}$
c. $\frac{24}{5}$
d. $\frac{5}{24}$

28. What percent of 96 is 8?

a. $1\frac{1}{2}$
b. $8\frac{1}{3}$
c. $8\frac{3}{8}$
d. 12

29. $7\frac{2}{5} - 3\frac{2}{3} =$

a. $4\frac{11}{15}$
b. $4\frac{4}{15}$
c. $3\frac{4}{15}$
d. $3\frac{11}{15}$

30. Annie buys 1 pack of gum every day of the week, except for Saturday, when she buys 2 packs of gum. If a pack of gum costs 75 cents, how much does Annie spend on gum every week?

a. $5.75
b. $6.00
c. $6.25
d. $2.25

31. On a certain map, 1 mile is represented by 2.5 inches. How long is a road that has a length of 12.5 inches on the map?

a. 0.2 miles
b. 5 miles
c. 7.5 miles
d. 10 miles

32. During a special sale, a dress originally priced for $80 was marked down by 30%. What was the price of the dress during the sale?

a. $79
b. $67
c. $56
d. $50

33. $\frac{16}{5} \times \frac{15}{8} =$

a. 6
b. 8
c. 9
d. 11

34. If $x^2 + 4 = 20$, then x could be

a. 3
b. 4
c. 5
d. 6

35. $5.2 \times 2.1 =$

a. 10.92
b. 10.22
c. 7.3
d. 3.1

36. Molly scored 86, 87, 93, and x on her four history tests. If her average for the four tests was 91, what is the value of x?

a. 91
b. 93
c. 96
d. 98

37. 25% of 80 is equal to 10% of what number?

a. 200
b. 2,000
c. 400
d. 4,000

38. Which of the following is equal to $\frac{1}{3} \div \frac{3}{7}$?

a. $\frac{1}{7}$
b. $\frac{7}{3}$
c. $\frac{7}{9}$
d. $\frac{9}{7}$

39. At a birthday party, there were 3 boxes of doughnuts. Each box contained 14 doughnuts. If the 12 party guests ate 3 doughnuts each, how many doughnuts were left over at the end of the party?

a. 4
b. 6
c. 8
d. 10

40. How many minutes will it take for an airplane traveling 400 miles per hour to travel 6,000 miles?

a. 15
b. 90
c. 900
d. 1,200

41. $4 - (5 - 2) + 3 \times 5 =$

a. 12
b. 16
c. 20
d. 23

42. Albert is twice as old as Bert, and Bert is 7 years younger than Carl. If Albert is 12 years old, how old will Carl be in 8 years?

a. 21
b. 18
c. 13
d. 6

43. If $4^x = 16^3$, then $x =$

a. 4
b. 5
c. 6
d. 8

44. If the ratio of tomatoes to cucumbers in David's garden is 2:6, and there are 72 cucumbers in the garden, how many tomatoes are there?

a. 6
b. 12
c. 18
d. 24

45. $6\frac{1}{4} \div 12\frac{1}{2} =$

a. $\frac{3}{4}$
b. $\frac{2}{3}$
c. $\frac{1}{2}$
d. $1\frac{1}{3}$

46. If $5x + 5 = 3x - 9$, then $x =$

a. −7
b. −5
c. 5
d. 7

47. Tabatha decided to save money to buy a plant. If the plant costs $20, and Tabatha saves $1.25 per day, how many days will she have to save in order to have enough money to buy the plant?

a. 16
b. 18
c. 22
d. 24

48. Alex has three times as many cards as David. If the average number of cards that Alex and David have is 20, how many cards does Alex have?

a. 30
b. 25
c. 20
d. 10

49. If a square has a perimeter of 40 feet, what is its area?

a. 16 ft^2
b. 64 ft^2
c. 100 ft^2
d. 124 ft^2

50. If $-5x - 1 < 9$, which of the following is true?

a. $x < -2$
b. $x > -2$
c. $x < -\frac{1}{2}$
d. $x > -\frac{1}{2}$

51. If a bus leaves city A at 9:45 A.M. and arrives in city B at 4:05 P.M. how long did it take the bus to travel from city A to city B?

a. 5 hours 40 minutes
b. 6 hours 20 minutes
c. 6 hours 40 minutes
d. 7 hours 20 minutes

52. If the average of 3, 8, and x is equal to the average of 7 and x, what is the value of x?

a. 1
b. 2
c. 3
d. 4

53. Kim put 40 blue beads and 20 red beads on a necklace. Approximately what percent of the beads on the necklace were red?

a. 25%
b. 30%
c. 33%
d. 40%

54. How many times greater is $2\frac{1}{4}$ than $\frac{3}{4}$?

a. 3
b. 5
c. 6
d. 8

55. If $\frac{1}{4x} + 3 = 6$, then $x =$

a. 12

b. 6

c. $\frac{1}{12}$

d. $\frac{1}{6}$

56. The price of a toy is reduced by $15. If the new price of the toy is 80% of the original price, what was the original price of the toy?

a. $30
b. $45
c. $75
d. $80

57. $\frac{.08 + .08 + .08 + .08}{4} =$

a. 0.08
b. 0.16
c. 0.02
d. 0.2

58. If Leslie can run 2 miles in 35 minutes, how long will it take her to run 16 miles at the same rate?

a. 3 hours 50 minutes
b. 4 hours 40 minutes
c. 5 hours 50 minutes
d. 6 hours 20 minutes

59. $2\sqrt{12} \times 2\sqrt{3} =$

a. 12

b. $2\sqrt{12}$

c. $4\sqrt{12}$

d. 24

60. $(55 - 62) \times 4 - 2^3 =$

a. –36
b. –28
c. 28
d. 36

61. Jason gets 35 cents for every weed he pulls from his neighbor's yard. He wants to earn enough money to buy a game that costs $52.50. How many weeds must he pull in order to earn enough money to buy the game?

a. 80
b. 100
c. 120
d. 150

62. At Davis High, 150 students take biology and 120 take physics. Of these students, 30 take both biology and physics. How many students take biology but do not take physics?

a. 20
b. 30
c. 120
d. 130

63. If $2(2x + 2) = 16$, then $x =$

a. 2
b. 3
c. 4
d. 5

64. Which of the following is not the product of two distinct prime numbers?

a. 3
b. 6
c. 10
d. 15

Language

Questions 1–60, 25 minutes

For questions 1–40, check the sentences for errors of usage, capitalization, or punctuation. If there is no error, choose (D).

1. Choose the sentence with the correct grammar.

a. Supermarkets try to make their food look as appetizing as possible.
b. The Tower of London is the city's most popular tourist attraction.
c. Many people enjoy listening to quiet music while they work.
d. No mistake.

2. Choose the sentence with the correct grammar.

a. There are three kinds of rooms at the Main Street Hotel.
b. Today's cars are most more powerful than cars of the past.
c. It is always important to read the directions very careful.
d. No mistake.

3. Choose the sentence with the correct grammar.

a. Lisa bought a silk dress from a store at the mall.
b. Jason left the cake in the oven and burned it.
c. Most seashells are made from calcium.
d. No mistake.

4. Choose the sentence with the correct punctuation.

a. I know some words, that my friends don't know.
b. Camels can travel for days, without stopping to drink.
c. My three favorite vegetables are carrots, spinach, and onions.
d. No mistake.

5. Choose the sentence with the correct capitalization.

a. Most of the food we eat is grown in Foreign Countries.
b. If you paint indoors, make sure that Your room is well ventilated.
c. Last year I saw an exhibition of modern American art at the museum.
d. No mistake.

6. Choose the sentence with the correct punctuation.

a. I jumped, when I heard a loud knock on the door.
b. "That's interesting," he said. "I never knew that."
c. There is more than one correct answer to Lukes question.
d. No mistake.

7. Choose the sentence with the correct grammar.

a. Jeff visited a cheese factory and learned how cheese is made.
b. I forgot to invite my brother's best friend to the party.
c. Though Mark is not a doctor, he knows a great deal about medicine.
d. No mistake.

8. Choose the sentence with the correct grammar.

a. Many people don't not know that snakes are reptiles.
b. He gave my brother and me a book.
c. Max go to the museum last week with his mother.
d. No mistake.

9. Choose the sentence with the correct punctuation.

a. Frogs lay their egg's in the water.
b. Julie had a hard time reading her sister's handwriting.
c. Franklin D Roosevelt was an expert politician.
d. No mistake.

10. Choose the sentence with the correct punctuation.

a. Everyone should read Shakespeare's play's.
b. The dog licked its paw after stepping on a sharp rock.
c. Since I didnt have enough money, I couldnt buy the book.
d. No mistake.

11. Choose the sentence with the correct grammar.

a. Martina are a naturally optimistic person.
b. David say, "I hope we find her soon."
c. My brother has a large number of baseball cards.
d. No mistake.

12. Choose the sentence with the correct grammar.

a. Some animals sleeps all winter.
b. My father take some great pictures of me.
c. Amy saw the cat and showed it to her sister.
d. No mistake.

13. Choose the sentence with the correct capitalization.

a. Peter is always late for School.
b. My doctor recommends that I eat more fruit.
c. Carpentry and Cabinetmaking are very different skills.
d. No mistake.

14. Choose the sentence with the correct punctuation.

a. David greatly enjoyed the new opera, that he saw last night.
b. "Isn't it beautiful?" asked Laurie when she saw her sister's new pet.
c. Pavlov won a Nobel Prize for his work with dog's.
d. No mistake.

15. Choose the sentence with the correct grammar.

a. I always wash my hands before eating.
b. Some people mistakenly believe that he knows how to fly an airplane.
c. After winning the race, the runner began to cry.
d. No mistake.

16. Choose the sentence with the correct grammar.

a. My father gave the car to my brother and me.
b. We never thought that they will arrive on time.
c. When it rains, the roads are become very slippery and dangerous.
d. No mistake.

17. Choose the sentence with the correct grammar.

a. Unless you finished your spinach, you won't be allowed to have cake.
b. Troy played the most brilliant game of his life last night.
c. Tom holded his breath and hoped that his brother would score a goal.
d. No mistake.

18. Choose the sentence with the correct punctuation.

a. Even after losing, David refused to give up hope.
b. Manny warmly greeted his guests at the door.
c. “Penelope,” Jason replied, “I don’t think you’re ready.”
d. No mistake.

19. Choose the sentence with the correct grammar.

a. They weren’t sure of the address, so they ask for directions.
b. Paul is a man who loves to play baseball in the park.
c. Abigail thank her teacher at the end of the school year.
d. No mistake.

20. Choose the sentence with the correct grammar.

a. Everyone thinks that he or she has the right answer.
b. When Ines arrived at school, she didn’t not know which classes to take.
c. Jan suddenly become very pale.
d. No mistake.

21. Choose the sentence with the correct grammar.

a. Jackson is born in a log cabin in North Carolina.
b. The audience, was obviously very pleased, with the performance.
c. The birds in the park by the lake sing beautifully.
d. No mistake.

22. Choose the sentence with the correct grammar.

a. Any citizen over 18 year old can vote in the election.
b. It is always important to read every pages of the book.
c. It is easier to learn to walk than to dance.
d. No mistake.

23. Choose the sentence with the correct grammar.

a. I am very worried about his failing health.
b. The most easiest way to move heavy cargo is by ship.
c. I would much rather take the bus to work than driving.
d. No mistake.

24. Choose the sentence with the correct grammar.

a. You need to try a mango to know whether you like it.
b. The jugglers attracted a large crowd.
c. Kim realized that she had forgotten to bring her lunch and her homework.
d. No mistake.

25. Choose the sentence with the correct grammar.

a. After beginning her career as a schoolteacher, Ida Tarbell became a writer.
b. Airplanes require frequent inspections to ensure that they are safe.
c. Early ice skates were made of wood and leather.
d. No mistake.

26. Choose the sentence with the correct grammar.

a. This puzzle is one of the more complicated ever made.
b. The fruit I ate yesterday was much better than the fruit I ate today.
c. Jack keep his trophies on a shelf in the basement.
d. No mistake.

27. Choose the sentence with the correct grammar.

a. While hiking in the forest, we eaten lunch near a small creek.
b. The greatest book I have ever read was written by Ernest Hemingway.
c. The mayor of the town is very concerned for pollution.
d. No mistake.

28. Choose the sentence with the correct grammar.

a. Matt wash the dishes while Alex dried them.
b. Tomorrow, Richard and his sister will go to the amusement park.
c. Woodrow, my pet hamster, escapes from his cage last night.
d. No mistake.

29. Choose the sentence with the correct grammar.

a. I was very impressed to seen him lift that heavy weight.
b. Nathan always carry a leather wallet in his back pocket.
c. I hardly ever drink coffee before noon.
d. No mistake.

30. Choose the sentence with the correct grammar.

a. It has been so long since I have seen them that I have forgotten what they look like.
b. Owen thought that his brother was not very nice toward his mother.
c. I need to buy some new strings for my guitar.
d. No mistake.

31. Choose the sentence with the correct grammar.

a. When I seen him again, I'll give him the message.
b. I have seen that book on the shelf just behind the counter.
c. Tammy plays the violin, but she prefer the flute.
d. No mistake.

32. Choose the sentence with the correct grammar.

a. Building a treehouse can be a very educational experience.
b. While chasing a squirrel, my cat bumped into the wall.
c. My parents told me that I am mature enough to have my own bank account.
d. No mistake.

33. Choose the sentence with the correct grammar.

a. Anis goes to Brattleborough every summers to study physics.
b. How many languages do Mr. Ferral speak?
c. I think that Ms. Walton is the most intelligent of all my teachers.
d. No mistake.

34. Choose the sentence with the correct grammar.

a. Barry was so impressed by the book that he decided to become a cook.
b. The Constitution of the United States was signed in September 1787.
c. The human body stores excess energy in the form of fat.
d. No mistake.

35. Choose the sentence with the correct grammar.

a. My mother said she thinks that I should drink more milk.
b. My friend Jim find a snake hiding in the grass behind his house.
c. Anna return her books to the library yesterday.
d. No mistake.

i love reese

36. Choose the sentence with the correct punctuation.

a. Max did not respond to Davids letter.
b. "Can you bring me a chair?" asked my sister.
c. The river, is on the other side of the hill.
d. No mistake.

37. Choose the sentence with the correct grammar.

a. Most people do not think of fish as dangerous, but the barracuda is an exception.
b. Each of the guests at the party was a professor.
c. Walter was excited to hear that his mother had gotten a promotion.
d. No mistake.

38. Choose the sentence with the correct grammar.

a. David will arrive at the airport sometime next week.
b. Vivian told me that she had never gone so far in the woods alone.
c. Everyone at the party received a note from the father of the bride.
d. No mistake.

39. Choose the sentence with the correct grammar.

a. The marbles, are in a jar, on the top shelf, of the closet.
b. Most of the people at the party think that he is 15 years old.
c. Sarah thinks her father's job wasn't very dull.
d. No mistake.

40. Choose the sentence with the correct grammar.

a. Yesterday my best friend David said he wants to be a policeman someday.
b. Harriet Tubman made nineteen trips to the South and guides more than 300 slaves to freedom.
c. Few people know that Massachusetts has the countries biggest crop of cranberries.
d. No mistake.

Spelling

For questions 41–50, look for errors in spelling.

41. Choose the incorrect spelling.

a. Martin was very happy with the toy he purchased.
b. Early automobiles had headlights made of brass.
c. He complemented her on her pretty dress.
d. No mistake.

42. Choose the incorrect spelling.

a. Some films are serious while others are merely for entertainment.
b. Lawrence walked for eight days in the dessert without finding any water.
c. Mr. Carter tried to improve the working conditions in his factory.
d. No mistake.

43. Choose the incorrect spelling.

a. Jennifer was a vigorous and effective public speaker.
b. There was very little difference between their two positions.
c. Most nations switched from sail to steam power at the turn of the century.
d. No mistake.

44. Choose the incorrect spelling.

a. Patrick thinks that he made the wrong descision the other day.
b. It is never easy to choose between two people who are so similar.
c. John has been a student of political science for over five years.
d. No mistake.

45. Choose the incorrect spelling.

a. Lonny likes to read magazines on the weekends.
b. Everyone can benefit from improvements in transportation.
c. The people cheered when the war was finally over.
d. No mistake.

46. Choose the incorrect spelling.

a. Last week Sally's father took her to the aquarium.
b. My essay was supposed to be fifty sentenses long.
c. Lindsay was the best musician of the group.
d. No mistake.

47. Choose the incorrect spelling.

a. Tina was worried that she could not pay off her debts.
b. The sun was shinning brightly and the birds were singing.
c. David's parents sat down and waited for the concert to begin.
d. No mistake.

48. Choose the incorrect spelling.

a. Modern farmers make good use of agricultural technology.
b. Our history teacher sent David to the principle's office.
c. There are several advantages to his method.
d. No mistake.

49. Choose the incorrect spelling.

a. Carol accomplished much less than she promised.
b. Many disasters are caused by poor management.
c. Both candidates agreed on most of the important political issues.
d. No mistake.

50. Choose the incorrect spelling.

a. Mr. Bowles helped to put these historical events into perspective for us.
b. Amelia is an ambitious woman who wants to become a lawyer someday.
c. The British goverment was unhappy with her performance.
d. No mistake.

Composition

51. Choose the sentence that is correct and most clearly written.

a. Yesterday five miles Alex ran around the track.

b. Around the track, yesterday Alex ran five miles.

c. Five miles was how far Alex ran around the track yesterday.

d. Alex ran five miles around the track yesterday.

52. Choose the sentence that is correct and most clearly written.

a. 21 years old was the age when Jonathan decided that he wanted to become a linguist.

b. Jonathan decided, at the age of 21 years old, that a linguist was what he wanted to become.

c. Jonathan decided to become a linguist when he was 21 years old.

d. When he was 21 years old, Jonathan decided that a linguist was what to be.

53. Choose the sentence that is correct and most clearly written.

a. To read the works of Shakespeare was what Dr. Thornton recommended to his students.

b. The works of Shakespeare was what Dr. Thornton recommended to his students to read.

c. Dr. Thornton suggested that his students read the works of Shakespeare.

d. The works of Shakespeare, suggested Dr. Thornton, were what his students should read.

54. Where should the following sentence be placed in the paragraph below?

Her career as an activist began when she was a schoolteacher.

1) Susan B. Anthony, born in 1820, was one of the strongest advocates for women's rights in America. 2) She was filled with horror when she realized that the male schoolteachers were being paid much more for performing the same job. 3) Shortly after that she began to fight for equality and for women's suffrage, or the right to vote. 4) She was never deterred by her many traditionalist opponents. 5) Before she died in 1906, Susan B. Anthony addressed the women's suffrage convention. 6) She urged them to fight on and not to surrender. 7) Just over ten years later, women were finally given the right to vote.

a. After sentence 1
b. After sentence 2
c. After sentence 3
d. After sentence 4

55. Where should the following sentence be placed in the paragraph below?

Nonetheless, they are powerful animals and some of the fastest birds in the air.

1) Hummingbirds are most commonly found in South America, but can be found in other parts of the Western Hemisphere. 2) They are extremely small in size, as small as 3 inches in length. 3) They can reach speeds of up to 60 miles per hour, and can beat their wings up to 75 times every second. 4) They expend so much energy that they have to constantly eat. 5) At night, when they cannot feed, they fall into a deep sleep similar to hibernation.

a. After sentence 1
b. After sentence 2
c. After sentence 3
d. After sentence 4

56. Fill in the blank.

Many dogs have natural hunting instincts; _______ retrievers enjoy fetching and carrying things in their mouths.

a. in contrast,
b. for example,
c. because,
d. likewise

57. Fill in the blank.

I was not able to go to the concert last week _______ I could not get tickets.

a. therefore
b. nevertheless
c. moreover
d. because

58. Fill in the blank.

Picking apples off the tree too early is not good for the tree; _______ the apples won't taste very good either.

a. however,
b. for example,
c. furthermore,
d. but,

59. Which sentence does not belong in the following paragraph?

1) My paternal grandfather worked for many years as a photographer's assistant. 2) In the evenings, he gave private dance lessons to actors. 3) Since he didn't have a lot of money, the apartment his family lived in was very small. 4) But he earned enough to send my father to college. 5) There were not many colleges in rural America in the 1950s. 6) It was very important to my grandfather to see that his son had a good education.

a. Sentence 2
b. Sentence 3
c. Sentence 4
d. Sentence 5

60. Which sentence does not belong in the following paragraph?

1) A few years ago, I was looking through some old photographs that my parents kept in the attic. 2) I uncovered pictures of my family as they stood in line at Ellis Island and looked at the Statue of Liberty. 3) The Statue of Liberty was a gift from the French government. 4) My grandparents spent a few days in a shelter that overlooked the Hudson River. 5) However, they did not stay in New York for long. 6) Thankfully their cousins in Chicago gave them jobs and so they moved to the Midwest to begin their new lives. 7) This is the story of how my family arrived in America.

a. Sentence 2
b. Sentence 3
c. Sentence 4
d. Sentence 5

Chapter 13
HSPT Practice Test 2: Answers and Explanations

ANSWER KEY

Verbal Skills

1.	A	38.	A
2.	B	39.	B
3.	B	40.	B
4.	C	41.	B
5.	B	42.	A
6.	D	43.	C
7.	B	44.	A
8.	C	45.	B
9.	D	46.	B
10.	C	47.	C
11.	B	48.	A
12.	B	49.	B
13.	C	50.	C
14.	C	51.	A
15.	A	52.	C
16.	D	53.	C
17.	B	54.	B
18.	C	55.	D
19.	B	56.	B
20.	C	57.	A
21.	C	58.	B
22.	A	59.	D
23.	D	60.	C
24.	D		
25.	B		
26.	A		
27.	B		
28.	B		
29.	C		
30.	D		
31.	C		
32.	B		
33.	A		
34.	D		
35.	A		
36.	D		
37.	C		

Quantitative Skills

1.	C	38.	B
2.	B	39.	C
3.	D	40.	B
4.	C	41.	C
5.	D	42.	C
6.	A	43.	B
7.	B	44.	B
8.	B	45.	D
9.	D	46.	D
10.	B	47.	B
11.	A	48.	C
12.	A	49.	C
13.	B	50.	A
14.	B	51.	B
15.	A	52.	D
16.	D		
17.	D		
18.	D		
19.	C		
20.	A		
21.	D		
22.	D		
23.	A		
24.	B		
25.	C		
26.	C		
27.	B		
28.	C		
29.	C		
30.	B		
31.	C		
32.	D		
33.	B		
34.	D		
35.	A		
36.	A		
37.	C		

Reading

1.	D	38.	A
2.	B	39.	C
3.	A	40.	C
4.	C	41.	B
5.	C	42.	A
6.	C	43.	D
7.	A	44.	B
8.	B	45.	C
9.	A	46.	A
10.	C	47.	C
11.	C	48.	B
12.	D	49.	D
13.	B	50.	A
14.	B	51.	B
15.	B	52.	D
16.	B	53.	B
17.	B	54.	B
18.	A	55.	A
19.	B	56.	D
20.	B	57.	A
21.	A	58.	C
22.	D	59.	B
23.	B	60.	C
24.	C	61.	C
25.	B	62.	B
26.	A		
27.	B		
28.	A		
29.	D		
30.	B		
31.	D		
32.	B		
33.	A		
34.	B		
35.	C		
36.	D		
37.	B		

Mathematics

1.	B	38.	C
2.	A	39.	B
3.	C	40.	C
4.	B	41.	B
5.	C	42.	A
6.	B	43.	C
7.	D	44.	D
8.	A	45.	C
9.	D	46.	A
10.	D	47.	A
11.	B	48.	A
12.	A	49.	C
13.	A	50.	B
14.	A	51.	B
15.	D	52.	A
16.	C	53.	C
17.	C	54.	A
18.	A	55.	C
19.	A	56.	C
20.	C	57.	A
21.	C	58.	B
22.	D	59.	D
23.	D	60.	A
24.	B	61.	D
25.	C	62.	C
26.	A	63.	B
27.	A	64.	A
28.	B		
29.	D		
30.	B		
31.	B		
32.	C		
33.	A		
34.	B		
35.	A		
36.	D		
37.	A		

Language Skills

1.	D	38.	D
2.	A	39.	B
3.	D	40.	A
4.	C	41.	C
5.	C	42.	B
6.	B	43.	D
7.	D	44.	A
8.	B	45.	D
9.	B	46.	B
10.	B	47.	B
11.	C	48.	B
12.	C	49.	D
13.	B	50.	C
14.	B	51.	D
15.	D	52.	C
16.	A	53.	C
17.	B	54.	A
18.	D	55.	B
19.	B	56.	B
20.	A	57.	D
21.	C	58.	C
22.	C	59.	D
23.	A	60.	B
24.	D		
25.	D		
26.	B		
27.	B		
28.	B		
29.	C		
30.	D		
31.	B		
32.	D		
33.	C		
34.	D		
35.	A		
36.	B		
37.	D		

ANSWERS AND EXPLANATIONS

Verbal Skills

1. **A**
2. **B** The U.S. as a country is led by a president; the army as a whole is led by a general.
3. **B** To fortify means to strengthen, so the opposite is weaken.
4. **C** Sad, lonely, and upset are all types of feelings.
5. **B**
6. **D** Gigantic means very large; hilarious means very funny.
7. **B** Opaque means hard to see or understand; the opposite is clear.
8. **C** Oregano, parsley, and pepper are all types of spices.
9. **D**
10. **C** We can diagram this as follows: $J > A$, $K > A$. We know that John and Kenny each have more than Alice, but we don't know whether John has more than Kenny.
11. **B**
12. **B** We can diagram this as follows: $J > L$, $L > M$. We know that Juanita finished before Lucy, so Lucy did not finish the race before Juanita.
13. **C**
14. **C** Touch, sight, and hearing are all types of senses.
15. **A** Abundant means plentiful; the opposite is meager.
16. **D**
17. **B** Feathers, beaks, and wings are all parts of a bird.
18. **C** We can diagram this as follows: $R > W$, $T > A$. We have no idea how Robert and Weston relate to Abigail and Tyrone, so we can't know whether Robert or Tyrone read first.
19. **B**
20. **C** A bird is kept in a cage; a prisoner is kept in a jail.
21. **C**
22. **A** Oceans, lakes, and rivers are all bodies of water.

23. **D** A paragraph is made up of sentences; a poem is made up of verses.

24. **D**

25. **B** Ruthless means without mercy; the opposite is merciful.

26. **A**

27. **B** Yard, mile, and foot are all measurements of length.

28. **B**

29. **C** Chaos means disorder, so the opposite is order.

30. **D** Sandal, slipper, and shoe are all worn on the foot; a glove is worn on the hand.

31. **C**

32. **B** Bread is made from grain; jam is made from fruit.

33. **A** A hat and a cap are both worn on the head; a shoe and a sneaker are both worn on the foot.

34. **D** Prevalent means common; the opposite is rare.

35. **A** Hammer, knife, and screwdriver are all types of tools.

36. **D**

37. **C** Pear, apple, and orange are all forms of fruit.

38. **A** Reprimand means to scold; the opposite is to praise.

39. **B** We can diagram this as follows: $A >$ Louise, Lisa $> A > J$. Since Lisa counts faster than Agnes, and Agnes can count faster than Jeremy, we know that Jeremy does not count faster than Lisa.

40. **B** A trunk is the base of a tree; a stem is the base of a flower.

41. **B** Dog, cat, and rabbit are all kinds of mammals.

42. **A**

43. **C** Peanuts, cashews, and walnuts all have shells.

44. **A** Mile is a measure of distance; pound is a measure of weight.

45. **B** We can diagram this as follows: $R\ E\ S > C$. Since Eric has the same number of cards as Steve, they both have more than Carl. Therefore it is false, that Steve has fewer cards than Carl.

46. **B** Erratic means unstable; the opposite is stable.

47. **C**

48. **A** We can diagram this as follows: $L > M > S$, $S > P$. Since Lanville has more inhabitants than Samtown, and Samtown has more than Pinton, we know that Lanville has more inhabitants than Pinton.

49. **B** Esteem means admiration or respect; the opposite is dislike.

50. **C** Speak, yell, and whisper all describe ways of making sounds.

51. **A** Indifferent means unconcerned; the opposite is concerned.

52. **C** Flute, violin, and cello are all instruments in an orchestra.

53. **C** We can diagram this as follows: *O* > *Q*, *O* > *J*, Sally > Stephen, Sally > *J*. All we know about Ollie and Sally is that they are each older than Joseph. But we don't know whether Ollie or Sally is older.

54. **B** A cook works in a kitchen; a doctor works in a hospital.

55. **D** Theater, stadium, and arena are all places where crowds gather.

56. **B** We can diagram this as follows: *E* > *H* > Bill, *A* > Becky, *A* > *E*. Since Adam can sing more songs than Enid, and Enid can sing more songs than Howard, we know that Adam cannot sing fewer songs than Howard.

57. **A** Cover, page, and spine are all parts of a book.

58. **B** We can diagram this as follows: *M* > Penelope > *U*, Petra > *M*. Since Petra has more cats than Michael, and Michael has more than Penelope, we know that Penelope does not have more cats than Petra.

59. **D** A group of trees is a forest; a group of stars is a constellation.

60. **C** Intentional means done on purpose; the opposite is accidental.

Quantitative Skills

1. **C** The series goes 4 (+ 8) 12 (+ 8) 20 (+ 8) 28 (+ 8) **36**.

2. **B** In a rectangle, the diagonals are always equal, and they are the longest lines.

3. **D** Divide 39 by 3 to get 13. That's $\frac{1}{3}$ of 39, so $\frac{2}{3}$ of 39 = 26. Divide each answer choice by 2 to see which one gives you 26.

4. **C** $\frac{1}{4}$ of 84 = 21. $\frac{1}{2}$ of 48 = 24. $\frac{1}{2}$ of 42 = 21. Therefore (1) and (3) are identical and smaller than (2).

5. **D** The series goes 3 (× 2) 6 (× 2) 12 (× 2) 24 (× 2) **48**.

6. **A** If we count the squares, we find that (A) has 12 squares, (B) has 12 squares, and (C) has 20 squares.

7. **B** The series goes 4 (+ 4) 8 (+ 4) 12 (+ 4) 16 (+ 4) **20**.

8. **B** 20% of 60 is the same as $\frac{20}{100} \times 60$, or 12. 60% of 20 is the same as $\frac{60}{100} \times 20$, or 12. 200% of 6 is the same as $\frac{200}{100} \times 6$, or 12.

9. **D** $5 \times 3 = 15$. Try taking 20% of each of the choices to see which gives you 15. When you get to (D), you'll see that 20% of 75 = $\frac{20}{100} \times 75$.

10. **B** The series goes 5 (+ 3) 8 (+ 4) 12 (+ 3) 15 (+ 4) 19 (+ 3) **22**.

11. **A** $3^3 = 3 \times 3 \times 3 = 27$. $4^2 = 4 \times 4 = 16$. $5^1 = 5 \times 1 = 5$. Choice (A) is the correct answer because, indeed $27 > 16 > 5$.

12. **A** The series goes 8 (– 3) 5 (+ 4) 9 (– 3) 6 (+ 4) 10 (– 3) **7**.

13. **B** $\frac{1}{2}$ of 24 = 12. Try taking $\frac{2}{3}$ of each answer choice to see which equals 12.

14. **B** The series goes 4 (+ 3) 7 (+ 2) 9 (+ 3) 12 (+ 2) 14 (+ 3) 17 (+ 2) **19**.

15. **A** The product of 3, 4, and 5 is 60. $\frac{3}{4} \times 60 = 45$.

16. **D** $\frac{5}{10} = 0.5$. $\frac{70}{100} = 0.7$. $\frac{8}{100} = 0.08$.

17. **D** The difference between 12 and 3 is 9. 200% of 9 = $\frac{200}{100} \times 9 = 18$.

18. **D** If you carry out the multiplications in (1), (2), and (3), you'll get 135 for each one. All three are equal, which makes (D) the answer.

19. **C** The series goes 12 (+ 6) 18 (+ 4) 22 (+ 6) 28 (+ 4) **32** (+ 6) 38.

20. **A** The product of 5 and 4 is 20. $\frac{5}{100} \times 20 = \frac{5}{5} = 1$.

21. **D** Since *O* is the center of the circle, *OA*, *OB*, and *OC* are all radii. All radii of a circle have the same lengths.

22. **D** 15% of 90 is the same as $\frac{15}{100} \times 90 = 13.5$. Try each answer choice to see which number divided by 4 is 13.5.

23. **A** The series goes 4 (× 2) 8 (+ 2) 10 (× 2) 20 (+ 2) 22 (× 2) **44** (+ 2) 46.

24. **B** The smallest prime number bigger than 4 is 5. The square root of 25 is 5. 75% of 8 is $\frac{75}{100} \times 8 = 6$.

25. **C** The product of 6 and 8 is 48. Add 20 to each of the choices to see which number gives you 48.

26. **C** Each number in the series is followed by its reciprocal.

27. **B** Each of the angles in a square is 90°, and each of the angles in an equilateral triangle is 60°. Therefore $a = 90°$, $b = 60°$, and $c = 60°$.

28. **C** The series goes 30 (– 2) 28 (– 3) 25 (– 4) 21 (– 5) **16**.

29. **C** Translate 140% of 40 as $\frac{140}{100} \times 40 = 56$.

30. **B** The series goes 2 (+ 2) 4 (– 1) 3 (+ 2) 5 (– 1) 4 (+ 2) 6 (– 1) 5 (+ 2) 7.

31. **C** The area of a square with sides 3 is $3 \times 3 = 9$. The area of a circle with radius 3 is 9π. You may not know how to solve for the area of an equilateral triangle with side 3, but you know that its area is smaller than that of a square with side 3.

32. **D** $3^3 = 3 \times 3 \times 3 = 27$. $3^4 = 3 \times 3 \times 3 \times 3 = 81$. The difference between 27 and 81 is 54. Two more than this is 56.

33. **B** Since angle *a* is on the same line with the angle 110°, we know that *a* must be 70°. Angle *c* must also be 110°, since it is across from 110°; angle *b* must be 70°, since it is across from angle *a*. Therefore $a + c$ and $b + c$ are each 180°, and are bigger than $a + c$, which is 70°.

34. **D** The series goes 11 (× 2) 22 (× 2) 44 (× 2) 88 (× 2) **176**.

35. **A** The series goes 15 (+ 15) 30 (+ 5) 35 (+ 15) 50 (+ 5) 55 (+ 15) **70** (+ 5) 75.

36. **A** Don't make this one too complicated; just translate this as $\frac{75}{100} \times \frac{20}{100} \times 200$. Once you cancel out all the zeros, you get $\frac{75}{10} \times 2 \times 2 = 30$.

37. **C** Choices (A) and (B) each have three parts shaded, while (C) has four parts shaded.

38. **B** Use the average formula to figure out this problem and find the average of 20, 25, and 45. The sum of these numbers is 90. Divide the sum by the number of items: $90 \div 3 = 30$. $\frac{3}{5}$ of 30 is 18.

39. **C** The series goes 20 (+ 10) 30 (+ 15) 45 (+ 20) 65 (+ 25) **90** (+ 30) 120.

40. **B** To figure out 6.5×10^{-3}, move the decimal 3 places to the left, and get 0.0065. Likewise, to solve 650×10^{-4}, move the decimal 4 places to the left, and get 0.065. Since (3) has a 6 in the hundredths place, it is the largest.

41. **C** The series goes $1^{(2)} = 1$, $2^{(2)} = 4$, $3^{(2)} = 9$, $4^{(2)} =$ **16**.

42. **C** If $x = 2$, then (1) = 8, (2) = 16, and (3) = 16.

43. **B** Translate this question as $\frac{40}{100} \times \frac{20}{100} \times 600$. If you cancel all the zeros, you get $4 \times 2 \times 6$, or 48.

44. **B** Plug in each answer choice. 25 divided by 4 is 6 with a remainder of 1, so cross off (A). 31 divided by 4 is 7 with a remainder of 3.

45. **D** The series goes 15 (+ 5) 20 (– 2) 18 (+ 5) 23 (– 2) 21 (+ 5) 26 (– 2) 24 (+ 5) **29**.

46. **D** The area of any rectangle is equal to its length × width. Since a square has equal sides, we use the same number for each. (1) is therefore 4, (2) is 9, and (3) is $4 \times 4 = 16$, but half of that is 8.

47. **B** The product of 15 and $\frac{1}{3}$ is 5, and 5 more than 5 is 10.

48. **C** The series goes 56 (– 5) 51 (– 3) 48 (– 5) 43 (– 3) 40 (– 5) **35** (– 3) 32.

49. **C** One diagonal of a square is always longer than one side of a square. But a diagonal is always shorter than two sides of a square. (Try measuring this if you want to prove it to yourself.) Since *BD* and *BF* are longer than *CD* and *CB*, we know that (2) is larger than (1). Since *BD* and *BF* are less than the sum of $BC + CD$ and $BA + AF$ we know that (3) is larger than (2).

50. **A** First we need to find the average of 18, 24, 25, and 29. To do this, we add them to get 96, and then divide by 4 to get 24. $\frac{1}{6}$ of 24 is 4.

51. **B** The series goes 110 (÷ 2) 55 (– 5) 50 (÷ 2) 25 (– 5) 20 (÷ 2) **10**.

52. **D** 6^2 is $6 \times 6 = 36$. 16 more is 52.

Reading

Comprehension

1. **D** The third sentence of the second paragraph states, "We stumbled down from the train...."

2. **B** The first paragraph says, "I had crossed so many rivers that I was dull to them." The best paraphrase of the idea is (B).

3. **A** Just before the word *roused*, we see that the narrator "had been sleeping."

4. **C** At the end of the first paragraph, the narrator says that Nebraska is remarkable because "it was still, all day long."

5. **C** In the sentences before the word *tongue*, the narrator hears people talking, shouting, and exclaiming.

6. **C** According to the last paragraph, the people were immigrants.

7. **A** Just before mentioning that he "stumbled down from the train," the narrator "had been sleeping."

8. **B** The last paragraph says that they had "two half-grown boys and a girl...and a little girl clung to her mother's skirts."

9. **A** The third paragraph says that he discovered something to help protect "houses, people, and ships."

10. **C** Choices (A), (B), and (D) are too narrow to be the main idea. The passage discusses Franklin, Volta, Faraday, and Edison. This makes (C) the best choice.

11. **C** Choice (A) is extreme, and there is no evidence to support (B) or (D) in the passage. The author does say in the last sentence, however, that electricity is important to the modern world.

12. **D** According to the fifth paragraph, Faraday invented the generator.

13. **B** The fifth paragraph says that Faraday's discovery helped create the first electric motor, and that today's generators are almost identical to his.

14. **B** According to the sixth paragraph, Edison and Tesla disagreed about whether to use direct or alternating current.

15. **B** The sixth paragraph states that the transformer can "change the voltage of an electrical current."

16. **B** In the sixth paragraph, the word *advocated* is used with the same meaning as argued for.

17. **B** The first sentence says that Lindbergh was the first person to make a transatlantic flight.

18. **A** The second paragraph says that Earhart was in a plane with two people "at the controls," who would be her colleagues or coworkers.

19. **B** The passage mostly talks about Amelia Earhart.

20. **B** The third paragraph says that Earhart wanted to fly "to show that aviation was not exclusive to men."

21. **A** This story is mostly about a person, Amelia Earhart, so (A) is the most logical choice.

22. **D** According to the fourth paragraph, the "widest point" of the world is the equator.

23. **B** The final sentence of the story says that "nobody is sure what became of Amelia Earhart."

24. **C** The fifth paragraph says that Fred Noonan was "her navigator."

25. **B** Choices (A), (C), and (D) are only details of the story.

26. **A** The second paragraph says that Pasteur encouraged people to use antiseptics, which reduced infection caused by germs.

27. **B** The second paragraph says that Pasteur wanted doctors to "wash their hands [and] their instruments."

28. **A** The third paragraph says that anthrax could live in sheep but not in chickens, whose body temperature is above 44 degrees Celsius. Therefore, the body temperature of sheep must be less than 44 degrees Celsius.

29. **D** In the second paragraph, the word *sterilize* is used to describe a cleaning process to eliminate germs.

30. **B** The third paragraph says that pasteurization refers to the process of heating "dairy products." The only choice that is a dairy product is cheese.

31. **D** The final sentence of the passage says that Pasteur helped to free people from diseases.

32. **B** In the fourth paragraph, the word *antibodies* is used to refer to something that can protect the body from disease.

33. **A** Choices (B), (C), and (D) are details of the story. The main idea discusses chocolate from the time it was used by the Aztecs through its use in Europe.

34. **B** The word *fashion* is used to describe how European's drank chocolate, which was using the same method that the Aztec's use ("hot, spicy, and unsweetened").

35. **C** According to the second paragraph, it was the Spanish who brought chocolate to Europe.

36. **D** Choice (A) is extreme, so it can be eliminated. There is no evidence in the passage to support (B) or (C). However, the final paragraph says that cocoa butter is part of solid chocolate.

37. **B** The third paragraph says, "At first, when cocoa was rare, chocolate was considered a delicacy."

38. **A** The first paragraph says that "cocoa beans were even used as a form of money."

39. **C** The third paragraph says that later, "chocolate became accessible to almost everyone." Therefore, at first, it must not have been available to everyone.

40. **C** The final paragraph discusses how chocolate was changed from a drink to solid form.

Vocabulary

41. **B**

42. **A**

43. **D**

44. **B**

45. **C**

46. **A**

47. **C**

48. **B**

49. **D**

50. **A**

51. **B**

52. **D**

53. **B**

54. **B**

55. **A**

56. **D**

57. **A**

58. **C**

59. **B**

60. **C**

61. **C**

62. **B**

Mathematics

Mathematical Concepts

1. **B** Try dividing each answer choice by 8. All of the choices except 56 leave a remainder.

2. **A** Use the Bowtie to see which fraction is largest. You can also Ballpark—only (A) and (D) are more than $\frac{1}{2}$.

3. **C** Try adding any two even whole numbers. 2 + 2 = 4, which is an even number.

4. **B** First, factor 18, which can be written as 1×18, 2×9, and 3×6. Of these, only 2 and 3 are prime.

5. **C** The circumference of a circle is equal to $2\pi r$. Since the circumference is equal to 16π, we know that $16\pi = 2\pi r$.

6. **B** Plug in the answer choices one at a time. Is 3 a multiple of 3 and 9? No. Is 9 a multiple of 3 and 9? Yes.

7. **D** 3.096 + 2.85 = 5.946, but don't forget to round to the nearest tenth.

8. **A** Draw a number line and find –2.4 on it. Now move to the left (less than –2.4), and find the largest integer.

9. **D** 10^2 means that you move the decimal two places to the right.

10. **D** All sides of an equilateral triangle are equal, and the perimeters for a triangle is the sum of all sides. Therefore, 3 + 3 + 3 = 9.

11. **B** You can either plot these points on a number line or find the difference between each and –4, –4.01 is only 0.01 away from –4.

12. **A** One easy way to test ratios is to try either reducing or expanding each number by the same power. For instance, if we test 3.5 and 2, we get 7 and 4. Now we can see that (B) and (D) won't work. If we double again, we get 14 and 8.

13. **A** Plug in the answers one at a time. If one of the numbers is 6, then the other must be 12, so that their sum is 18. Is their product also 72? Yes.

14. **A** The fractional part is always the part over the whole. Since there is one teacher, but a total of 19 people, the fractional part that represents teachers is $\frac{1}{19}$.

15. **D** Draw a number line and count the integer numbers between –5.2 and 3.4. You have –5, –4, –3, –2, –1, 0, 1, 2, and 3.

16. **C** If a square has an area of 36, each of its sides is 6. So its perimeter is 6 + 6 + 6 + 6 = 24.

17. **C** $3^3 = 3 \times 3 \times 3 = 27$. $9^1 = 9$, so cross off (A). $9^2 = 9 \times 9 = 81$, so cross off (B). $27^1 = 27$.

18. **A** Since reciprocals are numbers that when multiplied together become 1, try multiplying together the numbers in each choice: $\frac{1}{3} \times \frac{9}{3} = 1$.

19. **A** 0.16 is the same as $\frac{16}{100}$, which can be reduced to $\frac{4}{25}$.

20. **C** We can change this expression to $2\sqrt{4 \times 2}$ and take the square root of 4 out from under the root sign.

21. **C** The formula for the area of a triangle is area = $\frac{(\text{base} \times \text{height})}{2}$. We know the area is 30 and the height is 10, so we can plug these values into the equation to get $30 = \frac{(\text{base} \times 10)}{2}$. The base must be 6.

22. **D** We can multiply 4 by 20 to get 80. This means that there must be $2 \times 20 = 40$ piano students.

23. **D** The volume of a cube with side 3 is $3 \times 3 \times 3 = 27$. The volume of a cube with side 1 is $1 \times 1 \times 1 \times 1$. Therefore we can fit 27 of the smaller cubes into the larger cube.

24. **B** To make *sure* she gets a can of cola, she will have to remove all of the lemon-lime soda first. This means if on the first try she pulls out a can of lemon-lime soda, she will be certain to pull out a can of cola on the next try.

Problem Solving

25. **C** This is the same as $\frac{5}{\frac{1}{4}}$. To divide fractions, we flip and multiply: $5 \times \frac{4}{1} = 20$.

26. **A** Mary spent \$8 + \$12 + \$2 = \$22. Since she started with \$30, she had \$8 left at the end of the day.

27. **A** First subtract 3 from both sides of the equation, which becomes $5x = 18$. Now divide each side by 5.

28. **B** Translate this as $\frac{x}{100} \times 96 = 8$. Then solve for x.

29. **D** First, turn these into ordinary fractions. To solve the first fraction, multiply 5 times 7 and add two to get the numerator (37) and keep the same denominator (5). To solve the second fraction, multiply 3 times 3 and add 2 to get the numerator (11) and keep the same denominator (3). Then the problem becomes $\frac{37}{5} - \frac{11}{3}$. Now use the Bowtie to subtract them: $\frac{111}{15} - \frac{55}{15} = \frac{56}{15} = 3\frac{11}{15}$.

30. **B** If she buys 1 pack of gum every day except Saturday, that makes 6 packs of gum. If we add the 2 she buys on Saturday, we get a total of 8 packs for the week. Now we multiply by 75 cents to find out the total cost for the week.

31. **B** We can set up this problem as a ratio. If 1 mile = 2.5 inches, we want to know how many miles is shown by 12.5 inches: $\frac{1}{2.5} = \frac{x}{12.5}$. Cross-multiply, and we get 5 miles.

32. **C** First, take 30% of \$80: $\frac{30}{100} \times 80 = 24$. So the dress will be marked down by \$24. \$80 – \$24 = \$56.

33. **A** It will be easier if we reduce before we multiply. If we cross-reduce, the problem becomes 2 × 3 = 6.

34. **B** If we subtract 4 from each side of the equation, we get $x^2 = 16$. Now try plugging in the answer choices. Which choice squared equals 16? Choice (B) does.

35. **A** To multiply decimals, multiply the numbers without decimals: 52 × 21 = 1092. Now we put back the two decimal places.

36. **D** Since her average on 4 tests was 91, her total score on those four tests must have been 4 × 91 = 364. The sum of the other three tests is 86 + 87 + 93 = 266. The last test must be 364 – 266 = 98. You can also plug in the answer choices to get the same answer.

37. **A** Translate this as $\frac{25}{100} \times 80 = \frac{10}{100}x$. Now solve for x.

38. **C** To divide fractions, flip and multiply: $\frac{1}{3} \div \frac{3}{7} = \frac{1}{3} \times \frac{7}{3} = \frac{7}{9}$.

39. **B** If 3 boxes contained 14 doughnuts each, that makes 3 × 14 = 42 total doughnuts. If 12 guests ate 3 doughnuts each, there were 12 × 3 = 36 doughnuts eaten. 42 – 36 = 6 doughnuts left over.

40. **C** If the airplane goes 400 miles per hour, we divide 6,000 total miles by 400 to find out how many hours it will take. This makes 15 hours to complete the trip. But the answer asks for the number of minutes! Since 1 hour = 60 minutes, we need to multiply 15 by 60 to get the number of minutes.

41. **B** Remember order of operations! First, do the parentheses (5 – 2) = 3. Then multiply 3 × 5 = 15. Now it reads 4 – 3 + 15, which equals 16.

42. **A** If Albert is 12, and he is twice as old as Bert, then Bert is 6. We also know that Bert is 7 years younger than Carl, so Carl is 13. In 8 years, then, Carl will be 21.

43. **C** Try plugging in the answer choices. Could x be 4? Does $4^4 = 16^3$? The easy way to find out is to write it out longhand: $4^4 = 4 \times 4 \times 4 \times 4$. $16^3 = 16 \times 16 \times 16$, which is the same as 4 × 4 × 4 × 4 × 4 × 4. Therefore, (A) can't be right. But we've made an interesting discovery. We know that $16^3 = 4 \times 4 \times 4 \times 4 \times 4 \times 4$. Therefore we need a total of six 4s on the left side of the equation. This means the answer is (C).

44. **D** We can set up a proportion: $\frac{2}{6} = \frac{x}{72}$. Cross-multiply to find that $x = 24$.

45. **C** First let's convert these to normal fractions. This gives us $\frac{\frac{25}{4}}{\frac{25}{2}}$. To divide these fractions, we need to flip the second one and multiply: $\frac{25}{4} \div \frac{25}{2} = \frac{25}{4} \times \frac{2}{25} = \frac{1}{2}$.

46. **A** To solve for x, begin by getting the x's on one side of the equation. To do this, subtract $3x$ from each side, and get $2x + 5 = -9$. Now subtract 5 from each side, which gives us $2x = -14$. Now divide each side by 2.

47. **A** To find out how many days she will need to save $20, we divide $\frac{\$20}{\$1.25}$, which gives us 16.

48. **A** The easiest way to solve this is by plugging in the answer choices. Let's try (A). If Alex has 30 cards, and has three times as many as David, then David has 10 cards. Do their cards average 20? Yes.

49. **C** If the perimeter of a square is 40 feet, its sides are 10 (the perimeter of a square equals four times the length of one side). To find the area, square the length (s^2) of the sides: $10^2 = 10 \times 10 = 100$ ft^2.

50. **B** Let's try solving for x. If we add 1 to each side, we get $-5x < 10$. Now divide each side by -5. Remember that when dividing by a negative number, you have to change the direction of the inequality sign, changing the < into a > sign. So we get $x > -2$.

51. **B** From 9:45 A.M. to 10:05 A.M. is 20 minutes. From 10:05 A.M. to 4:05 P.M. is 6 hours.

52. **A** The easiest way to solve this is by plugging in the answer choices. Let's try (A) first. Could x be 1? Is the average of 3, 8, and 1 equal to the average of 7 and 1? Yes.

53. **C** There are a total of 60 beads on the necklace, and 20 of them are red. Therefore the percentage of red beads on the necklace is $\frac{20}{60} = 33\%$.

54. **A** To see how many times greater one number is than another, you divide: $\frac{2\frac{1}{4}}{\frac{3}{4}}$. If we change the fractions into normal fraction form, we get $\frac{\frac{9}{4}}{\frac{3}{4}}$. To divide, flip and multiply: $\frac{9}{4} \times \frac{4}{3} = 3$.

55. **C** First, move the numbers to the other side of the equation by subtracting 3 from each side. This gives us $\frac{1}{4x} = 3$. To get the x on top, we can invert both sides of the equation, which gives us $4x = \frac{1}{3}$. Now divide each side by 4.

56. **C** Since $15 is equal to 20% off the original price, we can translate: 15 is 20% of what number? $15 = \frac{20}{100}x$. If we solve for x, we get $x = 75$. You can also plug in the answer choices to get the same answer.

57. **A** Add the decimals on top to get 0.32 and divide by 4, or see that the fraction could be changed to $\frac{4 \times 0.08}{4}$ and cancel the 4s. Divide this, and we get 0.08.

58. **B** Let's set up a proportion: $\frac{2 \textit{ miles}}{35 \textit{ minutes}} = \frac{16 \textit{ miles}}{x \textit{ minutes}}$. Cross-multiply to get 280 minutes, which is the same as 4 hours 40 minutes.

59. **D** If we multiply these together, we get $4\sqrt{36}$. Since $\sqrt{36} = 6$, this becomes 4 × 6 = 24.

60. **A** Remember order of operations. We do parentheses and exponents first, to get – 7 × 4 – 8. Then, we do multiplication to get –28 – 8 = –36.

61. **D** To see how many 35-cent weeds he needs to pull, we can divide $\frac{\$52.50}{.35}$. To make this easier to divide, move the decimal point two places to the right: $\frac{5250}{35} = 150$.

62. **C** We know that 150 students take biology, but 30 of them take physics as well. To see how many take biology without taking physics, subtract 30 from 150.

63. **B** Try plugging in the answer choices. Let's start with (A). Could *x* be 2? Does 2(2(2) + 2) = 16? No. Try (B). Could *x* be 3? Does 2(2(3) + 2) = 16? Yes.

64. **A** 6 = 2 × 3, 10 = 5 × 2, and 15 = 5 × 3. Only 3 is not the product of two distinct prime numbers. (Remember that 1 is not prime!)

Language

Usage

1. **D**

2. **A** Since "three kinds" is plural, the sentence needs to begin "There are."

3. **D**

4. **C** Items in a list should be separated by commas.

5. **C** Adjectives that refer to nationalities should be capitalized.

6. **B** When someone is speaking, a comma should be placed before the closed quotation marks, when the sentence will continue after the person is done speaking.

7. **D**

8. **B** Since the book was given to me, "me" becomes the object pronoun.

9. **B** The word *sister's* is possessive and needs an apostrophe.

10. **B** The word *it's* is not possessive and should be spelled *its.*

11. **C** Since baseball cards are countable, we use the word "number."

12. **C** The sentence begins in the past tense with the verb *saw.* It should continue in the past tense with the verb *showed.*

13. **B** The word *doctor* is not a proper name and should not be capitalized.

14. **B** The sentence begins with a direct quotation, which requires quotation marks.

15. **D**

16. **A** "Me" is in the correct form because it's an indirect object.

17. **B** We are talking about the game, so we use the adjective *brilliant.*

18. **D**

19. **B** Since we are referring to a person, we use *who.*

20. **A** "Everyone" is singular, so it needs the singular: "he or she has the right answer."

21. **C** "The birds" is plural, so it needs the plural verb *sing.*

22. **C** The sentence maintains parallel form.

23. **A** The correct idiom is *worried about.*

24. **D**

25. **D**

26. **B** To keep the comparisons in this sentence parallel, we use the past tense, "ate."

27. **B** "Greatest" is the correct superlative form.

28. **B** Since the sentence discusses tomorrow, it should use the future tense *will go.*

29. **C** The adverbial phrase "hardly ever" describes how often I drink coffee before noon.

30. **D**

31. **B** "Seen" is an invalid verb form, the sentence should read "I have seen" or "I saw."

32. **D**

33. **C** Since Ms. Walton is being compared to all the other teachers, you use the superlative form "most intelligent."

34. **D**

35. **A** "She thinks" creates correct subject/verb agreement.

36. **B** A direct question should end with a question mark.

37. **D**

38. **D**

39. **B** "Most of the people" is plural and requires the plural verb form "think."

40. **A** "Yesterday" requires the past tense "said."

Spelling

41. **C** The word *complimented* is misspelled.

42. **B** The word *desert* is misspelled.

43. **D**

44. **A** The word *decision* is misspelled.

45. **D**

46. **B** The word *sentences* is misspelled.

47. **B** The word *shining* is misspelled.

48. **B** The word *principal's* is misspelled.

49. **D**

50. **C** The word *government* is misspelled.

Composition

51. **D** (A), (B), and (C) separate "five miles" and "around the track," which should be together.

52. **C** (A), (B), and (D) are wordy and awkward.

53. **C** (A), (B), and (D) are wordy and awkward.

54. **A** The sentence we need to place introduces the idea of her working as a schoolteacher.

55. **B** The sentence we need to place introduces a contrast by saying that they are powerful animals. Therefore it should follow a sentence that implies they are not powerful.

56. **B** Since the second phrase continues the idea of the first, we need a same-direction word such as (B) or (C). Choice (C), however, is not logical in this context.

57. **D** Since the second phrase continues the idea of the first, we need a same-direction word such as (A) or (D). When a second phrase explains the first, because is the best choice. Choice (D) is your answer.

58. **C** The second phrase continues the idea of the first, so we need a same-direction word such as (B) or (C). Since the second phrase gives additional information and not an example, (C) is best.

59. **D** The rest of the paragraph is about the narrator's grandfather.

60. **B** While the rest of the paragraph is about the arrival of a family in America, sentence 3 is only about the Statue of Liberty.

Chapter 14
HSPT
Practice Test 3

Verbal Skills

Questions 1–60, 15 Minutes

1. Diligent most nearly means

a. stable
b. lost
c. hardworking
d. original

2. Severe means the *opposite* of

a. buried
b. informative
c. historic
d. mild

3. Candle is to wax as tire is to

a. road
b. car
c. rubber
d. tread

4. Which word does *not* belong with the others?

a. spoon
b. food
c. knife
d. fork

5. Horse is to stable as chicken is to

a. farm
b. coop
c. sty
d. rooster

6. Which word does not belong with the others?

a. winter
b. season
c. fall
d. summer

7. Prohibit most nearly means

a. punish
b. disallow
c. locate
d. paint

8. Which word does *not* belong with the others?

a. shirt
b. dress
c. clothes
d. shorts

9. Famished is to hungry as arid is to

a. dry
b. desert
c. water
d. heat

10. Biased means the *opposite* of

a. original
b. neutral
c. merciful
d. closed

11. Suitcase is to clothes as briefcase is to

a. papers
b. business
c. leather
d. handle

12. Hinder means the *opposite* of

a. help
b. gather
c. decrease
d. blame

13. Content most nearly means

a. able to be heard
b. satisfied
c. precise
d. courteous

14. Rachel finished the test before Alice. Barry finished the test after Richard. Rachel finished the test before Richard. If the first two statements are true, the third is

a. True
b. False
c. Uncertain

15. Container is to lid as house is to

a. door
b. people
c. roof
d. window

16. Credible most nearly means

a. edible
b. lazy
c. believable
d. drinkable

17. Sincere means the *opposite* of

a. final
b. dishonest
c. common
d. complete

18. Ines stood ahead of Marcus in line. Larry stood after Marcus in line. Larry stood before Ines in line. If the first two statements are true, the third is

a. True
b. False
c. Uncertain

19. Contaminate most nearly means

a. infect
b. produce
c. learn
d. suggest

20. Bink had more balloons than David. David had fewer balloons than Alex and Carol. Alex had more balloons than Bink. If the first two statements are true, the third is

a. True
b. False
c. Uncertain

21. Which word does *not* belong with the others?

a. sail
b. mast
c. rudder
d. ship

22. Fortunate most nearly means

a. proud
b. hopeful
c. late
d. lucky

23. Zoologist is to animal as botanist is to

a. rock
b. plant
c. ocean
d. book

24. Which word does *not* belong with the others?

a. fruit
b. apple
c. peach
d. pear

25. John is taller than Bart and Evelyn. Mark is taller than John. Mark is taller than Evelyn. If the first two statements are true, the third is

a. True
b. False
c. Uncertain

26. Which word does *not* belong with the others?

a. water
b. liquid
c. oil
d. vinegar

27. Frank most nearly means

a. clean
b. honest
c. light
d. annoying

28. Famine is to food as drought is to

a. water
b. sound
c. bread
d. room

29. Olivia ate more apples than Jennifer. Jennifer ate fewer apples than Nancy. Nancy ate more apples than Olivia. If the first two statements are true, the third is

a. True
b. False
c. Uncertain

30. Which word does *not* belong with the others?

a. tree
b. trunk
c. branch
d. leaf

31. Immune means the *opposite* of

a. shared
b. complex
c. vulnerable
d. learned

32. Which word does *not* belong with the others?

a. tea
b. coffee
c. water
d. cereal

33. Elude most nearly means

a. escape
b. show
c. remain
d. shout

34. Frank has seen more films than Jonathan and Nicholas. Jonathan has seen the same number of films as Manny. Manny has seen fewer films than Frank. If the first two statements are true, the third is

a. True
b. False
c. Uncertain

35. Which word does *not* belong with the others?

a. sole
b. shoe
c. lace
d. heel

36. Mimic most nearly means

a. talk
b. study
c. imitate
d. search

37. Counterfeit means the *opposite* of

a. genuine
b. amusing
c. young
d. loose

38. Felix walked farther than Danielle but not as far as Kate. Amanda walked farther than Kate. Amanda walked farther than Felix. If the first two statements are true, the third is

a. True
b. False
c. Uncertain

39. Barbaric means the *opposite* of

a. equal
b. popular
c. civilized
d. embarrassed

40. Which word does *not* belong with the others?

a. dog
b. fish
c. hamster
d. pet

41. Conventional means the *opposite* of

a. usual
b. boring
c. strange
d. rough

42. Inspect most nearly means

a. practice
b. jump
c. stretch
d. examine

43. Varied means the *opposite* of

a. similar
b. finished
c. ironic
d. simple

44. Which word does *not* belong with the others?

a. milk
b. goat
c. cow
d. horse

45. Maple is to tree as apple is to

a. fruit
b. leaf
c. green
d. seed

46. Diminish most nearly means

a. announce
b. please
c. discover
d. reduce

47. Mindy read fewer books than Mike, but more than Walter. Rochelle read fewer books than Mike. Mindy read more books than Rochelle. If the first two statements are true, the third is

a. True
b. False
c. Uncertain

48. Which word does *not* belong with the others?

a. movie
b. book
c. fiction
d. play

49. Unbiased most nearly means

a. weak
b. neutral
c. helpful
d. realistic

50. Criticize means the *opposite* of

a. stare
b. praise
c. read
d. catch

51. Which word does *not* belong with the others?

a. mop
b. floor
c. broom
d. vacuum

52. Bird is to wing as fish is to

a. water
b. fin
c. salmon
d. gill

53. Permanent most nearly means

a. active
b. proud
c. unchanging
d. difficult

54. Sergio has more badges than Terence, but fewer than Wendy. Zack has fewer badges than Terence. Wendy has fewer badges than Zack. If the first two statements are true, the third is

a. True
b. False
c. Uncertain

55. Serene most nearly means

a. peaceful
b. tired
c. clever
d. thoughtful

56. Enlarge means the *opposite* of

a. greet
b. enjoy
c. reduce
d. expand

57. Which word does *not* belong with the others?

a. wind
b. rain
c. snow
d. coat

58. Hour is to day as month is to

a. year
b. time
c. week
d. calendar

59. Which word does *not* belong with the others?

a. brick
b. stone
c. house
d. wood

60. Authentic most nearly means

a. valuable
b. genuine
c. sharp
d. gradual

Quantitative Skills

Questions 1–52, 30 minutes

1. What number should come next in this series: 2, 4, 8, 16, ____?

a. 18
b. 24
c. 32
d. 36

2. Examine (A), (B), and (C) to find the best answer.

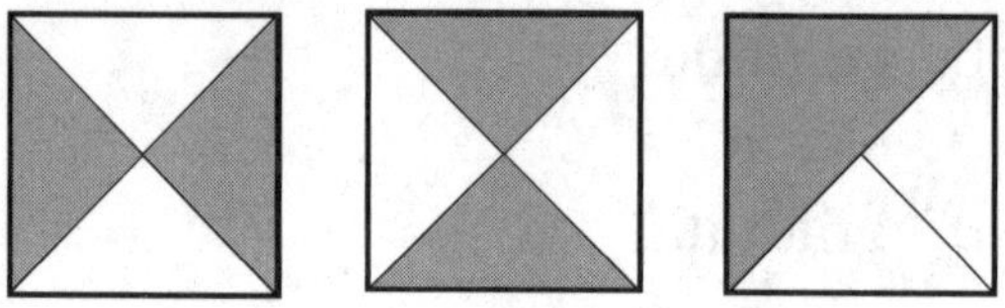

(A) (B) (C)

a. (A) is more shaded than (B)
b. (A) is less shaded than (B) and more shaded than (C)
c. (B) and (C) are both more shaded than (a)
d. (A), (B), and (C) are equally shaded

3. What number should come next in this series: 6, 15, 24, 33, ____?

a. 42
b. 4
c. 38
d. 36

4. 25% of what number is 3 times 5?

a. 15
b. 25
c. 50
d. 60

5. What number should come next in this series: 1, 3, 9, 27, ____?

a. 24
b. 36
c. 66
d. 81

6. Examine the following and find the best answer.

1. 40% of 80
2. 50% of 64
3. 150% of 16

a. 1 is greater than 2 or 3
b. 1, 2, and 3 are equal
c. 1 is equal to 2 and larger than 3
d. 2 is less than 1 and 3

7. What number divided by 3 is $\frac{1}{4}$ of 24?

a. 18
b. 14
c. 12
d. 6

8. What number should come next in this series: 100, 99, 97, 94, ____?

a. 90
b. 89
c. 88
d. 86

9. Examine the following to find the best answer.

1. $\frac{1}{4}$ of 96
2. 2×48
3. $\frac{1}{2}$ of 192

a. $1 > 2 > 3$
b. $1 = 2 = 3$
c. $2 = 3 > 1$
d. $2 > 1 > 3$

10. What number should come next in this series: 5, 8, 13, 16, 21, ____?

a. 22
b. 23
c. 24
d. 26

11. Examine the following and find the best answer.

1. 32^1
2. 2^5
3. 3^3

a. $1 > 2 > 3$
b. $1 = 2 > 3$
c. $2 > 1 = 3$
d. $2 > 1 > 3$

12. What number should come next in this series: 10, 7, 8, 5, 6 ____?

a. 2
b. 3
c. 5
d. 9

13. $\frac{4}{5}$ of what number is 10% of 40?

a. 3
b. 4
c. 5
d. 8

14. What number should come next in this series: 6, 9, 13, 16, 20, ____?

a. 21
b. 22
c. 23
d. 24

15. Examine the following and find the best answer.

1. 0.008
2. 0.0088
3. 0.08

a. $1 > 2 > 3$
b. $3 > 1 > 2$
c. $3 > 2 > 1$
d. $2 > 1 > 3$

16. What number should fill in the blank in this series: 2, 6, 12, 16, 22 ____?

a. 26
b. 28
c. 32
d. 34

17. What number is $\frac{1}{4}$ of the difference between 80 and 64?

a. 4

b. 8

c. 12

d. 16

18. Examine the following and find the best answer.

1. 3(4 + 9)
2. 12 + 27
3. 34 + 9

a. 1 is greater than 2 and 3

b. 1 is equal to 2 and less than 3

c. 2 and 3 are equal and greater than 1

d. 1, 2, and 3 are equal

19. What number is 18 more than $\frac{1}{5}$ of 15?

a. 18

b. 21

c. 23

d. 25

20. Look at the rectangles below. Find the best answer.

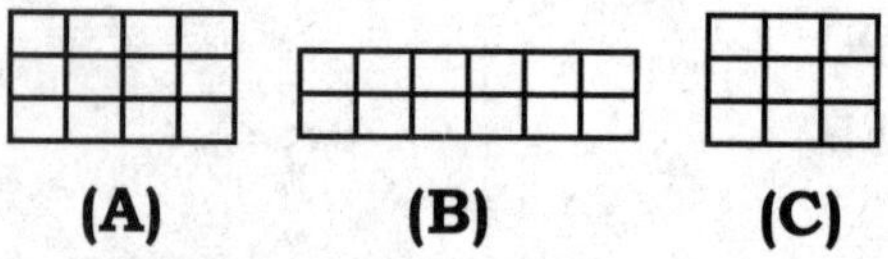

a. the perimeter of (A) < the perimeter of (B) < the perimeter of (C)

b. the perimeter of (C) < the perimeter of (A) < the perimeter of (B)

c. the perimeter of (A) < the perimeter of (C) < the perimeter of (B)

d. the perimeter of (A) = the perimeter of (C) < the perimeter of (B)

21. What number is 10% of 20% of 300?

a. 6

b. 9

c. 60

d. 90

22. What number should come next in this series: 8, 9, 16, 17, 24, 25, ____?

a. 31

b. 32

c. 33

d. 34

23. Examine the following and find the best answer.

1. 3.02×10^3
2. 32×10^2
3. 302×10^0

a. 1 is greater than 2 and 3
b. 2 is larger than 1, which is larger than 3
c. 2 and 3 are equal and greater than 1
d. 1, 2, and 3 are equal

24. What number leaves a remainder of 2 when divided by 7?

a. 24
b. 51
c. 60
d. 64

25. The figure below is a circle with center *O*. Find the best answer.

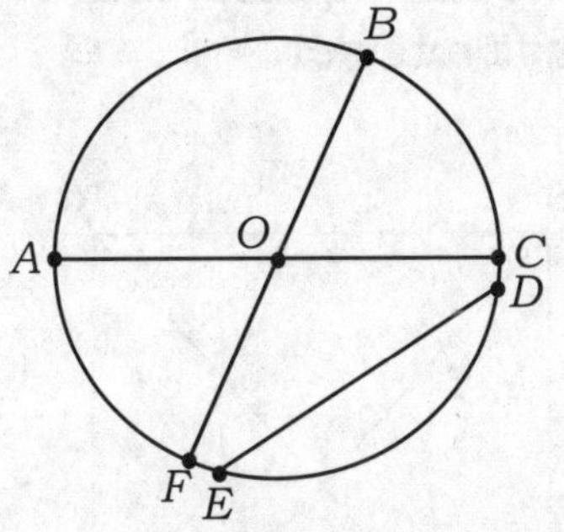

a. *AC* is equal to *FB* and larger than *ED*
b. *AC* is larger than *FB* and *ED*
c. *AC* is equal to *FB* and smaller than *ED*
d. *AC*, *FB*, and *ED* are equal

26. What number should fill the blank in this series: 1, 7, 3, 21, ____, 35?

a. 4
b. 5
c. 7
d. 28

27. Look at the rectangle below. Find the best answer.

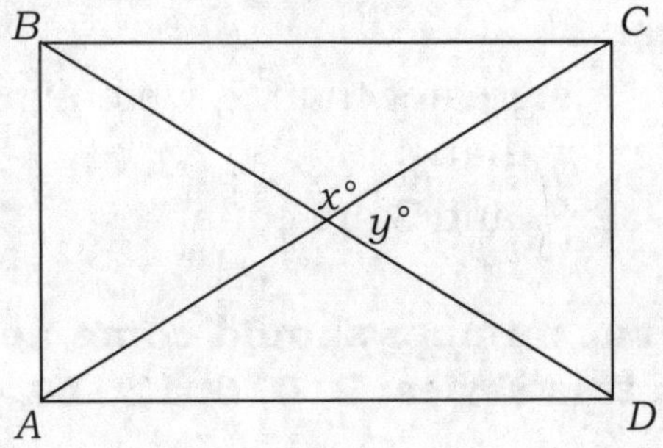

a. $x < y < 90°$
b. $x > 90° > y$
c. $x + y = 90°$
d. $90° > x > y$

28. Examine the following and find the best answer.

1. $\frac{7}{100} + \frac{6}{10} + 3$
2. $\frac{3}{100} + \frac{7}{10} + 6$
3. $\frac{6}{100} + \frac{3}{10} + 7$

a. 1 is greater than 2 and 3
b. 1 is greater than 2 and less than 3
c. 3 is greater than 2, which is greater than 1
d. 1, 2, and 3 are equal

29. What number should come next in this series: 2, 4, 6, 12, 14, 28, ____?

a. 30
b. 32
c. 48
d. 56

30. What number is 9 times more than 20% of 60?

a. 21
b. 63
c. 108
d. 180

31. What number should fill the blank in this series: 9, 7, 5, 9, 7, ____, 9?

a. 5
b. 7
c. 9
d. 11

32. What is 17 more than twice the difference between 15 and 17?

a. 19
b. 20
c. 21
d. 22

33. What number should come next in this series: 9, 20, 31, 42, ____?

a. 52
b. 53
c. 61
d. 84

34. Look at the square below. Find the best answer.

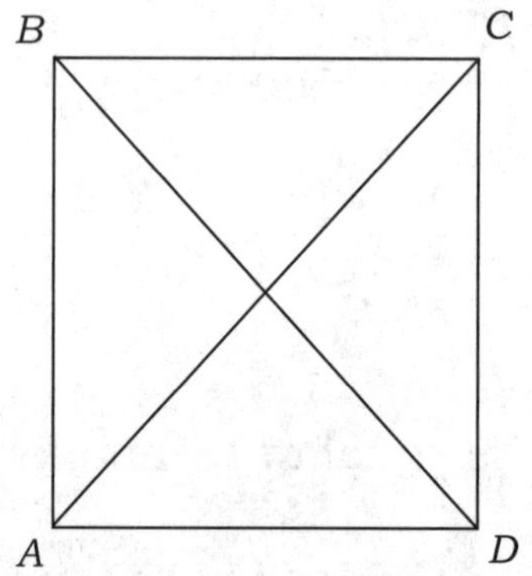

a. $AC = BC > AD$
b. $AC > AB > BD$
c. $AC > AB = BC$
d. $AC = BD = BC$

35. What number should come next in this series: 7, 14, 13 26, 25, ____?

a. 32
b. 37
c. 42
d. 50

36. The sum of 8 and what number is equal to $\frac{1}{11}$ of 121?

a. 2
b. 3
c. 5
d. 7

37. Examine the following and find the best answer.

1. the perimeter of a square with side 4
2. the area of a square with side 4
3. the area of half of a square with side 8

a. 2 > 1 > 3
b. 3 > 1 > 2
c. 3 > 2 = 1
d. 2 = 3 > 1

38. What number should fill the blank in this series: 2, 4, 6, 4, 6, 8, ____, 8, 10?

a. 2
b. 4
c. 6
d. 10

39. Examine the figure below and find the best answer.

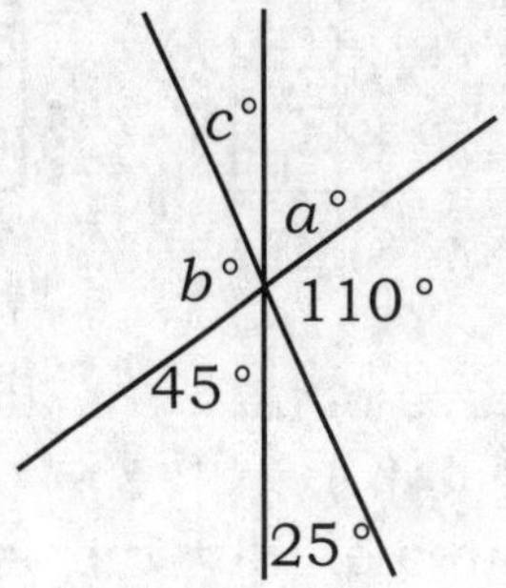

a. $b > a > c$
b. $c > a > b$
c. $c > b > a$
d. $b > c > a$

40. What is the difference between 23 and the average of 42, 45, and 39?

a. 17
b. 19
c. 21
d. 23

41. What number is $\frac{1}{4}$ the product of 8 and 18?

a. 6
b. 12
c. 18
d. 36

42. Examine (A), (B), and (C) and find the best answer.

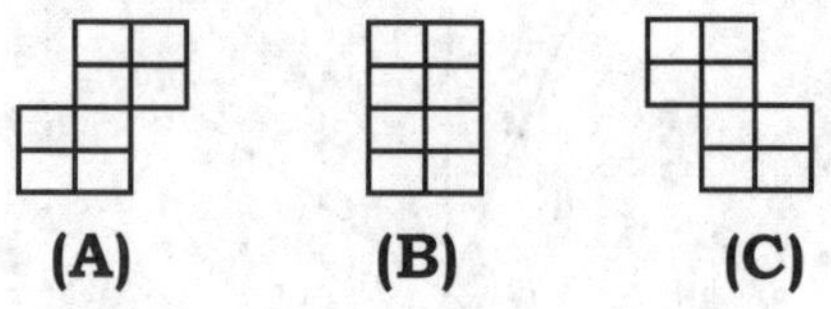

a. the area of (A) > the area of (B) = the area of (C)

b. the area of (B) > the area of (C) = the area of (A)

c. the area of (C) < the area of (A) = the area of (B)

d. the area of (A) = the area of (B) = the area of (C)

43. What number should come next in this series: 88, 85, 83, 80, 78, ____?

a. 77

b. 76

c. 75

d. 74

44. Examine the following and find the best answer.

1. –(8 – 10)
2. 8 – 10
3. –8 – 10

a. 1 is bigger than 2, which is bigger than 3

b. 2 is bigger than 3, which is bigger than 1

c. 1 and 2 are equal and bigger than 3

d. 1 and 3 are equal and bigger than 2

45. What number should fill the blank in this series: 49, 7, 81, ____, 121, 11?

a. 8

b. 9

c. 10

d. 79

46. What number is 50% greater than the product of 6 and 3?

a. 9

b. 14

c. 18

d. 27

47. What is the difference between 10% of 50 and 20% of 100?

a. 5

b. 10

c. 15

d. 20

48. What number should fill the blank in this series: 6, 8, 7, 9, ____, 10, 9, 11?

a. 7

b. 8

c. 9

d. 11

49. What is 4 less than $\frac{5}{3}$ of 9?

a. 5
b. 9
c. 11
d. 13

50. What number is 18 more than half the sum of 4, 9, and 11?

a. 12
b. 20
c. 30
d. 34

51. What number is 2 more than the average of 10, 15, and 8?

a. 9
b. 11
c. 13
d. 15

52. What number should come next in this series: 41, 11, 52, 22, 63, ____?

a. 27
b. 33
c. 37
d. 44

Reading

Questions 1–62, 25 minutes

Questions 1–8 refer to the following passage.

Passage 1 - Reminiscence on the River

This was our last watch fire of the year, and there were reasons why I should remember it better than any of the others. Next week the other boys were to file back to their old places in Sandtown High School, but I was to go up to the divide to teach my first country school in the Norwegian district. I was already homesick at the thought of <u>quitting</u> the boys with whom I had always played, of leaving the river and going up into a windy plain that was all windmills and cornfields and big pastures, where there was nothing willful or unmanageable in the landscape, no new island, and no chance of unfamiliar birds—such as often followed the watercourses.

Other boys came and went and used the river for fishing or skating, but we six were sworn to the spirit of the stream, and we were friends mainly because of the river. There were the two Hassler boys. Fritz and Otto, sons of the little German tailor. They were the youngest of us—ragged boys of ten and twelve, with sunburned hair, weather-strained faces, and pale blue eyes. Otto, the elder, was the best mathematician in school and clever at his books, but he always dropped out in the spring term as if the river could not get on without him. He and Fritz caught the fat, horned catfish and sold them about the town, and they lived so much in the water that they were as brown and sandy as the river itself.

There was Percy Pound, a fat, freckled boy with chubby cheeks, who took half a dozen 'boys' storypapers and was always being kept in for reading detective stories behind his desk. There was Tip Smith, destined by his freckles and red hair to be the buffoon in all our games, though he walked like a timid little old man and had a funny, cracked laugh. Tip worked hard at his father's grocery store every afternoon, and swept it out before school in the morning.

1. **The word <u>quitting</u>, as used in the passage, most nearly means**
   a. leaving
   b. cheating
   c. playing with
   d. feeding

2. **According to the story, the narrator belonged to a group that gathered**
   a. in the narrator's backyard
   b. in the gym after school
   c. near the river
   d. at Percy Pound's house

3. **It can be inferred from the passage that the narrator is**
   a. younger than 10 years old
   b. between 10 and 20 years old
   c. between 20 and 30 years old
   d. more than 30 years old

4. **This story mostly describes**
   a. the narrator's friends
   b. the narrator's teachers
   c. Otto Hassler
   d. the parents of the students at Sandtown High

5. **Why will the narrator remember this watch fire better than others?**
   a. It is the narrator's birthday.
   b. The narrator is going away soon.
   c. The narrator has just been born.
   d. The narrator has recently gotten a new job.

6. **It can be inferred from the passage that the narrator has recently become**
   a. a parent
   b. a police officer
   c. a teacher
   d. a journalist

7. According to the passage, who caught and sold catfish?

a. Otto and Tip
b. Otto and Fritz
c. Fritz and the narrator
d. Fritz and Percy

8. Tip's father was

a. a tailor
b. a grocer
c. a teacher
d. a fish merchant

Questions 9–17 refer to the following passage.

Passage 2 - Illuminating the Electric Eel

The electric eel is one of the most curious animals on the planet. It is found in the marshes of the Amazon Basin, and can grow up to almost eight feet in length—as long as some crocodiles. As the name implies, the electric eel has the ability to <u>generate</u> a strong electric field.

The electric eel uses this special ability in several ways. Mild electrical impulses can help the eel to sense different objects around it and to navigate the waters in which it lives. The eel can send out mild electrical signals, in much the same way as a bat uses sound waves, in order to find its way around.

When it comes time to feed, the eel relies on its electrical system for hunting. Because small animals have a different electrical "signature" than do plants or rocks, the electric eel effectively has a kind of radar that allows it to find fish. When the eel finds its prey, it delivers a strong electric <u>current</u> that can instantly kill smaller animals such as fish. The force of the charge is often strong enough to kill or stun even larger animals. A human could survive one or two shocks, but would probably not survive several. Eels, however, do not hunt humans and will only shock a human in self-defense.

How does the eel avoid hurting itself? The eel has evolved with a kind of insulation that protects its nervous system. This insulation acts as a <u>buffer</u> against the electricity that it generates.

There may be one more way in which the electric eel uses electricity. Some scientists believe that eels can communicate among themselves using electrical signals akin to the clicks and whistles of other animals such as dolphins. As this point, however, this theory has not yet been proven.

9. The word <u>generate</u>, as used in the passage, most nearly means

a. examine
b. create
c. protect
d. catch

10. The author of the passage is probably

a. a marine biologist
b. an electrician
c. a history teacher
d. a fisherman

11. The word <u>current</u>, as used in the passage, most nearly means

a. modern
b. charge
c. vision
d. river

12. Which of the following can be inferred from the passage?

a. Bats use electricity to help them see in the dark.
b. Electric eels are more like crocodiles than like fish.
c. Without electricity, electric eels would have a hard time feeding.
d. Electric eels kill many people each year.

13. The word <u>buffer</u>, as used in the passage, most nearly means

a. cleaner
b. protection
c. poison
d. source

14. Which of the following does the author probably believe?

a. Electric eels are the most dangerous creatures on earth.
b. Electric eels have as many teeth as do crocodiles.
c. We are not yet certain whether electric eels use electricity to communicate.
d. Bats can also generate electric fields.

15. The author uses each of the following animals to help describe the electric eel except

a. the bat
b. the dolphin
c. the crocodile
d. the horse

16. It can be inferred from the passage that the electricity is dangerous because it

a. damages the nervous system
b. interferes with breathing
c. deprives animals of food
d. causes animals to bleed

17. You could probably find this article in

a. a dictionary
b. a guide to an aquarium
c. a chemistry textbook
d. a photography magazine

Questions 18–24 refer to the following passage.

Passage 3 - Pavlov and His Reaction

Ivan Pavlov was a Russian physiologist born in 1849. Instead of becoming a doctor, he chose to work in a medical laboratory, where he worked on the function of the nervous system. It is said that his salary was so <u>meager</u> that he and his family had to live in an unheated apartment in St. Petersburg. Nonetheless, Pavlov was so dedicated to his work that he remained at the laboratory almost all his life.

Pavlov was best known for his research on <u>conditioned</u> reflexes. While some reflexes are <u>innate</u>, such as the knee-jerk response when a doctor strikes with a mallet just below the kneecap, Pavlov showed that other reflexes can be acquired through experience or training. To demonstrate this, Pavlov performed a series of experiments on dogs. For several days in a row, one of Pavlov's assistants rang a bell just before feeding his dogs. The dogs learned to associate the bell with food. Pavlov discovered that afterward, when he rang the bell, the dogs would begin to salivate in anticipation of a meal. Pavlov argued that humans, just like dogs, have many conditioned reflexes.

Following Pavlov's idea, a school of psychology called behaviorism arose. Behaviorists such as B. F. Skinner believe that almost all animal (including human) behavior could be explained in terms of conditioning. Though behaviorism cannot plausibly explain all of human behavior, it has deepened our understanding of the way in which we react to events in the world. For his work, Pavlov received the Nobel Prize in 1904.

18. The word <u>meager</u>, as used in the passage, most nearly means

a. funny
b. small
c. late
d. critical

19. It can be inferred from Pavlov's experiment that conditioned reflexes

a. can only be learned when hungry
b. depend on repeated experiences
c. can be found mostly in dogs
d. are stronger than innate reflexes

20. According to the passage, the knee-jerk response is

a. conditioned
b. innate
c. partially conditioned and partially innate
d. neither conditioned nor innate

21. The word <u>innate</u>, as used in the passage, most nearly means

a. violent
b. inborn
c. puzzling
d. large

22. The author mentions B. F. Skinner as someone who

a. disagreed with Pavlov's findings
b. gave Pavlov the Nobel Prize
c. believed in Pavlov's work and continued it
d. was one of Pavlov's students

23. According to what the author says in the passage, the author would probably agree that behaviorism

a. can explain all of human behavior
b. is an interesting but limited way of explaining behavior
c. was criticized by Pavlov
d. was wrong and should be forgotten about

24. The word conditioned, as used in the passage, most nearly means

a. electrical
b. unknown
c. mild
d. learned

Questions 25–29 refer to the following passage.

Passage 4 - Cousin Fanny

She was extraordinarily credulous—would believe anything on earth anyone told her—because, although she had plenty of humor, she herself never would deviate from the absolute truth a moment, even in jest. I do not think she would have told an untruth to save her life. Well, of course we used to play on her to tease her. Frank would tell her the most unbelievable and impossible lies such as that he thought he saw a mouse yesterday on the back of the sofa she was lying on (this would make her bounce up like a ball), or that he believed he heard—he was not sure—that Mr. Scroggs (the man who had rented her old home) had cut down all the old trees in the yard and pulled down the house because he wanted the bricks to make brick ovens. This would worry her excessively (she loved every brick in the old house, and often said she would rather live in the kitchen there than in a palace anywhere else), and she would get into such a state of depression that Frank would finally have to tell her that he was just "fooling" her.

She used to make him do a good deal of waiting on her in return, and he was the one she used to get to dress old Fashion's back when it was raw and to put drops in her eyes. He got quite expert at it. She said it was a penalty for his worrying her so.

She was a great musician of the connection. This is in itself no mean praise, for it was the fashion for every musical gift among the girls to be cultivated and every girl played or sang more or less, some of them very well. But cousin Fanny was not only this. She had a way of playing that used to make the old piano sound different from itself, and her voice was almost the sweetest I ever heard except one or two on the stage.

25. We can infer from the passage that the reason Fanny would "bounce up like a ball" is that

a. she is very energetic
b. she is afraid of mice
c. she likes to play games
d. her couch had very powerful springs

26. The word <u>credulous</u>, as used in the passage, most nearly means

a. dependable
b. trusting
c. intelligent
d. lazy

27. According to the passage, Fanny's musical talents include

a. the piano and the violin
b. her voice and the piano
c. the violin and the flute
d. her voice and the violin

28. The word <u>cultivated</u>, as used in the passage, most nearly means

a. beautiful
b. planted
c. encouraged
d. lonely

29. Which of the following can be inferred from the passage?

a. Fanny lived in a palace.
b. Mr. Scroggs's first name is Frank.
c. Frank liked to tease Fanny.
d. Fanny was often worried about her children.

Questions 30–35 refer to the following passage.

Passage 5 - Life of Caesar

Julius Caesar was perhaps the most important politician's leader of all time. It was his military and political genius that created the Roman Empire, a civilization so large and powerful that no other Western government could be considered its equal until the 1700s. Caesar's historical influence was so great that the German and Russian words for emperor (Kaiser and Czar) are derived from his name.

Caesar belonged to a family of many senators and other politicians. In spite of this, Caesar did not simply act in the interest of his family. Early in his life, Caesar not only championed the Roman people but also fought against abuse and corruption in the senate.

For ten years, between 58 and 49 B.C.E., Caesar led a series of campaigns known as the Gallic Wars. His armies conquered the Gauls in France, and he marched as far north as England. Thanks to Caesar's military skill, almost all of Europe was under Roman control. These battles showed Caesar to be one of the greatest military strategists of all time.

Around 50 B.C.E., Caesar's popularity and strength began to frighten Pompey, who used to be his friend and colleague. Pompey tried to convince the senate to disband Caesar's army. In response, Caesar marched his army into Rome, defeated Pompey, and declared himself dictator.

Caesar was famously killed on the Ides of March (March 15) by a band of conspirators including Brutus, whom Caesar had considered a friend.

30. The author gives us the German and Russian words for emperor to demonstrate

a. the similarities between the German and Russian languages
b. how words can change over time
c. the importance of Julius Caesar in Western history
d. that Julius Caesar spoke German and Russian

31. The author would probably agree that the Roman Empire

a. was one of the most powerful civilizations of the ancient world
b. was not as important as modern historians think it is
c. ended in the 1700s
d. was led by Pompey

32. It is somewhat surprising that Caesar was a champion of the people because he

a. did not like the Roman people
b. was too busy fighting
c. came from a family of senators and politicians
d. was not a very nice person

33. The word <u>campaigns</u>, as used in the passage, most nearly means

a. wars
b. stories
c. studies
d. games

34. According to the passage, Pompey became afraid of Caesar because Caesar

a. had a famous father
b. was rich
c. was powerful and popular
d. had a very big army

35. Which of the following is true based on the passage?

a. Caesar fought Pompey in the Gallic Wars.
b. The Gallic Wars took place in 58 to 49 B.C.E.
c. Caesar never left the city of Rome.
d. Caesar died in the month of May.

Questions 36–40 refer to the following passage.

Passage 6 - A Short History of Mary Shelley

Mary Shelley was born in 1797. Her parents, Mary Wollstonecraft and William Godwin, were both writers; Wollstonecraft's *A Vindication of the Rights of Woman* made her one of the most important early feminist thinkers. Shelley was surrounded as a child by some of the greatest literary figures of her day, including Samuel Coleridge and Charles Lamb. Her parents introduced her to these people because they believed that every child had the potential to develop a great intellect.

Shelley wrote her best-known work, *Frankenstein*, at the age of 19. She wrote it while staying at Lake Geneva with a group of young poets that included Lord Byron and Percy Shelley, whom she would later marry.

Frankenstein is not merely a horror story, but a brillant work of art. The dark, gloomy imagery in *Frankenstein* was probably in part a reflection of the calamities taking place in Mary Shelley's life, which included several suicides in her extended family. Certain feminist ideas inherited from her mother are also included, as is a romantic mistrust of modern technology.

Shelley's bad luck continued. Her first child died shortly after birth. Later, Percy drowned when Mary was just 24 years old. She continued to write and lived among other artists and literary figures for the rest of her life.

36. With which of the following would the author probably agree?

a. Mary Shelley was too young to be a writer.
b. Mary Shelley was the best writer of the nineteenth century.
c. Frankenstein is one of the great works of modern literature.
d. Shelley would never have written Frankenstein had it not been for Coleridge.

37. According to the passage, which one of the following influenced the way Shelley wrote *Frankenstein*?

a. the birth of her first child
b. her mother's feminist ideas
c. the works of Samuel Coleridge
d. a bad dream she had as a child

38. What is this passage mostly about?

a. the relationship between Mary Shelley and Lord Byron
b. a gathering of poets at Lake Geneva
c. Mary Shelley's life and work
d. why Frankenstein is so scary

39. In approximately what year did Shelley write *Frankenstein?*

a. 1805
b. 1811
c. 1816
d. 1820

40. The world calamities, as used in the passage, most nearly means

a. feelings
b. tragedies
c. suggestions
d. questions

Vocabulary

41. Choose the best definition of the underlined word.

an important <u>era</u>

a. place
b. time
c. story
d. person

42. Choose the best definition of the underlined word.

a <u>concise</u> explanation

a. pleasant
b. famous
c. short
d. proud

43. Choose the best definition of the underlined word.

to show great <u>compassion</u>

a. strength
b. interest
c. dislike
d. sympathy

44. Choose the best definition of the underlined word.

a dangerous <u>felon</u>

a. criminal
b. sport
c. vacation
d. shark

45. Choose the best definition of the underlined word.

a <u>mythical</u> creature

a. farm
b. surprising
c. imaginary
d. muscular

46. Choose the best definition of the underlined word.

a <u>weary</u> traveler

a. busy
b. difficult
c. famous
d. tired

47. Choose the best definition of the underlined word.

an <u>unorthodox</u> approach

a. happy
b. violent
c. unusual
d. marvelous

48. Choose the best definition of the underlined word.

to <u>conceal</u> the truth

a. sing
b. study
c. hide
d. display

49. Choose the best definition of the underlined word.

to <u>tremble</u> with joy

a. shake
b. skip
c. sit
d. pounce

50. Choose the best definition of the underlined word.

a dangerous <u>epidemic</u>

a. idea
b. flight
c. disease
d. package

51. Choose the best definition of the underlined word.

a museum <u>exhibition</u>

a. visitor
b. display
c. building
d. box

52. Choose the best definition of the underlined word.

to <u>reinforce</u> a building

a. decorate
b. examine
c. strengthen
d. project

53. Choose the best definition of the underlined word.

a <u>crucial</u> part

a. important
b. difficult
c. magnetic
d. wasted

54. Choose the best definition of the underlined word.

a <u>tedious</u> speech

a. loud
b. boring
c. received
d. sparse

55. Choose the best definition of the underlined word.

to <u>endorse</u> a candidate

a. write
b. criticize
c. plead
d. support

56. Choose the best definition of the underlined word.

the <u>arduous</u> task

a. school
b. finished
c. difficult
d. adult

57. Choose the best definition of the underlined word.

a <u>qualified</u> person

a. sick
b. capable
c. interesting
d. older

58. Choose the best definition of the underlined word.

to <u>decline</u> an invitation

a. refuse
b. send
c. paint
d. dream

59. Choose the best definition of the underlined word.

a <u>potent</u> chemical

a. strong
b. common
c. illegal
d. mixed

60. Choose the best definition of the underlined word.

to <u>perturb</u> someone

a. please
b. bother
c. introduce
d. hire

61. Choose the best definition of the underlined word.

rapid <u>respiration</u>

a. running
b. selling
c. breathing
d. change

62. Choose the best definition of the underlined word.

a moving <u>oration</u>

a. injury
b. decision
c. meal
d. speech

Mathematics

Questions 1–64, 45 Minutes

Mathematical Concepts

1. Which of the following is greatest?

a. 0.1042
b. 0.1105
c. 0.0288
d. 0.0931

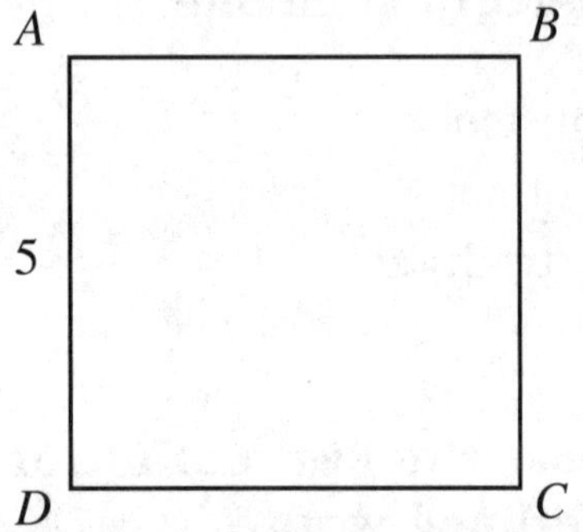

2. What is the area of the square *ABCD*?

a. 5
b. 20
c. 25
d. 50

3. What is the least positive integer divisible by 3, 4, and 5?

a. 30
b. 40
c. 50
d. 60

4. The decimal representation of $5 + 60 + \frac{5}{100}$ is

a. 65.05
b. 65.5
c. 56.05
d. 56.5

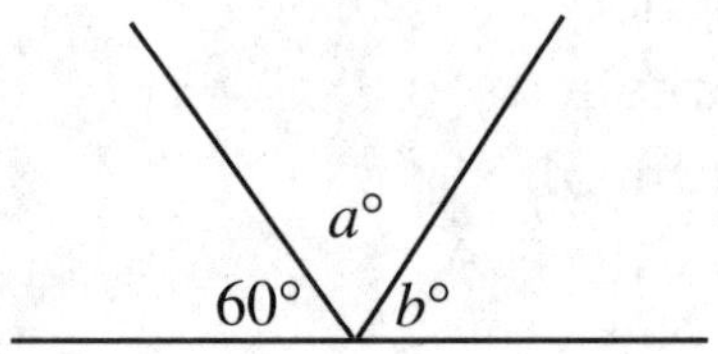

5. What is the sum of *a* + *b*?

a. 60°
b. 100°
c. 120°
d. 160°

6. The product of 0.28 and 100 is approximately

a. 0.3
b. 2.8
c. 2
d. 30

7. **What is the greatest prime factor of 45?**
   a. 2
   b. 3
   c. 5
   d. 9

8. **A store normally sells a certain dress for $160. During a special sale, the store reduces the price of the dress to $120. By what percent is the price of the dress reduced for the sale?**
   a. 20%
   b. 25%
   c. 30%
   d. 40%

9. $10^3 \times 10^5 =$
   a. 10^8
   b. 10^{15}
   c. 100^8
   d. 100^{15}

10. **All of the following are multiples of 8 except**
   a. 24
   b. 96
   c. 178
   d. 192

11. **What is the volume of a box with length 6, width 8, and height $\frac{1}{2}$?**
   a. 96
   b. 48
   c. 24
   d. $14\frac{1}{2}$

12. **If the ratio of boys to girls in a class is 3:4 and there are 124 girls in the class, how many boys are there in the class?**
   a. 33
   b. 93
   c. 103
   d. 109

13. $(4^2)^3 =$
   a. 4^5
   b. 4^6
   c. 5^4
   d. 3^{16}

14. **In the number 365, the product of the digits is how much greater than the sum of the digits?**
   a. 76
   b. 54
   c. 36
   d. 14

15. What is 2,847 rounded to the nearest tenth?

a. 2.84
b. 2.9
c. 2.8
d. 2.85

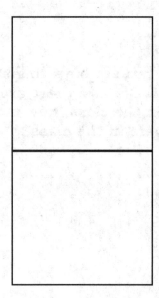

16. Each of the squares in the figure above has an area of 16. What is the perimeter of the figure?

a. 16
b. 24
c. 28
d. 32

17. If one of the angles inside a triangle measures 85 degrees, what could the other two angles measure?

a. 45° and 55°
b. 45° and 50°
c. 35° and 50°
d. 50° and 60°

18. $\sqrt{2^2}$

a. 1
b. 2
c. 4
d. 16

19. Juan has 5 blue marbles, 9 green marbles, and 3 red marbles. What fractional part of his marbles is blue?

a. $\frac{5}{9}$
b. $\frac{5}{17}$
c. $\frac{17}{5}$
d. $\frac{9}{5}$

20. Which of the following is true?

a. $2\sqrt{2} + 3\sqrt{3} = 5\sqrt{5}$
b. $2\sqrt{2} \times 3\sqrt{3} = 5\sqrt{5}$
c. $2\sqrt{2} + 3\sqrt{2} = 5\sqrt{2}$
d. $2\sqrt{2} \times 3\sqrt{2} = 6\sqrt{2}$

21. What is the smallest common multiple of 6 and 4?

a. 4
b. 6
c. 12
d. 24

22. Which of the following leaves a remainder of 4 when divided by 6?

a. 18
b. 22
c. 26
d. 32

23. If you multiply a negative even number by a positive odd number, the result will be

a. negative and even
b. negative and odd
c. positive and even
d. positive and odd

24. How many prime numbers are there between 0 and 10?

a. 3
b. 4
c. 5
d. 6

Problem Solving

25. $\frac{5}{15} + \frac{6}{13} =$

a. $\frac{11}{28}$
b. $\frac{31}{39}$
c. $\frac{6}{39}$
d. $\frac{13}{15}$

26. Maxine scored 42, 45, and 46 on her first three history tests. What score would she need on her fourth test to raise her average to 48?

a. 50
b. 55
c. 59
d. 62

27. 20% of 40% of 500 is

a. 20
b. 30
c. 40
d. 60

28. $6 - 3(2 - 4) + 5 =$

a. 9
b. 11
c. 17
d. 19

29. $\frac{20}{.02} =$

a. 0.1
b. 10
c. 100
d. 1,000

30. The price of a $25 comic book is decreased by 5%. What is the new price of the comic book?

a. $23.75
b. $22.75
c. $20.25
d. $20.00

31. On a certain map, 8 miles is represented by 1 inch. If two cities are 3.5 inches apart on the map, what is the distance between these two cities?

a. 8 miles
b. 16 miles
c. 24 miles
d. 28 miles

32. Which of the following is equal to 0.24?

a. $\frac{12}{5}$

b. $\frac{24}{10}$

c. $\frac{12}{50}$

d. $\frac{4}{10}$

33. Alice's Emporium discounts the price of a shirt by 20%, and then discounts it again by an additional 10%. The final price represents what percent decrease from the original price of the shirt?

a. 15%

b. 18%

c. 28%

d. 30%

34. Two positive integers have a ratio of 6:9. If the smaller of the two numbers is 18, what is the average of the two numbers?

a. 15

b. 22.5

c. 24

d. 27

35. $11 + 5 \times 6 \div 3 - (2 - 5) =$

a. 47

b. 41

c. 96

d. 102

36. A swimming pool has dimensions 4 feet by 10 feet by 12 feet. If the pool can be filled at a rate of 8 cubic feet per minute, how many minutes will it take to fill the pool?

a. 20

b. 24

c. 48

d. 60

37. At Joe's Burger Shop, two hamburgers and an order of french fries cost $3.55. If three hamburgers cost $4.05, what is the price of an order of french fries?

a. $0.50

b. $0.65

c. $0.85

d. $1.15

38. In a certain classroom, the ratio of boys to girls is 3:5. If there are 32 students in the class, how many girls are in the class?

a. 12

b. 14

c. 16

d. 20

39. The area of a circle with radius 8 is how much greater than its circumference?

a. 8π

b. 16π

c. 24π

d. 48π

40. $4^4 =$

a. 16^2
b. 31^1
c. 32^2
d. 64^2

41. If two-thirds of the 660 students at Middleburg Junior High attend the school dance, how many students do not atttend?

a. 220
b. 240
c. 400
d. 440

42. Which of the following is equal to $2\sqrt{2} \times 3\sqrt{2}$?

a. 24
b. $5\sqrt{2}$
c. $6\sqrt{2}$
d. 12

43. $18 + \frac{3}{4} + \frac{3}{6} + \frac{1}{4} =$

a. 19
b. $19\frac{1}{2}$
c. 20
d. $20\frac{1}{6}$

44. If $3x + 5 = 23$, then $x =$

a. 3
b. 4
c. 5
d. 6

45. $\frac{1}{2} \div \frac{1}{10} =$

a. 5
b. $\frac{1}{5}$
c. $\frac{1}{20}$
d. 20

46. If $zy + 18 = 36$, and $x = 2$, then $y =$

a. 6
b. 7
c. 8
d. 9

47. What is the area of a rectangle with length 15 feet and width 24 feet?

a. 240 ft^2
b. 280 ft^2
c. 320 ft^2
d. 360 ft^2

48. $\left(7 \times \frac{1}{100}\right) + \left(2 \times \frac{1}{10}\right) + \left(6 \times \frac{1}{1000}\right) + 4 =$

a. 4.267
b. 4.276
c. 4.726
d. 5.627

49. A pound of onions costs \$3.25 at the supermarket. What is the maximum number of pounds of onions that Larry can buy with \$13?

a. 4
b. 5
c. 6
d. 7

50. $5.5 \div 0.2 =$

a. 11
b. 13.5
c. 23.5
d. 27.5

51. Four years ago, Alex was half as old as he is now. How old is Alex now?

a. 4
b. 5
c. 6
d. 8

52. $5\frac{1}{2} \times 2\frac{1}{3} =$

a. $10\frac{1}{6}$
b. $12\frac{5}{6}$
c. $7\frac{1}{5}$
d. $5\frac{1}{3}$

53. If one gallon of paint can cover $2\frac{1}{2}$ square feet, how many gallons of paint will be needed to cover a rectangular wall that measures 20 feet by 12 feet?

a. 48
b. 64
c. 72
d. 96

54. If $2x^2 + y = 55$ and $y = 5$, what could x be?

a. 3
b. 5
c. 6
d. 7

55. $4\sqrt{18} \times 3\sqrt{2} =$

a. 72
b. $12\sqrt{18}$
c. $4\sqrt{32}$
d. 36

56. How many seconds are there in 4 hours?

a. 240
b. 2,400
c. 3,600
d. 14,400

57. In a group of 100 children, there are 24 more girls than boys. How many girls are in the group?

a. 62
b. 50
c. 38
d. 24

58. If $-4x - 3 < x + 2$, what is the range of possible values of x?

a. $x < -1$
b. $x < 1$
c. $x > -1$
d. $x > 1$

59. How many multiples of 5 and 6 are there between 1 and 100?

a. 3
b. 5
c. 7
d. 9

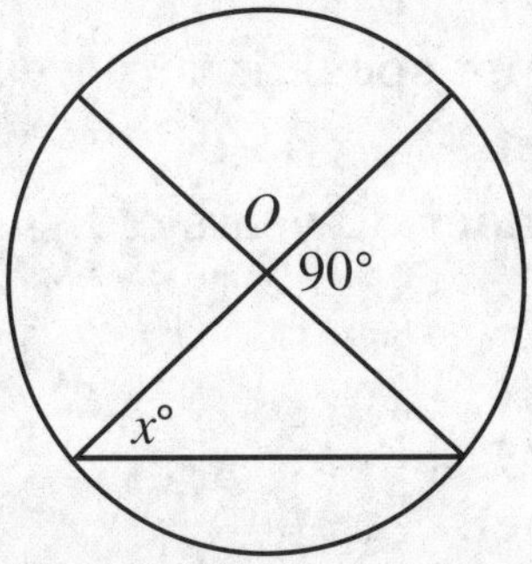

60. The figure above is a circle with center *O*. What is the value of *x*?

a. 30°
b. 45°
c. 60°
d. 90°

61. Emil can shape two cookies every minute. How long will it take him to shape 150 cookies?

a. 1 hour 15 minutes
b. 1 hour 25 minutes
c. 3 hours 15 minutes
d. 5 hours

62. Carl is twice as old as his brother Jim, who is five years older than Liz. If Carl is 15 years older than Liz, how old is Jim?

a. 20
b. 15
c. 10
d. 8

63. The diameter of a circle with a circumference of 8π is

a. 2
b. 8
c. 16
d. 64

64. Alex buys a gallon of soda for $8.50, and wants to split the cost among 5 people. How much will each person pay?

a. $1.70
b. $1.65
c. $1.50
d. $0.65

Language

Questions 1–60, 25 minutes

For questions 1–40, check the sentences for errors of usage, capitalization, or punctuation. If there is no error, choose (D).

1. Choose the sentence with the correct capitalization.

a. David studied French for many years but could not speak it very well.
b. Ophelia was a great singer as well as a gifted poet.
c. Some of the world's greatest chess players are under 30 years old.
d. No mistake

2. Choose the sentence with the correct grammar.

a. If I had a telescope, I will be able to see that planet.
b. Steve ran very quickly around the track.
c. We are all going to sing a songs after dinner.
d. No mistake

3. Choose the sentence with the correct punctuation.

a. The first typewriters were huge machines, that were difficult to operate.
b. I went home to help clean my parent's room.
c. We followed the river for three mile's before eating lunch.
d. No mistake

4. Choose the sentence with the correct grammar.

a. My uncle lived in houston while he was in college.
b. Belgium was neutral for years, but then it decided to join the war.
c. There are few things more enjoyable than a walk through the Park.
d. No mistake

5. Choose the sentence with the correct capitalization.

a. Last year we spent our vacation near Lake Michigan.
b. Alicia's Teacher is very well educated.
c. How many times have you seen Martin's Father?
d. No mistake

6. Choose the sentence with the correct grammar.

a. We were all so scared that nobody said a word.
b. "I don't know how you can eat that," said Ms. Carroll.
c. Each of us has at least three hundred baseball cards.
d. No mistake

7. Choose the sentence with the correct capitalization.

a. My Mother found a cat behind the grocery store.
b. I broke my arm on New Year's Eve.
c. How many times have you been to the Coast of California?
d. No mistake

8. Choose the sentence with the correct grammar.

a. Mary was an imaginative child who reads many books.
b. My teacher asked me if I knew whose backpack was left on the bus.
c. Cathryn spended her summer working with chimpanzees.
d. No mistake

9. Choose the sentence with the correct punctuation.

a. Jane sat at the front of the boat; and tried to catch a fish.
b. My brother, and I are going fishing this weekend.
c. Many great battles of the American Revolution took place around Boston, Massachusetts.
d. No mistake

10. Choose the sentence with the correct capitalization.

a. The Blueberries in Kai's backyard are always delicious.
b. I have never seen so many People at once.
c. My book report is due on Monday.
d. No mistake

11. Choose the sentence with the correct grammar.

a. The eruption of a volcano is a violent and frightening event.
b. Since the end of the school year, I have had little to do.
c. Do you think I should bring flowers to the party?
d. No mistake

12. Choose the sentence with the correct punctuation.

a. Nitrogen and oxygen, are the most common gases in our atmosphere.
b. The book was so popular, that the author became famous.
c. Sally asked, “Have you seen the new park?”
d. No mistake

13. Choose the sentence with the correct punctuation.

a. Annie’s letter was dated Saturday, July 5.
b. We were very impressed, by his playing.
c. Manny’s brother left for college, last week.
d. No mistake

14. Choose the sentence with the correct grammar.

a. Jane’s cat ran away two weeks ago, but it finally came back.
b. Mrs. Hendon greet her daughter and nephew when they arrived.
c. The Pulitzer Prize are named after the newspaper reporter Joseph Pulitzer.
d. No mistake

15. Choose the sentence with the correct grammar.

a. Dorothea Dix helps to change the way that ill prisoners were treated.
b. The story was written by my friend and me.
c. Graphs are useful tools to help organized and display information.
d. No mistake

16. Choose the sentence with the correct capitalization.

a. marion and I have not seen each other for months.
b. How many times have you seen this Movie?
c. My father and I went to see Chief Stanley at the firehouse.
d. No mistake

17. Choose the sentence with the correct grammar.

a. Alison had already taken her bath by the time I arrived.
b. There will be enough wind to fly a kites today.
c. Almost every culture has it’s own special kind of music.
d. No mistake

18. Choose the sentence with the correct grammar.

a. Paul went to the park after dinner to play with his Friends.
b. Everyone appreciated julia's hard work.
c. We went to the store together.
d. No mistake

19. Choose the sentence with the correct grammar.

a. The driver the only witness to the crime.
b. Paula is serving dinner on the patio.
c. Archaeology the study of early civilizations.
d. No mistake

20. Choose the sentence with the correct grammar.

a. Many of Picasso paintings were based on photographs of his friends.
b. Rachel's family is very happy for her.
c. I like white papers better then blue papers.
d. No mistake

21. Choose the sentence with the correct punctuation.

a. The cat was searching for its water dish.
b. Patricia want's to work for herself.
c. Laura has seen more films' than Jackie has.
d. No mistake

22. Choose the sentence with the correct grammar.

a. Each of my friends has a toy car.
b. Sarah was fascinate by the pictures.
c. Jason knows the names of almost all the instrument in a orchestra.
d. No mistake

23. Choose the sentence with the correct grammar.

a. Sarah is probably, very hungry.
b. She is not ready to finish the job.
c. Martins mother gave him two days to clean his room.
d. No mistake

24. Choose the sentence with the correct grammar.

a. I saw several stars in the sky, but my sister saw hardly any.
b. Charles go to the pool to practice every day after school.
c. Some believe that the helicopter is first drawn by Leonardo da Vinci.
d. No mistake

25. Choose the sentence with the correct grammar.

a. Libby begged her parents to let her go to the concert on a weeknight.
b. Alice and her parents are going to visit their friends at the beach.
c. Kathy grabbed her books and ran out the door.
d. No mistake

26. Choose the sentence with the correct grammar.

a. This box contains fewer cookies than the other box.
b. In my very first game I hit three home run.
c. David leave his notebook on the kitchen counter.
d. No mistake

27. Choose the sentence with the correct grammar.

a. Lidia's mother have a frown on her face.
b. The new librarian are very friendly.
c. Michael has as many pictures as his brother.
d. No mistake

28. Choose the sentence with the correct grammar.

a. Peter's cookies are better than Steve's.
b. She have no reason to be afraid.
c. Lisa's brother win the first race of the day.
d. No mistake

29. Choose the sentence with the correct grammar.

a. Unlike animals, plant can make their own food.
b. Mr. Jones is a intelligent and caring teacher.
c. My mother divided the sandwich between my sister and me.
d. No mistake

30. Choose the sentence with the correct grammar.

a. Paper make up almost half of the garbage in America.
b. My brother is heavier than I am.
c. I would rather seen a movie than go to the opera.
d. No mistake

31. Choose the sentence with the correct punctuation.

a. It is impossible to travel faster than the speed of light.
b. I was invited to his party, but I caught the flu and could not attend.
c. Frank is not only a great writer, but he can also draw cartoons.
d. No mistake

32. Choose the sentence with the correct punctuation.

a. Most bees live in hive's, but some live alone.
b. The member's of our team sold candy to raise money for a trip.
c. That collar belongs to my friend's dog Spot.
d. No mistake

33. Choose the sentence with the correct capitalization.

a. Alex and I played in the park after school the other day.
b. The punch served at Anna's party was delicious.
c. The dwarf planet Pluto is named after a Greek god.
d. No mistake

34. Choose the sentence with the correct capitalization.

a. Women played a very important role in the American Revolution.
b. Computers are now found in almost every home in the United States.
c. The first westerner to discover Hawaii was Captain James Cook.
d. No mistake

35. Choose the sentence with the correct grammar.

a. My teacher looked at my homework very closely and found several mistakes.
b. Penny looked out the window and seen a rainbow.
c. Martin was so worry that he couldn't sleep.
d. No mistake

36. Choose the sentence with the correct grammar.

a. There were fewer houses in my neighborhood than I remembered.
b. The ship was so bad damaged by the iceberg that it had to return to port.
c. Katrina give a presentation to the class on the origins of ballet.
d. No mistake

37. Choose the sentence with the correct grammar.

a. The greatest singer of the twentieth century was Frank Sinatra.
b. William the Conqueror invading England in 1066.
c. After hurting his knee, David begin to groan.
d. No mistake

38. Choose the sentence with the correct grammar.

a. Neither gunpowder nor the compass was invented in Europe.
b. Janet would believe almost anything that anyone told her.
c. Missy fell off her horse, but she was not injured.
d. No mistake

39. Choose the sentence with the correct grammar.

a. The computer is one of our most importantest educational tools.
b. The giant mouse ran through the house and escaped from the cat.
c. Did you know that Julie is an experience guide and mountaineer?
d. No mistake

40. Choose the sentence with the correct grammar.

a. Our parents often help us with our math homework.
b. Wallace has always wanted to visit Paris, but he has never has the time.
c. Rick go to the library every day after school to study.
d. No mistake

Spelling

For questions 41–50, look for errors in spelling.

41. Choose the incorrect spelling.

a. Everyone should have a good dictionary and thesaurus in the house.
b. He admited that he had never seen the play.
c. After years of neglect, the building finally collapsed.
d. No mistake

42. Choose the incorrect spelling.

a. Terry considered joining a traveling circus.
b. Drew usually exaggerates a bit when he tells a story.
c. He was seldom late to a party.
d. No mistake

43. Choose the incorrect spelling.

a. Many great discoveries happen entirely by accident.
b. If we don't show up on time, they're going to be very angry.
c. Winning the scholarship was a great oportunity for John.
d. No mistake

44. Choose the incorrect spelling.

a. His messy handwriting made his letter nearly illegible.
b. I think he was sincerely sorry for what he did.
c. We have a rehersal for the play almost every night.
d. No mistake

45. Choose the incorrect spelling.

a. His teacher was awed and very impressed by his artistic ability.
b. Mr. Worthington thought that Kathy looked upset.
c. I tried to learn to sew, but I wasn't very good at it.
d. No mistake

46. Choose the incorrect spelling.

a. The play was so long that it required two intermissions.
b. Uma prefered to sit on the couch.
c. Each tribe has a cloth with a distinctive pattern.
d. No mistake

47. Choose the incorrect spelling.

a. My sister practises the piano two hours a day.
b. John told me that he wants to be an astronaut.
c. His article was misleading, even if true.
d. No mistake

48. Choose the incorrect spelling.

a. The sheriff's deputy caught the thief later that night.
b. Paul was surprized to hear that he had won the award.
c. Agnes was very fond of her stuffed bear named Edward.
d. No mistake

49. Choose the incorrect spelling.

a. Justin was confused by the strange behavior of his pet frog.
b. Many people enjoy the challenge of an outdoor adventure.
c. Linus Pauling received the Nobel Prize for his many scientific accomplishments.
d. No mistake

50. Choose the incorrect spelling.

a. Ms. Davis teaches mathmatics and physics.
b. Cecil did not intend to insult his friend.
c. George was not sure how his friends would react to his talent.
d. No mistake

Composition

51. Choose the sentence that is correct and most clearly written.

a. Martin decided on the blue suit after several days.
b. The blue suit was decided upon by Martin after several days.
c. After several days, the blue suit was decided upon by Martin.
d. The blue suit, after several days, was what Martin decided on.

52. Choose the sentence that is correct and most clearly written.

a. Importantly, occasions such as birthdays should not be forgotten.
b. Occasions, such as birthdays, which are important, should not be forgotten.
c. Birthdays are important occasions which should not be forgotten.
d. Occasions should not be forgotten when they are as important as birthdays.

53. Choose the sentence that is correct and most clearly written.

a. Spinach is my favorite food it goes well with almost anything.
b. Spinach is my favorite food; it goes well with almost anything.
c. Spinach is my favorite food and spinach goes well with almost anything.
d. Spinach is my favorite food to go well with almost anything.

54. Where should the following sentence be placed in the paragraph below?

She was responsible for promoting sanitary surgical methods, a pure water supply, and other hygienic measures.

1) Born in Italy and raised in England, Florence Nightingale is recognized universally as the person who established the principles of modern nursing. 2) In 1854, Nightingale assembled a team of women to care for British soldiers during the Crimean War. 3) During her nearly two years of service, Nightingale stressed cleanliness and good medical care. 4) These measures led to a drop in the mortality rate from 60% to 2%, saving countless British lives. 5) When she returned from the war, she founded the Nightingale School to train the next generation of professional nurses.

a. After sentence 2
b. After sentence 3
c. After sentence 4
d. After sentence 5

55. Where should the following sentence be placed in the paragraph below?

The ash spread over hundreds of square miles, making the sky look black as night.

1) In 1980, Mount Saint Helens, in the state of Washington, became a volcano. 2) It exploded for the first time in thousands of years. 3) The explosion was felt as far north as Seattle and as far south as Los Angeles. 4) The mountain threw tons of ash into the air before it stopped exploding a few days later. 5) There was, however, no lava. 6) Most geologists believe that Mount Saint Helens will not explode again for many thousands of years to come. 7) But they admit that another explosion might occur at any time.

a. After sentence 2
b. After sentence 3
c. After sentence 4
d. After sentence 5

56. Fill in the blank.

Jason thought that he found a lump of gold, ______ it turned out to be a painted rock.

a. because
b. moreover
c. but
d. or

57. Fill in the blank.

Most people feel that it is worthwhile to buy a better product, ______ it might cost a little more.

a. therefore
b. even though
c. in fact
d. despite

58. Fill in the blank.

Brushing your teeth every day is important to prevent cavities; _______ it helps your gums stay healthy and prevents bad breath.

a. moreover,
b. nonetheless,
c. yet,
d. in contrast,

59. Which sentence does not belong in the following paragraph?

1) Many people think that rabbits are rodents, like rats and mice. 2) In fact, rabbits are not rodents at all. 3) Rodents scare many people because they have sharp teeth and claws. 4) Rabbits, along with hares, belong to a class of animals called lagomorphs. 5) Lagomorph is a Greek word that means "rabbit-shaped."

a. Sentence 2
b. Sentence 3
c. Sentence 4
d. Sentence 5

60. Which sentence does not belong in the following paragraph?

1) Of all the animals on earth, the one most suited to its environment is probably the camel. 2) Camels live in the desert, where water is scarce and breathing is difficult due to the sand in the air. 3) To cope with these conditions, camels can store several days' worth of water in their humps. 4) There are no higher animals on earth that can live without water. 5) Camels also have extra-long eyelashes and hairs that cover their noses to keep the sand out. 6) Furthermore, their large feet help them walk on the sand, which is difficult terrain for most other pack animals.

a. Sentence 2
b. Sentence 3
c. Sentence 4
d. Sentence 5

Fill in the Blank

[illegible]

a. [illegible]

8) Which word does not belong in the following passage?

1) Many [illegible] [illegible]

a. [illegible]
b. [illegible]
c. [illegible]

10) Which word does not belong in the following passage?

[illegible]

a. [illegible]
b. [illegible]
c. [illegible]
d. [illegible]

Chapter 15
HSPT Practice Test 3: Answers and Explanations

ANSWER KEY

Verbal Skills

1.	C	38.	A
2.	D	39.	C
3.	C	40.	D
4.	B	41.	C
5.	B	42.	D
6.	B	43.	A
7.	B	44.	A
8.	C	45.	A
9.	A	46.	D
10.	B	47.	C
11.	A	48.	C
12.	A	49.	B
13.	B	50.	B
14.	C	51.	B
15.	C	52.	B
16.	C	53.	C
17.	B	54.	B
18.	B	55.	A
19.	A	56.	C
20.	C	57.	D
21.	D	58.	A
22.	D	59.	C
23.	B	60.	B
24.	A		
25.	A		
26.	B		
27.	B		
28.	A		
29.	C		
30.	A		
31.	C		
32.	D		
33.	A		
34.	A		
35.	B		
36.	C		
37.	A		

Quantitative Skills

1.	C	38.	C
2.	D	39.	A
3.	A	40.	B
4.	D	41.	D
5.	D	42.	D
6.	C	43.	C
7.	A	44.	A
8.	A	45.	B
9.	C	46.	D
10.	C	47.	C
11.	B	48.	B
12.	B	49.	C
13.	C	50.	C
14.	C	51.	C
15.	C	52.	B
16.	A		
17.	A		
18.	B		
19.	B		
20.	B		
21.	A		
22.	B		
23.	B		
24.	B		
25.	A		
26.	B		
27.	B		
28.	C		
29.	A		
30.	C		
31.	A		
32.	C		
33.	B		
34.	C		
35.	D		
36.	B		
37.	C		

Reading

1.	A	38.	C
2.	C	39.	C
3.	B	40.	B
4.	A	41.	B
5.	B	42.	C
6.	C	43.	D
7.	B	44.	A
8.	B	45.	C
9.	B	46.	D
10.	A	47.	C
11.	B	48.	C
12.	C	49.	A
13.	B	50.	C
14.	C	51.	B
15.	D	52.	C
16.	A	53.	A
17.	B	54.	B
18.	B	55.	D
19.	B	56.	C
20.	B	57.	B
21.	B	58.	A
22.	C	59.	A
23.	B	60.	B
24.	D	61.	C
25.	B	62.	D
26.	B		
27.	B		
28.	C		
29.	C		
30.	C		
31.	A		
32.	C		
33.	A		
34.	C		
35.	B		
36.	C		
37.	B		

Mathematics

1.	B	38.	D
2.	C	39.	D
3.	D	40.	A
4.	A	41.	A
5.	C	42.	D
6.	D	43.	B
7.	C	44.	D
8.	B	45.	A
9.	A	46.	D
10.	C	47.	D
11.	C	48.	B
12.	B	49.	A
13.	B	50.	D
14.	A	51.	D
15.	C	52.	B
16.	B	53.	D
17.	B	54.	B
18.	B	55.	A
19.	B	56.	D
20.	C	57.	A
21.	C	58.	C
22.	B	59.	A
23.	A	60.	B
24.	B	61.	A
25.	B	62.	C
26.	C	63.	B
27.	C	64.	A
28.	C		
29.	D		
30.	A		
31.	D		
32.	C		
33.	C		
34.	B		
35.	A		
36.	D		
37.	C		

Language Skills

1.	D	38.	D
2.	B	39.	B
3.	B	40.	A
4.	B	41.	B
5.	A	42.	D
6.	D	43.	C
7.	B	44.	C
8.	B	45.	D
9.	C	46.	B
10.	C	47.	A
11.	D	48.	B
12.	C	49.	D
13.	A	50.	A
14.	A	51.	A
15.	B	52.	C
16.	C	53.	B
17.	A	54.	B
18.	C	55.	C
19.	B	56.	C
20.	B	57.	B
21.	A	58.	A
22.	A	59.	B
23.	B	60.	C
24.	A		
25.	D		
26.	A		
27.	C		
28.	A		
29.	C		
30.	B		
31.	D		
32.	C		
33.	D		
34.	D		
35.	A		
36.	A		
37.	A		

ANSWERS AND EXPLANATIONS

Verbal Skills

1. **C** Diligent means hardworking.
2. **D** Severe means serious; the opposite is mild.
3. **C** A candle is made of wax; a tire is made of rubber.
4. **B** A spoon, a knife, and a fork are utensils used to eat food.
5. **B** A horse lives in a stable; a chicken lives in a coop.
6. **B** Winter, fall, and summer are seasons of the year.
7. **B** Prohibit means to disallow.
8. **C** A shirt, a dress, and a pair of shorts are all articles of clothing.
9. **A** Famished means very hungry; arid means very dry.
10. **B** Biased means taking a position; the opposite is neutral.
11. **A** A suitcase holds clothes; a briefcase holds papers.
12. **A** Hinder means to hold back; the opposite is help.
13. **B** Content means happy or satisfied.
14. **C** We can diagram this as follows: Rachel > Alice, Richard > Barry. Since we don't know how Rachel and Alice relate to Richard and Barry, we don't know whether Rachel or Richard finished first.
15. **C** The top of a container is a lid; the top of a house is a roof.
16. **C** Credible means believable.
17. **B** Sincere means honest; the opposite is dishonest.
18. **B** We can diagram this as follows: $I > M > L$. Since Ines is before Marcus, who is before Larry, we know that Larry is not before Ines.
19. **A** To contaminate means to infect.
20. **C** We can diagram this as follows: $B > D$, $A > D$, $C > D$. All we know is that Alex and Bink had more balloons than David, but we don't know whether Alex or Bink had more.
21. **D** Sail, mast, and rudder are all parts of a ship.
22. **D** Fortunate means lucky.

23. **B** A zoologist studies animals; a botanist studies plants.

24. **A** Apples, peaches, and pears are all kinds of fruit.

25. **A** We can diagram this as follows: $J > B$, $J > E$, $M > J$. Since Mark is taller than John, who is taller than Evelyn, we know that Mark is taller than Evelyn.

26. **B** Water, oil, and vinegar are all types of liquid.

27. **B** Frank means honest.

28. **A** Famine means the lack of food; drought means the lack of water.

29. **C** We can diagram this as follows: $O > J$, $N > J$. All we know is that Olivia and Nancy each ate more than Jennifer, but we don't know whether Olivia or Nancy ate more.

30. **A** A trunk, a branch, and a leaf are all parts of a tree.

31. **C** Immune means not vulnerable to disease; the opposite is vulnerable.

32. **D** Tea, coffee, and water are all things you drink; you eat cereal.

33. **A** Elude means to get away or escape.

34. **A** We can diagram this as follows: $F > J$, $F > N$, $J = M$. Since Frank has seen more than Jonathan, who has seen the same number as Manny, we know that Manny has seen fewer films than Frank.

35. **B** Sole, lace, and heel are all parts of a shoe.

36. **C** To mimic means to imitate.

37. **A** Counterfeit means fake or false; the opposite is genuine.

38. **A** We can diagram this as follows: $K > F > D$, $A > K$. Since Amanda walked farther than Kate, who walked farther than Felix, we know that Amanda walked farther than Felix.

39. **C** Barbaric means rude or uncivilized; the opposite is civilized.

40. **D** Dog, fish, and hamster are all kinds of pets.

41. **C** Conventional means normal; the opposite is strange.

42. **D** To inspect means to examine closely.

43. **A** Varied means different; the opposite is similar.

44. **A** Goat, cow, and horse are all animals that produce milk.

45. **A** Maple is a type of tree; an apple is a type of fruit.

46. **D** To diminish means to reduce.

47. **C** We can diagram this as follows: Mike > Mindy > *W*, Mike > *R*. All we know is that both Mindy and Rochelle read fewer books than Mike. We don't know which of the two read more.

48. **C** Movie, book, and play are all kinds of works that can be fictional.

49. **B** Unbiased means without bias, or neutral.

50. **B** Criticize is the opposite of praise.

51. **B** Mop, broom, and vacuum are all tools used to clean the floor.

52. **B** A bird guides itself with its wings; a fish guides itself with its fins.

53. **C** Permanent means unchanging.

54. **B** We can diagram this as follows: $W > S > T > Z$. Since Wendy has more badges than Terence, who has more than Zack, we know that Wendy does not have fewer than Zack.

55. **A** Serene means calm or peaceful.

56. **C** Enlarge means to grow; the opposite is shrink or reduce.

57. **D** Wind, rain, and snow are all reasons to wear a coat.

58. **A** An hour is a part of the day; a month is a part of the year.

59. **C** Brick, stone, and wood are all materials used to make a house.

60. **B** Authentic means real or genuine.

Quantitative Skills

1. **C** The series goes 2 (× 2) 4 (× 2) 8 (× 2) 16 (× 2) **32**.

2. **D** Each of the figures has two parts out of four shaded.

3. **A** The series goes 6 (+ 9) 15 (+ 9) 24 (+ 9) 33 (+ 9) **42**.

4. **D** $3 \times 5 = 15$. Now try each choice to see which one, if you take 25% of it, gives you 15. $25\% \times 60 = 15$.

5. **D** The series goes 1 (× 3) 3 (× 3) 9 (× 3) 27 (× 3) **81**.

6. **C** Translate each of these: $\frac{40}{100}$ of $80 = 32$. $\frac{50}{100}$ of $64 = 32$. $\frac{150}{100}$ of $16 = 24$.

7. **A** $\frac{1}{4}$ of 24 is 6. What number divided by 3 is 6? 18.

8. **A** The series goes 100 (– 1) 99 (– 2) 97 (– 3) 94 (– 4) **90**.

9. **C** Let's calculate each of the choices: $\frac{1}{4} \times 96 = 24$. $2 \times 48 = 96$. $\frac{1}{2} \times 192 = 96$.

10. **C** The series goes 5 (+ 3) 8 (+ 5) 13 (+ 3) 16 (+ 5) 21 (+ 3) **24.**

11. **B** Let's calculate each of the choices: $32^1 = 32$. $2^5 = 32$. $3^3 = 27$.

12. **B** The series goes 10 (– 3) 7 (+ 1) 8 (– 3) 5 (+ 1) 6 (– 3) **3.**

13. **C** 10% of 40 is the same as $\frac{10}{100} \times 40 = 4$. Now we need to figure out $\frac{4}{5}$ of which number is 4. Try taking $\frac{4}{5}$ of each of the choices until you find the one that makes 4.

14. **C** The series goes 6 (+ 3) 9 (+ 4) 13 (+ 3) 16 (+ 4) 20 (+ 3) **23.**

15. **C** Since (3) has an 8 in the hundredths places, it is the largest number. (2) has an extra digit, and is greater than (1).

16. **A** The series goes 2 (+ 4) 6 (+ 6) 12 (+ 4) 16 (+ 6) 22 (+ 4) **26.**

17. **A** The difference between 80 and 64 is 16. $\frac{1}{4}$ of 16 = 4.

18. **B** Let's calculate these choices: 3(4 + 9) = 39. 12 + 27 = 39. 34 + 9 = 43.

19. **B** $\frac{1}{5}$ of 15 is 3. 18 more than 3 is 21.

20. **B** The perimeter of (A) is 14, the perimeter of (B) is 16, and the perimeter of (C) is 12.

21. **A** Translate this as $\frac{10}{100} \times \frac{20}{100} \times 300 = 6$.

22. **B** The series goes 8 (+ 1) 9 (+ 7) 16 (+ 1) 17 (+ 7) 24 (+ 1) 25 (+ 7) **32.**

23. **B** Let's calculate these choices. For (1), we move the decimal three places to the right to get 3,020. For (2), we move the decimal two places to the right to get 3,200. (3) is 302.

24. **B** Try dividing each number by 7. 51 ÷ 7 = 7 with a remainder of 2.

25. **A** Since *AC* and *FB* are both diameters, they are equal; *ED* is shorter than both of them.

26. **B** The series goes 1 (× 7) 7 | 3 (× 7) 21 | **5** (× 7) 35.

27. **B** *x* is larger than *y*. Since their sum is 180°, *x* must be larger than 90°, and *y* must be less than 90°.

28. **C** (1) = 3.67; (2) = 6.73; and (3) = 7.36.

29. **A** The series goes 2 (× 2) 4 (+ 2) 6 (× 2) 12 (+ 2) 14 (× 2) 28 (+ 2) **30.**

30. **C** Translate 20% of 60: $\frac{20}{100} \times 60 = 12$. What number is 9 times 12? 108.

31. **A** The series goes 9 (– 2) 7 (– 2) 5 (+ 4) 9 (– 2) 7 (– 2) **5** (+ 4) 9.

32. **C** Twice the difference between 15 and 17 is 4. 17 more than 4 is 21.

33. **B** The series goes 9 (+ 11) 20 (+ 11) 31 (+ 11) 42 (+ 11) **53.**

34. **C** Since this is a square, all the sides are equal and smaller than the diagonals.

35. **D** The series goes 7 (× 2) 14 (– 1) 13 (× 2) 26 (– 1) 25 (× 2) **50**.

36. **B** $\frac{1}{11}$ of 121 = 11. To make 11, you need to add 8 and 3.

37. **C** (1) = 16, (2) = 16, and (3) = 32.

38. **C** The series goes 2 (+ 2) 4 (+ 2) 6 (– 2) 4 (+ 2) 6 (+ 2) 8 (– 2) **6** (+ 2) 8 (+ 2) 10.

39. **A** Since they are vertical angles, a = 45°, b = 110°, and c = 25°.

40. **B** The average of 42, 45, and 39 is 42. The difference between 23 and 42 is 19.

41. **D** The product of 8 and 18 is 144. $\frac{1}{4}$ of 144 = 36.

42. **D** Choice (A) has an area of 8; (B) has an area of 8; (C) has an area of 8.

43. **C** The series should go 88 (– 3) 85 (– 2) 83 (– 3) 80 (– 2) 78 (– 3) **75**.

44. **A** (1) = 2, (2) = –2, and (3) = –18.

45. **B** The series goes 49 $(\sqrt{\ })$ 7 | 81 $(\sqrt{\ })$ **9** | 121 $(\sqrt{\ })$ 11.

46. **D** The product of 6 and 3 is 18. 50% more than 18 is 27.

47. **C** 10% of 50 = 5; 20% of 100 = 20. The difference between 5 and 20 is 15.

48. **B** The series goes 6 (+ 2) 8 (– 1) 7 (+ 2) 9 (– 1) **8** (+ 2) 10 (– 1) 9 (+ 2) 11.

49. **C** $\frac{5}{3}$ of 9 = 15. 4 less than 15 is 11.

50. **C** Half the sum of 4, 9, and 11 is 12. 18 more than 12 is 30.

51. **C** The average of 10, 15, and 8 is 11. 2 more than 11 is 13.

52. **B** The series goes 41 (– 30) 11 (+ 41) 52 (– 30) 22 (+ 41) 63 (– 30) **33**.

Reading

Comprehension

1. **A** The passage uses quitting in contrast to playing with his friends. It must therefore mean something like no longer playing with, or leaving.

2. **C** According to the passage, they gathered near the river.

3. **B** The first paragraph states that the narrator is going to take a job while the friends go back to the high school. The narrator is probably around 18 years old.

4. **A** Each paragraph of the passage describes the various friends of the narrator.

5. **B** According to the first paragraph, the narrator will "remember it better" because the narrator is about the leave.

6. **C** The first paragraph says that the author was going "to teach my first country school."

7. **B** The second paragraph says that Otto and Fritz "caught the fat, horned catfish."

8. **B** According to the last sentence, Tip's father worked in a "grocery store."

9. **B** Since the sentence following the mention of the word *generate* discuss the ways in which the eel uses electricity, the word *generate* must mean something like use or make.

10. **A** The author knows a great deal of detail about the electric eel, which is an animal that lives in the sea.

11. **B** The word *current* is right next to the word *electric*, so it must have something to do with electricity.

12. **C** According to the third paragraph, eels use their electricity "to find fish."

13. **B** In the sentence prior to the word *buffer*, we see that it is something that "protects its nervous system."

14. **C** The final sentence of the passage says that it is not certain whether eels use electricity to communicate because "this theory has not yet been proven."

15. **D** Each of these animals is mentioned somewhere in the passage except the horse.

16. **A** The fourth paragraph states that the eel has insulation that "protects its nervous system" from the electricity that it generates. Therefore we can infer that electricity harms the nervous system.

17. **B** The only choice listed that would describe an electric eel is (B).

18. **B** The word *meager* is explained by saying that his salary was so meager that they lived "in an unheated apartment." Evidently he didn't have enough money to afford heat, so the word meager must mean small.

19. **B** The second paragraph says that Pavlov worked on "conditioned reflexes" and showed that they "can be acquired through experience or training."

20. **B** According to the second paragraph, the knee-jerk response is an example of an "innate" reflex.

21. **B** Since the word *innate* is used in the second paragraph in contrast to the word *conditioned*, it must refer to something that is not learned and instead had at birth.

22. **C** The final paragraph says that Skinner was a behaviorist, which was a school of psychology that followed Pavlov's ideas. But we don't know if Skinner was one of Pavlov's students, so (C) is the best choice.

23. **B** In the final paragraph, the author says, "Though behaviorism cannot plausibly explain all of human behavior, it has deepened our understanding...."

24. **D** The second paragraph states that Pavlov worked on "conditioned reflexes" and showed that they "can be acquired through experience or training."

25. **B** The words "bounce up like a ball" are used to describe how Fanny acts when she thinks she sees a mouse.

26. **B** The word *credulous* in the passage is followed immediately by "would believe anything."

27. **B** The final paragraph states that she played the piano and sang.

28. **C** The word *cultivated* is used to describe the "musical gift" of people. Choices (A), (B), and (D) are therefore impossible.

29. **C** According to the first paragraph, "Frank would tell her the most unbelievable and impossible lies" and enjoyed "fooling her."

30. **C** The final sentence of the first paragraph states that "Caesar's historical influence was so great" that these words "are derived from his name."

31. **A** The second sentence says that the Roman Empire was "so large and powerful that no other Western government could be considered its equal."

32. **C** The second paragraph says that Caesar came from a family of politicians, but he "did not simply act in the interests of his family" but rather helped the people.

33. **A** The word *campaigns* is used to describe the Gallic Wars.

34. **C** The fourth paragraph states that "Caesar's popularity and strength began to frighten Pompey."

35. **B** This is stated in the first sentence of the third paragraph.

36. **C** The third paragraph says that *Frankenstein* is "a brilliant work of art."

37. **B** In the third paragraph, the author states that "feminist ideas inherited from her mother" influenced her writing.

38. **C** Choices (A) and (B) are only details of the passage, and (D) is not really discussed.

39. **C** According to the second paragraph, she wrote it at the age of 19. Since she was born in 1797, she must have written it around 1816.

40. **B** The word *calamities* is used to describe events that "included several suicides."

Vocabulary

41. **B**
42. **C**
43. **D**
44. **A**
45. **C**
46. **D**
47. **C**
48. **C**
49. **A**
50. **C**
51. **B**
52. **C**
53. **A**
54. **B**
55. **D**
56. **C**
57. **B**
58. **A**
59. **A**
60. **B**
61. **C**
62. **D**

Mathematics

Mathematical Concepts

1. **B** First, eliminate choices that have a zero in the tenths place. This leaves (A) and (B). Since (B) has a 1 in the hundredths place, whereas (A) has a 0, (B) is bigger.

2. **C** The area of a square is length × width. Since this is a square, its length and width are both 5, so the area is $5 \times 5 = 25$.

3. **D** Plug in each answer choice until you find one that can be divided by 3, 4, and 5. 30 cannot be divided by 4; 40 cannot be divided by 3; 50 cannot be divided by 3.

4. **A** Remember that the second place to the right of the decimal is called the hundredths place. Therefore, $\frac{5}{100} = 0.05$, so the sum = 65.05.

5. **C** Since $60° + a + b = 180°$, $a + b = 120°$.

6. **D** Remember that when you multiply by 100, you move the decimal point two places to the right: $0.28 \times 100 = 28$. The closest choice is (D).

7. **C** If we find the factors of 45, they are 1 and 45, 3 and 15, and 5 and 9. Since 9 is not prime, the biggest prime factor is 5.

8. **B** Percent decrease is calculated by taking $\frac{\textit{difference}}{\textit{original}}$. The difference in this case is \$40. The original amount of the dress was \$160. Therefore, we calculate $\frac{40}{160} = \frac{1}{4} = 25\%$.

9. **A** When in doubt, write exponents out longhand. $10^3 = 10 \times 10 \times 10$. $10^5 = 10 \times 10 \times 10 \times 10 \times 10$. This makes a total of eight 10s, or 10^8.

10. **C** Try dividing each choice by 8 until you find the one that cannot be divided evenly.

11. **C** The volume of his box is $6 \times 8 \times \frac{1}{2} = 24$.

12. **B** We can make this into a proportion: $\frac{3\ \textit{boys}}{4\ \textit{girls}} = \frac{x}{124\ \textit{girls}}$. If we cross multiply and solve for x, we get $x = 93$ boys.

13. **B** When in doubt, write out the exponents in longhand. $(4^2)^3$ is the same thing as $4^2 \times 4^2 \times 4^2 = 4 \times 4 \times 4 \times 4 \times 4 \times 4$. There are a total of six 4s, or 4^6.

14. **A** The product of the digits is $3 \times 6 \times 5 = 90$. The sum of the digits is $3 + 6 + 5 = 14$. $90 - 14 = 76$.

15. **C** Remember that the tenths place is the first to the right of the decimal. Since the next digit is 4, we round down to 2.8.

16. **B** Since the squares have an area of 16, their sides must equal 4. The perimeter of the figure covers 6 sides total, so the perimeter is $6 \times 4 = 24$.

17. **B** The angles inside a triangle must add up to 180°. If one of the angles measures 85°, then the other two must measure 180 – 85 = 95°. The only choice that adds up to 95° is (B).

18. **B** $\sqrt{2^2}$ is the same as $\sqrt{4} = 2$.

19. **B** Juan has a total of 17 marbles, and 5 of them are blue. Therefore, $\frac{5}{17}$ of his marbles are blue.

20. **C** You can add only similar roots together, so (C) is the only true statement.

21. **C** The first multiples of 4 are 4, 8, 12, 16, 20, and 24. The first multiples of 6 are 6, 12, 18, and 24. The smallest number that is common to each is 12.

22. **B** Try dividing each choice by 6. 22 ÷ 6 = 3 with a remainder of 4.

23. **A** Try taking a negative even number such as –2 and a positive odd number such as 3, and multiply them to get –6. This number is negative and even.

24. **B** Don't forget to memorize your primes! There are four: 2, 3, 5, and 7.

Problem Solving

25. **B** Use the Bowtie to get a common denominator. $\frac{5}{15} + \frac{6}{13} = \frac{65}{195} + \frac{90}{195} = \frac{155}{195}$ which reduces to $\frac{31}{39}$.

26. **C** To get an average of 48 on four tests, her total score would have to be 48 × 4, or 192. Maxine already has 42 + 45 + 46 = 133 points on the first three tests, so on her fourth she would need 192 – 133 = 59 points.

27. **C** Translate this as $\frac{20}{100} \times \frac{40}{100} \times 500 = 40$.

28. **C** Remember your order of operations! First do parentheses to get 6 – 3(– 2) + 5. Now do multiplication to get 6 + 6 + 5. Now add to get 17.

29. **D** To make this division easier, let's move the decimal point two places to the right. Now we can divide $\frac{2000}{2} = 1{,}000$.

30. **A** First, we need to find 5% of $25. $\frac{5}{100} \times 25 = \$1.25$. When you take this off the original price, we get $23.75.

31. **D** Let's set up the proportion: $\frac{8\ miles}{1\ inch} = \frac{x}{3.5\ inches}$. Cross-multiply to get x = 28 miles.

32. **C** Remember that the places after the decimal point are the tenths and hundredths. So 0.24 = $\frac{24}{100}$, which reduces to $\frac{12}{50}$.

33. **C** Let's plug in our own number to make this easier. Let's say that the shirt begins at $100. When the prices is discounted by 20%, it will go down to $80. When it is discounted by another 10%, it will go down to $72. This means that it went from $100 to $72, a discount of 28%.

34. **B** If two numbers have a ratio of 6:9, and the smaller one is actually 18, then we know that we need to multiply the ratio by 3 to get 18:27. The question then asks for the average of these two numbers. The average of 18 and 27 is 22.5.

35. **A** Remember your order of operations! First do parentheses to get $11 + 5 \times 6 \div 3 - (-3)$. Now multiply to get $11 + 30 + 3 - (-3)$. Now we can add and subtract to get 47.

36. **D** The volume of this pool is $4 \times 10 \times 12 = 480$. If it gets filled at 8 cubic feet per minute, it will take $\frac{480}{8} = 60$ minutes to fill.

37. **C** If three hamburgers cost \$4.05, then each hamburger costs \$1.35. This means that two hamburgers cost \$2.70. If two hamburgers and an order of french fries costs \$3.55, then an order of fries must cost \$3.55 – \$2.70 = \$0.85.

38. **D** If the ratio of boys to girls is 3:5, that means that for every 8 total students, 3 are boys and 5 are girls. If there are 32 total students, then there are 4 groups of 8 students. This means that there are 12 boys and 20 girls.

39. **D** The area of this circle is πr^2, or 64π. The circumference of this circle is $2\pi r$, or 16π. Therefore, the difference is 48π.

40. **A** To make this problem easier, let's write out the exponents. $4^4 = 4 \times 4 \times 4 \times 4$. Which one of the choices says the same thing? Let's try them. Choice (A) says 16×16, which is the same as $4 \times 4 \times 4 \times 4$.

41. **A** First, let's find how many do attend. $\frac{2}{3} \times 660 = 440$ students. This means that 220 do not attend.

42. **D** If we multiply these two numbers together, we get $6\sqrt{4}$. We can take 4 out of the root to get $6 \times 2 = 12$.

43. **B** To make this easier, let's add the fractions with common denominators together. This gives us $18 + 1 + \frac{3}{6}$. Since $\frac{3}{6}$ is the same as $\frac{1}{2}$, the sum is $19\frac{1}{2}$.

44. **D** Let's begin by subtracting 5 from each side. This gives us $3x = 18$. When we divide 3 from each side, we get $x = 6$.

45. **A** To divide fractions, flip and multiply: $\frac{1}{2} \times \frac{10}{1} = 5$.

46. **D** Since $x = 2$, we know that $2y + 18 = 36$. Now we can solve for y: $2y = 18$, so $y = 9$.

47. **D** The area of this rectangle is the same as length × width, or $15 \times 24 = 360$ ft^2.

48. **B** There is no need to work out the entire problem. Just one term is probably enough to get the right answer. The first terms says $7 \times \frac{1}{100}$. Seven-hundredths means a 7 in the hundredths place, or 0.07. Only (B) has a 7 in the hundredths place.

49. **A** By Ballparking, you can probably get this one right. Since 5 pounds would be at least \$15, (B), (C), and (D) are all too big. You can also solve by setting up a proportion. $\frac{1\text{ lb.}}{\$3.25} = \frac{x}{\$13}$. Cross-multiply to solve for x.

50. **D** To make the division easier, move the decimal point one place to the right. Now divide $\frac{55}{2} = 27.5$.

51. **D** Plug in the answer choices, starting with (A). If Alex is 4 years old, then 4 years ago, he was 0 years old. Does this make him half as old? No. How about (B)? If Alex is 5 years old, then 4 years ago, he was 1. Does this make him half as old? No. How about (C)? If Alex is 6 years old, then 4 years ago, he was 2. Still not half as old. How about (D)? If Alex is 8 years old, then 4 years ago, he was 4. This is half as old as he is now.

52. **B** First, change these into ordinary fractions, and then multiply: $\frac{11}{2} \times \frac{7}{3} = \frac{77}{6}$ *or* $12\frac{5}{6}$.

53. **D** A wall that is 20 feet by 12 feet has a total area of $20 \times 12 = 240$ square feet. One gallon will cover 2.5 square feet, so divide 240 by 2.5 to see how many gallons we will need.

54. **B** Since $y = 5$, we know that $2x^2 + 5 = 55$. If we subtract 5 from each side, we get $2x^2 = 50$. Now we can divide 2 from each side and get $x^2 = 25$, so x could be 5.

55. **A** We can multiply these numbers together to get $12\sqrt{36}$. Since $\sqrt{36} = 6$, this becomes $12 \times 6 = 72$.

56. **D** Since there are 60 seconds in a minute and 60 minutes in an hour, there are $60 \times 60 = 3{,}600$ seconds in an hour. So in 4 hours there are $4 \times 3{,}600 = 14{,}400$ seconds.

57. **A** This problem is best solved by plugging in the answer choices. Let's start with (A). Could there be 62 girls in the group? If there are 62 girls, there are $62 - 24 = 38$ boys. Does this make a total of 100 children? Yes.

58. **C** Let's solve for x. First, subtract x from each side to get $-5x - 3 < 2$. Now add 3 to each side and get $-5x < 5$. When we divide each side by -5, we have to change the direction of the sign, so $x > -1$.

59. **A** Multiples of 5 and 6 are multiples of 30. How many multiples of 30 are there between 1 and 100? Three: 30, 60, and 90.

60. **B** The triangles are formed from two radii, which must be the same length, so the triangle must be isosceles. Since the inside angle is 90°, the other two angles must be 45°.

61. **A** We can set up a proportion: $\frac{2\text{ cookies}}{1\text{ minutes}} = \frac{150\text{ cookies}}{x\text{ minutes}}$. Now we solve for x, which becomes 75 minutes, or 1 hour and 15 minutes.

62. **C** Plug in the answer choices to solve this problem. Start with (A). If Jim is 20 years old, then Carl is 40 and Liz is 15. Does this make Carl 15 years older than Liz? No. Let's try (B). If Jim is 15 years old, then Carl is 30 and Liz is 10. Does this make Carl 15 years older than Liz? No. Let's try (C). If Jim is 10, then Carl is 20 and Liz is 5. Does this make Carl 15 years older than Liz? Yes.

63. **B** If the circumference is 8π and circumference = $2\pi r$, then the radius of the circle must be 4, and the diameter is twice the radius.

64. **A** To divide \$8.50 among 5 people, we need to calculate $\frac{\$8.50}{5}$. To make it easier to divide, move the decimal points two places to the right: $\frac{850}{500} = \$1.70$.

Language

1. **D**

2. **B** Since quick describes the way in which Steve ran around the track, it should be the adverb *quickly.*

3. **B** The correct punctuation is parent's.

4. **B** Belgium is a country, which is a singular noun. Therefore, you would use the singular pronoun "it."

5. **A** Names of locations, such as Lake Michigan, should be capitalized.

6. **D**

7. **B** Names of holidays, such as New Year's Eve, should be capitalized.

8. **B** "Whose" is the possessive of "who."

9. **C** A comma should always separate city and state.

10. **C** Names of days of the week, such as Monday, should be capitalized.

11. **D**

12. **C** A comma should follow the word *asked.*

13. **A** Always use a comma in dates. A comma should follow the word Saturday.

14. **A** Since cat is singular, we need the singular pronoun "it."

15. **B** Since the phrase "my friend and me" is the object of a preposition, we use the objective pronoun "me" rather than the subject pronoun "I."

16. **C** Since it is a title accompanied by a proper name, Chief Stanley should be capitalized.

17. **A** "Taken" is the correct past tense verb form.

18. **C** When the subject of a sentence is a group of people, "we" is the correct pronoun.

19. **B** "Is" serves as the main verb in this sentence. The other two sentences are fragments.

20. **B** "Rachel's family" is singular and requires the singular verb form is.

21. **A** In this case we are showing possession, that the dish belongs to the cat, so we need "its."

22. **A** The word *each* is singular and needs the singular verb form *has.*

23. **B** When one person is the subject of the sentence, use the subject pronoun.

24. **A** "Saw" is the correct past tense verb.

25. **D**

26. **A** When counting items, the correct word is *fewer,* not less.

27. **C** The idiom is "as many as" his brother.

28. **A** This question is comparing people and their cookies. If you are unsure, you can read it as "Peter's cookies are better than Steve's cookies."

29. **C** Since the phrase "my sister and me" follows the preposition "between," the objective case is needed.

30. **B** "Heavier" is the comparative form of "heavy."

31. **D**

32. **C** Since Spot belongs to "my friend," friend is possessive, friend's is correct.

33. **D**

34. **D**

35. **A** Since the word *close* describes the way in which the teacher looked at the homework, it should be the adverb *closely.*

36. **A** Since we are counting, the word should be *fewer* not less.

37. **A** "Greatest" is the correct superlative form.

38. **D**

39. **B** The verbs should be parallel. Both should be in the past tense.

40. **A** "Our parents" is plural and requires the plural verb form "help."

Spelling

41. **B** The word *admitted* is misspelled.

42. **D**

43. **C** The word *opportunity* is misspelled.

44. **C** The word *rehearsal* is misspelled.

45. **D**

46. **B** The word *preferred* is misspelled.

47. **A** The word *practices* is misspelled.

48. **B** The word *surprised* is misspelled.

49. **D**

50. **A** The word *mathematics* is misspelled.

Composition

51. **A** Choices (B), (C), and (D) are all in the passive voice.

52. **C** Choices (A) and (B) are awkward; (D) is wordy.

53. **B** Some punctuation is required to avoid a run-on sentence.

54. **B** The sentence to be placed in the paragraph discusses measures that Nightingale proposed. Sentence 4 refers to "These measures," so the sentence should go before sentence 4.

55. **C** The sentence to be placed further discusses ash. Sentence 4 introduces the ash, so the sentence should follow sentence 4.

56. **C** The second phrase contrasts with the first, so an opposite-direction word such as (C) or (D) is needed. Choice (D) doesn't work here, so the answer should be (C).

57. **B** The second phrase is in contrast to the first, so we need an opposite-direction word such as (B).

58. **A** The second phrase gives more information about the first, so we need a same-direction word such as (A).

59. **B** All of the sentences in this paragraph discuss features of rodents, except sentence 3, which discusses people.

60. **C** All of the sentences in this paragraph discuss camels except sentence 4.

Part II
Cracking the COOP & TACHS

Chapter 16
What is the COOP? What is the TACHS?

The Cooperative Admissions Examination Program, or COOP, is given to students in certain New York and New Jersey counties who are planning to go to Catholic high schools. It is given to students in late October; check with your local diocese the summer before you plan to test for more precise information on the date of the test. Keep in mind, there is a 30% content change every year, so make sure to visit the site for the most updated information.

The TACHS (Test for Admission into Catholic High Schools) is similar to the COOP, but will test a few different skills. The TACHS is given to students in New York who plan to attend Catholic high school.

In this section of the book, we will review COOP material, and we will indicate what you might see on the TACHS.

Below is the format of the test at the time this book was published. The test does undergo changes from one year to the next, so your test may vary from the model you see here. To learn more about the most recent updates to the exam, go to **www.tachsinfo.com** or **coopexam.org**, depending on which test you're planning to take.

- Sequences
- Analogies
- Quantitative Reasoning
- Verbal Reasoning—Words
- Verbal Reasoning—Context
- Reading and Language Arts
- Mathematics

On the TACHS you will find:

- Reading: including Vocabulary and Language Arts
- Language Skills: including Spelling, Capitalization, Punctuation, and Usage
- Math:
  Ability (this tests your abject reasoning ability, and presents you with things like visual tasks and identifying patterns)

The following chapters cover the broad range of material found on both exams and review the types of problems you are likely to see.

A STUDY PLAN *

*If you're taking the HSPT, you can find your study guide on page 15!

COOP Study Plan

If you are taking the COOP, follow this nine-session study plan.

Session 1

- Before you do anything else, besides reading this introduction, take the first practice COOP test in this book. Correct it and pay particularly close attention to your mistakes.
- Write down anything you notice that you had difficulty with, such as "triangle problems." This will help you remember to pay extra attention to those concepts when you study those chapters.
- If you got more than 25 percent incorrect in any section, tell yourself to slow down and do fewer problems. You are much better off doing only 75 percent of the questions and getting more of them correct than doing all of the problems and getting many of them wrong.

Session 2

- Read Chapter 1: General Test-Taking Skills
- Read Chapter 2: Vocabulary

Session 3

- Read Chapter 16: What is the COOP?
- Read Chapter 17: Sequences

Session 4

- Read Chapter 18: Analogies
- Read Chapter 19: Quantitative Reasoning

Session 5

- Read Chapter 20: Verbal Reasoning—Words

Session 6

- Read Chapter 21: Verbal Reasoning—Context

Session 7

- Read Chapter 22: Reading and Language Arts

Session 8

- Read Chapter 23: Mathematics (You may find that you need to spread this chapter over two sessions—and that's okay.)

Session 9:

- Take the second practice COOP test. Correct the test, ooh and ahh over how much your score improved, and review the concepts in the book for the questions you answered incorrectly.
- Use any additional days before the test to continue to review the concepts and test-taking techniques covered in the book.

Chapter 17
Sequences

WHAT IS A SEQUENCE?

A sequence is a list of items that follows a pattern. In this section of the COOP, the questions will show you a sequence made up of pictures, numbers, or letters. You will be asked to figure out what picture(s) or number(s) should fill the blank in the sequence. Your job is to figure out the pattern in the sequence. For instance, the numbers 2, 4, 6, 8 make a sequence because each number is 2 more than the number before it.

First, let's look at the sequences made of pictures:

A B C D

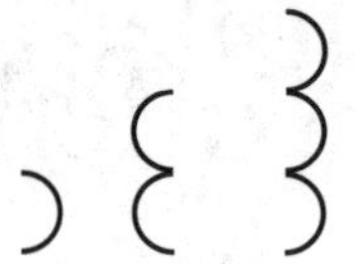

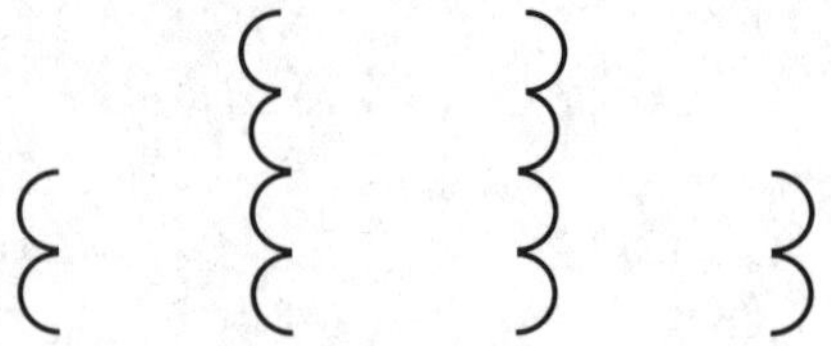

A B C D

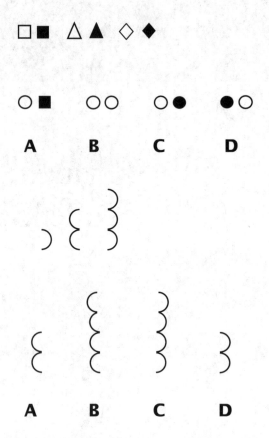

To answer these questions, look at what is similar and what changes from one picture to the next.

The first sequence is made up of pairs of similar shapes, where the first shape is white and the second shape is black: A white square with a black square, a white triangle with a black triangle, and a white diamond with a black diamond. Since all three pairs have two similar shapes, the correct answer will also be made up of similar shapes. Therefore we can eliminate choice (A). Since all three pairs have the white shape before the black shape, the answer must be (C).

The second sequence is made up of numbers of half-circles. You can see that the first picture has one, the second picture has two, and the third picture has three half-circles. Therefore the missing picture should continue the series and contain four half-circles. So we know that (A) and (D) can be eliminated. How can we decide between (B) and (C)? In the first picture, the half-circles are open on the left, in the second picture they are open on the right, and in the third picture they are open on the left. Since they change direction from one picture to the next, the missing picture will have half-circles that are open to the right. Therefore the answer is (B).

Other sequences will be made up entirely of numbers. In these examples there are three numbers in each grouping. All three groupings follow a pattern. You have to figure out what the pattern is in order to choose the correct number.

1

1 5 9 | 3 7 11 | 8 12 __

10	14	16	17
A	**B**	**C**	**D**

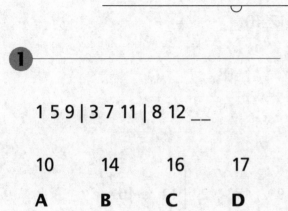

Here's How to Crack It

Between the first and second and the second and third numbers in each group, write the number that—by performing an operation like adding, subtracting, multiplying, or dividing—takes you from the first number to the next.

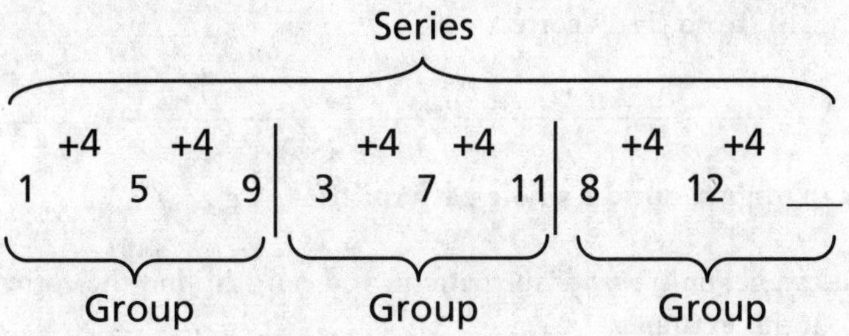

Because in the three groups each number is 4 more (+ 4) than the previous number, the next number in the series must be 16: 8 (+ 4) = 12 (+ 4) = 16. The answer is (C).

On more complicated problems, you'll need to use more than one kind of operation (multiplication, addition, division, subtraction) between each pair of numbers to figure out how the pattern works. You might have to subtract the first and second numbers in each group and then multiply to get the third. Here's an example.

2

7 5 12 | 19 17 24 | 12 10 __

8	14	17	18
F	**G**	**H**	**J**

	−2		+7			−2		+7			−2		+7	
7		5		12	19		17		24	12		10		___

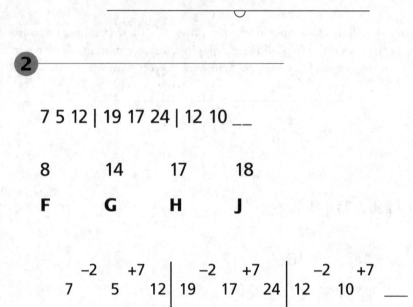

Here's How to Crack It

In this sequence problem, you have to *subtract* 2 from the first number to get the second number and then *add* 7 to the second number to get the third number. Look at the last group to see how easy it can be: 12 – 2 = 10 and 10 + 7 = 17. The pattern is 12, 10, 17, so (H) is correct.

What if I can't figure out the whole pattern?

Even if you can get only *part* of the pattern, you can still find the correct answer. Take a look at this example.

3

2 4 5 | 10 20 21 | 8 16 __

8	14	17	18
A	**B**	**C**	**D**

Here's How to Crack It

Suppose you have a hard time figuring out what operation you need to use to get from the first to the second number. In this problem, as long as you can figure out that you add 1 to the second number to get the third number, you can get the answer. (By the way, the first operation in this sequence was to multiply by 2.)

	+1		+1		+1
2	4	5 | 10	20	21 | 8	16 ___

Since 16 + 1 = 17, the answer is (C).

Sometimes the blank will be in the middle of the series rather than at the end. Follow the same technique, and double-check your answer by making sure that the number you put in the blank works with the number that follows.

4

3 5 10 | 9 11 22 | 12 __ 28

14	16	18	24
F	**G**	**H**	**J**

	+2	×2		+2	×2		+2	×2
3	5	10	9	11	22	12	___	28

Here's How to Crack It

In this example, the first operation is to add 2, and the second operation is to multiply by 2: 12 + 2 = 14 and 14 × 2 = 28. The answer is (F).

SUBSTITUTE NUMBERS FOR LETTERS TO CRACK LETTER SEQUENCES

The sequence problems toward the end of the section will probably combine letters and numbers or use all letters. These tend to be the most difficult problems on the test. If one of them stumps you, move on to the next one and go back. Try to do as many as you can. Don't forget that you can often solve the problem (or eliminate a few choices) by figuring out just one part of each group in the sequence. You don't always have to figure out the entire sequence. If you're completely stumped, don't forget to guess so that you haven't left anything blank.

One way to make the sequences that use letters easier to solve is to substitute the letters with numbers according to the location of each letter in the alphabet. This often helps you see the pattern of the sequences more easily. The first step is to write the following on your test booklet.

A	B	C	D	E	F	G	H	I	J	K	L	M	N	O	P	Q	R	S	T	U	V	W	X	Y	Z
1	2	3	4	5	6	7	8	9	10	11	12	13	14	15	16	17	18	19	20	21	22	23	24	25	26

This will help you change letters into numbers easily. Now look at the following problem.

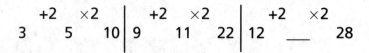

5

BDF | HJL | NPR | ______

SUW	TVX	RST	UWY
A	**B**	**C**	**D**

Here's How to Crack It

Look at the chart of numbers and letters above. B is 2, D is 4, F is 6, H is 8, and so on. By using numbers instead of letters, you should be able to figure out the pattern much more easily.

2 4 6 | 8 10 12 | 14 16 18 | ______

Now we can see the pattern. The numbers are all even and increase by 2: 2 + 2 = 4 and 4 + 2 = 6. The original question, before we made the substitution, would look like this:

+2 +2 | +2 +2 | +2 +2

B D F | H J L | N P R

The correct answer will also have even numbers that increase by 2. Substitute numbers for letters in the answer choices.

A SUW	**A** 19 21 23
B TVX	**B** 20 22 24
C RST	**C** 18 19 20
D UWY	**D** 21 23 25

Only (B) follows the pattern: 20 + 2 = 22 and 22 + 2 = 24. On our number and alphabet chart, 20 is T, 22 is V, and 24 is X, so you know the answer has to be TVX.

COOP Sequence Exercise

Answers can be found in Chapter 24.

For Numbers 1 through 3, choose the response that continues the pattern or sequence.

1

○○○●   ○○●●   ○●●●

○●○●   ●●●●   ○○○○   ●○○○

A   **B**   **C**   **D**

2

□ – □   □ + □   ○ – ○

□ + ○   ○ + □   ○ + ○   □ – □

F   **G**   **H**   **J**

3

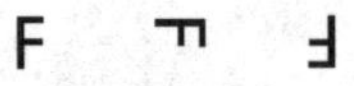

A   **B**   **C**   **D**

For Numbers 4 through 11, choose the response that continues the pattern or sequence.

4

4 8 12 | 11 15 19 | 21 25 ____

22	23	27	29
F	**G**	**H**	**J**

5

38 32 26 | 17 11 5 | 42 ____ 30

36	34	32	24
A	**B**	**C**	**D**

6

6 12 16 | 4 8 12 | 5 10 ____

8	14	15	20
F	**G**	**H**	**J**

7

10 5 15 | 13 8 18 | 22 _____ 27

15	17	22	25
A	**B**	**C**	**D**

8

8 16 20 | 4 8 12 | 20 ____ 44

24	28	35	40
F	**G**	**H**	**J**

9

20 18 25 | 23 21 28 | 30 28 ____

25	26	35	38
A	**B**	**C**	**D**

10

HFD | LJH | PNL | TRP | ____

RQP	XVT	VUT	YWV
F	**G**	**H**	**J**

11

A1FK | D2IN | G3LQ | J4OT | ____

M5RW	N5QS	N5ST	U6VW
A	**B**	**C**	**D**

Chapter 18
Analogies

WHAT IS AN ANALOGY?

An analogy is just a fancy word that means two pairs of objects have the same relationship. For instance, kittens/cats and puppies/dogs are analogies. Each pair of words has the same relationship: Kittens are baby cats, just as puppies are baby dogs. On the COOP, instead of making analogies with words, you will be asked to make them with pictures.

How to Approach Analogies

Here is what an analogy question will look like on the COOP:

1

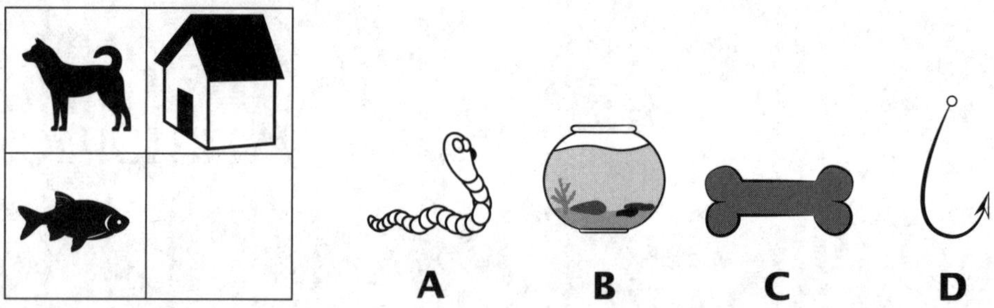

Here's How to Crack It

Even though the COOP asks you to make analogies with pictures, the best way to solve them is to turn those pictures into words. To figure out the relationship between two words, make a sentence using the words. Finally, use that *same sentence* for each of the answer choices, and see which one fits best.

The top two pictures show a dog and a doghouse. What sentence could we make with these two words?

A dog **lives in** a doghouse.

Now let's use that same sentence with the remaining picture and each of the answer choices.

A fish **lives in** a _________.

Does a fish live in a worm? No. Cross off (A). Does a fish live in a fish bowl? Yes. Let's leave (B) in the running. Does a fish live in a dog bone? No. Cross off (C). Does a fish live in a hook? No. Cross off (D). Since we have crossed off (A), (C), and (D), the best answer must be (B).

Let's try one more:

2

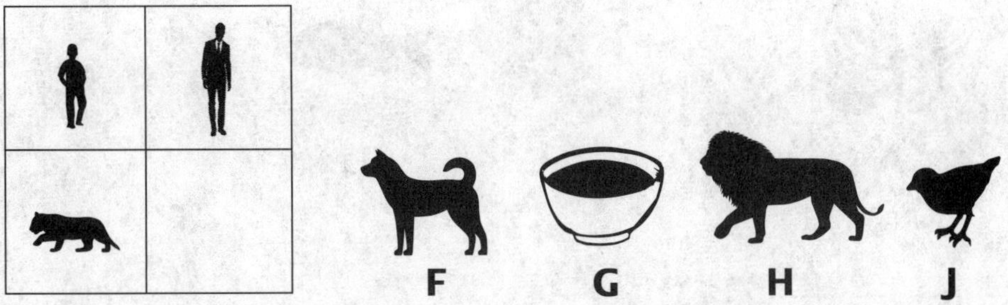

What kind of sentence could we make using the words boy and man?

A boy **is a small** man.

Here's How to Crack It

Now let's try that same sentence with the answer choices. Is a cat a small dog? No. Cross off (F). Is a cat a small bowl of milk? No. Cross off (G). Is a cat a small lion? Maybe. Let's leave H in the running. Is a cat a small bird? No. Cross off (J). This makes (H) the best choice.

As you can see, you should expect to use Process of Elimination on these questions. The one that fits best is the one you should pick.

Now let's put it all together.

COOP Analogy Exercise 1

Answers can be found in Chapter 24.

Choose the picture that would go in the empty box so that the bottom two pictures are related in the same way the top two are related.

1

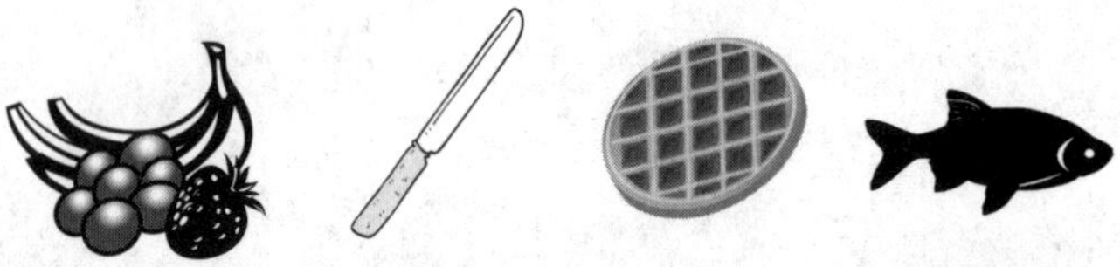

A B C D

2

F G H J

3

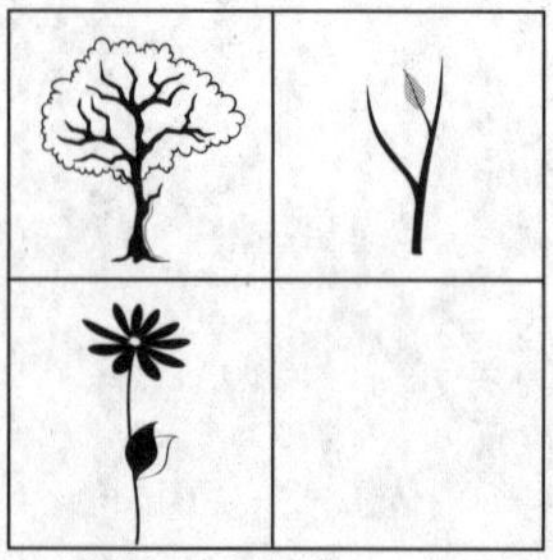

A B C D

4

F

G

H

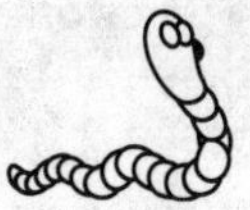
J

5

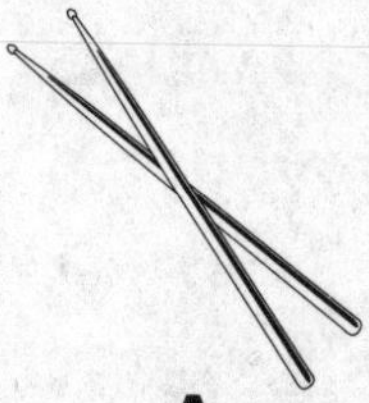
A

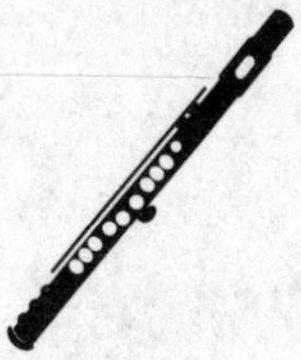
B

C

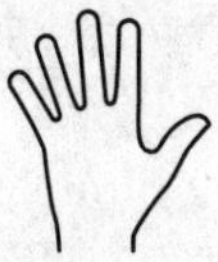
D

Timing

On the COOP, you have seven minutes to complete twenty analogies. This means that you have to move along fairly quickly. If you get stuck on one problem, move on to the next. There are probably easier ones later in the section, and you can always come back to a difficult problem if you have time left at the end. Now that you understand how to crack these questions, go back to the first practice test and rework any of the analogy problems that you found difficult.

Time to take a walk
and let all that info sink in!

Chapter 19
Quantitative Reasoning

The quantitative reasoning section of the COOP is designed to assess your ability to identify relationships. It is **not** testing your knowledge of mathematics! Rather, like the Sequences section, this portion of the COOP is measuring your ability to recognize relationships.

This section has several different kinds of questions:

- Number relationships
- Visual relationships
- Symbol relationships

NUMBER RELATIONSHIP QUESTIONS

The first set of questions in the quantitative reasoning section will ask you to identify the relationship between the numbers in the first column and the numbers in the second column. Then you must select the missing number from the answer choices.

Here is what a number relationship question will look like:

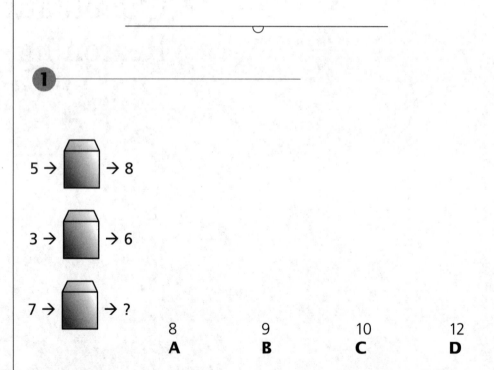

1

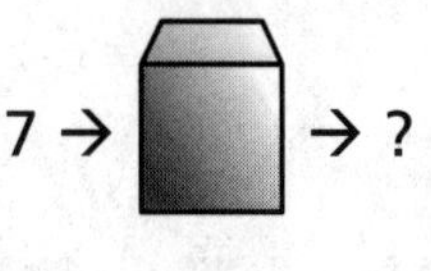

A	B	C	D
8	9	10	12

Here's How to Crack It

Look at the first row: 5 is in the first column and 8 is in the second column. What is the relationship? Well, if 3 is added to 5, 8 is the result. Does that same relationship apply to the second row? It does! If 3 is added to 3, then the result is 6.

Therefore, the relationship between the columns is to add 3 to the first column to produce the second column. Thus, the correct answer is 10, or choice (D), since 7 plus 3 equals 10.

Let's take a look at a second example:

2

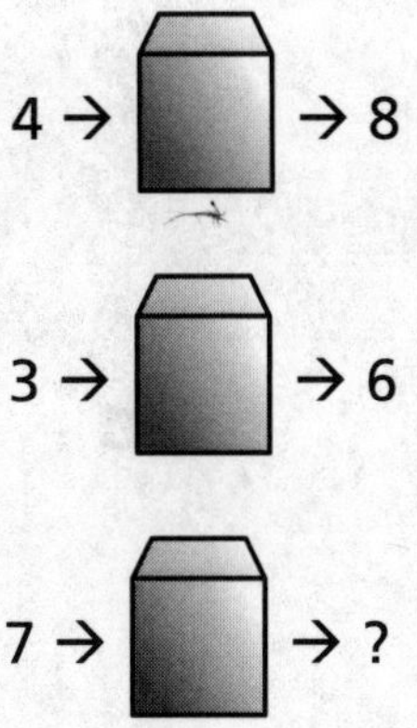

10	11	12	14
F	**G**	**H**	**J**

Here's How to Crack It

Notice how, in this example, adding the same number to the first column each time isn't the correct relationship. In this case, the two columns have a different kind of relationship. So what kind is it? Well, if 4 is multiplied by 2, 8 is the result. Does that same relationship apply to the second row? It does! If 3 is multiplied by 2, then the result is 6. Therefore, the relationship between the columns is to multiply the first column by two to get the value in the second column. Thus, the correct answer is 14, or choice (J), since 7 times 2 equals 14.

VISUAL RELATIONSHIP QUESTIONS

In the second set of questions on the quantitative reasoning section, you will be provided with a figure that is divided up into sections, some of which are shaded. You will be asked to choose the answer that represents the shaded region.

Here is what a visual relationship question will look like:

3

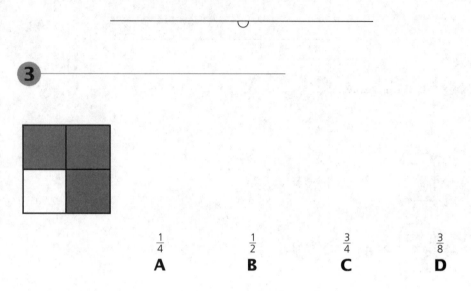

$\frac{1}{4}$	$\frac{1}{2}$	$\frac{3}{4}$	$\frac{3}{8}$
A	**B**	**C**	**D**

Here's How to Crack It

Remember that you're looking for the part of the figure that is shaded. The whole figure is divided into four smaller squares, so count up the number of smaller squares shaded. 3 of the 4 smaller squares are shaded, so that means 3 out of 4 (or $\frac{3}{4}$) is the answer, which is choice (C). If you picked choice (A), $\left(\frac{1}{4}\right)$, remember that on these problems, you are finding the shaded portion of the figure, not the unshaded portion.

Here's another example:

4

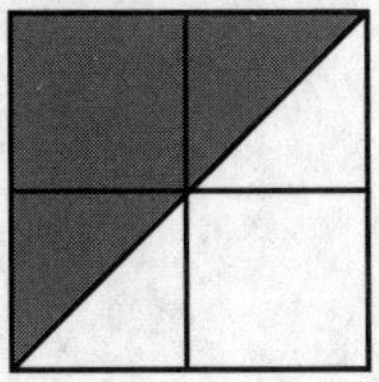

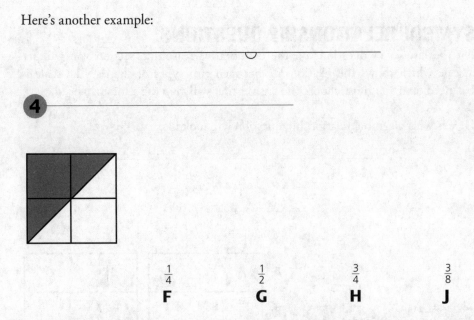

$\frac{1}{4}$	$\frac{1}{2}$	$\frac{3}{4}$	$\frac{3}{8}$
F	**G**	**H**	**J**

Here's How to Crack It

Remember that you're looking for the part of the figure that is shaded. The whole figure is divided into four smaller squares, but in this example two of the smaller squares are only half-shaded. Imagine if those two shaded pieces were put together. What do they make? Together they make a fully shaded smaller square. Therefore, there is a total of two smaller squares shaded. Since 2 of the 4 smaller squares are shaded, that means one half of the figure is shaded, which is choice (G).

SYMBOL RELATIONSHIP QUESTIONS

For the last set of questions on the quantitative reasoning section you will see a scale which shows the relationship between two types of shapes. The scale is balanced, and you must choose the answer that will *keep* the scales balanced.

Here is what a symbol relationship question will look like:

5

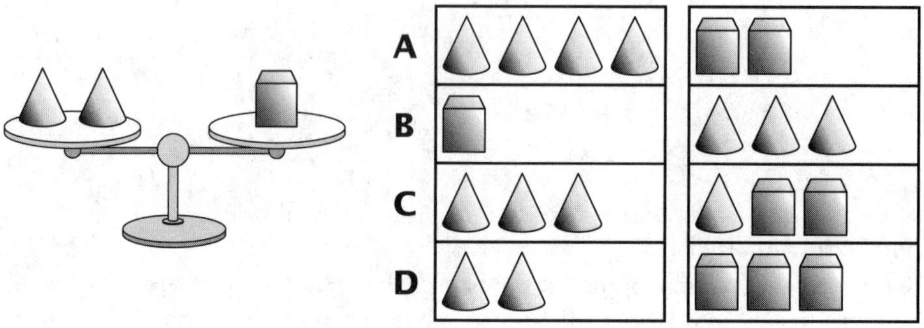

Here's How to Crack It

The goal of these questions is to find a balanced scale—one that uses the same relationship as the original set—so pay attention to how the shapes relate to each other. The correct answer won't necessarily have the same number of shapes as the original. For this example, the original scale shows that 2 cones are equal in weight to 1 cube. Thus, there is a 2:1 relationship between the shapes. The correct answer will also have a 2:1 relationship between cones and cubes. The scale in choice (A) has 4 cones on the left side and 2 cubes on the right side, which is equal to 2 cones to 1 cube, and is therefore the correct answer. The remaining choices would not result in a balanced scale. Remember: 1 cube is equal in weight to 2 cones.

Sometimes you may see two different shapes on one side of the scale in the answer choices. Remember to keep the original relationship in mind and look for a choice that maintains that relationship. Let's look at an example:

6

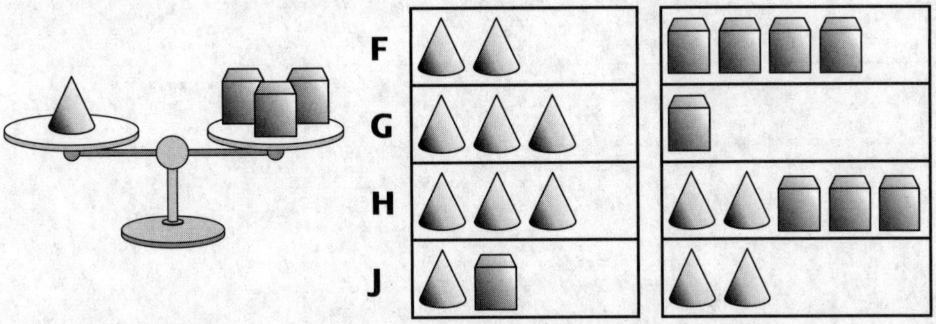

Here's How to Crack It

This question is a little trickier since the correct answer combines the two shapes on one side of the scale. In this example, one cone is equal in weight to 3 cubes. Thus, a cone could be substituted for 3 cubes on the right side of the scale. The scale in choice (H) has 3 cones on the left side of the scale, which is equivalent to 9 cubes. The right side of the scale in choice (H) has 2 cones and 3 cubes. Remember that 1 cone equals 3 cubes, so that means 2 cones are equal to 6 cubes. Add those 6 cubes to the other 3 cubes and that makes a total of 9 cubes. Since the two sides of the scale balance, choice (H) is the correct answer. The remaining choices would not result in a balanced scale.

COOP Quantitative Reasoning Exercise

Answers can be found in Chapter 24.

For Numbers 1-3, find the relationship of the numbers in one column to the numbers in the other column. Then find the missing number.

1

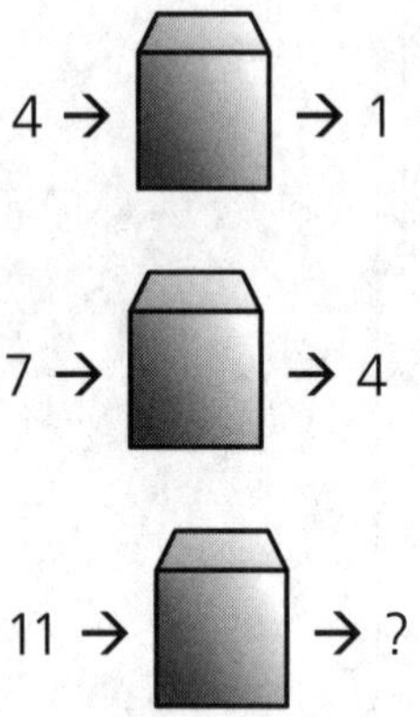

A	B	C	D
1	7	8	14

2

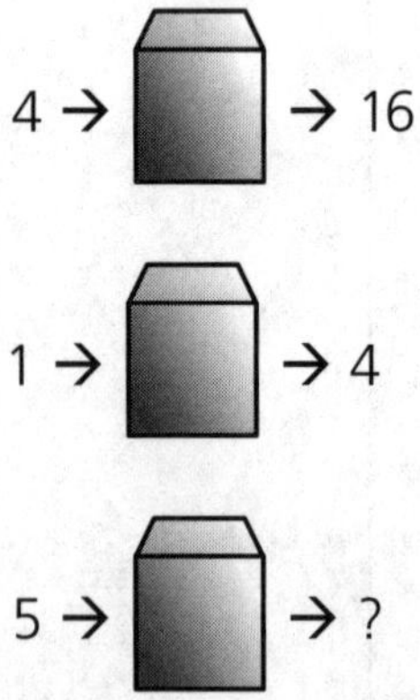

F	G	H	J
8	9	16	20

3

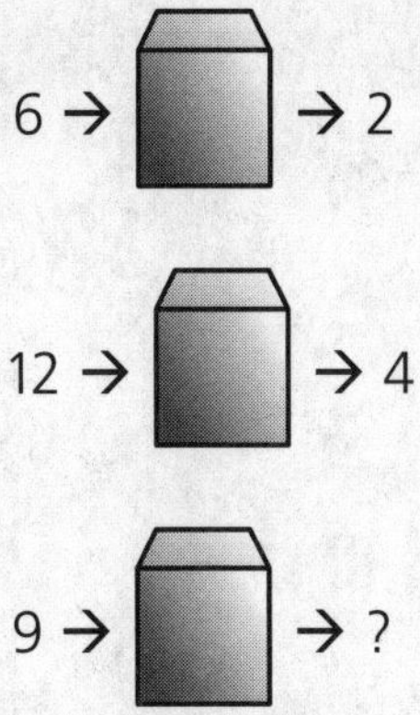

A	B	C	D
2	3	6	8

For Numbers 4–7, find the portion of the figure that is shaded.

4

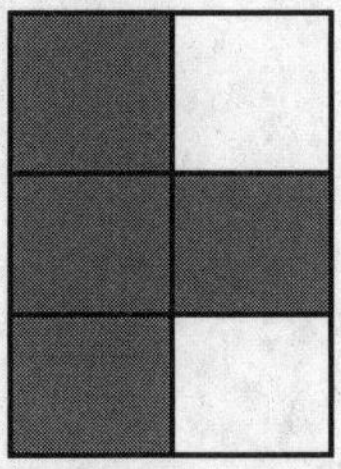

F	G	H	J
$\frac{1}{2}$	$\frac{1}{3}$	$\frac{2}{3}$	$\frac{4}{5}$

5

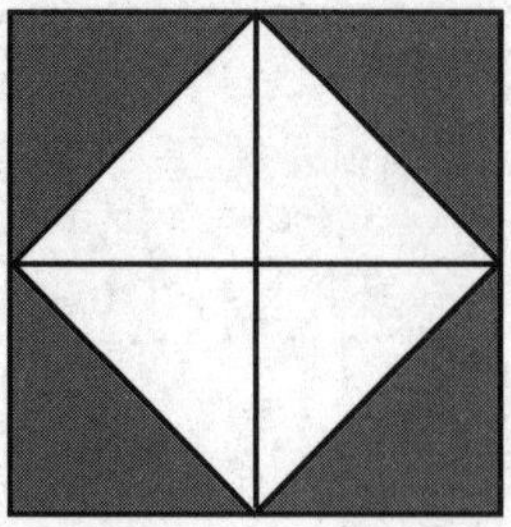

A	B	C	D
$\frac{1}{2}$	$\frac{1}{4}$	$\frac{3}{4}$	$\frac{5}{8}$

6

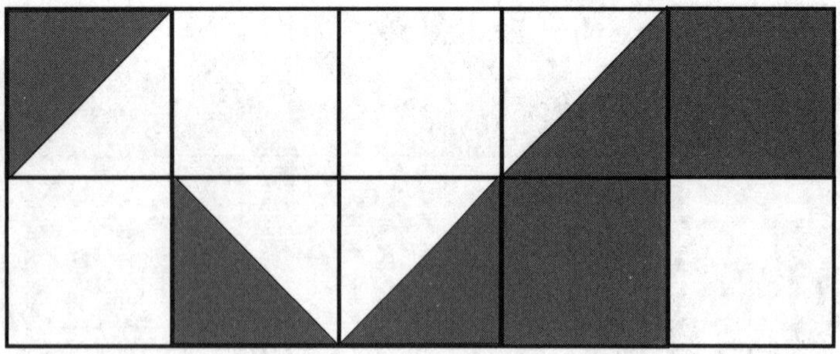

F	G	H	J
$\frac{3}{10}$	$\frac{4}{10}$	$\frac{5}{10}$	$\frac{6}{10}$

7

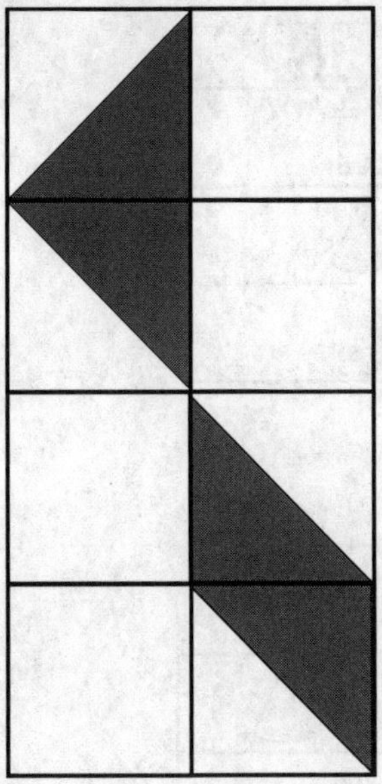

A	B	C	D
$\frac{2}{4}$	$\frac{2}{8}$	$\frac{4}{8}$	$\frac{6}{8}$

For Numbers 8–11, look at the scale showing sets of shapes of equal weight. Find an equivalent pair of sets that would also balance the scale.

8

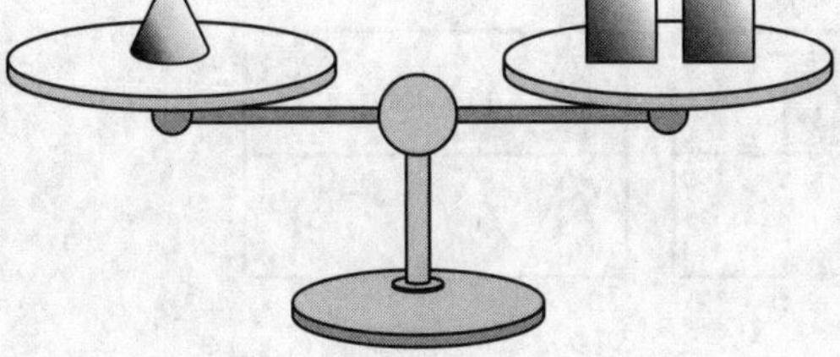

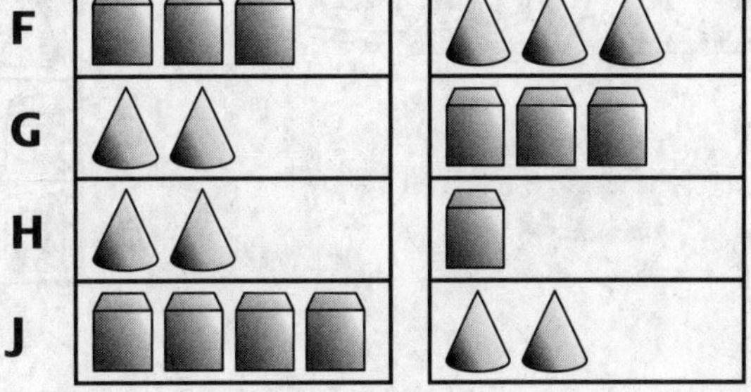

9

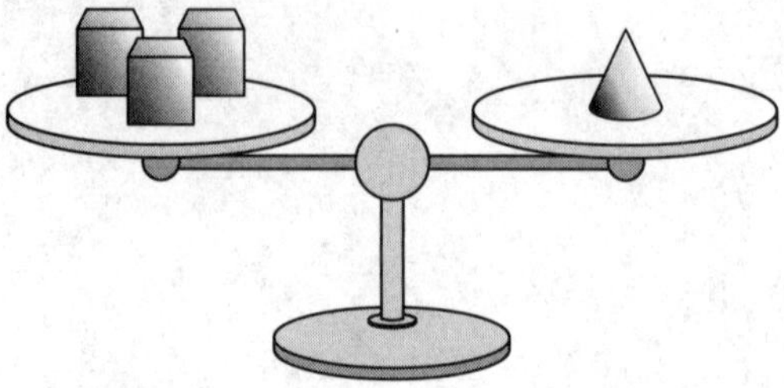

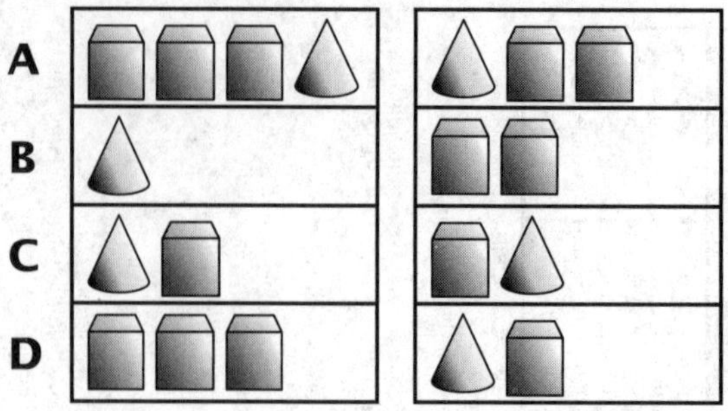

10

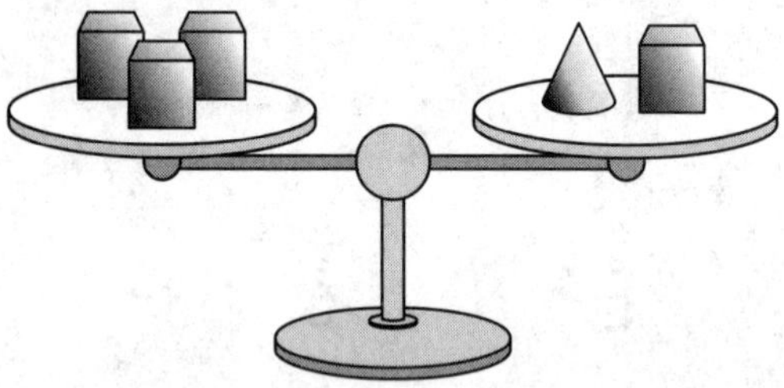

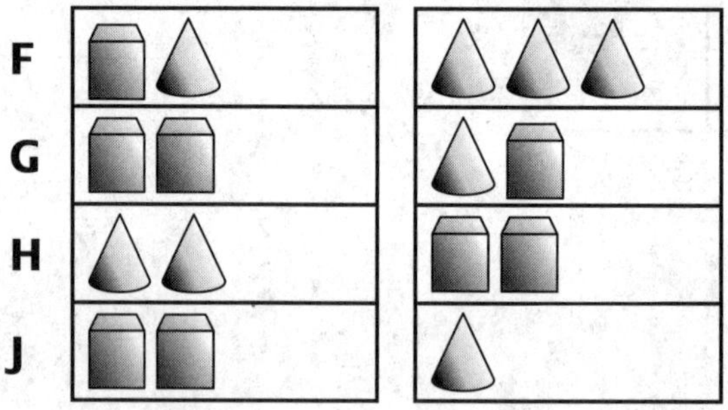

11

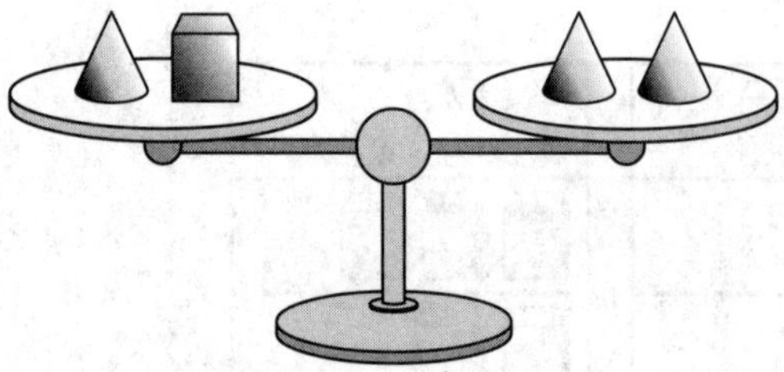

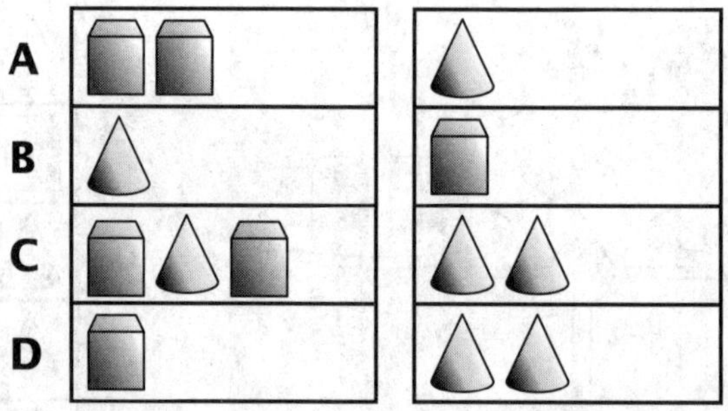

Chapter 20
Verbal Reasoning—Words

The verbal reasoning—words section of the COOP has several different kinds of questions:

- Necessary part
- Two-story analogies
- Must be true
- Mystery language

NECESSARY PART QUESTIONS

The first of the questions in the verbal reasoning section will ask you to think carefully about the meaning of a word and to find the answer choice that is a necessary part of the meaning of that word.

What does *necessary* mean? It means that you're looking for a choice that describes something that the word *cannot do without*. For instance, could you have an apple that was not red? Yes. Could you have an apple that did not have a stem? Yes. Could you have an apple that was not a piece of fruit? No. This means that the word *fruit* is something that is necessary to the idea of the word apple. You can't do without the word *fruit*.

Here is what a necessary part question will look like:

1

apple

A red

B fruit

C store

D stem

Here's How to Crack It

The best way to approach this is to look at the answer choices one at a time, and ask yourself, "Could you do without it?" If the answer is "No," you've found the correct choice. You could have an apple that wasn't red, that wasn't in a store, or that didn't have a stem. Therefore you can eliminate these choices. But you can't have an apple that is not a piece of fruit. You can't do without (B). Therefore (B) is the best answer.

Let's try another example:

2

<u>shirt</u>

F button

G blue

H chest

J sleeve

Here's How to Crack It

Does a shirt have to have a button? No. Cross off (F). Does a shirt have to be blue? No. Cross off (G). Does it have to cover your chest? Probably. Let's leave choice (H). Does it have to have sleeves? Well, most shirts do, but they don't have to. Therefore we can cross off (J). The best answer is (H).

Whenever you find a choice that you're sure is incorrect, cross it off. On more difficult problems, you may find that there are two choices, both of which seem necessary. If you're stuck, take your best guess and move on.

TWO-STORY ANALOGY QUESTIONS

Remember the analogy questions from Chapter 18? The next questions you will see are a bit more complicated. We'll call them two-story analogies.

These problems are trickier because the analogies may go in two directions. The words may relate to each other left to right (horizontally) or up and down (vertically). Let's look at an example of an analogy that relates left to right:

3

inch	**foot**	**yard**
ounce	**pound**	_____

A gallon

B ton

C ruler

D mile

Here's How to Crack It

As with the ordinary analogies, the best way to solve this type of problem is to make a sentence. In this case, we can make sentences with the words on top of the line.

> An **inch** is a smaller distance than a **foot**, and a **foot** is a smaller distance than a **yard**.

In this case, the words on top of the line represent sizes that go from smaller to larger. Now let's use that same idea with the words below the line.

> An **ounce** is a smaller amount than a **pound**, and a **pound** is a smaller amount than a ______________?

Is a pound a smaller amount than a gallon? Not really. A pound measures solid things, and a gallon measures liquids. Cross off (A). Is a pound smaller than a ton? Yes. Is a pound smaller than a ruler? This doesn't make any sense. Cross off (C). Is a pound smaller than a mile? This doesn't make sense, either. It's talking about distance, not weight. Cross off (D). The best answer is (B).

Here's an example of a two-story analogy that goes up and down:

4

dog	**pig**	**horse**
kennel	**sty**	____

F saddle

G hoof

H gallop

J stable

Here's How to Crack It

You can tell this analogy goes up and down, because there's no relation among the words above the line. We can make a sentence only between a word above the line and a word below the line.

A group of **dogs** lives in a **kennel**.

A group of **pigs** lives in a **sty**.

Now let's use that same sentence with the last pair. Does a group of horses live in a saddle? No. Does a group of horses live in a hoof? Definitely not. Does a group of horses live in a gallop? No. Does a group of horses live in a stable? Yes. This makes (J) the best answer. Neat, huh?

MUST-BE-TRUE QUESTIONS

For a must-be-true question, you will be asked to read a few sentences that describe people, places, or things. These sentences will be followed by four short statements. Your job is to find the choice that *must be true* based on the sentences you read.

What Does "Must Be True" Mean?

Look at these two statements.

Jason scored a 92 on his math test.

Lisa scored a 96 on her math test.

There are many things you might assume to be true, given these two statements. Here are some of them.

Lisa is a better student than Jason.

Lisa knows math better than Jason.

Lisa and Jason are in the same math class.

However, none of these choices **must** be true. Sure, they might be true, but we don't really know. Lisa might not be a better student than Jason—maybe she just got lucky on this test, or maybe in most other subjects she scores much worse than Jason. Lisa might not be better at math—maybe she's just taking an easier math class than Jason is taking. We don't know whether or not they're in the same math class. We don't even know whether they're in the same grade or the same school! Don't make any assumptions on must-be-true questions.

What is something that *must* be true given the information above? Only this:

Lisa scored higher on her math test than Jason scored on his math test.

That's the only statement that really *must* be true. It's something that we *know* for certain is true given the facts.

Must-Be-True Questions on the COOP

Here is an example of the way the COOP will give you a must-be-true problem.

Jason goes to math class for exactly two hours per day, English class for exactly one hour per day, and Science class for exactly three hours per day. Jason never takes math and science at the same time. If all of the information above is true, which of the following must also be true?

A Jason likes science class better than he likes math class.

B Jason never goes to history class.

C Jason spends more time in science class per day than in math class.

D For exactly two hours per day, Jason does not take math or science.

Here's How to Crack It

Take each choice one at a time, and ask yourself, "Does this *really* have to be true based on the information in the passage?"

Do we know anything about what Jason likes or does not like? The passage says nothing about this. Therefore we can cross off (A). Do we know that Jason never goes to history class? The passage doesn't say this. Cross off (B). Do we know that he spends more time each day in science class than in math class? Yes, since he spends three hours in science class and two hours in math class. Leave (C) in. Do we know Jason does not take math or science for exactly two hours per day? If we knew how many total hours were in Jason's school day, we might be able to figure it out. But as it stands, we can't know whether this is true or not, so we can cross off (D). The best answer is (C).

MYSTERY LANGUAGE QUESTIONS

Finally, you will see a couple questions that we call mystery language questions. These questions ask you to figure out the way to say something in an imaginary foreign language.

The following is an example of a mystery language question.

maxelipoti means science book
yipipoti means history book.
maxeligolub means science teacher

Which of the following could mean history teacher?

A *yipigolub*

B *maxeliyipi*

C *maxeligolub*

D *yipipoti*

Here's How to Crack It

Step 1: Find two mystery words that have one set of letters that are the same, and then see what English word they have in common. This is what that set of letters must mean.

In this case, we can see that the first two mystery words both have "poti" in them. These two words share the English word "book," so "poti" must mean "book."

We can also see that the first and third mystery words have the letters "maxeli" in them. These two words share the English word "science," so "maxeli" must mean "science."

Step 2: Use Process of Elimination to eliminate those parts of the mystery words that do not correspond with the English word you are asked for.

In this case, we are asked for the word that means "history teacher." We know that "poti" means "book" and that "maxeli" means "science." Therefore we can cross off any choice with "poti" or "maxeli" in it. This will allow us to cross off (B), (C), and (D). The correct answer is (A): "Yipi" means history and "golub" means teacher.

COOP Verbal Reasoning—Words Exercise

Answers can be found in Chapter 24.

For Numbers 1-2, find the word that names a necessary part of the underlined word.

1

pen

A letter

B ink

C hand

D black

2

book

F picture

G history

H page

J introduction

For Numbers 3-4, the words in the top row are related in a certain way. The words in the bottom row are related in the same way. Find the word that completes the bottom row of words.

3

walk	**skip**	**run**
tug	**pull**	____

A yank

B draw

C lift

D push

4

tie	**bracelet**	**belt**
neck	**wrist**	____

F watch

G waist

H joint

J jewelry

5

At a track meet, Irene ran in 8 races. She won one gold medal, two silver medals, and three bronze medals. After the track meet she saw a movie and had dinner with her parents.

According to the information above, which of the following must be true?

A Irene's family watched her win her medals at the track meet.

B Irene's favorite activity is running races.

C Irene set a record in one of the events.

D Irene won a greater number of silver medals than gold medals.

6

Paul can jump farther than David and Jeff. Jeff and Edwin can both jump farther than Larry.

Based on the information above, which of the following must be true?

F Larry cannot jump as far as Paul can.

G Paul can jump farther than anyone else at school.

H Larry does not practice jumping very often.

J Jeff jumps father than David.

7

uticitho means pear tree
oopicitho means pear juice
utilanno means orange tree

Which of the following could mean orange juice?

A *utioopi*

B *oopilanno*

C *oopicitho*

D *uticitho*

8

tolomaguni means front window
tolokala means back window
werimaguni means front door

Which of the following could mean back door?

F *werikala*

G *weritolo*

H *tolomaguni*

J *kalamaguni*

Chapter 21
Verbal Reasoning—Context

HOW TO THINK ABOUT VERBAL REASONING—CONTEXT

Reading the passages on the COOP is different from most other kinds of reading that you will do in school. You might think that you have to read slowly enough to learn all the information in the passage. But there is much more information in the passage than you can learn in a short time, and you will be asked about only a few facts from the passage. So trying to understand all of the facts in the passage is not the best use of your time.

Most importantly, you don't get points for understanding everything in the passage. You only get points for answering questions correctly. Therefore, we're going to teach you the best strategy to get the most correct answers.

There is one more important thing to know, which works to your advantage: The answer to every question can be found somewhere in the passage. All you've got to do is find it. This means that you should think of verbal reasoning—context like a treasure hunt: You need to use clues in the questions to find the answers in the passage and earn your points.

Strategy for Attacking Verbal Reasoning—Context

Step 1: Read the passage and label each paragraph. Don't try to learn every single fact in the passage; you can always go back later. It is important only to get a general idea of what each paragraph talks about.

Step 2: Answer the general questions based on your paragraph labels.

Step 3: Answer the specific questions by looking back at the passage and finding the answer.

Important! In steps 2 and 3, answer your questions by using Process of Elimination. The test writers will often try to disguise the correct answer by using different words that mean basically the same thing as the words used in the passage. You might not recognize these words right away as the ones used in the passage. Why do the test writers do this? If they gave you the exact same words straight out of the passage, that would be too easy. Your best bet is to cross off the choices that you know are wrong and pick from the choices that are left.

Now let's look at each step in more detail.

Step 1: Label Your Paragraphs

Every good treasure hunt needs a map, which will help you locate the answers in the passage. The best way to make a map is to label your paragraphs as you read. This will help you understand the main idea of the passage and at the same time make it easier to locate facts in the passage while you're reading.

After you finish each paragraph, stop for a moment and ask yourself, "What is this paragraph about?" Try to summarize the idea of this paragraph in seven or eight words, and quickly write this summary in the margin. This way you'll have a guide to important parts of the passage when you have to answer a question.

After you have read the entire passage, take a moment and ask yourself, "What is this whole passage about?" Write a one-sentence summary at the bottom of the page. This will help you answer any main-idea questions you may see. Try doing Step 1 for the following passage:

Contrary to popular belief, the first European known to lay eyes on America was not Christopher Columbus or Amerigo Vespucci, but a little-known Viking named Bjarni Herjolfsson. In the summer of 986, Bjarni sailed from Norway to Iceland, heading for the Viking settlement where his father Heriulf resided.

When he arrived in Iceland, Bjarni discovered that his father had already sold his land and estates and set out for the latest Viking settlement on the subarctic island called Greenland. Discovered by an <u>infamous</u> murderer and criminal named Erik the Red, Greenland lay at the limit of the known world. Dismayed, Bjarni set out for this new colony.

Since the Vikings traveled without a chart or compass, it was not uncommon for them to lose their way in the unpredictable northern seas. Beset by fog, the crew lost their bearings. When the fog finally cleared, they found themselves before a land that was level and covered with woods. They traveled farther up the coast, finding more flat, wooded country. Farther north, the landscape revealed glaciers and rocky mountains. Without knowing it, Bjarni had arrived in North America.

Though Bjarni realized this was an unknown land, he was no intrepid explorer. Rather, he was a practical man who had simply set out to find his father. Refusing his crew's request to go ashore, he promptly turned his bow back to sea. After four days' sailing, Bjarni landed at Herjolfsnes on the southwestern tip of Greenland, the exact place he had been seeking all along.

What is this whole passage about? ____________________

Your labels and passage summary should look something like this:

Paragraph 1: America was first visited by Bjarni Herjolfsson.

Paragraph 2: Herjolfsson wanted to follow his father to Greenland.

Paragraph 3: He got lost and ended up at America.

Paragraph 4: He turned around and finally reached Greenland.

Summary: How Bjarni Herjolfsson got lost and saw America before anyone else.

Now we have a good picture of the overall point of the passage, and we should be able to look back and find any details we need. So let's turn to the questions.

Step 2: Answer the General Questions

It's usually best to answer the general questions first. These questions ask you about the passage as a whole. There are several types of general questions, and they look like this.

Main Idea/Purpose

- The passage is mostly about
- The main idea of this passage is
- The best title for this passage would be
- The purpose of this passage is to
- The author wrote this passage in order to

Tone/Attitude

- The author's tone is best described as
- The attitude of the author is one of

General Interpretation

- The author would most likely agree that
- It can be inferred from the passage that
- The passage implies that
- You would probably find this passage in a
- This passage is best described as

To answer a main idea/purpose question, ask yourself, "What did the passage talk about most?" Look at the choices and cross off anything that was not discussed or that was only a detail of the passage.

To answer a tone/attitude question, ask yourself, "How does the author feel about the subject?" Cross off anything that doesn't agree with the author's view.

To answer a general interpretation question, ask yourself, "Which answer sounds most like what the author said?" Cross off anything that was not discussed in the paragraph or that does not agree with the author's view.

Let's take a look at some general questions for this passage:

1 **The passage is mostly about**

A the Vikings and their civilization

B the waves of Viking immigration

C sailing techniques of Bjarni Herjolfsson

D one Viking's glimpse of America

Here's How to Crack It

To answer this question, let's look back at our labels and our summary of the passage. We said that the main idea of the passage was how Bjarni Herjolfsson got lost and saw America before anyone else. Choices (A) and (B) are about the Vikings in general and not about Herjolfsson, so they can be eliminated. Choice (C) is about Herjolfsson, but his sailing techniques are not really discussed. This makes (D) the best choice.

2 **Which of the following can be inferred from the passage?**

F The word America was first used by Herjolfsson.

G Herjolfsson's discovery of America was an accident.

H Herjolfsson was helped by Native Americans.

J Greenland and Iceland were the Vikings' most important discoveries.

Here's How to Crack It

You should be able to make quick work of this problem by using Process of Elimination. The passage never says anything about Native Americans, so (H) can be eliminated. Also, it doesn't say that Herjolfsson ever used the word *America*, so you can cross off (F). (If you're not positive whether this is true or not, quickly skim back and double-check this in the passage.) We're already down to two choices. Choice (J) is an extreme choice—meaning it uses strong language that makes something absolutely true or false—due to the word most, so it probably is not the answer. If you check the passage, you can see that (J) is never stated. Therefore (G) is the best choice.

Step 3: Answer the Specific Questions

Specific questions ask you about a fact or detail mentioned in the passage. For these questions, look back at the passage to find your answer. These are the different kinds of specific questions.

Fact

- According to the passage
- According to the author
- Which of these questions is answered by the passage?

Vocabulary in Context

- The word <u>pilfer</u> probably means
- What does the passage mean by <u>pilfer</u>?

Specific Interpretation/ Purpose

- The author mentions Mother Goose in order to
- From the information in the passage, Mother Goose would probably

To answer a **Fact** question, look back at the passage and find the lines that mention the thing you are asked about. Use your passage labels to find the information quickly, or simply skim until you find it. Reread those lines to see exactly what the passage says. Then look for a choice that best restates what the passage says. Cross off anything that is never stated or that says the opposite of the information in the passage.

To answer a **Vocabulary in Context** question, look back at the passage and find the underlined word. It will probably be a word that you don't know. Cover the word with your finger. Reread the lines around that word, and think of the word that you would put there. Then look at the answer choices and see which comes closest to the word that you think should go there. If you can't think of the exact word, it's okay to simply note that the word should be a "positive word" or a "negative word."

To answer a **Specific Interpretation/ Purpose** question, look back at the passage and find the lines that discuss the thing you are asked about. Use your passage labels or skim the passage. Reread those lines to see exactly what the passage says. The correct answer will always be very closely based on the information in the passage. For instance, if a passage tells us that John likes to play tennis, we can infer that he will probably play tennis if he is given the chance. Cross off any choices that are not stated in the passage or sound very far off from what the passage says.

3 **According to the passage, Greenland was discovered by**

A Amerigo Vespucci

B Bjarni Herjolfsson's father

C Bjarni Herjolfsson

D Erik the Red

Here's How to Crack It

To answer this question, we should look back at the passage and find the line that talks about the discovery of Greenland. If you skim for the word *Greenland*, you'll find it in the second paragraph: "Discovered by an infamous murderer and criminal named Erik the Red, Greenland lay at the limit of the known world." Therefore the answer is (D).

4 **The word infamous probably means**

F lazy

G strong

H wicked

J intelligent

Here's How to Crack It

Let's reread the line that mentions the word *infamous*: "Discovered by an infamous murderer and criminal named Erik the Red…." Since the word *infamous* describes a *murderer* and *criminal*, it must be a word that describes someone who is bad. Choices (G) and (J) are positive words, so you can eliminate them. Choice (H) sounds much more like a description of a bad person than (F), so the best choice is (H).

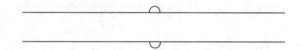

5 **According to the passage, Bjarni Herjolfsson left Norway to**

A start a new colony

B open a trade route to America

C visit his relatives

D map the North Sea

Here's How to Crack It

The end of the first paragraph discusses Herjolfsson's departure. There it states, "Bjarni sailed from Norway to Iceland, heading for the Viking settlement where his father Heriulf resided." The correct answer will use different words, but it should restate the same idea. Can we find anything here about starting a colony? No, so (A) can be eliminated. Does it mention opening a trade route to America? No, so (B) can also be eliminated. (It's true that he does eventually reach America, but that isn't the reason why he left.) Does it mention visiting his relatives? Well, it does say that he wanted to find his father. So let's leave (C). Does this sentence mention mapping the North Sea? No. Choice (D) is wrong, and (C) is the answer.

6 Bjarni's reaction upon landing in Iceland can best be described as

F disappointed

G satisfied

H amused

J fascinated

Here's How to Crack It

Where can we find a description of Bjarni Herjolfsson's arrival in Iceland? At the beginning of the second paragraph. There it states, "When he arrived in Iceland, Bjarni discovered that his father had already sold his land and estates and set out for the latest Viking settlement on the subarctic island called Greenland." Feeling "dismayed," Bjarni left to look for the new colony. Since he had missed his father, he was unhappy. Which word best states this idea? Choice (F).

7 **When the author says, "The crew lost their bearings," this probably means that**

A the ship was damaged beyond repair

B the sailors did not know which way they were going

C the sailors were very angry

D the sailors misplaced their clothes

Here's How to Crack It

Let's reread the lines around "the crew lost their bearings": "since the Vikings traveled without a chart or compass, it was not uncommon for them to lose their way in the unpredictable northern seas. Beset by fog, the crew lost their bearings." Since the story says that the crew would often "lose their way," the best answer is (B).

PROCESS OF ELIMINATION

If you're stuck on which answer is correct, remember to use Process of Elimination to cross off answers you know are wrong. On *general* questions, you'll usually want to cross off answers that

- are not mentioned in the passage
- are too detailed—if the passage mentions something in only one line, it is a detail, not a main idea
- go against, or say the opposite of, information in the passage
- are too big—you can't say much in four or five paragraphs; any answer that says something like, "The passage proves that the theory Einstein spent his entire life creating was right" is probably a wrong answer
- are too extreme—if a choice uses absolute terms such as "all," "every," "never," or "always," it's probably a wrong answer
- go against common sense

On *specific* questions, you should probably cross off answers that

- are extreme
- go against information in the passage
- are not mentioned in the passage
- go against common sense

If you look back at the questions in the sample reading comprehension passage above, you'll see that following these guidelines eliminates many of the wrong answer choices. Use these guidelines when you take the COOP!

What Kind of Answers Do I Keep?

Correct answers tend to be

- restatements or paraphrases of what is said in the passage
- traditional and conservative
- moderate, using words such as "may," "can," and "often."

COOP Verbal Reasoning—Context Exercise

Answers can be found in Chapter 24.

Try the following reading comprehension passage. Don't forget to label your paragraphs!

Although many people associate indoor lighting with modern electrical wiring, practical indoor lighting existed thousands of years before Thomas Edison invented the light bulb. Rudimentary oil lamps, a primitive ancestor of the gaslight, were used in the caves in which prehistoric humans lived.

Approximately 50,000 years ago, cave-dwelling humanoids fashioned a basic oil-based lamp out of animal fat that was kept inside a stone base as well as a wick made out of a cloth-like material. Due to the fact that animal fat smells awful when burned, the lamp gave off a terrible odor.

Thousands of years later, during the Egyptian era (around 1300 B.C.E.) the structure and design of the lamp changed. Instead of using only stone, the Egyptians used a form of decorated pottery with a papyrus-based wick and vegetable oil instead of the foul-smelling animal fat.

In times of need people burned whatever oil was plentiful. Because vegetable oil and animal fat are both edible, in times of hunger people did not burn lamps; they used the oil for food. But oil lamps brought with them other problems. Wicks for the lamps did not always burn away and had to be changed periodically. Soon the oil lamp gave way to the candle, which became a popular source of light in Rome during the first century B.C.E.

1 **What is this passage mostly about?**

- **A** how Egyptians lit their homes
- **B** why the candle is better than the oil lamp
- **C** the history of indoor lighting
- **D** why vegetable oil replaced animal fat in oil lamps

2 **It can be inferred that the author views the change from oil lamps to candles as**

- **F** the most important discovery of human history
- **G** a mistake made by the Romans
- **H** important to the discovery of electricity
- **J** a step in the development of indoor lighting

3 **The word rudimentary most likely means**

- **A** expensive
- **B** basic
- **C** colorful
- **D** handy

4 **The author mentions Thomas Edison in the passage in order to**

- **F** explain his discoveries
- **G** compare him with other modern inventors
- **H** introduce someone that the author will discuss later
- **J** show that Edison was not the first to discover indoor lighting

5 **The word foul probably means**

A awful

B sweet

C fruity

D clean

6 **People probably stopped burning animal fat in lamps because**

F vegetable oil was more plentiful

G they needed the animal fat for cooking

H animal fat smelled bad

J burning animal fat was against the law

7 **The author's tone can best be described as**

A angry

B unconcerned

C instructive

D critical

Chapter 22
Reading and Language Arts

USAGE QUESTIONS

Taking the TACHS? Then pay close attention to this section!

Most of the questions in the language expressions section of the COOP (and TACHS) will ask you to look at five sentences and figure out which one is correctly written. Some of the sentences can be eliminated because they violate the rules of English grammar. Others are wrong because they are awkward or hard to understand.

Follow this procedure for attacking usage questions.

Step 1: Read all five sentences, and eliminate any choice that breaks a rule of grammar.

Step 2: Reread the choices that are left, and cross off any that are awkward or don't make sense.

The sentence you are left with may not sound great, but you should always pick the one that is the best of the bunch—the one that makes the most sense. If you can't narrow it down to only one sentence, that's okay. Cross off what you can, and guess from among the remaining choices.

ERRORS

What kind of errors should you look for? The COOP tests only a few kinds of errors. Learn them, and you'll know what to look for, which can greatly increase your score.

Subject/ Verb Agreement

What is wrong with the following sentences?

1 **The cats in the house watches the bird.**

2 **A wild dingo from Sydney were caught last year.**

To spot subject/verb agreement errors, always find the subject and the verb in the given sentence. To find the subject, ask yourself, "Who or what is acting or being described?" To find the verb, find the action word by asking yourself, "What is the subject doing?" Then make sure that the subject and the verb agree. Subjects and verbs have to agree in both number (singular or plural) and person (I, she, we, you). You may have to read around other parts of the sentence to make it clear to yourself.

What is the subject in sentence 1? It's the cats who are watching the bird. Can you say, "The cats **watches** the bird"? No. *Cats*, in this case, is plural—more than one cat—so the verb has to agree. It should be: "The cats **watch** the bird."

What is the subject in sentence 2? A wild dingo is the thing being described. Can you say, "A wild dingo **were** caught last year"? No; in this case *dingo* is singular, and the verb has to agree with a singular subject. It should be "A wild dingo **was** caught last year."

Verb Form and Tense

What is wrong with the following sentences?

3 **Yesterday, John is going to the playground.**

4 **Patricia has took her hamster to the vet.**

Verb Tense

The word *yesterday* in sentence 3 tells us that the verb should be in the past tense. You can see that this sentence has an error because it clearly says that the action happened yesterday, but the verb "is going" is in the present tense. The sentence should read "Yesterday, John **went** to the playground." *Went* is the past tense of the infinitive verb *to go*. To spot tense problems, look for words and phrases that indicate present or past, such as

- today (present)
- now (present)
- yesterday (past)
- last week (past)
- in 1956 (past)
- once (past)
- a long time ago (past)
- during the Second World War (past)

Verb Form

Sometimes the error will be in the verb form, such as in sentence 4. Recognizing correct verb form is as simple as knowing the proper present, past, and future forms of verbs. The COOP will not ask you to identify and name verb forms, just to choose the correct version of the sentence. Usually, it should be obvious to you when a verb form is wrong because the sentence just won't make sense. The past tense form of the verb *to take* would be either *took* or *has taken.* You could say, "Patricia **took** her hamster to the vet" or "Patricia **has taken** her hamster to the vet." But *has took* is not a possible form. Make sure that you review proper verb forms as part of your preparation for the COOP.

Adjective/ Adverbs

What is wrong with the following sentence?

5 **Kim ran quick around the track.**

What is the word *quick* describing? The way that Kim ran around the track. If a word describes a person or a thing, it should be an adjective like *quick*. But if a word describes an action (verb), it should be an adverb like *quickly*. Don't forget: Most adverbs end in *-ly*.

Remember this rule: Adjectives modify nouns; adverbs modify everything else.

Comparison Words

What is wrong with the following sentences?

6 **He was one of the most greatest authors of his time.**

7 **She is intelligenter than he is.**

Some questions on the COOP will ask you to determine the correct form of a comparison word. In the sentences above, *greatest* and *more intelligent* are the correct forms of the comparison words. For most adjectives that have only one syllable, we make them into comparison words by adding *–er* and *–est* to the end of the word, such as big, bigger, biggest and great, greater, greatest.

For most adjectives with more than one syllable, we make the comparison using the words more and most, as with intelligent, more intelligent, most intelligent, and interesting, more interesting, most interesting.

Pronoun Agreement and Case

8 **The dog ran away, but they soon came back**

9 **Murray is a man which loves to play the piano.**

10 **Olivia gave the assignment to Peter and I.**

Pronouns are words such as *I, it, they, me,* and *she* that take the place of nouns. Whenever you see pronouns in a sentence, check to make sure that they agree with the nouns they stand for and that they are in the proper case. Pronoun *agreement* means that singular pronouns stand in for singular nouns, and plural pronouns stand in for plural nouns. In sentence 8, the subject is "the dog," which is singular, but the pronoun "they" is plural. The sentence should read "The dog ran away, but it soon came back."

Another important rule to remember is to use the pronoun *who* for people and *which* or *that* for things. Therefore sentence 9 should read "Murray is a man who loves to play the piano."

Pronoun *case* means that the subject of the sentence (the thing doing the acting) needs a subject pronoun, and the object of a sentence (the thing receiving the action) needs an object pronoun. In the sentence "Mary threw the ball to John." Mary is the subject and John is the object. Below is a chart that tells you how to use a pronoun, whether it is the subject or the object.

Subject	**Example**
I	I left the office.
You	You should get some rest.
He/she/it	He knew the best route to take.
We	We love to visit our grandparents.
They	They live in California.
Object	**Example**
Me	My boss told me to go home.
You	A good night's sleep would do you some good.
Him/her/it	Jenny refused to tell him the best route to take.
Us	Our grandparents love us.
Them	We visited them in California.

In sentence 10, does the word *I* describe someone who is giving the book (a subject) or someone to whom the book was given (an object)? Think about it this way: We say *I* gave it to *him*, but *he* gave it to *me.* In the example sentence, the word *I* describes someone who received the action, not someone who was doing the action. So the pronoun used should be the object pronoun, and the sentence should read "Olivia gave the assignment to Peter and **me**." If you are confused about the correct answer, try this trick: Take away the word *Peter* and see what is left. You wouldn't say, "Olivia gave the assignment to I," but you would say, "Olivia gave the assignment to me."

Important note: Whenever a pronoun follows a proposition (such as *to, of, in, at, around, between,* and *from*) the pronouns are *always* in the object case.

Here are some common pronoun mix-ups. Don't forget them! Recognizing pronouns is a simple way to rack up points on the COOP.

It's = it is	It's raining outside.
Its = belongs to it	The dog eats its bone.
You're = you are	You're a great friend.
Your = belongs to you	I love your shoes.
Who's = who is	Who's at the door?
Whose = belongs to who	Whose car is this?

Sentence Fragments

What is wrong with the following sentences?

11 **Told me that I would have to see the dentist.**

12 **The elephant, after eating dinner, walking around the zoo.**

Every sentence has to express a complete thought and have both a subject and a verb. What is the subject in sentence 11? Who or what told me to go to the dentist? There is no subject in this sentence, and therefore it is only a sentence fragment. Sentence fragments are not complete sentences and are never the correct answer on the COOP.

Sentence 12 has a subject—the elephant—but it has no true verb. It is also a fragment so we know it's an error!

Parallelism

What is wrong with the following sentences?

13 **Lawrence left the house and going to school.**

14 **Erica wanted to eat lunch, visit her friend, and to play soccer.**

Whenever you read a sentence that contains a list of actions or objects, check to make sure that the items in the list are all in the same form. For instance, in sentence 13 there are two actions. The first action is that Lawrence left the house. So the second action must be in the same form; however, *left* and *going* aren't in the same form. The second part of the sentence should read "Lawrence went to school" to make this a parallel sentence.

In sentence 14, there are three items that Erica wanted: to *eat* lunch, *visit* her friend, and to *play* soccer. Are these three items in the same form? No. The first and the third items in the list use the infinitive verb forms—*to eat* and *to play*—but the second does not. To be parallel and correct, the sentence should read "Erica wanted to eat lunch, to visit her friend, and to play soccer." You could also say, "Erica wanted to eat lunch, visit her friend, and play soccer." Make sure you check to see what your answer choices are.

Double Negative

What is wrong with the following sentence?

15 **Paul has hardly seen no birds today.**

In English, you should have only one negative word in the same phrase. When a sentence has two, it is called a double negative. All of the following are double negatives, and are always considered incorrect.

- can't hardly
- can't never
- barely none
- barely never
- won't never
- won't hardly
- hardly never
- hardly none
- hasn't got none

Errors Exercise

Answers can be found in Chapter 24.

1. **There is already many people in the auditorium.**

2. **Since my father's company has so much business, they are very busy.**

3. **My uncle often help my parents to make dinner.**

4. **Henry going to school, runs into his friend.**

5. **The giant mouse ran through the house and escaping from the cat.**

6. **Last year, Ines won the first prize and receives a beautiful trophy.**

7. **Roger finished his most biggest assignment.**

8. **Colin cleaned the bowl and gives it to his mother.**

SENTENCE COMPLETIONS

A few questions in the language expression section will ask you to complete a sentence by filling in a blank.

Check it out, TACHS takers! This one's for you!

Some of the questions in this section of the TACHS will test how well you can pick the correct word based on the "direction" of the sentence.

How would you fill in the blanks in the following sentences.

1 **I really like you _____ you are very friendly.**

2 **I really like you _____ you are a very nasty person.**

In sentence 1, you probably picked a word like "because." How did you know that this word was the right one to choose? Because the idea after the blank ("are very friendly") kept going in the *same direction* as the idea before the blank ("I really like you"). The sentence started out with a positive idea and continued with a positive idea.

In sentence 2, you probably picked something like "but," "although," or "even though." Why? Because the idea after the blank ("you are a very nasty person") went in the *opposite direction* from the idea before the blank ("I really like you"). The sentence started out with a positive idea and then changed to a negative idea.

Here are lists of same-direction and opposite-direction words:

Same-Direction

- and
- moreover
- in fact
- for instance
- for example
- so
- therefore
- because
- since

Opposite-Direction

- however
- but
- yet

- although
- though
- nevertheless
- nonetheless
- despite
- rather
- instead
- in contrast

Try the following example:

3 **Susie's mother wanted her to be a dancer; ______ Susie felt like becoming a doctor.**

A because,

B however,

C in fact,

D rather,

E in general,

Here's How to Crack It

In this case, the idea after the blank ("becoming a doctor") goes in the opposite direction from the idea before the blank ("be a dancer"). Therefore we can eliminate (A), (C), and (E). If you get no further, you have a great guess. The best choice is (B).

Other questions will test the same rules of grammar you have already learned earlier in this chapter—especially the rules of comparison words and double negatives.

Here is a sample problem.

4 **John is the _____ player on our soccer team.**

F more important

G most important

H much important

J importanter

K importantest

Here's How to Crack It

We've already learned that with comparison words that have more than one syllable we can only use more or most. Choices (H), (J), and (K) are not grammatically correct and can be eliminated. Since we are comparing John with all the other players on the team, we want to use most important, (G).

FIND THE SUBJECT/PREDICATE

You'll also see a set of questions that asks you for the simple subject of the sentence, while some questions will ask you for simple predicate (verb) of the sentence.

What is a simple subject? The simple subject is always the noun that is performing the action or being described in a sentence. This means that the simple subject

- must be a noun (person, place or thing) and
- is not describing something else

The latter part is tricky. Nouns can be used to describe things when they are used after words such as *in, on, at, around, under, after, when,* and *that.*

Look at the following sentences:

5 **The cat is on the mat.**

6 **The cat that belongs to John is on the mat.**

7 **After eating lunch in the kitchen, the cat took a bath.**

8 **When John came home, the cat began to run around the house.**

Here's How to Crack It

In sentence 5, the word *mat* is a noun, but it is part of the phrase "on the mat," which describes where the cat is sitting. Therefore *mat* cannot be the simple subject. In sentence 6, the word *John* is a noun, but it is part of the phrase "that belongs to John," which describes the cat. Therefore *John* cannot be the simple subject. In sentence 7, the words *lunch* and *kitchen* are nouns, but they are part of the phrase "After eating lunch in the kitchen," which describes what the cat did earlier in the day. In sentence 8, the words *John*, *home*, and *house* are nouns, but they are part of phrases that describe the cat.

In all four sentences, "the cat" is the simple subject.

Follow these steps to answer questions that ask you for the simple subject.

Step 1: Cross off any words that you know are not nouns—verbs, adjectives, and adverbs.

Step 2: Cross off any words that are not the simple subject—any noun that follows a preposition such as *in, at, of,* or *to* and any noun that appears in a phrase that begins with *if, when, since, after,* or *that.*

What is a simple predicate (verb)? The simple predicate is always the main verb in the sentence. This means that the simple predicate

- must be a verb (an action word) and
- is not describing something else

Again, the latter part is tricky. Just like nouns, verbs can be used to describe other things when they appear in phrases that begin with words such as *if, when, after,* and *that.*

9 **The cat slept on the mat that John made at school.**

10 **Since she was tired from running in the park, the cat slept on the mat.**

11 **While John cooked dinner, the cat slept on the mat.**

Here's How to Crack It

In sentence 9, the word *made* is a verb, but it is part of the phrase "that John made," which describes who made the mat. Therefore *made* cannot be the simple verb. In sentence 10, the word *was* is a verb, but it is part of the phrase "Since she was tired," which describes the cat. Therefore *was* cannot be the simple verb. In sentence 11, the word *cooked* is a verb, but it is part of the phrase "While John cooked dinner," which describes what John did while the cat was asleep.

In all three sentences, "slept" is the simple predicate.

Follow these steps to answer questions that ask you for the simple predicate.

Step 1: Cross off any words that you know are not verbs—nouns, adjectives, and adverbs.

Step 2: Cross off any words that are not simple verbs—any verb that follows a word such as *if, when, since, after,* or *that.*

Simple Subject Exercise

Answers can be found in Chapter 24.

1 **After many years, Jonathan finally found his favorite cat.**

2 **The most important part was probably the discovery of the Northwest Passage.**

3 **When she figured out the answer, her teacher was very pleased with her.**

4 **If he had known about his neighbor's collie, he never would have said that his dog was the fastest.**

Simple Predicate Exercise

Answers can be found in Chapter 24.

1 **Since his sister had already washed the dishes, Jonas volunteered to dry them.**

2 **In order to finish the race without falling down, Alexander drank a great deal of water.**

3 **Adrienne never imagined that she would be chosen to play the leading role in the production.**

4 **Because Laurie ate too much, she felt too sick to play soccer.**

STRUCTURE QUESTIONS

A few questions in this section will ask you to choose which sentences fit best with our other sentences in a paragraph. You may be asked to find

- the best topic sentence
- the sentences that best follow a topic sentence
- which sentence belongs in the paragraph
- which sentence does not belong in the paragraph

To answer all of these questions, make sure that the ideas are in a logical order from one sentence to the next.

What is a topic sentence? A topic sentence is the first sentence in a paragraph, and it is supposed to introduce the idea that will follow. The sentences that follow the topic sentence should talk more about the subject that is mentioned in the topic sentence. To answer a question that asks you to find the best topic sentence, you should read the sentences in the paragraph and ask yourself, "What are these sentences talking about?" Then look at the answer choices and find the one that best fits the idea.

To answer a question that asks you to find the sentences that should follow a topic sentence, read the topic sentence and ask yourself, "What is the main idea in this topic sentence?" Then find the sentences that describe this idea in more detail.

To answer a question that asks you which sentence belongs in the paragraph, read the sentences before and after the blank. You should find a sentence that discusses the same ideas as the sentences before and after it, while watching out for same-direction or opposite-direction words.

To answer a question that asks you which sentence does not belong, read the paragraph and ask yourself what the paragraph is about. Then reread it, and find the sentence that does not discuss this same idea or suddenly changes the topic.

Take a look at the following examples.

19 **Which of the following is the best topic sentence for this paragraph?**

________________________________. It was first made in China around 100 B.C.E. from bits of plants and tree bark. At first it was rough, and not very suitable for official documents. Soon, however, people found ways to make it flat and even. Over the next few hundred years, paper was introduced to the rest of Asia, where it was used to keep government documents and religious inscriptions.

A Today, many documents are stored electronically instead of on paper.

B The ancient Chinese discovered many useful things.

C Paper has a long and interesting history.

D Modern governments would not be able to survive without paper.

E One interesting kind of art is the making of beautiful paper.

Here's How to Crack It

If we read the paragraph, we see that it is mostly about the history of paper. Therefore, the topic sentence should introduce the idea. Choice (B) is not specifically about paper at all, and (A), (D), and (E) are not about the history of paper. Therefore, (C) is the best choice.

20 **Which of the following sentences does not belong in the paragraph?**

1) One of the most loved musical styles today is blues. 2) Blues originated in the early 1900s in America. 3) It was born from a combination of African-American work chants and gospel songs. 4) The blues got its name from the introduction of special "blue notes," which are created by "bending" normal notes up or down. 5) These blue notes give the song a certain sad sound that people recognize as part of the blues. 6) While some people like sad music, other people prefer happier songs. 7) In the 1920s, blues began to incorporate elements from jazz, dance music, and show tunes. 8) Today, blues has spread to many different countries and is one of the most popular types of music in the world.

F sentence 2

G sentence 3

H sentence 4

J sentence 5

K sentence 6

You've absorbed a lot of information! Now get outside and get some fresh air! Or eat a snack! Or listen to a song. Just give yourself a break.

Here's How to Crack It

If we read the paragraph, we see that it is about the musical style called blues. Each sentence talks about this idea except for sentence 6, which talks about whether people like happy or sad music. This makes (K) the best choice.

Chapter 23
Mathematics

Most of the questions in this section require you to do some amount of arithmetic. Let's take a moment to review the basics.

MATH VOCABULARY

Term	Definitions	Examples
integer	any number that does not contain either a fraction or a decimal	–4, –1, 0, 9, 15
positive number	any number greater than zero	$\frac{1}{2}$, 1, 4, 101
negative number	any number less than zero	$-\frac{1}{2}$, –1, –4, –101
even number	any number that is evenly divisible by two	–2, 0, 2, 8, 24 (*Note:* 0 is even)
odd number	any number that is not evenly divisible by two	–1, 1, 5, 35
prime number	any number that is evenly divisible only by one and itself	2, 3, 5, 7, 11, 13 (*Note:* 1 is not a prime number)
sum	the result of addition	The sum of 6 and 2 is 8.
difference	the result of subtraction	The difference between 6 and 4 is 2.
product	the result of multiplication	The product of 3 and 4 is 12.

COOP Math Vocabulary Exercise

Answers can be found in Chapter 24.

1. How many integers are there between –4 and 5?

2. How many positive integers are there between –4 and 5?

3. What is the sum of 6, 7, and 8?

4. What is the product of 2, 4, and 8?

ORDER OF OPERATIONS

How would you do the following problem?

$$4 + 5 \times 3 - (2 + 1)$$

Whenever you have a problem such as this, remember the rule.

Please **E**xcuse **M**y **D**ear **A**unt **S**ally

Believe it or not, this sentence tells you the order in which you should solve the above problem. This stands for:

Parentheses
Exponents
Multiplication and **D**ivision (from left to right)
Addition and **S**ubtraction (from left to right)

Therefore we need to solve the parentheses first.

$$4 + 5 \times 3 - (2 + 1)$$

becomes

$$4 + 5 \times 3 - 3$$

Next, we do multiplication and division to get

$$4 + 15 - 3$$

Finally, we add and subtract to get our final answer of 16.

COOP Order of Operations Exercise

Answers can be found in Chapter 24.

1 $15 - 5 + 3 =$ ____

2 $15 - 2 \times 3 =$ ____

3 $2 \times (2 + 3) - 5 =$ ____

4 $20 + 3 \times 5 + 10 =$ ____

5 $(3 + 6) \times 3 \times 4 =$ ____

FRACTIONS

A fraction is just another way of representing division. For instance, $\frac{2}{5}$ actually means two divided by five (which is 0.4 as a decimal). Another way to think of this is to imagine a pie cut into five pieces: $\frac{2}{5}$ means two out of the five pieces. The parts of the fraction are called the numerator and the denominator. The numerator is the number on top; the denominator is the number on the bottom.

$$\frac{\text{numerator}}{\text{denominator}}$$

Reducing Fractions

Often you'll need to reduce your fractions after you have made a calculation. This means that you want to make the numbers as small as possible. To reduce a fraction, simply divide top and bottom by the same number. Don't spend too long trying to figure out the best number to divide by; use 2, 3, or 5, and keep dividing until you can't divide anymore.

For example, if you have the fraction $\frac{42}{18}$, we can divide the top and the bottom each by 3 to get $\frac{14}{6}$. Then we can divide top and bottom by 2 and get $\frac{7}{3}$. It can't be reduced any further than this, so this is your final answer.

Adding and Subtracting Fractions

To add or subtract fractions, the fractions have to have a common denominator. This means that they have to have the same number on the bottom (the denominators need to be the same). If the fractions already have a common denominator, you can add or subtract them by adding or subtracting the numbers on top.

$$\frac{4}{7}+\frac{2}{7}=\frac{6}{7}$$

If the fractions do not have a common denominator, the easiest way to add or subtract them is to use the Bowtie.

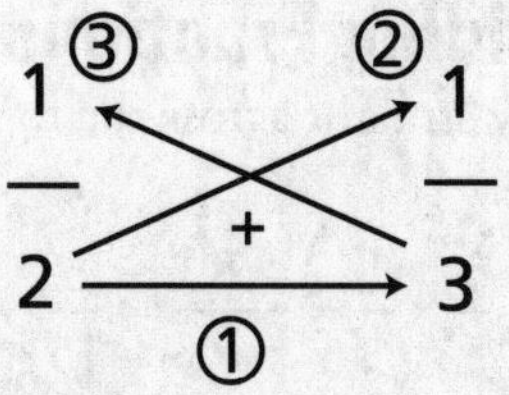

Step 1: Multiply the two bottom numbers together. Their product goes on the bottom of your two new fractions.

Step 2: Multiply diagonally from the bottom left to the top right. Write this product on the top right.

Step 3: Multiply diagonally from the bottom right to the top left. Write this product on the top left.

See—it looks like a bowtie! Now you have two fractions with a common denominator, and you can add or subtract them.

For example:

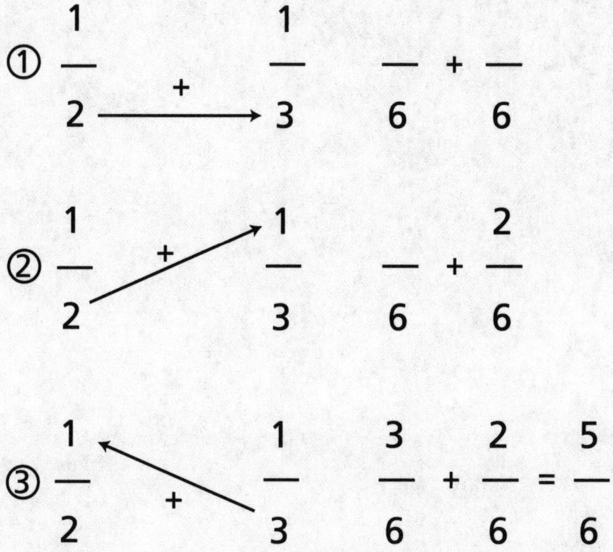

Multiplying and Dividing Fractions

To multiply fractions, multiply straight across the top and bottom.

$$\frac{3}{5} \times \frac{1}{3} = \frac{3 \times 1}{5 \times 3} = \frac{3}{15}$$

To divide fractions, flip the second fraction and multiply.

$$\frac{3}{5} \div \frac{1}{3} = \frac{3 \times 3}{5 \times 1} = \frac{9}{5}$$

COOP Fractions Exercise

Answers can be found in Chapter 24.

1 Reduce $\frac{12}{60}$ = ____

2 $\frac{3}{8}+\frac{2}{3}=$ ____

3 $\frac{3}{4}-\frac{2}{3}=$ ____

4 $\frac{3}{5}\times\frac{3}{2}=$ ____

5 $\frac{1}{3}\div\frac{1}{2}=$ ____

DECIMALS

Remember that decimals are just another way of writing fractions. Be sure to know the names of all the decimal places.

3 4 . 8 5 7

tens, units, tenths, hundredths, thousandths

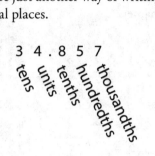

Adding Decimals

To add decimals, just line up the decimal places and add.

$$\begin{array}{r} 24.05 \\ +12.23 \\ \hline 36.28 \end{array}$$

Subtracting Decimals

To subtract decimals, just line up the decimal places and subtract.

$$\begin{array}{r} 24.05 \\ -12.23 \\ \hline 11.82 \end{array}$$

Multiplying Decimals

To multiply decimals, count the total number of digits to the right of the decimal point in the numbers you are multiplying. Then multiply the numbers without the decimal points. Once you have your answer, add back into the new number all of the decimal places you removed from the first two numbers.

To solve 0.2×3.4, remove two decimal places and multiply.

$$\begin{array}{r} 34 \\ \times\ 2 \\ \hline 68 \end{array}$$

Now put back the two decimal places we removed to get 0.68.

Dividing Decimals

To divide decimals, move the decimal places in both numbers the same number of places to the right until you are working with only integers. But unlike when you're multiplying decimals, you don't have to put the decimals back in when you're dividing.

$$3.4 \div 0.2 = 34 \div 2 = 17$$

Converting Decimals to Fractions

Remember that multiplying by 10 means the same thing as moving the decimal point one place to the right, and dividing by 10 means the same thing as moving the decimal points one place to the left.

$$9 \div 10 = \frac{9}{10} = 0.9$$

$$5 \div 100 = \frac{5}{100} = 0.05$$

This is why the first place to the right of the decimal is called "tenths" and the second place to the right is called "hundredths." Nine-tenths = 0.9 = $\frac{9}{10}$. Five-hundredths = 0.05 = $\frac{5}{100}$. So to convert a decimal to a fraction, all you need to do is change the numbers after the decimal to their fraction form.

$$5.24 = 5 + \frac{2}{10} + \frac{4}{100}$$

COOP Decimals Exercise

Answers can be found in Chapter 24.

1 $2.43 + 5.25 =$ ____

2 $5.75 - 3.12 =$ ____

3 $1.5 \times 3 =$ ____

4 $2.5 \times 0.5 =$ ____

5 $2.5 \div 0.5 =$ ____

6 What is 6.32 in fraction form? ____

EXPONENTS, SCIENTIFIC NOTATION, AND SQUARE ROOTS

Exponents are just a short way of writing multiplication. 3^2 means to multiply two 3s together: 3×3. Likewise, 3^4 means to multiply four 3s together: $3 \times 3 \times 3 \times 3$. On the COOP you will not see very complex exponents, so the best way to solve them is to write them out longhand and multiply.

Scientific notation is also a short way of writing big numbers. Whenever you see a number such as 3.44×10^2, this means that you should move the decimal point to the right the same number of places as the exponent to the 10. In this case, you move the decimal two places to the right (10^2), and you get 344. Likewise, 4.355×10^2 is just another way of writing 435.5.

Square root is just the opposite of raising a number to the second power. $\sqrt{4} = 2$, since $2^2 = 4$. On the COOP you will not have very big square roots. Your best bet is simply to memorize these common ones.

Since $2^2 = 4$, $\sqrt{4} = 2$

Since $3^2 = 9$, $\sqrt{9} = 3$

Since $4^2 = 16$, $\sqrt{16} = 4$

Since $5^2 = 25$, $\sqrt{25} = 5$

COOP Exponents, Scientific Notation, and Square Roots Exercise

Answers can be found in Chapter 24.

1 $4^3 =$ ____

2 $2^4 =$ ____

3 $3.4 \times 10^2 =$ ____

4 $5.23 \times 10^4 =$ ____

5 $\sqrt{4} + \sqrt{16} =$ ____

SOLVE FOR *X*

To solve an equation, you want to get the variable (the x) on one side of the equation and put everything else on the other side.

To get only the variable on one side, follow these two steps.

Step 1: Move elements around using addition and subtraction. Put the variables on one side of the equation and numbers on the other. As long as you do the same operation on both sides of the equal sign, you aren't changing the value of the variable.

Step 2: Divide both sides of the equation by the coefficient, which is the number in front of the variable. If that number is a fraction, multiply everything by the denominator.

For example:

$$3x + 5 = 17$$

Subtract 5 from each side.

$$\begin{array}{r}3x + 5 = 17 \\ -5 = -5 \\ \hline 3x = 12\end{array}$$

Divide 3 from each side

$$\begin{array}{rcr}3x & = & 12 \\ \div 3 & = & \div 3 \\ \hline x & = & 4\end{array}$$

Always remember the rule of equations: *Whatever you do to one side of the equation, you must also do to the other side.*

COOP Solve for *x* Exercise

Answers can be found in Chapter 24.

1 If $4x = 20$ then $x =$ ____

2 If $4x + 3 = 31$ then $x =$ ____

3 If $6 = 8x + 4$ then $x =$ ____

4 If $4x - 3 = 3x$ then $x =$ ____

PERCENT TRANSLATION

Everyone knows how easy it is to make a simple mistake on a percent problem. Should you write "5% of 100" as $\frac{5}{100}$ or as $\frac{100}{5}$ or as something else? To make sure to avoid silly mistakes, here's a foolproof method for solving percent questions.

Any percent problem can be translated word for word into an equation if you know the mathematical equivalent of the English words. For instance, "percent" means the same thing as "divided by 100," and "of" means the same thing as "multiply." Therefore, "5% of 100" can be written as $\frac{5}{100} \times 100$, which equals 5.

The chart below shows you the mathematical translation of the English words you will probably see. To solve any percent question, read the problem back to yourself and replace the words on the left side of the chart with the math symbols on the right. Then you can easily solve.

Percent	$\div$ 100
Of	$\times$
What	x (or any variable)
Is, Are, Equals	=

Here are two examples:

20% of 50 is?

20% of 50

↓ ↓ ↓

$$\frac{20}{100} \times 50$$

5 is what percent of 80?

5 is what percent of 80

↓ ↓

$$5 = \frac{x}{100} \times 80$$

$$5 = \frac{x}{100} \times 80$$

COOP Percent Translation Exercise

Answers can be found in Chapter 24.

1 30% of 60 = ____

2 40% of 200 = ____

3 15 is what percent of 60? ____

4 What is 25% of 10% of 200? ____

RATIOS AND PROPORTIONS

What Is a Ratio?

A ratio is a way of stating the relationship of two numbers in a reduced form. For instance, if there are 50 boys and 25 girls in a room, we can say that the ratio of boys to girls is 50 to 25. But we can also reduce this ratio just like a fraction: $\frac{50}{25} = \frac{2}{1}$. So we can also say that the ratio of boys to girls is 2 to 1. This is sometimes written as "The ratio of boys to girls is 2:1."

Of course, if we say that the ratio of boys to girls is 2 to 1, this doesn't tell us exactly how many boys and girls there are. The actual number could be 8 boys and 4 girls, or 10 boys and 5 girls, or 200 boys and 100 girls. Each of these can be reduced to the ratio 2 to 1.

But if we know one of the actual values, we can always solve for the other one. For instance, if we know that the ratio of boys to girls is 2 to 1, and there are 200 boys, we know that there must be 100 girls. Most of you can probably do that in your heads. But how do you calculate it?

Solving Ratio and Proportion Problems

The way you solve almost all ratio and proportion questions is by setting up two fractions and cross-multiplying.

$$\frac{A}{B} = \frac{C}{D}$$

Whenever you set up two equal fractions, you know that $A \times D$ is equal to $B \times C$. The only thing you have to make sure to do is keep the same thing on top and bottom of each fraction.

In this case, if we know that the ratio of boys to girls is 2 to 1 and that there are 200 boys, we can figure out the number of girls by setting up these fractions.

$$\frac{\text{boys } 2}{\text{girls } 1} = \frac{200}{x}$$

Now we can cross multiply: We know that $2x = 1 \times 200$. This means that $x = 100$

Take a look at the following problem.

10 John has a bowl of red and blue marbles. The ratio of red to blue marbles is 5 to 4. If there are 35 red marbles in the bowl, how many blue marbles are in the bowl?

F 16

G 20

H 28

J 39

Here's How to Crack It

Let's set up our fractions with red marbles on top and blue marbles on the bottom.

$$\frac{\text{red}}{\text{blue}}\frac{5}{4} = \frac{35}{x}$$

Now we can cross-multiply. We know that $5x = 4 \times 35$. After we multiply, $5x = 140$. We can solve for x by dividing both sides by 5 to get $x = 28$. Therefore there are 28 blue marbles in the bowl, which is (H).

AVERAGES

The formula we use to figure out the average is

$$\text{average} = \frac{\text{sum total}}{\text{\# of things}}$$

For instance, if you take three tests on which you score 50, 55, and 57, the sum total of your scores is 50 + 55 + 57, or 162. Since the number of tests was 3, the average on these tests must be $\frac{162}{3} = 54$.

Try the following problem.

11 During a certain month, David counted the number of apples he ate each week. He ate 2 apples during the first week, 4 apples during the second week, and 2 apples during the third week. The fourth week he ate no apples. On average, how many apples did David eat each week of the month.

A 2

B $2\frac{1}{2}$

C $3\frac{1}{3}$

D 7

Here's How to Crack It

The total number of apples David ate was 2 + 4 + 2 + 0, or 8. This sum total, over the number of weeks, will give us the average: $\frac{8}{4} = 2$.

PLUGGING IN THE ANSWER CHOICES

Very often you may think that you need to do a lot of complicated math to set up a problem. This is especially true on those long, wordy problems that give everyone a headache.

You know, however, that one of the answer choices given has to be the correct answer. All you've got to do is figure out which one. Therefore, the easiest way to solve many problems is by simply plugging in each answer choice until you find the one that works. Plugging in just means substituting numbers to figure out the answer quickly.

Take a look at the following problem.

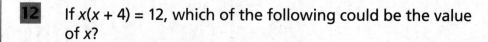

12 If $x(x + 4) = 12$, which of the following could be the value of x?

F –1

G 0

H 1

J 2

Here's How to Crack It

You might think that you have to do some complicated algebra to solve this problem, but you really don't. Let's just try plugging in each answer choice for the value of x and see which one makes the equation work.

If we plug in –1 for x, does $-1(-1 + 4) = 12$? No. Cross off (F). If we plug in 0 for x, does $0(0 + 4) = 12$? No. Cross off (G). If we plug in 1 for x, does $1(1 + 4) = 12$? No. Cross off (H). If we plug in 2 for x, does $2(2 + 4) = 12$? Yes, so (J) is the answer.

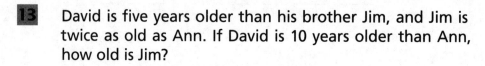

13 David is five years older than his brother Jim, and Jim is twice as old as Ann. If David is 10 years older than Ann, how old is Jim?

A 20

B 15

C 10

D 8

Here's How to Crack It

The question asks how old Jim is, so this is what we'll be plugging in for. Let's start with (A). Could Jim be 20? We know that David is five years older than Jim, so if Jim is 20, then David is 25. We also know that Jim is twice as old as Ann, so Ann must be 10. But the last sentence says that David should be 10 years older than Ann, which he's not. Therefore (A) can't be the answer.

How about (B)? Could Jim be 15? We know that David is five years older than Jim, so if Jim is 15, then David must be 20. We also know that Jim is twice as old as Ann, so Ann must be $7\frac{1}{2}$. But the last sentence says that David should be 10 years older than Ann, which he's not. Therefore (B) can't be the answer.

Let's try (C). Could Jim be 10? We know that David is five years older than Jim, so if Jim is 10, then David is 15. We also know that Jim is twice as old as Ann, so Ann must be 5. Does this make David 10 years older than Ann? Yes. So (C) is the answer.

Here's a slightly harder problem. Trying to solve it using algebra is difficult, but by plugging in the answer choices, it becomes very easy.

---

14 If the average of 4 and x is equal to the average of 5, 4, and x, what is the value of x?

F 1

G 2

H 6

J 8

Here's How to Crack It

Let's start with (F), and plug 1 in for x. Does the average of 4 and 1 (which is 2.5) equal the average of 5, 4, and 1 (which is $\frac{10}{3}$)? No, so (F) can be eliminated. Let's try (G). Does the average of 4 and 2 (which is 3) equal the average of 5, 4, and 2 (which is $\frac{11}{3}$)? No. Choice (G) can also be eliminated. How about (H)? Does the average of 4 and 6 (which is 5) equal the average of 5, 4, and 6 (which is 5)? Yes. Choice (H) is the answer.

PLUGGING IN YOUR OWN NUMBERS

The problem with doing algebra is that it's just too easy to make a mistake. Whenever you see a problem with variables (x's) in the answer choices, PLUG IN. Start by picking a number for the variable in the problem (or for more than one variable, if necessary); solve the problem using that real number; then see which answer choice gives you the correct answer.

Have a look at the following problem:

15 If x is a positive integer, then 20 percent of $5x$ equals

A x

B $2x$

C $5x$

D $15x$

Here's How to Crack It

Let's start by picking a number for x. Let's plug in the nice round number 10. When we plug in 10 for x, we change every x in the whole problem into a 10. Now the problem reads:

16 If 10 is a positive integer, then 20 percent of 5(10) equals

F 10

G 2(10)

H 5(10)

J 15(10)

Here's How to Crack It

Look how easy the problem becomes! Now we can solve: 20 percent of 50 is 10. Which answer says 10? Choice (F) does.

Let's try it again.

17 If $0 < x < 1$, then which of the following is true?

A $x > 0$

B $x > 1$

C $x > 2$

D $2x > 2$

Here's How to Crack It

This time when we pick a number for *x*, we have to make sure that it is between 0 and 1, because that's what the problem states. So let's try $\frac{1}{2}$. If we make every *x* in the problem into $\frac{1}{2}$, the answer choices now read:

(A) $\frac{1}{2} > 0$

(B) $\frac{1}{2} > 1$

(C) $\frac{1}{2} > 2$

(D) $1 > 2$

Which one of these is true? Choice (A). Plugging In is such a great technique that it makes even the hardest algebra problems easy. *Anytime you can, plug in for the variable!*

GEOMETRY

Lines and Angles

On every line, all the angles must add up to a total of 180°.

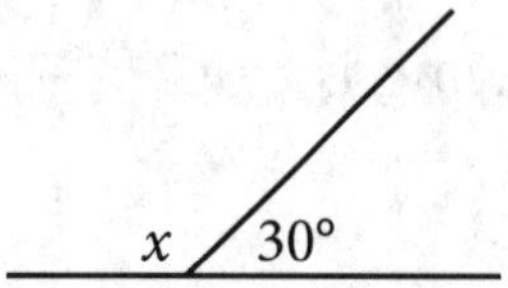

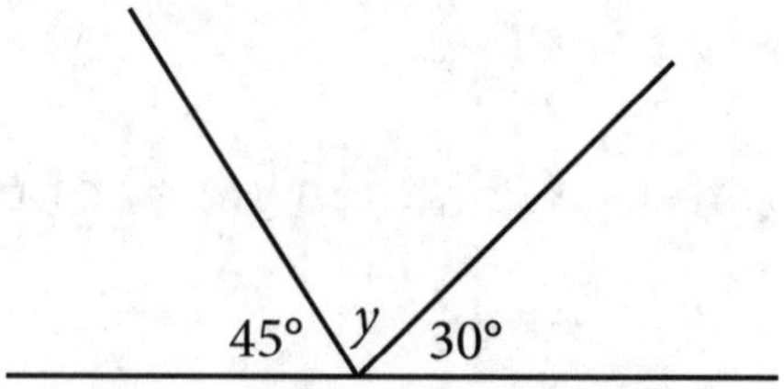

Since x and 30° must add up to 180°, we know that x must measure 180° – 30°, or 150°. Since 45°, y, and 30° must add up to 180°, we know that y must measure 180° – 45° – 30°, or 105°.

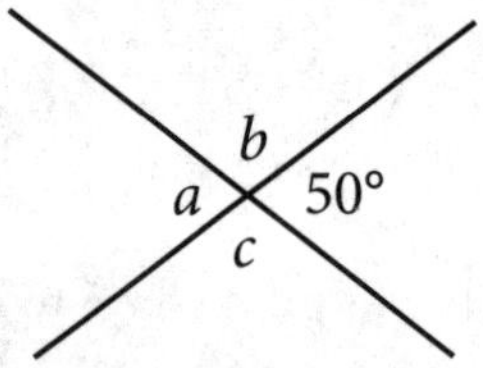

In this case, b and the angle measuring 50° are on a line together. This means that b must measure 130° (180° – 50° = 130°). Also, c and the angle measuring 50° are on a line together. This means that c must also measure 130° (180° – 50° = 130°). Finally, a must measure 50°, because $a + b$ (and we already know that b = 130°) must measure 180° (50° + 130° = 180°).

This explains why vertical angles (the angles opposite each other when two lines cross) are always equal. Angles b and c are both 130°, and angle a (which is opposite the angle 50°) is 50°.

In a triangle, all the angles must add up to 180°. In a four-sided figure, all the angles must add up to 360°.

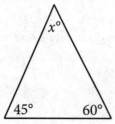

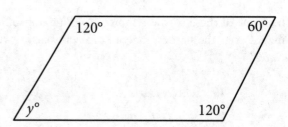

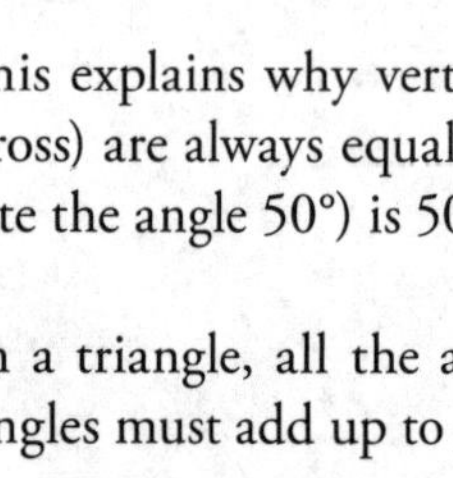

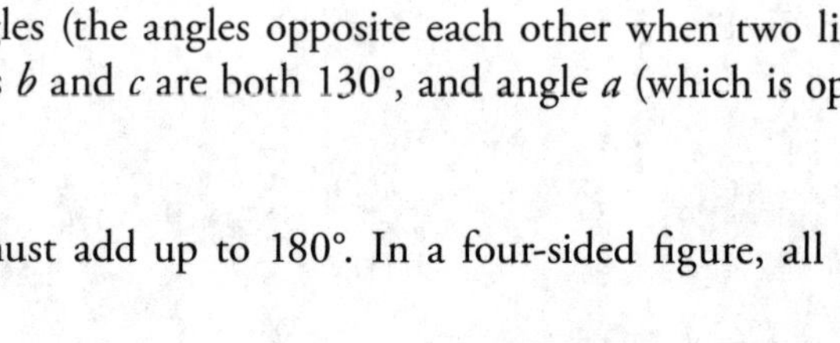

In this triangle, two of the angles are 45° and 60°. They make a total of 105°. The sum of the angles needs to equal 180°. Therefore angle *x* must be 180° – 105°, or 75°.

In the figure on the right, three of the angles have a total of 300°. Therefore *y* must be equal to 360° – 300°, or 60°.

A triangle is isosceles if it has two equal sides. This means that the two opposite angles are also equal. A triangle is *equilateral* if it has three equal sides. This means that all three angles are equal. Since these angles must equally divide 180°, they must each be 60°.

The triangle on the left is isosceles, so the two bottom angles must each be 35°. This makes a total of 70° for the two bottom angles. Since all of the angles must add up to 180°, we know that *x* is equal to 180° – 70°, or 110°.

Area, Perimeter, and Circumference

The area of a square or rectangle is length × width.

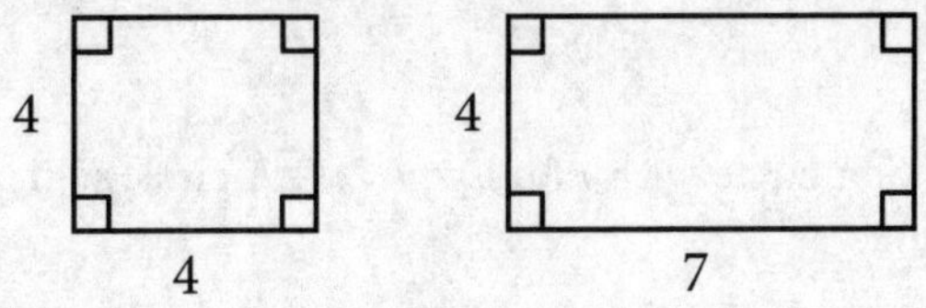

The area of this square is 4 × 4, or 16. The area of the rectangle is 4 × 7, or 28.

The area of a triangle is $\frac{1}{2}$ base × height.

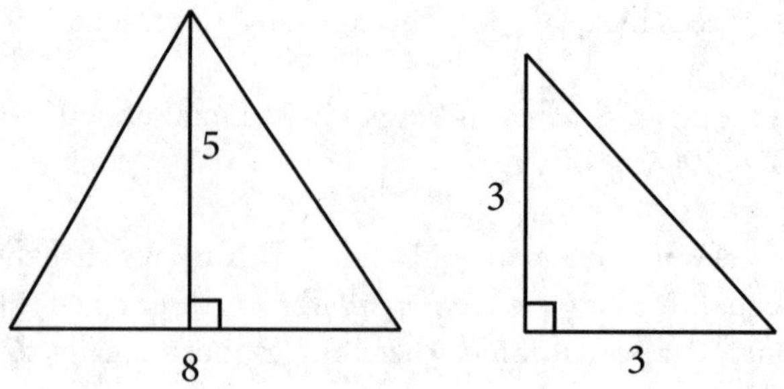

The area of the triangle on the left is $\frac{1}{2} \times 5 \times 8$, or 20.

The area of the triangle on the right is $\frac{1}{2} \times 3 \times 3$, or $4\frac{1}{2}$.

The perimeter of any object is the sum of the lengths of its sides.

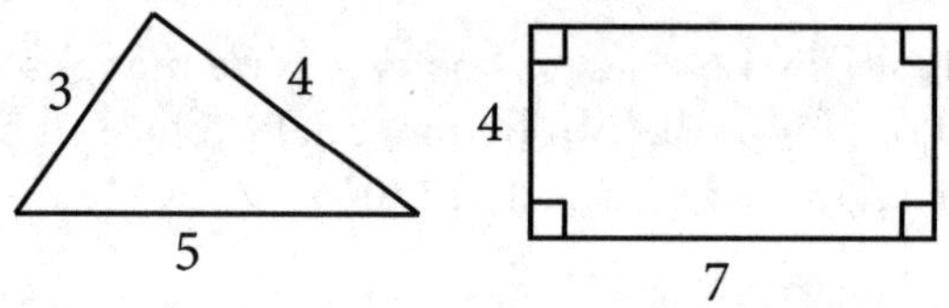

The perimeter of the triangle is 3 + 4 + 5, or 12. The perimeter of the rectangle is 4 + 7 + 4 + 7, or 22 (opposite sides are always equal to each other in a rectangle or a square).

The circumference of a circle with radius r is $2\pi r$. A circle with a radius of 5 has a circumference of 10π.

The area of a circle with radius r is πr^2. A circle with a radius of 5 has an area of 25π.

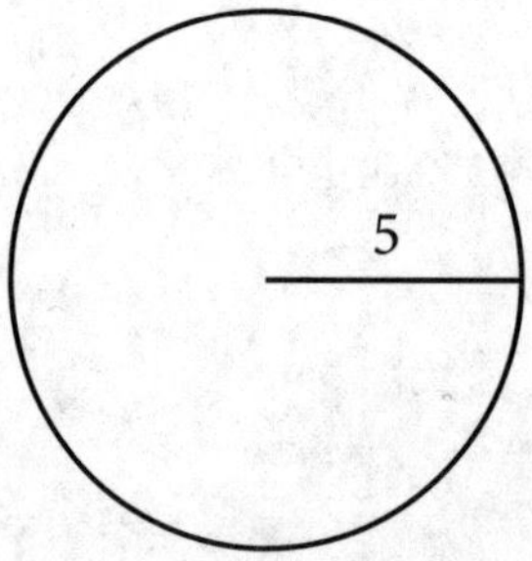

COOP Geometry Exercise

Answers can be found in Chapter 24.

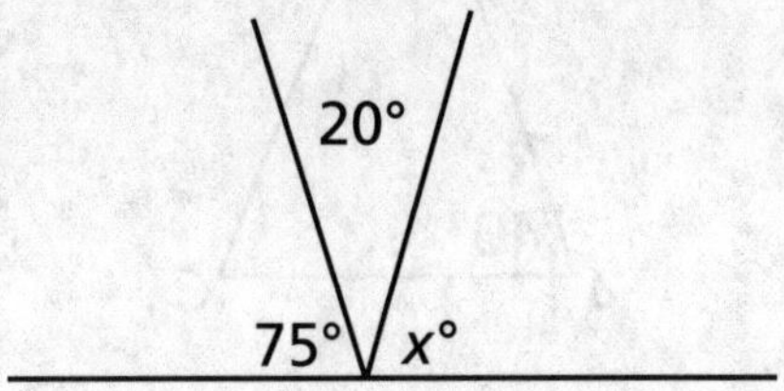

1 In the figure above, what is the value of x?

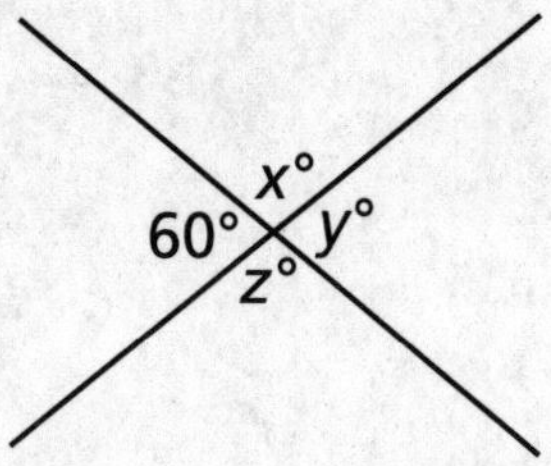

2 In the figure above, what is the value of $y + z$?

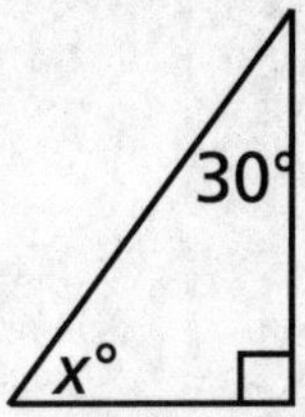

3 In the figure above, what is the value of x?

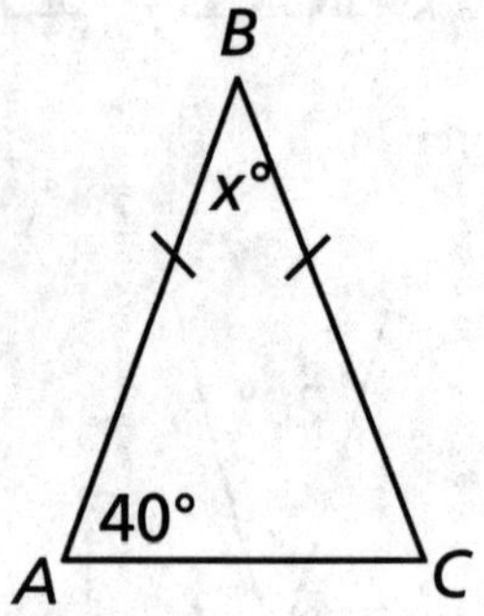

4 If triangle *ABC* is isosceles, what is the value of *x*?

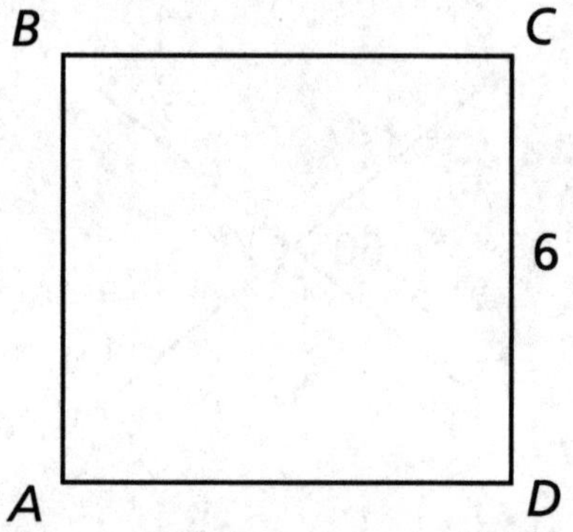

5 What is the area of square *ABCD* above?

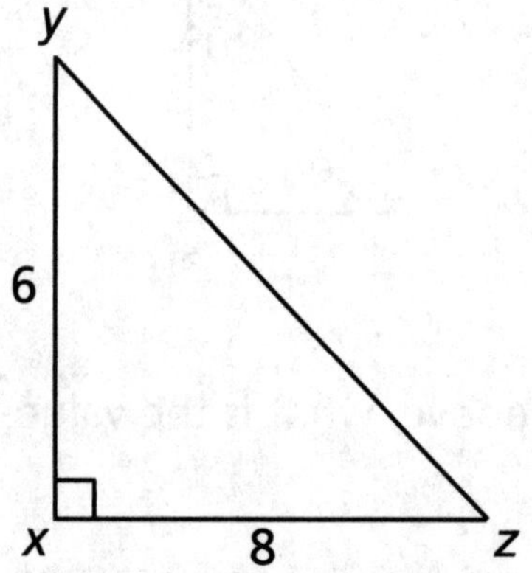

6 What is the area of triangle *XYZ* above?

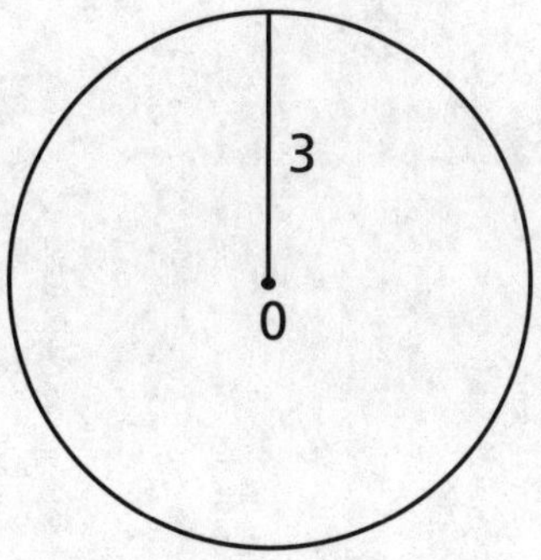

7a What is the area of the circle above with center *O*?

7b What is its circumference?

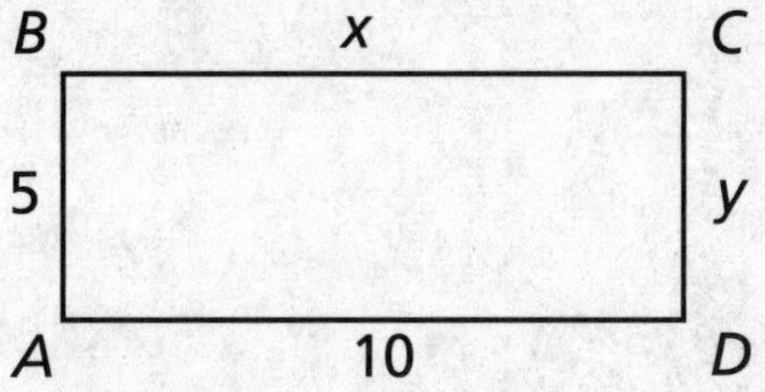

8a If *ABCD* is a rectangle, $x =$ ____ and $y =$ ____.

8b What is the perimeter of rectangle *ABCD*?

Now that you've reviewed all the elements of the test, time to go take a Practice Test and see where you are, as far as content you need to review again and content that you know cold. The next chapters contain COOP Practice Tests and a TACHS Practice Test. Enjoy!

Chapter 24
Answers to COOP Exercises

CHAPTER 17

COOP Sequence Exercise

1. **B** The first element has 1 black dot, the second has 2, and the third has 3, so the fourth should have 4 black dots.

○○○● ○○●● ○●●●

○●○● ●●●● ○○○○ ●○○○

A B C D

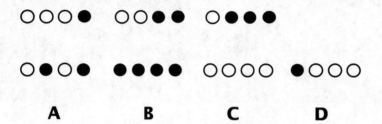

2. **H** The middle of each element should follow the pattern – + – +, so (D) can be eliminated. The first two groups have all squares, so the final two elements should have all circles.

□ – □ □ + □ ○ – ○

□ + ○ ○ + □ ○ + ○ □ – □

F G H J

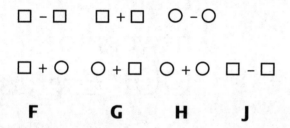

3. **A** In each element the letter "F" makes a quarter-turn. Therefore the missing element should be a quarter-turn more.

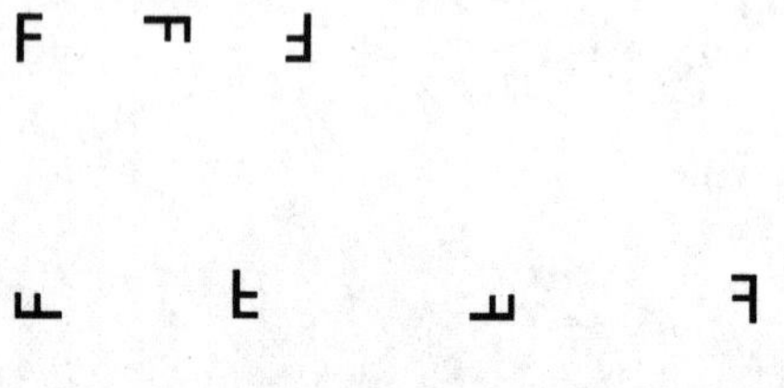

A B C D

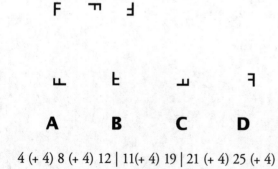

4. **J** 4 (+ 4) 8 (+ 4) 12 | 11(+ 4) 19 | 21 (+ 4) 25 (+ 4) 29

4 8 12 | 11 15 19 | 21 25 ___

22 23 27 29

F G H J

5. **A** 38 (– 6) 32 (– 6) 26 | 17 (– 6) 11 (– 6) 5 | 42 (– 6) 36 (– 6) 30

38 32 26 | 17 11 5 | 42 ____ 30

36	34	32	24
A	**B**	**C**	**D**

6. **G** 6 (× 2) 12 (+ 4) 16 | 4 (× 2) 8 (+ 4) 12 | 5 (× 2) 10 (+ 4) 14

6 12 16 | 4 8 12 | 5 10 ____

8	14	15	20
F	**G**	**H**	**J**

7. **B** 10 (– 5) 5 (+ 10) 15 | 13 (– 5) 8 (+ 10) 18 | 22 (– 5) 17 (+ 10) 27

10 5 15 | 13 8 18 | 22 ____ 27

15	17	22	25
A	**B**	**C**	**D**

8. **J** 8 (× 2) 16 (+ 4) 20 | 4 (× 2) 8 (+ 4) 12 | 20 (× 2) 40 (+ 4) 44

8 16 20 | 4 8 12 | 20 ____ 44

24	28	35	40
F	**G**	**H**	**J**

9. **C** 20 (– 2) 18 (+ 7) 25 | 23 (– 2) 21 (+ 7) 28 | 30 (– 2) 28 (+ 7) 35

20 18 25 | 23 21 28 | 30 28 ____

25	26	35	38
A	**B**	**C**	**D**

10. **G** If you transform the letters into numbers, you see that they decreased by 2. For instance, HFD is the same as 8 6 4; 8 (– 2) 6 (– 2) 4. The only choice that also does this is XVT: 24 22 20; 24 (– 2) 22 (– 2) 20.

HFD | LJH | PNL | TRP | ____

RQP	XVT	VUT	YWV
F	**G**	**H**	**J**

11. **A** Since the number in each group increased by 1 from each group to the next, the missing group should contain the number 5. This will allow us to eliminate (C) and (D) because the only number in those groups is 6. If you change the letters into numbers, you see that they increase by 5. For instance, AFK is the same as 1 6 11; 1(+ 5) 6 (+ 5) 11. The only choice whose letters are each separated by 5 is MRW: 13 18 23; 13 (+ 5) 18 (+ 5) 23.

A1FK | D2IN | G3LQ | J4OT | ____

M5RW	N5QS	N5ST	U6VW
A	**B**	**C**	**D**

CHAPTER 18

COOP Analogy Exercise

1. **A** Bread is made from grain; jam is made from fruit.
2. **H** A dress hat is more formal than a baseball cap; a dress shoe is more formal than a sneaker.
3. **B** A tree grows from its trunk (or the bottom part of a tree is a trunk); a flower grows from its stem (or the bottom part of a flower is a stem).
4. **F** A fish moves with its fins; a bird moves with its wings.
5. **D** A violin is played with a bow; a piano is played with a hand.

CHAPTER 19

COOP Quantitative Reasoning Exercise

1. **C** Subtract 3 from the number in the first column to get the number in the second column: 4 minus 3 equals 1, 7 minus 3 equals 4, and 11 minus 3 equals 8.

2. **J** Multiply the number in the first column by 4 to get the number in the second column: 4 times 4 equals 16, 1 times 4 equals 4, and 5 times 4 equals 20.

3. **B** Divide the number in the first column by 3 to get the number in the second column: 6 divided by 3 equals 2, 12 divided by 3 equals 4, and 9 divided by 3 equals 3.

4. **H** There are 6 squares total. Four of the six squares are shaded. $\frac{4}{6}$ is equal to $\frac{2}{3}$.

5. **A** The square is cut into fourths. Half of each fourth is shaded. Combine the halves together. That makes 2 full shaded squares, which means that $\frac{1}{2}$ of figure is shaded. Alternatively, the square is divided into 8 equal triangles. Four of the eight triangles are shaded. $\frac{4}{8}$ is equal to $\frac{1}{2}$.

6. **G** The rectangle is divided into 10 squares. 2 full squares are shaded and 4 other squares are half-shaded. The 4 halves make 2 whole squares. Therefore, $\frac{4}{10}$ of the rectangle is shaded.

7. **B** Combine the half-shaded pieces together to make two full shaded squares. The figure is divided into 8 squares, so $\frac{2}{8}$ of the figure is shaded.

8. **J** For every one cone, there should be 2 cubes. Choice (J) has 4 cubes and 2 cones: 2 cubes for the first cone and 2 cubes for the second cone.

9. **C** For every 3 cubes, there should be 1 cone. However, 1 cone (or 3 cubes) on the left side would balance 1 cone (or 3 cubes) on the right side. If 1 cube is added to the left side (making a total of 4 cubes) and 1 cube is added to the right side (making a total of 4 cubes), the scale is balanced.

10. **J** If there are 3 cubes on the left side and 1 cube and 1 cone on the right side, then 1 cube on the left goes with 1 cube on the right, making the remaining 2 cubes on the left side equal to the 1 cone on the right side. Since 2 cubes are equal to 1 cone, the correct choice is (J).

11. **B** If there is 1 cube and 1 cone on the left side and 2 cones on the right side, then the 1 cone on the left goes with 1 of the cones on the right, making the 1 cube on the left side equal to the remaining 1 cone on the right side. Therefore, 1 cube and 1 cone weigh the same, making (B) correct.

CHAPTER 20

COOP Verbal Reasoning—Words Exercise

1. **B**
2. **H**
3. **A**
4. **G**
5. **D**
6. **F**
7. **B**
8. **F**

CHAPTER 21

COOP Verbal Reasoning—Context Exercise

1. **C** If you summarized the passage well, you probably wrote something like, "People have had lights for a long time in different ways." Choice (A) is too precise, since the Egyptians are discussed in only one paragraph. Choices (B) and (D) are just details that are discussed in only one or two lines.

2. **J** In the final paragraph, the author says that "oil lamps brought with them other problems." Therefore, the Romans began to use candles. Choices (G) and (H) are not stated in the paragraph, so they can be eliminated. Choice (F) is incorrect because the wording is extreme, and there is no indication the author thinks that candles are the most important discovery in human history.

3. **B** If we reread the line that mentions the word *rudimentary,* it states, "Rudimentary oil lamps, a primitive ancestor of the gaslight..." Therefore the word rudimentary must be something like primitive, or basic. This will eliminate (A), (C), and (D).

4. **J** If we skim the passage looking for Edison, we can find him mentioned in the first paragraph. There it states that "practical indoor lighting existed thousands of years before Thomas Edison invented the light bulb." Now we need to find the choice that best restates this idea. Does this sentence explain his discoveries or mention other inventors? No, so we can eliminate (F) and (G). Does the author later discuss Edison? No, so (H) can also be eliminated.

5. **A** The passage says that "the lamp gave off a terrible odor," and "foul-smelling" is used to describe the odor of the lamp.

6. **H** There is no evidence in the passage to support (F), (G), or (J). the passage does say that the "animal fat smells awful when burned," so (H) is the best answer.

7. **C** Nothing in the passage sounds angry, so we can eliminate (A). Choice (B) probably isn't right, since someone who was unconcerned wouldn't have written the passage. If that's as far as you get, take a guess between (C) and (D). Critical means that the author disagrees with something, but there's nothing in the passage that shows disagreement, which rules out (D).

CHAPTER 22

Errors Exercise

1. Since "many people" is plural, it needs the plural verb form "are": "There are already many people in the auditorium."

2. Since "my father's company" is singular, the pronoun and verb should be the singular "it is" instead of the plural "they are": "Since my father's company has so much business, it is very busy."

3. "My uncle" is singular, so it needs the singular verb form "helps": "My uncle often helps my parents to make dinner."

4. This is a sentence fragment. A complete sentence would read: "On his way to school, Henry ran into his friend."

5. The first verb, "ran," is in the past tense; to maintain parallel form, the second verb, "escaping," should also be in the past tense: "The giant mouse ran through the house and escaped from the cat."

6. The first verb, "won," is in the past tense, and the second verb, "receives," is in the present tense. You know the sentence should be in the past tense because of the clue words "last year." To maintain parallel form, the verbs should both be in the same tense: "Last year, Ines won the first prize and received a beautiful trophy."

7. "Most biggest" is not a valid comparative form. The sentence should simply read: "Roger finished his biggest assignment."

8. The first verb, "cleaned," is in the past tense, but the second verb, "gives," is in the present tense. To maintain parallel form, these verbs should both be in the same tense: "Colin cleaned the bowl and gave it to his mother."

Simple Subject Exercise

1. Jonathan
2. part
3. her teacher
4. he

Simple Predicate Exercise

1. volunteered
2. drank
3. imagined
4. felt

CHAPTER 23

COOP Math Vocabulary Exercise

1. –3, –2, –1, 0, 1, 2, 3, 4 are all integers. That makes a total of 8.
2. 1, 2, 3, 4, are all positive integers. That makes a total of 4.
3. $6 + 7 + 8 = 21$
4. $2 \times 4 \times 8 = 64$

COOP Order of Operations Exercise

1. 13
2. 9 (Do multiplication first!)
3. 5 (Do parentheses, then multiplication!)
4. 45 (Do multiplication first!)
5. 108 (Do parentheses first!)

COOP Fractions Exercise

1. $\frac{1}{5}$ (Divide the top and bottom by 12.)

2. $\frac{3}{8} + \frac{2}{3} = \frac{9}{24} + \frac{16}{24} = \frac{25}{24}$

3. $\frac{3}{4} - \frac{2}{3} = \frac{9}{12} - \frac{8}{12} = \frac{1}{12}$

4. $\frac{3}{5} \times \frac{3}{2} = \frac{9}{10}$

5. $\frac{1}{3} \div \frac{1}{2} = \frac{1}{3} \times \frac{2}{1} = \frac{2}{3}$

COOP Decimals Exercise

1. 7.68

2. 2.63

3. 4.5

4. 1.25

5. 5

6. $\frac{632}{100}$

COOP Exponents, Scientific Notation, and Square Roots Exercise

1. $4 \times 4 \times 4 = 64$

2. $2 \times 2 \times 2 \times 2 = 16$

3. 340

4. 52,300

5. This becomes $2 + 4 = 6$

COOP Solve for *x* Exercise

1. $x = 5$
2. $x = 7$
3. $x = \frac{1}{4}$
4. $x = 3$

COOP Percent Translation Exercise

1. $\frac{30}{100} \times 60 = 18$
2. $\frac{40}{100} \times 200 = 80$
3. $15 = \frac{x}{100} \times 60 = 25$
4. $x = \frac{25}{100} \times \frac{10}{100} \times 200 = 5$

COOP Geometry Exercise

1. Since these angles must add up to 180°, $x = 85°$.
2. x and z must be 120° and y must be 60° so $y + z = 180°$.
3. The angles in a triangle must add up to 180°. Since we already have angles 90° and 30°, the remaining angle must be 60°.
4. Since this triangle is isosceles, the two bottom angles measure 40° each. To make a total of 180°, $x = 100°$.
5. The area of this square is 6×6, or 36.
6. The area of a triangle is $\frac{1}{2}$ base × height, or $\frac{1}{2} \times 8 \times 6 = 24$.

7a. The area of this circle is $3^2\pi$, or 9π.

7b. The circumference of this circle is $2(3)\pi$, or 6π.

8a. Since this figure is a rectangle, $x = 10$ and $y = 5$.

8b. The perimeter is $10 + 5 + 10 + 5 = 30$.

Chapter 25
COOP
Practice Test 1

Test 1

Sequences

(20 questions, 15 minutes)

Choose the letter that shows what should fill the blank in the sequence

1

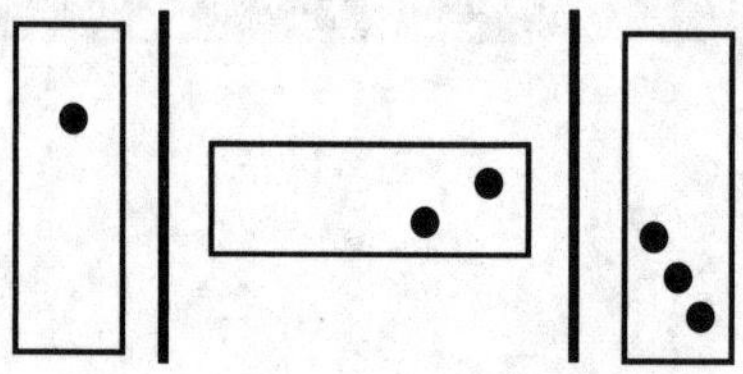

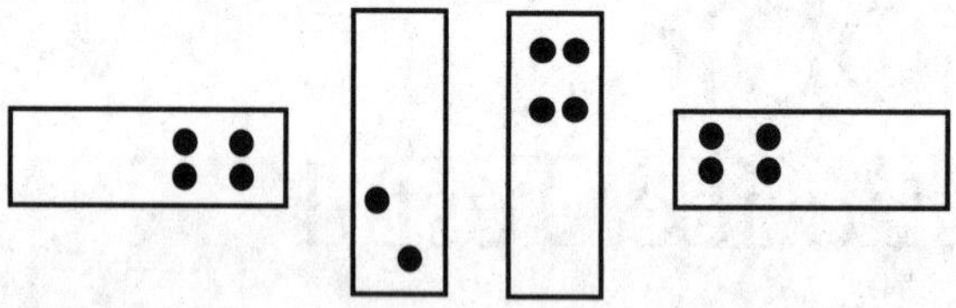

A B C D

2

△○□△ | △□○△ | ·○□· | ___

·○□△   △□○△   ·□○·   △○□·

F G H J

3

XOX | OXO | XXO | ___

OOX   OXO   XOX   OOO

A B C D

4

F G H J

5

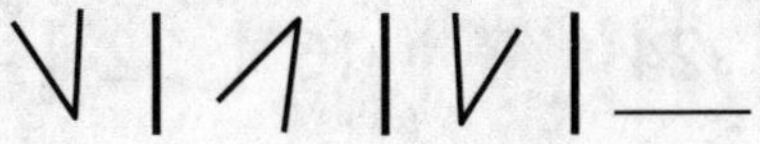

A **B** **C** **D**

6

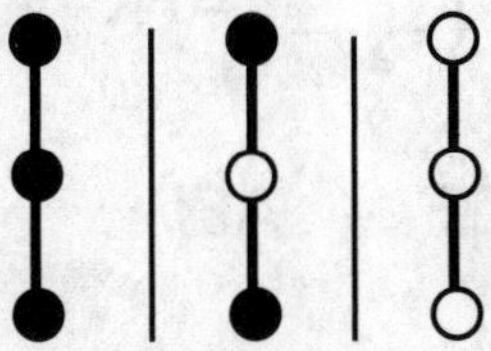

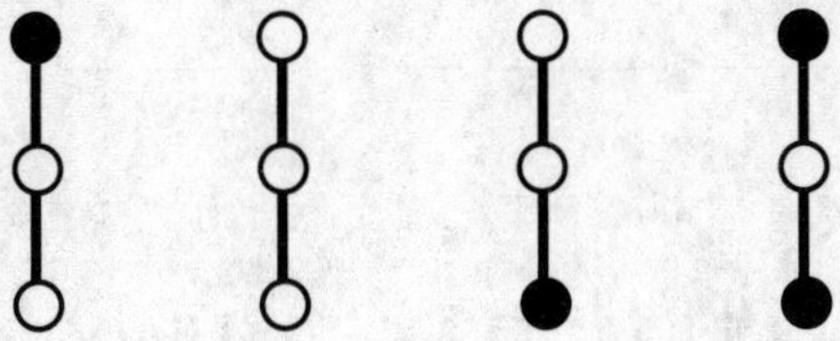

F **G** **H** **J**

7

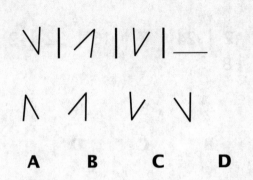

21 | 32 | 28 | 56 | 67 | 73 | 16 | ___ | 33

22	27	31	32
A	**B**	**C**	**D**

8

63 | 65 | 63 | 18 | 20 | 18 | 52 | 54 | ___

5	8	2	52
F	**G**	**H**	**J**

9

32 | 16 | 8 | 52 | 26 | 13 | 24 | ___ | 6

16	12	10	8
A	**B**	**C**	**D**

10

2 | 8 | 32 | 3 | 12 | 48 | 1 | ___ | 16

F	G	H	J
3	4	8	12

11

5 | 6 | 18 | 2 | 3 | 9 | 8 | ___ | 27

A	B	C	D
9	12	24	26

12

15 | 15 | 5 | 24 | 24 | 8 | 9 | 9 | ___

F	G	H	J
3	6	9	12

13

6 | 12 | 24 | 8 | 16 | 32 | 2 | ___ | 8

A	B	C	D
2	4	6	8

14

ABC | ACE | ADG | ___ | AFK

F	G	H	J
ABD	ACF	ADF	AEI

15

EGI | IKM | MOQ | ___ | UWY

A	B	C	D
QSU	RTU	MPT	LMO

16

J1L | M2O | P3R | ____ | V5X

S4U	A1C	L3M	T4V
F	**G**	**H**	**J**

17

CB2 | ED4 | GF8 | ____ | KJ32

JK10	IH16	MN16	PQ32
A	**B**	**C**	**D**

18

VWXY | RSTU | NOPQ | ____ | FGHI

CDEF	GHIK	KMNO	JKLM
F	**G**	**H**	**J**

19

AZBY | CXDW | EVFU | ____ | IRJQ

GTHB	XATB	GSHT	KTLS
A	**B**	**C**	**D**

20

CEHL | EGJN | GILP | ____ | KMPT

MOPQ	JLOP	IKNR	SUVY
F	**G**	**H**	**J**

Test 2

Analogies

(20 questions, 7 minutes)

For the following questions, look at the pictures in the top two boxes. Then choose the picture that should go in the empty box so that the bottom two pictures have the same relationship as the top two pictures.

1

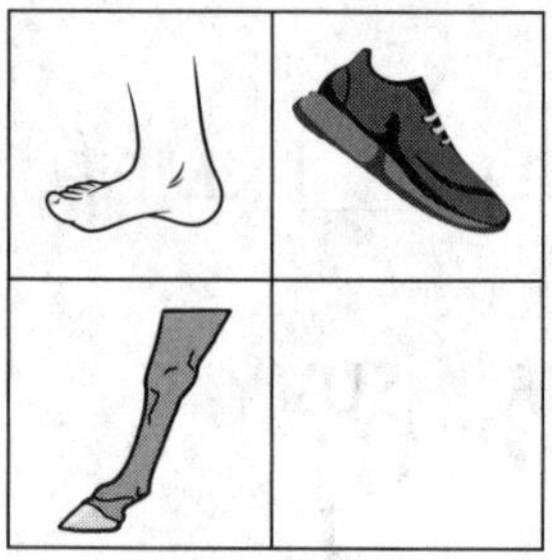

A

B

C

D

2

F

G

H

J

3

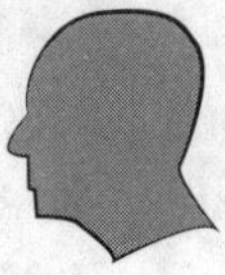

A

B

C

D

4

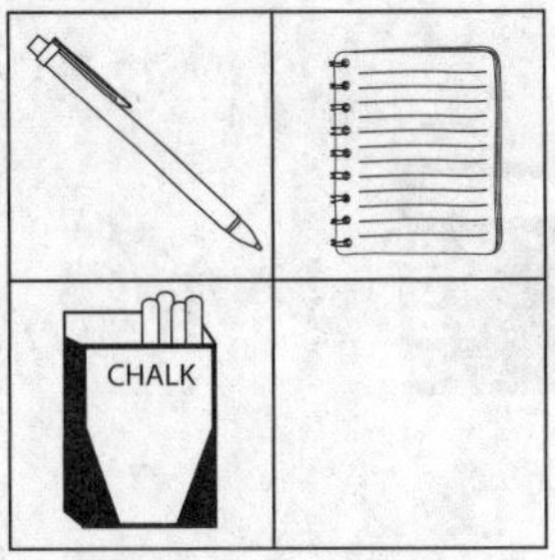

F

G

H

J

5

A

B

C

D

6

F

G

H

J

7

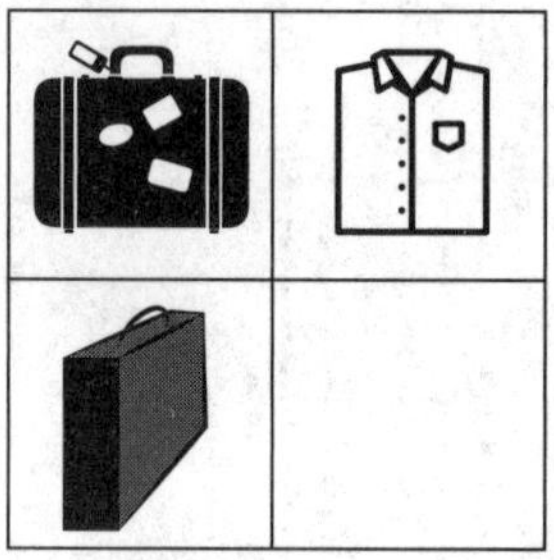

A

B

C

D

8

F

G

H

J

9

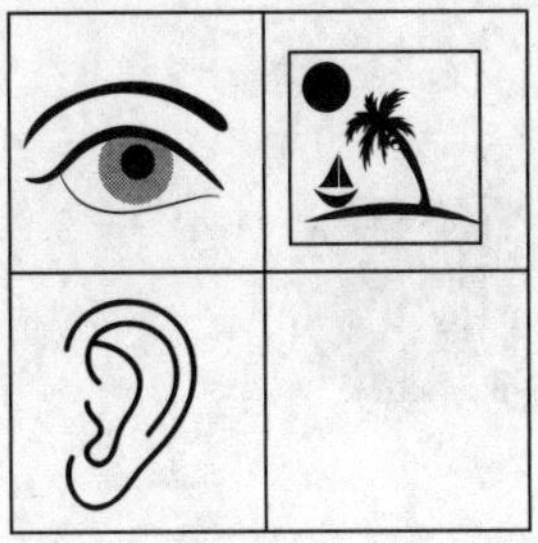

A B C D

10

F G H J

11

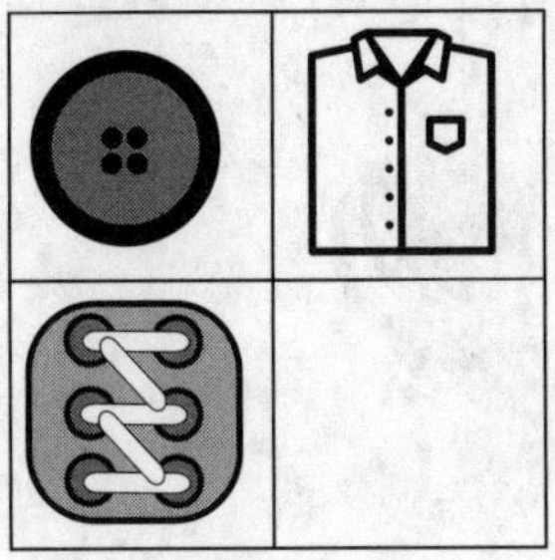

A B C D

12 ______________________________

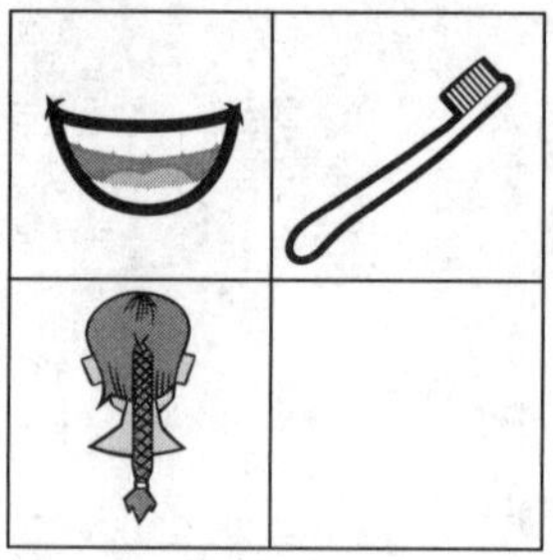

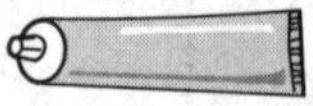
F

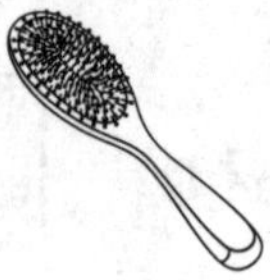
G

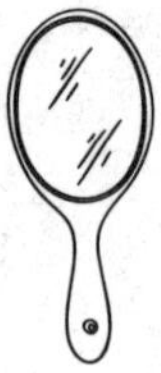
H

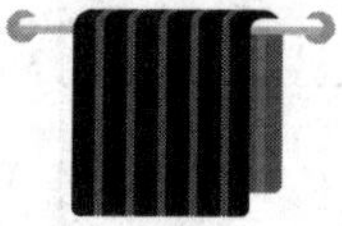
J

13 ______________________________

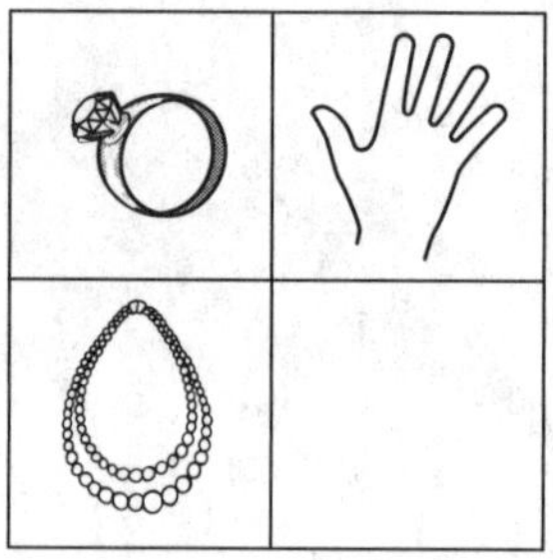

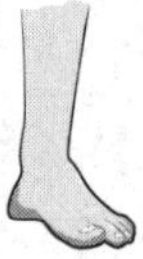
A

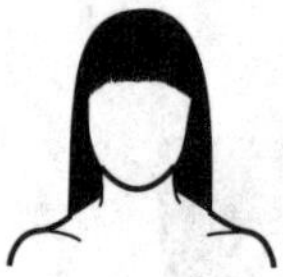
B

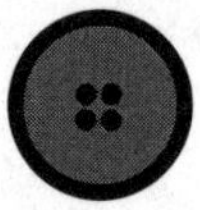
C

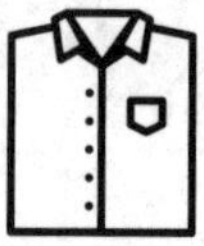
D

14 ______________________________

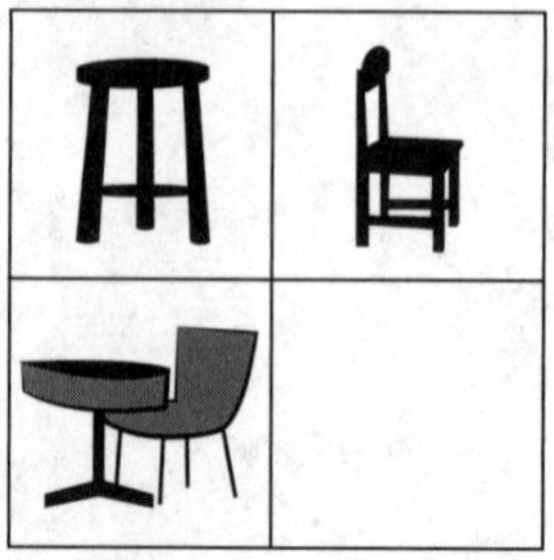

F

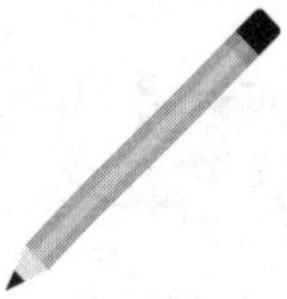
G

H

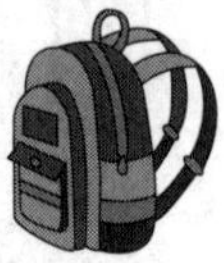
J

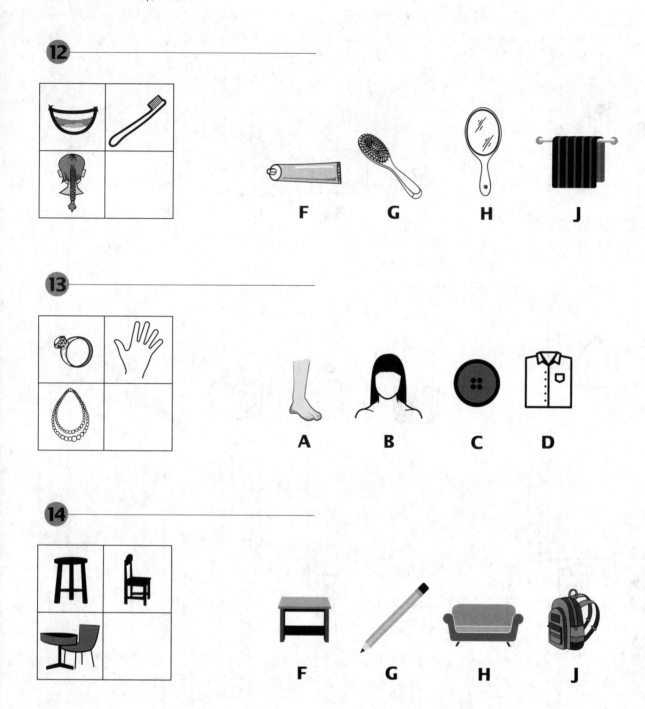

15

A

B

C

D

16

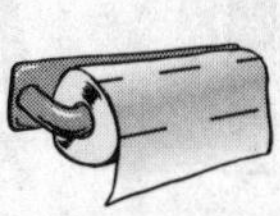
F

G

H

J

17

A

B

C

D

18

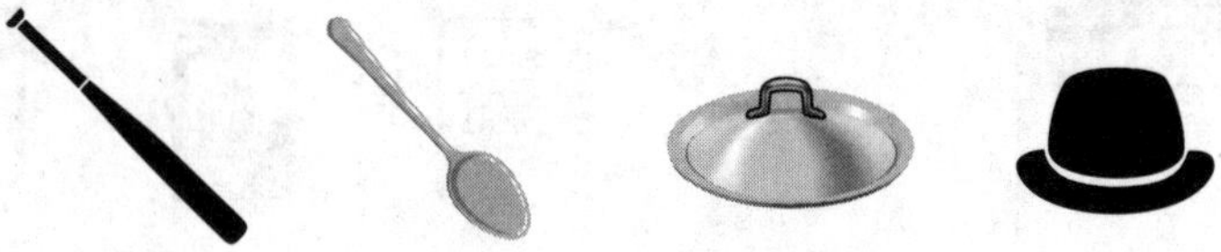

F G H J

19

A B C D

20

F G H J

Test 3

Quantitative Reasoning

(20 questions, 5 minutes)

For questions 1–7, find the relationship of the numbers in one column to the numbers in the other column. Then find the missing number.

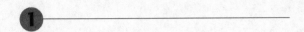

1

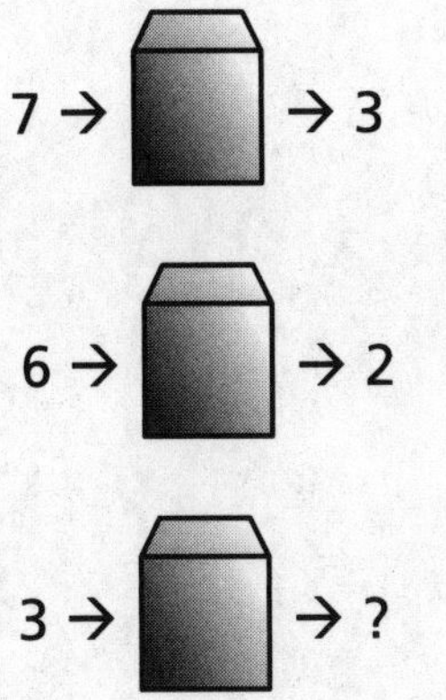

4	1	0	–1
A	**B**	**C**	**D**

2

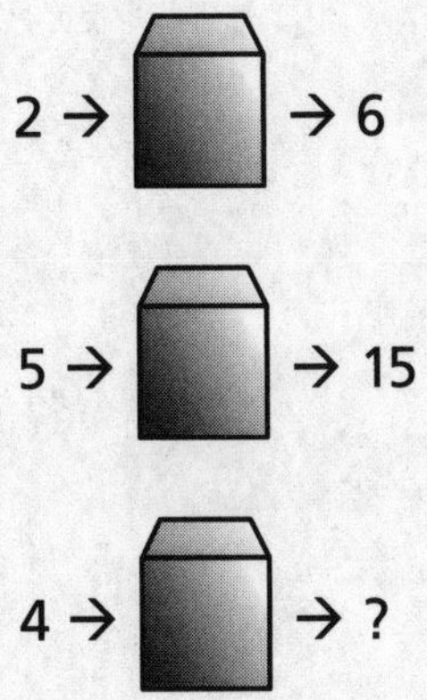

3	8	10	12
F	**G**	**H**	**J**

3

6 →  → 8

9 →  → 12

3 →  → ?

4	5	6	8
A	**B**	**C**	**D**

4

3.5 →  → 4

5 →  → 5.5

–2 →  → ?

–2.5	–1.5	1.5	2.5
F	**G**	**H**	**J**

5

$\frac{4}{6} \rightarrow \square \rightarrow \frac{2}{3}$

$\frac{14}{8} \rightarrow \square \rightarrow \frac{7}{4}$

$\frac{10}{6} \rightarrow \square \rightarrow ?$

A	B	C	D
$\frac{5}{4}$	$\frac{5}{3}$	$\frac{4}{2}$	$\frac{6}{2}$

6

$24 \rightarrow \square \rightarrow 6$

$12 \rightarrow \square \rightarrow 3$

$-8 \rightarrow \square \rightarrow ?$

F	G	H	J
–4	–2	2	4

7

$\frac{1}{2} \rightarrow$  $\rightarrow \frac{3}{4}$

$-\frac{1}{2} \rightarrow$  $\rightarrow -\frac{1}{4}$

$\frac{6}{8} \rightarrow$  $\rightarrow ?$

A $\frac{1}{2}$

B $\frac{7}{8}$

C 1

D $\frac{5}{4}$

For Numbers 8–14, find the portion of the figure that is shaded.

8

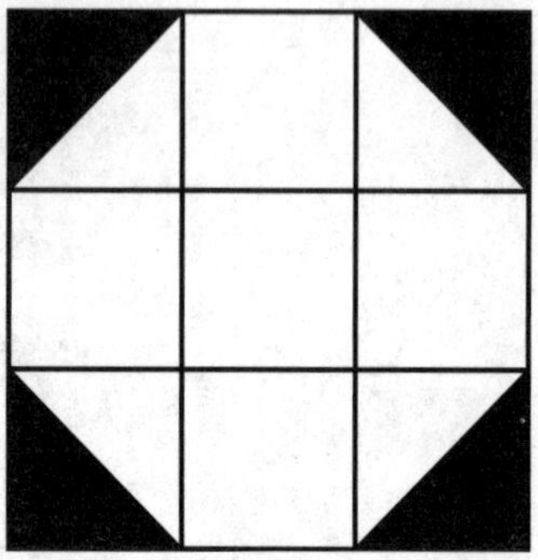

F $\frac{2}{9}$

G $\frac{2}{7}$

H $\frac{4}{9}$

J $\frac{4}{7}$

9

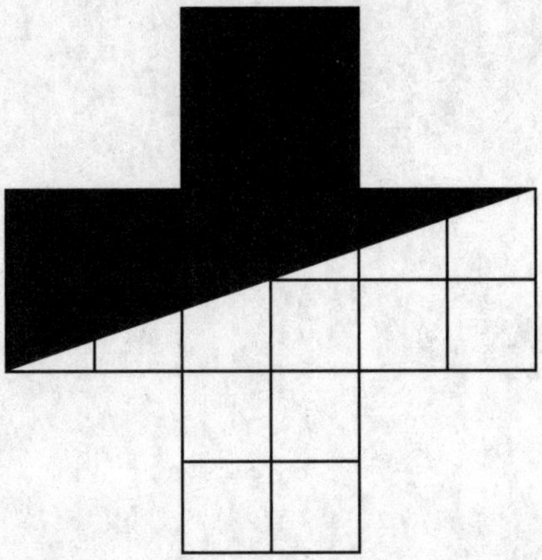

$\frac{2}{5}$	$\frac{1}{2}$	$\frac{3}{5}$	$\frac{2}{3}$
A	**B**	**C**	**D**

10

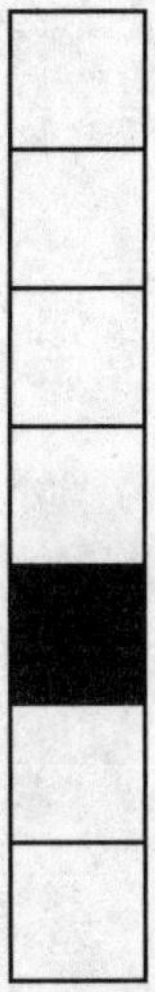

$\frac{1}{5}$	$\frac{1}{6}$	$\frac{1}{7}$	$\frac{1}{8}$
F	**G**	**H**	**J**

11

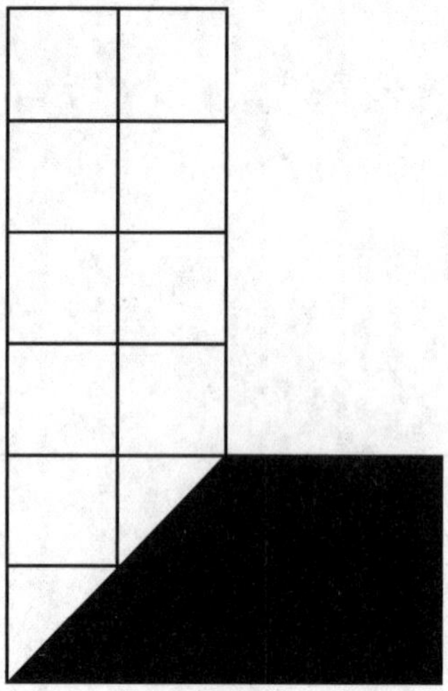

$\frac{5}{16}$	$\frac{1}{3}$	$\frac{3}{8}$	$\frac{6}{8}$
A	**B**	**C**	**D**

12

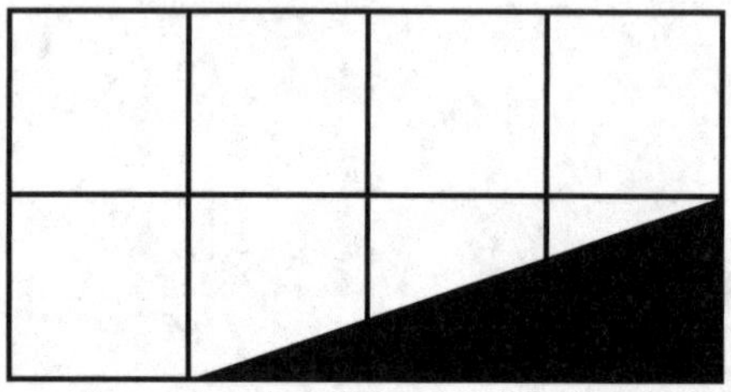

$\frac{3}{16}$	$\frac{1}{5}$	$\frac{1}{4}$	$\frac{3}{8}$
F	**G**	**H**	**J**

13

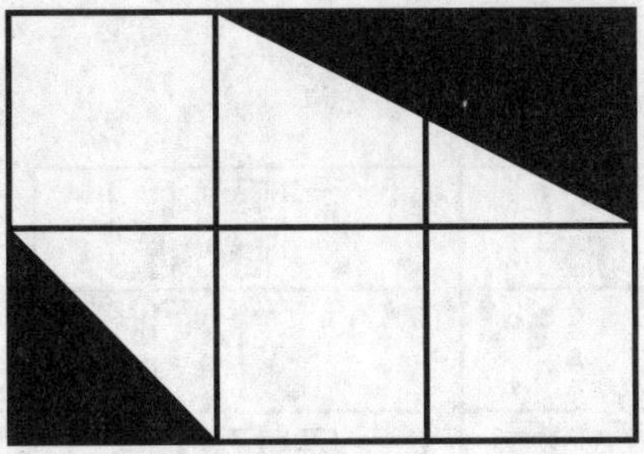

$\frac{1}{6}$	$\frac{1}{4}$	$\frac{1}{3}$	$\frac{1}{2}$
A	**B**	**C**	**D**

14

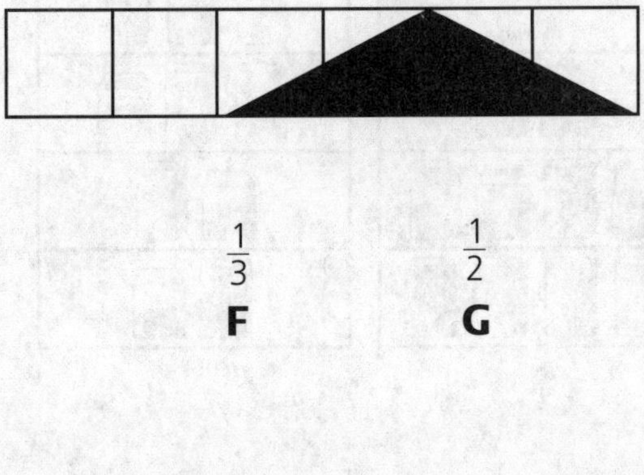

$\frac{1}{3}$	$\frac{1}{2}$	$\frac{2}{3}$	$\frac{5}{6}$
F	**G**	**H**	**J**

For Numbers 15–20, look at the scale showing sets of shapes of equal weight. Find an equivalent pair of sets that would also balance the scale.

15

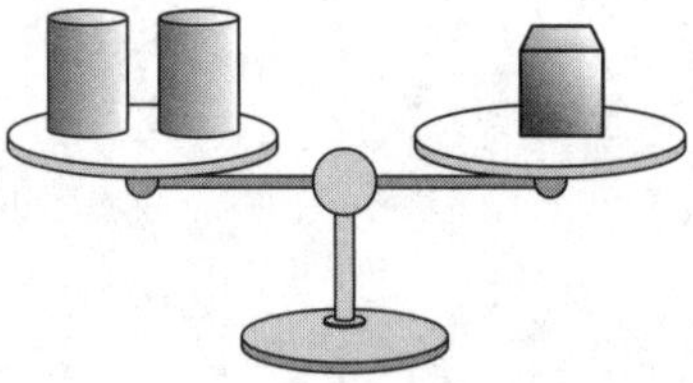

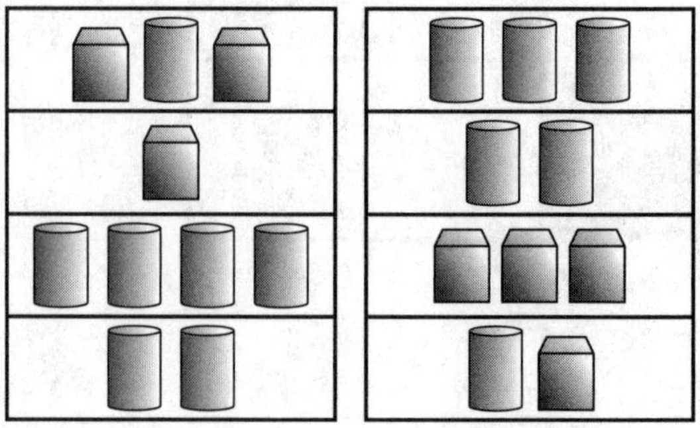

A

B

C

D

16

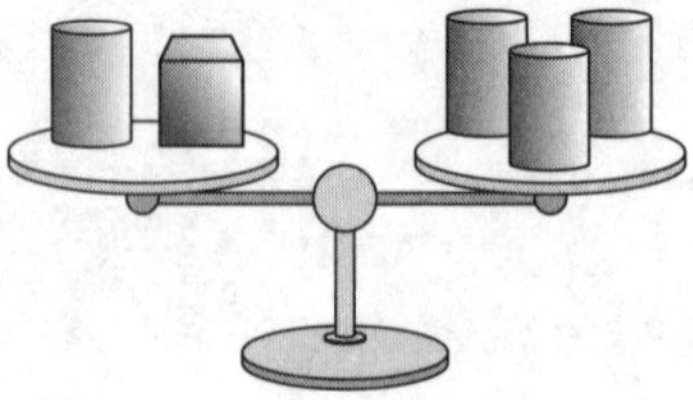

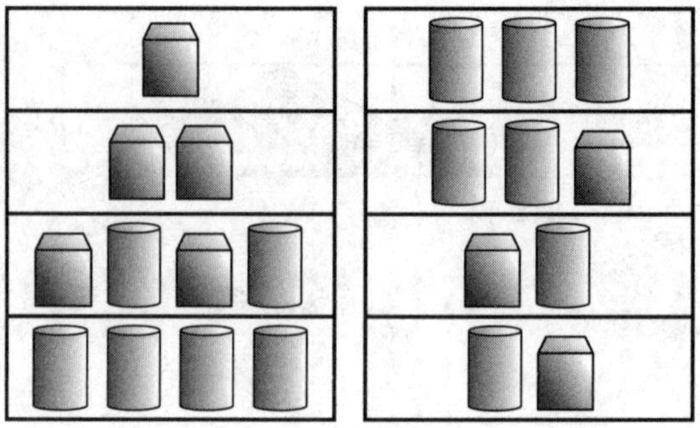

F

G

H

J

17

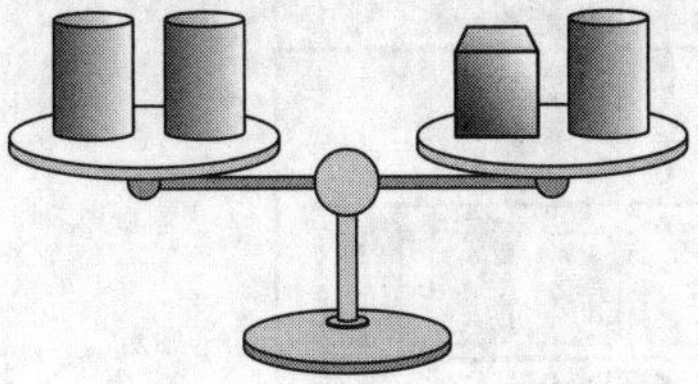

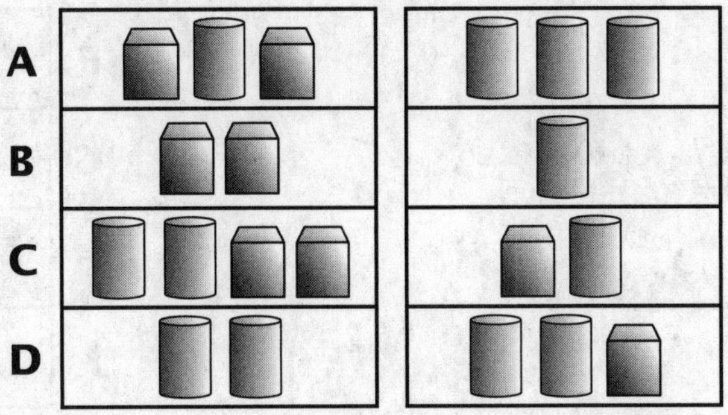

18

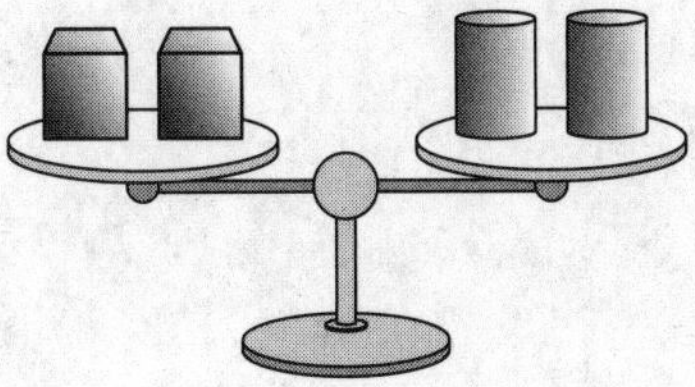

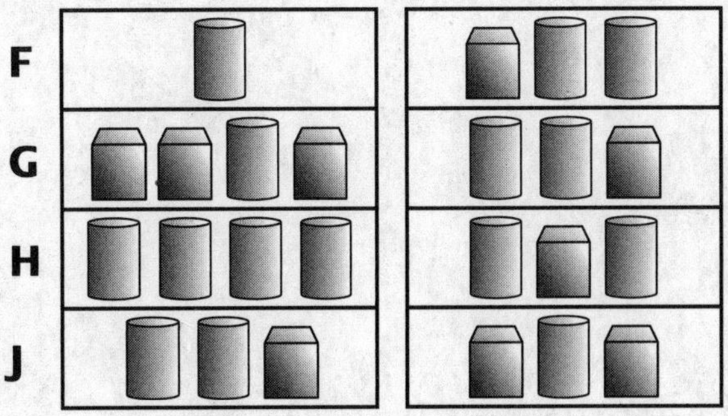

19

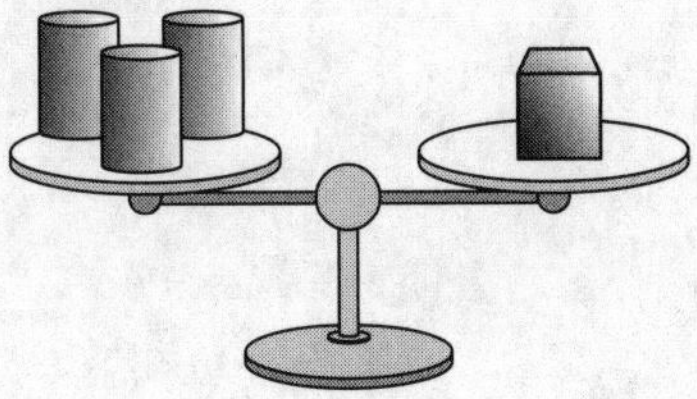

20

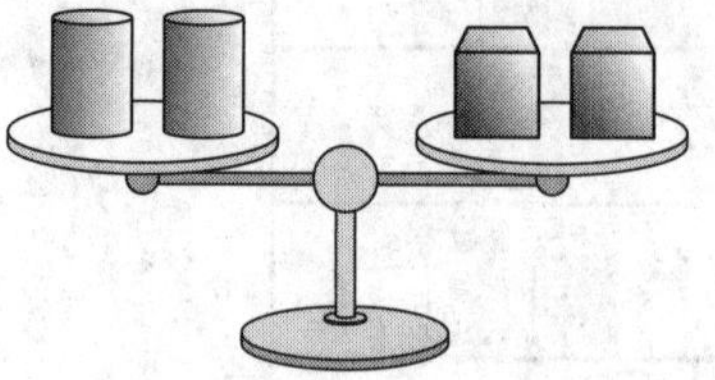

F 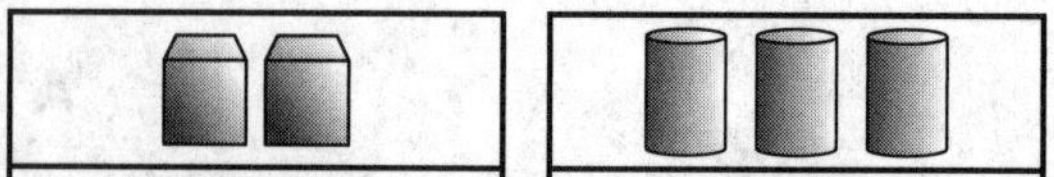

G 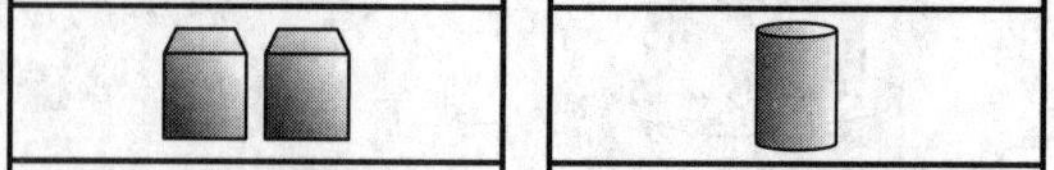

H 

J 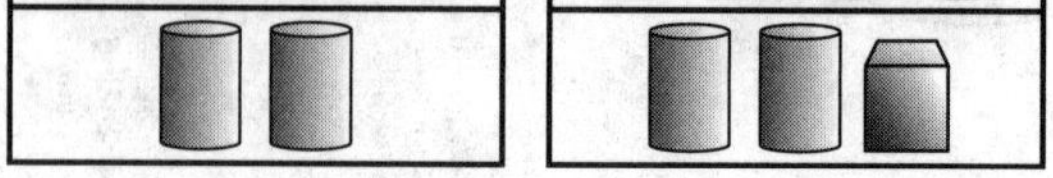

Test 4

Verbal Reasoning—Words
(20 Questions, 15 Minutes)

For questions 1–6 find the word that is a necessary part of the underlined word.

1

<u>oven</u>

A heat

B stone

C bread

D rack

2

<u>scissors</u>

F paper

G hair

H cut

J office

3

<u>hat</u>

A black

B felt

C head

D cowboy

4

<u>knife</u>

F metal

G edge

H steak

J kitchen

5

<u>**microphone**</u>

A cord

B music

C announcement

D sound

For questions 6–10, find the word that is most like the underlined words.

6

<u>**coax**</u> <u>**encourage**</u> <u>**persuade**</u>

F force

G entice

H dissuade

J drive

7

<u>**volleyball**</u> <u>**basketball**</u> <u>**soccer**</u>

A badminton

B tennis

C baseball

D bowling

8

<u>**turtle**</u> <u>**snake**</u> <u>**crocodile**</u>

F lizard

G frog

H fish

J salamander

9

<u>**pacify**</u> <u>**soothe**</u> <u>**comfort**</u>

A baby

B calm

C cradle

D sweet

10

<u>**letter**</u> <u>**email**</u> <u>**manuscript**</u>

F speech

G lecture

H message

J memo

For questions 11–15, three of the words in the group belong together. Find the word that does not belong.

11

A Bulldog

B Poodle

C Dog

D Labrador

12

F Eye

G Squint

H Blink

J Wink

13

A Astronomy

B Astronaut

C Astrology

D Astrobiology

14

F Count

G Tally

H Numbers

J List

15

A Recall

B Designate

C Appoint

D Assign

For questions 16–20, the words in the top row are related in a certain way. The words in the bottom row are related in the same way. Find the word that completes the bottom row of words.

16

breeze	**gust**	**hurricane**
drizzle	**rain**	______

F weather

G downpour

H sun

J snow

17

cup	**quart**	**gallon**
ounce	______	**pound**

A mile

B flour

C measure

D ton

18

tie	**bracelet**	**belt**
neck	**wrist**	______

F watch

G waist

H joint

J jewelry

19

ankle	**knee**	**elbow**
foot	**leg**	______

A arm

B finger

C muscle

D bone

20

feline	**lion**	**cat**
canine	**wolf**	______

F mouse

G jungle

H dog

J fur

Test 5

Verbal Reasoning—Context

(10 Questions, 7 Minutes)

For questions 1–10, find the statement that is true according to the information given.

1

John is taller than both Sam and Trudy. Trudy is taller than Cindy but not as tall as Eric. Cindy is taller than Walter and Alice.

A Trudy is taller than Sam.

B Sam is not as tall as Eric.

C Walter is taller than Alice.

D Alice is not as tall as Trudy.

2

Martina spent 3 hours studying the night before the math test. Carol did not study at all, but Carol always does her homework on time.

F Martina will do better on the math test than Carol.

G Martina studied more than Carol did the night before the math test.

H Martina does not always turn in her homework on time.

J Carol is better at math than Martina is.

3

Bob will either buy an ice cream cone or a cup of frozen yogurt. But he only buys frozen yogurt if he can have chocolate sprinkles. The store is out of chocolate sprinkles.

A Bob will not buy anything.

B Bob will buy an ice cream cone.

C Bob will buy a frozen yogurt with chocolate syrup.

D Bob will buy an ice cream with chocolate syrup.

4

Peter and Karen went to the movie theater. They bought their tickets before the movie started and went right into the theater. Peter bought some popcorn and a soda and then sat down to watch the movie. Halfway through the movie, Peter left the theater and did not return.

F Peter was ill and went to the hospital.

G Peter did not like the movie.

H Peter did not see the end of the movie.

J The popcorn gave Peter a stomach ache.

5

Ron can type 13 pages per hour. Sylvia and Jean can type 8 pages per hour. Alex can type 4 pages per hour.

A Jean cannot type as fast as Ron can.

B Alex makes lots of mistakes when he types.

C Ron likes to type more than Sylvia does.

D Alex only types with two fingers, while Sylvia uses all ten fingers.

6

Taylor and Emily are competitive swimmers for their high school swim team. Taylor can swim 60 laps in 30 minutes. Emily can swim 55 laps in 30 minutes.

F Taylor can swim farther than Emily.

G Taylor can swim faster than Emily.

H Emily will never swim faster than Taylor.

J Taylor is the fastest swimmer on the team.

7

Everyone who wants to see a movie rated PG-13 is required to be at least 13 years old. Alex is 13 ½ years old and is planning to go see a movie at Cinema World where PG-13 movies are playing.

A Alex will see a PG-13 rated movie at Cinema World.

B Alex will be able to see any movie playing at Cinema World.

C If age is the only restriction to see a movie rated PG-13, Alex will be permitted to do so.

D Alex will not see any other movie at Cinema World except for a PG-13 movie.

8

Luisa got a horse for her 15th birthday. She's considering the following names: Applejack, Princess Sophia, or Luna. Luisa's sister thinks Luna would be the most appropriate name since the horse is white and black speckled.

F Luisa was 14 years old two weeks ago.

G Luisa's sister gave Luisa the horse.

H Luisa considered at least ten other names for the horse.

J The only present Luisa received for her 15th birthday was the horse.

9

If Ila auditions for the annual ice skating show, then Khadijah does as well. If Khadija auditions for the annual ice skating show, then Kemisa does not audition.

A If Kemisa auditions, Ila does not audition.

B If Kemisa does not audition, Khadijah does audition.

C If Khadijah does not audition, Kemisa does audition.

D If Khadijah auditions, Ila auditions.

10

Currently, everyone who plays guitar at Goldberg Variations Studio is right-handed. One of the two teachers is right-handed. Sharon and Ted are left-handed. Katy and Peter are right-handed.

F Katy plays guitar at this studio.

G Ted does not play guitar at this studio.

H Sharon is not a teacher at this studio.

J Goldberg Variations Studio does not accept guitar students who are left-handed.

Test 6

Reading and Language Arts

(40 Questions, 40 minutes)

Kangaroos are fascinating creatures because they are so different from other mammals. Unlike most mammals, kangaroos rear their young in a pouch and hop to get around. Their long, powerful hind legs are used for jumping, and their thick tail gives them balance. Their forelimbs are used almost like human hands. Despite these well-known characteristics, prevalent among all kangaroos, there are many lesser-known variations; some kangaroo species differ tremendously in such characteristics as habitat, color, social patterns, and size. For example, various species range in size from nine inches to more than eight feet.

The explanation often given for these odd features is that kangaroos are marsupials, and marsupials are a primitive form of mammal. This explanation, which may or may not be correct, is particularly popular among people who live in the Northern Hemisphere. Their view is reflected in the statements they make about the Virginia opossum, the only marsupial native to North America. The opossum is frequently described as a primitive animal, little changed since the time of the dinosaurs.

But even if the opossum can in some ways be considered a "living fossil," the same cannot be said of the kangaroo. These Australian marsupials have changed recently in order to adapt to a changing environment. Kangaroos evolved from small forest animals into creatures that live mainly in open spaces. This development was probably related to the spread of grassland areas in Australia between ten and fifteen million years ago.

1 **Which of the following best describes what this passage is about?**

A a comparison of the opossum and the kangaroo

B the competition between marsupials and dinosaurs

C the evolutionary background of kangaroos

D why kangaroos are not really mammals

2 **The author of the passage would most likely believe that**

F opossums are smarter than kangaroos

G dinosaurs ate kangaroo meat

H kangaroos were once extinct

J kangaroos are interesting animals

3 **The author of this passage is most likely**

A a scientist

B a hunter

C an Australian

D a physicist

4 **According to the passage, kangaroos use their tails primarily to**

F defend themselves against predators

G help them balance while they jump

H communicate with other kangaroos

J grasp small objects

5 **The author says that kangaroos "range in size from nine inches to more than eight feet" in order to**

A shock the reader

B demonstrate one way in which species of kangaroos can differ from each other

C contradict earlier research on kangaroos

D prove that not all kangaroos are important

Abraham Lincoln was born in 1809 in a log cabin in Kentucky. In his early years he lived in Kentucky and Indiana. He did not attend many years of formal schooling, but he was very ambitious and taught himself through reading. Partly due to his poor upbringing, Lincoln was determined to promote equal economic opportunity for all people. When he was older, Lincoln moved to New Salem, Illinois, where he studied law and served in the state legislature. After he became a lawyer, he moved to Springfield, where he became an important and wealthy attorney.

Lincoln returned to politics with the repeal of the Missouri Compromise, which meant the threat of the expansion of slavery. In part due to the national attention he gained through a series of debates with Stephen A. Douglas, he moved to the forefront of the new Republican Party, and was soon elected President of the United States.

The Civil War began shortly after Lincoln took office. Despite his inexperience in military matters, he showed a keen understanding of military strategy. Lincoln always insisted that his main objective was to save the Union, but as it became clear that abolishing slavery would weaken the South, he began to give serious attention to the issue of emancipation.

Shortly after the Union victory and his re-election to office, Lincoln's life was cut short by an assassin's bullet. Lincoln remains, nevertheless, one of our greatest presidents. His rise from poverty to the White House exemplifies the American dream. He was a skillful politician, a natural leader, and bravely bore the weight of a war that almost ended the Union for which so many people had fought.

6 **The passage is mostly about**

F how the Civil War was won by the North

G the life of one of the presidents of the United States

H where Abraham Lincoln was born

J why Abraham Lincoln abolished slavery

7 **According to the passage, Abraham Lincoln worked for equality in part because of**

A his religious beliefs

B his poverty as a child

C the advice of his wife

D his dislike of the English monarchy

8 **The author probably believes that Lincoln**

F was one of our most important presidents

G lost the debates with Stephen Douglas

H had an unhappy childhood

J was the wealthiest person in Springfield, Illinois

9 **According to the passage, Lincoln returned to politics from practicing law because of**

A the start of the Civil War

B the repeal of the Missouri Compromise

C the emancipation of the slaves

D the Union victory

10 **It can be inferred from the passage that Lincoln**

F had no sisters or brothers

G did not like public speaking

H did not command an army before the Civil War

J wanted to return to Kentucky after his presidency

11 **Which of the following questions is answered in the passage?**

A In what year was Lincoln elected President?

B Which political party did Lincoln belong to?

C Why did the Civil War begin?

D In what year did Lincoln die?

An Inuit navigating in polar darkness and whiteouts makes use of many clues to find his way. When traveling on ice in the fog, the Inuit uses the voices of seabirds against the cliffs and the sound of the surf at the end of the ice. When he begins to travel over open terrain, he marks the angle of the wind and aligns the fur of his parka with the breeze. He notes the trend of any cracks in the ice as he crosses them. Sea ice cracks can reveal the presence of a cape or headland invisible in the distance, or they may confirm one's arrival at a known area.

Constant attention to such details, memories of the way the land looks, and stories told by other travelers are used together with the movements of animals to keep the traveler on course. Searching for small but crucial clues can be exhausting for a person who does not know what to look for.

These navigational tools are still part of village life in the Arctic, used just as often today while traveling long distances by snowmobile as they were once by people traveling on foot. Such skills are still more critical for the success of a journey than even the best maps and navigation aids. Fogs and blizzards hide the reference points needed to navigate by map. Even compasses can't be relied on so close to the magnetic pole: the compass needle wanders aimlessly due to the proximity of the magnetic field. The most dependable sources of direction for most Inuit, therefore, are the behavior of the wind and ocean currents, and such subtle clues as the flow of a river.

12 **The passage is mostly**

F a comparison of modern and traditional methods of navigation

G a description of traditional navigational techniques used by Inuit

H an explanation of the purpose of the migration of Inuit

J a discussion of advances in navigational equipment

13 **Which of the following is not mentioned as a technique the Inuit use for navigating?**

A consulting with the elders of the Inuit community

B examining cracks in the ice along the route

C learning from the experiences of earlier travelers

D using the angle of the wind to judge direction

14 **According to the author, traditional navigational skills are still used by the Inuit because**

F traditional techniques are always superior to modern technology

G the Inuit prefer not to travel too far from home

H modern navigational equipment is too expensive for most Inuit

J traditional methods are sometimes more effective than sophisticated equipment

15 **The last paragraph suggests that in the polar region navigation is complicated by the fact that**

A objects in the sky, such as stars, do not provide useful information

B the summer moon affects ocean currents in unpredictable ways

C accurate compass readings are difficult to obtain

D wind and ocean currents change too quickly to be reliable

16 **It can be inferred from the passage that**

F Inuit live in the Antarctic.

G Inuit parkas are sometimes made with fur.

H Inuit do not have maps of their territory.

J Inuit always live in total darkness.

It may seem to you as you gaze up into the night sky that the stars move from one night to the next. While the position of a star may vary a bit over the years, in general the movement of the stars is due to the rotation of the Earth, not the movement of the stars. The Earth rotates on its axis from west to east every day. Because you are not aware of the movement of the Earth, it looks to you as though the stars are moving from east to west in the sky. The only star that does not appear to have any motion is Polaris, or what is commonly called the North Star. The reason it does not appear to move is that it lies almost directly above the North Pole. Because its position is fixed, the North Star has long been used as a tool for navigation. No matter where you are, if you can locate the North Star, you can figure out which direction is North. Sailors out on the sea used it to find their way. Polaris is a very bright star, so it can be located easily.

17 **The word appear in this passage most nearly means**

A seem

B show up

C reveal

D occur

18 **According to the passage, the reason we think that the stars move is due to**

F the distance between the Earth and the stars

G the effect of the Sun

H gravity

J the rotation of the Earth

19 **The North Star can be used for navigation because it**

A is very bright

B is easy to locate

C has a fixed position in the sky

D is low on the horizon

20 **According to the passage, the reason Polaris does not appear to move is that**

F it moves more slowly than the other stars

G it is brighter than the other stars

H it lies above the North Pole

J it is farther away than other stars

21 **According to the passage, most stars appear to move**

A from east to west

B from west to east

C toward the north

D from north to south

A yurt is a kind of tent that the Mongols lived in year-round. It was designed specifically for the particular needs of the Mongol people. It was portable enough that it could be carried by a single pack animal. It could be set up or taken down in half an hour. And it could retain enough heat to keep its inhabitants warm during the <u>frigid</u> Mongolian winters.

The frame of a yurt is made from wooden poles laced together with leather straps. The tops of these poles fit into slots in a wooden ring that forms the top of the structure. The ring is open in the center to allow air to flow in and smoke to flow out. When it rains, this hole can be covered with a piece of felt or animal skin.

To complete the yurt, large pieces of felt or animal hides are placed over the wooden frame. During especially cold months, several layers might be used to ensure warmth. These pieces of felt are then <u>secured</u> to the frame using ropes.

If you ever meet a Mongol, however, don't ask to see his yurt. In fact, the word "yurt" is Russian; the Mongols themselves called the structure a "ger," which means "home."

22 **The word <u>frigid</u> probably means**

F boring

G frightening

H very cold

J dangerous

23 **It can be inferred from the way the yurt is fashioned that the Mongols**

A had a large number of possessions

B were a very peaceful people

C moved around a great deal

D grew up in large families

24 **The yurts were probably warmed by using**

F the body heat of people who lived in them

G hot water from nearby hot springs

H a fire made inside the tent

J heated rocks

25 **The word <u>secured</u> probably means**

A attached

B rescued

C found

D dried

The digestive system of the cow is complex and interesting. Unlike humans, who have a simple stomach, the cow has a large four-chambered stomach. Cows eat plants, primarily grasses, which are only partly digested in one of the four chambers, called the rumen. The cow will then regurgitate, or bring back up, the partially digested plant fibers in a small mass called "cud." The cud is chewed further and swallowed again, this time into the second chamber, called the reticulum. It passes then to the third and fourth chambers, until it is completely digested. It may sound unpleasant, but the cow is able to extract a maximum of nutrients from its food by digesting in this manner. The whole process may take more than three days.

26 **The best title for this passage might be**

F The Cow's Great Gift to Man: Milk

G Digestive Systems and their Purposes

H The Diet of the Cow

J The Digestive System of the Cow

27 **According to the passage, the primary benefit of the cow's digestive system is that it**

A allows the cow to eat more slowly

B doesn't require as much food as other digestive systems do

C allows the cow to absorb more nutrients

D is complex and original

28 **The passage suggests that humans**

F depend on cows

G do not have four-chambered stomachs

H do not eat grass

J require the same nutrients as cows do

The first old "horseless carriages" of the 1880s may have been worthy of a snicker or two, but not the cars of today. The progress that has been made over the last one hundred years has been phenomenal. In fact, much progress was made even in the first twenty years—in 1903 cars could travel 70 mph. The major change from the old cars to today is the expense. Whereas cars were once a luxury that only the rich could afford, today people of all income levels own cars.

In fact, today there are so many cars that if they were to line up end to end, they would touch the moon. Cars are used for everyday transportation for millions of people, for recreation, and for work. Many people's jobs depend on cars—police officers, healthcare workers, and taxi drivers, to name a few.

One thing that hasn't changed is how cars are powered. The first cars ran on gas and diesel fuel just as today's cars do. Scientists have recently done a great deal of research on how to improve the design of cars, and this has made modern cars much more fuel efficient and less polluting than older cars.

29 **The author uses the word progress to refer to**

- **A** the ability of a car to move forward
- **B** technological advancements
- **C** new types of fuel
- **D** the low cost of the car

30 **Which of the following is answered by the passage?**

- **F** What jobs involve the use of cars?
- **G** How much money is spent on cars today?
- **H** Where will the fuels of the future come from?
- **J** When will cars completely stop polluting?

31 **This passage is primarily concerned with**

- **A** the problem of fuel consumption
- **B** the invention of the car
- **C** the development of the car from past to present
- **D** the future of automobiles

32 **Scientists devote much of their research today to**

- **F** making cars that run faster
- **G** making more cars
- **H** making cars more affordable
- **J** making cars more fuel efficient

33 **When discussing the early advances of the automobile, the author's tone could best be described as**

A proud

B hesitant

C doubtful

D angry

34 **Choose the sentence that is written correctly.**

F Remaining independent until the late 1800s, the U.S. took Hawaii as a territory in 1900.

G Hawaii remains independent until the late 1800s, and they became a U.S. territory in 1900.

H Hawaii remained independent until the late 1800s, and it became a U.S. territory in 1900.

J Becoming a U.S. territory in 1900, Hawaii was keeping its independence up until the late 1800s.

35 **Choose the sentence that is written correctly.**

A Rachel received the Premier Physicist award, which did outstanding work in the lab this year.

B Rachel received the Premier Physicist award, whose work in the lab was outstanding this year.

C The Premier Physicist award was given to Rachel this year, her work having been outstanding in this.

D For her outstanding work in the lab this year, Rachel received the Premier Physicist award.

36 **Choose the sentence that is written correctly.**

F Not understanding its importance, wrist pain is a symptom most people ignore.

G Wrist pain is ignored by most people because of their not understanding its importance.

H Most people ignore wrist pain because they do not understand its importance.

J A symptom ignored by most people not understanding its importance is wrist pain.

37 **Choose the sentence that is written correctly.**

A A great deal of natural talent and grace belongs to Beverly, which are important qualities for figure skaters.

B Beverly has what are important qualities for figure skaters, which are a great deal of natural talent and grace.

C A great deal of natural talent and grace, which are important qualities for figure skaters, belong to Beverly.

D Beverly has a great deal of natural talent and grace, which are important qualities for figure skaters.

38 **Choose the best topic sentence for the paragraph.**

> ______________________ *She supplied soldiers with bandages and medical supplies, food, and clean water. She helped search for survivors and cared for the wounded. Later, when she discovered the work of the Red Cross, she was instrumental in establishing the American chapter in 1881.*

F Clara Barton, an American humanitarian, cared a great deal for victims of natural disasters.

G During the Civil War, Clara Barton performed deeds that earned her the title "Angel of the Battlefield."

H In her early years, Clara Barton worked as a schoolteacher before taking a job with the U.S. Patent Office.

J During the civil war, soldiers did not receive very good health care.

39 **Choose the best topic sentence for the paragraph.**

> ______________________ *First, frogs have long hind legs with webbed feet. This makes it easy for them to hop or swim. Toads, on the other hand, have short and stubby legs that are better for walking. Moreover, frogs have smooth and slimy skin, because they tend to live in a wet environment. Toads, instead, have warty dry skin and prefer to live in arid environments.*

A Living in the water has caused some animals to develop special features.

B Frogs are some of the most interesting creatures in the world.

C Animals that live both in water and on land are called amphibians.

D Though they may look similar, there are many differences between frogs and toads.

40 **Choose the sentence that best combines the two italicized sentences into one.**

I wanted to go to the zoo on Sunday with my brother.

So I did all my chores.

F Because I wanted to go the zoo on Sunday with my brother, I did all my chores.

G Because I wanted to go to the zoo, I did all my chores on Sunday with my brother.

H Because I did all my chores, I wanted to go to the zoo on Sunday with my brother.

J I did all my chores on Sunday, I wanted to go to the zoo with my brother.

Test 7—Mathematics

(40 Questions, 35 minutes)

1 Which of the following is equal to $3 + 60 + \frac{2}{1000}$?

A 63.002

B 63.02

C 36.02

D 2063

2 For delivering newspapers, Polly earns \$20 per month during the months of January through October. During the months of November and December, she earns \$32 per month. What is Polly's average monthly income for the year?

F \$20

G \$21.50

H \$22

J \$22.50

3 A negative even number multiplied by a positive odd number will be

A positive and odd

B positive and even

C negative and odd

D negative and even

4 $\frac{0.246}{0.12} =$

F 0.205

G 2.05

H 20.5

J 205

5 $(3.0 \times 10^3) \times (5.3 \times 10^2) =$

A 1.59×10^6

B 1.59×10^5

C 8.3×10^5

D 8.3×10^6

6 What is the area of a circle with radius 5?

F 5π

G 10π

H 25

J 25π

7 The price of a notebook is reduced from $85.00 to $56.00. By what percent is the price of the notebook decreased?

A 15%

B 23%

C 29%

D 34%

8 If the average of 2, 5, and x is equal to the average of 3 and x, what is the value of x?

F 2

G 3

H 4

J 5

9 Alicia receives $3.00 for every 50 papers she delivers on her paper route. If in the month of July she delivered 420 papers, how much money did she make?

A $25.20

B $27.00

C $32.30

D $33.30

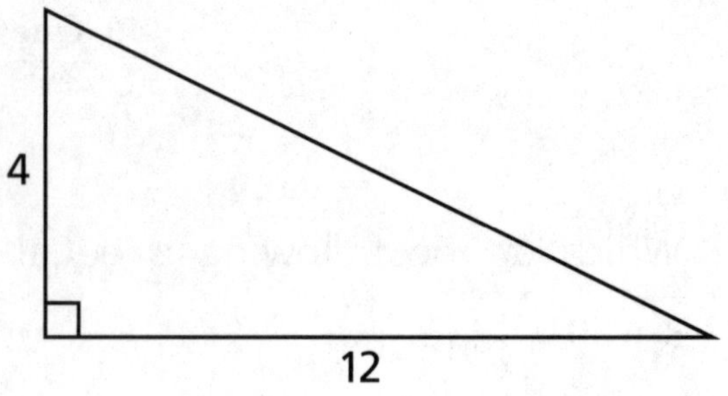

10 What is the area of the triangle above?

F 16

G 18

H 22

J 24

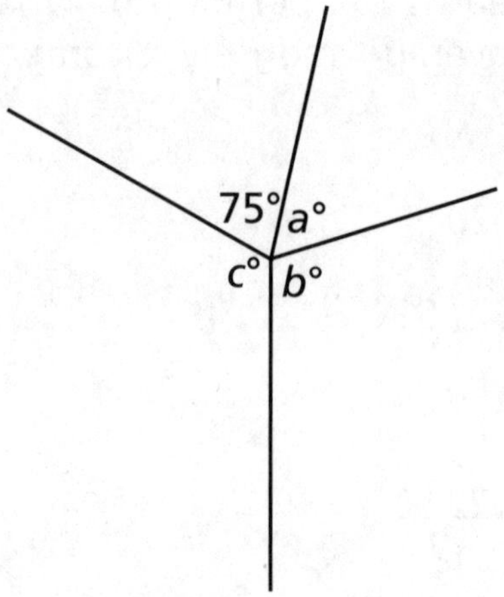

11 In the figure above, what is the value of $a + b + c$?

A 105

B 125

C 235

D 285

12 A record store increases the price of a \$15 record by 20%. This new price is later reduced 10%. What is the final price of the record?

F \$15.80

G \$16.20

H \$16.80

J \$18.00

13 Which of the following is the greatest?

A $\frac{5}{11}$

B $\frac{7}{13}$

C $\frac{1}{3}$

D $\frac{6}{15}$

14 How many factors do 16 and 56 have in common?

F 2

G 3

H 4

J 5

15 If $2x - 5 > 5x + 1$, which of the following gives the possible value of x?

A $x < -2$

B $x > -2$

C $x < 2$

D $x > 2$

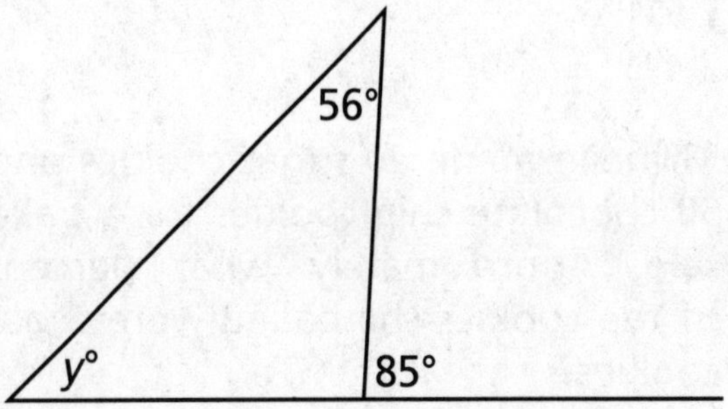

16 In the triangle above, what is the value of y?

F 29

G 39

H 24

J 66

17 How many multiples of 3 and 4 are between 1 and 50?

A 2

B 4

C 6

D 9

18 How many cubes with an edge of 1 inch can fit into a box of dimensions 5 inches by 8 inches by 3 inches?

F 15

G 24

H 40

J 120

19 Michelle made 20 sugar cookies and 50 chocolate chip cookies for a bake sale. Approximately what percent of the cookies she baked were sugar cookies?

A 20%

B 30%

C 35%

D 40%

20 If one gallon of paint can cover 3 square feet, how many gallons of paint will be needed to cover a rectangular wall that measures 12 feet by 18 feet?

F 10

G 24

H 56

J 72

21 Peter is packing oranges into 2 large and 8 small boxes. He can put 12 oranges into each small box, and 18 oranges into each large box. Which of the following shows how many total oranges Peter can pack?

A $(2 \times 12) + (8 \times 18)$

B $(12 \times 8) + (18 \times 2)$

C $(2 \times 8) + (12 \times 18)$

D $2(12 + 8 + 18)$

22 Louise has 8 pairs of socks in her drawer. 2 pairs are blue, 2 pairs are black, 2 pairs are red, and 1 pair is white. If she chooses one pair of socks at random from the drawer, what is the chance that the pair she draws will be black?

F $\frac{1}{8}$

G $\frac{1}{4}$

H $\frac{3}{8}$

J $\frac{1}{3}$

23 If $3x - 5 = 4x + 3$, what is the value of x?

A −8

B −5

C 5

D 8

24 $\dfrac{\frac{3}{4}}{\frac{3}{5}} =$

F $\frac{4}{5}$

G $\frac{5}{4}$

H $\frac{9}{20}$

J $\frac{9}{5}$

25 John has 18 marbles and Ken has 44. How many marbles must Ken give to John such that they have the same number of marbles?

A 13

B 18

C 24

D 32

26 Which of the following is equivalent to multiplying a number *x* by 5?

F multiplying *x* by $\frac{10}{5}$

G dividing *x* by $\frac{1}{5}$

H multiplying *x* by $\frac{1}{5}$

J dividing *x* by $\frac{5}{1}$

27 Which of the following leaves a remainder of 2 when divided by 3?

A 25

B 37

C 44

D 51

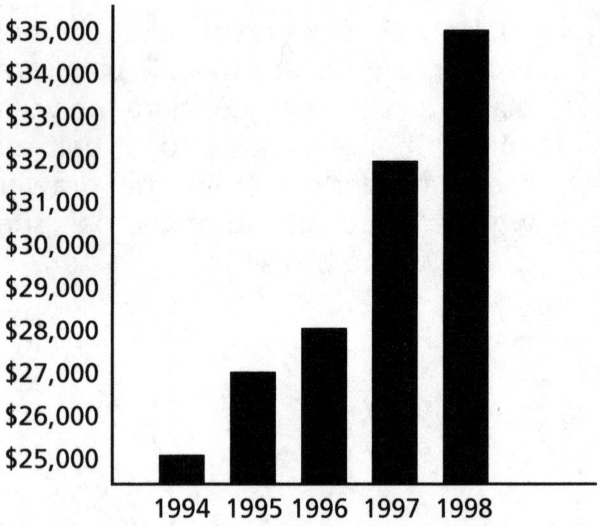

28 According to the chart above Amanda's salary increased by approximately what percent from 1994 to 1997?

F 28%

G 22%

H 14%

J 7%

29 In the figure above, the distance between points *B* and *C* is 5. If *B* is the midpoint of *AC* and *C* is the midpoint of *BD*, what is the distance between *A* and *D* ?

A 5

B 10

C 15

D 20

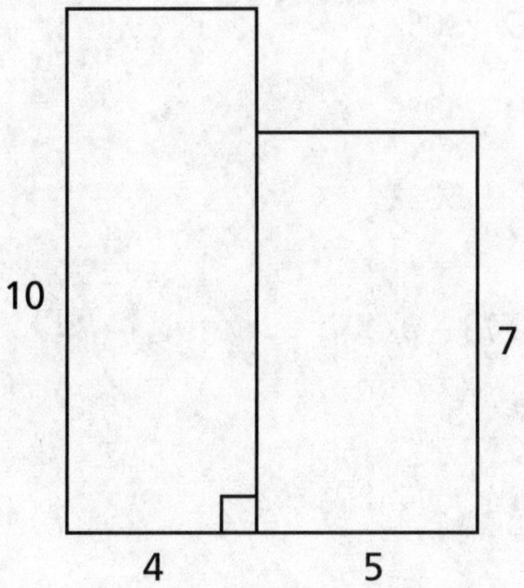

30 What is the perimeter of the figure above?

F 26

G 32

H 38

J 42

31 In a group of 50 adults and children, there are 18 more adults than children. How many adults are in the group?

A 34

B 32

C 16

D 18

32 If $2^x + 3^x = 97$, then $x =$

F 2

G 3

H 4

J 5

33 What is the sum of the distinct positive factors of 12?

A 20

B 27

C 28

D 36

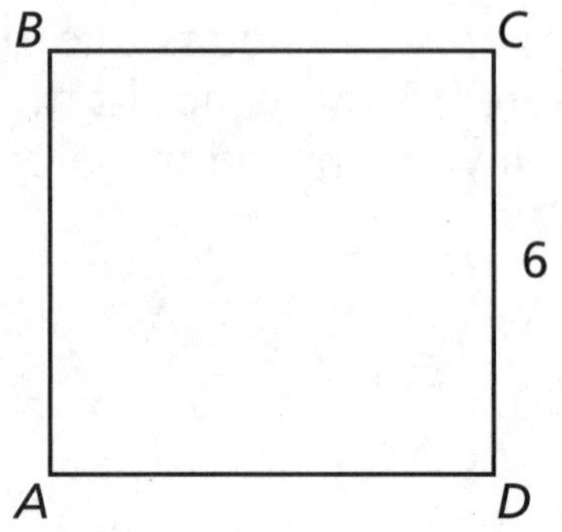

34 Figure *ABCD* above is a square. What is the difference between the area of *ABCD* and the perimeter of *ABCD*?

F 8

G 12

H 16

J 18

35 If $\frac{1}{5}$ of a number is 14, then $\frac{1}{2}$ of that number is

A 35

B 32

C 30

D 28

36 On Main Street, there are 2 red houses, 3 blue houses, and 5 white houses. What fractional part of the houses are blue?

F 20%

G 30%

H 40%

J 50%

37 $2\sqrt{3} + 3\sqrt{3}$?

A 5

B $5\sqrt{3}$

C $6\sqrt{3}$

D 15

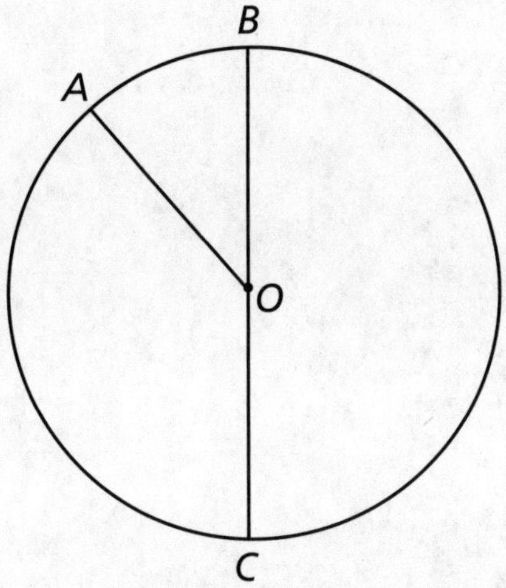

38 The figure above shows a circle with center *O*. If *AO* = 14, what is the measure of *BC* ?

F 14

G 24

H 28

J 32

39 If $-5 + 2(3a + 2b) = 4b - 2$ then $a =$

A $\frac{1}{2}$

B 2

C 6

D –1

40 $\frac{5^6}{5^2} =$

F 4^5

G 5^3

H 5^4

J 25^4

Chapter 26
COOP Practice Test 1: Answers and Explanations

ANSWER KEY

Test 1	Test 2	Test 3	Test 4	Test 5	Test 6	Test 7
1. D	1. B	1. D	1. A	1. D	1. C	1. A
2. H	2. H	2. J	2. H	2. G	2. J	2. H
3. A	3. A	3. A	3. C	3. B	3. A	3. D
4. H	4. G	4. G	4. G	4. H	4. G	4. G
5. A	5. C	5. B	5. D	5. A	5. B	5. A
6. G	6. G	6. G	6. G	6. G	6. G	6. J
7. B	7. A	7. C	7. D	7. C	7. B	7. D
8. J	8. H	8. F	8. F	8. F	8. F	8. J
9. B	9. A	9. C	9. B	9. D	9. B	9. A
10. G	10. J	10. H	10. J	10. G	10. H	10. J
11. A	11. A	11. C	11. C		11. B	11. D
12. F	12. G	12. F	12. F		12. B	12. G
13. B	13. B	13. B	13. B		13. F	13. B
14. J	14. F	14. F	14. H		14. D	14. H
15. A	15. D	15. B	15. A		15. H	15. A
16. F	16. G	16. G	16. G		16. B	16. F
17. B	17. A	17. A	17. D		17. A	17. B
18. J	18. J	18. J	18. G		18. J	18. J
19. A	19. A	19. D	19. A		19. C	19. B
20. H	20. G	20. H	20. H		20. H	20. J
					21. A	21. B
					22. C	22. G
					23. H	23. A
					24. C	24. G
					25. F	25. A
					26. D	26. G
					27. H	27. C
					28. B	28. F
					29. B	29. C
					30. F	30. H
					31. C	31. A
					32. J	32. H
					33. F	33. C
					34. C	34. G
					35. D	35. A
					36. H	36. G
					37. D	37. B
					38. B	38. H
					39. J	39. A
					40. F	40. H

ANSWERS AND EXPLANATIONS

Test 1—Sequences

1. **D** The sequence goes 1, 2, 3 and rotates from top to right to bottom, so the missing element should have four spots on the left.

2. **H** The first two elements have triangles on the outside and reversed inside shapes. Therefore the missing element should have spots on the outside and reversed shapes on the inside.

3. **A** From the first to second element, all the Os change to Xs and Xs change to Os. Therefore the missing element should have OOX.

4. **H** The first element has two lines, the next has three lines, and the next has four lines. The missing element should have five lines.

5. **A** The second element is what you should get if you flipped the first element upside down. The final element should be what you would get if you flipped the third element upside down.

6. **G** The first element has three black circles, the second has two black circles, and the third has one black circle. Therefore the missing element should have no black circles.

7. **B** The sequence should go 21 (+ 11) 32 (+ 6) 28 | 56 (+ 11) 67 (+ 6) 73 | 16 (+ 11) 27 (+ 6) 33.

8. **J** The sequence should go 62 (+ 2) 65 (– 2) 63 | 18 (+ 2) 20 (– 2) 18 | 52 (+ 2) 54 (– 2) 52.

9. **B** The sequence should go 32 (÷ 2) 16 (÷ 2) 8 | 52 (÷ 2) 26 (÷ 2) 13 | 24 (÷ 2) 12 (÷ 2) 6.

10. **G** The sequence should go 2 (× 4) 8 (× 4) 32 | 3 (× 4) 12 (× 4) 48 | 1 (× 4) 4 (× 4) 16.

11. **A** The sequence should go 5 (+ 1) 6 (× 3) 18 | 2 (+ 1) 3 (× 3) 9 | 8 (+ 1) 9 (× 3) 27.

12. **F** The sequence should go 15 (+ 0) 15 (÷ 3) 5 | 24 (+ 0) 24 (÷ 3) 8 | 9 (+ 0) 9 (÷ 3) 3.

13. **B** The sequence should go 6 (× 2) 12 (× 2) 24 | 8 (× 2) 16 (× 2) 32 | 2 (× 2) 4 (× 2) 8.

14. **J** Substitute numbers for letters to make it easier. The sequence should go 1 (+ 1) 2 (+ 1) 3 | 1 (+2) 3 (+ 2) 5 | 1 (+ 3) 4 (+ 3) 7 | 1 (+ 4) 5 (+4) 9, or ABC | ACE | ADG | AEI.

15. **A** Each element in the sequence begins with a letter that was the last letter in the previous element, so the missing element must begin with Q. You can also substitute numbers for letters; start with 5 because E is the fifth letter of the alphabet. The sequence should go 5 (+ 2) 7 (+ 2) 9 | 9 (+ 2) 11 (+ 2) 13 | 13 (+ 2) 15 (+ 2) 17 | 17 (+ 2) 19 (+ 2) 21, or EGI | IKM | MOQ | QSU | UWY.

16. **F** The number in the center increased by 1, so the missing element must have a 4 in it. The letters follow this pattern: 10 (+ 2) 12 | 13 (+ 2) 15 | 16 (+ 2) 18 | 19 (+ 2) 21 | 22 (+ 2) 24, or JL | MO | PR | SU | VX.

17. **B** The number at the end goes up by the power of 2 each time, so the missing element should have a 16 in it. The letters follow this pattern: 3 (– 1) 2 | 5 (– 1) 4 | 7 (– 1) 6 | 9 (– 1) 8 | 11 (– 1) 10, or CB | ED | GF | IH | KJ.

18. **J** The sequence goes backward through the alphabet in blocks of four letters.

19. **A** The first and third letters of the sequence start with A and go down the alphabet; the second and fourth letters start with Z and go backward through the alphabet.

20. **H** The second letter in each element becomes the first letter in the next element, so the missing element should begin with IK.

Test 2—Analogies

1. **B** A shoe is worn on a foot; a horseshoe is worn on a hoof.
2. **H** Bees live in a hive; fish live in a fish tank.
3. **A** Goggles protect the eyes; a helmet protects the head.
4. **G** A pencil is used to write on paper; chalk is used to write on a blackboard.
5. **C** A bus is a large car; a lion is a large cat.
6. **G** An apple grows on a tree; a raspberry grows on a bush.
7. **A** A suitcase is used to hold a shirt; a briefcase is used to hold a file.
8. **H** Bread is made from grain; jam is made from fruit.
9. **A** You use your eyes to look at a painting; you use your ear to hear music.
10. **J** An axe is used to cut a tree; a knife is used to cut a carrot.
11. **A** A button holds a shirt closed; laces hold a shoe closed.
12. **G** You use a toothbrush to brush your teeth; you use a hairbrush to brush your hair.
13. **B** A ring is worn around a finger; a necklace is worn around the neck.
14. **F** A stool is a kind of chair; a desk is a kind of table.
15. **D** A typewriter was used to write letters, but now people use computers; a carriage was used for transportation, but now people use cars.
16. **G** An umbrella protects against the rain; sunglasses protect against the sun.
17. **A** A vacuum is a machine that does the work of a broom; a sewing machine is a machine that does the work of a needle and thread.
18. **J** A pot is a type of kettle; a cap is a type of hat.
19. **A** A wristwatch is a small clock; a house is a small skyscraper.
20. **G** A caterpillar becomes a butterfly; an acorn becomes a tree.

Test 3—Quantitative Reasoning

1. **D** In this problem, the numbers are decreasing, so the number must be less than 2 in the second line, eliminating (A). Evaluate how much the numbers decrease from 7 to 3 and 6 to 2: in each case, the difference is 4. Since the difference in both these cases is consistent, you know the pattern must be to subtract 4 from the left-hand number, so $3 - 4 = -1$, (D).

2. **J** Here, the numbers do not change in a uniform way, so look for relationships in the number pairs. $2 + 4 = 6$, but so too does $2 \times 3 = 6$. This relationship works as well in the second pair, as $5 \times 3 = 15$. Therefore, $4 \times 3 = 12$, making (J) correct.

3. **A** The numbers change at different rates, and both are increasing. $\frac{6}{8} = \frac{9}{12}$, meaning that these numbers are related to each other in the form of a ratio. As a result, $\frac{6}{8} = \frac{9}{12} = \frac{3}{4}$, (A).

4. **G** Decimal points usually look more intimidating, but continue to look for relationships between the numbers. $3.5 + 0.5 = 4$, which also works for $5 + 0.5 = 5.5$. Since this difference is common to both number pairs, use this to find the third number, remembering that as you add a positive number to a negative number, the result will get closer to zero instead of further away. $-2 + 0.5$ will therefore equal -1.5, (G).

5. **B** $\frac{4}{6}$ to $\frac{2}{3}$ is the same number reduced by a factor of 2. The same applies to $\frac{7}{4}$ from $\frac{14}{8}$. Therefore, reduce $\frac{10}{6}$ by dividing the by 2 in the numerator and denominator to find $\frac{5}{3}$, (B). Be careful to divide by 2 instead of subtract, or else you might fall into the trap of $\frac{5}{4}$, (A) or $\frac{6}{2}$, (D).

6. **G** 24 is a multiple of 6, and 12 is a multiple of 3. $\frac{24}{4} = 6$, and $\frac{12}{4} = 3$. Therefore, divide -8 by 4 and the result is -2, (G). Remember the negative sign for -8 will result in a negative quotient, eliminating (H) and (J).

7. **C** $\frac{1}{2} + \frac{1}{4} = \frac{3}{4}$. Check to see if this relationship is the same in the second pair. $-\frac{1}{2} + \frac{1}{4} = -\frac{1}{4}$ as well, so add $\frac{1}{4}$ to $\frac{6}{8}$. $\frac{6}{8}$ is the same as $\frac{3}{4}$, so $\frac{3}{4} + \frac{1}{4} = \frac{4}{4}$, or 1. Make sure to have a common denominator when adding fractions.

8. **F** Count up the shaded triangles. There are 4 triangles, each taking the space of half a square. Therefore, $4 \times \frac{1}{2} = 2$, out of the total 9 squares. This makes (F) correct.

9. **C** Use the unshaded portions of the cross to figure out the dimensions of the remaining portions. You may assume that the figure is to scale, and you can use the uncovered squares to find the dimensions of other portions of the cross. The shaded portion is more than half the figure, eliminating (A) and (B).

10. **H** There are 7 squares in total, and only 1 square is shaded. Be sure to count the full amount in the denominator as in (H), not the ratio of shaded to unshaded as in (G).

11. **C** Use the unshaded portion to deduce how many squares are shaded. The shaded portion consists of one section 2 squares by 2 squares, along with a triangle formed by a 2 square by 2 square portion. Therefore, the full 2 by 2 section consists of 4 squares and the triangle will be half that amount. Therefore, the total number of squares in the shaded portion is 6, and the number of squares in the figure is 16. $\frac{6}{16}$ reduces to $\frac{3}{8}$.

12. **F** There are 8 total squares in the figure. The shaded triangle has a base of 3 and a height of 1. Therefore the area of the triangle is $\left(\frac{1}{2}\right)(3)(1) = \frac{3}{2}$. $\frac{\left(\frac{3}{2}\right)}{8}$ can be simplified to $\frac{3}{16}$, since the expression can also be written $\left(\frac{3}{2}\right)\left(\frac{1}{8}\right)$. Choice (F) is correct.

13. **B** There are 6 total squares in the figure. The small triangle in the bottom left corner comprises half of a square, while the larger triangle in the top right corner has an area of 1, using the area formula for a triangle: $A = \left(\frac{1}{2}\right)(2)(1) = 1$. The total shaded area, therefore, is 1.5, or $\frac{3}{2}$. $\frac{\left(\frac{3}{2}\right)}{5} = \frac{3}{12}$, or $\frac{1}{4}$, (B).

14. **F** The shaded triangle is can be found by using the area formula: $A = \left(\frac{1}{2}\right)bh$. The base is 4 units long and the height is 1, so the formula should read $A = \left(\frac{1}{2}\right)(4)(1) = 2$. The total area of the figure is 6, so the fraction of the shaded portion should read $\frac{2}{6}$, which reduces to $\frac{1}{3}$, (F).

15. **B** The scale shows two cylinders on the left and one cube on the right. This means that for every cube, two cylinders must balance it out on the other side. In (A), the one cylinder on either side will cancel each other out, leaving two cubes on the left and two on the right. This is not the same ratio as above, so eliminate (A). Choice (B) shows a cube on the opposite side, balanced out by two cylinders on the right. Since this is the same ratio to keep the scale balanced, it must be the correct answer. Choice (C) is incorrect because the 2 cylinders:1 cube ratio is not there. Choice (D) is also incorrect because one cylinder on either side will cancel, leaving a 1:1 ratio between the remaining cylinder on the left and cube on the right.

16. **G** One cylinder on either side will cancel each other out. The remaining ratio is one cube to two cylinders. Choice (F) has a ratio of one cube to three cylinders, which is incorrect. In (G), one cube on either side will cancel, leaving one cube to two cylinders, the correct ratio. In (H), a cube and a cylinder will cancel on either side, leaving only two cubes on the left, which is incorrect. In (J), a cylinder on either side will cancel, leaving a ratio of three cylinders to one cube instead of the 2:1 ratio necessary.

17. **A** There are two shapes on either side of the scale, meaning that the cylinder and cube are the same weight (you could think of a cylinder cancelling on either side, leaving a cylinder and a cube on either side). Therefore, the choice that has an equal number of shapes on either side will be the correct answer, regardless of shape. In this case, that answer is (A).

18. **J** There are two shapes on either side of the scale, meaning that the cylinder and cube are the same weight. Therefore, the answer choice that has an equal number of shapes on either side will be the correct answer, regardless of shape. In this case, that answer is choice (J).

19. **D** The ratio of cylinders to cubes in this case is 3:1. Therefore, the correct answer will contain that same ratio. In (A), cancel a cylinder on either side, and you will find that the ratio is 2 cylinders to 1 cube, so it may be eliminated. Choice (B) contains a ratio of 3 cylinders to 2 cubes, so eliminate this choice as well. Choice (C) is the inverse of what we are looking for, since the cubes are supposed to be the heavier object here. Cancel a cylinder on either side in (D), and you will find the desired ratio of 3 cylinders to 1 cube in the remaining shapes.

20. **H** There are two shapes on either side of the scale, meaning that the cylinder and cube are the same weight. Therefore, the answer choice that has an equal number of shapes on either side will be the correct answer, regardless of shape. In this case, that answer is (H).

Test 4—Verbal Reasoning—Words

1. **A** An oven is used to heat things. It does not necessarily have to be made of stone, heat bread, or have a rack.

2. **H** Scissors are used to cut things. They can cut things besides paper and hair, and they do not have to be in an office.

3. **C** A hat is worn on the head. It may or may not be black, felt, or a cowboy hat.

4. **G** A knife has an edge for cutting. It may or may not be metal, used for steak, or found in a kitchen.

5. **D** A microphone is used to capture sound. It may or may not have a cord, capture music, or be used to make an announcement.

6. **G** Coax, encourage, persuade, and entice are synonyms and mean to cause (someone) to do something through reasoning or argument.

7. **D** Volleyball, basketball, soccer, and bowling are sports that involve a ball without the use of a racquet or bat.

8. **F** A turtle, snake, crocodile, and lizard are all types of reptiles.

9. **B** Pacify, soothe, comfort, and calm are synonyms and mean to gently quiet or relax a person.

10. **J** A letter, email, manuscript, and memo are all types of written messages.

11. **C** Bulldog, poodle, and Labrador are all breeds of dogs.

12. **F** To squint, blink, and wink are all actions perform by an eye.

13. **B** Astronomy, Astrology, Astrobiology are all areas of science that involve the study space and/or celestial objects. An astronaut is a person, not a type of science.

14. **H** Numbers can be counted, tallied, or listed.

15. **A** Designate, appoint, and assign are synonyms that mean to give someone a specific task or position.

16. **G** A breeze is a mild gust, and a gust is a mild hurricane. Drizzle is a light rain, and rain is a light downpour.

17. **D** Cup, quart, and gallon are measures of volume; ounce, pound, and ton are measures of weight.

18. **G** A tie goes around the neck; a bracelet goes around the wrist; a belt goes around the waist.

19. **A** An ankle is a joint in the foot; a knee is a joint in the leg; an elbow is a joint in the arm.

20. **H** A lion and a cat are kinds of feline; a wolf and a dog are kinds of canine.

Test 5—Verbal Reasoning—Context

1. **D** We know that Trudy is taller than Cindy, and Cindy is taller than Alice, so we know that Trudy is taller than Alice.

2. **G** All we know is that Martina studied for three hours and Carol did not study at all, so Martina studied more than Carol. None of the other choices are certain.

3. **B** We know that Bob will not buy a frozen yogurt since the store is out of sprinkles. Since we also know that he buys either an ice cream cone or frozen yogurt, we know he will buy an ice cream cone.

4. **H** All we know is that Peter left the movie theater and did not return, so he didn't see the end of the movie. None of the other choices are certain.

5. **A** We know that Jean types 8 pages per hour and Ron types 13 pages per hour. Therefore Jean types more slowly than Ron.

6. **G** Because Taylor can swim more laps in the same amount of time than Emily, his pace is faster. Therefore, (G) is correct. The other choices go beyond the information in the question stem.

7. **C** Just because Alex is 13 does not mean that she will see a PG-13 movie, eliminating (A). She also would not be allowed to to see an R-rated film yet, so we do not know if she would be able to see any movie at Cinema World, which eliminates (B) as well. Choice (C) works because Alex will be permitted to see a PG-13 movie if she chooses, since age is the only restriction. Choice (D) is incorrect because she might want to see something other than a PG-13 movie.

8. **F** If Luisa had her 15th birthday, then she must have been 14 previously. The question does not state that her sister gave her the horse, so eliminate (G). We do not know how many other names, if any, Luisa considered, eliminating (H). Finally, the horse may have been only one of many presents, so eliminate (J). Choice (F) is the correct answer.

9. **D** If Ila auditions, then Khadijah does as well. Therefore, if Khadijah is auditioning, it must mean that Ila is auditioning since that is the condition on which Khadijah would audition. This makes (D) correct.

10. **G** Because all of the guitar players at the studio are right-handed, Ted must not be a guitar player at that studio because he is left-handed, (G). Katy does not have to play guitar just because she is right-handed, though she could be. Eliminate (F) since it does not have to be true. Similarly, Katy might be a teacher at the studio, but it is not necessarily true, eliminating (H). Choice (J) is not true.

Test 6—Reading Comprehension

1. **C** Each paragraph of the passage discusses some aspect of the evolution of kangaroos.

2. **J** There is no evidence in the passage to support (F), (G), or (H).

3. **A** The only person listed who would know about fossils and dinosaurs is a scientist.

4. **G** The first paragraph says that "their thick tail gives them balance."

5. **B** The quotation appears as an example for how "some kangaroo species differ."

6. **G** Choices (F), (H), and (J) are only details of the passage. The whole passage discusses Lincoln's life, from his birth to his death.

7. **B** The passage says that "due to his poor upbringing, Lincoln was determined to promote equal economic opportunity for all people."

8. **F** There is no evidence to support (G), (H), or (J). The passage says, however, that Lincoln was "one of our greatest presidents."

9. **B** According to the passage, "Lincoln returned to politics with the repeal of the Missouri Compromise."

10. **H** The third paragraph says that Lincoln was inexperienced in military matters. We can therefore infer that he did not have the experience of commanding an army.

11. **B** According to the passage, he was a member of the Republican Party.

12. **B** Every paragraph discusses how an Inuit can navigate without sight or tools.

13. **F** Every choice is mentioned somewhere in the passage except (F).

14. **D** Choice (A) is extreme, and there is no support in the passage for (B) or (C). It does say in the final paragraph, however, that Inuit methods sometimes work when modern technology is ineffective.

15. **H** According to the last paragraph, "compasses can't be relied on."

16. **B** There is no evidence in the passage to support (A), (C), or (D). However, it does say that an Inuit "aligns the fur of his parka with the breeze." Therefore, some parkas must be made with fur.

17. **A** Since the passage begins by saying that the stars "seem" to move and then uses the word *appear* in the same way, the word *appear* in this passage must mean "seem."

18. **J** The second sentence of the passage says that "the movement of the stars is due to the rotation of the earth."

19. **C** The passage says that it can be used for navigation because "its position is fixed."

20. **H** According to the passage, Polaris "lies almost directly above the North Pole."

21. **A** The passage says that it seems "as though the stars are moving from east to west in the sky."

22. **C** The word *frigid* follows a mention of a need "to keep its inhabitants warm." Therefore *frigid* must mean "very cold."

23. **H** According to the first paragraph, the yurt was designed to be "portable" and to be "carried by a single pack animal."

24. **C** The second paragraph says that the yurt was designed to allow "smoke to flow out." This means that there is smoke inside the yurt.

25. **F** The word *secured* is used to discuss how the pieces of felt are attached to the frame of the yurt.

26. **D** Since milk is never mentioned, (A) can be eliminated. Choice (B) does not mention cows and is too general; (C) is only a detail of the passage.

27. **H** According to the passage, "the cow is able to extract a maximum amount of nutrients from its food" with its special digestive system.

28. **B** The passage says that cows are "unlike humans, who have a simple stomach."

29. **B** The word *progress* is used to describe the technological developments in the last hundred years.

30. **F** The second paragraph says that police officers and taxi drivers make use of cars on the job.

31. **C** Choices (A) and (B) are only details, and (D) is not really discussed.

32. **J** According to the final sentence of the passage, they devote research to making cars "more fuel-efficient and less polluting."

33. **F** The authors says in the first paragraph that the advances have been "phenomenal."

34. **C** Choice (D) is awkward, (B) uses two different verb tenses, and (A) suggests that the U.S. remained independent instead of Hawaii.

35. **D** Choices (A) and (B) suggest that the award was doing the work. Choice (C) contains a comma splice and is awkward.

36. **H** Choices (G) and (J) are awkward. Choice (F) suggests that the wrist pain (rather than the person experiencing the wrist pain) doesn't understand its importance.

37. **D** Choices (A) and (B) are awkward and contain misplaced modifiers. In (C), the main subject (deal) and verb (belong) do not agree.

38. **B** The following sentences discuss ways in which Clara Barton helped soldiers during a particular war. Therefore, the opening sentence should introduce this. Choice (A) is too broad, (C) is too specific and not directly related to the following sentences, and (D) doesn't introduce who "she" is.

39. **J** The rest of the paragraph discusses the differences between frogs and toads, so the first sentence should introduce this discussion.

40. **F** Choices (G) and (H) change the meaning of the original sentences, and (J) is a comma splice.

Test 7—Math

1. **A** 3 + 60 alone makes 63, so (C) and (D) can be eliminated. Since the thousandth place is the third to the right of the decimal, $\frac{2}{1000} = 0.002$.

2. **H** First, let's find Polly's total income for the year. She earns \$20 per month for 10 months, or \$200. Add to that her \$32 from November and \$32 from December, and her total income for the year is \$264. To find the average, we divide this amount by 12 (the number of months).

3. **D** Let's use –4 as our negative even number and 3 as our positive odd number. If we multiply them together we get –12, which is negative and even.

4. **G** The easiest way to solve this is to move the decimals three places to the right, and we get $\frac{246}{120}$. If you like, you can estimate and see that this is just larger than 2, or you can do long division.

5. **A** To solve 3.0×10^3 we move the decimal three places to the right, and get 3,000. To solve 5.3×10^2 we move the decimal two places to the right, and get 530. If we multiply these numbers together, we get 1,590,000. Already we can eliminate (C) and (D). Which of (A) or (B) says 1,590,000? Take 1.59 and move the decimal point 6 places to the right.

6. **J** The formula for the area of a circle is πr^2. Since the radius is 5, the area is 25π.

7. **D** Percent decrease is always $\frac{\textit{difference}}{\textit{original}}$. The difference beween the two prices is $29, and the original price of the notebook is $85. So the percent difference is $\frac{29}{85} = 0.34$, or 34%.

8. **J** One easy way to solve this problem is to plug in the answer choices. Could x be 2? Is the average of 2, 5, and 2 equal to the average of 3 and 2? No. Could x be 3? Is the average of 2, 5, and 3 equal to the average of 3 and 3? No. Could x be 4? Is the average of 2, 5, and 4 equal to the average of 3 and 4? No. Could x be 5? Yes, because the average of 2, 5, and 5 is 4, and the average of 3 and 5 is 4.

9. **A** We can set this up as a proportion: $\frac{50\ \textit{papers}}{\$3} = \frac{420\ \textit{papers}}{x}$. To solve for x, solve $\frac{420 \times 3}{50}$.

10. **J** The area of a triangle is $\frac{1}{2}$ base $\times$ height. The base is 12 and the height is 4, so the area is 24.

11. **D** We know that $a + b + c + 75 = 360$, so $c + b + c = 285$.

12. **G** First we need to find 20% of $15. Translate this as $\frac{20}{100} \times 15 = 3$. That means that the price is inc-treased to $18. If that price is then reduced by 10%, that's $1.80 off.

13. **B** We can figure out which fraction is greatest by comparing them in pairs using the Bowtie. $\frac{7}{13}$ is larger than $\frac{5}{11}$, so (A) can be eliminated. $\frac{7}{13}$ is also larger than $\frac{1}{3}$. Finally, $\frac{7}{13}$ is larger than $\frac{6}{15}$.

14. **H** Let's begin by listing all the factors of 16 and 56. 16 can be factored as 1×16, 2×8, and 4×4. 56 can be factored as 1×56, 2×28, 4×14, and 7×8. They have the factors 1, 2, 4, and 8 in common.

15. **A** We can solve for x by first subtracting $5x$ from each side. This gives us $-3x - 8 > 1$. If we add 5 to each side, this becomes $-3x > 6$. Now we need to divide each side by -3. When you divide by a negative number, you need to change the direction of the inequality.

16. **F** The angle inside the triangle next to 85 must be 95 degrees because their sum is 180. Now the angles inside the triangle are 95 and 56. The sum of the angles inside a triangle must equal 180, so the third angle must be 29.

17. **B** It's very hard to count multiples up to 50. There must be an easier way. What are the first multiples of 3? 3, 6, 9, 12, and 15. What are the first multiples of 4? 4, 8, 12, and 16. What do you notice? Their first common multiple is 12. Therefore the question is really asking how many 12s there are between 1 and 50. This is a much simpler question: 12, 24, 36, 48.

18. **J** The easiest way to solve this is to find the volume of the large box. Volume is length × width × height = 5 × 8 × 3 = 120. Each small cube has volume of 1 × 1 × 1 = 1.

19. **B** Michelle made 70 cookies. Of those 70 cookies, 20 were sugar. The question is what percent of the total cookies were sugar? You can translate the question as $\frac{x}{100} \times 70 = 20$. To solve for *x*, multiply each side by 100 and divide by 70. This gives you 28%. The closest is (B).

20. **J** First we need to find out how many square feet the wall measures: 12 × 18 = 216 square feet. Each gallon of paint covers 3 square feet, so we will need $\frac{216}{3}$ gallons of paint.

21. **B** Let's take the small boxes first. We have 8 small boxes with 12 oranges each. That makes 8 × 12 oranges in the small boxes. Only (B) has (8 × 12) in it.

22. **G** Since Louise has 8 total pairs of socks, and we want to know the probability of drawing one of the 2 black pairs, we set up the fraction $\frac{2}{8}$, which is the same as $\frac{1}{4}$.

23. **A** To get all the *x*'s on one side, subtract 4*x* from each side. This gives us $-x - 5 = 3$. Now let's add 5 to each side: $-x = 8$.

24. **G** You can rewrite this as: $\frac{3}{4} \div \frac{3}{5}$. To divide fractions, flip the second fraction and multiply them: $\frac{3}{4} \times \frac{5}{3} = \frac{5}{12} = \frac{5}{4}$

25. **A** The best way to solve this problem is by plugging in the answer choices. Start with (A). If Ken gives 13 marbles to John, then Ken will lose 13 marbles and John will gain 13 marbles. Ken will then have 31, and John will have 31.

26. **G** Plug In a number for *x* to make the problem easier. Say that *x* is 10. The question now reads, "Which of the following is equivalent to multiplying 10 by 5?" Find a target by solving: 10 × 5 = 50, so the answer should be 50 when 10 is plugged into the answer choices. (B) works because 10 divided by $\frac{1}{5}$ is the same as 10 times $\frac{5}{1}$, which equals 50.

27. **C** Plug in the answer choices until we find the one that leaves a remainder of 2. 25 divided by 3 leaves a remainder of 1, so (A) isn't the answer. 37 divided by 3 leaves a remainder of 1, so (B) isn't the answer. 44 divided by 3 leaves a remainder of 2, so (C) is the answer.

28. **F** Amanda's salary increased from \$25,000 to \$32,000. Percent increase is calculated by $\frac{\textit{difference}}{\textit{original}}$. In this case the difference in salary is \$7,000 over the original \$25,000: $\frac{7{,}000}{25{,}000} = 28\%$.

29. **C** If *BC* is 5 and B is the midpoint of *AC*, then *AB* is also 5. Likewise, if *C* is the midpoint of *BD*, then *CD* is also 5.

30. **H** The side of the rectangle opposite side 4 must also be 4; the side of the rectangle opposite side 5 must also be 5, and the remaining side must be 3 because the two sides on the right of the figure make 10.

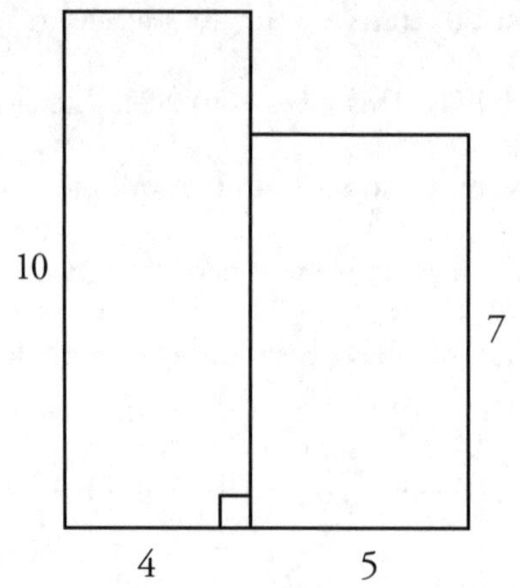

Therefore the perimeter of the whole figure is $5 + 4 + 10 + 4 + 3 + 5 + 7 = 38$.

31. **A** Plug in the answer choices until we find the right answer. Could the number of adults be 34? The problem says that there are 18 more adults than children, so if there are 34 adults, there will be 16 children. Does this make a total of 50? Yes.

32. **H** Plug in the answer choices until we find the value for x that works in the equation. Could x be 2? $2^2 + 3^2$ is 13, not 97. Let's try 3: $2^3 + 3^3$ is 35. How about 4? $2^4 + 3^4$ is 97.

33. **C** Let's begin by finding the factors 12. 12 can be written 1×12, 2×6, and 3×4. Now we need to find the sum of these factors: $1 + 1 + 2 + 2 + 6 + 3 + 4 = 28$.

34. **G** Since this is a square, the perimeter is $6 + 6 + 6 + 6$, or 24, and the area is 6×6, or 36. The difference between 24 and 36 is 12.

35. **A** If $\frac{1}{5}$ of a number is 14, then that number must be 14×5, or 70. Now the problem wants us to take $\frac{1}{2}$ of 70, which is 35.

36. **G** There are a total of 10 houses, of which 3 are blue. If 3 out of 10 are blue, then $\frac{3}{10}$, or 30%, are blue.

37. **B** When the number under the root symbol is the same, you can add them together: $2\sqrt{3} + 3\sqrt{3} = 5\sqrt{3}$.

38. **H** Any line from the center to the edge of the circle is a radius. Therefore, *AO, BO,* and *CO* are all radii. If the radius is 14, then the diameter (which is twice the radius) is 28.

39. **A** First, let's multiply out the left side of the equation. This gives us $-5 + 6a + 4b = 4b - 2$. If we subtract $4b$ from each side, we get $-5 + 6a = -2$. Now we can add 5 to each side, which gives us $6a = 3$. By dividing 6 from each side, we get $a = \frac{1}{2}$.

40. **H** Let's write these exponents out and then reduce. 5^6 is the same as $5 \times 5 \times 5 \times 5 \times 5 \times 5$. 5^2 is the same as 5×5. So we can rewrite the expression as $\frac{5 \times 5 \times 5 \times 5 \times 5 \times 5}{5 \times 5}$. If we reduce, we are left with $5 \times 5 \times 5 \times 5$, or 5^4.

Chapter 27
COOP
Practice Test 2

Test 1

Sequences

(20 questions, 15 minutes)

Choose the letter that shows what should fill the blank in the sequence

1

$\frac{x}{y}$ | $\frac{y}{x}$ | $\frac{p}{q}$ | ___

A	B	C	D
$\frac{p}{x}$	$\frac{p}{y}$	$\frac{q}{p}$	$\frac{q}{x}$

2

BBBA | BBAA | BAAA | ___

F	G	H	J
BABA	AAAA	ABBB	ABBA

3

△○○△ | ○△△○ | +□□+ | ___

A	B	C	D
□++□	□+□+	□○○□	△++△

4

F G H J

5

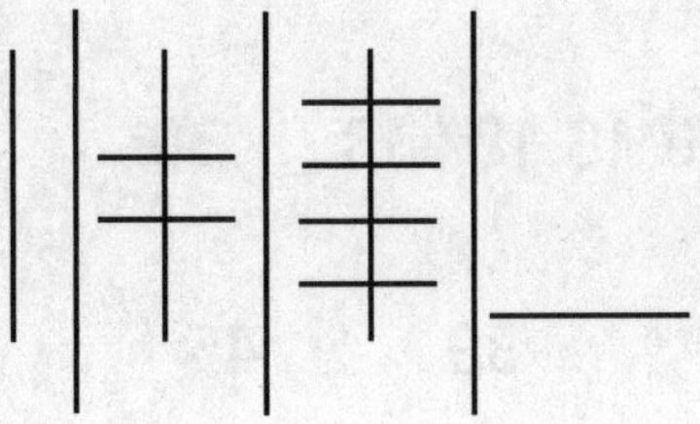

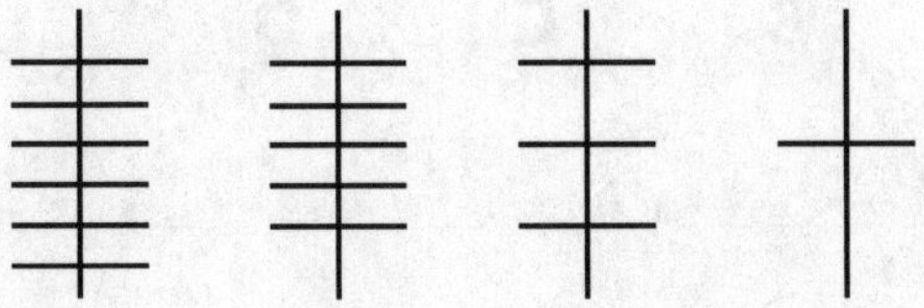

A **B** **C** **D**

6

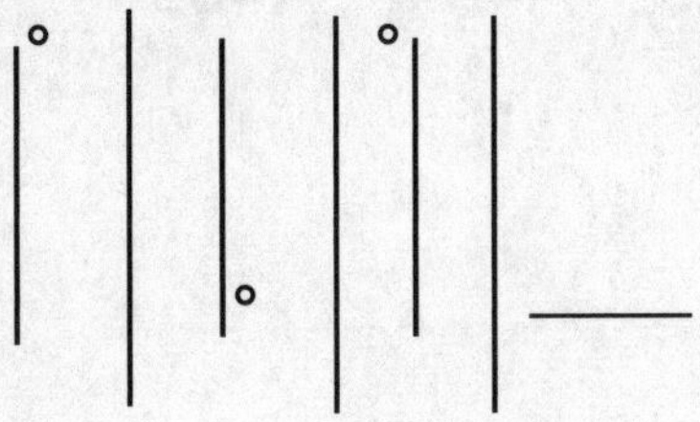

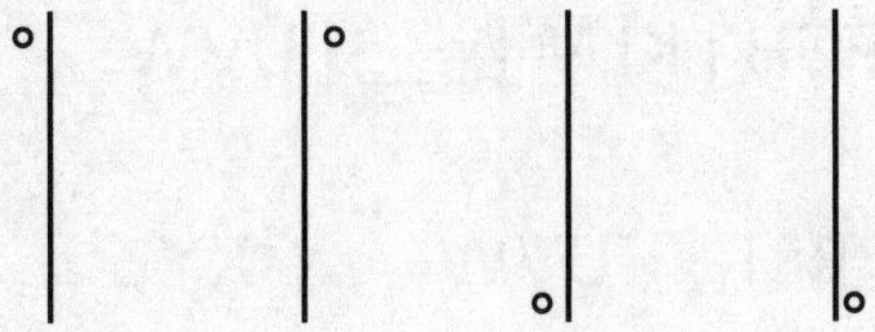

F **G** **H** **J**

7

34 46 49 | 8 20 23 | 57 __ 72

63	65	69	70
A	**B**	**C**	**D**

8

31 28 35 | 17 14 21 | 36 __ 40

30	33	35	39
F	**G**	**H**	**J**

9

66 66 22 | 18 18 6 | 27 __ 9

5	9	27	53
A	**B**	**C**	**D**

10

8 6 12 | 17 15 30 | 6 __ 8

4	6	8	12
F	**G**	**H**	**J**

11

6 18 19 | 3 9 10 | 4 __ 13

8	12	16	20
A	**B**	**C**	**D**

12

3 12 6 | 12 48 24 | 8 __ 16

12	24	32	36
F	**G**	**H**	**J**

13

11 33 33 | 6 18 18 | 13 __ 39

13	18	39	45
A	**B**	**C**	**D**

14

A1B2 | A2B3 | A3B4 | ___ | A5B6

A5B5	A5C6	A4B4	A4B5
F	**G**	**H**	**J**

15

ABC | FGH | KLM | ___ | UVW

PQR	RST	UVW	XYZ
A	**B**	**C**	**D**

16

AZA | BYB | CXC | ____ | EVE

DYD DWD WDW XDX

F **G** **H** **J**

17

GHF | IJH | KLJ | ___ | OPN

LMN NML MNL KML

A **B** **C** **D**

18

ABDE | FGIJ | KLNO | ____ | UVXY

MNPR PRST PQST MNRS

F **G** **H** **J**

19

BDFH | FHJL | JLNP | ____ | RTVX

MPRT NPRT NPTV MNRV

A **B** **C** **D**

20

B9LG | C12MH | D15NI | __ | F21PK

E16OI E18OJ E19PL E20QJ

F **G** **H** **J**

Test 2

Analogies

(20 questions, 7 minutes)

For the following questions, look at the pictures in the top two boxes. Then choose the picture that should go in the empty box so that the bottom two pictures have the same relationship as the top two pictures.

1

A

B

C

D

2

F

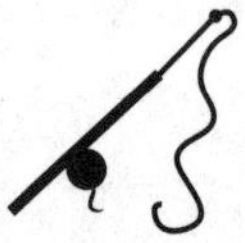
G

H

J

3

A B C D

4

F G H J

5

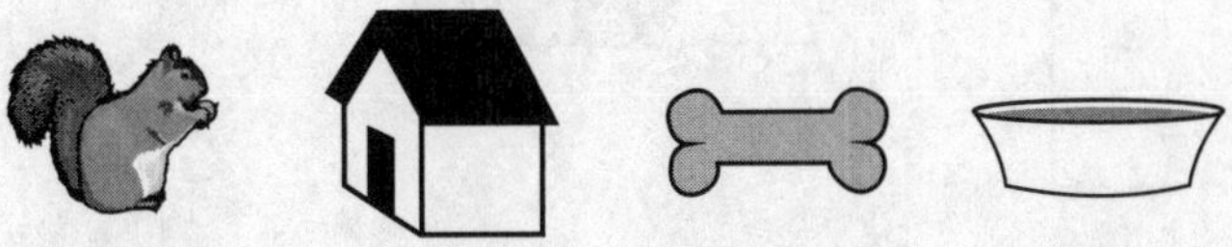

A B C D

6

F

G

H

J

7

A

B

C

D

8

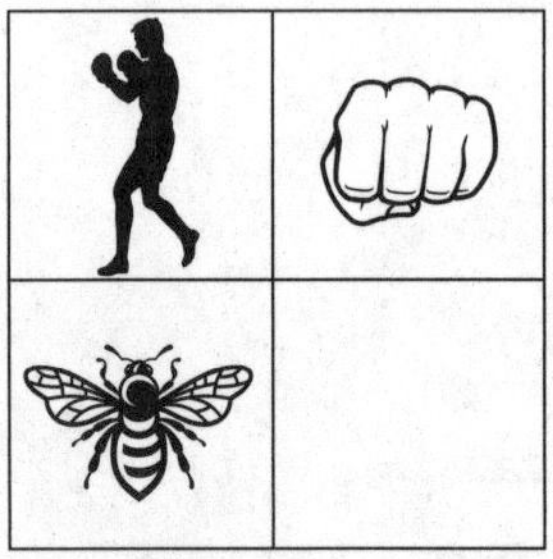

F

G

H

J

9

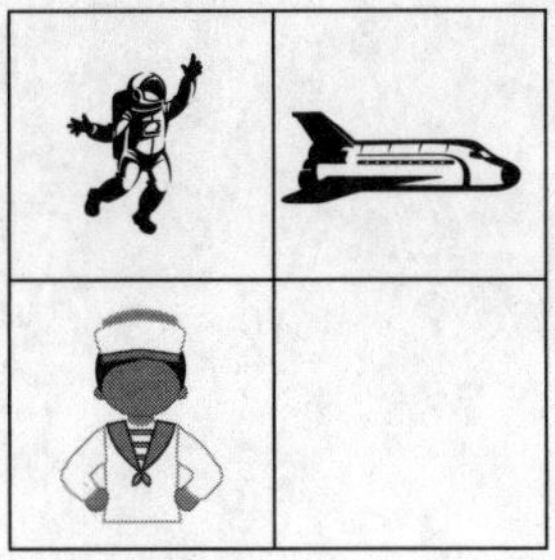

A **B** **C** **D**

10

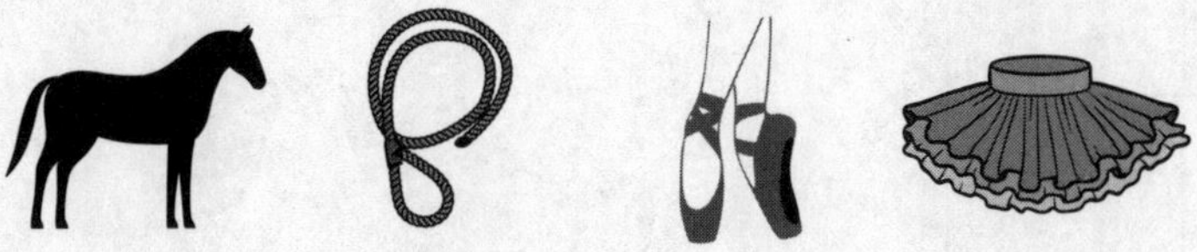

F **G** **H** **J**

11

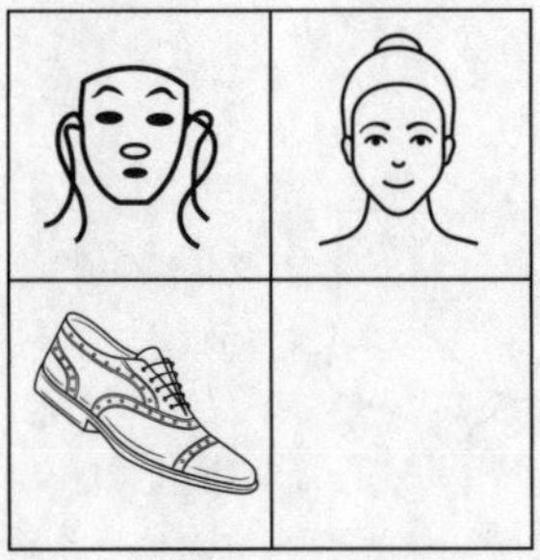

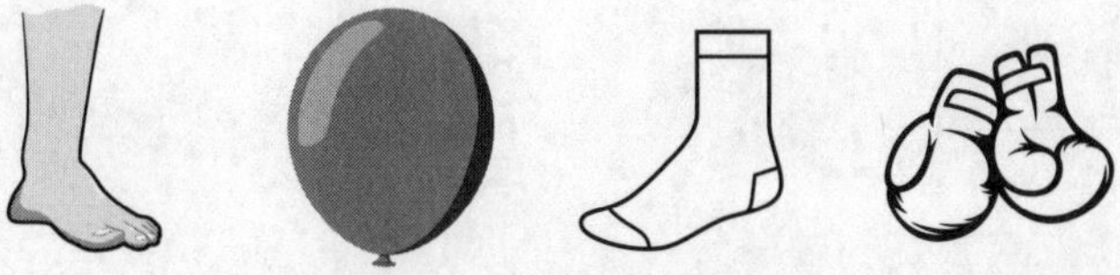

A **B** **C** **D**

12

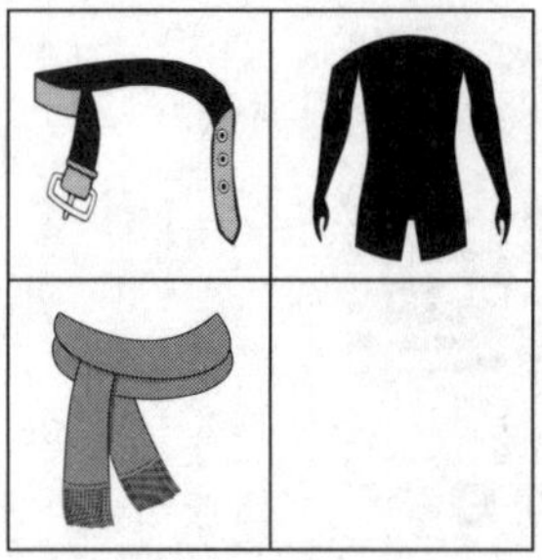

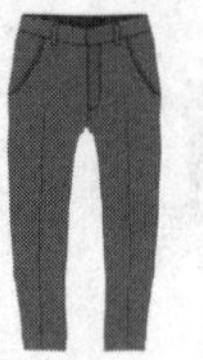

F

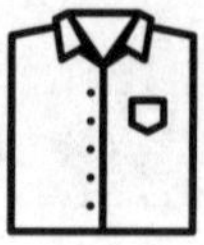

G

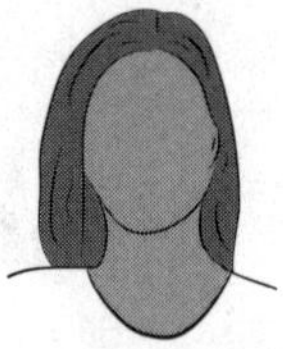

H

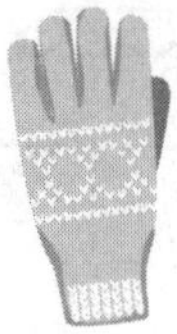

J

13

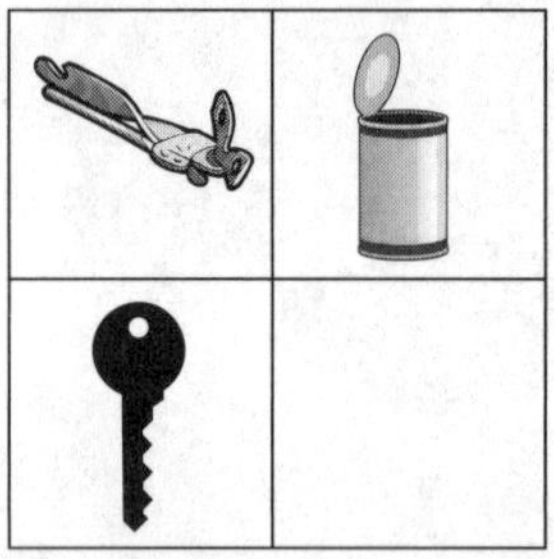

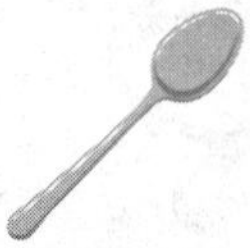

A

B

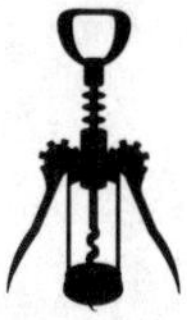

C

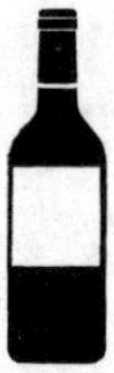

D

14

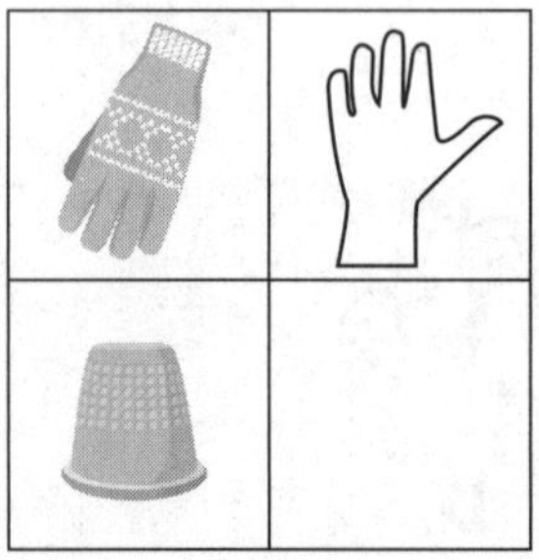

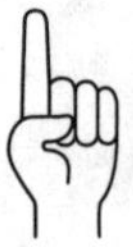

F

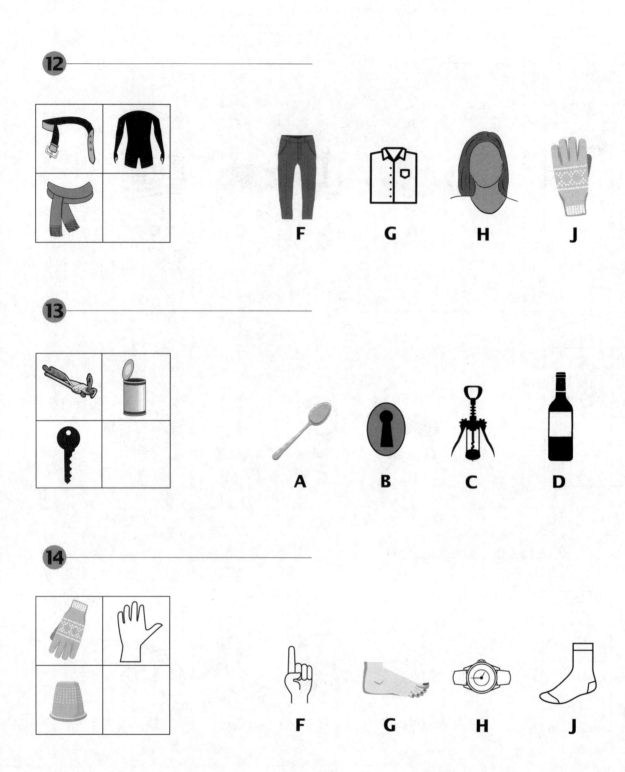

G

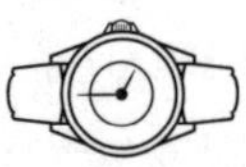

H

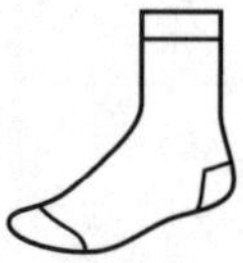

J

15

A B C D

16

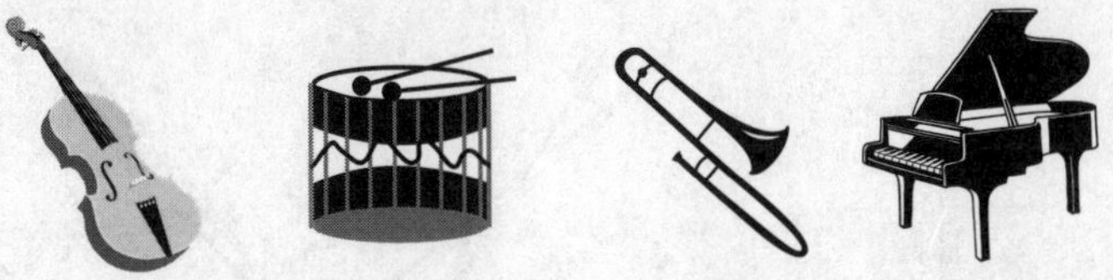

F G H J

17

A B C D

18

F

G

H

J

19

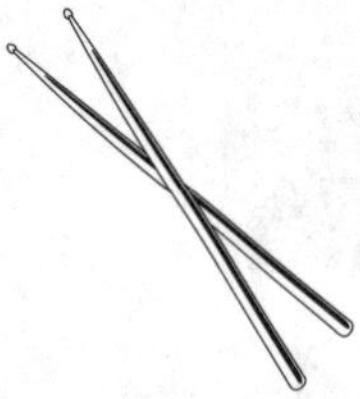
A

B

C

D

20

F

G

H

J

Test 3

Quantitative Reasoning

(20 questions, 5 minutes)

For questions 1–7, find the relationship of the numbers in one column to the numbers in the other column. Then find the missing number.

1

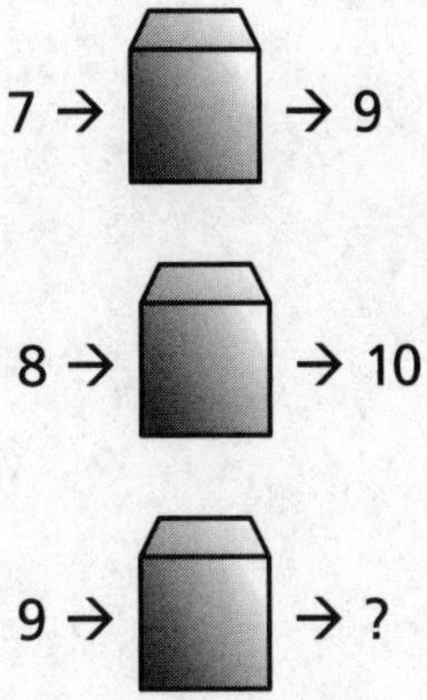

9	10	11	12
A	**B**	**C**	**D**

2

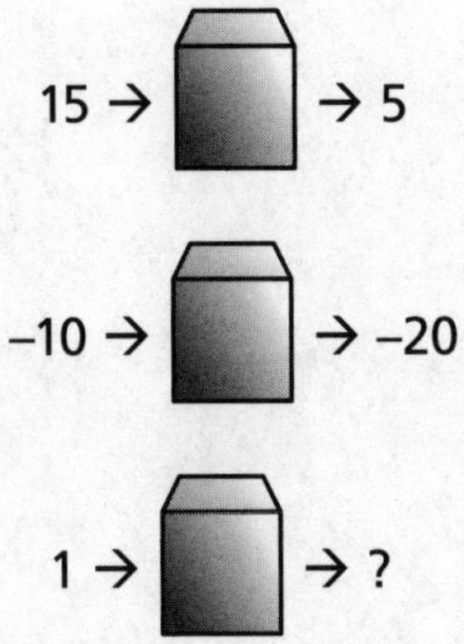

11	10	–10	–9
F	**G**	**H**	**J**

3

4 → ☐ → 6

3 → ☐ → $\frac{9}{2}$

2 → ☐ → ?

A	B	C	D
4	$\frac{5}{2}$	3	$\frac{3}{2}$

4

–8 → ☐ → –4

6 → ☐ → 3

–12 → ☐ → ?

F	G	H	J
6	3	–4	–6

5

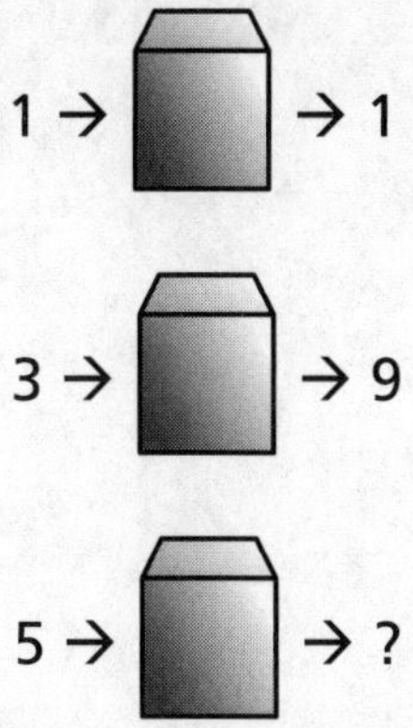

5	10	11	25
A	**B**	**C**	**D**

6

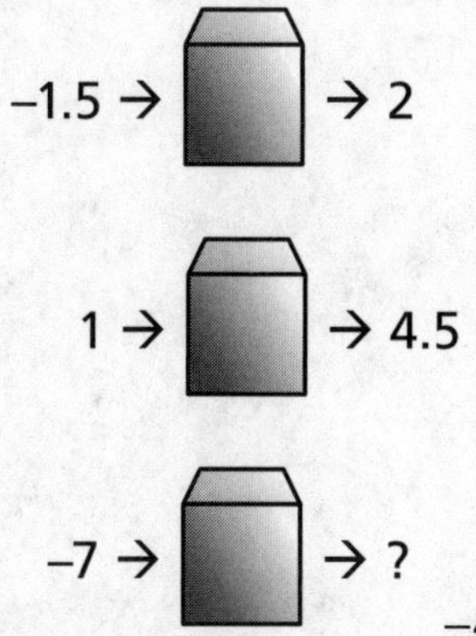

–4.5	–3.5	–1.5	2.5
F	**G**	**H**	**J**

7

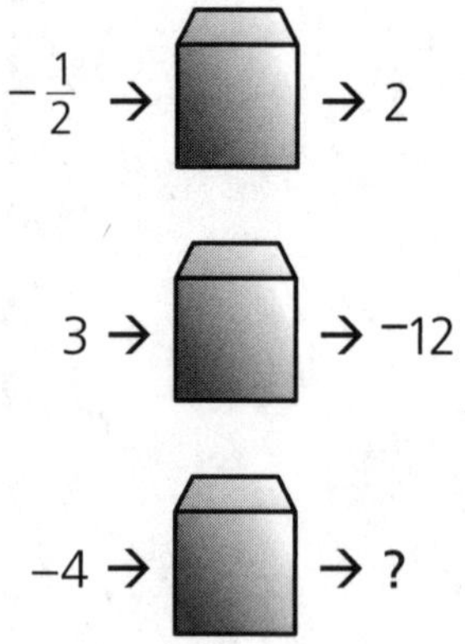

A	B	C	D
16	5	4	$\frac{1}{2}$

For Numbers 8–14, find the portion of the figure that is shaded.

8

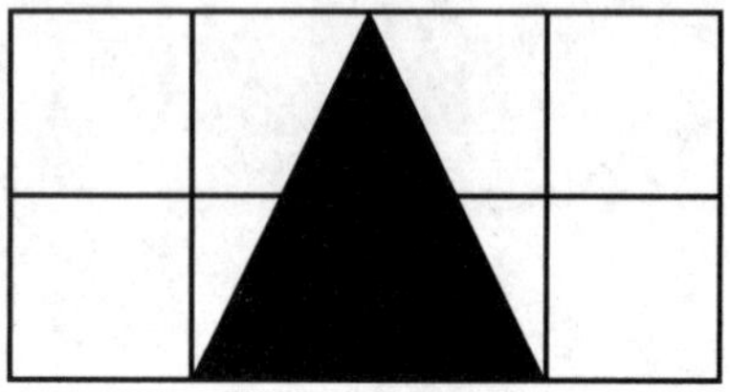

F	G	H	J
$\frac{1}{8}$	$\frac{1}{4}$	$\frac{1}{3}$	$\frac{3}{8}$

9

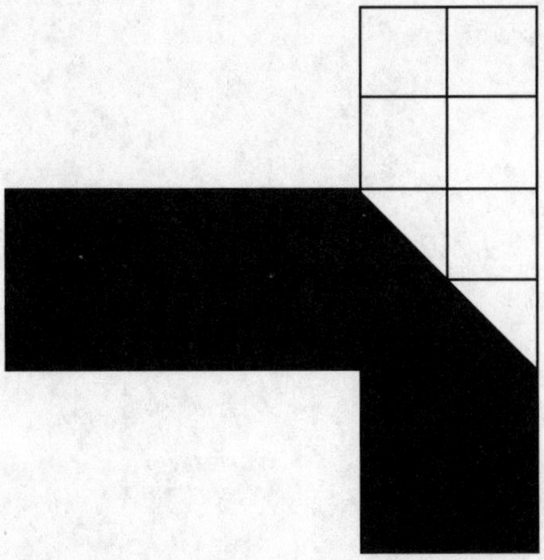

$\frac{1}{2}$	$\frac{3}{5}$	$\frac{4}{5}$	$\frac{7}{10}$
A	**B**	**C**	**D**

10

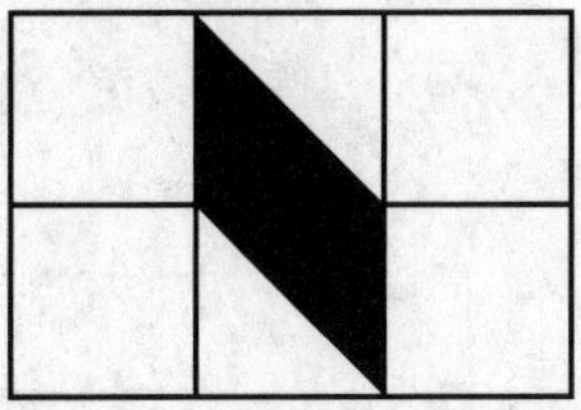

$\frac{1}{8}$	$\frac{1}{6}$	$\frac{1}{4}$	$\frac{1}{3}$
F	**G**	**H**	**J**

11

A	B	C	D
$\frac{1}{4}$	$\frac{5}{12}$	$\frac{1}{2}$	$\frac{7}{12}$

12

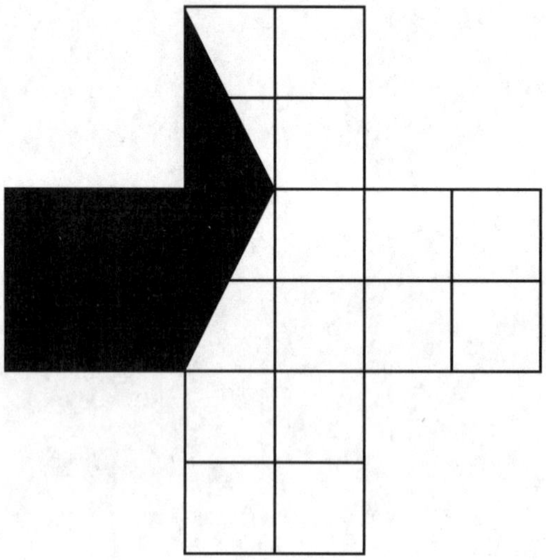

F	G	H	J
$\frac{5}{20}$	$\frac{3}{10}$	$\frac{4}{10}$	$\frac{7}{20}$

13

A	B	C	D
$\frac{1}{4}$	$\frac{1}{3}$	$\frac{4}{9}$	$\frac{5}{9}$

14

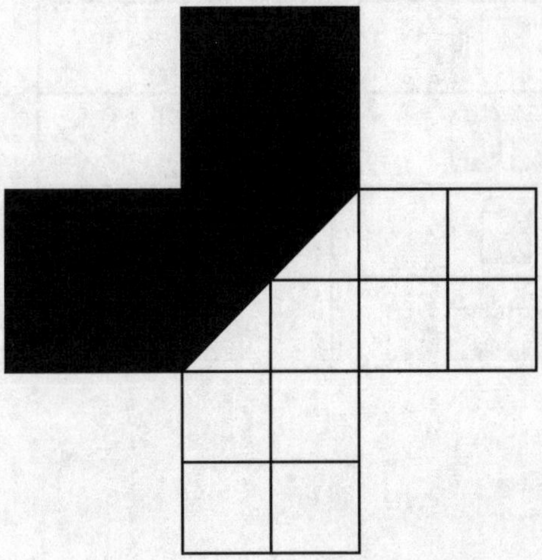

F	G	H	J
$\frac{1}{3}$	$\frac{1}{2}$	$\frac{12}{20}$	$\frac{4}{5}$

For Numbers 15–20, look at the scale showing sets of shapes of equal weight. Find an equivalent pair of sets that would also balance the scale.

15

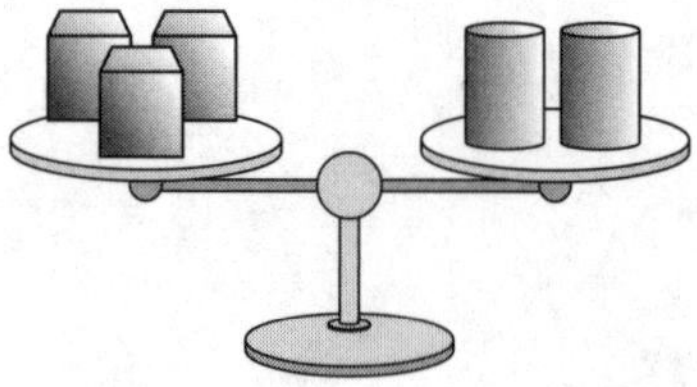

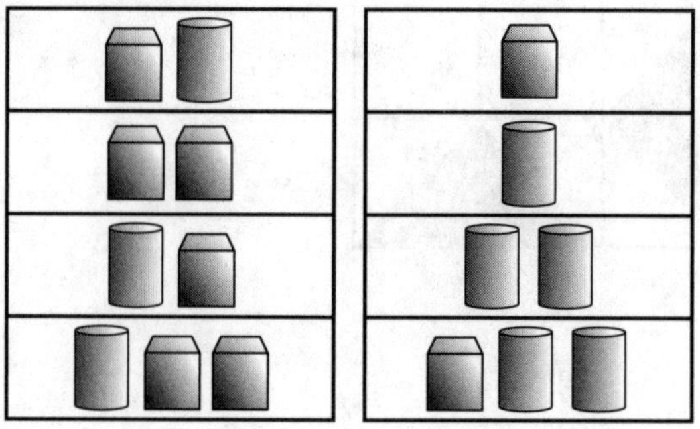

A
B
C
D

16

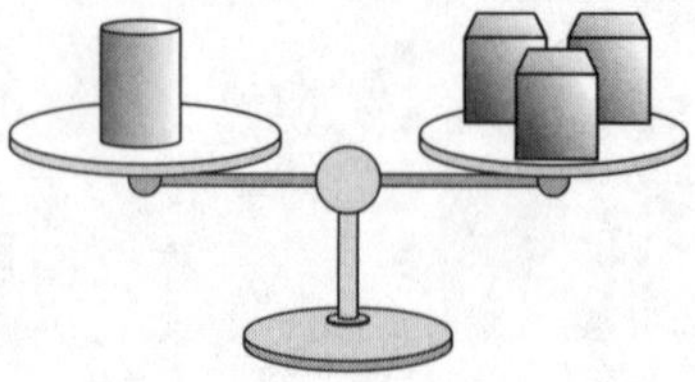

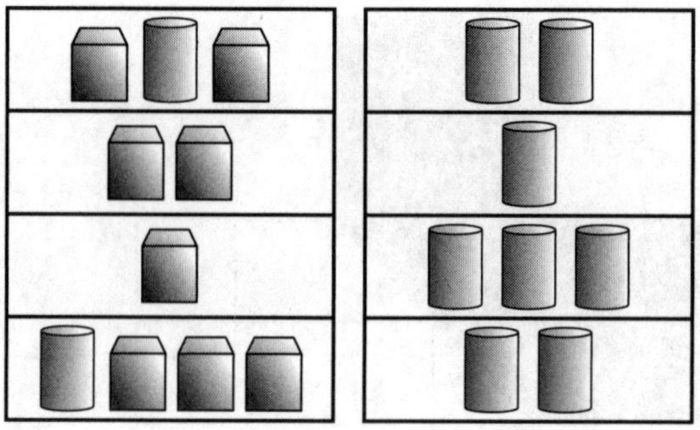

F
G
H
J

17

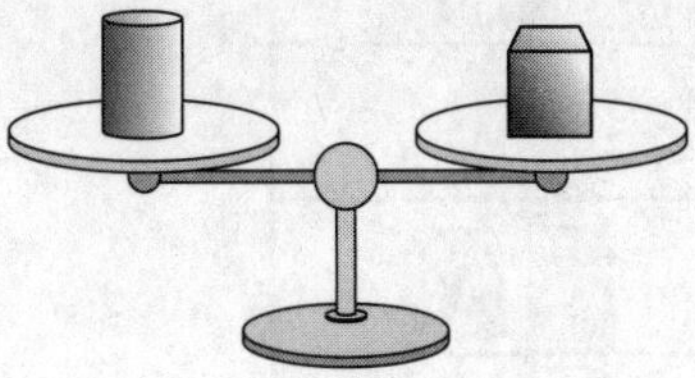

A
B
C
D

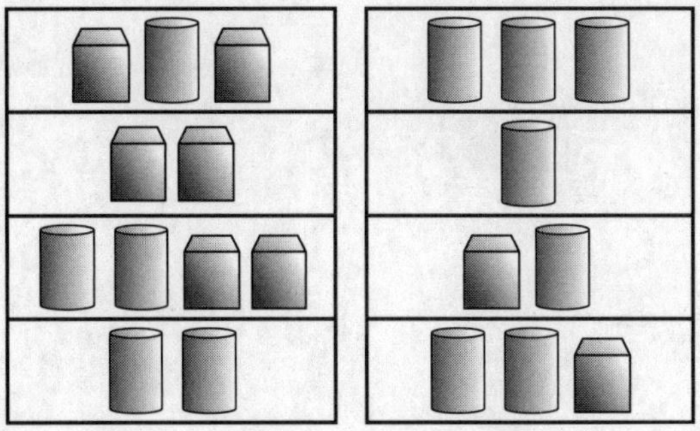

18

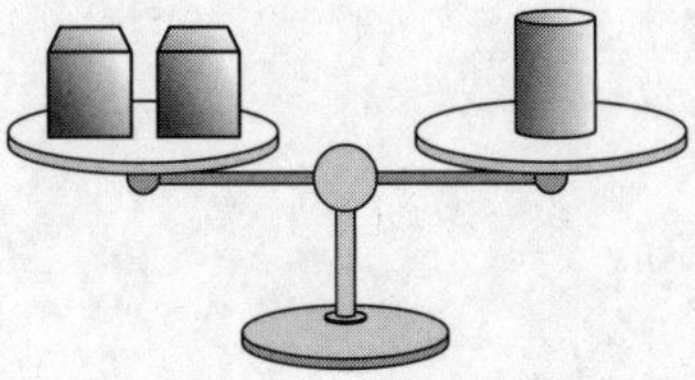

F
G
H
J

19

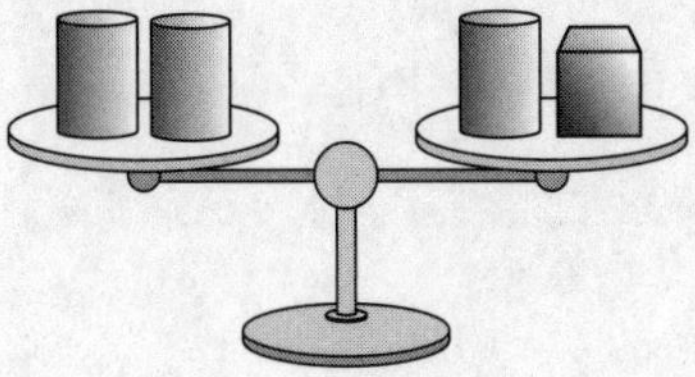

A
B
C
D

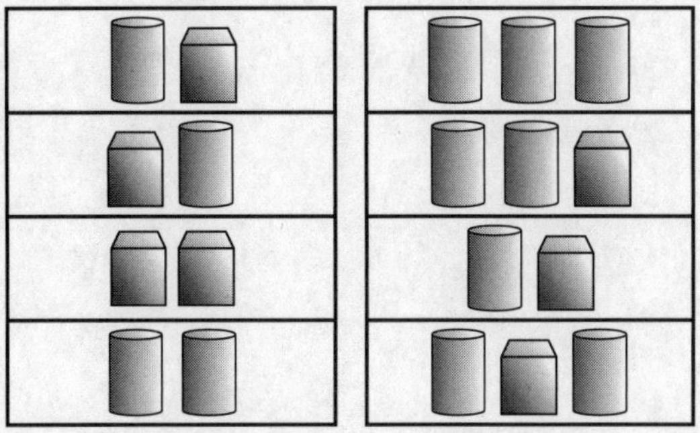

20

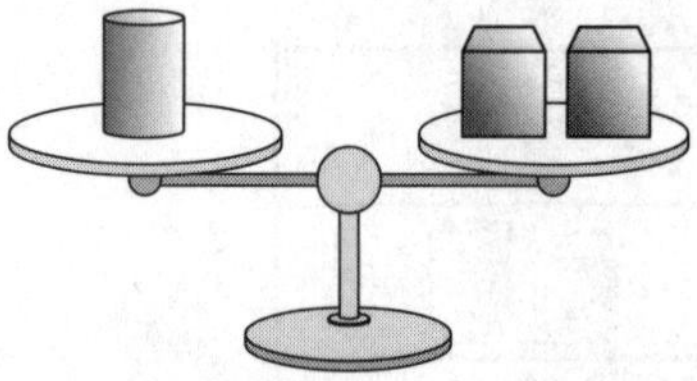

F
G
H
J

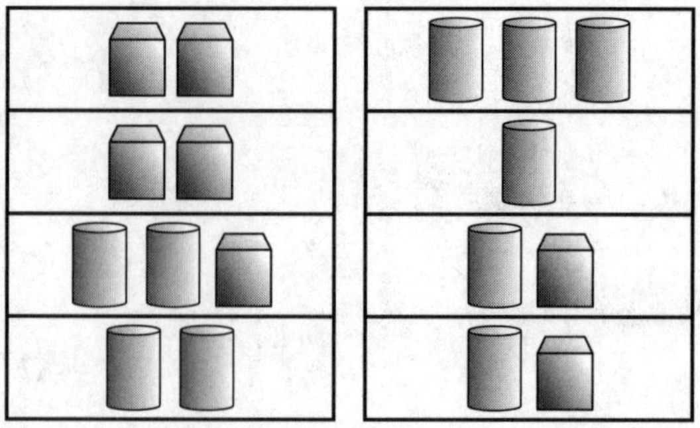

Test 4

Verbal Reasoning—Words

(20 Questions, 15 Minutes)

For questions 1–6, find the word that is a necessary part of the underlined word.

1

<u>dictionary</u>

A picture

B word

C history

D bookshelf

2

<u>refrigerator</u>

F cold

G ice

H food

J kitchen

3

<u>melody</u>

A sound

B piano

C beauty

D orchestra

4

<u>feline</u>

F jungle

G attack

H speed

J cat

5

<u>**humidity**</u>

A summer

B thermometer

C water

D cleanliness

For questions 6–10, choose the word that should go below the line such that the words above the line and the words below the line have the same relationship.

6

<u>**woof**</u> <u>**quack**</u> <u>**purr**</u>

F squawk

G squirm

H slither

J sprint

7

<u>**coach**</u> <u>**instruct**</u> <u>**direct**</u>

A lecture

B teach

C bossy

D nurture

8

<u>**log**</u> <u>**timber**</u> <u>**trunk**</u>

F limb

G paper

H leaves

J wood

9

<u>**rowing**</u> <u>**canoeing**</u> <u>**kayaking**</u>

A swimming

B paddling

C lake

D propelling

10

scholar **student** **tutee**

F teacher

G study

H pupil

J instructor

For questions 11–15, three of the words in the group belong together. Find the word that does not belong.

11

A loot

B raid

C rob

D borrow

12

F colt

G horse

H pony

J foal

13

A understanding

B command

C intelligence

D comprehension

14

F drop

G hang

H float

J suspend

15

A March

B April

C May

D August

For questions 16–20, the words in the top row are related in a certain way. The words in the bottom row are related in the same way. Find the word that completes the bottom row of words.

16

cool	**cold**	**frigid**
warm	**hot**	______

F temperature

G scalding

H air

J water

17

second	**minute**	**hour**
day	**month**	______

A clock

B year

C time

D holiday

18

bush	**vine**	**tree**
berry	**grape**	______

F carrot

G apple

H raisin

J leaf

19

feathers	**fur**	**scales**
bird	**bear**	______

A fur

B animal

C dog

D fish

20

annoyed	**angry**	**enraged**
content	**happy**	______

F ecstatic

G feeling

H sad

J bored

Test 5

Verbal Reasoning—Context

(10 Questions, 7 Minutes)

For questions 1–10, find the statement that is true according to the information you are given.

1

Martin's class can go to Europe this summer only if they get a group rate. To get a group rate, at least 20 people must sign up for the trip. Martin's class is eventually able to go to Europe this summer.

A More than 30 people signed up for the trip.

B Group rates are common for class trips.

C No fewer than 20 people signed up for the trip.

D Martin had to convince many of his friends to sign up for the trip.

2

David, Alice, and Marsha belong to their high school's track team. Alice can run 6 miles per hour. David can run 7 miles per hour. Marsha can run 7 miles per hour.

F David and Alice are the fastest runners on the team.

G Alice is a better student than Marsha.

H David and Marsha tied for first place at last week's race.

J Marsha can run faster than Alice.

3

John has more marbles than Tabatha. Cindy has fewer marbles than Larry. Peter has more marbles than Tabatha. Julie has more marbles than Larry.

A Julie has more marbles than Cindy.

B John has more marbles than Larry.

C Tabatha has more marbles than Julie.

D Cindy has more marbles than Tabatha.

4

To be allowed to swim in the pool during recess, each student has to pass a swim test. To pass the test, a student must be able to swim 3 laps of the pool. Carlos can swim 4 laps of the pool, John can swim 5 laps, and Erwin can swim 2 laps.

F Carlos likes to swim more than Erwin.

G Carlos, John, and Erwin can swim during recess.

H Carlos may swim during recess but Erwin cannot.

J John can swim faster than Carlos but not as fast as Erwin.

5

On a recent math test, Alex got a higher score than Scott and Lucy. Scott got a higher score than Petra and Janice. Lucy got a higher score than Marcus and Wendy.

A Janice got a higher score than Lucy.

B Wendy and Petra got the same score.

C Petra got a failing grade on the math test.

D Wendy got a lower score than Alex.

6

Julia spent time with three of her friends on the same day. She went ice-skating with Elise, and went to coffee with Laura, and had lunch with Shelton. Julia never skates before she eats.

F Julia spent the same amount of time with Laura and Shelton.

G Immediately after Julia went skating with Elise, she went to lunch with Shelton.

H Julia went to Lunch with Shelton before she skated with Elise.

J Julia likes Elise more than more than she likes Laura or Shelton.

7

Five friends (Reggie, Oscar, Yuri, Greg, and Barry) each have a different favorite color. The colors are red, orange, yellow, green, and blue. If Reggie likes blue, Yuri must like orange. If Oscar does not like yellow, Yuri does not like red. Neither Greg nor Barry like green.

A Oscar's favorite color is green.

B Oscar's favorite color is orange.

C Greg and Barry have the same favorite color.

D Yuri's favorite color is yellow.

8

Stephen, Max, David, and Adam all prefer different movie genres. Stephen likes horror movies or documentaries, while Max likes either romantic comedies or action movies. If David likes romantic comedies, Adam does not like documentaries.

F Adam likes horror movies.

G Max likes romantic comedies.

H Neither Max nor David like action movies.

J Stephen likes horror movies.

9

At a One-Act Play competition, the longest play performed was 60 minutes long. The shortest play was 20 minutes long. The play performed by Parkview High School was 40 minutes long.

A The school that performed the 20-minute play did not prepare enough for the One-Act Competition.

B Parkview High School's play was neither the longest not the shortest play performed.

C The play performed by Parkview High School was one-third the length of the longest play performed.

D Parkview High School's play was the second longest one performed.

10

The bank is directly south of the hospital and directly east from police station. The police station is directly north of the fire station.

F The fire station is southeast of the bank.

G The bank is south of the police station.

H The fire station is southwest of the hospital.

J The police station is north of the hospital.

Test 6

Reading and Language Arts

(40 Questions, 40 minutes)

Most people know that the ancient Egyptians mummified their dead. But few people know the details of how or why a mummy was made.

The point of mummification was to remove all of the parts of the body that could decompose to ensure that the remaining parts lasted forever. This was important to the Egyptians, who believed that parts of a person's soul needed a body to live in. If the body were to rot and disappear, the soul would be left homeless for eternity. To prevent the body from rotting, all the water had to be removed and all the bacteria had to be killed.

The process of embalming took more than sixty days. First, most of the internal organs had to be removed. The embalmer would break the corpse's nose and pull out the brain. He would then make an incision in the abdomen to remove the stomach, intestines, lungs, and liver. These were then salted, dried, and placed in jars that were buried with the body. The heart, which the Egyptians believed to be the source of consciousness, was often salted, dried, and placed back inside the body.

After the organs were removed, the body was doused with alcohol. This served to kill the bacteria in the body. The body was then salted, which dried out the skin. Finally, the whole body was wrapped in waxed bandages to form a waterproof casing around the body.

1 **The word decompose in the passage most nearly means**

A sing

B rot

C get wet

D frighten

2 **According to the passage, about how long did it take to make a mummy?**

F less than one month

G one month

H two months

J a year

3 **This passage is mostly about**

A the process of mummification

B the organs of the human body

C Egyptian religious beliefs

D why mummies are so small

4 **It can be inferred from the passage that another word for mummification is**

F salting

G embalming

H dousing

J incision

5 **According to the passage, the Egyptians mummified their dead in order to ensure that**

A the dead person would be protected from wolves

B the dead person's soul would have a home

C nobody would rob the dead person's grave

D the dead person's organs would not be lost

Like so many of his famous compatriots, Phineas Taylor Barnum came from good old New England <u>stock</u>. His ancestors were among the builders of the colonies of Massachusetts and Connecticut. His father's father, Ephraim Barnum, was a captain in the War of the Revolution, and was distinguished for his valor and fervent patriotism. His mother's father, Phineas Taylor, was locally noted as a wag and practical joker. His father, Philo Barnum, was in turn a tailor, a farmer, a storekeeper, and a country tavernkeeper, and was not particularly prosperous in any of these callings.

Philo Barnum and his wife, Irena Taylor, lived in Bethel, Connecticut, and there, on July 5, 1810, their first child was born. He was named Phineas Taylor Barnum after his maternal grandfather, and the latter, in return for the compliment, bestowed upon his first grandchild at his christening the title-deeds of a "landed estate," five acres in extent known as Ivy Island and situated in that part of Bethel known as the "Plum Trees."

In his early years, the boy led the life of the average New England farmer's son of that period. He drove the cows to and from the pasture, shelled corn, weeded the garden, and "did up chores." As he grew older, he rode the horse in plowing corn, raked hay, wielded the shovel and the hoe, and chopped wood. At six years old, he began to go to school—the typical district school. "The first date," he once said, "I remember inscribing upon my writing-book was 1818." The ferule, or birch-rod, was in those days the assistant schoolmaster, and young P.T. Barnum made its acquaintance. He was, however, an apt and ready scholar, particularly excelling in mathematics. One night, when he was ten years old, he was called out of bed by his teacher, who had made a wager with a neighbor that Barnum could calculate the number of feet in a load of wood in five minutes. Barnum did it in less than two minutes, to the delight of his teacher and the astonishment of the neighbor.

6 **The word <u>stock</u> in this passage most nearly means**

F soup

G merchandise

H ancestors

J money

7 **P.T. Barnum's paternal grandfather was**

A a soldier in the Revolutionary War

B a practical joker

C a farmer

D a shopkeeper

8 **According to the passage, P.T. Barnum's father**

F did many things and was not very good at any of them

G was one of the best teachers in the state

H was a farmer

J was a captain

9 **According to the passage, Barnum was particularly good at**

A physics

B mathematics

C biology

D chemistry

10 **It can be inferred from the passage that Barnum was named after**

F his father

G his mother

H his mother's father

J his father's father

11 **Barnum's early years were spent primarily learning**

A how to become a farmer

B how to be a mathematician

C how to lead a circus

D how to be a soldier

Alfred Wegener was one of many scientists whose theories were proven only after his death. Wegener was born in 1880 in Berlin. Wegener loved the outdoors and was always fascinated by the formation of the continents. However, in his early years he chose to study the stars.

Shortly after receiving his doctorate in astronomy, Wegener started studying the more <u>mundane</u> topic of the weather. He experimented with kites and balloons, even setting a world record for staying <u>aloft</u> for fifty-two hours straight. His appointment to the University of Marburg brought him considerable attention and status in the academic community.

Wegener, however, never lost interest in the formation of the continents. He noticed that though they were now far apart, it looked as if the continents fit together like puzzle pieces. Perhaps, he theorized, they were parts of one large continent at some point in the distant past. In 1912, he proposed his theory of continental drift. According to this theory, the continents broke apart millions of years ago and have drifted apart ever since then.

Many scientists at the time rejected Wegener's ideas. It was only in the 1960s, approximately thirty years after his death, that other scientists finally proved the correctness of Wegener's theory.

12 **The word <u>mundane</u> in this passage most nearly means**

F loud

G rare

H ordinary

J complicated

13 **It can be inferred from the passage that Wegener died in approximately what year?**

A 1880

B 1930

C 1950

D 1960

14 **According to the passage, Wegener first came to believe that the continents were all part of one large land mass because**

F he read a book by a famous scientist that said so

G the continents all had similar names

H the outlines of the continents seemed to fit together

J most scientists rejected the idea

15 **It can be inferred from the passage that astronomy is the study of**

A weather

B stars

C continents

D oceans

16 **The word <u>aloft</u> in this passage most nearly means**

F airborne

G asleep

H flat

J quiet

Bison and buffalo are not the same animal. For years, the American bison were mistakenly referred to as buffalo. Buffalo are actually found in Asia, Africa, and South America. Bison roamed the Northern American western plains by the millions just a couple of centuries ago. Because they were so widely hunted, however, their numbers fell greatly. In fact, as of a century ago, there were only about 500 left. They were deemed near extinction, but due to conservation efforts, their numbers have increased. There are approximately 50,000 bison living today in protected parks. Though they may never be as abundant as they once were, they are not in danger of extinction as long as they remain protected.

17 **The passage implies that the primary difference between buffalo and bison is**

A their geographic location

B their size

C their number

D when they lived

18 **The primary purpose of this passage is to**

F discuss the origin of the word *buffalo*

G promote conservation efforts

H describe some of the history of the American bison

J explain why people confuse bison and buffalo

19 **According to the passage, the reason that American bison are no longer near extinction is**

A lack of interest in hunting them

B conservation efforts

C loss of value of their fur

D the migration of the animals

20 **The word deemed in this passage most closely means**

F found

G rarely

H thought

J eaten

During the early years of the twentieth century, large cities such as London and Paris had short-haul stagecoaches to carry passengers to and from the suburbs. These vehicles were, however, not well adapted to the needs of a short journey. The coaches were difficult to enter and exit, and would often ruin passengers' clothing. One French visitor to London complained bitterly after a two-hour trip in such a coach in 1810, "I never saw anything so ill managed." To add insult to injury, the fares were exorbitantly high.

An improved vehicle was finally invented by another Frenchman, Stanislaus Baudry, who entered the transport business more by accident than by design. In 1823, he was the owner of a bathhouse in the suburb of Nantes, and to oblige his customers he ran a coach from the town center out to his establishment. Before long Baudry found that many of his passengers had no intention of bathing, but simply wanted a ride to the outskirts of the city. This gave him the idea of starting regular suburban services with vehicles designed to allow passengers to get on and off without stepping too much on each other's toes. Baudry's original coach started its journey from outside the shop of M. Omnes, whose motto "Omnes omnibus"—"Omnes for everyone"—is generally supposed to have resulted in the name "omnibus" being chosen for the name of the new vehicle.

21 **Which of the following is the main idea of this passage?**

A the differences in public transport in Paris and London

B the future of public transportation

C the early history of public vehicles

D the disadvantages of travel by coach

22 **Which of the following is a reason for the unpopularity of short-haul stagecoaches?**

F the unpleasant appearance of the coaches

H the difficulty of stopping the coaches once they started

J the way in which the coaches hurt the horses that pulled them

K the difficulty of getting in and out of the coaches

23 **This passage probably comes from**

A a dictionary

B a textbook on small business

C a history of urban transportation

D the diary of a nineteenth-century Frenchman

24 **According to the passage, Stanislaus Baudry is best described as a**

F patriotic Englishman

G perceptive businessman

H social reformer

J city planner

Krakatau, earlier misnamed Krakatoa, an island located in the Sundra Strait between Sumatra and Java, disappeared on August 27, 1883. It was destroyed by a series of powerful volcanic eruptions. The most violent blew upward with an estimated force of 100–150 megatons of TNT. The sound of the explosion traveled around the world, reaching the opposite end of the earth near Bogota, Colombia, whereupon it bounced back to Krakatau and then back and forth for seven recording passes over the earth's surface. The audible sounds, resembling the distant cannonade of a ship in distress, carried southward across Australia to Perth, northward to Singapore, and westward 4,600 kilometers to Rodriques Island in the Indian Ocean. This was the longest record distance traveled by any airborne sound in history.

The eruptions lifted more than 18 cubic kilometers of rock and other material into the air. Most of the tephra, as it is called by geologists, quickly rained back down to earth, but a residue of sulfuric-acid aerosol and dust boiled upward as high as 50 kilometers. It remained in the stratosphere, where for several years it created brilliant red sunsets and "Bishop's rings," visible circles surrounding the sun.

25 **This passage is mostly**

A an explanation of the atmospheric phenomenon of Bishop's rings

B a comparison of a volcanic eruption to the force of a bomb

C a discussion of a volcanic eruption of enormous power

D a discussion of the effect of volcanic activity on the stratosphere

26 **The author mentions "the distant cannonade of a ship in distress" in order to**

F describe a ship damaged by a volcanic eruption

G show that sound travels very quickly over water

H help illustrate the sound made by the Krakatau eruption

J illustrate the distance traveled by the volcano's heat wave

27 **The author's tone in the passage can best be described as**

A scientific

B critical

C optimistic

D annoyed

28 **The brilliant sunsets mentioned in the passage were caused by**

F gas and dust drifting in the stratosphere

G the detonation of 100 megatons of TNT

H an increase in the sun's temperature after the eruption

J vibrations from the sound waves created by the explosion

William, Duke of Normandy, conquered England in 1066. One of the first tasks he undertook as king was the building of a fortress in the city of London. Begun in 1066 and completed seve ral years later by William's son, William Rufus, this structure was called the White Tower.

The Tower of London is not just one building, but an 18-acre complex of buildings. In addition to the White Tower, there are nineteen other towers. The Thames River flows by one side of the complex, and a large moat, or shallow ditch, surrounds it. Once filled with water, the moat was drained in 1843 and is now covered with grass.

The Tower of London is the city's most popular tourist attraction. A great deal of fascinating history has taken place within its walls. The Tower has served as a fortress, a royal residence, a prison, the royal mint, a public records office, an observatory, a military barracks, a place of execution, and a city zoo. Today, it houses the crown jewels and a great deal of English history.

29 **The primary purpose of this passage is to**

A discuss the future of the Tower of London

B explain why the Tower was used as a royal residence

C argue that the Tower is an inappropriate place for the crown jewels.

D discuss the history of the Tower of London

30 **The Tower of London was used for all of the following except**

F a place where money was minted

G a royal residence

H a place of religious pilgrimage

J a place where executions were held

31 **Which of the following questions is answered by the passage?**

A How much money does the Tower of London collect from tourists each year?

B In what year did construction of the Tower begin?

C What type of stone was used to make the Tower of London?

D Who was the most famous prisoner in the Tower?

32 **The author's tone in this passage can best be described as**

F confused

G objective

H emotional

J envious

33 **The author would probably agree that**

A the Tower of London is useful only as a tourist attraction

B the Tower of London could never be built today

C the Tower of London has a complex history

D the prisoners at the Tower were generally well treated

34 **Choose the sentence that is written correctly.**

F Many people learn best by reading, while others learn best by listening.

G Many people learn better by reading as others who learn by listening.

H Many people who learn best by reading are others who learn best by listening.

J Many people learn best by reading than others learn best by listening.

35 **Choose the sentence that is written correctly.**

A A green salad, for lunch everyday, is what Miranda likes to eat.

B For lunch everyday, a green salad is eaten by Miranda.

C Miranda likes to eat a green salad every day for lunch.

D Miranda likes for lunch to eat green salad every day.

36 **Choose the sentence that is written correctly.**

F Many historians believe that the first helicopter was drawn by Leonardo da Vinci.

G Leonardo da Vinci, it is believed by many historians, was the one who drew the first helicopter.

H The first helicopter, believed by many historians, was drawn by Leonardo da Vinci.

J The one who drew the first helicopter, which was believed by many historians, was Leonardo da Vinci.

37 **Choose the best topic sentence for the paragraph.**

> ______________________________
> *At adulthood they will often grow to weigh 7 tons. The only animals bigger than the elephant live in the water, which helps to support their weight and regulate their body temperatures.*

A Aquatic animals have fewer problems than land animals.

B Few animals are more social than the elephant.

C The elephant is the largest animal that lives on land.

D One of the challenges for any animal is to stay warm in the winter and cool in the summer.

38 **Choose the best topic sentence for the paragraph.**

> *Crocodiles have longer and thinner jaws than alligators do. Alligators live in fresh water in lakes, rivers, or marshes. Crocodiles, on the other hand, prefer to live in salty or brackish water. While both animals need warm climates, the crocodile is very sensitive to cold and therefore lives in tropical regions.*

F Crocodiles and alligators are some of the fiercest animals on earth.

G Crocodiles differ from alligators in a number of ways.

H The southern regions of the United States are home to many interesting creatures.

J Alligators and crocodiles have many similar features.

39 **Choose the sentence that best combines the two italicized sentences into one.**

Patricia practiced the piano.

Later, Patricia watched a movie.

A Patricia practiced the piano and later watched a movie.

B Patricia practiced the piano, and then later Patricia watched a movie.

C Patricia practiced the piano, watched a movie.

D Patricia practiced the piano while she watched a movie.

40 **Choose the sentence that best combines the two italicized sentences into one.**

My mother was born in Illinois.

My mother is a doctor.

F My mother was born in Illinois and my mother is a doctor.

G In Illinois my mother was born and is a doctor.

H My mother, who was born in Illinois, is a doctor.

J My mother, is a doctor, was born in Illinois.

Test 7

Mathematics

(40 Questions, 35 minutes)

1 During the month of March, Nancy ran $14\frac{1}{2}$ miles. During the month of April, she ran $8\frac{3}{4}$ miles. What is the difference between the distance she ran during the month of March and the distance she ran during the month of April?

A $5\frac{3}{4}$ miles

B 6 miles

C $6\frac{1}{4}$ miles

D $6\frac{3}{4}$ miles

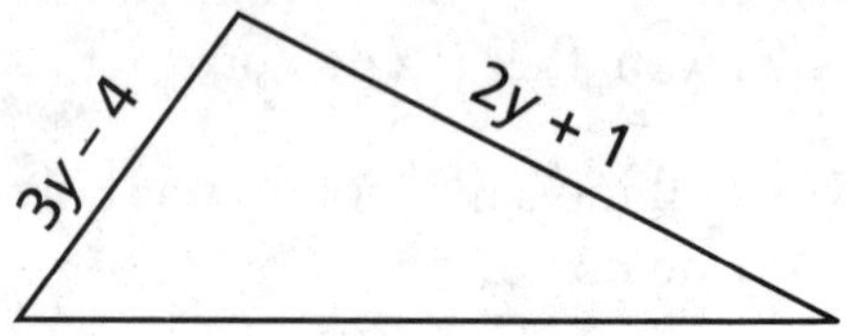

2 What is the perimeter of the triangle above?

F $10y + 2$

G $10y - 2$

H $7y + 2$

J $4y - 2$

3 $2\frac{1}{2}$ is how many times greater than $1\frac{1}{2}$?

A $1\frac{2}{3}$

B 1

C 2

D $2\frac{1}{2}$

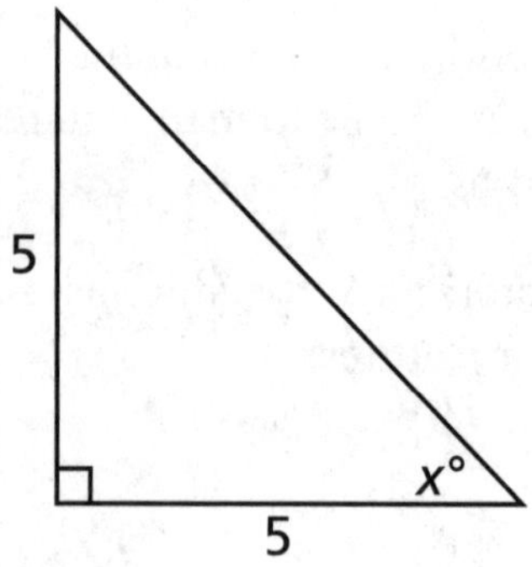

4 What is the value of x in the figure above?

F 90

G 60

H 45

J 30

5 A telephone call costs \$2.35 for the first minute and 15 cents for each additional minute. What is the cost of an 8-minute call?

A \$3.55

B \$3.40

C \$3.25

D \$3.10

6 What is the sum of the distinct prime factors of 48?

F 5

G 6

H 12

J 36

7 Which of the following is equal to $42.2678 \times 1{,}000$?

A 4.22678×10^3

B 4.22678×10^4

C 4.22678×10^5

D 4.22678×10^6

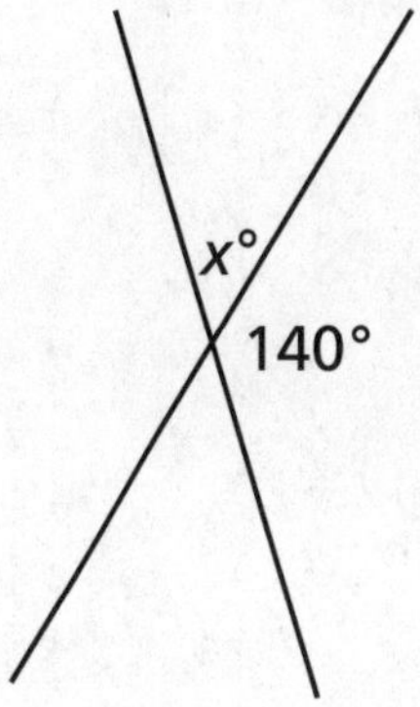

8 What is the value of *x* in the figure above?

F 30

G 40

H 45

J 60

9 $\left(4 \times \frac{1}{100}\right) + \left(3 \times \frac{1}{10}\right) + \left(2 \times \frac{1}{1000}\right) + 5 =$

A 4.325

B 5.234

C 5.342

D 5.432

10 If $2(x + 2x) > -6$, what is the range of possible values of x ?

F $x > -1$

G $x > 1$

H $x < -1$

J $x < 1$

11 $4^4 \times 4^5 =$

A 4^1

B 4^9

C 4^{20}

D 169

12 $\frac{25}{27} \times \frac{9}{5} =$

F $\frac{34}{32}$

G $\frac{5}{4}$

H $\frac{5}{3}$

J $\frac{3}{5}$

13 John puts $5,000 into a savings account that gives him 4% simple interest every year. If John makes no deposits or withdrawals, how much money will be in John's account at the end of one year?

A $5,004

B $5,040

C $5,020

D $5,200

14 While driving to the amusement park, the Claffey's car travels an average of $\frac{1}{2}$ mile every minute. At this rate, how many hours will it take to drive 40 miles?

F $1\frac{1}{3}$

G $2\frac{1}{2}$

H 20

J 80

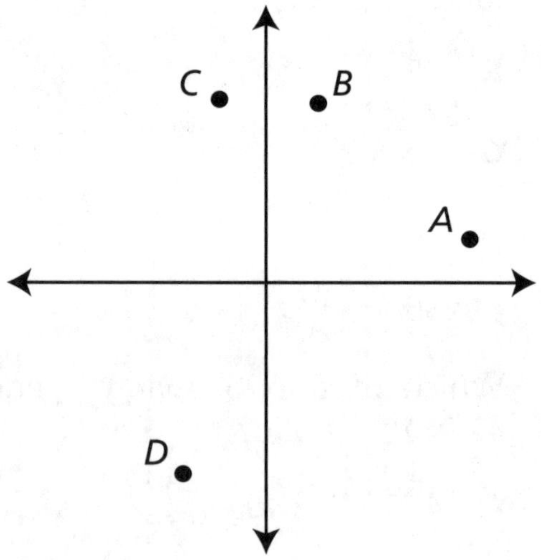

15 Which of the points on the graph above could have the coordinates (2,7)?

A point A

B point B

C point C

D point D

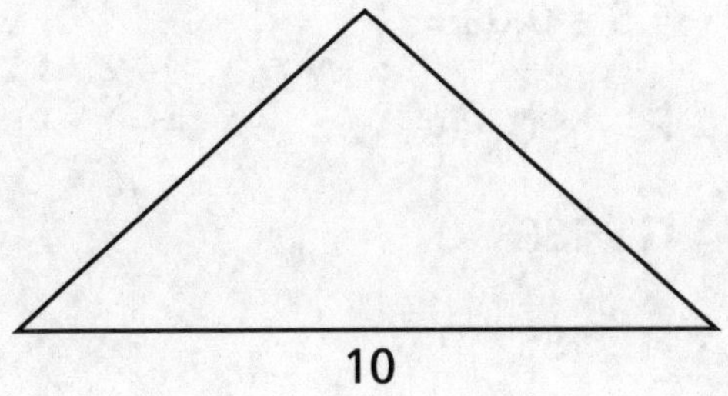

16 If the area of the triangle above is 40, what is its height?

F 4

G 8

H 10

J 12

17 If $4x - 9 = x + 6$, then $x =$

A 1

B 3

C 4

D 5

18 A basket of 5 apples costs \$8. How much will it cost to buy 60 apples at the same rate?

F \$40

G \$60

H \$86

J \$96

19 $13 + 2 \times 9 + 1 - (2 - 8) =$

A 26

B 38

C 76

D 84

20 Nine years ago, Mack was half as old as he is now. How old is Mack now?

F 9

G 12

H 15

J 18

21 At a local clothing store, two shirts and a pair of shorts cost \$19.25. If five shirts cost \$28.50, what is the price of a pair of shorts?

A \$5.50

B \$7.65

C \$7.75

D \$7.85

22 $3\frac{3}{4}\ \% =$

F 3.75

G 0.0375

H 0.00375

J 0.000375

23 If $x = 3$, then $3x^2$ is how much less than $(3x)^2$?

A 0

B 6

C 36

D 54

24 Walter's card collection contains football cards and baseball cards. If he has 120 football cards and 80 baseball cards, what fractional part of his collection is made up of baseball cards?

F 15%

G 20%

H 40%

J 66%

25 What is the volume of a cube with sides that are 3 inches?

A 3 in^3

B 6 in^3

C 9 in^3

D 27 in^3

26 $4.5 \div 0.02 =$

F 90

G 180

H 185

J 225

27 A grain silo has dimensions 25 feet by 6 feet by 12 feet. If the silo can be filled with grain at a rate of 4 cubic feet per minute, how many minutes will it take to fill the silo?

A 120

B 250

C 450

D 600

28 $3\frac{1}{2} \times 6\frac{1}{2} =$

F $9\frac{1}{2}$

G 18

H $22\frac{3}{4}$

J $27\frac{1}{4}$

29 If a circle has a radius of 4, what is the ratio of its area to its circumference?

A 2:1

B 3:1

C 4:1

D 5:3

30 In 1997, Cindy sold 120 newspapers. In 1998, she sold 200. The number of newspapers Cindy sold increased by approximately what percent from 1997 to 1998?

F 40%

G 50%

H 66%

J 80%

31 If $\frac{1}{3}$ of a number is 32, then $\frac{3}{4}$ of that number is

A 16

B 32

C 64

D 72

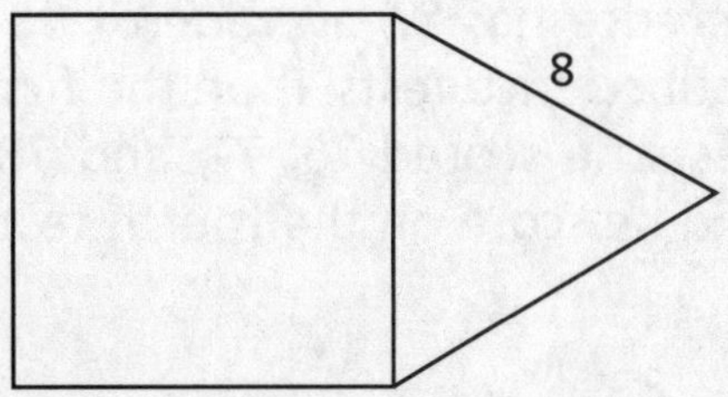

32 The figure above consists of a square and an equilateral triangle. What is the perimeter of the figure above?

F 24

G 40

H 64

J 80

33 How many multiples of 3 and 5 are between 1 and 32?

A 0

B 1

C 2

D 3

34 Terence has an average of 80 on his four science tests. If on the first three tests he scored 76, 77, and 78, what did he score on the fourth test?

F 83

G 85

H 87

J 89

35 If one of the angles in a right triangle is 65, what is the measure of the smallest angle in the triangle?

A 15

B 25

C 35

D 65

36 Lewis has a bowl of red and blue marbles. The ratio of blue marbles to red marbles is 5:2. If he has a total of 70 marbles in the bowl, how many blue marbles does he have?

F 20

G 30

H 40

J 50

37 Maryann gets 75 cents for every cake she sells at the bake sale. She wants to earn enough money to buy a book that costs $18. How many cakes will she need to sell in order to earn enough money to buy the book?

A 12

B 20

C 24

D 32

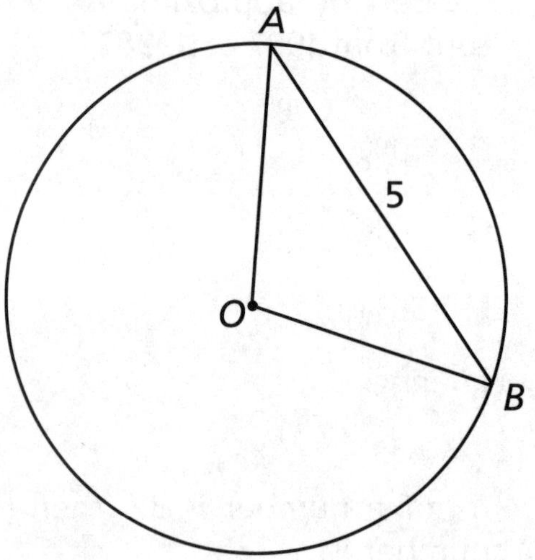

38 The figure above shows a circle with center *O*. If *OA* = 4, what is the perimeter of triangle *OAB*?

F 9

G 11

H 13

J 15

39 If $x + x = x \times x$, which of the following could be the value of x ?

A 1

B 2

C 3

D 4

40 If $\frac{1}{\frac{1}{x}} = \frac{3}{4}$ then $x =$

F $\frac{3}{4}$

G $\frac{4}{3}$

H 3

J 4

Chapter 28
COOP Practice Test 2: Answers and Explanations

ANSWER KEY

Test 1	Test 2	Test 3	Test 4	Test 5	Test 6	Test 7
1. C	1. C	1. C	1. B	1. C	1. B	1. A
2. G	2. F	2. J	2. F	2. J	2. H	2. G
3. A	3. D	3. C	3. A	3. A	3. A	3. A
4. G	4. F	4. J	4. J	4. H	4. G	4. H
5. A	5. B	5. D	5. C	5. D	5. B	5. B
6. H	6. H	6. G	6. F	6. H	6. H	6. F
7. C	7. A	7. A	7. B	7. A	7. A	7. A
8. G	8. G	8. G	8. J	8. F	8. F	8. G
9. C	9. A	9. D	9. B	9. B	9. B	9. C
10. F	10. H	10. G	10. H	10. H	10. H	10. F
11. B	11. A	11. B	11. D		11. A	11. B
12. H	12. H	12. G	12. G		12. C	12. H
13. C	13. B	13. B	13. C		13. G	13. D
14. J	14. F	14. G	14. F		14. C	14. F
15. A	15. B	15. B	15. D		15. G	15. B
16. G	16. H	16. J	16. G		16. A	16. G
17. C	17. D	17. A	17. B		17. A	17. D
18. H	18. G	18. J	18. G		18. H	18. J
19. B	19. A	19. C	19. D		19. B	19. B
20. G	20. G	20. G	20. F		20. H	20. J
					21. H	21. D
					22. D	22. G
					23. H	23. D
					24. B	24. H
					25. C	25. D
					26. H	26. J
					27. A	27. C
					28. F	28. H
					29. J	29. A
					30. C	30. H
					31. G	31. D
					32. B	32. G
					33. H	33. C
					34. F	34. J
					35. C	35. B
					36. F	36. J
					37. C	37. C
					38. G	38. H
					39. A	39. B
					40. H	40. F

ANSWERS AND EXPLANATIONS

Test 1—Sequences

1. **C** The second element reverses the top and bottom of the first, so the missing element should reverse the top and bottom of the third.

2. **G** The first element has one A, the second has two As, and the third has three As, so the missing element should have four As.

3. **A** The second element reverses the elements of the first—the triangles change to circles and the circles to triangles. Therefore, the missing element should reverse the elements of the third.

4. **G** The second element is the same as the first but fills in one-quarter of the figure. Therefore, the missing element should be the same as the third, with one-quarter filled in.

5. **A** The first element has one line, the second has three lines, and the third has five lines, so the missing element should have seven lines to follow the pattern of adding two lines.

6. **H** The second element moves the dot from top to bottom on the right side, so the missing element should move the dot from top to bottom on the left side.

7. **C** The sequence should go 34 (+ 12) 46 (+ 3) 49 | 8 (+ 12) 20 (+ 3) 23 | 57 (+ 12) **69** (+ 3) 72

8. **G** The sequence should go 31 (– 3) 28 (+ 7) 35 | 17 (– 3) 14 (+ 7) 21 | 36 (– 3) **33** (+ 7) 40

9. **C** The sequence should go 66 (+ 0) 66 (÷ 3) 22 | 18 (+ 0) 18 (÷ 3) 6 | 27 (+ 0) **27** (÷ 3) 9

10. **F** The sequence should go 8 (– 2) 6 (× 2) 12 | 17 (– 2) 15 (× 2) 30 | 6 (– 2) **4** (× 2) 8

11. **B** The sequence should go 6 (× 3) 18 (+ 1) 19 | 3 (× 3) 9 (+ 1) 10 | 4 (× 3) **12** (+ 1) 13

12. **H** The sequence should go 3 (× 4) 12 (÷ 2) 6 | 12 (× 4) 48 (÷ 2) 24 | 8 (× 4) **32** (÷ 2) 16

13. **C** The sequence should go 11 (× 3) 33 (+ 0) 33 | 6 (× 3) 18 (+ 0) 18 | 13 (× 3) **39** (+ 0) 39

14. **J** The A and B do not change; only the numbers increase: 1 2 | 2 3 | 3 4 | **4 5** | 5 6

15. **A** The sequence gives three letters, then skips two, then gives the next three letters. The letters follow this pattern: 1 2 3 | 6 7 8 | 11 12 13 | 16 17 18 | 21 22 23, or ABC | FGH | KLM | **PQR** | UVW.

16. **G** The outside letters start with A and go forward through the alphabet; the inside letter starts with Z and goes backward through the alphabet.

17. **C** The middle letter of each element becomes the last letter of the next element. So the last letter of the missing element must be L, and the middle letter must be N. Use numbers in place of letters to make it clearer: 7 8 6 | 9 10 8 | 11 12 10 | 13 14 12 | 15 16 14, or GHF | IJH | KLJ | **MNL** | OPN.

18. **H** The sequence has a missing letter in the middle of each element. Again, numbers will help clarify: 1 2 4 5 | 6 7 9 10 | 11 12 14 15 | 16 17 19 20 | 21 22 24 25, or ABDE | FGIJ | KLNO | **PQST** | UVXY.

19. **B** The last two letters of one element become the first two letters of the next element. So the missing element must being with **NP** and end with **RT**.

20. **G** The number in the middle goes up by 3. Therefore, the missing element must have an 18 in the middle.

Test 2—Analogies

1. **C** A puppy is a young dog; a kitten is a young cat.
2. **F** A net is used to catch a fish; a baseball glove is used to catch a baseball.
3. **D** A crab holds things with a claw; a human holds things with a hand.
4. **F** A vase is used to hold flowers; a pot is used to hold a plant.
5. **B** A horse lives in a stable; a dog lives in a doghouse.
6. **H** You put on skates to travel on ice; you put on skis to travel on snow.
7. **A** You use a hammer to make a house; you use a paintbrush to make a painting.
8. **G** A boxer attacks with his fists; a bee attacks with its stinger.
9. **A** An astronaut travels in a rocket; a sailor travels on a ship.
10. **H** A cowboy wears cowboy boots; a ballet dancer wears ballet shoes.
11. **A** A mask is worn on the face; a shoe is worn on the foot.
12. **H** A belt is worn around the waist; a scarf is worn around the neck.
13. **B** A can opener is used to open a can; a key is used to open a lock.
14. **F** A glove protects the hand; a thimble protects a finger.
15. **B** You use a spoon to eat soup; you use a fork to eat pasta.
16. **H** A guitar and a banjo are both stringed instruments; a trumpet and a trombone are both brass instruments.
17. **D** A cactus is a plant that lives in the desert; a camel is an animal that lives in the desert.
18. **G** A motorcycle is a motorized bicycle; a propeller plane is a motorized airplane.
19. **A** You play a violin with a bow; you play a drum with a mallet.
20. **G** A digital clock is a modern wind-up clock; a light bulb is a modern oil lamp.

Test 3—Quantitative Reasoning

1. **C** Think about the relationship between 7 and 9. 7 + 2 = 9, so check this same relationship with the next pair: 8 + 2 = 10 works, so this must be the relationship. Therefore, 9 + 2 = 11, (C).

2. **J** 15 and 5 are related in a few ways: 15 – 10 = 5, or $\frac{15}{3} = 5$. Try these relationships on the next pair to see what works. –10 – 10 = –20, which works, so this must be the relationship. Therefore, 1 – 10 = –9. Choice (J) is correct.

3. **C** 4 + 2 = 6, but 3 + 2 does not equal $\frac{9}{2}$, so think of another way these numbers might be related. $4 \times x = 6$, so solve for x to find that $x = \frac{6}{4} = \frac{3}{2}$. $3\left(\frac{3}{2}\right) = \frac{9}{2}$, so this must be the relationship. Therefore, $2\left(\frac{3}{2}\right) = 3$, (C).

4. **J** –8 and –4 are related in a couple different ways. –8 + 4 = –4, or $-\frac{8}{2} = -4$. 6 – 4 does not equal 3, but $\frac{6}{2} = 3$ works, so the rule must be to divide by 2. Therefore, $-\frac{12}{2} = -6$, (J).

5. **D** 1 and 1 are difficult to decipher, but 3 and 9 have a few relationships possible. 3 + 6 = 9, but this does not work for 1 and 1. 3 × 3 = 9, but this does not work for 1 and 1. Finally, $3^2 = 9$, which works because $1^2 = 1$. Therefore, $5^2 = 25$, (D).

6. **G** $-1.5 + x = 2$, so $x = 3.5$, Check to see if this works for the next pair: 1 + 3.5 = 4.5, so this is, in fact, the correct relationship. Therefore, –7 + 3.5 = –3.5, (G).

7. **A** Perhaps it is easier to start with 3 and –12. The difference between the two is –15, which clearly is not the case in the other pair of numbers. 3 × –4 = –12, and that also works for the other pair, as $\left(-\frac{1}{2}\right)(-4) = 2$. Therefore, (–4)(–4) = 16.

8. **G** There are 8 total squares in the figure. The shaded figure is a triangle with dimensions of base 2 and a height of 2, so the area of the triangle = $\left(\frac{1}{2}\right)bh = \left(\frac{1}{2}\right)(2)(2) = 2$. Therefore, the fraction shaded is $\frac{2}{8}$, or $\frac{1}{4}$. Choice (G) is correct.

9. **D** Use the unshaded portion of the figure to find the total number of squares in the shape. 13 full squares are shaded, along with two half squares, making a total of 14 shaded squares out of a possible 20. $\frac{14}{20}$ can be reduced to $\frac{7}{10}$, (D).

10. **G** There are six squares in total, and there are two half squares shaded, which add up to one full square. Therefore, the area of the shaded portion is $\frac{1}{6}$, (G).

11. **B** There are six squares in the figure in total, and there are two triangular shaded portions, each with an area formula $\left(\frac{1}{2}\right)bh$. One triangle has a base of 3 and height of 1, so its area is $\left(\frac{1}{2}\right)(3)(1) = \frac{3}{2}$, and the other has a base of 2 and height of 1, so its area is $\left(\frac{1}{2}\right)(2)(1) = 1$. $\frac{3}{2} + 1 = \frac{5}{2}$, so $\frac{\frac{5}{2}}{6} = \frac{5}{12}$, (B).

12. **G** The total area here is 20. One of the four spokes of the cross is entirely shaded, and each of those contains 4 squares. The remaining portion is a triangle with dimensions 4 and 1, so $\left(\frac{1}{2}\right)(4)(1) = 2$. $\frac{4+2}{20} = \frac{6}{20} = \frac{3}{10}$. The correct answer is (G).

13. **B** There are 9 squares in total, and 3 equal triangles, each with a base of 2 and a height of 1. Each of the triangles has an area of 1, so the 3 total shaded portions would total $\frac{3}{9}$, or $\frac{1}{3}$ of the total area.

14. **G** Two of the four cross spokes are completely shaded, as is half of the central square. Therefore, half of the figure is shaded, making (G) correct.

15. **B** Cancel a cylinder on either side of the scale since they are equal in weight. You will find that the remaining shapes show a ratio of two cubes to 1 cylinder. In (A), eliminate a cube on either side to find a lone cylinder on the left. Eliminate (A). Choice (B) is the exact ratio that you are looking for, making it the correct answer. In (C), eliminate a cylinder on either side, and there is only a 1 : 1 ratio between the cube and the cylinder left over. In (D), cancel a cylinder and cube on either side, leaving a ratio of 1 : 1 as well, making it incorrect. Choice (B) is the correct answer.

16. **J** The ratio of the scale of cubes to cylinders is 3 : 1. Cancel a cylinder from either side of (F), and the remaining ratio of cubes to cylinders is 2 : 1. Choice (G) also contains a ratio of 2 : 1, making both choices incorrect. Choice (H) is the opposite of the of the ratio on the scale because the cylinder is the heavier object in this example. Eliminate (H), and check (J). Cancel a cylinder on either side, and the remaining ratio is three cubes to one cylinder, making (J) correct.

17. **A** There are two shapes on either side of the scale, meaning that the cylinder and cube are the same weight. Therefore, the answer choice that has an equal number of shapes on either side will be the correct answer, regardless of shape. In this case, that answer is (A).

18. **J** The ratio in this example is one cube to two cylinders. In (F), cancel a cylinder and a cube from either side, and you will be left with a lone cylinder on the right, making this choice incorrect. Cancel two cylinders from either side in (G), and you will be left with a lone cube on the right, making it incorrect as well. In (H), cancel two cylinders and a cube from either side, and you will be left with a lone cylinder on the left, making it incorrect. In (J), cancel a cylinder from either side, and you will be left with the correct ratio of two cubes to one cylinder.

19. **C** There are two shapes on either side of the scale, meaning that the cylinder and cube are the same weight. Therefore, the answer choice that has an equal number of shapes on either side will be the correct answer, regardless of shape. In this case, that answer is (C).

20. **G** The ratio in this example is one cylinder to two cubes. In (F), the ratio is three cylinders to two cubes, so it may be eliminated. Choice (G) is the correct ratio, just in the opposite order shown on the scale. In (H), cancel a cylinder and a cube from either side, and you will be left with a lone cylinder on the left, making it incorrect. Finally, cancel a cylinder from either side of (J), and the remaining ratio is 1 : 1, making this choice incorrect. Choice (G) is the only choice with the correct ratio.

Test 4—Verbal Reasoning—Words

1. **B** A dictionary gives definitions of words. It may or may not have pictures or sit on a bookshelf, and it does not give information on history.

2. **F** A refrigerator keeps things cold. It may or may not make ice, have food in it, or be in the kitchen.

3. **A** A melody is a series of sounds. It may or may not be played on a piano, be beautiful, or be played by an orchestra.

4. **J** Feline means having to do with cats. It has nothing to do with jungles, attacks, or speed.

5. **C** Humidity means have a lot of water. It may or may not occur in summer and has nothing to do with thermometers or cleanliness.

6. **F** Woof, quack, purr, and squawk are all sounds that different animals make. Squirm, slither, and sprint are not sounds animals make.

7. **B** Coach, instruct, direct, and teach are synonyms and mean to teach or educate.

8. **J** Log, timber, and trunk are all pieces of, or made from, large pieces of wood. Limbs are typically small, leaves are not made out of wood, and paper is material made from the pulp of wood.

9. **B** Rowing, canoeing, kayaking, and paddling all involve moving through water in a water vehicle using a paddle or paddles.

10. **H** Scholar, student, tutee, and pupil are all people who are involved in learning or being taught by someone.

11. **D** Loot, raid, and rob all mean to steal or take something that belongs to someone else. Borrow suggests the intent to return the object to the owner.

12. **G** Colt, pony, and foal are all names for a young horse.

13. **C** Understanding, command, and comprehension all mean the ability to understand something.

14. **F** Hang, float, and suspend all mean to be dangling above ground. Drop suggests that the object is falling and not remaining suspended in the air.

15. **D** March, April, and May are all spring months. August is a summer month.

16. **G** Something very cool is cold and extremely cold is frigid. Something very warm is hot and extremely warm is scalding.

17. **B** Seconds make up a minute, and minutes make up an hour. Days make up a month, and months make up a year.

18. **G** A berry is a fruit that grows on a bush, a grape is a fruit that grows on a vine, and an apple is a fruit that grows on a tree.

19. **D** A bird has feathers, a bear has fur, and a fish has scales.

20. **F** Angry means very annoyed, and enraged means very angry. Happy means very content, and ecstatic means very happy.

Test 5—Verbal Reasoning—Context

1. **C** Since Martin's class does go to Europe, they must have gotten the group rate, so they must have at least 20 people signed up for the trip. None of the other choices are certain.

2. **J** Since Alice can run 6 miles per hour and Marsha can run 7 miles per hour, Marsha can run faster than Alice. None of the other choices are certain.

3. **A** Since Julie has more marbles than Larry and Larry has more marbles than Cindy, we know that Julie has more marbles than Cindy.

4. **H** Since Carlos can swim more than 3 laps and Erwin can only swim 2, we know that Carlos can swim during recess but Erwin cannot.

5. **D** Since Alex got a higher score than Lucy and Lucy got a higher score than Wendy, we know that Alex got a higher score than Wendy.

6. **H** If Julia never skates before she eats, then she must have skated with Elise after she had lunch with Shelton. No information is given about the amount of time she spends with each friend nor if she prefers one friend more than any other friend, so (F) and (J) are incorrect. The order that she sees her friends is not provided, so eliminate (G).

7. **A** If Reggie likes blue, Yuri likes orange. Eliminate (B) and (D). Greg and Barry do not like green. Since each person has a different favorite color, then Oscar must like green.

8. **F** Draw a chart.

	Stephen	Max	David	Adam
doc	+			x
rom com		+	+	
horror	+			
action		+		

Since each person likes a different movie genre and David only likes romantic comedies, then Max must like action movies, eliminate (G) and (H). Since Adam does not like documentaries, then he must like horror movies, which means Stephen likes documentaries. Therefore, (F) must be true.

9. **B** There is not enough information provided to determine whether (A) and/or (D) are true. 40 is two-thirds of 60, not one-third, so eliminate (C). Since 40 is less than 60 and greater than 20, (B) must be true.

10. **H** Draw a picture. Since the bank is south of the hospital, draw a B and then an H directly above the B. The bank is east from the police station, so write a P directly to the left of the B. Since the police station is directly north of the fire station, write a F directly below the P. The drawing indicates that only (H) is true.

Test 6—Reading and Language Arts

1. **B** The word *decompose* is used in the passage in contrast to "lasted forever."

2. **H** The passage says that it took "more than sixty days." The closest choice is (H).

3. **A** Every paragraph in the passage discusses some aspect of making a mummy.

4. **G** The beginning of the third paragraph calls this process "embalming."

5. **B** The second paragraph states the "a person's soul needed a body to live in."

6. **H** In the first paragraph, the word *stock* is followed immediately by "His ancestors."

7. **A** According to the passage, he was "a captain in the War of the Revolution."

8. **F** The first paragraph says that he was "a tailor, a farmer, a storekeeper, and a country tavern-keeper, and was not particularly prosperous in any of these callings."

9. **B** The third paragraph says that he excelled "in mathematics."

10. **H** According to the second paragraph, he was named "after his maternal grandfather."

11. **A** At the beginning of the third paragraph it states that he "drove the crows to and from the pasture, shelled corn," and performed other farming duties.

12. **C** In the passage, the word *mundane* is used to describe the weather as opposed to astronomy. This makes (C) the most likely choice.

13. **G** We can infer that Wegener died in 1930 because the passage says, "It was only in the 1960s, approximately thirty years after his death, that other scientists finally proved the correctness of Wegener's theory."

14. **C** In the third paragraph it states that Wegener noticed that "the continents fit together like puzzle pieces."

15. **G** The end of the first paragraph says the Wegener "chose to study the stars;" the next sentence states that he got his degree in astronomy.

16. **A** In the second paragraph, the word *aloft* is used to describe a balloon.

17. **A** According to the passage, bison live in North America while buffalo live in Asia and Africa.

18. **H** The paragraph discusses how bison were originally plentiful in America, that they faced extinction, and how they are now protected. This best supports (H).

19. **B** The passage states that "due to conservation efforts, their numbers have increased."

20. **H** The sentence is stating that bison were believed to be nearly extinct, so the correct answer should mean something similar to "believed." The only choice that works is (H).

21. **H** The first sentence of this passage mentions transportation in the early years of large cities, and the rest of the passage discusses this idea.

22. **D** According to the first paragraph, they "were difficult to enter and exit."

23. **H** Only (H) would discuss developments in transportation in cities.

24. **B** The second paragraph says that he was a businessman who owned a bathhouse and took advantage of a need for short-distance transportation.

31. **C** The passage discusses the eruption at Krakatau and its results.

32. **H** The end of the first paragraph talks about how loud and powerful the sound of the explosion was.

33. **A** There is no evidence for (B), (C), or (D).

34. **F** According to the second paragraph, they were caused by "a residue of sulfuric-acid aerosol and dust."

36. **J** The passage begins with the origin of the Tower and discusses its uses through the years.

37. **C** Choices (A), (B), and (D) are mentioned in the passage.

38. **G** The first paragraph says that construction on the Tower was begun in 1066.

39. **B** There is no evidence to support (A), (C), or (D). The author simply describes the facts of the Tower.

40. **H** Choices (F) and (G) are extreme and can be eliminated. Choice (J) is never discussed.

42. **F** All the other choices are awkward or illogical.

43. **C** Choice (B) is in the passive voice, and (A) and (D) are awkward.

44. **F** All the other choices use passive voice and/or are awkward.

47. **C** The rest of the paragraph discusses the size of elephants, so the first sentence should discuss their size.

48. **G** This paragraph mentions how crocodiles and alligators differ. The first sentence should introduce this idea.

49. **A** Choice (B) is redundant, (C) is awkward, and (D) changes the meaning of the original sentences.

50. **H** Choices (G) and (J) are awkward. Choice (F) is a run-on sentence.

Test 7—Mathematics

1. **A** To find the difference between $14\frac{1}{2}$ and $8\frac{3}{4}$, first subtract the whole number portion: 14 – 8 = 6. Now subtract the fractional part. To solve $\frac{1}{2} - \frac{3}{4}$, use the Bowtie. Multiply the bottom numbers together to get 8, which goes on the bottom of each of the new fractions. Then we multiply up and diagonally: 2 × 3= 6 and 4 × 1 = 4. Our problem now becomes $\frac{4}{8} - \frac{6}{8}$, which is equal to $-\frac{2}{8}$, or $-\frac{1}{4}$. When we subtract this from 6, we get $5\frac{3}{4}$.

2. **G** The perimeter is the sum of the sides, or $(3y - 4) + (2y + 1) + (5y + 1)$.

3. **A** You could solve this by dividing $2\frac{1}{2}$ by $1\frac{1}{2}$, but there is an easier way. Plug in the answer choices starting with (A), and see which choice times $1\frac{1}{2}$ gives us $2\frac{1}{2}$. Is $1\frac{2}{3}$ times $1\frac{1}{2}$ equal to $2\frac{1}{2}$? Yes.

4. **H** The right angle in the triangle measures 90 degrees. Therefore, the other two angles must measure a total of 90 degrees. Since the triangle is isosceles, the two remaining angles must split the 90 degrees evenly. They are both therefore 45 degrees.

5. **B** The first minute will cost \$2.35. The other 7 minutes will cost 15 cents each, or 7 × 0.15 = \$1.05.

6. **F** First, find the factors of 48: 1 × 48, 2 × 24, 3 × 16, 4 × 12, and 6 × 8. How many of these are prime? Only 2 and 3.

7. **A** To multiply by 1,000, you move the decimal three places to the right: 42.2678 × 1,000 becomes 42,267.8. Now figure out which choice is equal to this. For (A), move the decimal three places to the right to match the exponent of 10, and you get 4,2267.8. Choice (A) is the right answer.

8. **G** Since x and 140 are on the same line, their sum must be 180: 180 – 140 = 40.

9. **C** Let's break this down into pieces. The first term is $\left(4 \times \frac{1}{100}\right)$. This is the same as 4 in the hundredths place, or 0.04. We could figure out the decimal equivalents of the other parts, but we don't have to do that much work: The only choice that has a 4 in the hundredths place is (C).

10. **F** To solve for x, first we need to multiply out the left side, which gives us $2x + 4x = 6x$. The inequality now reads $6x > -6$. Now divide each side by 6.

11. **B** 4^4 is the same as $4 \times 4 \times 4 \times 4$. 4^5 is the same as $4 \times 4 \times 4 \times 4 \times 4$. If we multiply them together we get $4 \times 4 \times 4 \times 4 \times 4 \times 4 \times 4 \times 4 \times 4$, or 4^9.

12. **H** To make this math work easier, don't forget to reduce first. We can reduce 25 and 5, as well as 9 and 27, and we get $\frac{5}{3} \times \frac{1}{1}$, or $\frac{5}{3}$.

13. **D** To find the amount of interest, we need to calculate 4% of \$5,000. This translates as $\frac{4}{100} \times 5000$. Cancel out two zeros, and you get 4×50, or \$200. Add this to his original deposit.

14. **F** If the car travels $\frac{1}{2}$ mile every minute, then it travels 1 mile every 2 minutes. To travel 40 miles will take them 80 minutes, or $1\frac{1}{3}$ hours.

15. **B** Coordinate (2,7) must have a positive x- and positive y-coordinate. This eliminates (C) and (D). Since the x-coordinate is smaller than the y-cooridnate, the point will be high on the y-axis.

16. **G** The area of a triangle $= \frac{1}{2}$ base $\times$ height. We know that the base is 10. If the area is 40, then $40 = \frac{1}{2} 10 \times$ height. So $40 = 5 \times h$. Divide each side by 5 to solve for the height.

17. **D** First put all the x's on the left side of the equation. We can do this by subtracting x from each side, which leaves us with $3x - 9 = 6$. Now add 9 to each side, to get $3x = 15$. Finally, we divide each side by 3 to get $x = 5$.

18. **J** To solve this, set up a proportion. $\frac{5 \text{ apples}}{\$8} = \frac{60 \text{ apples}}{x}$. To solve, we cross-multiply 60×8 and then divide by 5.

19. **B** For this question, make sure to follow the order of operations. First, do what is in parentheses: $2 - 8 = -6$. Now we have $13 + 2 \times 9 + 1 - (-6)$. Next, solve $2 \times 9 = 18$. This gives us $13 + 18 + 1 - (-6)$. Now add straight across. (Don't forget that $-(-6)$ is the same as $+6$!)

20. **J** Solve this by plugging in the answer choices. If Mack is 9, then 9 years ago he was 0 years old. Does that make him half as old as he is now? No. If Mack is 12, then 9 years ago he was 3. Does that make him half as old as he is now? No. If Mack is 15, then 9 years ago he was 6. Does that make him half as old as he is now? No. If Mack is 18, then 9 years ago he was 9. This makes him half as old as he is now.

21. **D** If five shirts cost \$28.50, then each shirt costs one-fifth of that, so divide \$28.50 by 5 to get \$5.70. Multiply that number by 2 to see that two shirts cost \$11.40. Since two shirts and a pair of shorts cost \$19.25, then the shorts must cost \$19.25 – \$11.40, or \$7.85.

22. **G** $3\frac{3}{4}\%$ is the same as 3.75%. Remember that % is the same as dividing by 100. Therefore, this equals $\frac{3.75}{100}$. To divide by 100, we move the decimal two places to the left.

23. **D** Let's put 3 in place of x and solve for each expression: $3(3^2) = 27$ and $(3 \times 3)^2 = 81$. The difference is $81 - 27 = 54$.

24. **H** Walter has a total of 120 + 80 = 200 baseball cards. Of these cards, 80 of them are baseball cards. Therefore, the fractional part of his collection that are baseball cards is $\frac{80}{200}$, which can be reduced to $\frac{40}{100}$, or 40%.

25. **D** The volume of a cube is length × width × height. The length, width, and height of this cube are each 3, so the volume is $3 \times 3 \times 3 = 27$.

26. **J** Rewrite this expression as $\frac{04.5}{0.02}$. If we move the decimal on the top and on bottom two places to the right, we get $\frac{450}{2} = 225$.

27. **C** First, let's find the volume of the silo, which will tell us how much grain it can hold. It can hold a total of $25 \times 6 \times 12 = 1{,}800$ cubic feet of grain. If it is being filled at a rate of 4 cubic feet every minute, divide 1,800 by 4 to find how many minutes it will take to fill the silo.

28. **H** To make it easier to multiply these fractions, put them in standard form. $3\frac{1}{2}$ is the same as $\frac{7}{2}$ $(2 \times 3 + 1 = 7)$, and $6\frac{1}{2}$ is the same as $\frac{13}{2}$ $(2 \times 6 + 1 = 13)$. Now multiply $\frac{7}{2} \times \frac{13}{2} = \frac{91}{4}$, or $22\frac{3}{4}$.

29. **A** The area of a circle is πr^2 and the circumference is $2\pi r$. If a circle has a radius of 4, its area is 16π and its circumference is 8π. The ratio of 16π to 8π is the same as 2:1.

30. **H** Percent increase is always figured by taking the difference over the original amount. The difference between the number of papers that Cindy sold in 1997 and 1998 is 80. The original number she sold in 1997 was 120. Therefore her percentage increase was $\frac{80}{120} = \frac{2}{3}$, or 66%.

31. **D** If $\frac{1}{3}$ of a number is 32, then the original number must be $3 \times 32 = 96$. $\frac{3}{4}$ of 96 is 72.

32. **G** Since the triangle is equilateral, all of its sides are 8. Since one of its sides is also a side of the square, the square must also have sides of 8. Therefore the perimeter is equal to 3 sides of the square plus 2 sides of the triangle, each of which are 8. $5 \times 8 = 40$.

33. **C** First, look at the multiples of 5. They are 5, 10, 15, 20, 25, and 30. How many of these are also multiples of 3? Only 15 and 30 are.

34. **J** Use the average formula: $\text{average} = \dfrac{\text{sum total}}{\#\text{ of things}}$ to figure out this problem. If Terence averaged 80 on 4 tests, the sum total of his results on his tests must have been 4×80, or 320. The three tests given have a sum of 231, so 320–231 is his score on his final test.

35. **B** Since the triangle is a right triangle, one of the angles is 90 degrees. If the other angle is 65 degrees, then the sum of these two angles is 155 degrees. Since there are 180 degrees in a triangle, the third angle must measure 25 degrees.

36. **J** If the ratio of blue to red marbles is 5:2, this means that 5 out of every 7 is blue and 2 of every 7 is red. This means that we can set up a proportion: $\dfrac{\textit{blue}\ 5}{\textit{total}\ 7} = \dfrac{x}{70}$. By cross multiplying we see that there must be 50 blue marbles out of the 70 total marbles.

37. **C** To find how many 75-cent cakes she needs to sell to make $18, divide $18 by $0.75. To make the division easier, move the decimal point two places to the right: $\dfrac{1800}{75} = 24$.

38. **H** Since $OA = 4$, the OB is also 4, since all radii are the same length. This makes the perimeter $4 + 4 + 5$.

39. **B** Plug in the answer choices, starting with A. When $x = 1$, is $1 + 1 = 1 \times 1$? No. When $x = 2$, is $2 + 2 = 2 \times 2$? Yes.

40. **F** $\dfrac{1}{\frac{1}{x}}$ is the same as $1 \div \dfrac{1}{x}$, which is the same as $1 \times \dfrac{x}{1}$, or just x.

Chapter 29
TACHS Practice Test

Reading

Part 1
(5 minutes)

For each question, decide which one of the four possible answers has most nearly the same meaning as the underlined word above it.

1. **<u>Launch</u> the program**

   (A) start

   (B) rocket

   (C) plan

   (D) uplift

2. **<u>Trying</u> times**

   (J) applying

   (K) hard

   (L) good

   (M) fun

3. **Maximum <u>value</u>**

   (A) change

   (B) performance

   (C) worth

   (D) praise

4. **<u>Intersecting</u> lines**

   (J) parallel

   (K) curved

   (L) boldfaced

   (M) crossing

5. **<u>Cold</u> expression**

   (A) unfeeling

   (B) smiling

   (C) shocking

   (D) happy

6. **<u>Turbulent</u> flight**

   (J) smooth

   (K) bumpy

   (L) quick

   (M) long

7. **To <u>champion</u> a cause**

(A) win

(B) defeat

(C) challenge

(D) support

8. **<u>Superb</u> performance**

(J) bad

(K) excellent

(L) live

(M) silent

9. **<u>Merciful</u> fighter**

(A) cruel

(B) tough

(C) friendly

(D) forgiving

10. **<u>Idle</u> hands**

(J) large

(K) inactive

(L) shaking

(M) smooth

Reading

Part 2
(15 minutes)

Read the passages below and then answer the questions. Four possible answers are given for each question. You are to choose the answer that you think is better than the others.

Kangaroos are fascinating creatures because they are so different from other mammals. Unlike most mammals, kangaroos rear their young in a pouch and hop to get around. Their long, powerful hind legs are used for jumping, and their thick tail gives them balance. Their forelimbs are used almost like human hands. Despite these well-known characteristics, prevalent among all kangaroos, there are many lesser-known variations; some kangaroo species differ tremendously in such characteristics as habitat, color, social patterns, and size. For example, various species range in size from nine inches to more than eight feet.

The explanation often given for these odd features is that kangaroos are marsupials, and marsupials are a primitive form of mammal. This explanation, which may or may not be correct, is particularly popular among people who live in the Northern Hemisphere. Their view is reflected in the statements they make about the Virginia opossum, the only marsupial native to North America. The opossum is frequently described as a primitive animal, little changed since the time of the dinosaurs.

But even if the opossum can in some ways be considered a "living fossil," the same cannot be said of the kangaroo. These Australian marsupials have changed recently in order to adapt to a changing environment. Kangaroos evolved from small forest animals into creatures that live mainly in open spaces. This development was probably related to the spread of grassland areas in Australia between ten and fifteen million years ago.

11. Which of the following best describes what this passage is about?

(A) a comparison of the opossum and the kangaroo

(B) the competition between marsupials and dinosaurs

(C) the evolutionary background of kangaroos

(D) why kangaroos are not really mammals

12. The author of this passage is most likely

(J) a scientist

(K) a hunter

(L) an Australian

(M) a physicist

An Inuit navigating in polar darkness and whiteouts makes use of many clues to find his way. When traveling on ice in the fog, the Inuit uses the voices of seabirds against the cliffs and the sound of the surf at the end of the ice. When he begins to travel over open terrain, he marks the angle of the wind and aligns the fur of his parka with the breeze. He notes the trend of any cracks in the ice as he crosses them. Sea ice cracks can reveal the presence of a cape or headland invisible in the distance, or they may confirm one's arrival at a known area.

Constant attention to such details, memories of the way the land looks, and stories told by other travelers are used together with the movements of animals to keep the traveler on course. Searching for small but crucial clues can be exhausting for a person who does not know what to look for.

These navigational tools are still part of village life in the Arctic, used just as often today while traveling long distances by snowmobile as they were once by people traveling on foot. Such skills are still more critical for the success of a journey than even the best maps and navigation aids. Fogs and blizzards hide the reference points needed to navigate by map. Even compasses can't be relied on so close to the magnetic pole: the compass needle wanders aimlessly due to the proximity of the magnetic field. The most dependable sources of direction for most Inuit, therefore, are the behavior of the wind and ocean currents, and such subtle clues as the flow of a river.

13. According to the author, traditional navigational skills are still used by the Inuit because

(A) traditional techniques are always superior to modern technology

(B) the Inuit prefer not to travel too far from home

(C) modern navigational equipment is too expensive for most Inuit

(D) traditional methods are sometimes more effective than sophisticated equipment

14. The last paragraph suggests that in the polar region navigation is complicated by the fact that

(J) objects in the sky, such as stars, do not provide useful information

(K) the summer moon affects ocean currents in unpredictable ways

(L) accurate compass readings are difficult to obtain

(M) wind and ocean currents change too quickly to be reliable

It may seem to you as you gaze up into the night sky that the stars move from one night to the next. While the position of a star may vary a bit over the years, in general the movement of the stars is due to the rotation of the Earth, not the movement of the stars. The Earth rotates on its axis from west to east every day. Because you are not aware of the movement of the Earth, it looks to you as though the stars are moving from east to west in the sky. The only star that does not appear to have any motion is Polaris, or what is commonly called the North Star. The reason it does not appear to move is that it lies almost directly above the North Pole. Because its position is fixed, the North Star has long been used as a tool for navigation. No matter where you are, if you can locate the North Star, you can figure out which direction is North. Sailors out on the sea used it to find their way. Polaris is a very bright star, so it can be located easily.

15. According to the passage, the reason we think that the stars move is due to

(A) the distance between the Earth and the stars

(B) the effect of the Sun

(C) gravity

(D) the rotation of the Earth

16. According to the passage, the reason Polaris does not appear to move is that

(J) it moves more slowly than the other stars

(K) it is brighter than the other stars

(L) it lies above the North Pole

(M) it is farther away than other stars

Most people know that the ancient Egyptians mummified their dead. But few people know the details of how or why a mummy was made.

The point of mummification was to remove all of the parts of the body that could decompose to ensure that the remaining parts lasted forever. This was important to the Egyptians, who believed that parts of a person's soul needed a body to live in. If the body were to rot and disappear, the soul would be left homeless for eternity. To prevent the body from rotting, all the water had to be removed and all the bacteria had to be killed.

The process of embalming took more than sixty days. First, most of the internal organs had to be removed. The embalmer would break the corpse's nose and pull out the brain. He would then make an incision in the abdomen to remove the stomach, intestines, lungs, and liver. These were then salted, dried, and placed in jars that were buried with the body. The heart, which the Egyptians believed to be the source of consciousness, was often salted, dried, and placed back inside the body.

After the organs were removed, the body was doused with alcohol. This served to kill the bacteria in the body. The body was then salted, which dried out the skin. Finally the whole body was wrapped in waxed bandages to form a waterproof casing around the body.

17. According to the passage, about how long did it take to make a mummy?

(A) less than one month

(B) one month

(C) two months

(D) a year

18. This passage is mostly about

(J) the process of mummification

(K) the organs of the human body

(L) Egyptian religious beliefs

(M) why mummies are so small

Like so many of his famous compatriots, Phineas Taylor Barnum came from good old New England stock. His ancestors were among the builders of the colonies of Massachusetts and Connecticut. His father's father, Ephraim Barnum, was a captain in the War of the Revolution, and was distinguished for his valor and fervent patriotism. His mother's father, Phineas Taylor, was locally noted as a wag and practical joker. His father, Philo Barnum, was in turn a tailor, a farmer, a storekeeper, and a country tavernkeeper, and was not particularly prosperous in any of these callings.

Philo Barnum and his wife, Irena Taylor, lived in Bethel, Connecticut, and there, on July 5, 1810, their first child was born. He was named Phineas Taylor Barnum after his maternal grandfather, and the latter, in return for the compliment, bestowed upon his first grandchild at his christening the title-deeds of a "landed estate," five acres in extent known as Ivy Island and situated in that part of Bethel known as the "Plum Trees."

In his early years, the boy led the life of the average New England farmer's son of that period. He drove the cows to and from the pasture, shelled corn, weeded the garden, and "did up chores." As he grew older, he rode the horse in plowing corn, raked hay, wielded the shovel and the hoe, and chopped wood. At six years old he began to go to school—the typical district school. "The first date," he once said, "I remember inscribing upon my writing-book was 1818." The ferule, or birch-rod, was in those days the assistant schoolmaster, and young P.T. Barnum made its acquaintance. He was, however, an apt and ready scholar, particularly excelling in mathematics. One night, when he was ten years old, he was called out of bed by his teacher, who had made a wager with a neighbor that Barnum could calculate the number of feet in a load of wood in five minutes. Barnum did it in less than two minutes, to the delight of his teacher and the astonishment of the neighbor.

19. According to the passage, P.T. Barnum's father

(A) did many things and was not very good at any of them

(B) was one of the best teachers in the sate

(C) was a farmer

(D) was a captain

20. When the passage says "The ferule, or birch-rod, was in those days the assistant schoolmaster," this probably means that in the early 1800s

(J) the birch-rod was the subject of much scientific study

(K) school assignments were written on birch-rods

(L) birch-rods were used to punish students who misbehaved

(M) assistant schoolmasters resembled birch-rods

Language

Part 1

(25 minutes)

This is a test of how well you can find mistakes in writing. For the questions with mistakes in spelling, capitalization, and punctuation, choose the answer with the same letter as the line containing the mistake. For the questions with mistakes in usage and expression, choose the answer with the same letter as the line containing the mistake, or choose the word, phrase, or sentence that is better than the others. When there is no mistake or no change needed, choose the last answer choice.

1. **(A)** sellfish
   (B) sharing
   (C) friendly
   (D) popular
   (E) *(No mistakes)*

2. **(J)** lynx
   (K) tyger
   (L) panther
   (M) cougar
   (N) *(No mistakes)*

3. **(A)** factory
   (B) convey
   (C) presentation
   (D) occupashun
   (E) *(No mistakes)*

4. **(J)** nail
   (K) maintain
   (L) pledge
   (M) align
   (N) *(No mistakes)*

5. **(A)** messenger
   (B) persuade
   (C) brayce
   (D) coerce
   (E) *(No mistakes)*

6. **(J)** interview
   (K) toffee
   (L) appliance
   (M) pertane
   (N) *(No mistakes)*

7. **(A)** oboe
 (B) symfany
 (C) flute
 (D) trombone
 (E) *(No mistakes)*

8. **(J)** pride
 (K) friend
 (L) obtayne
 (M) adhere
 (N) *(No mistakes)*

9. **(A)** wacher
 (B) mellow
 (C) whole
 (D) while
 (E) *(No mistakes)*

10. **(J)** whistle
 (K) shriek
 (L) fright
 (M) wrestle
 (N) *(No mistakes)*

11. **(A)** Tom shops at the
 (B) produce market on
 (C) wall street.
 (D) *(No mistakes)*

12. **(J)** The united states leads
 (K) all other nations in many
 (L) economic categories.
 (M) *(No mistakes)*

13. **(A)** Extracurricular activities, test
 (B) scores, and grade point average are
 (C) the basis of College applications.
 (D) *(No mistakes)*

14. **(J)** The cowboys stood out
 (K) in the field talking and
 (L) chewing toothpicks.
 (M) *(No mistakes)*

15. **(A)** When learning to juggle,
 (B) one needs to practice,
 (C) tossing gently.
 (D) *(No mistakes)*

16. **(J)** The only way to
(K) have a friend is
(L) to be one.
(M) *(No mistakes)*

17. **(A)** The directions clearly
(B) say to stop, look,
(C) and, listen.
(D) *(No mistakes)*

18. **(J)** Bob's knees started to
(K) tremble while He was
(L) staring down the ski slope.
(M) *(No mistakes)*

19. **(A)** Each of the dogs
(B) has been cared
(C) for, by the owners.
(D) *(No mistakes)*

20. **(J)** Pop rocks will rot
(K) Your teeth and may
(L) cause your stomach pain.
(M) *(No mistakes)*

Language

Part 2
(25 minutes)

For questions 21–30, choose the best answer based on the following paragraphs.

1) One of the most widespread musical instruments in the Middle Ages was the lute, a stringed instrument in the same family as the guitar. 2) The lute took many different forms over the years, and also of varying sizes and shapes. 3) Two variations on the lute were the chitarrone and the theorbo. 4) The chitarrone took its name from the Italian word chitarra, meaning guitar. 5) In later years, the chitarrone and theorbo were mainly used to accompany vocal groups and for the theater.

21. What is the best way to write the underlined part of sentence 2?

(A) but

(B) In spite of,

(C) years, of varying

(D) (No change)

22. What is the best way to write the underlined part of sentence 5?

(J) In, later years

(K) In later years;

(L) In later years:

(M) (No change)

1) One of the most amazing natural events that you can witness is a cyclone. 2) Cyclones can begin to be developing when air begins to spiral inward around a low-pressure area, creating a kind of whirlpool of air. 3) Without air, most land animals could not survive. 4) Some strong tropical cyclones pick up such speed, and power that they become hurricanes. 5) These are the most violent kind of cyclones, and they can do a great deal of damage when they encounter an inhabited island or coastline. 6) They can cause floods and wind damage, and may even be deadly.

23. What is the best way to write the underlined part of sentence 2?

(A) Cyclones are starting to develop

(B) Cyclones develop

(C) Cyclones are developing

(D) (No change)

24. What is the best way to write the underlined part of sentence 4?

(J) pick up such, speed and power

(K) pick up: such speed and power

(L) pick up such speed and power

(M) (No change)

1) It wasn't never Ella Fitzgerald's intention to become a jazz singer. 2) She had originally planned to be a dancer. 3) The arts of dancing and singing go back very far in human history. 4) But one day when she planned to dance in a talent show, she was so scared that she couldn't stand up straight. 5) She decided to sing instead, and her outstanding voice was noticed by a musician in the audience. 6) From there, she became famous very quickly, and is thought to be the greatest jazz singer of our time.

25. What is the best way to write the underlined part of sentence 1?

(A) It was never Ella Fitzgerald's intention

(B) It was never Ella Fitzgeralds intention

(C) It was never ella fitzgerald's intention

(D) (No change)

26. What is the best way to write the underlined part of sentence 3?

(J) go back, very

(K) go, back very

(L) go back very,

(M) (No change)

1) In 1980 Mount Saint Helens, in the state of Washington, became a volcano. 2) It exploded for the first time in thousands of years. 3) The explosion was felt as far north as Seattle and as far south as Los Angeles. 4) The mountain thru tons of ash into the air. 5) Most geologists believe that Mount Saint Helens will not explode for many thousands of years to come. 6) But they admit that another explosion might occur at any time.

27. What is the best way to write the underlined part of sentence 1?

(A) In 1980: Mount Saint Helens

(B) In 1980 Mount Saint Helen's

(C) In 1980 Mount Saint Helens'

(D) (No change)

28. What is the best way to write the underlined part of sentence 4?

(J) through tons

(K) threw tons

(L) thorough tons

(M) (No change)

1) Nicolaus Copernicus was born on <u>February 19, 1474.</u> 2) He first studied in Cracow, and then was sent to Italy to continue his education. 3) At first he studied law, but soon he became a scientist. 4) <u>In the middle ages</u> it was very easy to be a lawyer and a scientist at the same time. 5) Copernicus's most important contribution to science was the heliocentric (sun-centered) view of the universe. 6) This theory finally succeeded in displacing the old geocentric (earth-centered) view of the universe that had persisted since the time of the Greeks.

29. What is the best way to write the underlined part of sentence 4?

(A) In the Middle Ages

(B) In The Middle Ages

(C) In the middle Ages

(D) (No change)

30. What is the best way to write the underlined part of sentence 1?

(J) February, 19, 1474

(K) February 19 1474

(L) February, 19 1474

(M) (No change)

Math

Part 1
(30 minutes)

Choose the best answer.

1. Which of the following is *not* a factor of 45?

 (A) 2

 (B) 5

 (C) 9

 (D) 15

2. The fraction $\frac{3}{4}$ is approximately equal to which of the following?

 (J) 34.75

 (K) 0.75

 (L) 0.34

 (M) $\frac{4}{3}$

3. Which of the following is a prime number?

 (A) 51

 (B) 49

 (C) 27

 (D) 17

4. Which of the following is *not* a multiple of 4?

(J) 14

(K) 24

(L) 64

(M) 84

5. What is the difference between 82 and 20?

(A) 4.1

(B) 62

(C) 102

(D) 1,640

6. The number 0.0007 is equal to which of the following?

(J) $\frac{7}{10,000}$

(K) $\frac{7}{1,000}$

(L) $\frac{7}{100}$

(M) $\frac{7}{10}$

7. Which of the following is equivalent to 2^4?

(A) 2×4

(B) $2 \times 2 \times 2 \div 2$

(C) 10

(D) 16

8. What is the sum of $\frac{3}{4} + \frac{10}{8} + \frac{6}{6}$?

(J) 1

(K) 2

(L) 3

(M) $3\frac{3}{4}$

9. What is the sum (2 × 2) + (3 × 3) + (4 × 4)?

(A) 18

(B) 24

(C) 29

(D) 234

10. Which of the following represents 2.4 in reduced form?

(J) $\frac{48}{20}$

(K) $\frac{24}{10}$

(L) $2\frac{4}{10}$

(M) $2\frac{2}{5}$

11. Dixie has 5 pencils in her backpack. Geoffrey has in his backpack three times as many pencils as Dixie. Karen has in her backpack three times as many pencils as Geoffrey and Dixie combined. How many pencils does Karen have crammed into her backpack?

(A) 60

(B) 45

(C) 20

(D) 15

12. Jeremy wanted to restock the soda supply in his restaurant. The vat in his store room can hold 22 barrels of soda. His supplier sells soda in half-barrel units. How many half-barrel units will Jeremy need to purchase in order to fill the vat?

(J) 44

(K) 33

(L) 22

(M) 11

13. Christine currently has $7. Her parents pay her a monthly allowance of $30. How many months will it take Christine to save enough money to buy a skateboard that costs $127?

(A) 3 months

(B) 4 months

(C) 5 months

(D) Not given

14. Sonali is in a store that sells candy for $10 per pound, and she has a bag that holds 5 pounds of candy. If Sonali wants to fill her bag to $\frac{4}{5}$ of its capacity, how much can she expect it to cost?

(J) $20

(K) $30

(L) $40

(M) $50

15. The crossbar on an ice hockey net is 4 feet above the ice. If a player hit the crossbar with the puck 8 times, what is the sum of the distances the puck would travel between the crossbar and the ice below?

(A) 12

(B) 32

(C) 48

(D) Not given

16. If every bicycle on Bike Path 18 has two wheels, and there are currently 81 bicycles on Bike Path 18, how many wheels are currently touching the surface on Bike Path 18?

(J) 36

(K) 72

(L) 162

(M) 324

17. Joshua drives at 40 miles per hour. Elissa drives 20% faster than Joshua. How many miles does Elissa drive in 14 hours?

(A) 560

(B) 624

(C) 672

(D) Not given

18. Uncle Fred has 8 dozen model cars in his collection. He would like a total of 300 to complete his collection. How many new model cars should he purchase at the model car expo to reach his goal of 300 model cars for his collection?

(J) 216

(K) 204

(L) 96

(M) 74

19. Mr. Kim and Mrs. Adams are carpeting the rectangular floors of a few classrooms. They have five classrooms to carpet, and each floor is the same size. The floors are each 10 feet long and 11 feet wide. How many square feet of floors should they plan to carpet if they are going to carpet all five classrooms?

(A) 110

(B) 220

(C) 440

(D) 550

20. A student is awake for approximately 365,000 minutes each year. For approximately how many minutes is the student awake each day?

(J) 365

(K) 1,000

(L) 10,000

(M) Not given

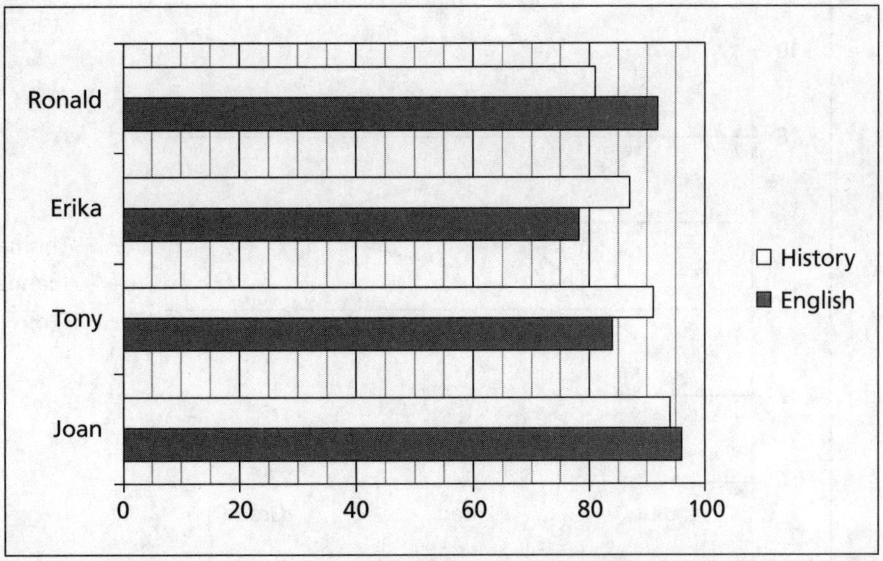

21. **A school recently gave an English test and a History test. Based on the information in the chart above, which student scored the highest on the History test.**

(A) Ronald

(B) Erika

(C) Tony

(D) Joan

22. **Based on the information in the chart above, which student score 11 more points on the English test than they did on the History test?**

(J) Ronald

(K) Erika

(L) Tony

(M) Joan

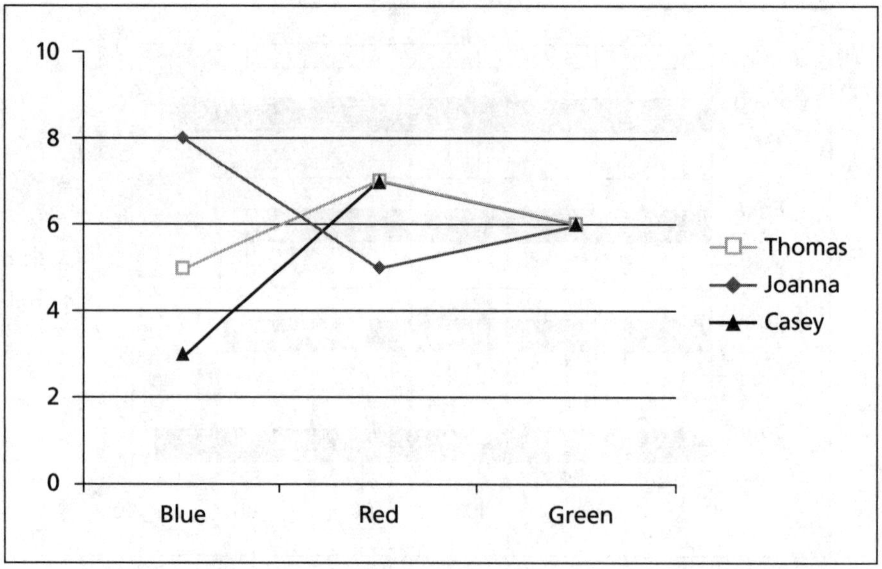

23. Three friends go to a toy store to buy marbles. The chart indicates the purchases made by the friends from their visit. Based on the information in the chart above, which of the friends collected the most blue and red marbles combined?

(A) Thomas

(B) Joanna

(C) Casey

(D) Thomas and Casey

24. Based on the information above, what was the total number of green marbles purchased by the three friends?

(J) 63

(K) 18

(L) 12

(M) 6

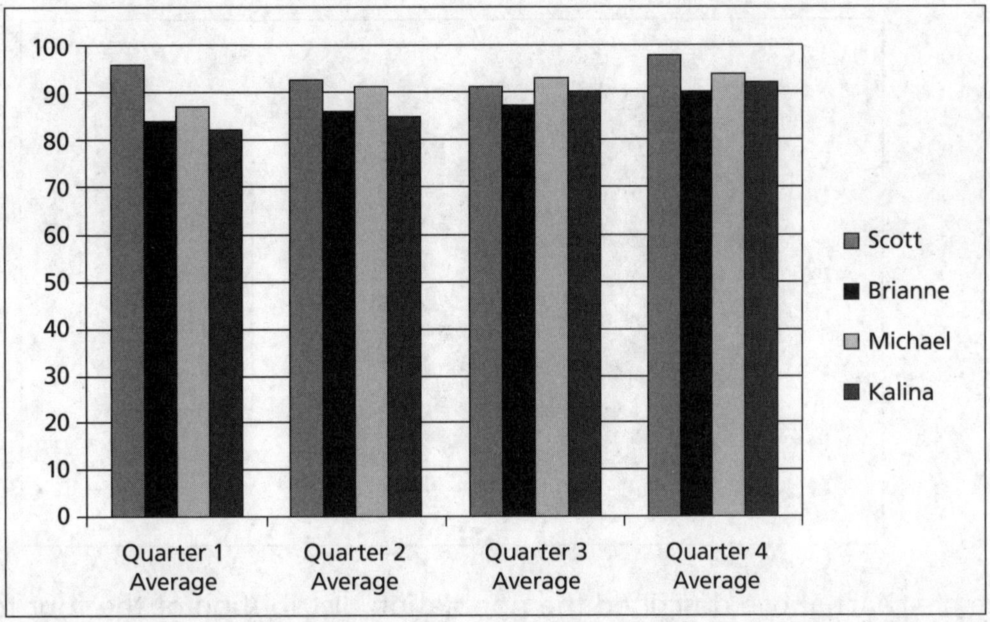

25. According to the bar graph above that expresses quarterly averages for four students in a given school year, which student experienced the greatest average improvement from Quarter 1 to Quarter 4?

(A) Scott

(B) Brianne

(C) Michael

(D) Kalina

26. According to the bar graph above, what was the approximate Brianne's approximate average for Quarter 4

(J) 84

(K) 86

(L) 88

(M) 90

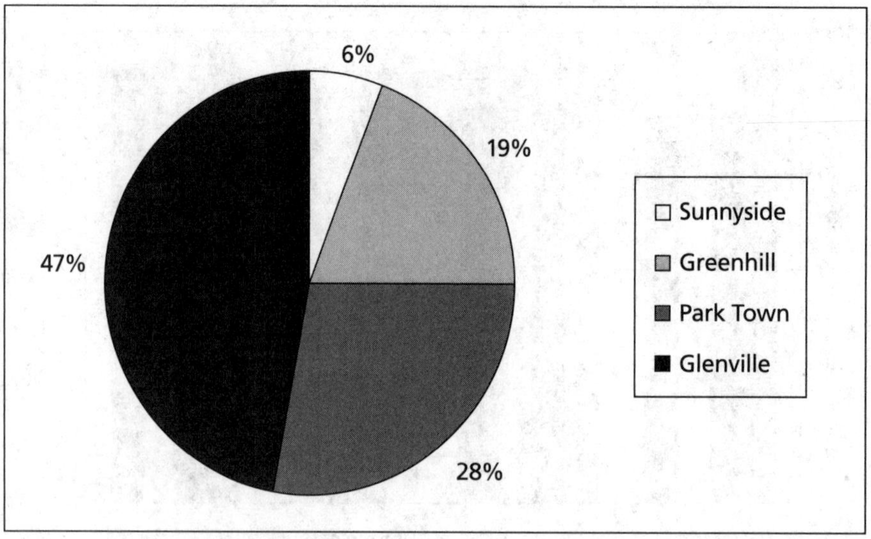

27. **The pie chart above described the population distribution of the four towns in Riviera County. Based on the information in the chart, what is the most populous town in Riviera County?**

    (A) Sunnyside

    (B) Greenhill

    (C) Park Town

    (D) Glenville

28. **Which two towns in Riviera County when added together equal the population of Glenville?**

    (J) Sunnyside and Greenhill

    (K) Glenville and Greenhill

    (L) Greenhill and Park Town

    (M) Sunnyside and Park Town

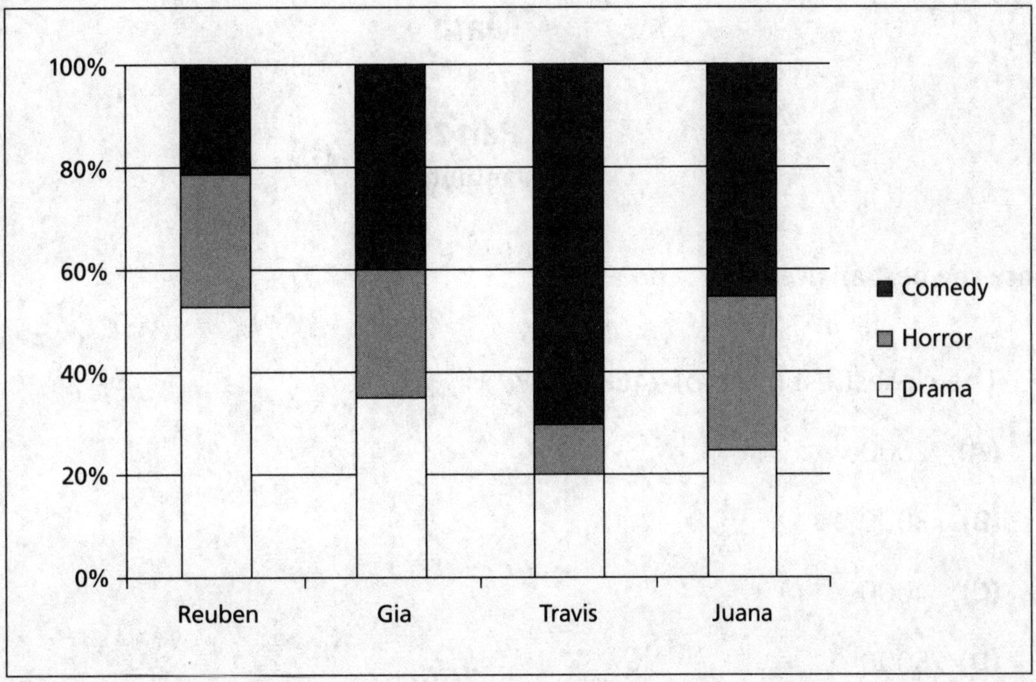

29. **The chart above shows the DVD collections of four students. Based on the information in the chart, which student has a DVD collection made up of about 70% comedy.**

(A) Reuben

(B) Gia

(C) Travis

(D) Juana

30. **Based on the information in the chart above, if the DVD collections of all four students are the same size, which student seems to prefer drama to both horror and comedy?**

(J) Reuben

(K) Gia

(L) Travis

(M) Juana

Math

Part 2
(10 minutes)

Choose the best answer.

31. The closest estimate of 7466 – 2377 is ______.

(A) 2000

(B) 3000

(C) 4000

(D) 5000

32. The closest estimate of 56,246 ÷ 8049 is ______.

(J) 7

(K) 70

(L) 700

(M) 7000

33. The average aisle in the model train store, O'Donnell's Toots, displays 21 trains. There are 20 aisles in the store. About how many trains are displayed in the O'Donnell's Toots?

(A) 200

(B) 300

(C) 400

(D) Not given

34. The closest estimate of 4992 + 3134 is ______.

(J) 8500

(K) 8000

(L) 7500

(M) 7000

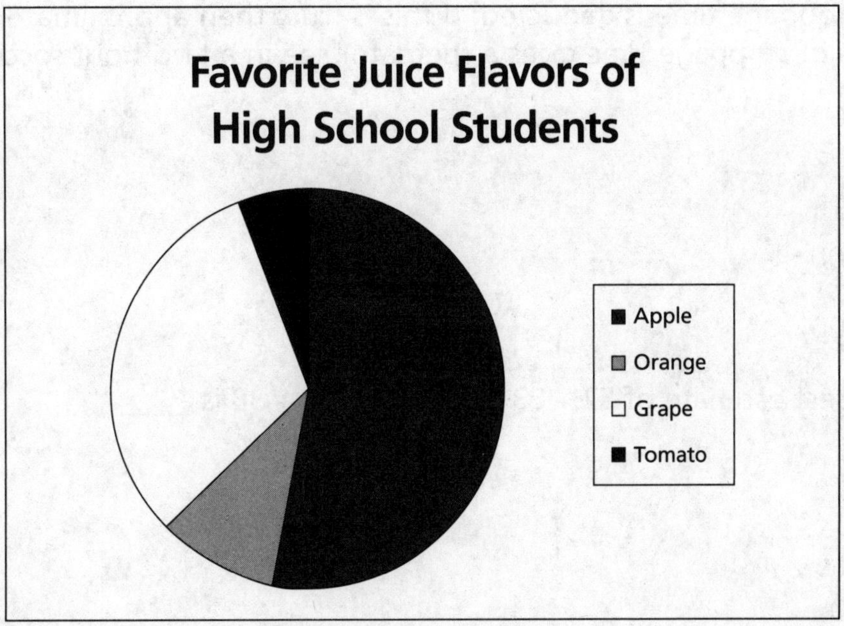

35. According to the information in the chart above, what percent of high school students prefer apple juice?

(A) 10%

(B) 30%

(C) 50%

(D) 70%

36. According to chart, if 100 students were surveyed, about how many would prefer grape juice?

(J) 10

(K) 33

(L) 50

(M) Not given

37. A soccer game that lasts a total of two hours is actually only 90 minutes long when stoppage time is deducted. If this is true, then approximately how many seconds of stoppage time does a spectator see in a two-hour soccer game?

(A) 2000

(B) 3000

(C) 4000

(D) 5000

38. The closest estimate of 52 + 83 + 17 + 59 + 22 + 38 is _______.

(J) 190

(K) 210

(L) 230

(M) 270

39. The closest estimate of 48,988 ÷ 6,993 is _______.

(A) 512

(B) 70

(C) 7

(D) Not given

40. The closest estimate of 305 – 198 + 197 – 103 + 214 – 205 is _____.

(J) 0

(K) 200

(L) 400

(M) 600

Ability

(5 minutes)

In questions 1–3, the first three figures are alike in certain ways. Choose the answer choice that corresponds to the first three figures.

1. 

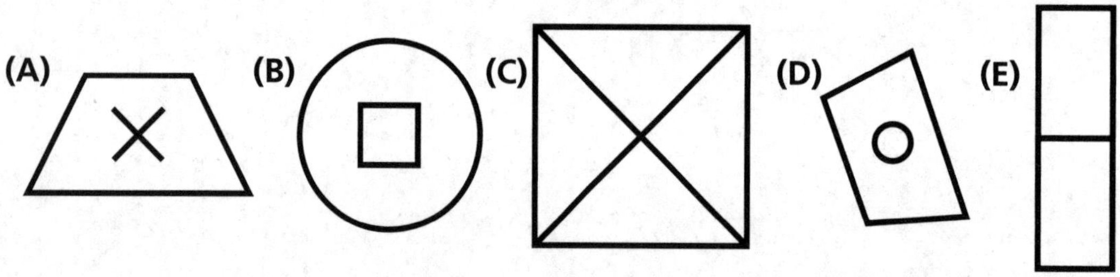

2. 

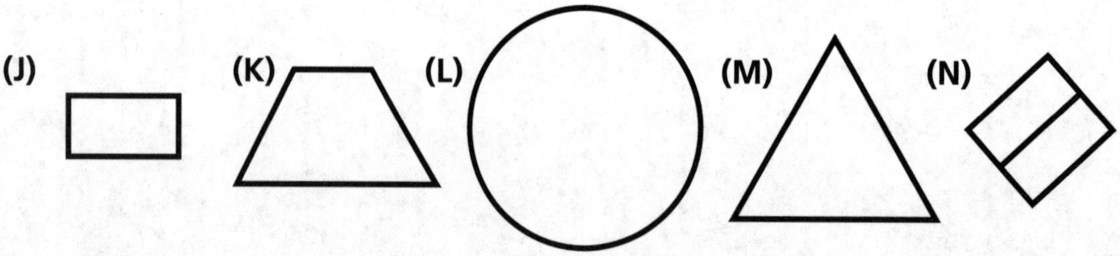

3.

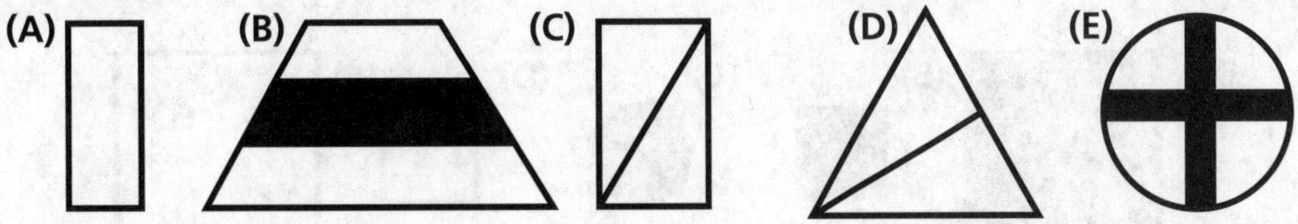

In questions 4–7, the first figure is related to the second figure. Determine that relationship. The third figure is changed in the same way to make one of the answer choices. Choose the answer choice that relates to the third figure.

4.

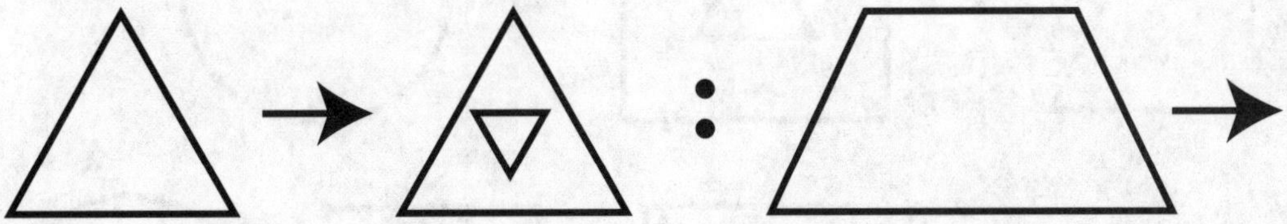

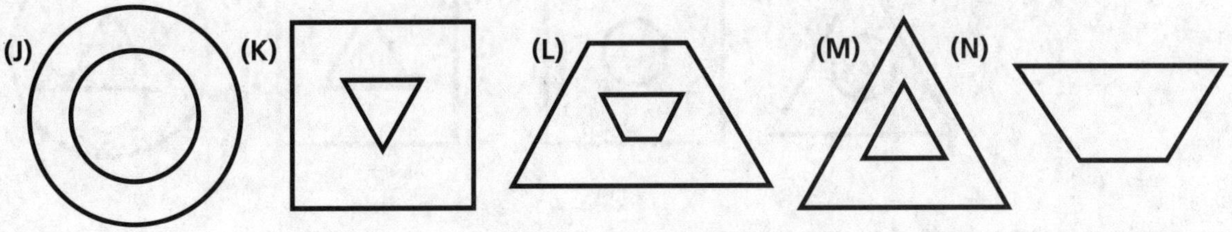

5.

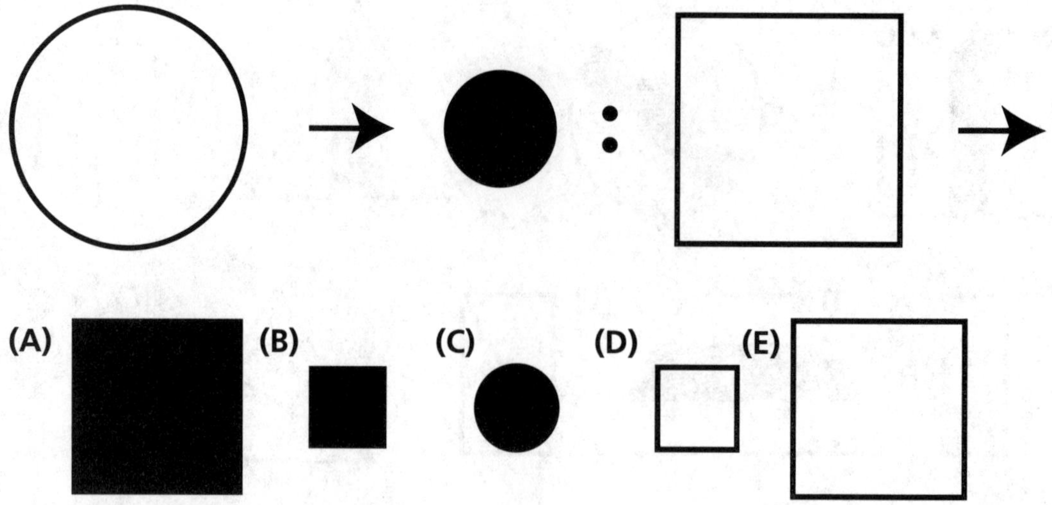

6.

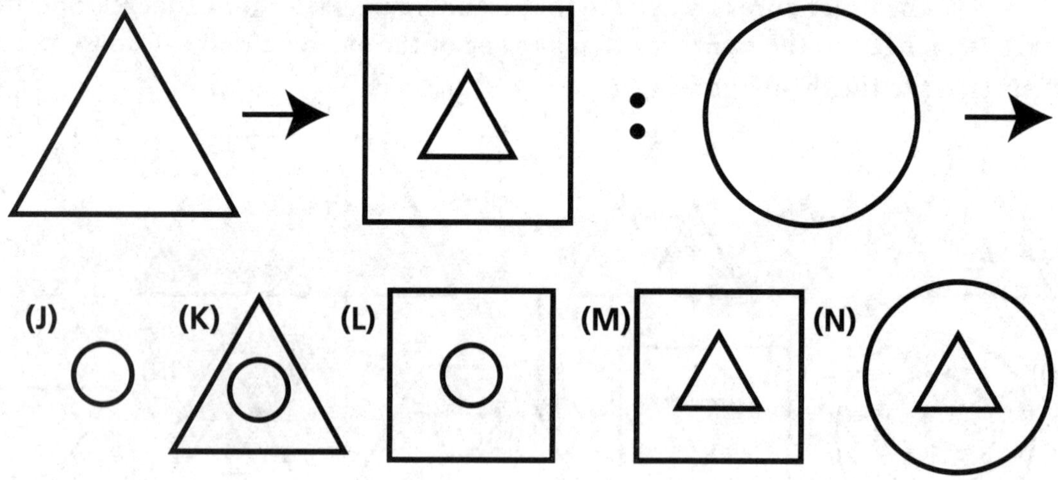

---

7. 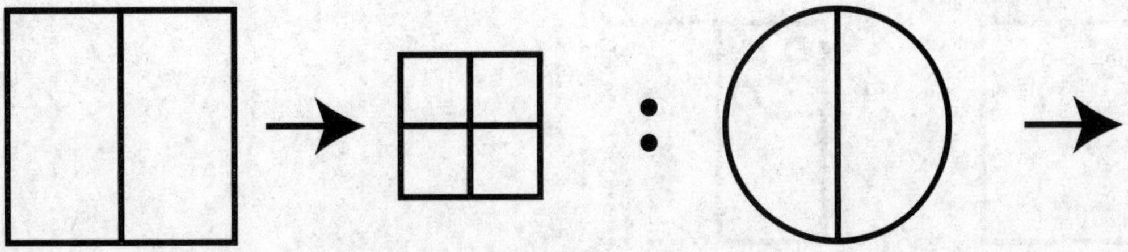

(A) 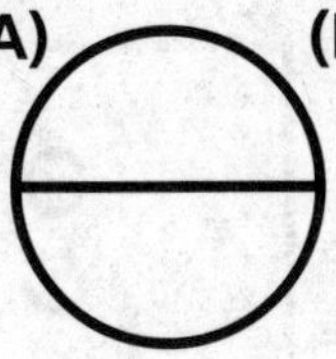
(B) 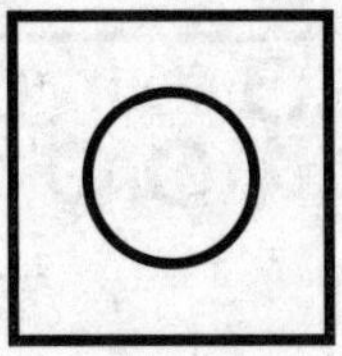
(C) 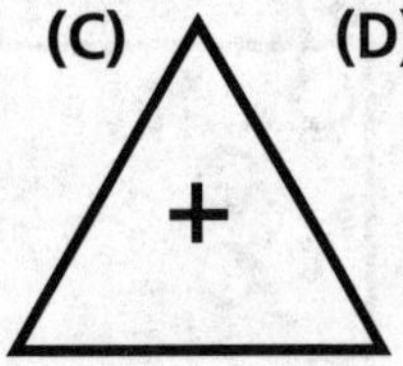
(D) 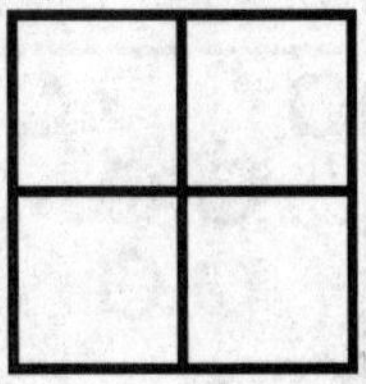
(E) 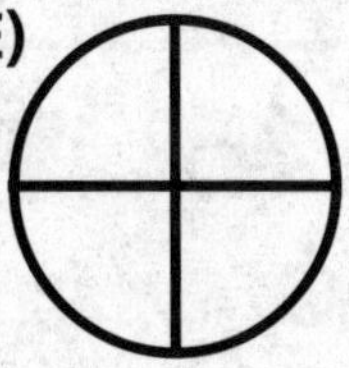

In questions 8–10, look at the top row to see how a square piece of paper is folded and where holes are punched into it. Then look at the bottom row to decide which answer choice shows how the paper will look when it is completely unfolded.

8. 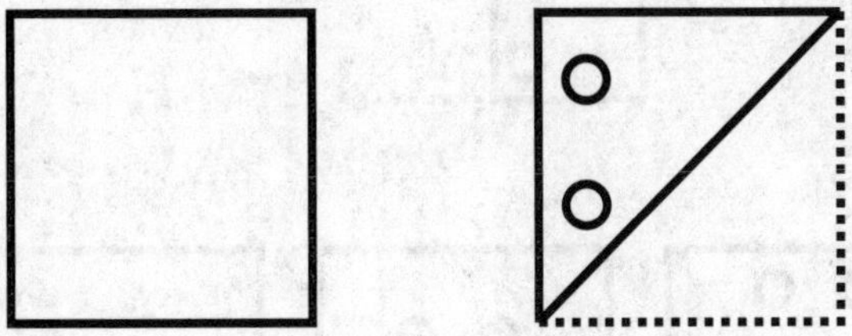

(J) 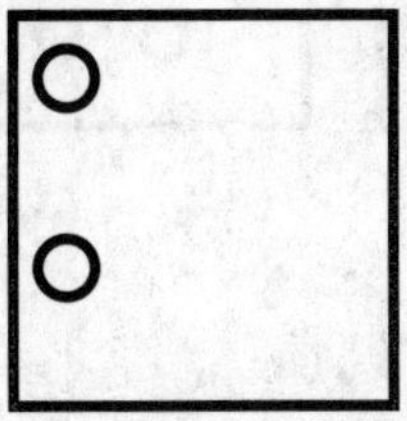
(K) 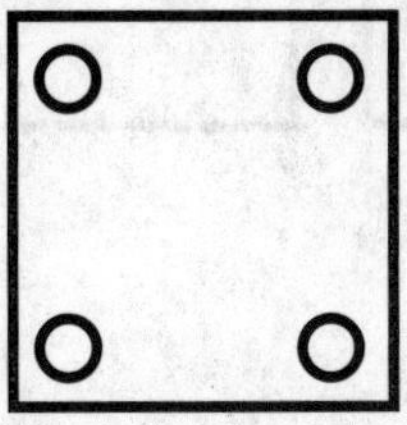
(L) 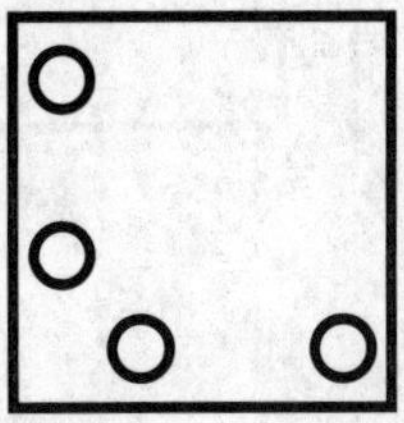
(M) 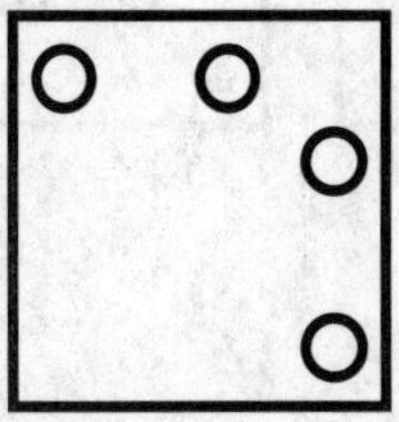
(N) 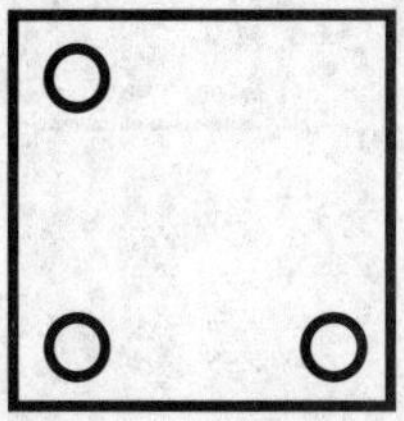

9.

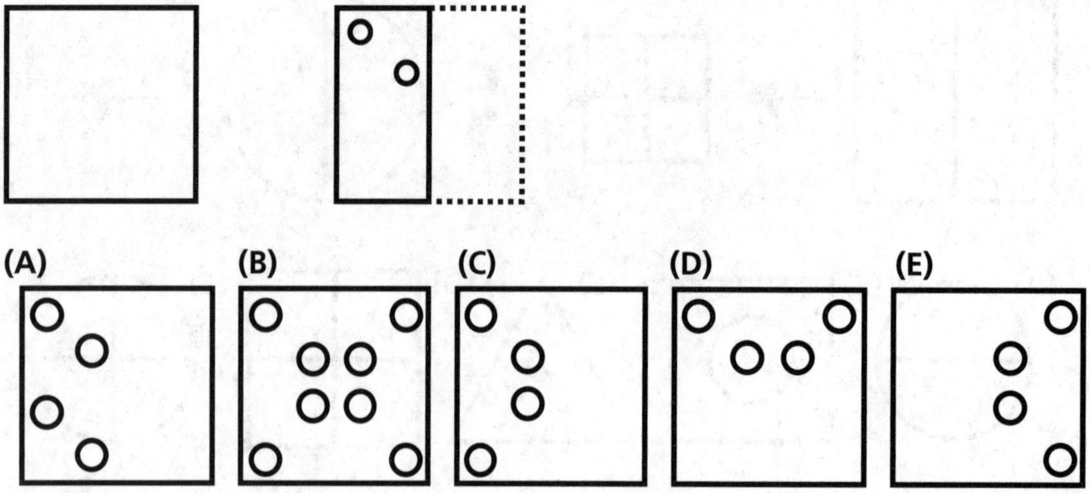

10.

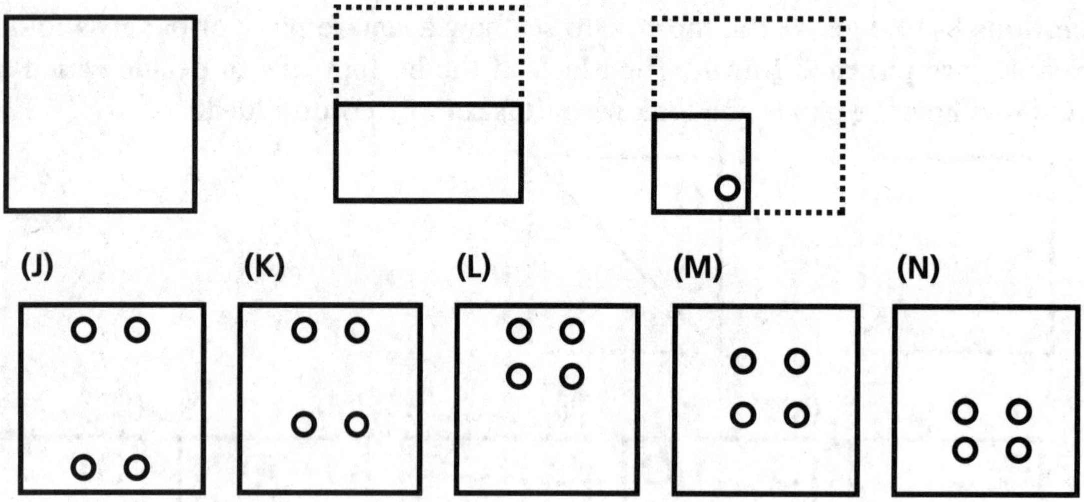

Chapter 30 TACHS Practice Test: Answers and Explanations

ANSWER KEY

Reading Part 1

1. A
2. K
3. C
4. M
5. A
6. K
7. D
8. K
9. D
10. K

Reading, Part 2

11. C
12. J
13. D
14. L
15. D
16. L
17. C
18. J
19. A
20. L

Language, Part 1

1. A
2. K
3. D
4. N
5. C
6. M
7. B
8. L
9. A
10. N
11. C
12. J
13. C
14. M
15. B
16. M
17. C
18. K
19. C
20. K

Language, Part 2

21. C
22. M
23. B
24. L
25. A
26. M
27. D
28. K
29. A
30. M

Math, Part 1

1. A
2. K
3. D
4. J
5. B
6. J
7. D
8. L
9. C
10. M
11. A
12. J
13. B
14. L
15. B
16. L
17. C
18. K
19. D
20. K
21. D
22. J
23. B
24. K
25. D
26. M
27. D
28. L
29. C
30. J

Math, Part 2

31. D
32. J
33. C
34. K
35. C
36. K
37. A
38. M
39. C
40. K

Ability

1. A
2. J
3. B
4. L
5. B
6. L
7. E
8. L
9. D
10. J

ANSWERS AND EXPLANATIONS

Reading, Part 1

1. **A** Other synonyms include "start," "begin," and "commence."
2. **K** Other synonyms include "difficult," "tough," and "stressful."
3. **C** Other synonyms include "usefulness," "merit," "significance."
4. **M** Other synonyms include "crisscross," "bisect," and "divide."
5. **A** Other synonyms include "unwelcoming," "unfriendly," and "unemotional."
6. **K** Other synonyms include "unstable," "chaotic," and "stormy."
7. **D** Other synonyms include "promote," "stand up for," and "defend."
8. **K** Other synonyms include "outstanding," "marvelous," and "remarkable."
9. **D** Other synonyms include "compassionate," "kind," and "softhearted."
10. **K** Other synonyms include "unused," "disused," and "nonfunctioning."

Reading, Part 2

11. **C** Each paragraph of the passage discusses some aspect of the evolution of kangaroos.
12. **J** The only person listed who would know about fossils and dinosaurs is a scientist.
13. **D** Choice (A) is extreme, and there is no support in the passage for (B) or (C). It does say in the final paragraph, however, that Inuit methods sometimes work when modern technology is ineffective.
14. **L** According to the last paragraph, "compasses can't be relied on."
15. **D** The second sentence of the passage says that "the movement of the stars is due to the rotation of the earth."
16. **L** According to the passage, Polaris "lies almost directly above the North Pole."
17. **C** The passage says that it took "more than sixty days." The closest choice is (C).
18. **J** Every paragraph in the passage discusses some aspect of making a mummy.
19. **A** The first paragraph says that he was "a tailor, a farmer, a storekeeper, and a country tavern-keeper, and was not particularly prosperous in any of these callings."
20. **L** This phrase is used in contrast to the sentence that follows, which says that Barnum "was, however, an apt and ready scholar." Therefore, the "birch-rod" must refer to something to do with bad students.

Language, Part 1

1. **A** The correct spelling is selfish.
2. **K** The correct spelling is tiger.
3. **D** The correct spelling is occupation
4. **N** *(No mistakes)*
5. **C** The correct spelling is brace.
6. **M** The correct spelling is pertain.
7. **B** The correct spelling is symphony.
8. **L** The correct spelling is obtain.
9. **A** The correct spelling is watcher
10. **N** *(No mistakes)*
11. **C** Names of streets, roads, or avenues are to be capitalized but not when used as common nouns like "the winding street."
12. **J** The name of a country needs to be capitalized as it is a proper name.
13. **C** "College" by itself does not need to be capitalized unless it is part of a proper name such as "Boston College."
14. **M** *(No mistakes)*
15. **B** There is no comma necessary after practice.
16. **M** *(No mistakes)*
17. **C** There is no comma necessary after "and."
18. **K** The pronoun "he" does not need to be capitalized.
19. **C** No comma is necessary after "for."
20. **K** "Your" does not require capitalization.

Language, Part 2

21. **C** The underlined part of Sentence 2 has unnecessary words, and can be simplified.

22. **M** This sentence is correct.

23. **B** Sentence 2 has a tense problem. That is fixed with (B).

24. **L** There is no need for a comma in Sentence 4, since we are not listing things.

25. **A** Sentence 1 is a double negative. Choice (A) is correct. Choices (B) and (D) have incorrect punctuation and capitalization.

26. **M** This sentence is correct.

27. **D** This sentence is correct.

28. **K** The word "thru" in the sentence and choices (J) and (K) are homophones. Choice (L) sounds similar.

29. **A** "Middle Ages" is an historical time period, and should be capitalized.

30. **M** This sentence is correct.

Math, Part 1

1. **A** A factor is a number that can divide evenly with no remainder. 45 ÷ 5 is 9 with no remainder, 45 ÷ 9 is 5 with no remainder, and 45 ÷ 15 is 3 with no remainder, so 5, 9, and 15 are all factors of 45. However, 45 ÷ 2 is 22 with a remainder of 1. Since there is a remainder when 45 is divided by 2, 2 is not a factor of 45. The answer is (A).

2. **K** Choice (M) is the only fraction, so start with this. To determine whether two fractions are equal, use the Bowtie method. Write the two fractions next to each other and draw two arrows as shown below.

$$\frac{3}{4} \times \frac{4}{3}$$

Now multiply across each arrow like below.

$$\overset{9}{\frac{3}{4}} \times \frac{4}{3}$$

Since the two products are not equal, neither are the two fractions. Eliminate (M). This means the answer must the one of the remaining choices, all of which are decimals. To convert a fraction to a decimal, do long division. Set up

$$4\overline{)3.00}$$

Add 0's after the decimal place as needed. Since none of the remaining choices have more than two digits after the decimal, only two 0's after the decimal will be needed. 4 does not go into 3, so write a 0 above the 3. Bring up the decimal. Now divide 4 into 30. 4 goes into 30 7 times, so write a 7 above the first zero. 4 × 7 = 28, but write 28 under the 3 and the first 0. Subtract to get 2. Then pull down the second 0 to get 20. 4 goes into 20 5 times with no remainder. Therefore, the result is shown below.

$$\begin{array}{r} 0.75 \\ 4\overline{)3.00} \\ \underline{2\,8} \\ 20 \end{array}$$

The answer is (K).

3. **D** A prime number is one that can only be divided evenly by 1 and itself. Go through each choice and eliminate any that can be divided by another number. Since 51 ÷ 3 = 17, 51 can be divided by 3, so it is not prime. Eliminate (A). Since 49 ÷ 7 = 7, 49 can be divided by 7, so it is not prime. Eliminate (B). Since 27 ÷ 3 = 9, 27 can be divided by 3, so it is not prime. Eliminate (C). There does not appear to be a number that divides 17 evenly other than 1 and 17, so keep (D). The answer is (D).

4. **J** A multiple of 4 is one that can be divided evenly by 4 with no remainder. Go through each choice. For (J), divide 14 by 4 to get

$$\begin{array}{r} 3 \\ 4\overline{)14} \\ \underline{12} \\ 2 \end{array}$$

Since there is a remainder, this appears not to be a multiple of 4. Check the others to be sure. For (K), divide 24 by 4 to get

$$\begin{array}{r} 6 \\ 4\overline{)24} \\ \underline{24} \\ 0 \end{array}$$

Since there is no remainder, this is a multiple of 4. Eliminate it. For (L), divide 64 by 4 to get

$$\begin{array}{r} 16 \\ 4\overline{)64} \\ \underline{64} \\ 0 \end{array}$$

Since there is no remainder, this is a multiple of 4. Eliminate (L). For (M), divide 84 by 4 to get

$$\begin{array}{r} 21 \\ 4\overline{)84} \\ \underline{84} \\ 0 \end{array}$$

Since there is no remainder, this is a multiple of 4. Eliminate (M). The answer is (J).

5. **B** In math, the word *difference* refers to subtraction. Therefore, *the difference between 82 and 20* is $82 - 20 = 62$. The answer is (B).

6. **J** All of the choices are fractions. To convert a decimal into a fraction, put the decimal over 1. In this case, put 0.0007 over 1 to get $\frac{0.0007}{1}$. Now, add a decimal after 1 and as many zeros after the decimal needed to make it so that the numerator and denominator have an equal number of digits after the decimal. Since 0.0007 has 4 digits after the decimal, write 1 as 1.0000 to get $\frac{0.0007}{1.0000}$. Now drop the decimals (and remove any 0s in the beginning) to get $\frac{7}{10,000}$. The answer is (J).

7. **D** When the number is raised to an exponent, multiply the number by itself a number of times equal to the exponent. Therefore, $2^4 = 2 \times 2 \times 2 \times 2$. Multiply this out to get $2 \times 2 \times 2 \times 2 = 4 \times 2 \times 2 = 8 \times 2 = 16$. The answer is (D).

8. **L** First, reduce the second and third fractions. The numerator and denominator in $\frac{10}{8}$ are both divisible by 2, so divide both by 2 to get $\frac{5}{4}$. The numerator and denominator in $\frac{6}{6}$ are equal, so the fraction is equal to 1. Thus, $\frac{3}{4} + \frac{10}{8} + \frac{6}{6} = \frac{3}{4} + \frac{5}{4} + 1$. Add $\frac{3}{4}$ and $\frac{5}{4}$. Since the denominators are the same, add the numerators to get $\frac{3+5}{4} = \frac{8}{4}$. Since the numerator and denominator in $\frac{8}{4}$ are both divisible by 4, divide both by 4 to get $\frac{8}{4} = 2$. Therefore, $\frac{3}{4} + \frac{10}{8} + \frac{6}{6} = \frac{3}{4} + \frac{5}{4} + 1 = \frac{8}{4} + 1 = 2 + 1$. Since $2 + 1 = 3$, the answer is (L).

9. **C** Remember in order of operations, start with the parentheses. $2 \times 2 = 4$, $3 \times 3 = 9$, and $4 \times 4 = 16$, so $(2 \times 2) + (3 \times 3) + (4 \times 4) = 4 + 9 + 16$. Add 4 and 9 to get 13. Then, add 13 and 16 to get 29. The answer is (C).

10. **M** To convert a decimal into a fraction, put the decimal over 1. In this case, put 2.4 over 1 to get $\frac{2.4}{1}$. Now, add a decimal after 1 and as many zeros after the decimal needed to make it so that the numerator and denominator have an equal number of digits after the decimal. Since 2.4 has 1 digit after the decimal, write 1 as 1.0 to get $\frac{2.4}{1.0}$. Now drop the decimals to get $\frac{24}{10}$. Although this is

(K), (K) is not the answer, because the question asks for *reduced form*. Since 24 and 10 are both divisible by 2, divide the numerator and denominator by 2 to get $\frac{12}{5}$. However, this is not a choice. Two of the choices, (L) and (M), are written as mixed numbers. To convert an improper fraction into a mixed number, divide and take the remainder. Divide 12 by 5 to get 2 remainder 2 as shown below.

$$\begin{array}{r} 2 \\ 5\overline{)12} \\ \underline{10} \\ 2 \end{array}$$

To get the mixed number, keep the denominator, use the quotient as the whole number, and use the remainder as the denominator to get $2\frac{2}{5}$. Since $\frac{2}{5}$ is a reduced fraction, the answer is (M).

11. **A** The question says that Dixie has 5 pencils and that Geoffrey has three times as many pencils as Dixie. Therefore Geoffrey has 3 × 5 =15 pencils. Karen has three times as many pencils as Geoffrey and Dixie combined. Geoffrey and Dixie combined have 15 + 5 = 20, so Karen has 3 × 20 = 60 pencils. The answer is (A).

12. **J** Since the question involves units, set up a proportion. One unit contains a half-barrel, so how many units contain 22-barrels. Set up $\frac{1\ unit}{\frac{1}{2}\ barrel} = \frac{x\ units}{22\ barrels}$. Cross multiply to get $\frac{1}{2}x = 2$. Divide both sides by $\frac{1}{2}$ to get $x = \frac{22}{\frac{1}{2}}$. When dividing by a fraction, multiply by the reciprocal, so $x = \frac{22}{1} \times \frac{2}{1} = \frac{44}{1} = 44$. The answer is (J).

13. **B** Since the answer choices aren't large, go through the problem one month at a time. She starts with $7 and her allowance is $30 per month. After 1 month, she has $37. After 2 months, she has $67. After 3 months, she has $97. After 4 months, she has $127. Since this is the amount she needs for her skateboard, stop here. The answer is (B).

14. **L** The question asks for the total cost. To get the total cost, multiply the cost per pound by the number of pounds. The cost per pound is $10, so determine the number of pounds. Sonali wants to fill her bag to $\frac{4}{5}$ of its capacity. The capacity is 5 pounds, so she wants to buy $\frac{4}{5} \times 5 = \frac{4}{5} \times \frac{5}{1} = \frac{20}{5} = 4$ pounds of candy. Four pounds of candy at $10 per pound will cost 4 × $10 = $40. The answer is (L).

15. **B** The question asks for the sum of the distances the puck travels between the crossbar and the ice. The puck hits the crossbar eight times. Since *sum* refers to addition, the sum of the distances is 4 + 4 + 4 + 4 + 4 + 4 + 4 + 4. A number added to itself eight times is the same as multiplying by 8, so this is 4 × 8 = 32. The answer is (B).

16. **L** There are currently 81 bicycles on the bike path, each of which has 2 wheels. To determine the total number of wheels, multiply the number of bicycles by the number of wheels on each bicycle to get 81 × 2 = 162. To avoid trap answers, make sure to note that there are 2 wheels instead of 4. Also, note that the bike path is numbered 18, but otherwise the number 18 has no effect on the problem. The answer is (L).

17. **C** Elissa drives 20% faster than Joshua. To determine how fast Elissa drives, start by taking 20% of 40. Mutiply $\frac{20}{100}$ by 40 to get $\frac{20}{100} \times \frac{40}{1} = \frac{800}{100} = 8$. Thus, Elissa drives 8 miles per hour faster than Joshua, so she drives 40 + 8 = 48. To determine the distance, multiply the speed by the time. Since the time is 14 hours, multiply 48 by 14 to get 48 × 14 = 672. The answer is (C).

18. **K** To determine the number of model cars Uncle Fred needs to complete his collection, subtract the number of model cars he currently has from the number of model cars in a complete collection. He currently has 8 dozen model cars. A dozen means 12, so 8 dozen is 8 × 12 = 96. Since he would 300 to complete his collection, subtract 96 from 300 to get 300 – 96 = 204. The answer is (K).

19. **D** The question asks for how many square feet they should plan to carpet. Determine the area of each floor. The area of a rectangle can be determined using the formula $A = lw$. Each floor is 10 feet long and 11 feet wide, so A = (10)(11)= 110. There are 5 classrooms, so to get the total number, multiply by 5 to get 110 × 5 = 550. The answer is (D).

20. **K** The question asks for the number of minutes a student is awake each day and gives the number of minutes the student is awake in a year. Divide the number of minutes the student is awake in a year by the number of days in a year. Divide 365,000 by 365. This looks difficult, but note that 365,000 = 365 × 1,000, so $\frac{365{,}000}{365} = \frac{365 \times 1{,}000}{365} = \frac{1{,}000}{1} = 1{,}000$. The answer is (K).

21. **D** The question asks for which student scored highest on the History test. Look at the key on the right side of the graph a notice that the white bar represents history. The student with the highest score on this history test is the one with the longest white bar, which belongs to Joan. Therefore, the answer is (D).

22. **J** The question asks for which student scores 11 more points on the History test than on the English test. First eliminate any choice with a student who has a higher score on English than History. According to the key on the right, English is represented by the dark gray bar and History is represented by the white bar. Since Erika and Tony have a longer white bar than dark gray bar, eliminate (K) and (L). Ronald and Joan both have a longer dark gray bar, and thus a higher score on the History test. Determine which has a difference of 11. The number markings are 20 apart and there are four segments between each number marking. Therefore, each segment is $\frac{20}{4} = 5$. Therefore, the correct answer should be the one whose dark bar is a little over two segments longer than the white bar. For Joan, the white bar is only slightly longer than the dark gray bar, so eliminate (M). For Ronald, the dark gray bar is about two segments longer than the white bar, so the answer is (J).

23. **B** The question asks for who had the most blue and red marbles combined. For each of the students, add the number of blue and red marbles. For Thomas, there are 5 blue marbles and 7 red marbles, so there is a total of 5 + 7 = 12. For Joanna, there are 8 blue marbles and 5 red marbles, so there is a total of 8 + 5 = 13. For Casey, there are 3 blue marbles and 7 red marbles, so there is a total of 3 + 7 = 10. The largest is Joanna. Notice that Thomas and Casey both have the most red and green marbles combines, so (D) is a trap. The answer is (B).

24. **K** Get the total green marbles purchased by each of the three friends bought and add them together. Thomas bought 6 green marbles, Joanna bought 6 green marbles, and Casey bought 6 green marbles, so there were a total of 6 + 6 + 6 = 18 green marbles. The answer is (K).

25. **D** Look at each students score for Quarter 1 and Quarter 4 and determine the increase of each. Scott's bar for average in Quarter 1 was about half way between the 90 line and the 100 line, so his average was about 95. Scott's bar for average in Quarter 4 is between the 90 line and 100 line but closer to 100, so his average in Quarter 4 was about 98. This is an increase of about 98 – 95 = 3. Brianne's bar for average in Quarter 1 is between the 80 line and the 90 line but closer to 80, so her average was about 83. Brianne's bar for average in Quarter 4 is at the 90 line, so her average in Quarter 4 was about 90. This is an increase of about 90 – 83 = 7. Michael's bar for average in Quarter 1 was between the 80 line and the 90 line but closer to 90, so his average was about 87. Michael's bar for average in Quarter 4 is between the 90 line and 100 line but closer to 90, so his average in Quarter 4 was about 93. This is an increase of about 93 – 87 = 6. Kalina's bar for average in Quarter 1 was between the 80 line and the 90 line but closer to 80, so her average was about 82. Kalina's bar for average in Quarter 4 is between the 90 line and 100 line but closer to 90, so her average in Quarter 4 was about 92. This is an increase of about 92 – 82 = 10. Kalina's increase is the greatest, so the answer is (D).

26. **M** Find the bar that matches the shade for Brianne in Quarter 4. The bar goes up to and reaches the 90 lines. Therefore, the average score is 90. The answer is (M).

27. **D** The pie chart gives the population distribution, so the town most populous town is the one with the largest piece of the pie and with the largest percentage labelled. Either way, this is Glenville, so the answer is (D).

28. **L** The population of Glenville makes up 47% of Riviera County. Go through the answer choices and find the choice whose towns add up to 47%. Choice (J) is Sunnyside and Greenhill. Sunnyside is 6%, and Greenhill is 19%, so the sum is 6% + 19% = 25%. Eliminate (J). Choice (K) is Glenville and Greenhill. Clearly Glenville and another town will have a higher population that just Glenville, so eliminate (K). Choice (L) is Greenhill and Park Town. Greenhill is 19%, and Park Town is 28%, so the sum is 19% + 28% = 47%, which is the same as the population of Glenville, so this choice is correct. The answer is (L).

29. **C** The type of bar graph shown stacks values on top of each other. Thus, the top of any section on a bar graph represents not just the amount for that section but rather the sum of the amounts of that section and every section underneath it. Therefore, in order to get the amount of a particular section, take the difference between the top of the section and the bottom. The question asks for which student had a collection made up of about 70% comedy. Comedy is the top section on each bar. Since the top of each bar is 100%, the difference between the bottom of the comedy section and the 100% must be about 70%. Therefore the bottom of the comedy section must be 30%. The top section of Travis's bar ends about halfway between 20% and 40%, so it is the closest to 70%. Therefore, the answer is (C).

30. **J** The question asks for the student that prefers drama to both horror and comedy. Since drama is represented by the bottom section of each bar, just look at the bottom section of each bar. For Rueben, the top of the drama section between the lines for 40% and 60%, slightly closer to 60%. Therefore, slightly over 50% of Reuben's collection is drama. Since it is over 50%, it must be higher than both horror and drama. Therefore, the answer is (J).

Math, Part 2

31. **D** The question asks for the closest estimate, so round off. 7,466 is about 7,000, and 2,377 is about 2,000. 7,000 – 2,000 = 5,000. The answer is (D).

32. **J** The question asks for the closest estimate, so round off. 56,246 is about 56,000 and 8,049 is about 8,000. Now divide 56,000 by 8,000. Remember that, in division, 0s cancel, so 56,000 ÷ 8,000 is the same as 56 ÷ 8, which is 7. The answer is (J).

33. **C** To determine the total number of trains, multiply the average number of trains per aisle by the number of aisles. The number of aisles is 20 and the number of trains per aisle is about 21. Since the question only asks for an estimate, round 21 to 20. Therefore, the total number of trains is about 20 × 20 = 400. The answer is (C).

34. **K** The question asks for the closest estimate, so round off. 4,992 is about 5,000, and 3,134 is about 3,000. 5,000 + 3,000 = 8,000. The answer is (K).

35. **C** Find apple juice on the chart. According to the key, apple is represented by the dark gray portion of the graph. The dark gray portion makes up about half the pie chart, so apple represents about 50%. The answer is (C).

36. **K** According to the key on the chart, grape is represented by the white portion of the graph. The white portion makes up about one-third of the pie chart, so grape represents about 33%. Since the question says 100 people were in the poll, each person represents 1%. Therefore 33% is 33 people. The answer is (K).

37. **A** A soccer game lasts a total of two hours. Since there are 60 minutes in one hour, there are 2 × 60 = 120 minutes in 2 hours, so the game lasts 120 minutes. The game is 90 minutes without stoppage times, so there are 120 – 90 = 30 minutes of stoppage time. Since there are 60 seconds in a minute, 30 minutes is 30 × 60 = 1,800. (To get 1,800, multiply 3 by 6 and add the two total 0s from 30 and 60.) Round this answer to 2,000. The answer is (A).

38. **M** To get the closet estimate of the answer, round off the numbers in the question. 52 rounds to 50, 83 rounds to 80, 17 rounds to 20, 59 rounds to 60, 22 rounds to 20, and 38 rounds to 40. Therefore, the question becomes 50 + 80 + 20 + 60 + 20 + 40 = 130 + 20 + 60 + 20 + 40 = 150 + 60 + 20 + 40= 210 + 20 + 40 = 230 + 40 = 270. The answer is (M).

39. **C** To get the closet estimate of the answer, round off the two numbers in the question. 48,988 rounds to 49,000, and 6,993 rounds to 7,000. Divide 49,000 by 7,000. In division, if each number ends with the same number of 0's, cancel the 0's. Therefore, 49,000 ÷ 7,000 = 49 ÷ 7 = 7. The answer is (C).

40. **K** To get the closet estimate of the answer, round off the numbers in the question. 305 rounds to 300, 198 rounds to 200, 197 rounds to 200, 103 rounds to 100, 214 rounds to 200, and 205 rounds to 200. Therefore, the question becomes 300 – 200 + 200 – 100 + 200 – 200 = 100 + 200 – 100 + 200 – 200 = 300 – 100 + 200 – 200 = 200 + 200 – 200 = 400 – 200 = 200. The answer is (K).

Ability

1. **A** All shapes have an "X" inside.
2. **J** All shapes are rectangles.
3. **B** All shapes have one stripe inside.
4. **L** The first shape is empty and the second has the flipped first shape inside. Choice (L) follows the same pattern.
5. **B** The first shape is large and empty. The second shape is smaller and filled yet still the same shape. Choice (B) follows the same pattern.
6. **L** The first shape is large and empty and the second shape is a large square with a smaller scale of the first shape inside. Choice (L) follows the same pattern.
7. **E** The first shape is a large square with a vertical line. The second shape is the same shape with a horizontal line added to it. Choice (E) follows the same pattern.
8. **L** After the figure is folded diagonally, two punches are made along the left side. Unfolding reveals two more holes along the bottom as well.
9. **D** After the figure is folded vertically, two punches are made from the top left toward the center. Unfolding reveals this to be mirrored on the other half of the paper.
10. **J** After the figure is folded twice, one punch is created on the bottom left corner. Unfolding reveals another hole on the bottom, then two more up top.

To access more bubble sheets as printable PDFs,
visit your online Student Tools.

The Princeton Review®

HSPT® TEST 1

Completely darken bubbles with a No. 2 pencil. If you make a mistake, be sure to erase mark completely. Erase all stray marks.

1.
YOUR NAME: ______________________ (Print) Last First M.I.

SIGNATURE: ______________________ DATE: / /

HOME ADDRESS: ______________________ (Print) Number and Street

______________________ City State Zip Code

PHONE NO.: ______________________ (Print)

IMPORTANT: Please fill in these boxes exactly as shown on the back cover of your test book.

2. TEST FORM

____

3. TEST CODE

0	A	J	0	0
1	B	K	1	1
2	C	L	2	2
3	D	M	3	3
4	E	N	4	4
5	F	O	5	5
6	G	P	6	6
7	H	Q	7	7
8	I	R	8	8
9			9	9

4. REGISTRATION NUMBER

0	0	0	0	0	0
1	1	1	1	1	1
2	2	2	2	2	2
3	3	3	3	3	3
4	4	4	4	4	4
5	5	5	5	5	5
6	6	6	6	6	6
7	7	7	7	7	7
8	8	8	8	8	8
9	9	9	9	9	9

5. YOUR NAME

First 4 letters of last name					FIRST INIT	MID INIT
A	A	A	A		A	A
B	B	B	B		B	B
C	C	C	C		C	C
D	D	D	D		D	D
E	E	E	E		E	E
F	F	F	F		F	F
G	G	G	G		G	G
H	H	H	H		H	H
I	I	I	I		I	I
J	J	J	J		J	J
K	K	K	K		K	K
L	L	L	L		L	L
M	M	M	M		M	M
N	N	N	N		N	N
O	O	O	O		O	O
P	P	P	P		P	P
Q	Q	Q	Q		Q	Q
R	R	R	R		R	R
S	S	S	S		S	S
T	T	T	T		T	T
U	U	U	U		U	U
V	V	V	V		V	V
W	W	W	W		W	W
X	X	X	X		X	X
Y	Y	Y	Y		Y	Y
Z	Z	Z	Z		Z	Z

6. DATE OF BIRTH

Month	Day		Year	
JAN				
FEB	0	0	0	0
MAR	1	1	1	1
APR	2	2	2	2
MAY	3	3	3	3
JUN	4	4	4	4
JUL	5	5	5	5
AUG	6	6	6	6
SEP	7	7	7	7
OCT	8	8	8	8
NOV	9	9	9	9
DEC				

7. SEX

MALE

FEMALE

The Princeton Review®

Test 1

Start with number 1 for each new section.
If a section has fewer questions than answer spaces, leave the extra answer spaces blank.

Verbal Skills

1. A B C D
2. A B C D
3. A B C D
4. A B C D
5. A B C D
6. A B C D
7. A B C D
8. A B C D
9. A B C D
10. A B C D
11. A B C D
12. A B C D
13. A B C D
14. A B C D
15. A B C D
16. A B C D
17. A B C D
18. A B C D
19. A B C D
20. A B C D
21. A B C D
22. A B C D
23. A B C D
24. A B C D
25. A B C D
26. A B C D
27. A B C D
28. A B C D
29. A B C D
30. A B C D
31. A B C D
32. A B C D
33. A B C D
34. A B C D
35. A B C D
36. A B C D
37. A B C D
38. A B C D
39. A B C D
40. A B C D
41. A B C D
42. A B C D
43. A B C D
44. A B C D
45. A B C D
46. A B C D
47. A B C D
48. A B C D
49. A B C D
50. A B C D
51. A B C D
52. A B C D
53. A B C D
54. A B C D
55. A B C D
56. A B C D
57. A B C D
58. A B C D
59. A B C D
60. A B C D

Quantitative Skills

1. A B C D
2. A B C D
3. A B C D
4. A B C D
5. A B C D
6. A B C D
7. A B C D
8. A B C D
9. A B C D
10. A B C D
11. A B C D
12. A B C D
13. A B C D
14. A B C D
15. A B C D
16. A B C D
17. A B C D
18. A B C D
19. A B C D
20. A B C D
21. A B C D
22. A B C D
23. A B C D
24. A B C D
25. A B C D
26. A B C D
27. A B C D
28. A B C D
29. A B C D
30. A B C D
31. A B C D
32. A B C D
33. A B C D
34. A B C D
35. A B C D
36. A B C D
37. A B C D
38. A B C D
39. A B C D
40. A B C D
41. A B C D
42. A B C D
43. A B C D
44. A B C D
45. A B C D
46. A B C D
47. A B C D
48. A B C D
49. A B C D
50. A B C D
51. A B C D
52. A B C D

The Princeton Review

HSPT® TEST 1

Completely darken bubbles with a No. 2 pencil. If you make a mistake, be sure to erase mark completely. Erase all stray marks.

Test 1 Start with number 1 for each new section.
If a section has fewer questions than answer spaces, leave the extra answer spaces blank.

Reading

1. (A) (B) (C) (D)
2. (A) (B) (C) (D)
3. (A) (B) (C) (D)
4. (A) (B) (C) (D)
5. (A) (B) (C) (D)
6. (A) (B) (C) (D)
7. (A) (B) (C) (D)
8. (A) (B) (C) (D)
9. (A) (B) (C) (D)
10. (A) (B) (C) (D)
11. (A) (B) (C) (D)
12. (A) (B) (C) (D)
13. (A) (B) (C) (D)
14. (A) (B) (C) (D)
15. (A) (B) (C) (D)
16. (A) (B) (C) (D)
17. (A) (B) (C) (D)
18. (A) (B) (C) (D)
19. (A) (B) (C) (D)
20. (A) (B) (C) (D)
21. (A) (B) (C) (D)
22. (A) (B) (C) (D)
23. (A) (B) (C) (D)
24. (A) (B) (C) (D)
25. (A) (B) (C) (D)
26. (A) (B) (C) (D)
27. (A) (B) (C) (D)
28. (A) (B) (C) (D)
29. (A) (B) (C) (D)
30. (A) (B) (C) (D)
31. (A) (B) (C) (D)
32. (A) (B) (C) (D)
33. (A) (B) (C) (D)
34. (A) (B) (C) (D)
35. (A) (B) (C) (D)
36. (A) (B) (C) (D)
37. (A) (B) (C) (D)
38. (A) (B) (C) (D)
39. (A) (B) (C) (D)
40. (A) (B) (C) (D)
41. (A) (B) (C) (D)
42. (A) (B) (C) (D)
43. (A) (B) (C) (D)
44. (A) (B) (C) (D)
45. (A) (B) (C) (D)
46. (A) (B) (C) (D)
47. (A) (B) (C) (D)
48. (A) (B) (C) (D)
49. (A) (B) (C) (D)
50. (A) (B) (C) (D)
51. (A) (B) (C) (D)
52. (A) (B) (C) (D)
53. (A) (B) (C) (D)
54. (A) (B) (C) (D)
55. (A) (B) (C) (D)
56. (A) (B) (C) (D)
57. (A) (B) (C) (D)
58. (A) (B) (C) (D)
59. (A) (B) (C) (D)
60. (A) (B) (C) (D)
61. (A) (B) (C) (D)
62. (A) (B) (C) (D)

Mathematics

1. (A) (B) (C) (D)
2. (A) (B) (C) (D)
3. (A) (B) (C) (D)
4. (A) (B) (C) (D)
5. (A) (B) (C) (D)
6. (A) (B) (C) (D)
7. (A) (B) (C) (D)
8. (A) (B) (C) (D)
9. (A) (B) (C) (D)
10. (A) (B) (C) (D)
11. (A) (B) (C) (D)
12. (A) (B) (C) (D)
13. (A) (B) (C) (D)
14. (A) (B) (C) (D)
15. (A) (B) (C) (D)
16. (A) (B) (C) (D)
17. (A) (B) (C) (D)
18. (A) (B) (C) (D)
19. (A) (B) (C) (D)
20. (A) (B) (C) (D)
21. (A) (B) (C) (D)
22. (A) (B) (C) (D)
23. (A) (B) (C) (D)
24. (A) (B) (C) (D)
25. (A) (B) (C) (D)
26. (A) (B) (C) (D)
27. (A) (B) (C) (D)
28. (A) (B) (C) (D)
29. (A) (B) (C) (D)
30. (A) (B) (C) (D)
31. (A) (B) (C) (D)
32. (A) (B) (C) (D)
33. (A) (B) (C) (D)
34. (A) (B) (C) (D)
35. (A) (B) (C) (D)
36. (A) (B) (C) (D)
37. (A) (B) (C) (D)
38. (A) (B) (C) (D)
39. (A) (B) (C) (D)
40. (A) (B) (C) (D)
41. (A) (B) (C) (D)
42. (A) (B) (C) (D)
43. (A) (B) (C) (D)
44. (A) (B) (C) (D)
45. (A) (B) (C) (D)
46. (A) (B) (C) (D)
47. (A) (B) (C) (D)
48. (A) (B) (C) (D)
49. (A) (B) (C) (D)
50. (A) (B) (C) (D)
51. (A) (B) (C) (D)
52. (A) (B) (C) (D)
53. (A) (B) (C) (D)
54. (A) (B) (C) (D)
55. (A) (B) (C) (D)
56. (A) (B) (C) (D)
57. (A) (B) (C) (D)
58. (A) (B) (C) (D)
59. (A) (B) (C) (D)
60. (A) (B) (C) (D)
61. (A) (B) (C) (D)
62. (A) (B) (C) (D)
63. (A) (B) (C) (D)
64. (A) (B) (C) (D)

Language

1. (A) (B) (C) (D)
2. (A) (B) (C) (D)
3. (A) (B) (C) (D)
4. (A) (B) (C) (D)
5. (A) (B) (C) (D)
6. (A) (B) (C) (D)
7. (A) (B) (C) (D)
8. (A) (B) (C) (D)
9. (A) (B) (C) (D)
10. (A) (B) (C) (D)
11. (A) (B) (C) (D)
12. (A) (B) (C) (D)
13. (A) (B) (C) (D)
14. (A) (B) (C) (D)
15. (A) (B) (C) (D)
16. (A) (B) (C) (D)
17. (A) (B) (C) (D)
18. (A) (B) (C) (D)
19. (A) (B) (C) (D)
20. (A) (B) (C) (D)
21. (A) (B) (C) (D)
22. (A) (B) (C) (D)
23. (A) (B) (C) (D)
24. (A) (B) (C) (D)
25. (A) (B) (C) (D)
26. (A) (B) (C) (D)
27. (A) (B) (C) (D)
28. (A) (B) (C) (D)
29. (A) (B) (C) (D)
30. (A) (B) (C) (D)
31. (A) (B) (C) (D)
32. (A) (B) (C) (D)
33. (A) (B) (C) (D)
34. (A) (B) (C) (D)
35. (A) (B) (C) (D)
36. (A) (B) (C) (D)
37. (A) (B) (C) (D)
38. (A) (B) (C) (D)
39. (A) (B) (C) (D)
40. (A) (B) (C) (D)
41. (A) (B) (C) (D)
42. (A) (B) (C) (D)
43. (A) (B) (C) (D)
44. (A) (B) (C) (D)
45. (A) (B) (C) (D)
46. (A) (B) (C) (D)
47. (A) (B) (C) (D)
48. (A) (B) (C) (D)
49. (A) (B) (C) (D)
50. (A) (B) (C) (D)
51. (A) (B) (C) (D)
52. (A) (B) (C) (D)
53. (A) (B) (C) (D)
54. (A) (B) (C) (D)
55. (A) (B) (C) (D)
56. (A) (B) (C) (D)
57. (A) (B) (C) (D)
58. (A) (B) (C) (D)
59. (A) (B) (C) (D)
60. (A) (B) (C) (D)

The Princeton Review

HSPT® TEST 2

Completely darken bubbles with a No. 2 pencil. If you make a mistake, be sure to erase mark completely. Erase all stray marks.

1.
YOUR NAME: ______ (Print) Last First M.I.

SIGNATURE: ______ DATE: / /

HOME ADDRESS: ______ (Print) Number and Street

______ City State Zip Code

PHONE NO.: ______ (Print)

IMPORTANT: Please fill in these boxes exactly as shown on the back cover of your test book.

2. TEST FORM

3. TEST CODE

0 1 2 3 4 5 6 7 8 9

A B C D E F G H I

J K L M N O P Q R

4. REGISTRATION NUMBER

0 1 2 3 4 5 6 7 8 9

5. YOUR NAME

First 4 letters of last name | FIRST INIT | MID INIT

A B C D E F G H I J K L M N O P Q R S T U V W X Y Z

6. DATE OF BIRTH

Month: JAN FEB MAR APR MAY JUN JUL AUG SEP OCT NOV DEC

Day: 0 1 2 3 4 5 6 7 8 9

Year: 0 1 2 3 4 5 6 7 8 9

7. SEX

MALE

FEMALE

Test 2

Start with number 1 for each new section.
If a section has fewer questions than answer spaces, leave the extra answer spaces blank.

Verbal Skills

1. A B C D
2. A B C D
3. A B C D
4. A B C D
5. A B C D
6. A B C D
7. A B C D
8. A B C D
9. A B C D
10. A B C D
11. A B C D
12. A B C D
13. A B C D
14. A B C D
15. A B C D
16. A B C D
17. A B C D
18. A B C D
19. A B C D
20. A B C D
21. A B C D
22. A B C D
23. A B C D
24. A B C D
25. A B C D
26. A B C D
27. A B C D
28. A B C D
29. A B C D
30. A B C D
31. A B C D
32. A B C D
33. A B C D
34. A B C D
35. A B C D
36. A B C D
37. A B C D
38. A B C D
39. A B C D
40. A B C D
41. A B C D
42. A B C D
43. A B C D
44. A B C D
45. A B C D
46. A B C D
47. A B C D
48. A B C D
49. A B C D
50. A B C D
51. A B C D
52. A B C D
53. A B C D
54. A B C D
55. A B C D
56. A B C D
57. A B C D
58. A B C D
59. A B C D
60. A B C D

Quantitative Skills

1. A B C D
2. A B C D
3. A B C D
4. A B C D
5. A B C D
6. A B C D
7. A B C D
8. A B C D
9. A B C D
10. A B C D
11. A B C D
12. A B C D
13. A B C D
14. A B C D
15. A B C D
16. A B C D
17. A B C D
18. A B C D
19. A B C D
20. A B C D
21. A B C D
22. A B C D
23. A B C D
24. A B C D
25. A B C D
26. A B C D
27. A B C D
28. A B C D
29. A B C D
30. A B C D
31. A B C D
32. A B C D
33. A B C D
34. A B C D
35. A B C D
36. A B C D
37. A B C D
38. A B C D
39. A B C D
40. A B C D
41. A B C D
42. A B C D
43. A B C D
44. A B C D
45. A B C D
46. A B C D
47. A B C D
48. A B C D
49. A B C D
50. A B C D
51. A B C D
52. A B C D

The Princeton Review® **HSPT® TEST 2**

Completely darken bubbles with a No. 2 pencil. If you make a mistake, be sure to erase mark completely. Erase all stray marks.

Test 2 Start with number 1 for each new section.
If a section has fewer questions than answer spaces, leave the extra answer spaces blank.

Reading

1. (A) (B) (C) (D)
2. (A) (B) (C) (D)
3. (A) (B) (C) (D)
4. (A) (B) (C) (D)
5. (A) (B) (C) (D)
6. (A) (B) (C) (D)
7. (A) (B) (C) (D)
8. (A) (B) (C) (D)
9. (A) (B) (C) (D)
10. (A) (B) (C) (D)
11. (A) (B) (C) (D)
12. (A) (B) (C) (D)
13. (A) (B) (C) (D)
14. (A) (B) (C) (D)
15. (A) (B) (C) (D)
16. (A) (B) (C) (D)
17. (A) (B) (C) (D)
18. (A) (B) (C) (D)
19. (A) (B) (C) (D)
20. (A) (B) (C) (D)
21. (A) (B) (C) (D)
22. (A) (B) (C) (D)
23. (A) (B) (C) (D)
24. (A) (B) (C) (D)
25. (A) (B) (C) (D)
26. (A) (B) (C) (D)
27. (A) (B) (C) (D)
28. (A) (B) (C) (D)
29. (A) (B) (C) (D)
30. (A) (B) (C) (D)
31. (A) (B) (C) (D)
32. (A) (B) (C) (D)
33. (A) (B) (C) (D)
34. (A) (B) (C) (D)
35. (A) (B) (C) (D)
36. (A) (B) (C) (D)
37. (A) (B) (C) (D)
38. (A) (B) (C) (D)
39. (A) (B) (C) (D)
40. (A) (B) (C) (D)
41. (A) (B) (C) (D)
42. (A) (B) (C) (D)
43. (A) (B) (C) (D)
44. (A) (B) (C) (D)
45. (A) (B) (C) (D)
46. (A) (B) (C) (D)
47. (A) (B) (C) (D)
48. (A) (B) (C) (D)
49. (A) (B) (C) (D)
50. (A) (B) (C) (D)
51. (A) (B) (C) (D)
52. (A) (B) (C) (D)
53. (A) (B) (C) (D)
54. (A) (B) (C) (D)
55. (A) (B) (C) (D)
56. (A) (B) (C) (D)
57. (A) (B) (C) (D)
58. (A) (B) (C) (D)
59. (A) (B) (C) (D)
60. (A) (B) (C) (D)
61. (A) (B) (C) (D)
62. (A) (B) (C) (D)

Mathematics

1. (A) (B) (C) (D)
2. (A) (B) (C) (D)
3. (A) (B) (C) (D)
4. (A) (B) (C) (D)
5. (A) (B) (C) (D)
6. (A) (B) (C) (D)
7. (A) (B) (C) (D)
8. (A) (B) (C) (D)
9. (A) (B) (C) (D)
10. (A) (B) (C) (D)
11. (A) (B) (C) (D)
12. (A) (B) (C) (D)
13. (A) (B) (C) (D)
14. (A) (B) (C) (D)
15. (A) (B) (C) (D)
16. (A) (B) (C) (D)
17. (A) (B) (C) (D)
18. (A) (B) (C) (D)
19. (A) (B) (C) (D)
20. (A) (B) (C) (D)
21. (A) (B) (C) (D)
22. (A) (B) (C) (D)
23. (A) (B) (C) (D)
24. (A) (B) (C) (D)
25. (A) (B) (C) (D)
26. (A) (B) (C) (D)
27. (A) (B) (C) (D)
28. (A) (B) (C) (D)
29. (A) (B) (C) (D)
30. (A) (B) (C) (D)
31. (A) (B) (C) (D)
32. (A) (B) (C) (D)
33. (A) (B) (C) (D)
34. (A) (B) (C) (D)
35. (A) (B) (C) (D)
36. (A) (B) (C) (D)
37. (A) (B) (C) (D)
38. (A) (B) (C) (D)
39. (A) (B) (C) (D)
40. (A) (B) (C) (D)
41. (A) (B) (C) (D)
42. (A) (B) (C) (D)
43. (A) (B) (C) (D)
44. (A) (B) (C) (D)
45. (A) (B) (C) (D)
46. (A) (B) (C) (D)
47. (A) (B) (C) (D)
48. (A) (B) (C) (D)
49. (A) (B) (C) (D)
50. (A) (B) (C) (D)
51. (A) (B) (C) (D)
52. (A) (B) (C) (D)
53. (A) (B) (C) (D)
54. (A) (B) (C) (D)
55. (A) (B) (C) (D)
56. (A) (B) (C) (D)
57. (A) (B) (C) (D)
58. (A) (B) (C) (D)
59. (A) (B) (C) (D)
60. (A) (B) (C) (D)
61. (A) (B) (C) (D)
62. (A) (B) (C) (D)
63. (A) (B) (C) (D)
64. (A) (B) (C) (D)

Language

1. (A) (B) (C) (D)
2. (A) (B) (C) (D)
3. (A) (B) (C) (D)
4. (A) (B) (C) (D)
5. (A) (B) (C) (D)
6. (A) (B) (C) (D)
7. (A) (B) (C) (D)
8. (A) (B) (C) (D)
9. (A) (B) (C) (D)
10. (A) (B) (C) (D)
11. (A) (B) (C) (D)
12. (A) (B) (C) (D)
13. (A) (B) (C) (D)
14. (A) (B) (C) (D)
15. (A) (B) (C) (D)
16. (A) (B) (C) (D)
17. (A) (B) (C) (D)
18. (A) (B) (C) (D)
19. (A) (B) (C) (D)
20. (A) (B) (C) (D)
21. (A) (B) (C) (D)
22. (A) (B) (C) (D)
23. (A) (B) (C) (D)
24. (A) (B) (C) (D)
25. (A) (B) (C) (D)
26. (A) (B) (C) (D)
27. (A) (B) (C) (D)
28. (A) (B) (C) (D)
29. (A) (B) (C) (D)
30. (A) (B) (C) (D)
31. (A) (B) (C) (D)
32. (A) (B) (C) (D)
33. (A) (B) (C) (D)
34. (A) (B) (C) (D)
35. (A) (B) (C) (D)
36. (A) (B) (C) (D)
37. (A) (B) (C) (D)
38. (A) (B) (C) (D)
39. (A) (B) (C) (D)
40. (A) (B) (C) (D)
41. (A) (B) (C) (D)
42. (A) (B) (C) (D)
43. (A) (B) (C) (D)
44. (A) (B) (C) (D)
45. (A) (B) (C) (D)
46. (A) (B) (C) (D)
47. (A) (B) (C) (D)
48. (A) (B) (C) (D)
49. (A) (B) (C) (D)
50. (A) (B) (C) (D)
51. (A) (B) (C) (D)
52. (A) (B) (C) (D)
53. (A) (B) (C) (D)
54. (A) (B) (C) (D)
55. (A) (B) (C) (D)
56. (A) (B) (C) (D)
57. (A) (B) (C) (D)
58. (A) (B) (C) (D)
59. (A) (B) (C) (D)
60. (A) (B) (C) (D)

The Princeton Review®

HSPT® TEST 3

Completely darken bubbles with a No. 2 pencil. If you make a mistake, be sure to erase mark completely. Erase all stray marks.

1.
YOUR NAME: (Print) ______ Last ______ First ______ M.I.

SIGNATURE: ______ DATE: ___ / ___ / ___

HOME ADDRESS: (Print) ______ Number and Street

______ City ______ State ______ Zip Code

PHONE NO.: (Print) ______

IMPORTANT: Please fill in these boxes exactly as shown on the back cover of your test book.

2. TEST FORM

______

3. TEST CODE

0	A	J	0	0
1	B	K	1	1
2	C	L	2	2
3	D	M	3	3
4	E	N	4	4
5	F	O	5	5
6	G	P	6	6
7	H	Q	7	7
8	I	R	8	8
9			9	9

4. REGISTRATION NUMBER

0	0	0	0	0	0
1	1	1	1	1	1
2	2	2	2	2	2
3	3	3	3	3	3
4	4	4	4	4	4
5	5	5	5	5	5
6	6	6	6	6	6
7	7	7	7	7	7
8	8	8	8	8	8
9	9	9	9	9	9

5. YOUR NAME

First 4 letters of last name				FIRST INIT	MID INIT
A	A	A	A	A	A
B	B	B	B	B	B
C	C	C	C	C	C
D	D	D	D	D	D
E	E	E	E	E	E
F	F	F	F	F	F
G	G	G	G	G	G
H	H	H	H	H	H
I	I	I	I	I	I
J	J	J	J	J	J
K	K	K	K	K	K
L	L	L	L	L	L
M	M	M	M	M	M
N	N	N	N	N	N
O	O	O	O	O	O
P	P	P	P	P	P
Q	Q	Q	Q	Q	Q
R	R	R	R	R	R
S	S	S	S	S	S
T	T	T	T	T	T
U	U	U	U	U	U
V	V	V	V	V	V
W	W	W	W	W	W
X	X	X	X	X	X
Y	Y	Y	Y	Y	Y
Z	Z	Z	Z	Z	Z

6. DATE OF BIRTH

Month	Day		Year	
JAN				
FEB	0	0	0	0
MAR	1	1	1	1
APR	2	2	2	2
MAY	3	3	3	3
JUN	4	4	4	4
JUL	5	5	5	5
AUG	6	6	6	6
SEP	7	7	7	7
OCT	8	8	8	8
NOV	9	9	9	9
DEC				

7. SEX

MALE

FEMALE

The Princeton Review®

Test 3 Start with number 1 for each new section.
If a section has fewer questions than answer spaces, leave the extra answer spaces blank.

Verbal Skills

1. A B C D
2. A B C D
3. A B C D
4. A B C D
5. A B C D
6. A B C D
7. A B C D
8. A B C D
9. A B C D
10. A B C D
11. A B C D
12. A B C D
13. A B C D
14. A B C D
15. A B C D
16. A B C D
17. A B C D
18. A B C D
19. A B C D
20. A B C D
21. A B C D
22. A B C D
23. A B C D
24. A B C D
25. A B C D
26. A B C D
27. A B C D
28. A B C D
29. A B C D
30. A B C D
31. A B C D
32. A B C D
33. A B C D
34. A B C D
35. A B C D
36. A B C D
37. A B C D
38. A B C D
39. A B C D
40. A B C D
41. A B C D
42. A B C D
43. A B C D
44. A B C D
45. A B C D
46. A B C D
47. A B C D
48. A B C D
49. A B C D
50. A B C D
51. A B C D
52. A B C D
53. A B C D
54. A B C D
55. A B C D
56. A B C D
57. A B C D
58. A B C D
59. A B C D
60. A B C D

Quantitative Skills

1. A B C D
2. A B C D
3. A B C D
4. A B C D
5. A B C D
6. A B C D
7. A B C D
8. A B C D
9. A B C D
10. A B C D
11. A B C D
12. A B C D
13. A B C D
14. A B C D
15. A B C D
16. A B C D
17. A B C D
18. A B C D
19. A B C D
20. A B C D
21. A B C D
22. A B C D
23. A B C D
24. A B C D
25. A B C D
26. A B C D
27. A B C D
28. A B C D
29. A B C D
30. A B C D
31. A B C D
32. A B C D
33. A B C D
34. A B C D
35. A B C D
36. A B C D
37. A B C D
38. A B C D
39. A B C D
40. A B C D
41. A B C D
42. A B C D
43. A B C D
44. A B C D
45. A B C D
46. A B C D
47. A B C D
48. A B C D
49. A B C D
50. A B C D
51. A B C D
52. A B C D

The Princeton Review

HSPT® TEST 3

Completely darken bubbles with a No. 2 pencil. If you make a mistake, be sure to erase mark completely. Erase all stray marks.

Test 3 Start with number 1 for each new section.
If a section has fewer questions than answer spaces, leave the extra answer spaces blank.

Reading

1. (A) (B) (C) (D)
2. (A) (B) (C) (D)
3. (A) (B) (C) (D)
4. (A) (B) (C) (D)
5. (A) (B) (C) (D)
6. (A) (B) (C) (D)
7. (A) (B) (C) (D)
8. (A) (B) (C) (D)
9. (A) (B) (C) (D)
10. (A) (B) (C) (D)
11. (A) (B) (C) (D)
12. (A) (B) (C) (D)
13. (A) (B) (C) (D)
14. (A) (B) (C) (D)
15. (A) (B) (C) (D)
16. (A) (B) (C) (D)
17. (A) (B) (C) (D)
18. (A) (B) (C) (D)
19. (A) (B) (C) (D)
20. (A) (B) (C) (D)
21. (A) (B) (C) (D)
22. (A) (B) (C) (D)
23. (A) (B) (C) (D)
24. (A) (B) (C) (D)
25. (A) (B) (C) (D)
26. (A) (B) (C) (D)
27. (A) (B) (C) (D)
28. (A) (B) (C) (D)
29. (A) (B) (C) (D)
30. (A) (B) (C) (D)
31. (A) (B) (C) (D)
32. (A) (B) (C) (D)
33. (A) (B) (C) (D)
34. (A) (B) (C) (D)
35. (A) (B) (C) (D)
36. (A) (B) (C) (D)
37. (A) (B) (C) (D)
38. (A) (B) (C) (D)
39. (A) (B) (C) (D)
40. (A) (B) (C) (D)
41. (A) (B) (C) (D)
42. (A) (B) (C) (D)
43. (A) (B) (C) (D)
44. (A) (B) (C) (D)
45. (A) (B) (C) (D)
46. (A) (B) (C) (D)
47. (A) (B) (C) (D)
48. (A) (B) (C) (D)
49. (A) (B) (C) (D)
50. (A) (B) (C) (D)
51. (A) (B) (C) (D)
52. (A) (B) (C) (D)
53. (A) (B) (C) (D)
54. (A) (B) (C) (D)
55. (A) (B) (C) (D)
56. (A) (B) (C) (D)
57. (A) (B) (C) (D)
58. (A) (B) (C) (D)
59. (A) (B) (C) (D)
60. (A) (B) (C) (D)
61. (A) (B) (C) (D)
62. (A) (B) (C) (D)

Mathematics

1. (A) (B) (C) (D)
2. (A) (B) (C) (D)
3. (A) (B) (C) (D)
4. (A) (B) (C) (D)
5. (A) (B) (C) (D)
6. (A) (B) (C) (D)
7. (A) (B) (C) (D)
8. (A) (B) (C) (D)
9. (A) (B) (C) (D)
10. (A) (B) (C) (D)
11. (A) (B) (C) (D)
12. (A) (B) (C) (D)
13. (A) (B) (C) (D)
14. (A) (B) (C) (D)
15. (A) (B) (C) (D)
16. (A) (B) (C) (D)
17. (A) (B) (C) (D)
18. (A) (B) (C) (D)
19. (A) (B) (C) (D)
20. (A) (B) (C) (D)
21. (A) (B) (C) (D)
22. (A) (B) (C) (D)
23. (A) (B) (C) (D)
24. (A) (B) (C) (D)
25. (A) (B) (C) (D)
26. (A) (B) (C) (D)
27. (A) (B) (C) (D)
28. (A) (B) (C) (D)
29. (A) (B) (C) (D)
30. (A) (B) (C) (D)
31. (A) (B) (C) (D)
32. (A) (B) (C) (D)
33. (A) (B) (C) (D)
34. (A) (B) (C) (D)
35. (A) (B) (C) (D)
36. (A) (B) (C) (D)
37. (A) (B) (C) (D)
38. (A) (B) (C) (D)
39. (A) (B) (C) (D)
40. (A) (B) (C) (D)
41. (A) (B) (C) (D)
42. (A) (B) (C) (D)
43. (A) (B) (C) (D)
44. (A) (B) (C) (D)
45. (A) (B) (C) (D)
46. (A) (B) (C) (D)
47. (A) (B) (C) (D)
48. (A) (B) (C) (D)
49. (A) (B) (C) (D)
50. (A) (B) (C) (D)
51. (A) (B) (C) (D)
52. (A) (B) (C) (D)
53. (A) (B) (C) (D)
54. (A) (B) (C) (D)
55. (A) (B) (C) (D)
56. (A) (B) (C) (D)
57. (A) (B) (C) (D)
58. (A) (B) (C) (D)
59. (A) (B) (C) (D)
60. (A) (B) (C) (D)
61. (A) (B) (C) (D)
62. (A) (B) (C) (D)
63. (A) (B) (C) (D)
64. (A) (B) (C) (D)

Language

1. (A) (B) (C) (D)
2. (A) (B) (C) (D)
3. (A) (B) (C) (D)
4. (A) (B) (C) (D)
5. (A) (B) (C) (D)
6. (A) (B) (C) (D)
7. (A) (B) (C) (D)
8. (A) (B) (C) (D)
9. (A) (B) (C) (D)
10. (A) (B) (C) (D)
11. (A) (B) (C) (D)
12. (A) (B) (C) (D)
13. (A) (B) (C) (D)
14. (A) (B) (C) (D)
15. (A) (B) (C) (D)
16. (A) (B) (C) (D)
17. (A) (B) (C) (D)
18. (A) (B) (C) (D)
19. (A) (B) (C) (D)
20. (A) (B) (C) (D)
21. (A) (B) (C) (D)
22. (A) (B) (C) (D)
23. (A) (B) (C) (D)
24. (A) (B) (C) (D)
25. (A) (B) (C) (D)
26. (A) (B) (C) (D)
27. (A) (B) (C) (D)
28. (A) (B) (C) (D)
29. (A) (B) (C) (D)
30. (A) (B) (C) (D)
31. (A) (B) (C) (D)
32. (A) (B) (C) (D)
33. (A) (B) (C) (D)
34. (A) (B) (C) (D)
35. (A) (B) (C) (D)
36. (A) (B) (C) (D)
37. (A) (B) (C) (D)
38. (A) (B) (C) (D)
39. (A) (B) (C) (D)
40. (A) (B) (C) (D)
41. (A) (B) (C) (D)
42. (A) (B) (C) (D)
43. (A) (B) (C) (D)
44. (A) (B) (C) (D)
45. (A) (B) (C) (D)
46. (A) (B) (C) (D)
47. (A) (B) (C) (D)
48. (A) (B) (C) (D)
49. (A) (B) (C) (D)
50. (A) (B) (C) (D)
51. (A) (B) (C) (D)
52. (A) (B) (C) (D)
53. (A) (B) (C) (D)
54. (A) (B) (C) (D)
55. (A) (B) (C) (D)
56. (A) (B) (C) (D)
57. (A) (B) (C) (D)
58. (A) (B) (C) (D)
59. (A) (B) (C) (D)
60. (A) (B) (C) (D)

The Princeton Review

COOP® TEST 1

Completely darken bubbles with a No. 2 pencil. If you make a mistake, be sure to erase mark completely. Erase all stray marks.

1.
YOUR NAME: (Print) ____ Last ____ First ____ M.I.

SIGNATURE: ____ DATE: __/__/__

HOME ADDRESS: (Print) ____ Number and Street

____ City ____ State ____ Zip Code

PHONE NO.: (Print) ____

IMPORTANT: Please fill in these boxes exactly as shown on the back cover of your test book.

2. TEST FORM

3. TEST CODE

0	A	J	0	0
1	B	K	1	1
2	C	L	2	2
3	D	M	3	3
4	E	N	4	4
5	F	O	5	5
6	G	P	6	6
7	H	Q	7	7
8	I	R	8	8
9			9	9

4. REGISTRATION NUMBER

0	0	0	0	0	0
1	1	1	1	1	1
2	2	2	2	2	2
3	3	3	3	3	3
4	4	4	4	4	4
5	5	5	5	5	5
6	6	6	6	6	6
7	7	7	7	7	7
8	8	8	8	8	8
9	9	9	9	9	9

5. YOUR NAME

First 4 letters of last name | FIRST INIT | MID INIT

A B C D E F G H I J K L M N O P Q R S T U V W X Y Z (each column)

6. DATE OF BIRTH

Month	Day		Year	
JAN				
FEB	0	0	0	0
MAR	1	1	1	1
APR	2	2	2	2
MAY	3	3	3	3
JUN	4	4	4	4
JUL	5	5	5	5
AUG	6	6	6	6
SEP	7	7	7	7
OCT	8	8	8	8
NOV	9	9	9	9
DEC				

7. SEX

MALE

FEMALE

The Princeton Review

Test 1 Start with number 1 for each new section.
If a section has fewer questions than answer spaces, leave the extra answer spaces blank.

Test 1— Sequences

1. A B C D
2. A B C D
3. A B C D
4. A B C D
5. A B C D
6. A B C D
7. A B C D
8. A B C D
9. A B C D
10. A B C D
11. A B C D
12. A B C D
13. A B C D
14. A B C D
15. A B C D
16. A B C D
17. A B C D
18. A B C D
19. A B C D
20. A B C D

Test 2— Analogies

1. A B C D
2. A B C D
3. A B C D
4. A B C D
5. A B C D
6. A B C D
7. A B C D
8. A B C D
9. A B C D
10. A B C D
11. A B C D
12. A B C D
13. A B C D
14. A B C D
15. A B C D
16. A B C D
17. A B C D
18. A B C D
19. A B C D
20. A B C D

Test 3— Quantitative Reasoning

1. A B C D
2. A B C D
3. A B C D
4. A B C D
5. A B C D
6. A B C D
7. A B C D
8. A B C D
9. A B C D
10. A B C D
11. A B C D
12. A B C D
13. A B C D
14. A B C D
15. A B C D
16. A B C D
17. A B C D
18. A B C D
19. A B C D
20. A B C D

The Princeton Review

COOP® TEST 1

Completely darken bubbles with a No. 2 pencil. If you make a mistake, be sure to erase mark completely. Erase all stray marks.

Test 1 Start with number 1 for each new section.
If a section has fewer questions than answer spaces, leave the extra answer spaces blank.

Test 4— Verbal Reasoning— Words

1. A B C D
2. A B C D
3. A B C D
4. A B C D
5. A B C D
6. A B C D
7. A B C D
8. A B C D
9. A B C D
10. A B C D
11. A B C D
12. A B C D
13. A B C D
14. A B C D
15. A B C D
16. A B C D
17. A B C D
18. A B C D
19. A B C D
20. A B C D

Test 5— Reasoning—Context

1. A B C D
2. A B C D
3. A B C D
4. A B C D
5. A B C D
6. A B C D
7. A B C D
8. A B C D
9. A B C D
10. A B C D

Test 6— Reading and Language Arts

1. A B C D
2. A B C D
3. A B C D
4. A B C D
5. A B C D
6. A B C D
7. A B C D
8. A B C D
9. A B C D
10. A B C D
11. A B C D
12. A B C D
13. A B C D
14. A B C D
15. A B C D
16. A B C D
17. A B C D
18. A B C D
19. A B C D
20. A B C D
21. A B C D
22. A B C D
23. A B C D
24. A B C D
25. A B C D
26. A B C D
27. A B C D
28. A B C D
29. A B C D
30. A B C D
31. A B C D
32. A B C D
33. A B C D
34. A B C D
35. A B C D
36. A B C D
37. A B C D
38. A B C D
39. A B C D
40. A B C D

Test 7— Mathematics

1. A B C D
2. A B C D
3. A B C D
4. A B C D
5. A B C D
6. A B C D
7. A B C D
8. A B C D
9. A B C D
10. A B C D
11. A B C D
12. A B C D
13. A B C D
14. A B C D
15. A B C D
16. A B C D
17. A B C D
18. A B C D
19. A B C D
20. A B C D
21. A B C D
22. A B C D
23. A B C D
24. A B C D
25. A B C D
26. A B C D
27. A B C D
28. A B C D
29. A B C D
30. A B C D
31. A B C D
32. A B C D
33. A B C D
34. A B C D
35. A B C D
36. A B C D
37. A B C D
38. A B C D
39. A B C D
40. A B C D

The Princeton Review

COOP® TEST 2

Completely darken bubbles with a No. 2 pencil. If you make a mistake, be sure to erase mark completely. Erase all stray marks.

1.
YOUR NAME: ______________________________ (Print) Last First M.I.

SIGNATURE: ______________________________ DATE: / /

HOME ADDRESS: ______________________________ (Print) Number and Street

______________________________ City State Zip Code

PHONE NO.: ______________________________ (Print)

IMPORTANT: Please fill in these boxes exactly as shown on the back cover of your test book.

2. TEST FORM

3. TEST CODE

0	A	J	0	0
1	B	K	1	1
2	C	L	2	2
3	D	M	3	3
4	E	N	4	4
5	F	O	5	5
6	G	P	6	6
7	H	Q	7	7
8	I	R	8	8
9			9	9

4. REGISTRATION NUMBER

0	0	0	0	0	0
1	1	1	1	1	1
2	2	2	2	2	2
3	3	3	3	3	3
4	4	4	4	4	4
5	5	5	5	5	5
6	6	6	6	6	6
7	7	7	7	7	7
8	8	8	8	8	8
9	9	9	9	9	9

5. YOUR NAME

First 4 letters of last name				FIRST INIT	MID INIT
A	A	A	A	A	A
B	B	B	B	B	B
C	C	C	C	C	C
D	D	D	D	D	D
E	E	E	E	E	E
F	F	F	F	F	F
G	G	G	G	G	G
H	H	H	H	H	H
I	I	I	I	I	I
J	J	J	J	J	J
K	K	K	K	K	K
L	L	L	L	L	L
M	M	M	M	M	M
N	N	N	N	N	N
O	O	O	O	O	O
P	P	P	P	P	P
Q	Q	Q	Q	Q	Q
R	R	R	R	R	R
S	S	S	S	S	S
T	T	T	T	T	T
U	U	U	U	U	U
V	V	V	V	V	V
W	W	W	W	W	W
X	X	X	X	X	X
Y	Y	Y	Y	Y	Y
Z	Z	Z	Z	Z	Z

6. DATE OF BIRTH

Month	Day		Year	
JAN				
FEB	0	0	0	0
MAR	1	1	1	1
APR	2	2	2	2
MAY	3	3	3	3
JUN	4	4	4	4
JUL	5	5	5	5
AUG	6	6	6	6
SEP	7	7	7	7
OCT	8	8	8	8
NOV	9	9	9	9
DEC				

7. SEX

- MALE
- FEMALE

The Princeton Review

Test 2

Start with number 1 for each new section.
If a section has fewer questions than answer spaces, leave the extra answer spaces blank.

Test 1—Sequences

1. (A) (B) (C) (D)
2. (A) (B) (C) (D)
3. (A) (B) (C) (D)
4. (A) (B) (C) (D)
5. (A) (B) (C) (D)
6. (A) (B) (C) (D)
7. (A) (B) (C) (D)
8. (A) (B) (C) (D)
9. (A) (B) (C) (D)
10. (A) (B) (C) (D)
11. (A) (B) (C) (D)
12. (A) (B) (C) (D)
13. (A) (B) (C) (D)
14. (A) (B) (C) (D)
15. (A) (B) (C) (D)
16. (A) (B) (C) (D)
17. (A) (B) (C) (D)
18. (A) (B) (C) (D)
19. (A) (B) (C) (D)
20. (A) (B) (C) (D)

Test 2—Analogies

1. (A) (B) (C) (D)
2. (A) (B) (C) (D)
3. (A) (B) (C) (D)
4. (A) (B) (C) (D)
5. (A) (B) (C) (D)
6. (A) (B) (C) (D)
7. (A) (B) (C) (D)
8. (A) (B) (C) (D)
9. (A) (B) (C) (D)
10. (A) (B) (C) (D)
11. (A) (B) (C) (D)
12. (A) (B) (C) (D)
13. (A) (B) (C) (D)
14. (A) (B) (C) (D)
15. (A) (B) (C) (D)
16. (A) (B) (C) (D)
17. (A) (B) (C) (D)
18. (A) (B) (C) (D)
19. (A) (B) (C) (D)
20. (A) (B) (C) (D)

Test 3—Quantitative Reasoning

1. (A) (B) (C) (D)
2. (A) (B) (C) (D)
3. (A) (B) (C) (D)
4. (A) (B) (C) (D)
5. (A) (B) (C) (D)
6. (A) (B) (C) (D)
7. (A) (B) (C) (D)
8. (A) (B) (C) (D)
9. (A) (B) (C) (D)
10. (A) (B) (C) (D)
11. (A) (B) (C) (D)
12. (A) (B) (C) (D)
13. (A) (B) (C) (D)
14. (A) (B) (C) (D)
15. (A) (B) (C) (D)
16. (A) (B) (C) (D)
17. (A) (B) (C) (D)
18. (A) (B) (C) (D)
19. (A) (B) (C) (D)
20. (A) (B) (C) (D)

Completely darken bubbles with a No. 2 pencil. If you make a mistake, be sure to erase mark completely. Erase all stray marks.

Test 2 Start with number 1 for each new section.
If a section has fewer questions than answer spaces, leave the extra answer spaces blank.

Test 4— Verbal Reasoning— Words

1. (A) (B) (C) (D)
2. (A) (B) (C) (D)
3. (A) (B) (C) (D)
4. (A) (B) (C) (D)
5. (A) (B) (C) (D)
6. (A) (B) (C) (D)
7. (A) (B) (C) (D)
8. (A) (B) (C) (D)
9. (A) (B) (C) (D)
10. (A) (B) (C) (D)
11. (A) (B) (C) (D)
12. (A) (B) (C) (D)
13. (A) (B) (C) (D)
14. (A) (B) (C) (D)
15. (A) (B) (C) (D)
16. (A) (B) (C) (D)
17. (A) (B) (C) (D)
18. (A) (B) (C) (D)
19. (A) (B) (C) (D)
20. (A) (B) (C) (D)

Test 5— Reasoning—Context

1. (A) (B) (C) (D)
2. (A) (B) (C) (D)
3. (A) (B) (C) (D)
4. (A) (B) (C) (D)
5. (A) (B) (C) (D)
6. (A) (B) (C) (D)
7. (A) (B) (C) (D)
8. (A) (B) (C) (D)
9. (A) (B) (C) (D)
10. (A) (B) (C) (D)

Test 6— Reading and Language Arts

1. (A) (B) (C) (D)
2. (A) (B) (C) (D)
3. (A) (B) (C) (D)
4. (A) (B) (C) (D)
5. (A) (B) (C) (D)
6. (A) (B) (C) (D)
7. (A) (B) (C) (D)
8. (A) (B) (C) (D)
9. (A) (B) (C) (D)
10. (A) (B) (C) (D)
11. (A) (B) (C) (D)
12. (A) (B) (C) (D)
13. (A) (B) (C) (D)
14. (A) (B) (C) (D)
15. (A) (B) (C) (D)
16. (A) (B) (C) (D)
17. (A) (B) (C) (D)
18. (A) (B) (C) (D)
19. (A) (B) (C) (D)
20. (A) (B) (C) (D)
21. (A) (B) (C) (D)
22. (A) (B) (C) (D)
23. (A) (B) (C) (D)
24. (A) (B) (C) (D)
25. (A) (B) (C) (D)
26. (A) (B) (C) (D)
27. (A) (B) (C) (D)
28. (A) (B) (C) (D)
29. (A) (B) (C) (D)
30. (A) (B) (C) (D)
31. (A) (B) (C) (D)
32. (A) (B) (C) (D)
33. (A) (B) (C) (D)
34. (A) (B) (C) (D)
35. (A) (B) (C) (D)
36. (A) (B) (C) (D)
37. (A) (B) (C) (D)
38. (A) (B) (C) (D)
39. (A) (B) (C) (D)
40. (A) (B) (C) (D)

Test 7— Mathematics

1. (A) (B) (C) (D)
2. (A) (B) (C) (D)
3. (A) (B) (C) (D)
4. (A) (B) (C) (D)
5. (A) (B) (C) (D)
6. (A) (B) (C) (D)
7. (A) (B) (C) (D)
8. (A) (B) (C) (D)
9. (A) (B) (C) (D)
10. (A) (B) (C) (D)
11. (A) (B) (C) (D)
12. (A) (B) (C) (D)
13. (A) (B) (C) (D)
14. (A) (B) (C) (D)
15. (A) (B) (C) (D)
16. (A) (B) (C) (D)
17. (A) (B) (C) (D)
18. (A) (B) (C) (D)
19. (A) (B) (C) (D)
20. (A) (B) (C) (D)
21. (A) (B) (C) (D)
22. (A) (B) (C) (D)
23. (A) (B) (C) (D)
24. (A) (B) (C) (D)
25. (A) (B) (C) (D)
26. (A) (B) (C) (D)
27. (A) (B) (C) (D)
28. (A) (B) (C) (D)
29. (A) (B) (C) (D)
30. (A) (B) (C) (D)
31. (A) (B) (C) (D)
32. (A) (B) (C) (D)
33. (A) (B) (C) (D)
34. (A) (B) (C) (D)
35. (A) (B) (C) (D)
36. (A) (B) (C) (D)
37. (A) (B) (C) (D)
38. (A) (B) (C) (D)
39. (A) (B) (C) (D)
40. (A) (B) (C) (D)

The Princeton Review

TACHS® TEST 1

Completely darken bubbles with a No. 2 pencil. If you make a mistake, be sure to erase mark completely. Erase all stray marks.

1.
YOUR NAME: ______________________________ (Print) Last First M.I.

SIGNATURE: ______________________________ DATE: ___/___/___

HOME ADDRESS: ______________________________ (Print) Number and Street

______________________________ City State Zip Code

PHONE NO.: ______________________________ (Print)

IMPORTANT: Please fill in these boxes exactly as shown on the back cover of your test book.

2. TEST FORM

____

3. TEST CODE

0	A	J	0	0
1	B	K	1	1
2	C	L	2	2
3	D	M	3	3
4	E	N	4	4
5	F	O	5	5
6	G	P	6	6
7	H	Q	7	7
8	I	R	8	8
9			9	9

4. REGISTRATION NUMBER

0	0	0	0	0	0
1	1	1	1	1	1
2	2	2	2	2	2
3	3	3	3	3	3
4	4	4	4	4	4
5	5	5	5	5	5
6	6	6	6	6	6
7	7	7	7	7	7
8	8	8	8	8	8
9	9	9	9	9	9

5. YOUR NAME

First 4 letters of last name					FIRST INIT	MID INIT
A	A	A	A		A	A
B	B	B	B		B	B
C	C	C	C		C	C
D	D	D	D		D	D
E	E	E	E		E	E
F	F	F	F		F	F
G	G	G	G		G	G
H	H	H	H		H	H
I	I	I	I		I	I
J	J	J	J		J	J
K	K	K	K		K	K
L	L	L	L		L	L
M	M	M	M		M	M
N	N	N	N		N	N
O	O	O	O		O	O
P	P	P	P		P	P
Q	Q	Q	Q		Q	Q
R	R	R	R		R	R
S	S	S	S		S	S
T	T	T	T		T	T
U	U	U	U		U	U
V	V	V	V		V	V
W	W	W	W		W	W
X	X	X	X		X	X
Y	Y	Y	Y		Y	Y
Z	Z	Z	Z		Z	Z

6. DATE OF BIRTH

Month	Day		Year	
JAN				
FEB	0	0	0	0
MAR	1	1	1	1
APR	2	2	2	2
MAY	3	3	3	3
JUN	4	4	4	4
JUL	5	5	5	5
AUG	6	6	6	6
SEP	7	7	7	7
OCT	8	8	8	8
NOV	9	9	9	9
DEC				

7. SEX

MALE

FEMALE

The Princeton Review

Test 1

Start with number 1 for each new section.
If a section has fewer questions than answer spaces, leave the extra answer spaces blank.

Reading

1.	A	B	C	D
2.	J	K	L	M
3.	A	B	C	D
4.	J	K	L	M
5.	A	B	C	D
6.	J	K	L	M
7.	A	B	C	D
8.	J	K	L	M
9.	A	B	C	D
10.	J	K	L	M
11.	A	B	C	D
12.	J	K	L	M
13.	A	B	C	D
14.	J	K	L	M
15.	A	B	C	D
16.	J	K	L	M
17.	A	B	C	D
18.	J	K	L	M
19.	A	B	C	D
20.	J	K	L	M

Language

1.	A	B	C	D	E
2.	J	K	L	M	N
3.	A	B	C	D	E
4.	J	K	L	M	N
5.	A	B	C	D	E
6.	J	K	L	M	N
7.	A	B	C	D	E
8.	J	K	L	M	N
9.	A	B	C	D	E
10.	J	K	L	M	N
11.	A	B	C	D	
12.	J	K	L	M	
13.	A	B	C	D	
14.	J	K	L	M	
15.	A	B	C	D	
16.	J	K	L	M	
17.	A	B	C	D	
18.	J	K	L	M	
19.	A	B	C	D	
20.	J	K	L	M	
21.	A	B	C	D	
22.	J	K	L	M	
23.	A	B	C	D	
24.	J	K	L	M	
25.	A	B	C	D	
26.	J	K	L	M	
27.	A	B	C	D	
28.	J	K	L	M	
29.	A	B	C	D	
30.	J	K	L	M	

Math

1.	A	B	C	D	21.	A	B	C	D
2.	J	K	L	M	22.	J	K	L	M
3.	A	B	C	D	23.	A	B	C	D
4.	J	K	L	M	24.	J	K	L	M
5.	A	B	C	D	25.	A	B	C	D
6.	J	K	L	M	26.	J	K	L	M
7.	A	B	C	D	27.	A	B	C	D
8.	J	K	L	M	28.	J	K	L	M
9.	A	B	C	D	29.	A	B	C	D
10.	J	K	L	M	30.	J	K	L	M
11.	A	B	C	D	31.	A	B	C	D
12.	J	K	L	M	32.	J	K	L	M
13.	A	B	C	D	33.	A	B	C	D
14.	J	K	L	M	34.	J	K	L	M
15.	A	B	C	D	35.	A	B	C	D
16.	J	K	L	M	36.	J	K	L	M
17.	A	B	C	D	37.	A	B	C	D
18.	J	K	L	M	38.	J	K	L	M
19.	A	B	C	D	39.	A	B	C	D
20.	J	K	L	M	40.	J	K	L	M

Ability

1.	A	B	C	D	E
2.	J	K	L	M	N
3.	A	B	C	D	E
4.	J	K	L	M	N
5.	A	B	C	D	E
6.	J	K	L	M	N
7.	A	B	C	D	E
8.	J	K	L	M	N
9.	A	B	C	D	E
10.	J	K	L	M	N

NOTES

NOTES

NOTES

NOTES

NOTES

NOTES

NOTES